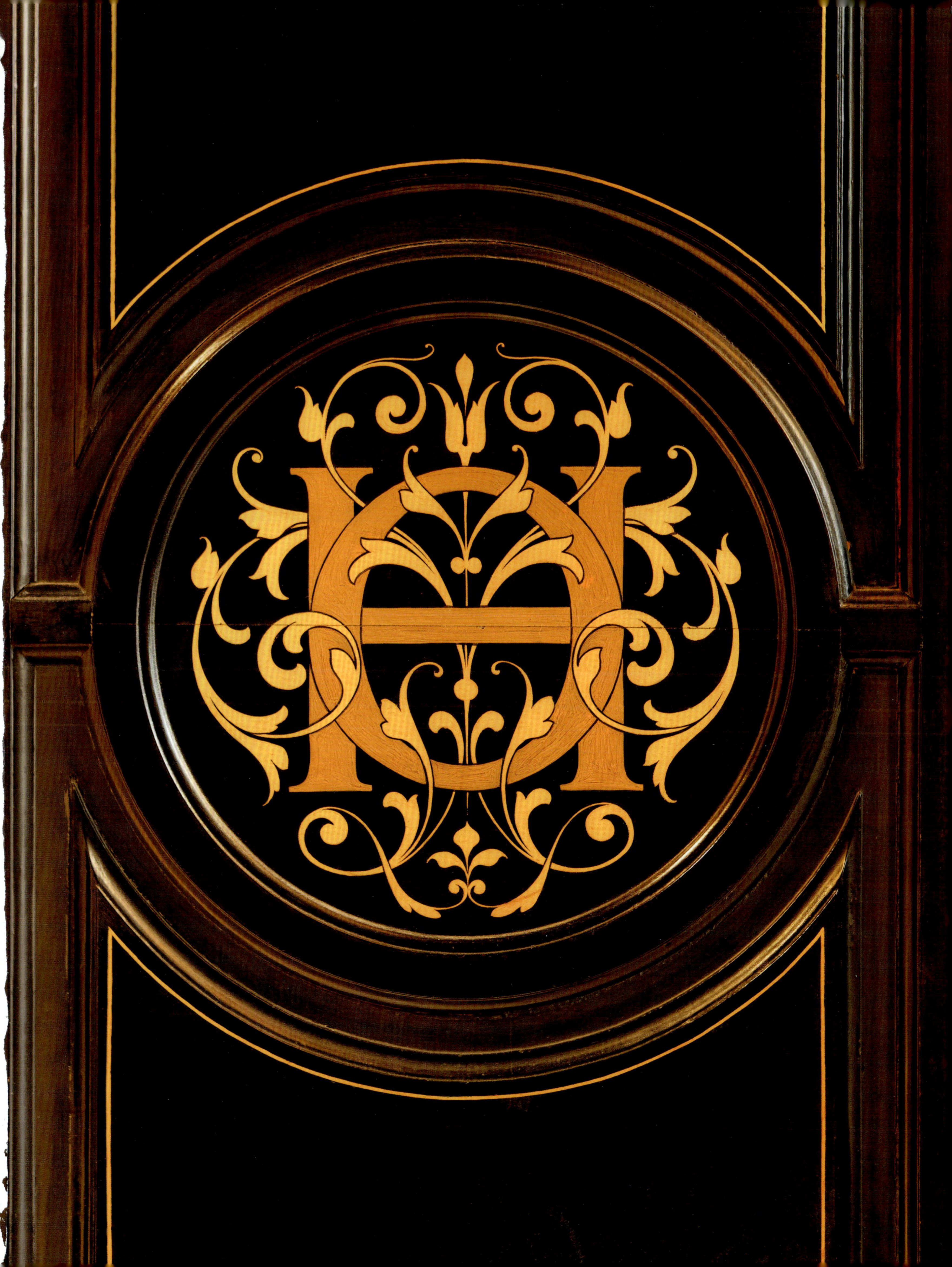

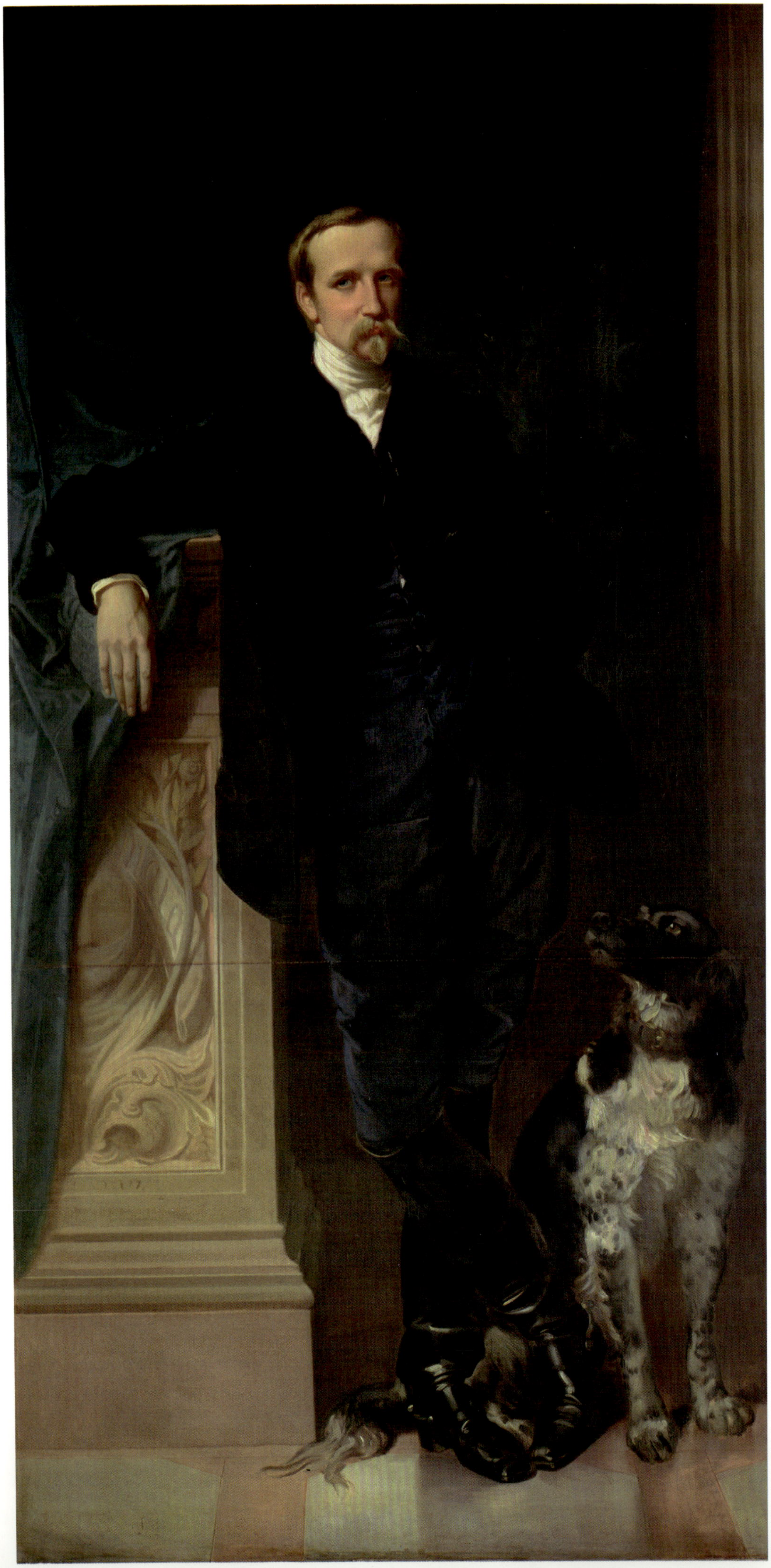

THE CONDÉ MUSEUM AT THE CHÂTEAU DE CHANTILLY

THE PAINTINGS COLLECTION

Nicole Garnier-Pelle

Introduction by **Stéphane Guégan**

DOMAINE DE CHANTILLY

Flammarion

This book received support from La Fondation pour la Sauvegarde et le Développement du Domaine de Chantilly.

The Crédit Agricole Brie Picardie provides support in the development of the heritage of the Château de Chantilly.
The publication of this book was made possible thanks to the support of the Caisses Locales of Chantilly, Senlis, Pont-Sainte-Maxence, Creil, Neuilly-en-Thelle, Crépy-en-Valois and Nanteuil-le-Haudouin.

EXECUTIVE DIRECTOR
Suzanne Tise-Isoré

EDITORIAL COORDINATION
Delphine Storelli

EDITORIAL ASSISTANTS
Delphine Montagne and François de Sailly

TRANSLATED FROM THE FRENCH BY
Deke Dusinberre

GRAPHIC DESIGN
Bernard Lagacé
Assisted by Marc Armand

PROOFREADING
Helen Woodhall

PRODUCTION
Carine Ruault

COLOR SEPARATION
Bussière

PRINTED BY
Zanardi, Italy

Distributed in North America by Rizzoli International Publications, Inc.

Simultaneously published in French as *Les Tableaux de Chantilly – La collection du Duc d'Aumale*

English-language edition

Éditions Skira Flammarion Paris
87 quai Panhard et Levassor
75647 Paris Cedex 13
France
editions.flammarion.com

09 10 11 3 2 1
Paperback
ISBN: 9782081232600
Hardcover
ISBN: 9782081225817
Dépôt légal: 10/2009

COVER Jean Auguste Dominique Ingres, *Self-Portrait, Aged Twenty-Four*, 1804 (see p. 238).
PAGE 1 Detail of wood paneling with monogram of Henri d'Orléans, duc d'Aumale.
PAGE 2 Victor Louis Mottez (1809–1897), *Portrait of Henri d'Orléans, duc d'Aumale, at Claremont*, 1850. Oil on canvas. Inv. 496, Musée Condé, Chantilly.

KEY TO THE ABBREVIATIONS IN THE CAPTIONS

H.: height	d.: date	c.: center
W.: width	b.: bottom	l.: left
S.: signature	t.: top	r.: right

PHOTOGRAPHIC CREDITS

© **Luc Camino, musée de Senlis**: 8–9, 19 – © **musée Condé, Chantilly**: 6 (left), 10 (top and bottom, right), 16–17, 23, 32, 110–113, 184–185, 197–198 – © **musée Condé, Chantilly/ Bridgeman Giraudon**: 2, 49, 77, 79–81, 91–92, 129 (left), 153, 188 – © **Hermine Cléret**: 208-209 – © **Francis Hammond**: 1, 12–14, 22, 24–31, 35, 288–296 – © **Matthieu Lombard**: 83 – © **RMN - D. Amaudet**: 21 (top) – © **RMN - M. Beck-Coppola**: 48, 62–63, 88, 189, 210 (right), 221 – © **RMN - G. Blot**: 11 (left), 168, 191–193, 225–229, 237, 249, 267, 269, 272, 275, 277, 287 – © **RMN - H. Bréjat**: 6 (bottom), 7 (bottom left), 7 (top right), 10 (right), 37, 41–42, 45, 50, 55, 57, 59, 64, 69–71, 73, 76, 78, 93–94, 97, 99–102, 106–107, 117–120, 125, 129 (right), 134, 141–143, 146–149, 155–159, 163–167, 171–181, 196, 201–203, 206, 217–219, 230, 232–235, 239–247, 250–266, 279–285 – © **RMN / Bulloz** : 20 – © **RMN - R.-G. Ojeda**: 7 (top left), 7 (bottom right), 11 (top right), 18, 21 (bottom), 36, 38–39, 52–53, 60–61, 65–67, 72, 75, 82, 87, 89, 98, 103–105, 109, 115, 122–123, 126–127, 131–133, 135–139, 151, 161, 169, 183, 187, 195, 205, 207, 210 (left), 213–215, 220, 222–223, 231, 271, 273–274, 282 – © **RMN - F. Raux** : 43, 47, 56, 58, 85, 95, 121, 145.

CONTENTS

THE MANY FACES OF CHANTILLY

THE LE BOUTEILLER DE SENLIS

END OF TENTH CENTURY
The Chantilly domain belongs to Rothold, lord of Senlis and Ermenonville.

1358
The château of the Le Bouteiller de Senlis is plundered during the Peasants' Revolt.

THE ORGEMONTS

1386
Pierre d'Orgemont buys Chantilly from the heirs of the Le Bouteillers and rebuilds the Grand Château. The domain will never again be sold.

THE MONTMORENCYS

1484
Pierre III d'Orgemont leaves Chantilly to his nephew, Guillaume de Montmorency.

1522
Guillaume de Montmorency passes Chantilly to his son, Anne.

1528–1530
Anne de Montmorency (1493–1567) entrusts the rebuilding of the medieval Grand Château to Pierre Chambiges (d. 1544).

1540
The Emperor Charles V (1500–1558) goes to Chantilly.

1558
The *connétable* (military commander-in-chief) Anne de Montmorency entrusts to Jean Bullant (1515–1578) the construction of the Petit Château on an island to the south of the Grand Château.

1567
Anne de Montmorency dies at the battle of Saint-Denis, aged seventy-three.

1632
Grandson of Anne, the *connétable* Henri II de Montmorency (born 1595) is beheaded at Toulouse for his rebellion against Richelieu. Chantilly is confiscated by Louis XIII (1601–1643).

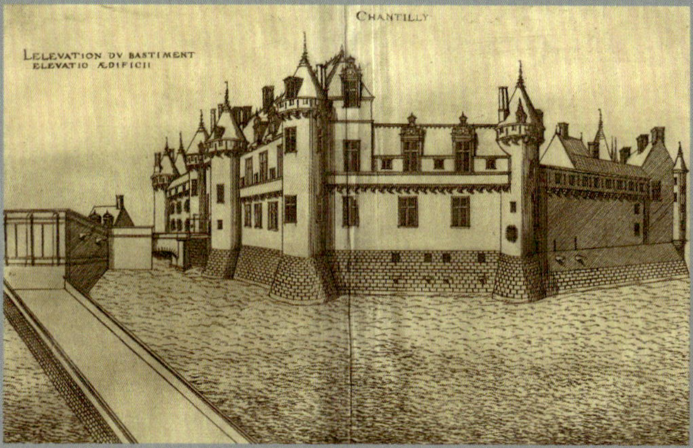

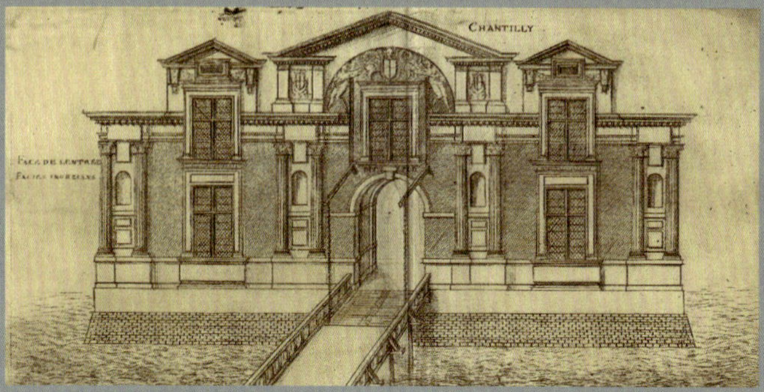

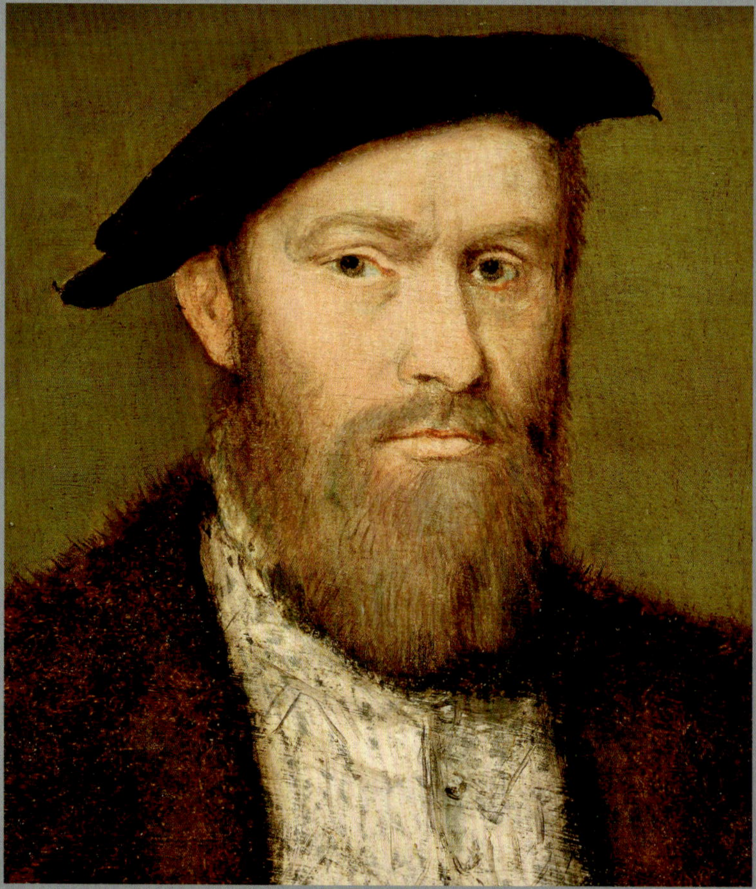

ABOVE Chantilly in the 16th century, etchings by Androuet du Cerceau, 1579. Musée Condé, Chantilly.
RIGHT Anne de Montmorency, by Corneille de Lyon (detail, see p. 134).

THE CONDÉS

1643
Death of Louis XIII.
Louis II de Bourbon, prince of Condé, known as the Great Condé (1621–1686), saves France from invasion by the Spanish. The regent, Anne of Austria, returns Chantilly to his mother, Charlotte Marguerite de Montmorency (1594–1650), sister of Henri II de Montmorency.

1648
The Fronde (civil war).
The Great Condé, who had supported the young king Louis XIV (1638–1715), rebels against the rise of absolutism.

1654
The Great Condé puts himself in the service of Spain and fights against France. He is condemned to death and his property confiscated.

1659
The Treaty of the Pyrenees means that Chantilly is returned to the Great Condé, and he retires there, far from the court.

1662
The Great Condé entrusts the creation of the gardens at Chantilly to André Le Nôtre (1613–1700).

1684
The Great Condé commissions the painter Sauveur Le Conte to decorate the Galerie des Actions de M. le Prince or the Gallery of Battles (p. 182–85).

1686
The Great Condé is succeeded by his son, Henry Jules (1643–1709).

1687
Jules Hardouin-Mansart (1646–1708) reconstructs the Grand Château.

1718
Great-grandson of the Great Condé, Louis Henri de Bourbon-Condé (1692–1740), duc de Bourbon, has the great apartments of the Petit Château decorated under the direction of the architect Jean Aubert (1680–1741).

1719–1735
Construction of the Grandes Écuries (Large Stables) by Jean Aubert.

1735
Christophe Huet paints *The Little Singerie* for the duc de Bourbon (p. 207).

1737
Christophe Huet paints *The Large Singerie* for the duc de Bourbon (p. 206).

1740
On the death of Louis Henri, his younger son, Louis Joseph de Bourbon-Condé (1736–1818), assumes the title of prince of Condé.

1769
Construction of the château of Enghien by the architect Jean-François Leroy (1729–1791).

1775
Construction of the Hameau by the architect Jean-François Leroy: his inspiration is the Hameau of Marie-Antoinette at Trianon (1783).

JULY 1789
July 14, the taking of the Bastille.
The princes of Condé leave the country.

1793
The château de Chantilly is turned into a prison.

1799
Demolition of the Grand Château.

1804
Louis Antoine de Bourbon-Condé (born 1772), son of Louis Henri Joseph and the last duke of Enghien, is executed in the moat of the Château de Vincennes.

1814
The prince of Condé, Louis Joseph, and his son, Louis Henri Joseph (1756–1830), duc de Bourbon, return to Chantilly.

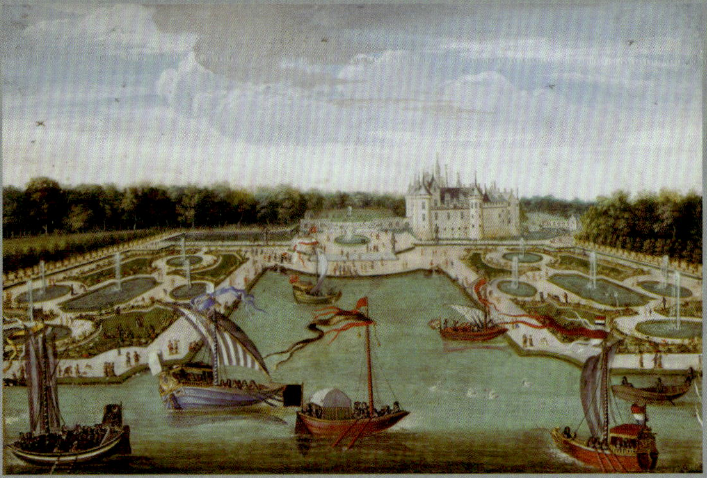

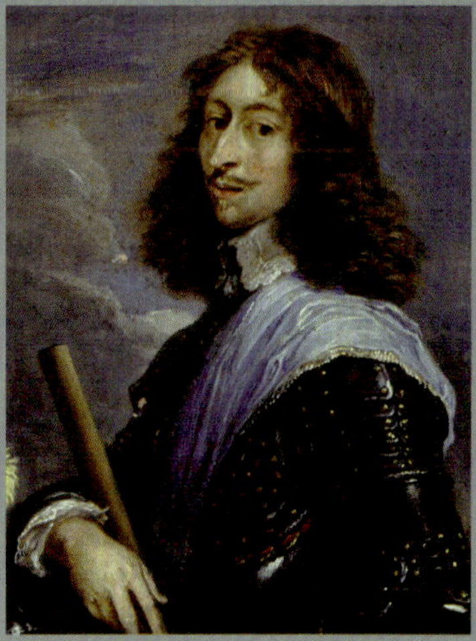

LEFT, TOP Chantilly in the late 17th century (French school, 17th century).
LEFT, BOTTOM *The Grand Château and the Petit Château as Seen from the Pool*, by Adam Perelle (1638–1695).
RIGHT *The Great Condé*, by David Teniers the Younger (detail, see p. 147).
BELOW The château de Chantilly in the 18th century, by Jean-Baptiste Lallemand (1716–1803). Gouache. Musée Condé, Chantilly.

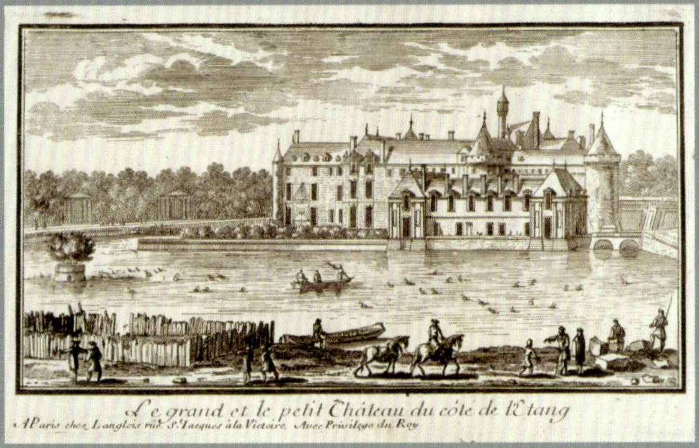

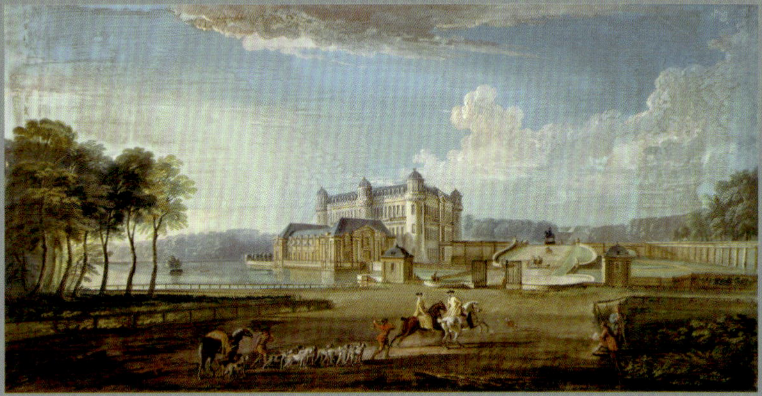

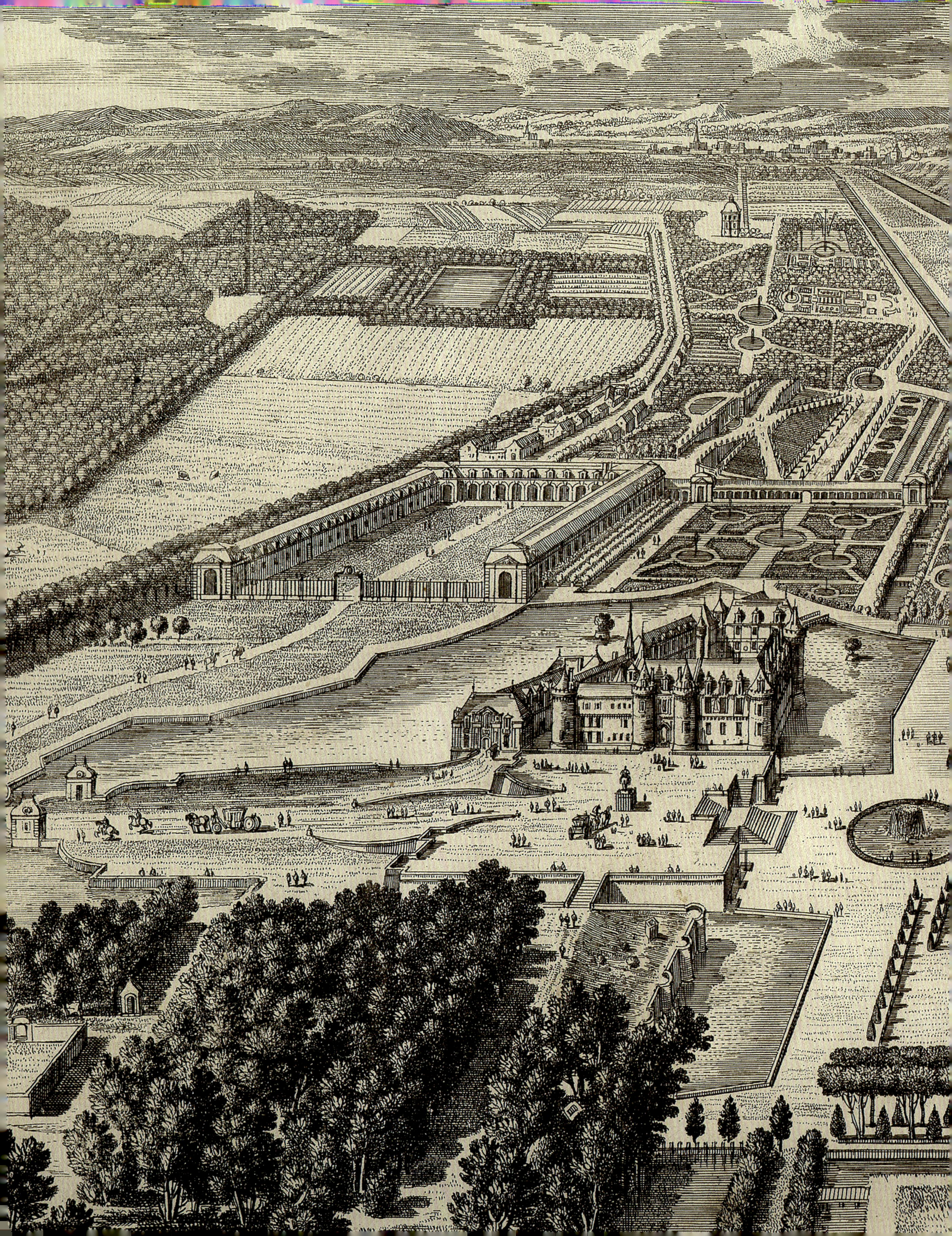

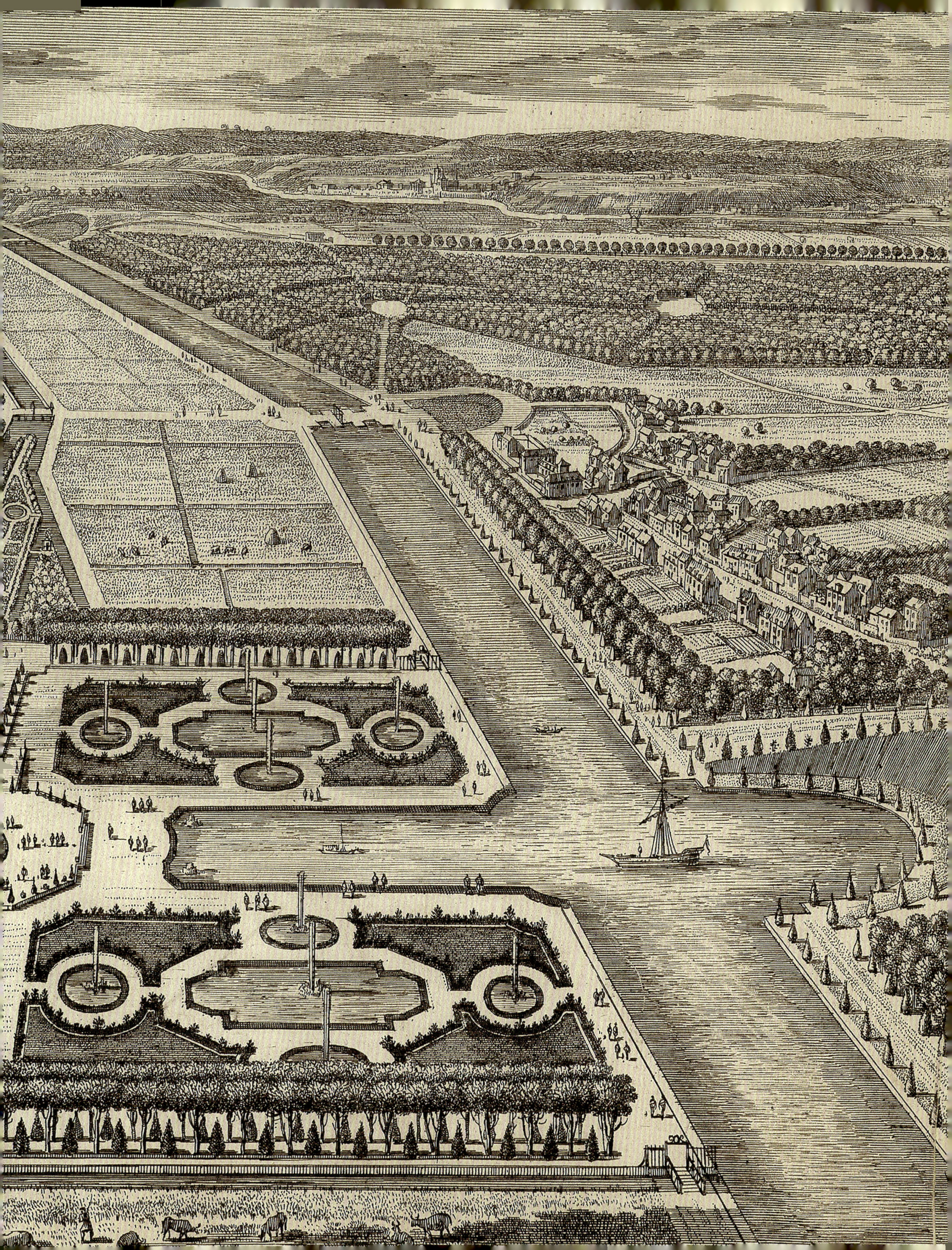

THE MANY FACES OF CHANTILLY

THE DUC D'AUMALE

1830
The duc de Bourbon leaves Chantilly and all his property to his great-nephew and godson, then aged eight, Henri d'Orléans, duc d'Aumale (1822–1897), son of King Louis-Philippe.

1843
The tribe of Abd el-Kader is taken by the duc d'Aumale in Algeria.

1844
The duc d'Aumale marries his first cousin, Maria Carolina de Bourbon-Sicily (1822–1869). He commissions the Romantic painter Eugène Lami to decorate his personal apartments and those of his wife, and buys portraits by Largillierre (p. 176–81) and Duplessis (p. 219–21) to decorate the salons.

1847
The duc d'Aumale is appointed governor general of Algeria.

1848
After the deposition of Louis-Philippe, the duc d'Aumale goes into exile in England for twenty-three years.

1854
The duc d'Aumale buys the collection of his uncle and father-in-law Leopold, prince of Salerno, which constitutes more than half of the Italian paintings at Chantilly: Raphael (p. 70), Carracci (p. 96), Guido Reni (p. 94), Salvator Rosa (p. 100, 105), Il Guercino (p. 99), as well as some beautiful antiques. He acquires *The Massacre of the Innocents* by Nicolas Poussin (p. 158) at public sale.

1856
The duc d'Aumale acquires the *Très Riches Heures du duc de Berry* in Genoa from a convent for young girls.

1861
The duc d'Aumale buys the collection of drawings of Frédéric Reiset (1815–1891), curator of drawings at the Musée du Louvre (Raphael, Dürer, Poussin, Lorrain).

1866
The duc d'Aumale inherits from his mother, Queen Maria-Amelia, the portrait of Gaston d'Orléans by Van Dyck. He loses his son Louis d'Orléans, prince of Condé, aged twenty-one.

1868
The duc d'Aumale buys the collection of the Marquis Maison: Watteau (p. 196), Greuze (p. 228), and the Orientalists Decamps (p. 262 and 264) and Marilhat (p. 266).

1869
The duc d'Aumale buys the *The Madonna of the House of Orléans* at the Delessert sale in Paris. Death of the duchess d'Aumale.

1871
The duc d'Aumale returns to France and is admitted to the Académie Française.

1872
The duc d'Aumale loses the second and last survivor of his seven sons, François d'Orléans, duc of Guise (born 1854).

1875
The duc d'Aumale entrusts the reconstruction of the Grand Château to the architect Honoré Daumet (1826–1911) in order to house his collections.

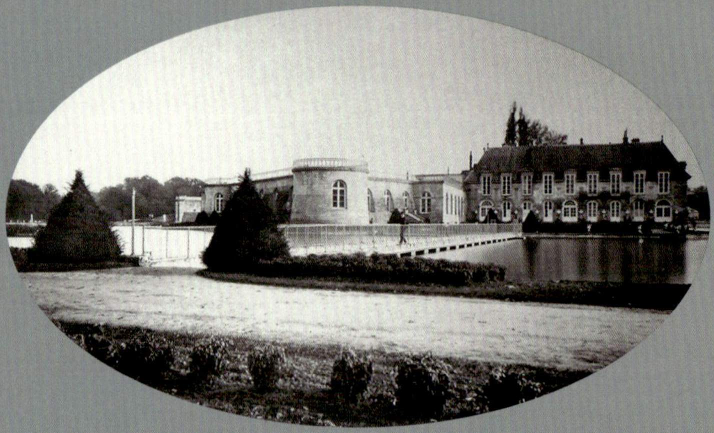

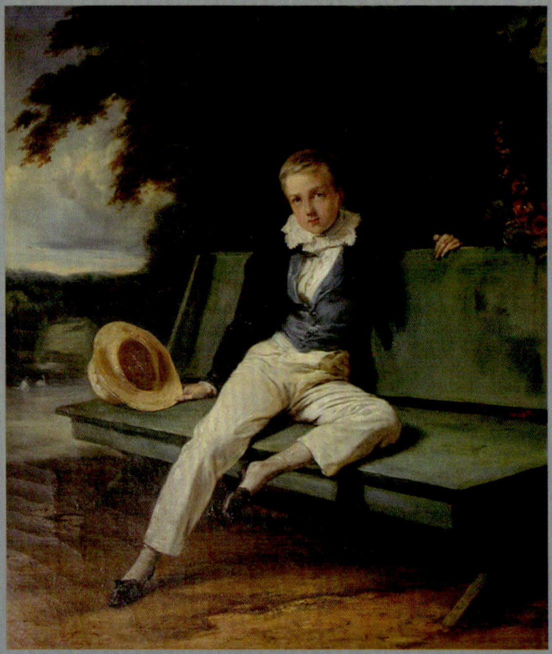

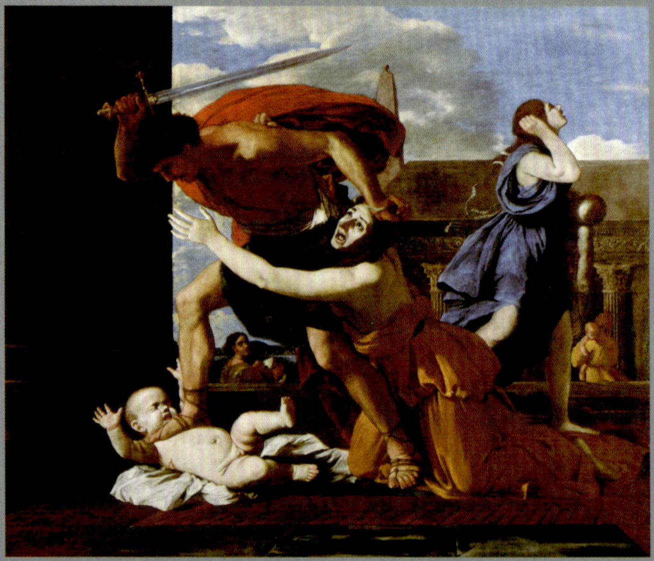

PRECEDING PAGES The château de Chantilly and its grounds in the late 17th century, by Adam Perelle.
ABOVE The Petit Château and the Volière Bridge in 1872. Photograph by Claudius Couton. Musée Condé, Chantilly.
RIGHT *The duc d'Aumale, Aged Nine*, by Joseph-Nicolas Robert-Fleury, 1831. Oil on canvas. Musée Condé, Chantilly.
FAR RIGHT Nicolas Poussin, *The Massacre of the Innocents*, bought by the duke in 1854 (see pp. 158–159).

1876

The duc d'Aumale buys in England, from the duke of Sutherland at Stafford House, the collection of French historical portraits gathered by Alexandre Lenoir (1761–1839), the first curator of museums of the Monuments Français, including paintings by Clouet (p. 126–33) and Corneille de Lyon (p. 134–35), the portrait of Molière by Mignard (p. 166), those of Mother Arnauld by Philippe de Champaigne (p. 170), of Marie-Antoinette Dauphine (p. 216) and of Mme de Pompadour (p. 216–18) by Drouais.

1879

The duc d'Aumale buys the collection of forty paintings by Frédéric Reiset, curator of paintings at the Musée du Louvre: Maso di Banco (p. 36), Fra Angelico (p. 38), Quarton (p. 122), Piero di Cosimo (p. 50), Sassetta (p. 44), Poussin (p. 156–65), Gérard (p. 232), Ingres (p. 240 and 246).

1881

The duc d'Aumale buys from Lord Carlisle in England three hundred and eleven portraits by Clouet and his school, originally in the collection of Queen Catherine de' Medici.

1884

The duc d'Aumale wills Chantilly and its collections to the Institut de France with the aim of opening the Musée Condé to the public, on condition that its collections will never be loaned and their presentation never modified.

1885

The duc d'Aumale buys Raphael's *Three Graces* (p. 66).

1886

The duc d'Aumale is affected by the laws of exile for a second time. He gives Chantilly and its collections to the Institut de France, as a life interest.

1889

The duc d'Aumale returns to France and completes the refurbishment of Chantilly.

1890

The duc d'Aumale buys Corot's *Le Concert champêtre* (Rustic Concert) (p. 256).

1891

The duc d'Aumale buys forty illuminations by Jean Fouquet from the *Livre d'heures d'Étienne Chevalier*.

1892

The duc d'Aumale buys Filippino Lippi's *King Ahasuerus Choosing Esther* (p. 52), at the Leclanché sale.

1897

The duc d'Aumale dies in Sicily on May 7.

1898

The Musée Condé is opened to the public.

1939

Poncins-Biencourt Donation (painted sixteenth-century portraits by Clouet and Corneille de Lyon).

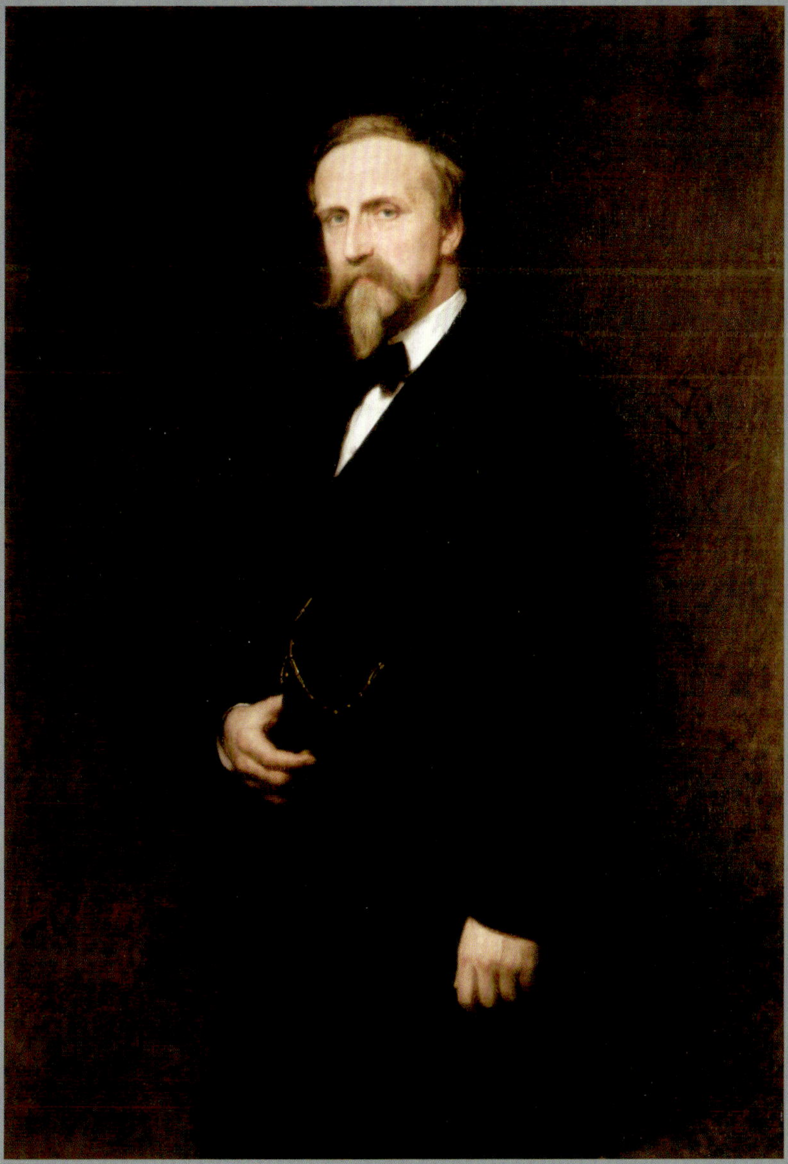

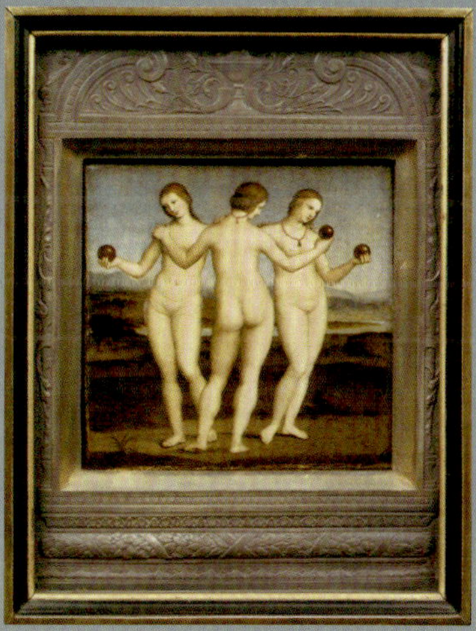

LEFT The duc d'Aumale during his exile at Twickenham in 1866, portrait by Charles François Jalabert (see p. 286).
RIGHT Raphael, *The Three Graces*, bought by the duke in 1885 (see p. 66).
BELOW The château de Chantilly today.

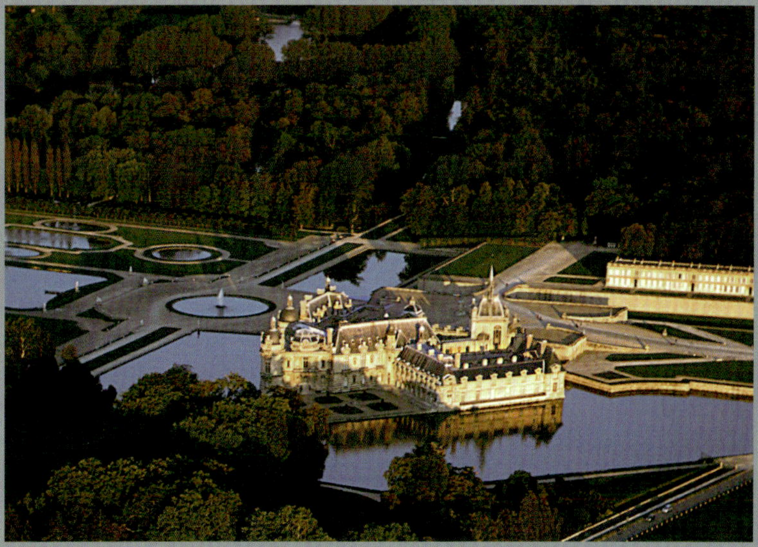

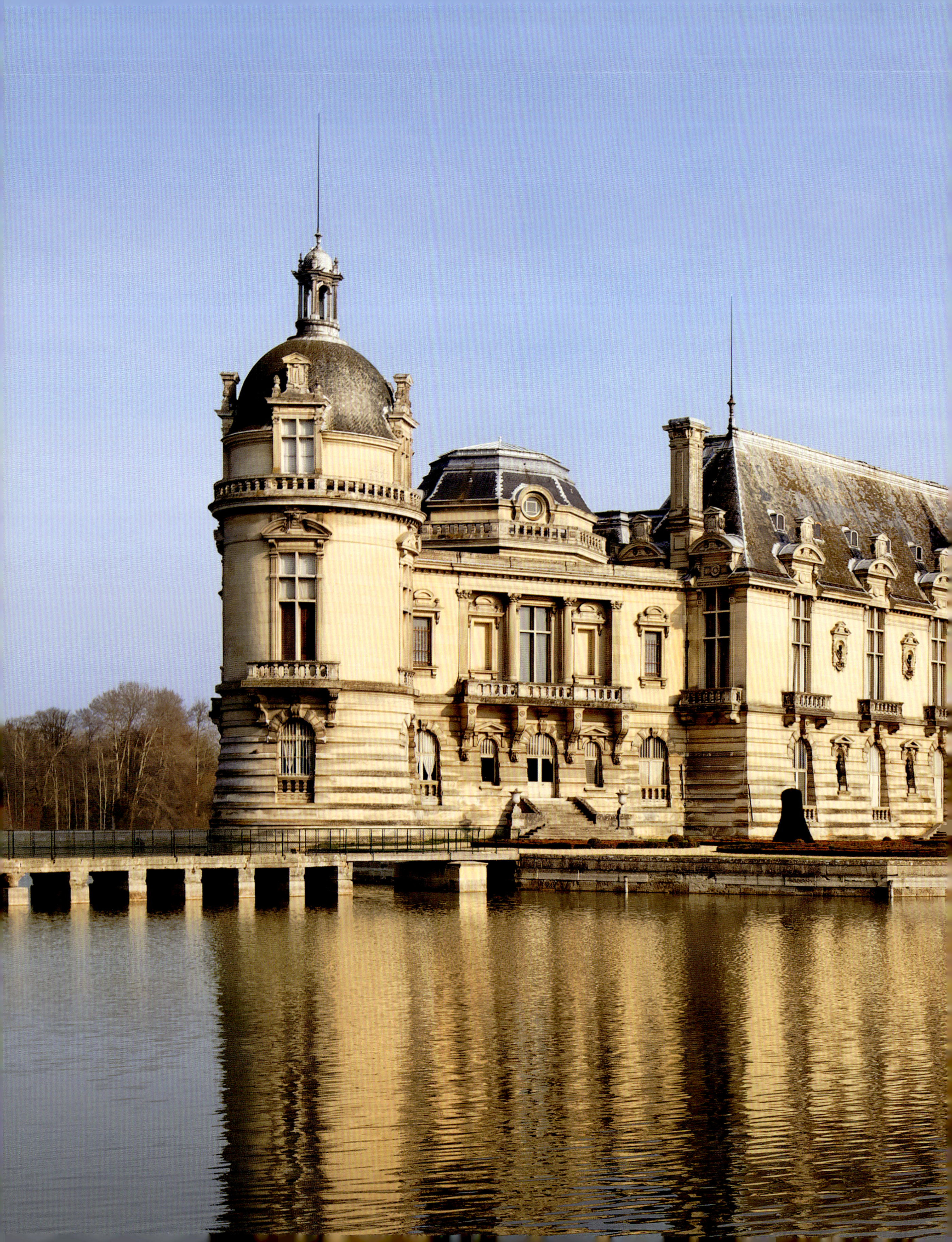

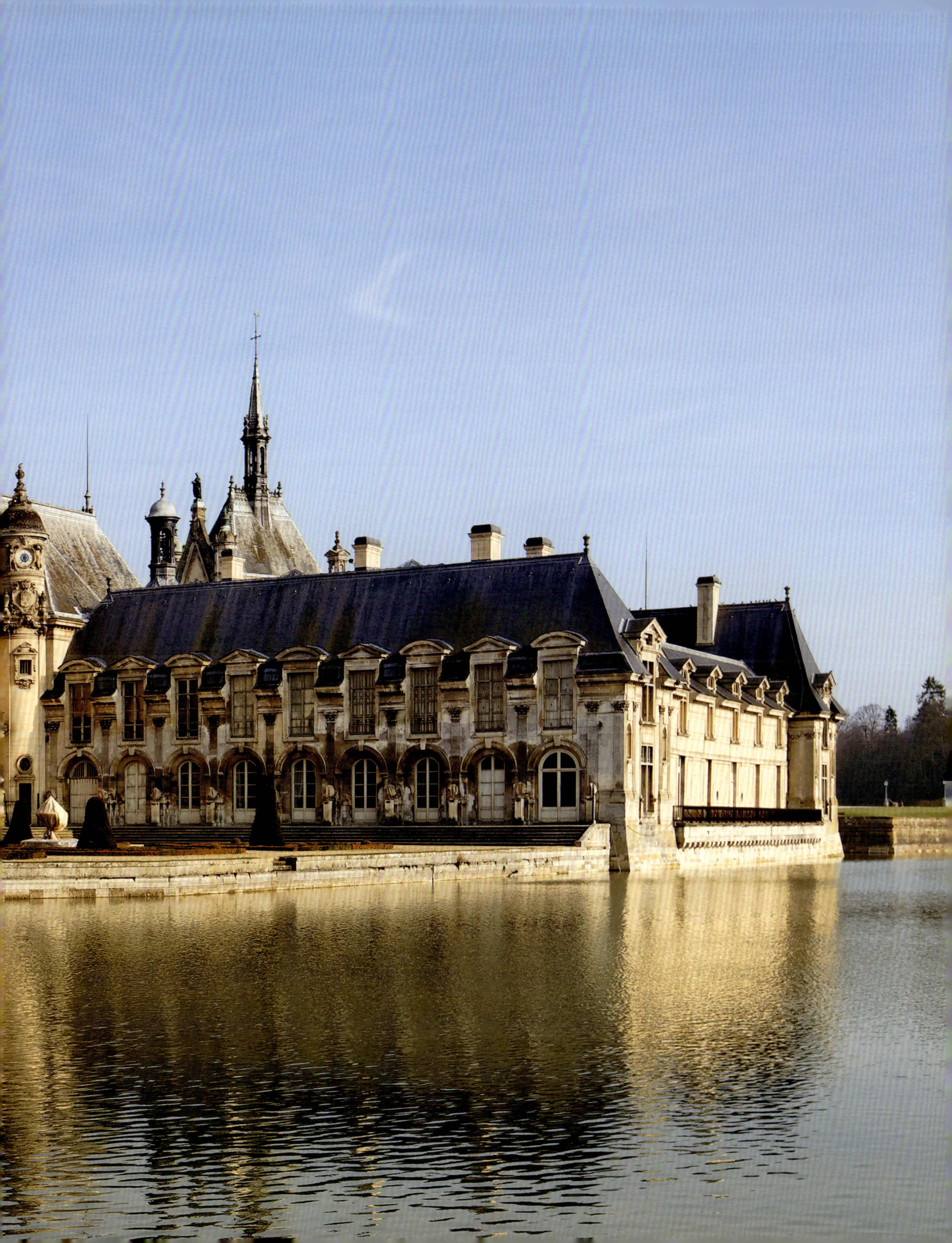

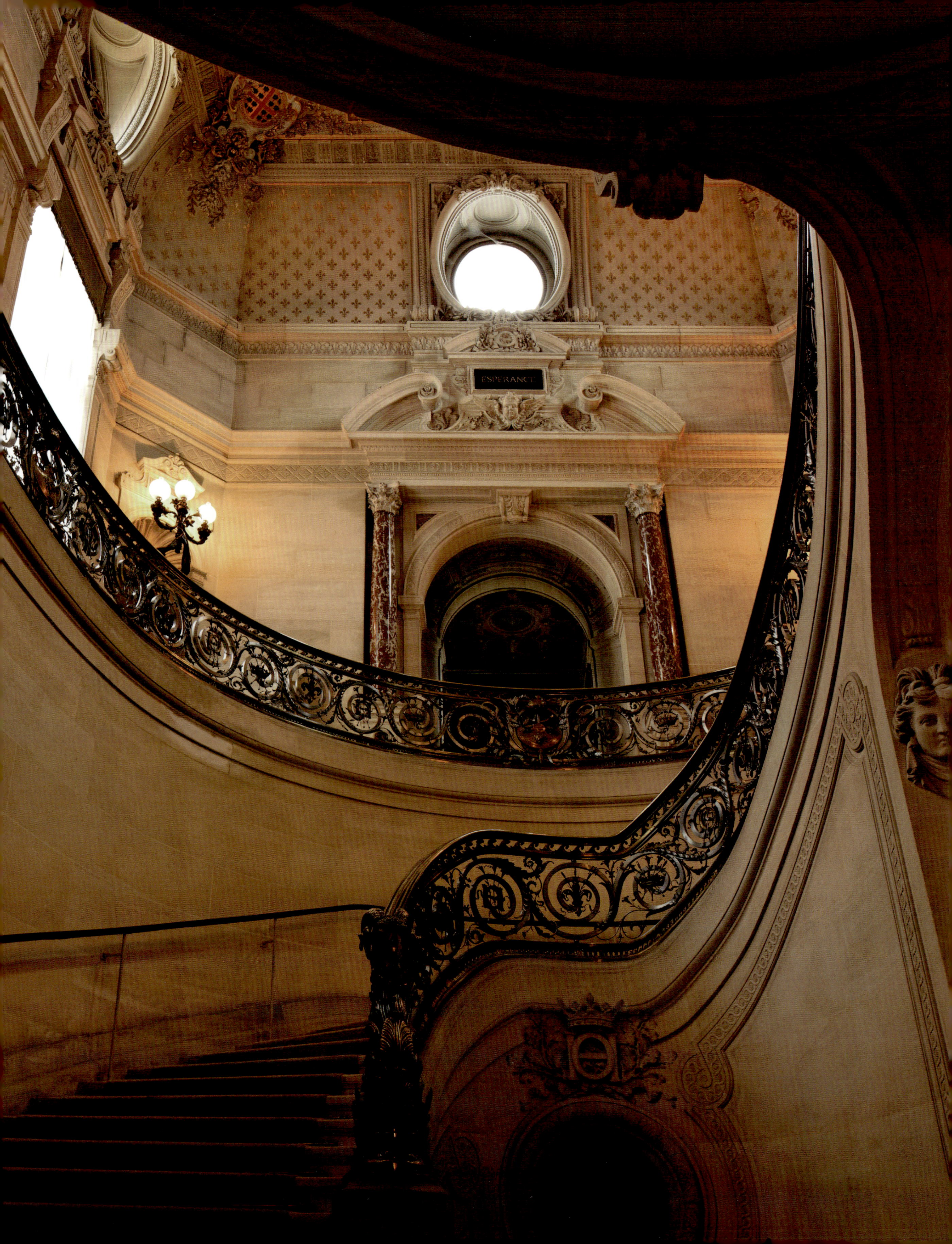
ESPERANCE

TO ARMS, TO ARTS

For Emmanuel Ducamp

"THE DAY BEFORE YESTERDAY I WENT TO THE BOURBON MUSEUM. I CAME OUT EXHAUSTED, BUT GREATLY PLEASED BY EVERYTHING I SAW."

The duc d'Aumale to his mother, Naples, November 8, 1843

Some collectors start with nothing. Their only asset is their desire for future conquest. Such was not the case with the duc d'Aumale, who was hardly a bargain hunter or "second-hand goods dealer" (as he cruelly described the notorious collector, Cardinal Mazarin). This son of King Louis-Philippe did not view collecting primarily as a question of personal choices—instead, collecting art was an ancestral practice that dated back, unbroken, to the early seventeenth century. Nothing seem more natural to him, more part of a deep-seated family tradition, than to pursue that practice by surrounding himself with artworks, by supporting painters, and by displaying their treasures. Ever aware of history, the duc d'Aumale also acknowledged the catastrophes that accompanied it: as a member of the house of Orléans—the younger branch of France's ruling Bourbon family—his forebears had known both fame and shame in the preceding two hundred years. Indeed, it was impossible to overlook his ancestors' uneven record when it came to art versus politics. Whereas they had long been frustrated in their hopes of reigning, having been regularly thwarted by the Bourbons since 1692, they had few rivals among royal princes when it came to the realm of art. This domain was their uncontested prerogative, a realm where they could excel without restraint (or almost). The collection of Philippe d'Orléans, Regent of France from 1715 to 1723 (who could turn his nose up at the rest of Europe in those days), still symbolizes the power of art versus the power of arms, of sovereign taste versus legitimate birth. The product of several generations of effort, the family collection abounded in the greatest old master paintings in Europe when Philippe d'Orléans' grandson, Philippe-Égalité, decided to guillotine the collection in the revolutionary days of 1791 by putting several hundred of them up for sale, including works by Raphael, Rubens, and Poussin (notably the latter's *Seven Sacraments*, once owned by seventeenth-century collector Paul Fréart de Chantelou, and a popular subject of engravings in the eighteenth century). Philippe-Égalité supported the beheading of his Bourbon cousin, King Louis XVI, but lost his own head shortly thereafter. This double loss largely governed the behavior of the house of Orléans in the nineteenth century: that is to say, the duc d'Aumale's unique collection can best be understood as a way of addressing the past, the present, and the future of his own family. Even before the duke's collection became a museum, history was the inner god that governed it.

PAGES 12–13
The château's multiple facets: on the left is the section built by the duc d'Aumale, on the right is the Renaissance wing built by the Montmorency family.
FACING PAGE
A wrought-iron handrail by the Moreau brothers adorns the main staircase at Chantilly, whose design is allegedly based on the one in the Palais-Royal.

Fortunes to restore

Among the ghosts haunting the duc d'Aumale (and still present for today's visitors to Chantilly), special mention should be made of his great-great grandfather, the Regent (1674–1723). The duke made a point of re-establishing a long-extinguished claim by buying several Italian paintings that once belonged to his ancestor, snapping them up under the nose of the Louvre during the Second Empire period (1852–70). He thereby came to own key works such as Domenichino's *Stoning of Saint Stephen* (p. 93) and Raphael's *Madonna of the House of Orléans* (p. 68), purchased in 1860 and 1869, respectively. The Regent was the son of Louis XIV's brother, simply known as "Monsieur" (1640–1701), and he inherited his father's exuberantly loose morals and enthusiasm for "rarities." Monsieur had been another great patron of the arts who reigned from his château in Saint Cloud, where he summoned painters such as Pierre Mignard and Antoine Coypel, who were not in favor with Louis XIV. Above all, Monsieur had numerous small rooms, called "cabinets," where he displayed exceptional paintings and objects of all kinds (including early pieces of chinoiserie). The Regent, meanwhile, occupied the Palais Royal in Paris where he concentrated and augmented his father's collection, orchestrating portraits with other works of pure delectation (a term that best suits the Regent's penchant for sensual delights and racy language). Coypel considered the Regent to be the ideal art lover, because more receptive to the beauties than to the defects of paintings that "set him dreaming pleasant dreams." The well-kept treasures accumulated by the Orléans family from the

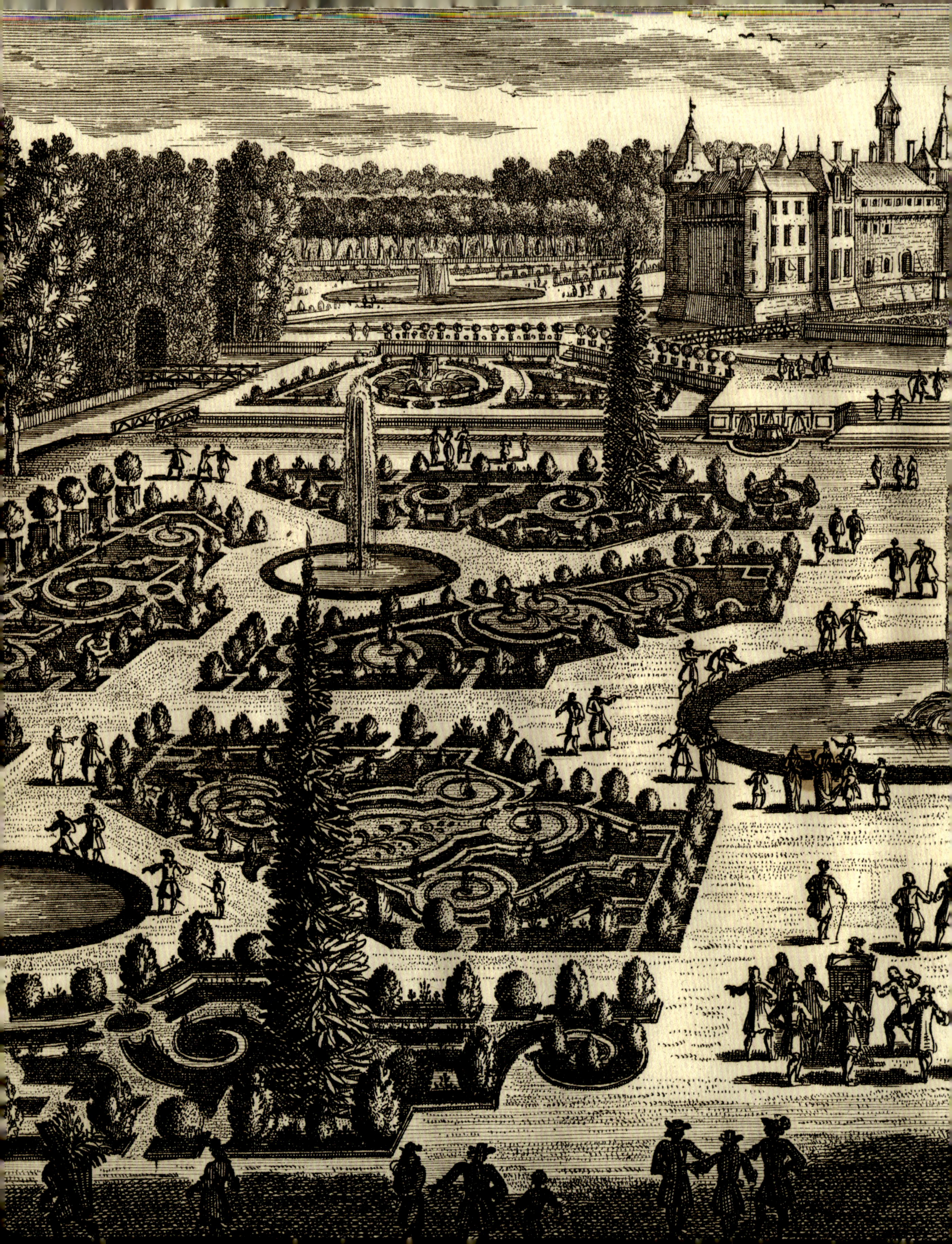

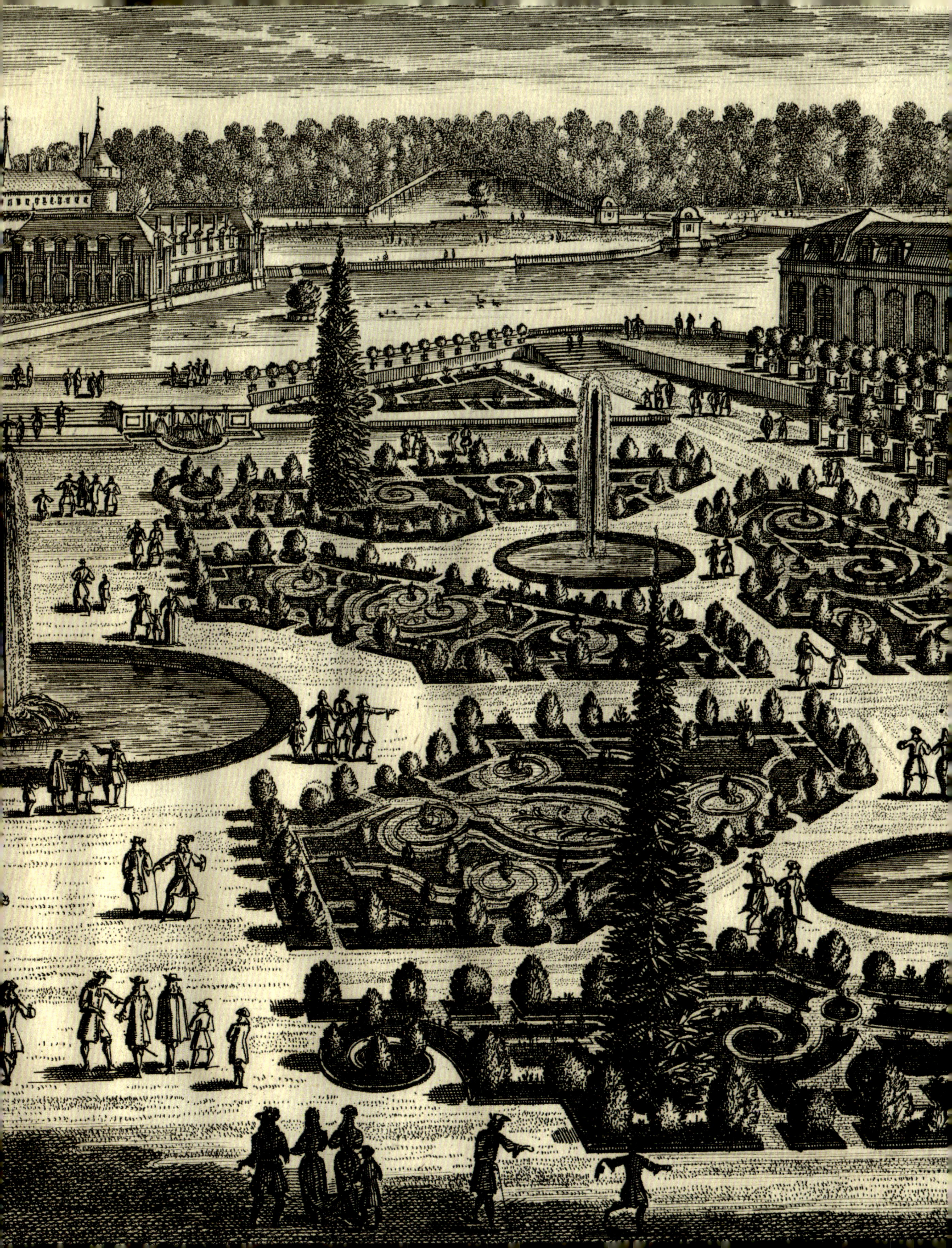

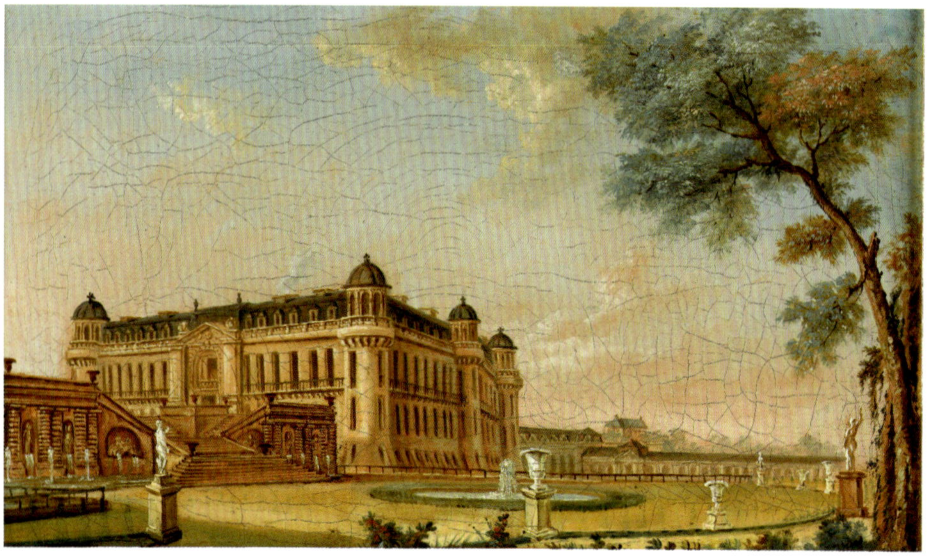

"YOU HAVE LONG BEEN AWARE, SIR, OF MY SORROW THAT THE PALAIS ROYAL NO LONGER HOSTS THE HANDSOME PAINTINGS THAT ONCE ADORNED IT, AND OF MY INTENTION TO RECTIFY THIS LOSS BY CONSTITUTING A NEW ART GALLERY, TO THE BEST OF MY ABILITIES."

Louis-Philippe to the artist François Gérard

Regent to Philippe-Égalité inspired admiration and covetousness from all refined art lovers. Once the collection was dispersed at auction in 1791, most of it crossed the channel to England, where the duc d'Aumale later recovered the wonderful remnants mentioned above.

The dispersal of the collection obviously left a big void at the Palais Royal. Filling this void became a family mission: it was the duc d'Aumale's father, Louis-Philippe (1773–1850), who began reconstituting the Orléans collection once he returned to France, prior to mounting the French throne. As the great-grandson of Louis XIV on his mother's side, Louis-Philippe was imbued with Enlightenment ideals—indeed, early revolutionary aspirations—by his father, Philippe-Égalité. He joined the radical Jacobin club at the age of seventeen, and fought under the republican flag at Jemmapes and Valmy in 1792. (Louis-Philippe later commissioned Horace Vernet to paint the battle of Valmy, a picture that obviously includes the dashing young officer.) A firm believer in constitutional monarchy, Louis-Philippe ultimately left France once revolutionary Terror set in. For twenty-five years he lived a nomadic, exile's life, as a cosmopolitan prince who already spoke four languages thanks to the encouragement of his "spiritual mother," Madame de Genlis. Louis-Philippe's sons would inherit his sense of wanderlust and fascination with exoticism.

A palace in need of refurbishment

Louis-Philippe's travels inoculated him against all forms of political absolutism. The English constitution served as an instructive counter-example to France, as did his years spent in Sicily, of which he became prince in 1809 upon marrying Maria Amelia de Bourbon (Marie-Antoinette's niece through her mother). Louis-Philippe thereby became the son-in-law of King Ferdinand IV of the Two Sicilies (a grand title for a minor monarch, sometimes simply known as the king of Naples), whose somewhat archaic government he observed at close hand. (Ferdinand was nicknamed "Nasone" for his big nose, which was matched by his short-sightedness.) Of Ferdinand's numerous off-spring, it is worth noting that his fifteenth child, Leopold de Bourbon-Sicily, prince of Salerno, was the father of Maria Carolina, who later married the duc d'Aumale. On October 13, 1815, having regained a throne that Napoleon had briefly awarded to his own brother-in-law, Joachim Murat, Ferdinand had the usurper executed by firing squad; at the same time he appropriated a few remnants of Murat's collection, no less than Gérard's *Three Ages of Man* (p. 233) and Ingres' early version of *Paolo and Francesca* (p. 242). In an ironic twist, the duc d'Aumale acquired these two paintings forty years later; the kiss of Dante's two famous lovers, Paolo and Francesca, depicted with subtle eroticism by Ingres, seems a long way from the Napoleonic upheavals that led to the Murat's own downfall in Naples in 1814.

When Napoleon first surrendered, Louis-Philippe hastened back to Paris, hoping to supplant a gouty Louis XVIII, who was already embroiled in the contradictions of restoring the Bourbons to the French throne. But Napoleon's surprising march back to power sent Louis XVIII scrambling to Ghent, while Louis-Philippe retreated to London. Once Napoleon was permanently defeated at Waterloo, Louis XVIII reclaimed the French crown again; Louis-Philippe decided to bide his time, not joining the hoards of returnees at a time when reactionary forces were sweeping France and Cossacks were camped along the Champs-Élysées—Louis-Philippe's liberal convictions were stronger than his dynastic loyalty. It was not until April 1817 that he left London with his large family, which already numbered two sons and three daughters. At that time, his main goal was to recover the estates, property, and prerogatives of the house of Orléans, which were being meanly restricted by Louis XVIII. Above all, Louis-Philippe reclaimed

PAGES 16–17

The formal gardens by the orangery, château de Chantilly. Print by Adam Pérelle. 17th century. Musée Condé, Chantilly.

FACING PAGE

View of the château de Chantilly, circa 1775–85. Artist unknown. Oil on canvas. Musée Condé, Chantilly.

BELOW

Cannon taken from Chantilly to Paris on August 9, 1789. Engraving by Pierre Gabriel Berthault, after Jean Louis Prieur the Younger. Musée Condé, Chantilly.

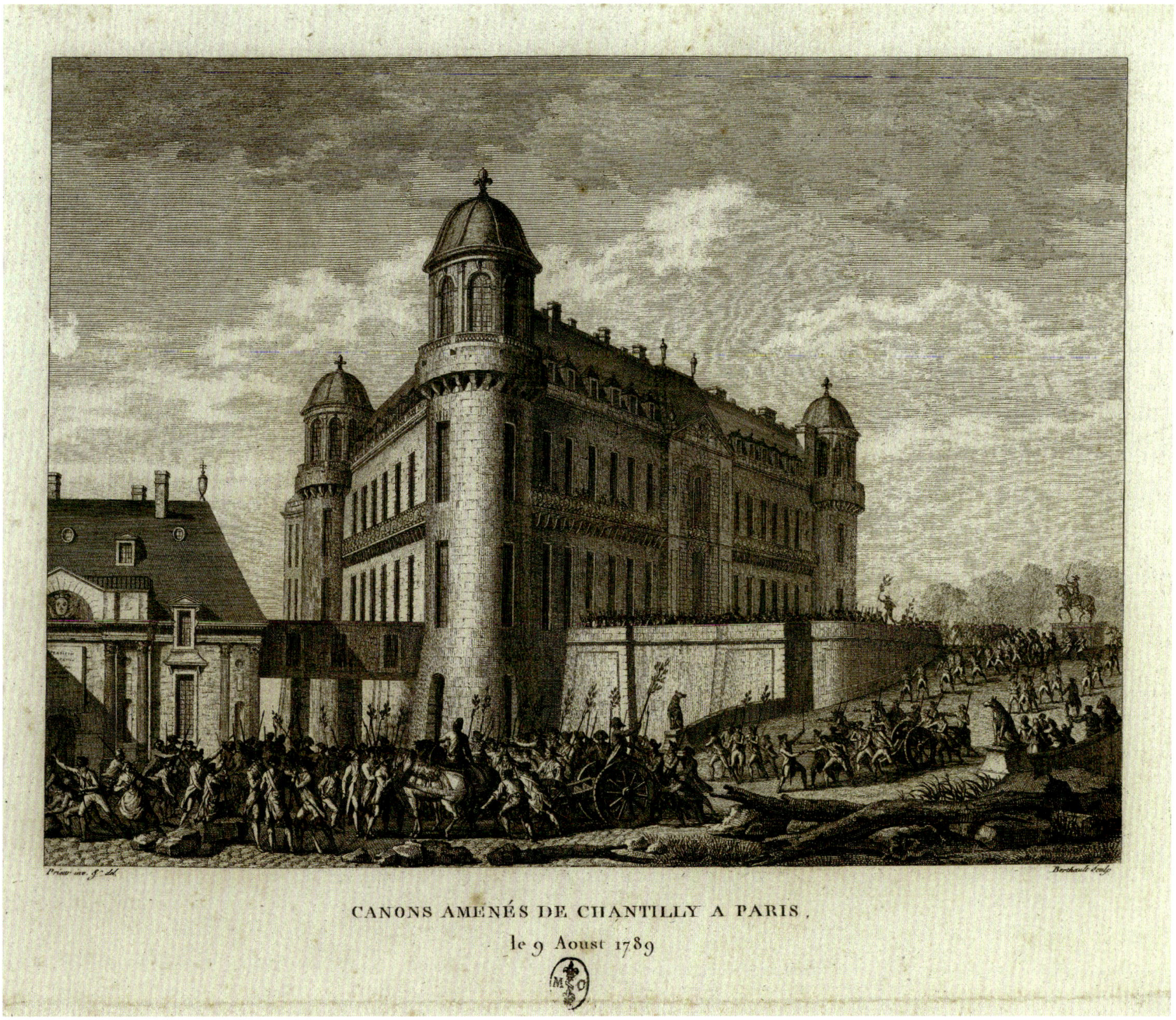

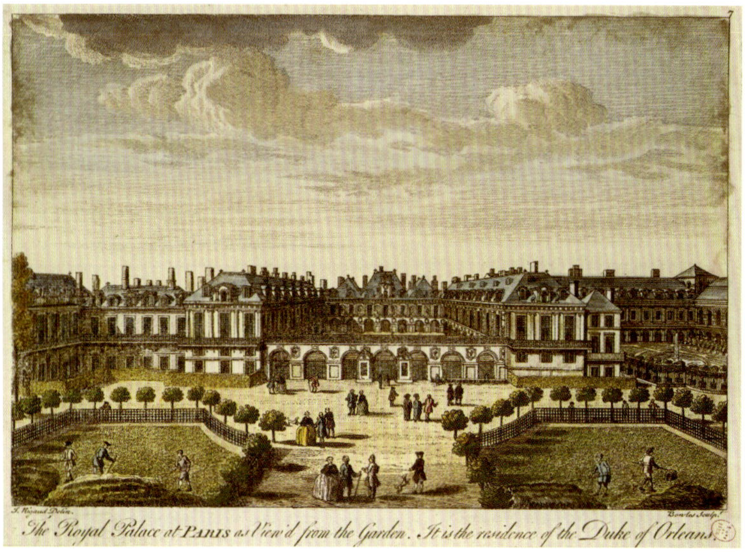

the highly symbolic Palais Royal in Paris, a palace that had fallen on hard times, having lost both its art collection and its glamour. The restoration of the Palais Royal thus competed with the restoration of the Bourbon monarchy, just as a child-bearing competition occurred between Maria Amelia and the duchesse de Berry, wife of the legitimate Bourbon heir to the throne. The future of the French throne hung in the balance. As long as the duchesse de Berry failed to produce a son, Maria Amelia could dream of some day seeing her eldest son, Ferdinand d'Orléans, mount the throne of France. Meanwhile, the Palais Royal was recovering both its original glitter and the aspirations of its regal name.

Up-and-coming France

While Maria Amelia and the duchesse de Barry engaged in a child-bearing contest, Louis-Philippe and the duc de Berry went head-to-head on another battlefield: contemporary art. A shrewd artist like the young Eugène Delacroix was able to profit from this situation, remaining on good terms with administrators of the Royal Museums without having to worry about Louis-Philippe's growing propensity for artists who showed what they thought of the restoration by nostalgically depicting national, republican, Napoleonic, and other subjects. A visit to the Salon of 1817 came as a revelation to the duc d'Orléans, who was not very familiar with contemporary art: he suddenly realized that he was not obliged to rebuild a collection of old masters identical to the one constituted by his forebears. He outlined his new strategy in a brilliant letter to the artist François Gérard (whose works would also be bought by his son, the duc d'Aumale). Although Gérard, an early proponent of David's neoclassicism, had already been appointed Painter to the King by Louis XVIII (and would be ennobled two years later), Louis-Philippe was addressing himself primarily to an advocate of the new school of painting:

> You have long been aware, Sir, of my sorrow that the Palais Royal no longer hosts the handsome paintings that once adorned it, and of my intention to rectify this loss by constituting a new art gallery, to the best of my abilities. The recent Salon show has convinced me that the French school of the nineteenth century can rival Italian art of the sixteenth. I therefore thought that a selection of paintings of our modern school might profitably replace the one we lost at the Palais Royal. The constitution of a gallery of such works would also be an encouragement to the arts.

His finances being at a low ebb, the thrifty Louis-Philippe was forced to turn to "up-and-coming" members of the French school. Year by year, the Palais Royal began filling up with art by flaming new artists. Works by Couder, Steuben, Blondel, and Granet hung alongside names that are more familiar today, such as Gérard, Gros, Girodet, Vernet, and, above all, Géricault, whose *Wounded Cuirassier* and *Charging Chasseur*, bagged by Louis-Philippe, were political and artistic icons of the emerging Romantic movement. Meanwhile, the works specifically commissioned by Louis-Philippe sought to evoke the "good old days" at the Palais Royal, going all the way back to the time when Cardinal Richelieu built it under Louis XIII. Delacroix, for example, was commissioned to paint *Richelieu Saying Mass* (destroyed during the fire of February 24, 1848), for which the Musée Condé still holds a precious preparatory drawing. Later, the duc d'Aumale received from his mother a painting she had commissioned from the young Delaroche, a *Descent from the Cross* (Musée Condé), a work in the Bolognese style that she placed in her private chapel. This commission, made in 1819, was perhaps related to the early death of Françoise, Maria Amelia's third daughter. The choice of the young Delaroche was probably suggested by Horace Vernet; although still unknown at the time, Delaroche had trained in Gros's studio and hence could not be suspected of Bourbon sympathies. In short, contemporary critics, notably writing in the liberal papers, were not mistaken when they described the Palais Royal art gallery as a "national museum."

A family of artists

Louis-Philippe's collection grew steadily, reaching nearly 450 items by 1824 and requiring a catalog. It was soon decided to reproduce part of the collection in engravings, and to open it to the public under certain conditions. This publicity enhanced the popularity of the collection among art lovers and patriots. Inevitably, the new gallery was designed to serve a dynasty seeking a chance to ascend the throne. For that matter, the collection of

ABOVE
Palais-Royal, the Paris residence of the duc d'Orléans, 18th century. Print after Jacques Rigaud (circa 1681–1754). Musée Carnavalet, Paris

FACING PAGE, TOP
At the Palais-Royal in 1830, the Chamber of Deputies presents Louis-Philippe, duc d'Orléans, with the Charter offering him the French throne, 1834. Oil on canvas by François Joseph Heim. Musée National du Château de Versailles.

FACING PAGE, BOTTOM
Nicolas Alexandre Barbier, *The Château de Chantilly as Seen from the Landscape Garden*, 1845. Oil on canvas. Musée Condé, Chantilly.

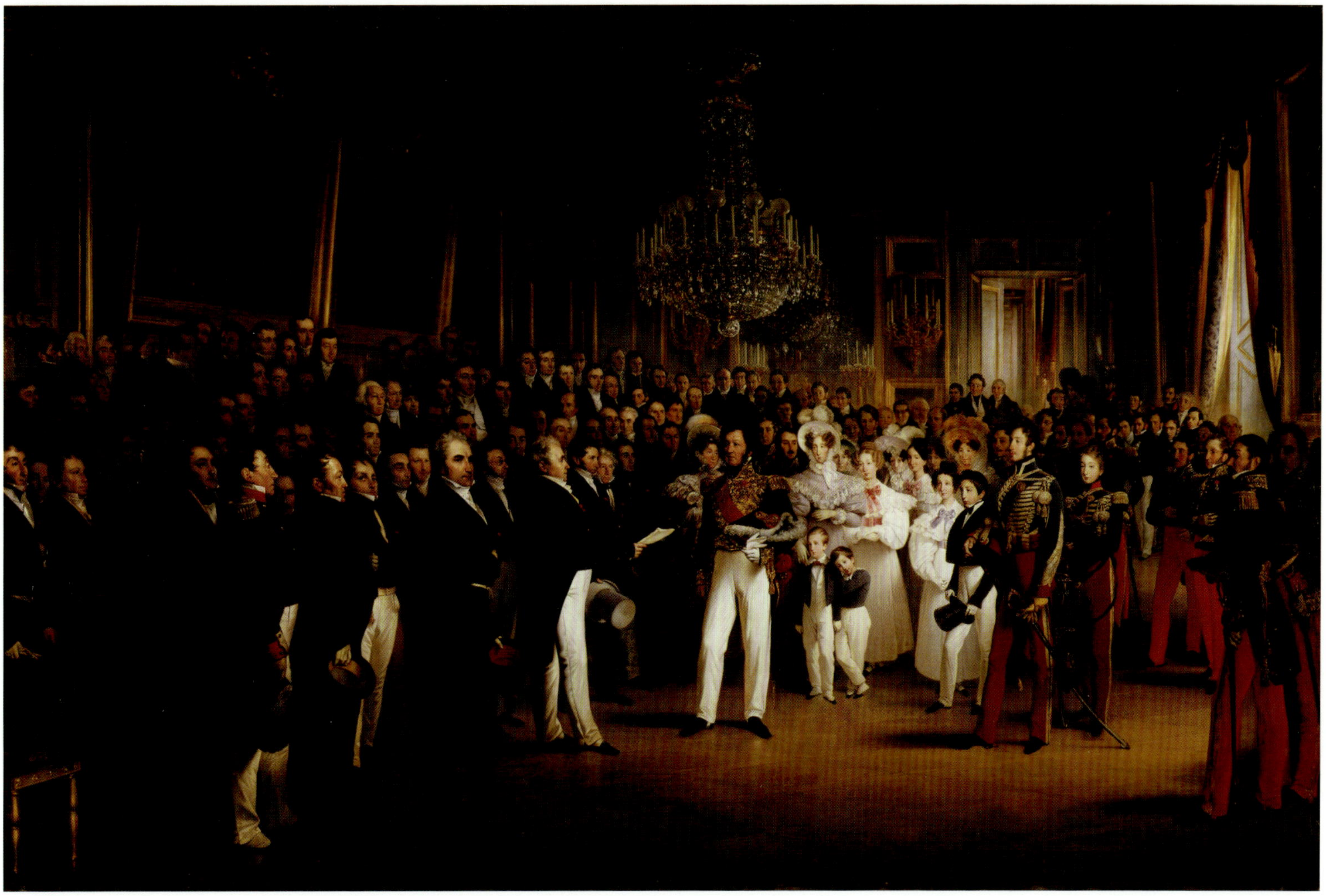

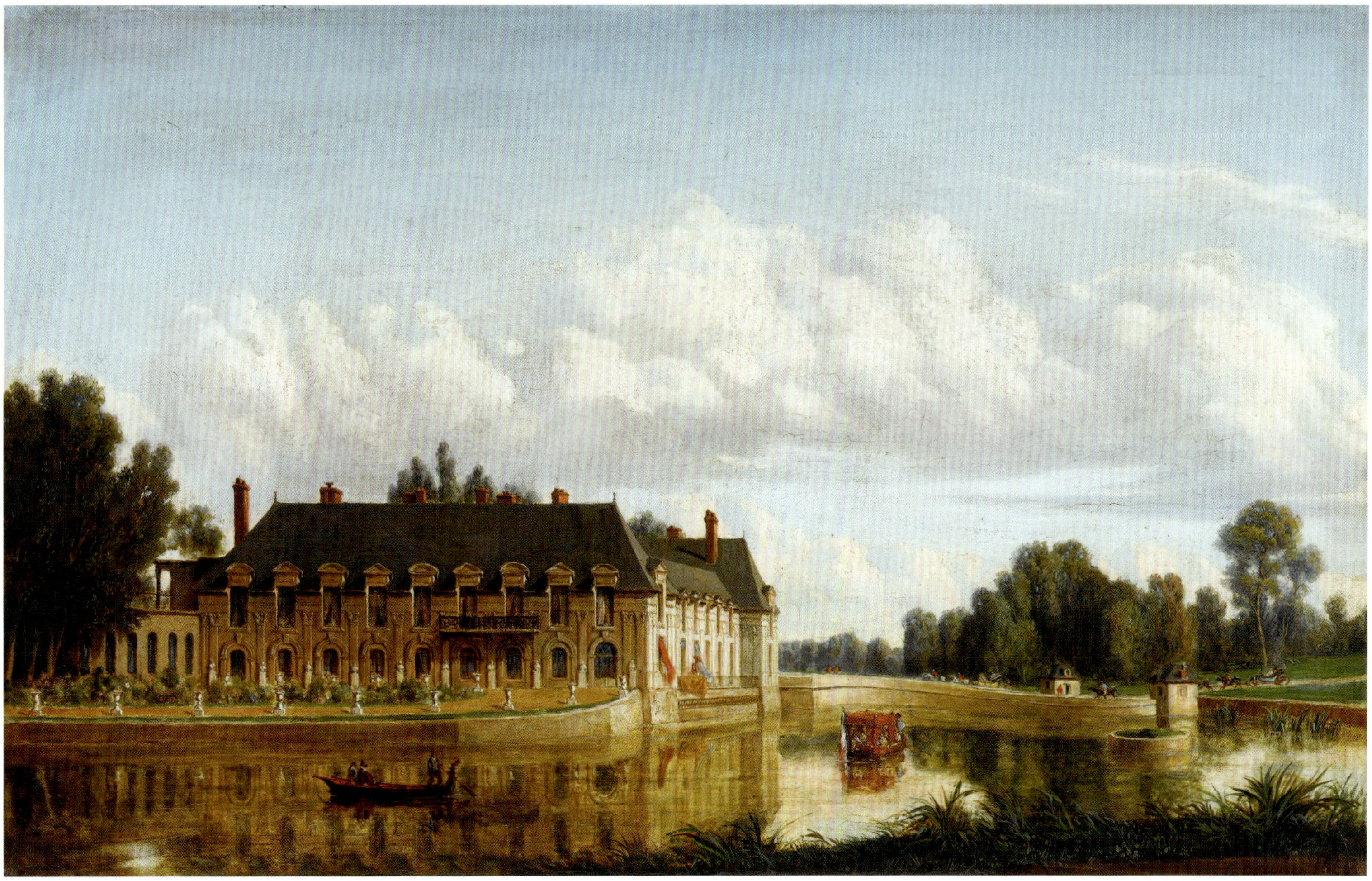

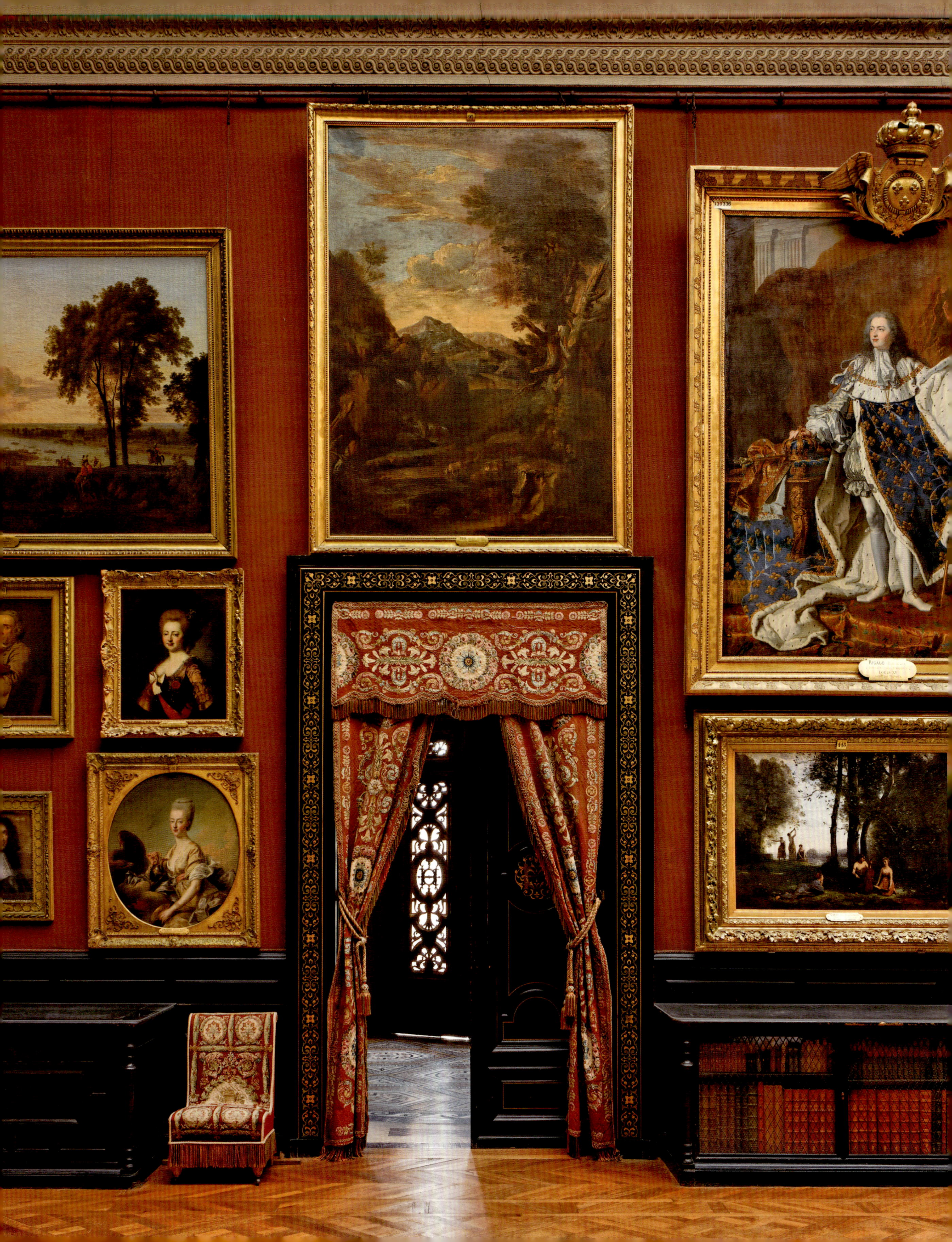

FACING PAGE
The gallery of paintings at Chantilly.
RIGHT
The duc d'Aumale (left) with his brother, the prince of Joinville, at Claremont in 1848. Photograph by Antoine Claudet. Musée Condé, Chantilly.
FAR RIGHT
The château as seen from the road, circa 1900. Unknown photographer. Musée Condé, Chantilly.

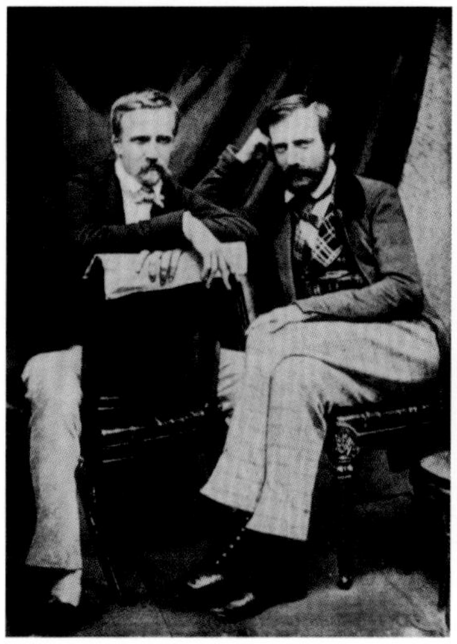

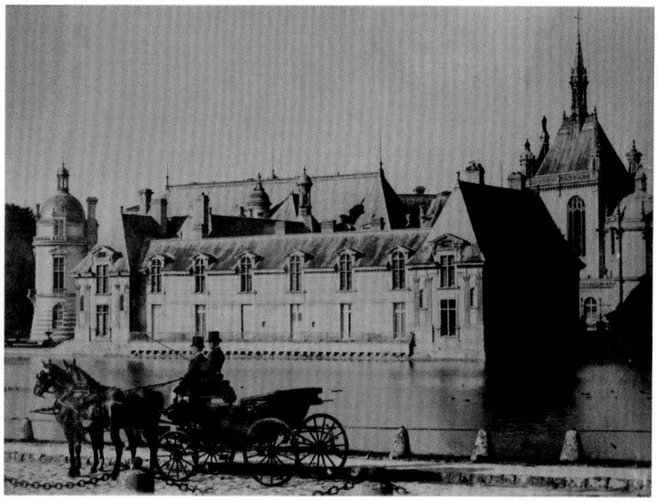

modern paintings was interspersed with three hundred portraits (including copies). This unusual museum still retained the features of a time-honored "reliquary" of "sacred treasures." But the "sanctity" it indirectly pointed to had evolved in the nineteenth century, being henceforth based on the significance of history. It was the era of men, the fates of the French monarchy, and the Orléans family that were being hallowed by these faded faces and outmoded fashions, whether Austrian, Sicilian, or English.

No better school could be imagined for the children of Louis-Philippe and Maria Amelia, whose numbers continued to grow during the Bourbon restoration. The Orléans children were sent to public schools, in a spirit of modernity as well as from political considerations. Whereas Ferdinand (duc d'Orléans), Louise, Marie, Louis (duc de Nemours), and Françoise were born abroad, Clementine, François (prince of Joinville), Charles (duc de Penthièvre), and Antoine (duc de Montpensier) were all born on French soil. All of Louis-Philippe's children—including the second-youngest son, Henri, the duc d'Aumale, born in the Palais Royal itself in 1822—received a basic education in art at an early age; most became outstanding collectors, but few became real artists apart from Marie, whose sculpting talents are just now being rediscovered. Marie's premature death in 1839, aged twenty-five, was a traumatic experience for the family, so it is not surprising that the duc d'Aumale piously installed vestiges of her all-too-brief career in Chantilly. Shortly after the Bourbon regime was toppled in 1830 (finally bringing Louis-Philippe to the head of an English-style constitutional monarchy), Marie began mingling with artists of her day, becoming an elegant standard bearer of Romantic sculpture alongside the likes of Duseigneur, Barye, Moine, and Henri de Triqueti (who later served the duc d'Aumale as a shrewd art scout).

Ferdinand, meanwhile, was a fine draftsman but was expected to mount the throne someday, so he merely frequented and patronized the most famous artists of the new school, which was another way of rejecting the gerontocracy typical of the Bourbon restoration. Having studied, like Marie, under Ary Scheffer, Ferdinand bought Scheffer's *Scenes of the July Revolution* at the Salon of 1831; it was the first of a series of paintings that would turn the family's new residence—the Tuileries Palace—into a precocious museum of Romanticism. The crown prince was not only friendly with Delacroix, Barye, and Musset (having attended the Lycée Henri IV with the latter), he was also an earnest patron of the artist he called "old Ingres." As a pendant to Delaroche's *Assassination of the Duc de Guise* (p. 253), Ferdinand commissioned Ingres, then head of the Académie de France in Rome, to paint *Antiochus and Stratonica* (p. 244). Ingres later executed an inspired portrait of the prince in a red-and-black uniform; a forerunner of Manet's *Fife Player,* this painting was recently acquired by the Louvre, where the ghosts of Orléans art patronage haunt many rooms.

A baptism of fire

Crown Prince Ferdinand was killed in a coaching accident on July 13, 1842. At the death of his elder brother, the duc d'Aumale made a revealing comment that prefigures his future determination to live among his deceased brother's artworks:

> I no longer feel alive. The dear departed was the soul of my life—I was merely his arm. Without him, I have no thoughts, no will; I am useless to this world, and would like to leave it.... But I know my duty: all my life I will be, like my poor [brother], like all my brothers, a perhaps obscure but passionate servant of France, devoted body and soul to the fine cause of the nation. We shall be its apostles and, if necessary, its martyrs.

The mourned man was thirty-two; the mourner was twelve years younger. In several respects, the duc d'Aumale felt he was the repository of his elder brother's "final wishes." Henri, like his brother Ferdinand, was raised to be tough yet was also an excellent student at Lycée Henri IV; he was an experienced horseman, a ladykiller, and a soldier as early as 1837, fighting in the Algerian campaign in 1840. Thus in more ways than one he was the last Condé, that other French family that had been the junior branch of a royal line. Henri was just eight years old when his godfather, the last prince of Condé, made the boy his sole heir. When the prince died a few months later, his estates, châteaus, and collections represented a considerable legacy despite his debts and his largesse toward his insatiable mistress. The bequest included the Chantilly estate,

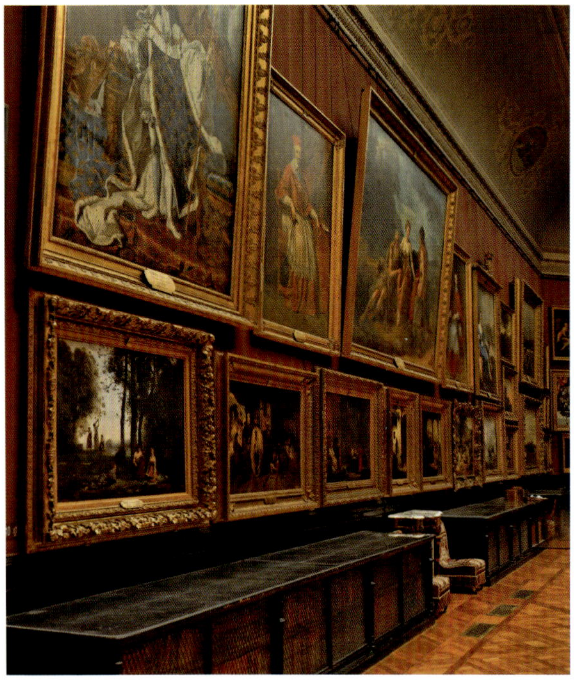

LEFT AND FACING PAGE
The highlight of the duc d'Aumale's renovation campaign for Chantilly was this gallery of paintings, based a design popular from the 1870s onward. The large, windowless volume was the only space not architecturally expressed on the architectural exterior of the château, being masked by symbolic features such as porch, chapel, apartments, and towers. It was lit by an overhead glass structure based on a metallic framework, testifying to the duke's innovative spirit—just below the roof, a horizontal plane of glass served as the ceiling. The vast hall with its angled corners is 9.5 meters (31 feet) high and covers a surface of 273 square meters (2900 square feet). The works are densely hung on the dark red walls; on the left-hand wall the duke hung works by the Italian school (including Italy-based Frenchmen such as Poussin and Dughet), while on the right he hung the French school, the large portraits and Orientalist subjects of which he was fond.

which, although seriously amputated by the acquisition-hungry French Revolution, would become the seat of a new reconquest. Although history never repeats itself, it presented the duc d'Aumale with a challenge similar to the one his father faced on returning from exile. Re-establishing a "house," in the aristocratic sense of the term, immediately called for a certain manner and style of life. Although never giving up his amorous adventures, Henri decided to settle down and to flaunt the military decorations on his uniform. The full-length portrait of him done by Franz Winterhalter in 1843 not only glitters with such decorations, it stresses the sitter's fair Austrian coloring while skillfully understating his large Sicilian nose and his Habsburg chin. Indeed, Henri was a dashing prince who acted the part. When he came of age in 1843 his most spectacular military feat was the routing of the camp of Abd el-Kader, the great military chief of the local resistance in Algeria. A few items now in Chantilly, notably a superb saber, recall the young duke's military service, which was impressive enough to earn him the title of governor general of Algeria after August 1847. This appointment did not prevent him from drawing up a mixed assessment of the colonization process and from adopting de Tocqueville's attitude toward the Arabs, previously under the Ottoman yoke. It was the duc d'Aumale who had the honor of accepting his staunch enemy's surrender. The year 1843 was also the moment when the matrimonial policies of the house of Orléans began to conflict with the duke's rather turbulent love life—he had been enjoying the efficient charms of Alice Ozy, a minor actress but top-rank mistress (who would later go on to charm the likes of writer Théophile Gautier and artist Théodore Chassériau). The duke's marriage to Maria Carolina de Bourbon-Sicily on November 25, 1844, constituted a break even as it cemented links to the Neapolitan branch of the family.

Princely collector

The duc d'Aumale immediately launched a major building campaign for the benefit of his young bride, who was the grand-daughter of King Ferdinand IV and niece of the duke's mother, Maria Amelia. The five-hundred-year-old Condé château was just a shadow of its former self, and its new master had not yet shown much interest in it, apart from the adjoining racetrack. In a matter of months, everything changed. Aumale hired good artists who shared his sense of historical continuity—the so-called "Louis-Philippe style" was not so much a product of indecisive bastardization as an attempt at historical reconciliation. The last Condé felt it was important to preserve the memory of the dynasties that preceded his own, from the medieval Orgemonts to the unfortunate Montmorency family. Chantilly suddenly became the focus of an extraordinary reunion of families, concretized through architecture and pictures. In an attempt to update things, the redecoration of the apartments of the Petit Château (the only building to survive the Revolution) was assigned to the fashionable artist Eugène Lami and his friends. The youthful Romanticism of the 1840s, as expressed by Henri Baron and Narcisse Díaz, blossomed amid furnishings and woodwork that shunned all austerity. A few works by Nicolas Largillierre (p. 176–81) completed an interior designed to evoke the "delightful lifestyle" of the past. Luck was with the newlyweds: in 1845 a son was born, styled the prince of Condé, in the Tuileries Palace; meanwhile, the ancestral art collection was making its way out to Chantilly. The duke reinforced his own collection with the help of his father, King Louis-Philippe, a regular supplier of modern paintings. As Baudelaire himself pointed out, it was a time when the French king endowed the nation with the various museums housed within the Louvre, notably his famous "Spanish Gallery." But the king's brilliant cultural policy was not matched by political astuteness: he had become inflexible and had surrounded himself with ministers deaf to the approaching thunder (as even his children quietly admitted). By 1847, even the ears of de Tocqueville had detected the rumbling.

Thus another revolution in February 1848 overthrew Louis-Philippe, who fled to England and temporarily lost all his property. The first days of exile were financially difficult for the fallen king and his children. These straitened circumstances explain why the duc d'Aumale—the richest of the children—temporarily reined in his appetite for old books and artworks. The revolution sent him back to Algeria, where he moved with his wife and his son Louis. Once circumstances permitted,

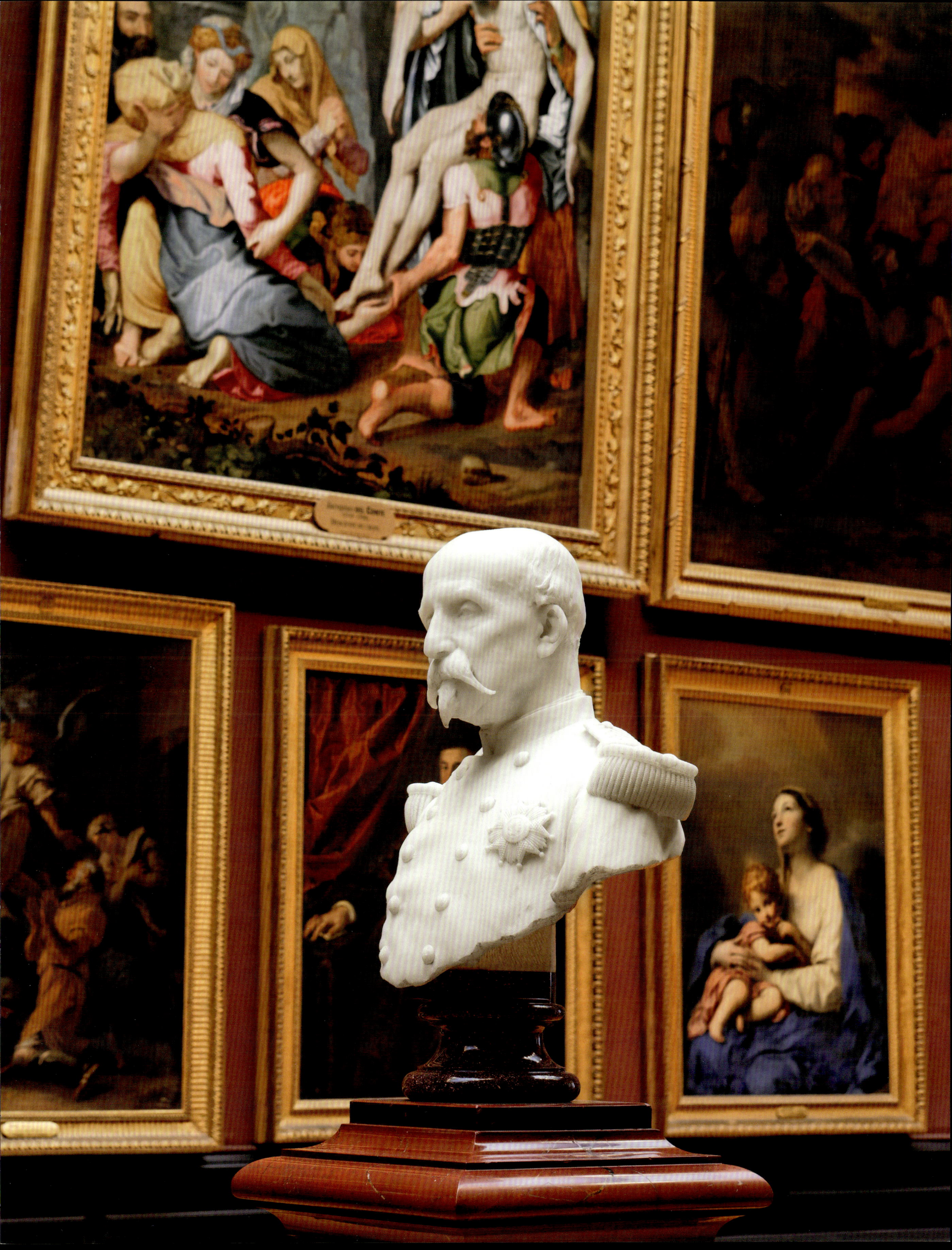

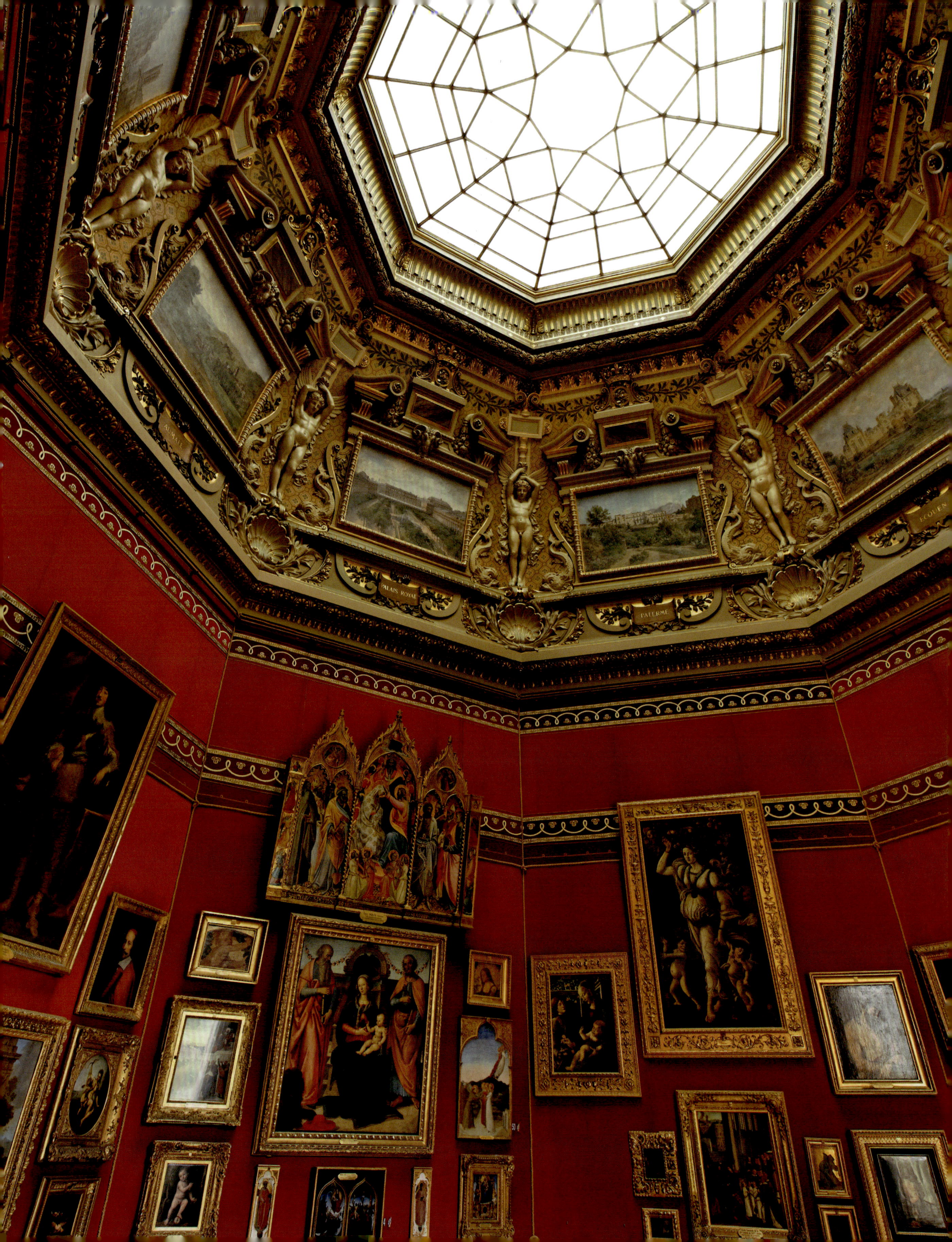
PALAIS ROYAL
PALERME
ECOUEN

FACING PAGE
The Tribune, based on and named after the room in the Uffizi Gallery in Florence where the grand duke of Tuscany hung his masterpieces, was one of the rooms of the first museum designed by architect Honoré Daumat. Here the duc d'Aumale hung his favorite paintings. In the lofty vault, eight paintings commissioned from Armand Bernard depict places dear to the duke, such as the Palais-Royal, the Lycée Henri-IV (where he completed his secondary education), and the château d'Ecouen built by the Montmorency and Condé families.

BELOW
The painting gallery leads into the Rotunda, where the duke placed a statue of Joan of Arc by sculptor Henri Chapu—a highly symbolic gesture at a time when France had just lost Alsace and Lorraine to Germany.

FOLLOWING PAGES
In 1844–45, the duc d'Aumale had Romantic artist Eugène Lami decorate the château's private apartments, where he intended to live with his new bride. Whereas the Guise Salon (left) was allocated to the duchess, the Condé Salon (right) was designed for the duke. The Renaissance-style chimney-piece (copied from one in the château de Villeroy) features a bust of the duc de Bourbon, the last member of the Condé family, who bequeathed his property to the duc d'Aumale.

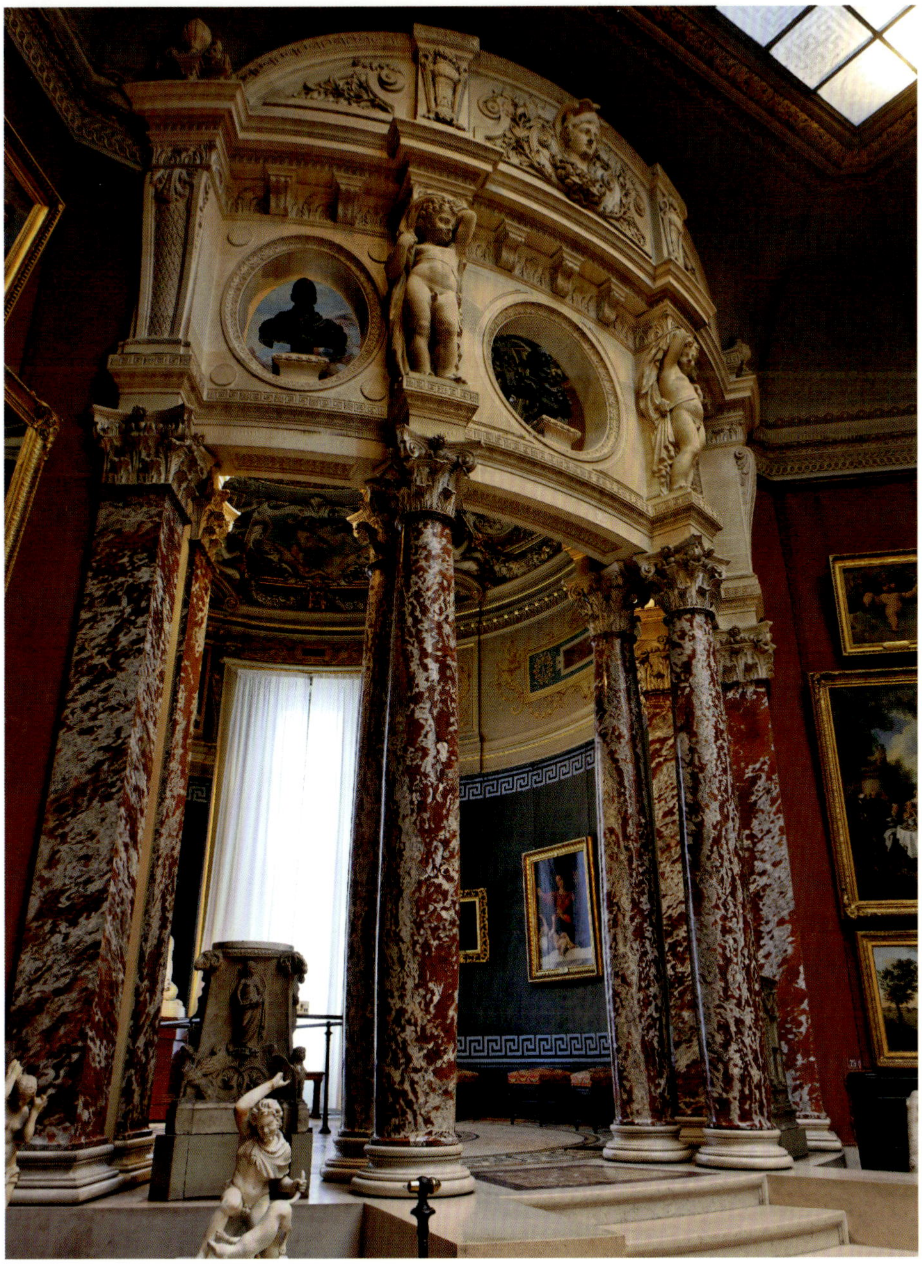

the family was reunited at Claremont House outside London, soon joined by the paintings owned by various family members, which the new French Republic deigned to restore to them. Although artworks crossed the English Channel, funds did not immediately follow, because the Orléans properties were still sequestered. Aumale therefore remained inactive until he managed to lift the ban on his personal property and recovered liquidity following the auctions that Napoleon III imposed on him in 1852. He had allowed the Louvre to acquire the large Géricault paintings that were placed on sale following the death of his father, Louis-Philippe, in 1850; they were greeted in Paris as manifestos of the new era. The only Géricault bought by Aumale was *Black Horse Leaving the Stables* (p. 248), an acquisition that simultaneously symbolized his filial loyalty, his penchant for Géricault's art, and his enthusiasm for horses. Two years later, it was the turn of his sister-in-law, the duchesse d'Orléans, to sell her late husband's paintings; Aumale was thus able to add Delaroche's *Assassination of the Duc de Guise* (p. 253) to his collection in memory of his brother.

Once he recovered substantial funds, the duc d'Aumale was able to rebuild his collection. He was also able to leave the gloomy atmosphere of Claremont House, associated with so much mourning: two children had been born and died since he and his wife had arrived in England. So in the summer of 1852 they moved to Twickenham, where the "soldier without an army" threw himself heart and soul into acquiring art, books, antiques, and learning. This was a lifestyle appropriate to a French royal prince concerned about his rank and eager to do battle with the Second Empire back home. His books and archives made their way to England, obviously, as did his paintings, for which he provided a worthy setting in the form of a fine gallery (the first of several). Even as he was writing a history of the princes of Condé, the duc d'Aumale was an active buyer at auctions, assisted by his advisers and agents. When his father-in-law, the prince of Salerno, died in 1854, the duke purchased part of the prince's collection, representing the heritage of the kings of Naples. Thus Aumale shipped to England a glamorous set of Italian paintings that included Raphael's *Madonna of Loreto* (p. 70). His gallery

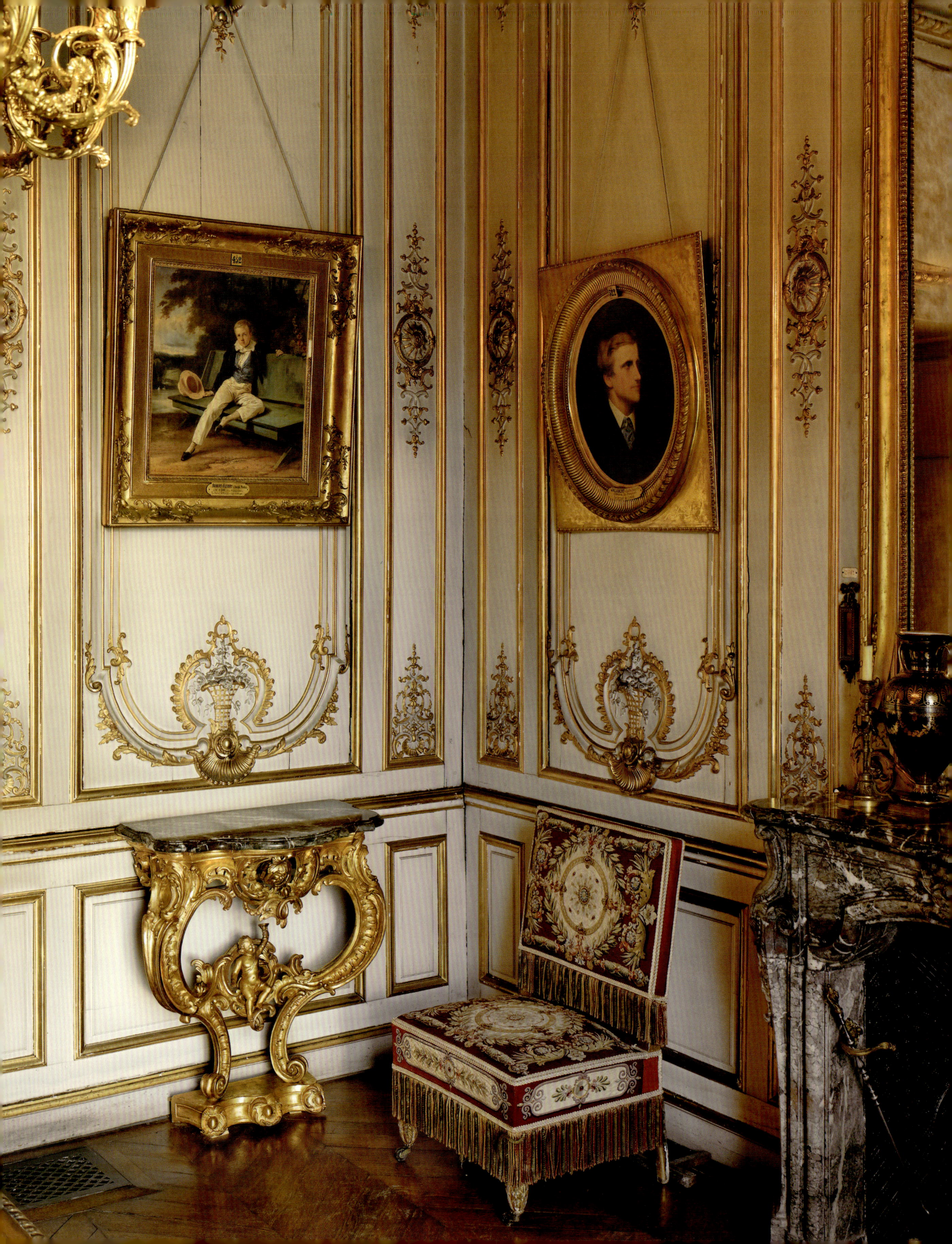

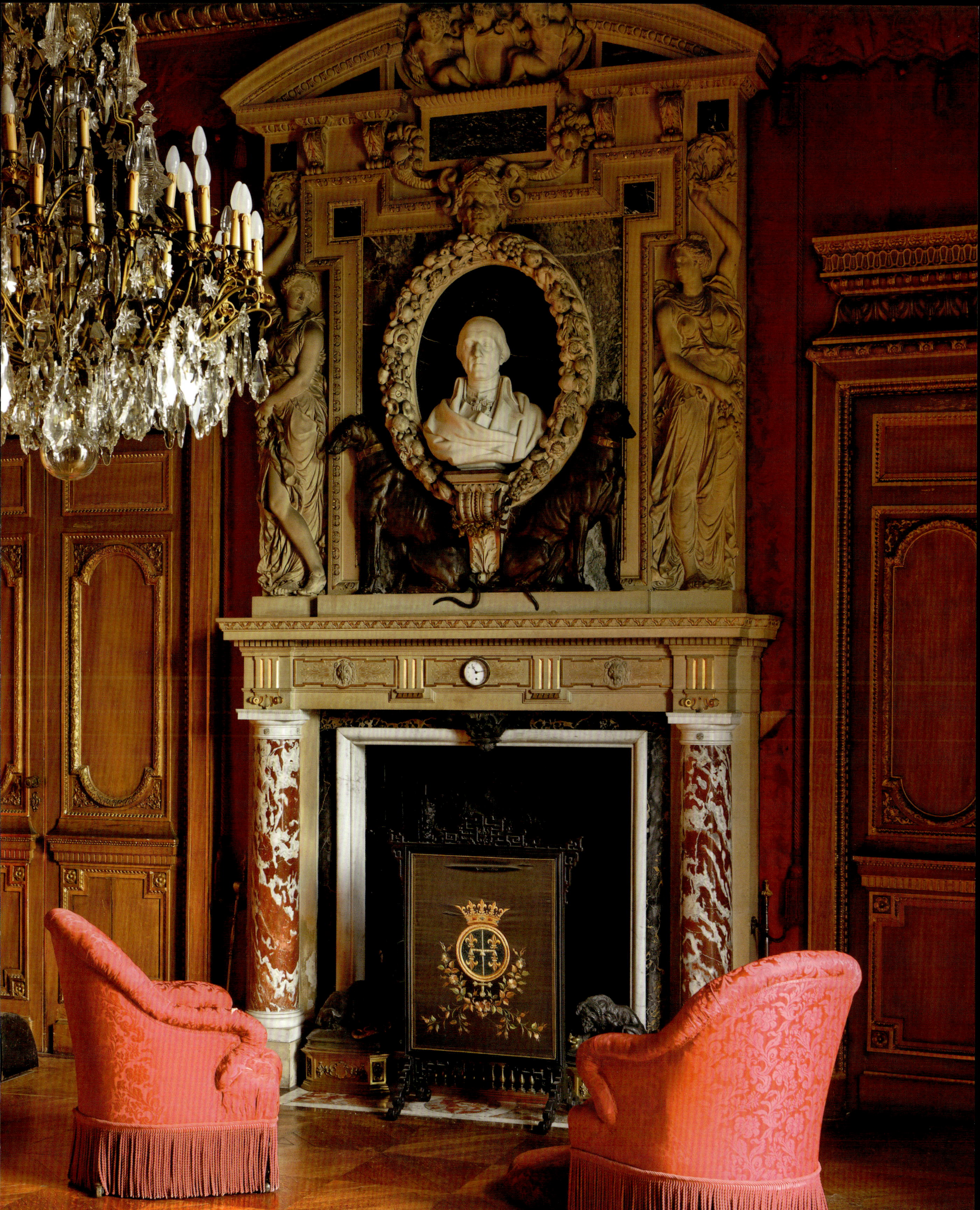

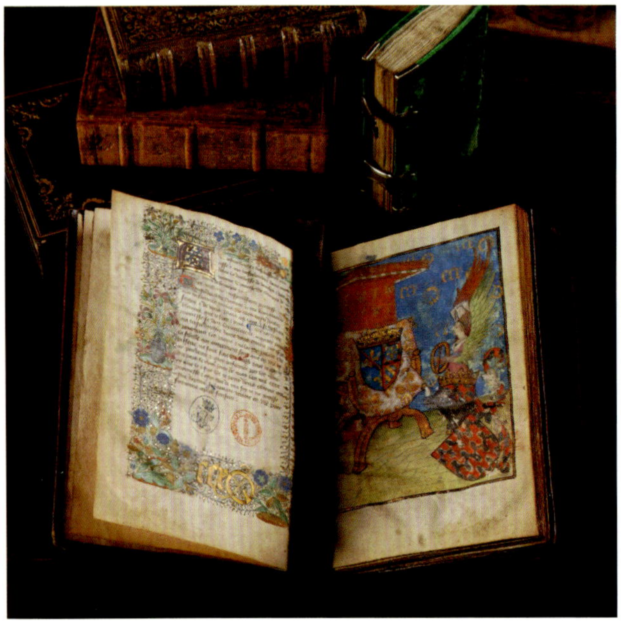

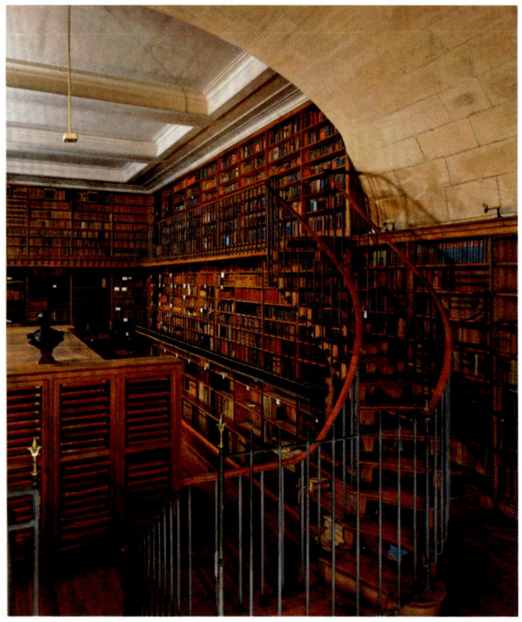

suddenly glittered with the greatest names of Italian baroque art—eleven works by Carracci (p. 86–92) and eight by Rosa (p. 100–06)—recalling the great days of the Regent. Five years later, his collection of Italian paintings was enhanced by further purchases (on the recommendation of Henri de Triqueti) at the Lord Northwick estate auction. These moves can only be seen as the duke's attempt to "get his own back"—an act of patriotism at a distance, of loyalty to the homeland where the duke would tirelessly seek to erect a temple to the treasures of French art and history.

Bequeathing art

The duke's many restorative purchases cannot be divorced from the anti-Bonapartism that spurred him to publish a "Letter on the History of France" in 1861. Behind his defense of his father's reign, the duke was giving Napoleon III a piece of his mind. Paris began to worry about a prince who had the means to finance his vindictive claims. Furthermore, the duke remained active and aggressive when it came to the English art market. In 1854, Colnaghi sold him one of the most beautiful and unique Poussins available, *The Massacre of the Innocents* (p. 158). This work had a delightful provenance, having passed through the hands of Lucien Bonaparte after having been part of the prestigious Giustiniani collection. Meanwhile a Genoese baron decided to sell another French gem, namely the illuminated manuscript of *Les Très Riches Heures du Duc de Berry.* There was no lack of prospective buyers, so the duc d'Aumale hastened to Italy, and one month later he came away with his prize. The precious manuscript reached England in 1856 and was later incorporated into the duke's library in Chantilly. A year later he snapped up one of Gérôme's best paintings from right under the Parisians' noses (it being exhibited at the Salon), then pursued his acquisition of his father's former possessions by buying two masterpieces of French art, *Dining on Oysters* by Jean-François de Troy (p. 202) and *Dining on Ham* by Nicolas Lancret (p. 204), which he believed depicted his ancestors. In 1860, the duke bought a Domenichino (p. 93), as mentioned above, and a Veronese (p. 84), both of which had hung in the family's Palais Royal until 1791. At the Demidoff sale in 1863, Aumale bought the *Stratonica* (p. 244) once owned by his brother, constituting a double relic with its sprightly Greek-revival colors. The mourned brother was flamboyantly commemorated again in 1867 when the duke commissioned Léon Perrault to execute a replica (p. 275) of a large painting by Horace Vernet that showed King Louis-Philippe and his sons leaving the château of Versailles on horseback. The weaving of past and present was not merely a question of flaunting justifiable pride, for in addition to the sorrow of losing two more children in 1861 and 1864, the duke and duchess suffered the death of their eldest son, the prince of Condé, felled by yellow fever in far-off lands in 1866. They never recovered from the blow. The only survivor among all their children was the twelve-year-old François, duc de Guise, whose health was fragile. The boy and father were struck with more misfortune when the duchess, Maria Carolina, died in 1869 after a lifetime marked by death—sorrows that left their trace on the surviving pictures of her. Charles-François Jalabert had begun a portrait of the duchess when news of the prince of Condé's death plunged the Twickenham household into the blackest depression. As the artist described it:

> Sorrow eventually lifts here, as elsewhere—the house is becoming somewhat gayer. Only [the duchess] remains constantly sad. The duke sometimes adopts the cheerful air that comes from his strong character, but then suddenly takes his head between his hands; he frequently discusses politics as a distraction.

Life carried on, and collecting probably helped the duke to hang on. The paintings he bought in 1868 from Marquis Maison, son of a minister to Louis-Philippe, brought him four works by Watteau (p. 196) and four by Greuze (p. 228), confirming his attachment not only to eighteenth-century painting but also to the idea of a comprehensive gallery of French art (Dr. La Caze's fine collection, with its Chardins and Fragonards, had already been promised to the Louvre). It is no coincidence, but rather additional proof, of the shrewd assessment that Aumale made of the public's growing curiosity and the political leverage it represented—his acquisition of twenty-two paintings from the Maison collection thus reinforced the Orientalist appeal of his gallery, including seven works by Decamps (p. 262 and 264) and three by Marilhat (p. 266), an unexpected boon

ABOVE AND FACING PAGE
As a learned, enthusiastic, and wealthy book lover, the duc d'Aumale was one of the major collectors of his day. The Bibliothèque du Théâtre (above), which housed recent books, was a place of work. Meanwhile, the Cabinet des Livres (right) was where the duke kept his most precious books and illuminated manuscripts; endowed with an upper gallery, this library embodies a design typical of the late 19th century. The metal shelving is sheathed in leather.

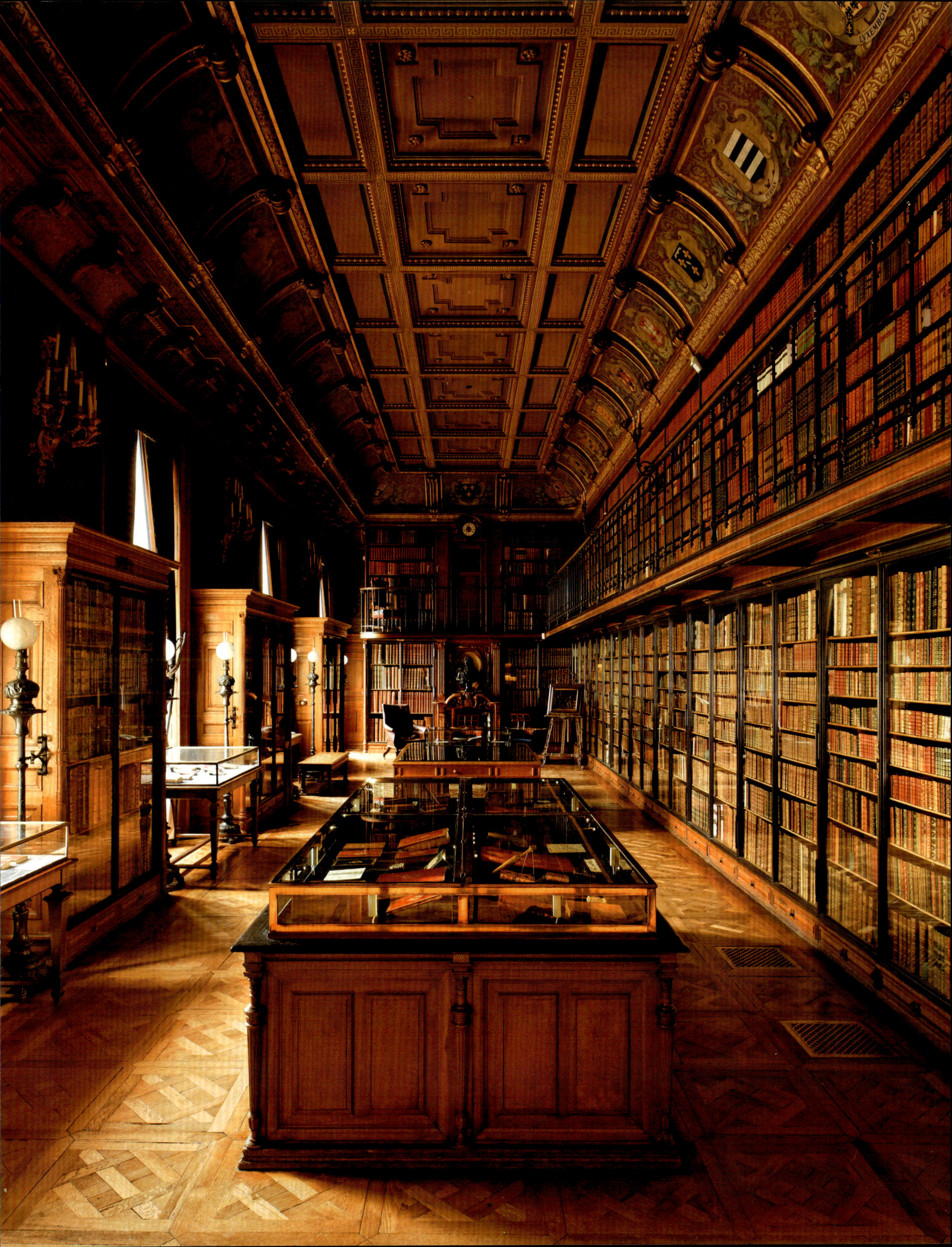

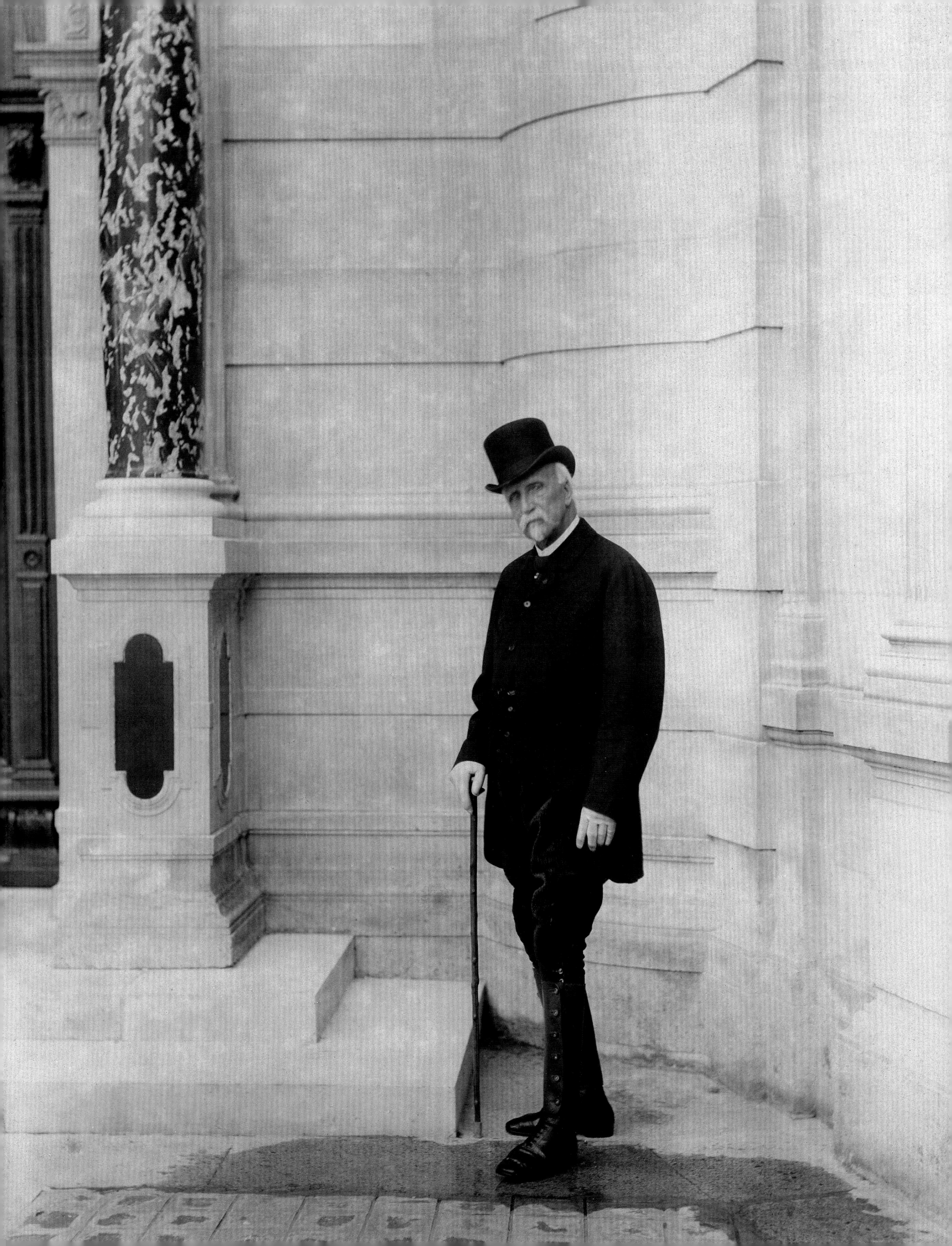

FACING PAGE
The duc d'Aumale in the courtyard of the château in 1896. Taken by Robert d'Orléans, duc de Chartres, this is the last photograph of Aumale at Chantilly, six months before his death. Musée Condé, Chantilly.

FOLLOWING PAGES
This antechamber, where the duke displayed busts and portraits of members of the Condé family, leads to the State Apartments of the princes of Condé.

"WANTING FRANCE TO RETAIN THE CHANTILLY ESTATE ... AN ENTIRE ENSEMBLE THAT CONSTITUTES A COMPLETE AND VARIED MONUMENT TO FRENCH ART ... AND TO THE HISTORY OF MY COUNTRY IN ITS DAYS OF GLORY, I HAVE DECIDED TO ENTRUST IT TO AN ILLUSTRIOUS BODY THAT HONORED ME BY WELCOMING ME AMONG ITS RANKS."

The duc d'Aumale's last will, dated June 3, 1884, bequeathing Chantilly to the Institut de France.

that even the Louvre still cannot match. As a former trooper in Algeria, the duke appreciated more than just the intense light and exotic landscapes of these Orientalist works—his nostalgia was furthermore reflected in one of his final purchases of drawings, a set by Auguste Raffet now in the Musée Condé in Chantilly.

Napoleon III's defeat at Sedan saddened the duke as a loyal French soldier but liberated him as a political exile—twenty-two years of estrangement came to an end. Although the new government expressed no desire to see the Orléans family come home, Aumale returned to France and was soon elected to the legislative assembly; some people began to view him as a potential candidate for the presidency of the new republic. The Paris uprising known as the Commune prevented him from returning to the capital until June 1871—an emotional return, obviously. Not having assumed the leadership of a weakened, humiliated France, the duke had himself handily elected to the Académie Française, that bastion of Orléans support in the days of empire. In September of that year, however, he became more concerned about his sole surviving child's education and erratic health. The lad died on July 25, 1872, the day of his Baccalaureat exam; his death "broke his father's heart forever." After such tragedy, life perhaps becomes impossible—one merely survives.

Henceforth with no direct heir, the duc d'Aumale—for whom the concept of "passing things on" was sacred—decided to take appropriate action concerning his collections. Another four years would nevertheless pass before he launched the project of returning Chantilly to its former glory. Architect Honoré Daumet, a winner of the Prix de Rome able to work in a sixteenth-century style, was commissioned to bring the château of the Montmorency and Condé families back to life, modeled on the château d'Ecouen. Work lasted twenty years. Although in running conflict with the French Republic, which entailed yet another period of exile from 1886 to 1889, the old duke continued to consolidate his collection. The museum he was establishing reflected the scale of his ambitions and his regrets. In 1876 he had bought, in England, the collection assembled by Alexandre Lenoir, which boasted hundreds of works by the Clouets (p. 126–33) and Corneille de Lyon (p. 134–135). In 1879, without haggling, he accepted the inflated prices quoted by Frédéric Reiset (the director of the French national museum administration from whom the duke had bought drawings in 1861) for a masterpiece by Ingres, *Venus Anadyomene* (p. 246) and a good number of early Italian paintings of which the rarest item is a portrait called *Simonetta Vespucci* (p. 50). The duc d'Aumale did not feel he was betraying his youthful Romanticism when he summoned Delaunay, Baudry, and Olivier Merson to work at the château. Nor is it a surprise that he did not welcome the likes of Courbet and Manet. A potentially universal museum was in the works. In 1884, having transcended the "extremely sudden upheavals" that had wracked France since his birth, the duke decided to bequeath his collection to the Intitut de France, that steady ship "in the midst of political fluctuations." And he remained an insatiable collector, snapping up a Raphael, Fouquet, or Lippi every time a priceless masterpiece surfaced. One exceptional purchase followed another. And so the years followed one another until, in 1897, the duc d'Aumale passed away. The Musée Condé opened just one year later. Today we can still appreciate the way the duc d'Aumale arranged the works on his walls, defying chronology and national groupings in favor of an eighteenth-century-style tapestry that weaves subtle relationships and correspondences, which he felt were more important than scholarly classifications—allowing this worthy heir to the Regent to rest in peace.

STÉPHANE GUÉGAN

THE CONDÉ MUSEUM AT THE CHÂTEAU DE CHANTILLY

THE PAINTINGS COLLECTION

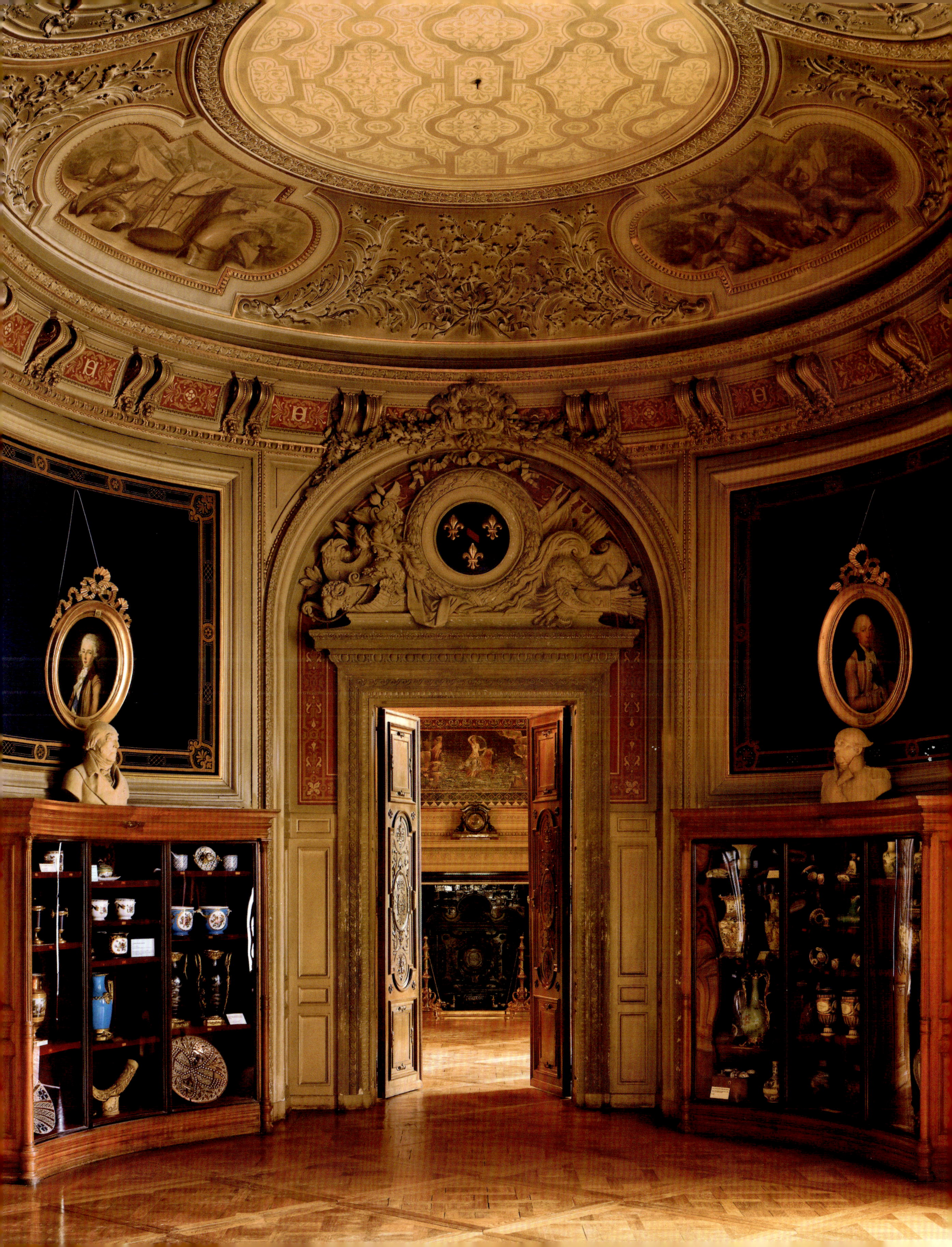

MASO DI BANCO

(active in Florence 1320 to 1353)

The Dormition of the Virgin

Wood. H. 44 cm (1 ft. 5 ½ in.); W. 48 cm (1 ft. 7 in.)
Inv. 1 (Cabinet du Giotto)

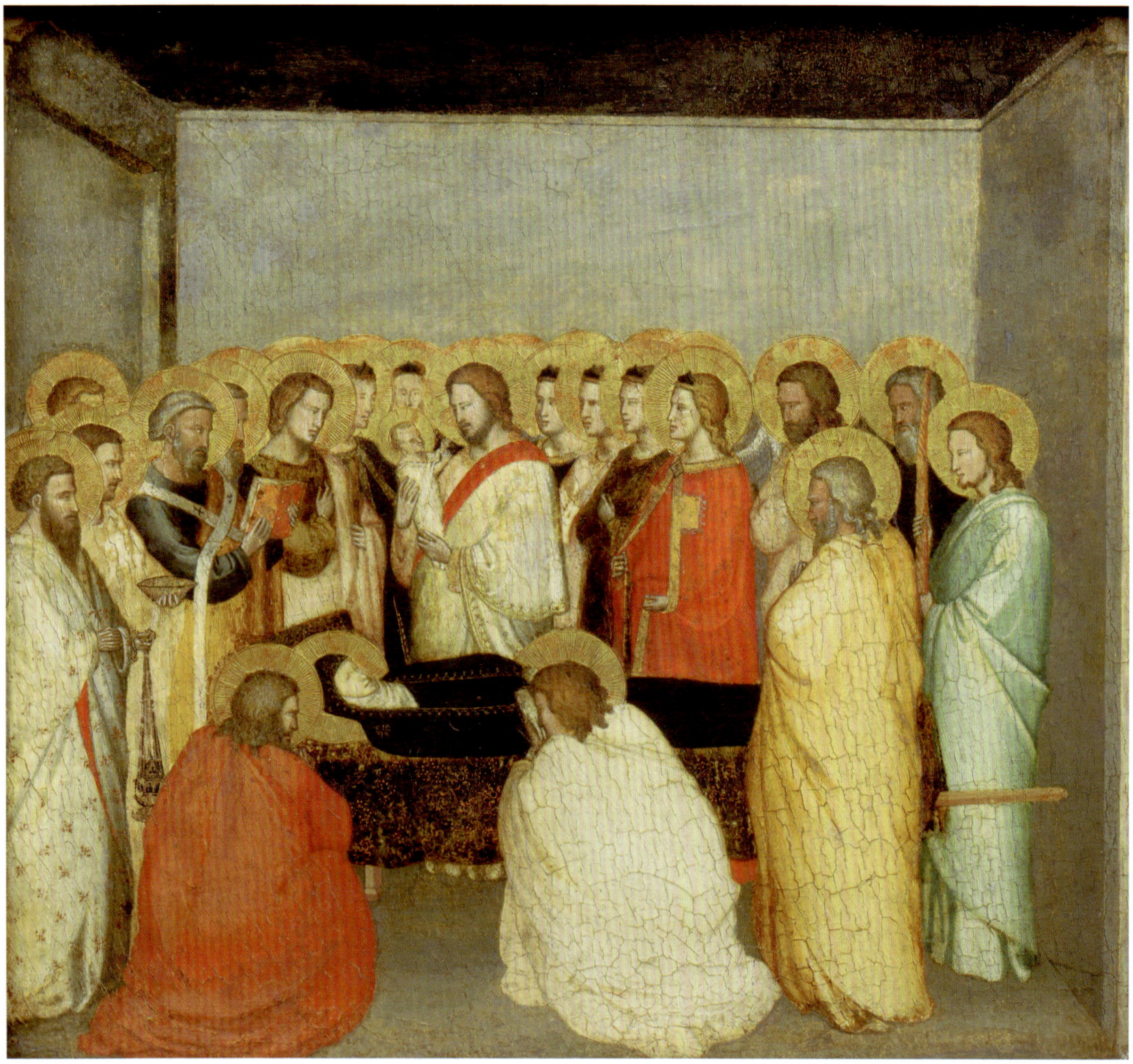

This painting depicts the dormition—that is to say, the death—of the Virgin. Her son, Christ, is seen standing at the side of her death bed to receive her soul (represented as a haloed, swaddled infant with outstretched arms). The Apostles stand in a semicircle around the bed, in a gray-walled room with strong perspective effect.

When the duc d'Aumale bought this painting in 1879 as part of the Frédéric Reiset collection (*see p. 33*), it was thought to be the work of Giotto, and therefore gave its name to the room where it was hung—the "Cabinet du Giotto." Today it is attributed to a follower of Giotto, Maso di Bianco, who was invited along with his master to the court of Robert of Anjou in Naples between 1329 and 1332, where he painted the chapel of Castelnuovo, several surviving fragments of which are attributed to Maso. It was after his return to Florence that Maso apparently executed *The Dormition of the Virgin,* prior to painting the frescoes (circa 1335) in the Bardi chapel in the church of Santa Croce.

This panel is thought to be part of the altar of the girdle of the Virgin in the cathedral of Prato, for which Maso received payments in 1337–38; the right-hand panel would correspond to *The Coronation of the Virgin* (National Museum, Budapest) while the central was constituted by *The Virgin Bestowing the Girdle on Saint Thomas* (Gemäldegalerie, Berlin). The three panels comprised either a tabernacle or, more probably, the predella of an altarpiece dedicated to the Virgin. Maso drew inspiration from a work by Giotto on the same subject, painted circa 1310 for the church of Ognissanti (now in Berlin), whose more traditional composition aligns the figures in a frieze set against a gold ground.

FRA ANGELICO (GUIDO DI PIETRO)

(Vicchio Mugello, circa 1395–1400; Rome, 1455)

Saint Mark

Wood. H. 36 cm (1 ft. 2 in.); W. 11 cm (4 ½ in.)
Inv. 4 (Tribune)

Saint Matthew

Wood. H. 32 cm (1 ft. ½ in.); W. 11 cm (4 ½ cm.)
Inv. 5 (Tribune)

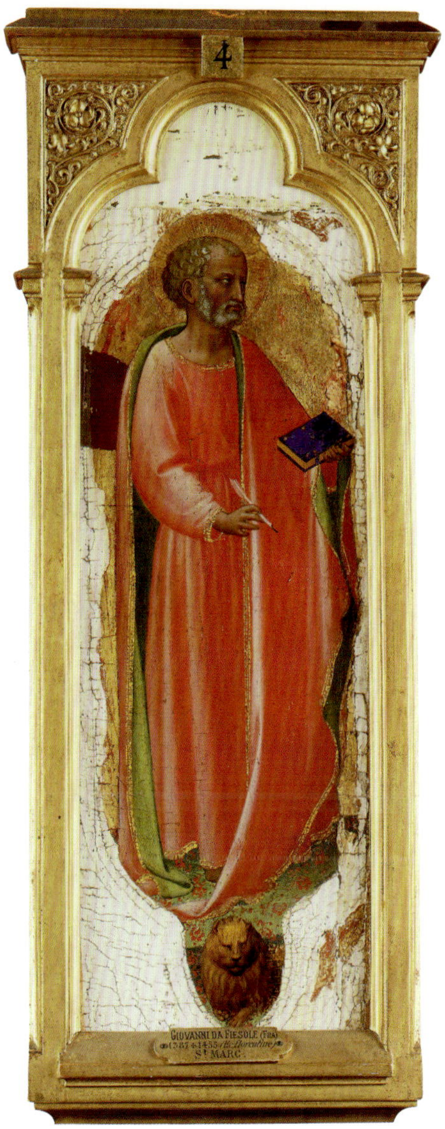

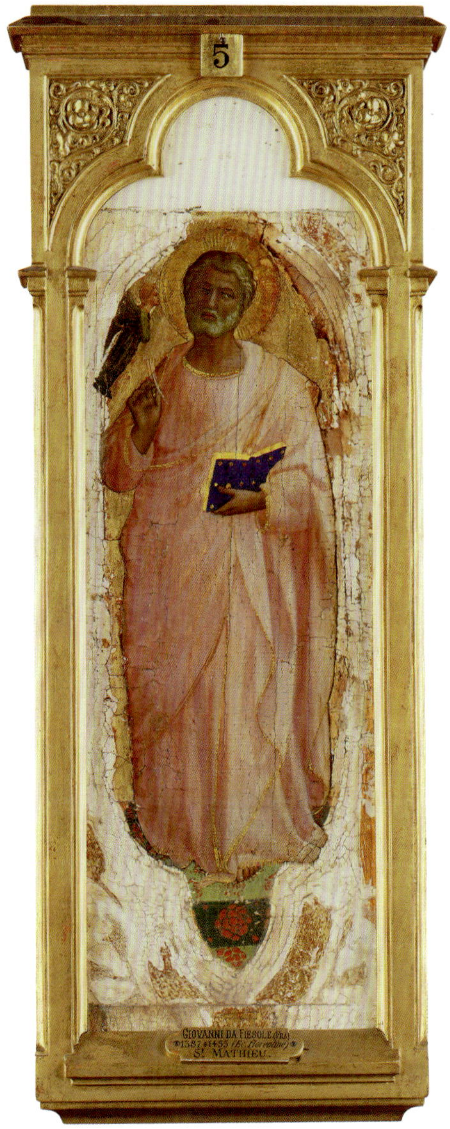

These portraits of two evangelists adorned the pilasters of a large altarpiece executed circa 1423–25 by Fra Angelico for the church of the friary of San Domenico at Fiesole, where he lived. In 1501 Lorenzo di Credi modified the original triptych, uniting the various elements in a single panel of the altarpiece, painting a landscape in the background on the gold background, and placing a canopy over the throne of the Virgin, as reported by Vasari in 1568. It was probably at this time that Lorenzo modified the figures of the two evangelists here, setting them against a gray ground that imitated a building in *pietra serena* (local greenish-gray stone); this background was removed during restoration in 1965.

The altarpiece was dismantled between 1792 and 1827 by the monks of San Domenico. The main panel, *Virgin and Child with Four Saints*, unified by Lorenzo di Credi, is still in Fiesole, but the predella depicting *Christ Glorified in the Court of Heaven* is now in the National Gallery in London. The panels here were placed on the lateral pilasters of the altarpiece, as were two similar panels now at the Rau Foundation (*Saint Michael* and *Saint Nicholas*) and others that are apparently lost. Since we have two of the evangelists here, recognizable from their attributes (the lion for Saint Mark and the angel for Saint Matthew, in addition to a book), it is possible that they were accompanied by Saint John and a Saint Luke, now lost. The altarpiece for San Domenico was the first major work by Fra Angelico, then at the start of his career. He was still under the influence of the international Gothic movement, yet was already evolving toward a new style.

FRA ANGELICO (GUIDO DI PIETRO)

(Vicchio Mugello, circa 1395–1400; Rome, 1455)

Saint Benedict in the Wilderness

Wood. H. 185 cm (6 ft. 1 in.); W. 283 cm (9 ft. 3 in.)
Inv. 6 (Cabinet du Giotto)

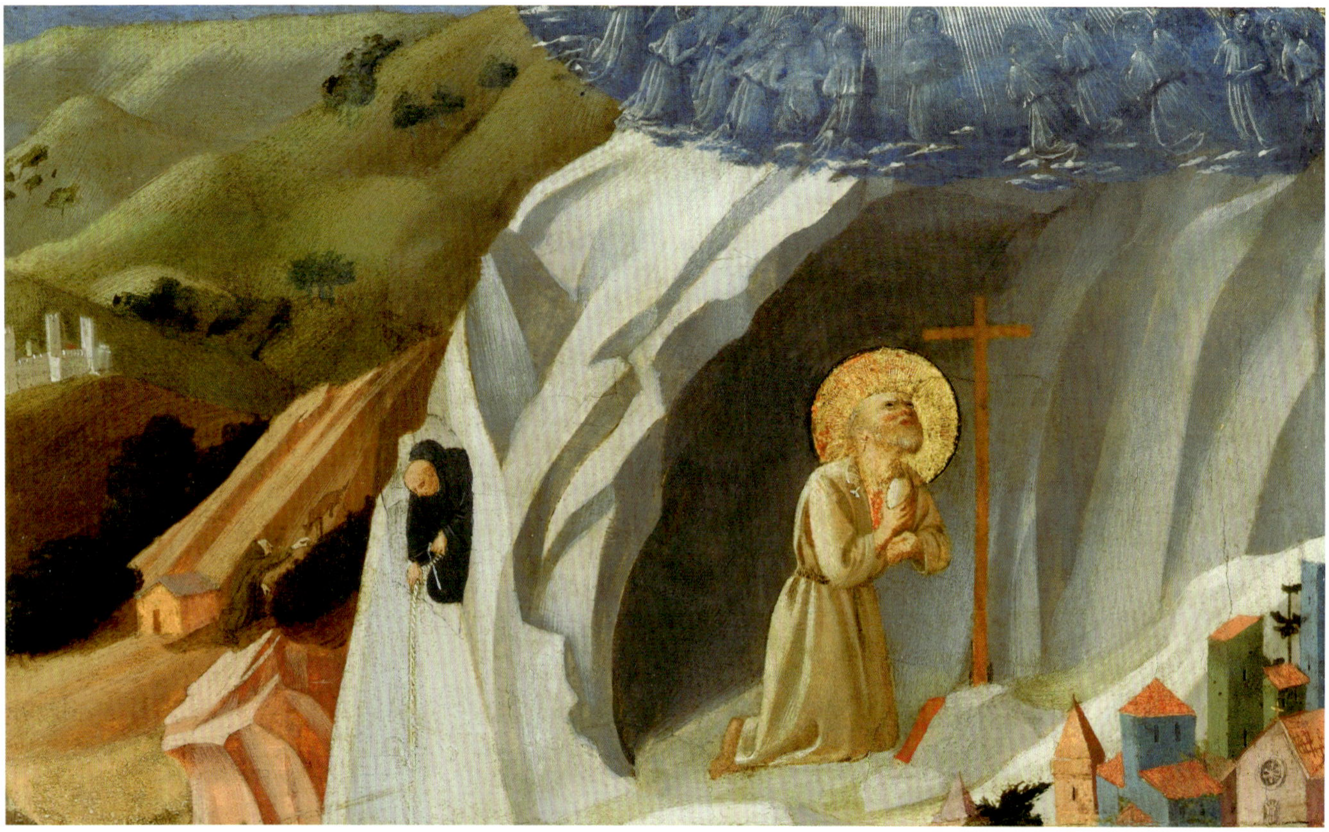

Saint Benedict is shown kneeling in his cave in the wilderness of Subiaco, praying before the Cross when he has an ecstatic vision of a choir of angels, seen in the upper section. It has now been established, thanks to a transversal groove at the top of the panel, that this piece was part of an ensemble also composed of elements now in the Musée Thomas Henry in Cherbourg (*Saint Augustine at Prayer*), in the Musée Royal des Beaux-Arts in Antwerp (*Saint Romuald Appearing to Otto III*), and the Philadelphia Museum of Art (the lower part, showing *The Papacy Offered to Saint Gregory the Great*). The ensemble was originally thought to have been a predella, but the discovery of a fifth panel, *The Solitary* (private collection), has revealed that it was a panel showing the lives of hermit saints on two levels. The composition was cut up for commercial reasons, and one fragment is still missing. The Philadelphia panel extends the village seen on the lower right here, which recent restoration has brought to light. The basket being lowered by the monk on the end of a rope is also visible on the Philadelphia panel.

The work is generally attributed to followers of Fra Angelico rather than to the artist himself. It was bought by the duc d'Aumale as part of the Frédéric Reiset collection in 1879 (*see p. 33*).

VECCHIETTA (PIETRO DI LORENZO) or FRANCESCO DI GIORGIO

(Siena, 1410; Siena, 1480) or (Siena, 1439; Siena, 1501)

Two Kneeling Flagellants

Wood. H. 29 cm (11 1/2 in.); W. 19 cm (7 1/4 in.)
Inv. 8 (Tribune)

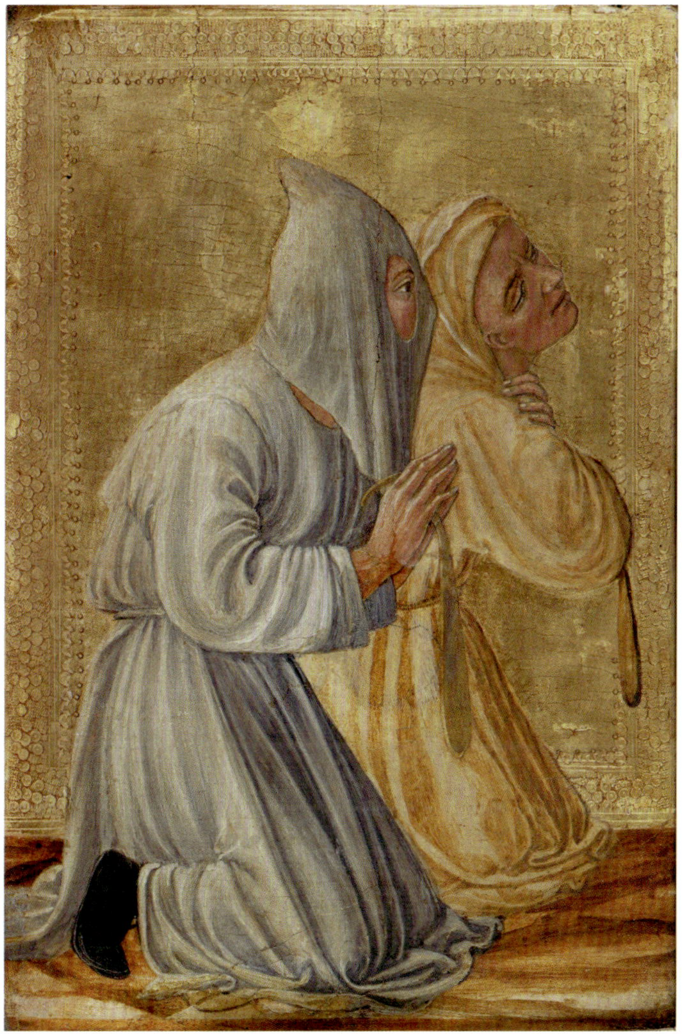

This little fragment was brought to France from Italy by Ingres. As a great admirer of the Italian Primitives, Ingres acquired it during his stay at the Académie de France in Rome (legend holds that his students chipped in to buy it for him). Ingres gave the painting to Frédéric Reiset in 1849 and the duc d'Aumale bought it along with the rest of the collection of Reiset, who had been director of France's national museums (*see p. 33*).

The panels are sometimes attributed to Vecchietta, sometimes to Francesco di Giorgio, who might have painted them in his youth when still in his master's workshop. Both artists were sculptors as well as painters, di Giorgio also being an architect.

These *Two Kneeling Flagellants* have a pendant showing the same subject matter, now in the Musée Bonnat in Bayonne; also related are two paintings of Saint Francis held by the Alte Pinakothek in Munich—*Saint Francis Embracing Poverty* and *Saint Francis Imposing the Rule of His Order*—because all have the same dimensions, a gold ground punched with a similar border, and marble flooring, which indicates that they belonged to the same group. They have sometimes been identified with a reliquary-wardrobe made for a Franciscan confraternity, but now they are felt rather to be part of a large altarpiece where they alternated with longer panels, following an approach seen in other Sienese religious works of the latter half of the fifteenth century. According to this hypothesis, the panels would have been commissioned from Vecchietta and partly executed in his workshop, along with three related paintings: *The Miracle of the Sandal* (Munich), *Saint Bernardino Preaching* (Walker Art Gallery, Liverpool), and *The Miracle of Saint Louis of Toulouse* (Pinacoteca Vaticana, Rome).

GIOVANNI DAL PONTE (GIOVANNI DI MARCO)

(Florence, 1385; Florence, 1438)

The Coronation of the Virgin

Wood. H. 178 cm (5 ft. 10 in.)
Inv. 3 (Tribune)

This work is a complete polyptych, which is rare outside of Italy. It comes from the church of Santa Maria Abovina in Val di Sieve near Florence, and dates from the 1420s. The frame was made in the early nineteenth century, in 1810, on the orders of the church prior, Zenobi. The attribution to Giovanni dal Ponte now seems assured. Dal Ponte, who did the frescoes for the church of Santa Trinita in Florence in 1434, drew inspiration here from a painting on the same subject by Lorenzo Monaco (1413, Uffizi, Florence). Dal Ponte painted many triptychs in which the saints are clearly identifiable through their attributes. Here the central panel shows the Virgin being crowned by Christ, with the Holy Trinity and angelic musicians; the left panel shows Saint Anthony Abbot, Saint Peter, Saint Zenobius, and a hermit saint; the right panel features John the Baptist, Saint Thomas, Saint Nicholas of Bari, and Saint Blaise. The round panels in the gables depict the Angel of the Annunciation (left) and the Virgin of the Annunciation (right). At the top of the lateral pilasters we see the sacrifice of Isaac (left) and Moses presenting the tablets of the law (right), while below them are angelic musicians. The painting entered the Chantilly collection in 1879 with the rest of the Frédéric Reiset collection (*see p. 33*).

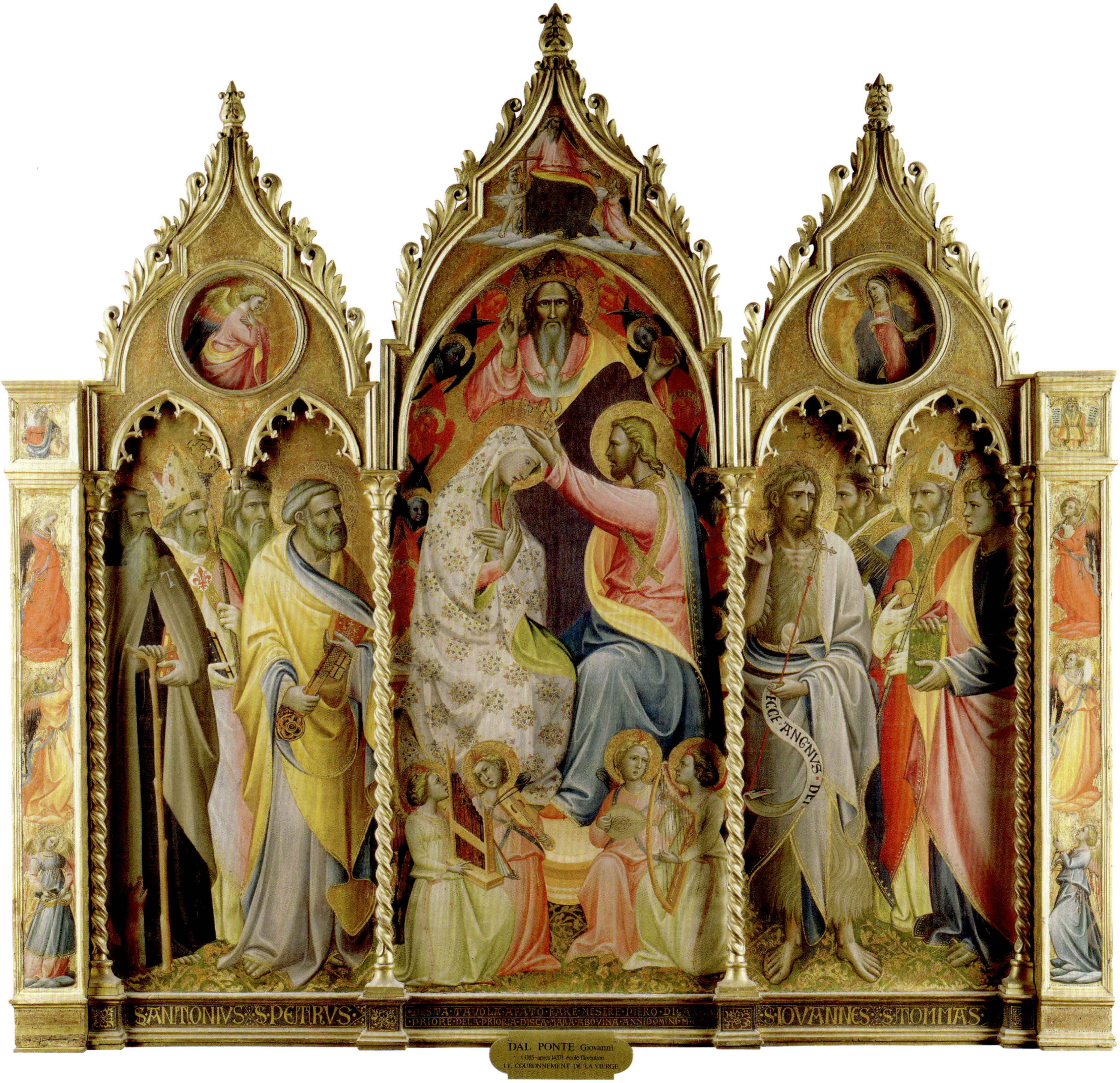

S·ANTONIVS·S·PETRVS·
PRIORE·DELA·PRIORIA·DISCA·MARIA·ABOVINA·ANNIDOMINI
S·IOVANNES·S·TOMMAS·
ECCE·ANGNVS·DEI
DAL PONTE Giovanni
(1385-après 1437) école florentine
LE COURONNEMENT DE LA VIERGE

GIOVANNI DI PAOLO

(active in Siena from 1417 to 1482)

Five Dancing Angels

Wood. H. 54 cm (1 ft. 9 ¼ in.); W. 66 cm (2 ft. 2 in.)
Inv. 9 (Cabinet du Giotto)

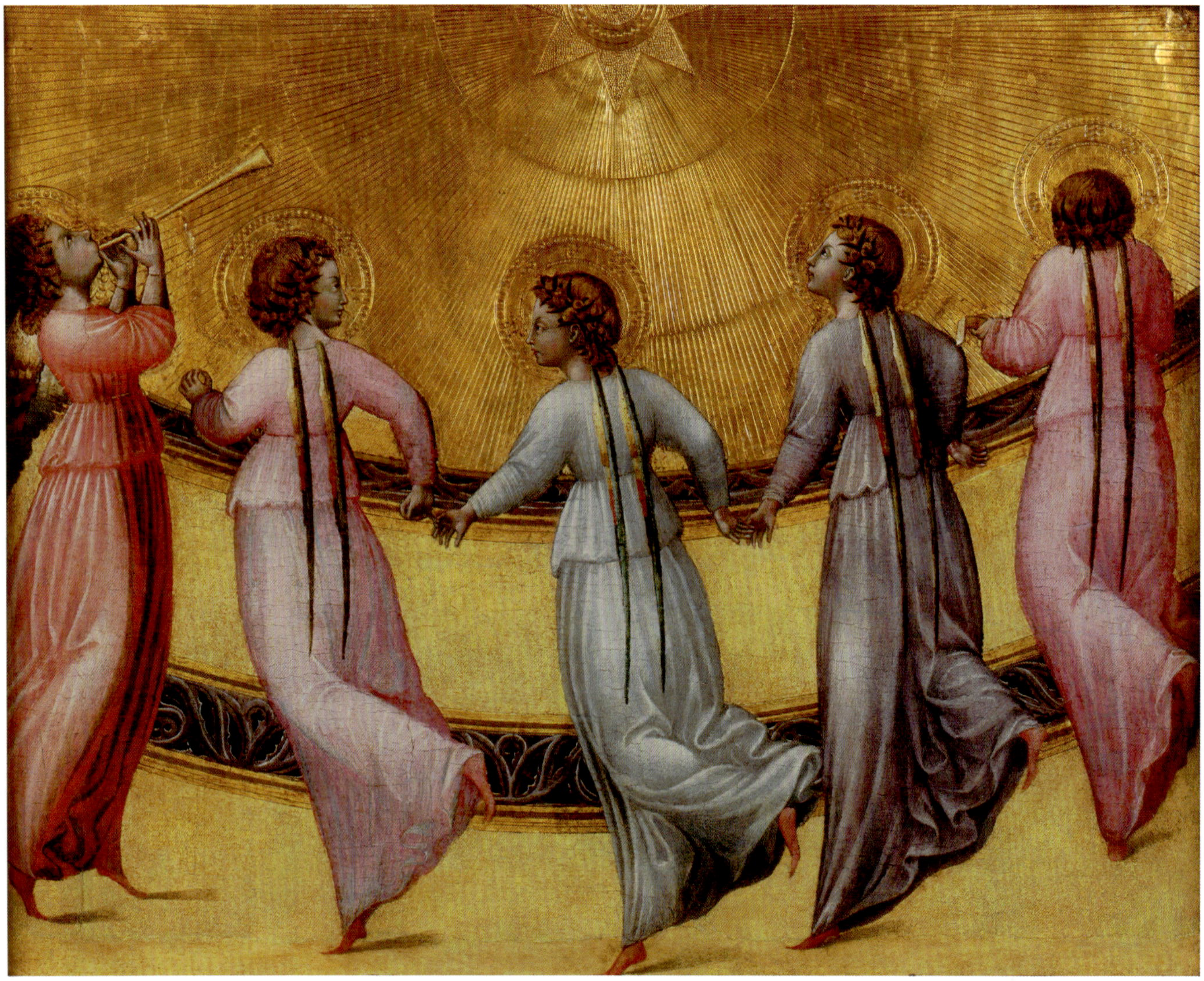

This panel is a mutilated fragment of a larger composition that showed a holy figure—probably the Madonna with Child—sitting on a throne flanked by dancing angels, as revealed by radiographic analysis. The five angels raise their heads toward the central character, while the curving steps of the throne, marked by scrolling decoration, can still be seen. X-ray analysis reveals the existence of an earlier, diamond-patterned motif, with drapery probably representing the Madonna's cloak. The restoration, which probably dates from the nineteenth century, replaced these elements with a gold background and a sun—iconography alien to fifteenth-century Italian primitives—in order to lend coherence to the scene. Henceforth the angels dance before a divine light. Despite these mutilations, the attribution to Giovanni di Paolo can stand: the iconography of angels at the foot of the Madonna's throne is also seen in his *Assumption of the Virgin* in the cathedral of Asciano.

The duc d'Aumale bought this painting, then attributed to Giotto, at the 1859 estate sale following the death of Lord Northwick, whose collection included several pre-Raphael works, some of which were acquired by the National Gallery (London) and the Louvre.

PESELLINO (FRANCESCO DI STEFANO)

(Florence, 1422[?]; Florence, 1457)

The Adoration of the Magi

Wood. H. 25 cm (9 ¾ in); W. 41 cm (1 ft. 4 in.)
Inv. 12 (Cabinet du Giotto)

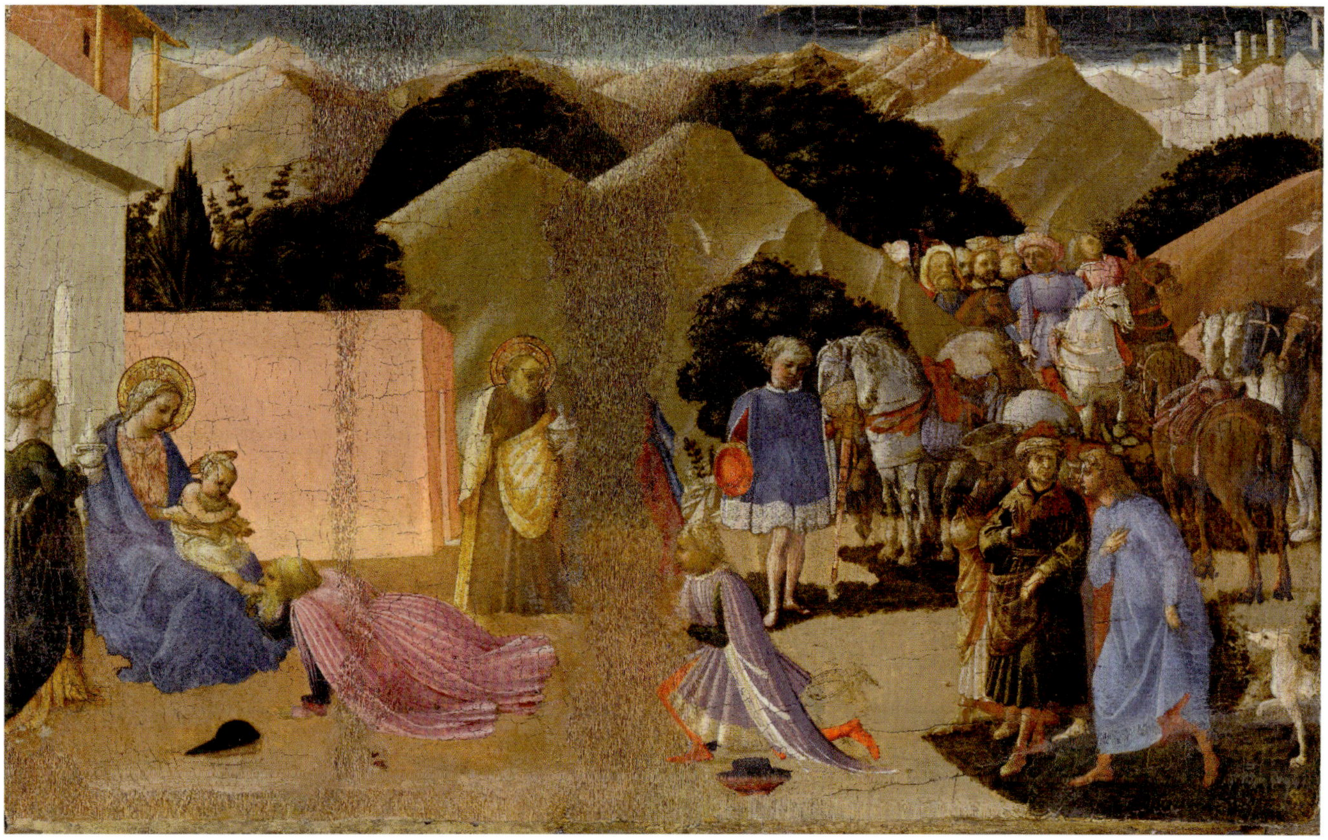

Francesco Pesellino, who died young, was one of Filippo Lippi's favorite pupils. This painting can be confidently attributed to Pesellino. It was a private devotional work rather than a predella for an altarpiece. The center of the panel contains a large gap that was previously filled by a somewhat rash restoration, which has been recently removed. The panel still reflects the International Gothic style, but perspective is already handled confidently. In the background is a landscape of a city and hills. Here Pesellino was moving away from Filippo Lippi and closer to Fran Angelico and Domeninco Veneziano. The painting can most likely be dated to 1450 or so.

According to an inscription on the back, this *Adoration of the Magi* came from Lucca. It was probably purchased in France by Frédéric Reiset, as were the other works in his collection (*see p. 33*).

SASSETTA (STEFANO DI GIOVANNI)

(Siena, 1392[?]; Siena, 1450)

The Mystic Marriage of Saint Francis of Assisi

Wood. H. 94.5 cm (3 ft. 1 ½ in.); W. 56 cm (1 ft. 10 in.)
Inv. 10 (Tribune)

In 1437 the Franciscan friars in Borgo San Sepolcro in Tuscany, not far from Umbria, commissioned from Sassetta a double-sided altarpiece for the high altar of the church of San Francesco, at a cost of 510 florins. The work was only installed on the high altar seven years later, in 1444. Composed of some sixty panels, the altarpiece was apparently dismantled by the late sixteenth century, being replaced by a tabernacle commissioned from Alberto Alberti subsequent to changes in the liturgy. As early as 1583 some of the panels of the altarpiece were placed in the side chapels of the church. The high altar was completely removed in 1752, and in 1810 when the monastery was closed down certain fragments, including the one here, were sold by Father Sereni to Cavaliere Sergiulano of Arezzo, later passing to the Angelucci family in Arezzo. The Chantilly fragment was purchased in Italy by Mantion and Wagner who sold it in 1840 to Frédéric Reiset, from whom the duc d'Aumale bought it in 1879 (*see p. 33*).

Various reconstructions of the large polyptych have been proposed. The front was devoted to a *Virgin and Child* (Louvre) and saints (Villa I Tatti, Settignano; Louvre), whereas as parts of the predella are now in the Louvre and in Berlin. On the back of the altarpiece, facing the monks' choir, were the panel here plus several other panels depicting the life of Saint Francis (National Gallery, London) which flanked a *Saint Francis Triumphant* in the middle (Villa I Tatti, Settignano). The episode shown here was taken from the life of the saint by Thomas of Celano, as related by Saint Bonaventura. However, while the texts mention the apparition of the saint's three favorite virtues—Poverty, Obedience, and Chastity—they make no reference to a mystic marriage with Poverty, which was therefore invented by Sassetta. The artist depicts the three virtues flying off with their attributes; Poverty looks back at the last moment. The unreal handling of the scene (notably the model-like city of Siena and the landscape in the background) make this panel a masterpiece by Sassetta and a wonderful example of Sienese painting.

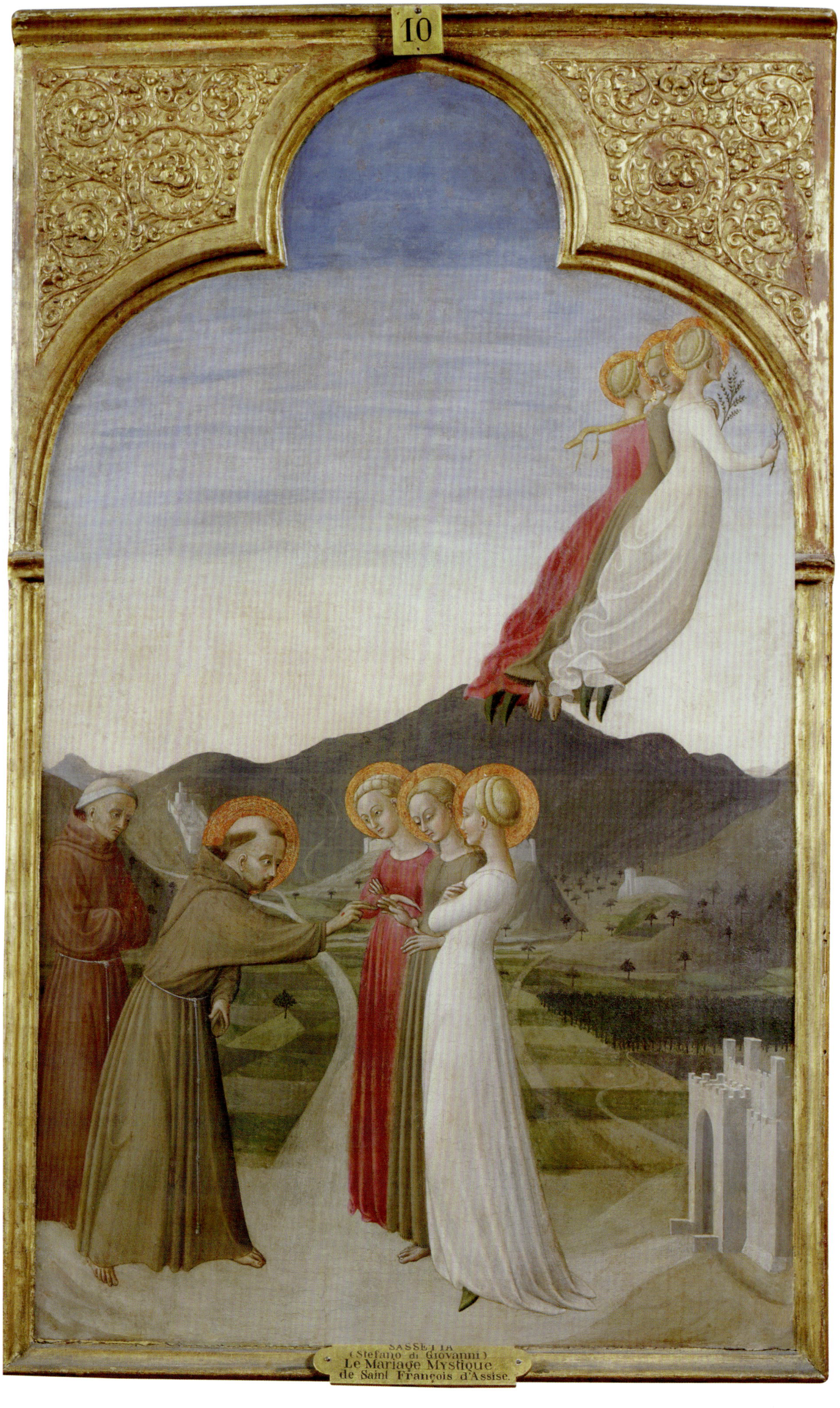
10
SASSETTA
(Stefano di Giovanni)
Le Mariage Mystique
de Saint François d'Assise.

NICCOLO PISANO

(active in Pisa, then Ferrara, from 1484 to 1538)

Virgin and Child Enthroned between Saint Francis, Saint Anthony, and Two Donors

Wood. H. 200 cm (6 ft. 7 in.); W. 112 cm (3 ft. 8 in.)
Inv. 50 (Galerie de Peinture)

This painting made its way to Rome by 1693, where it became part of the collection of Giovan Battista Borghese, heir to Olympia Aldobrandini. Despite not being mentioned in Aldobrandini's estate inventory in 1682, it probably came from Ferrara, a hypothesis supposed by its recent attribution to an artist from Ferrara, Niccolo Pisano. Indeed, part of the Aldobrandini collection originated there, because Cardinal Pietro Aldobrandini had inherited works belonging to Lucretia d'Este. This *Virgin and Child Enthroned* was bought between 1800 and 1802 by Cavaliere Domenico Venuti for the king of Naples, Ferdinand IV, then entered the collection of the prince of Salerno, which was acquired by his son-in-law, the duc d'Aumale, after his death in 1854 (*see p. 27*).

Attributed in the past to Pietro Perugino, then to Luca Longhi, this panel is now attributed to Niccolo Pisano, an artist who was mainly active in Ferrara. Toward 1499, he worked with L. Costa and B. Boccaccino to decorate the choir of the cathedral. His major work is the large altarpiece of the *Virgin with Child with Saint Helen and Saint James* (Pinacoteca di Brera, Milan); a *Saint Sebastian* (Pinacoteca, Ferrara) is also attributed to him.

The composition is a *sacra conversazione* in several hierarchical registers. At the top, the Virgin and Child are enthroned; toward the middle, the saints are depicted full-length, each with their attributes: the monk's robe, cross, and stigmata for Saint Francis of Assisi and the lily and the book for Saint Anthony. They are joined by a charming angel playing a lute, the only representative of the traditional choir of angels. Finally, the donors are represented at the base, their heads and upper bodies emerging from the lower corners. The different registers of the composition are linked by the architecture.

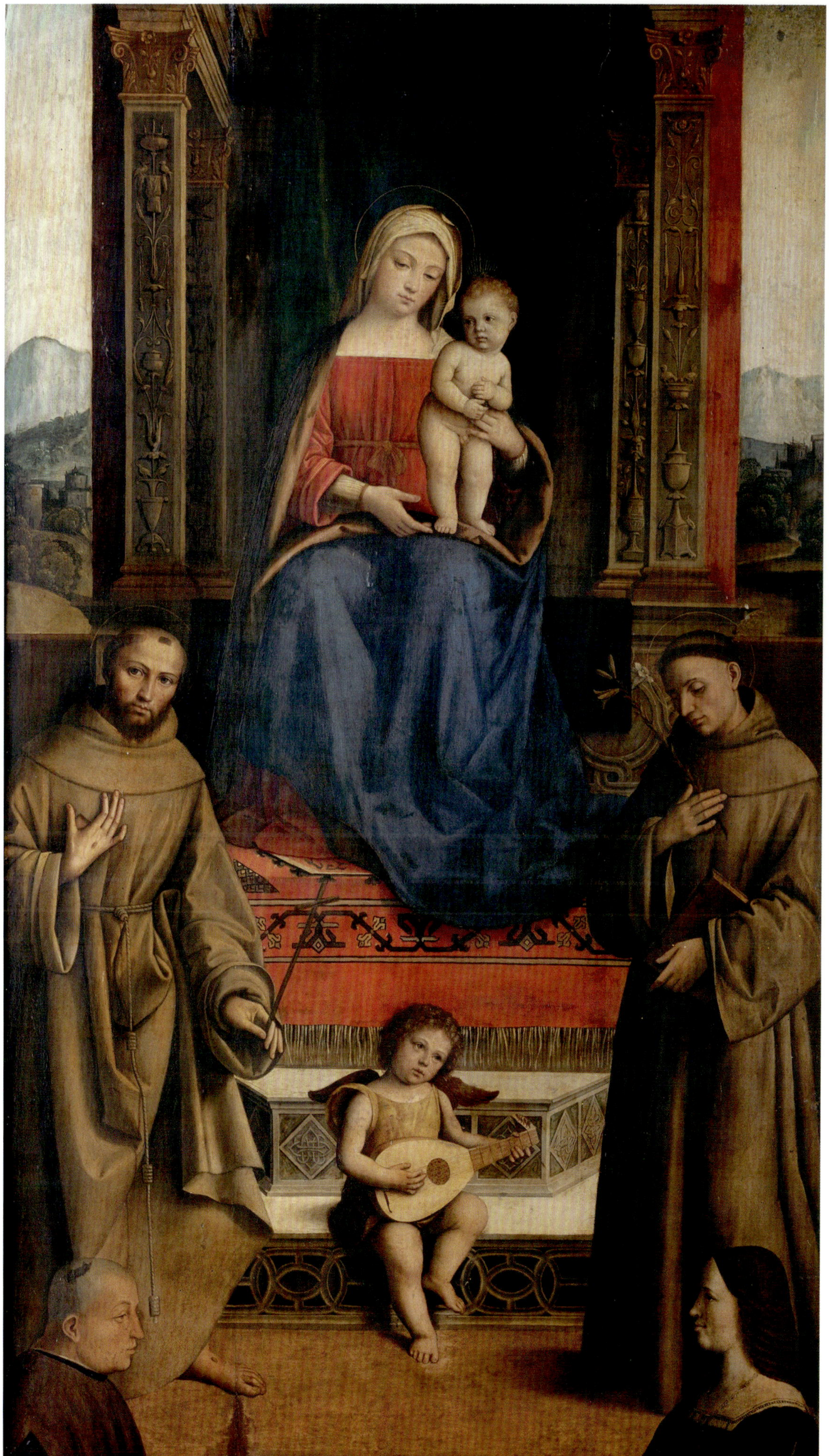

FRA CARNEVALE (BARTOLOMEO DI GIOVANNI CORRADINI DA URBINO) (?)

(active in Florence in 1445 and in Urbino from 1451 onward)

Virgin and Child Flanked by Six Angels and Two Saints

Wood. H. 20 cm (7 ½ in.); W. 16 cm (6 ¼ in.)
Inv. 11 (Tribune)

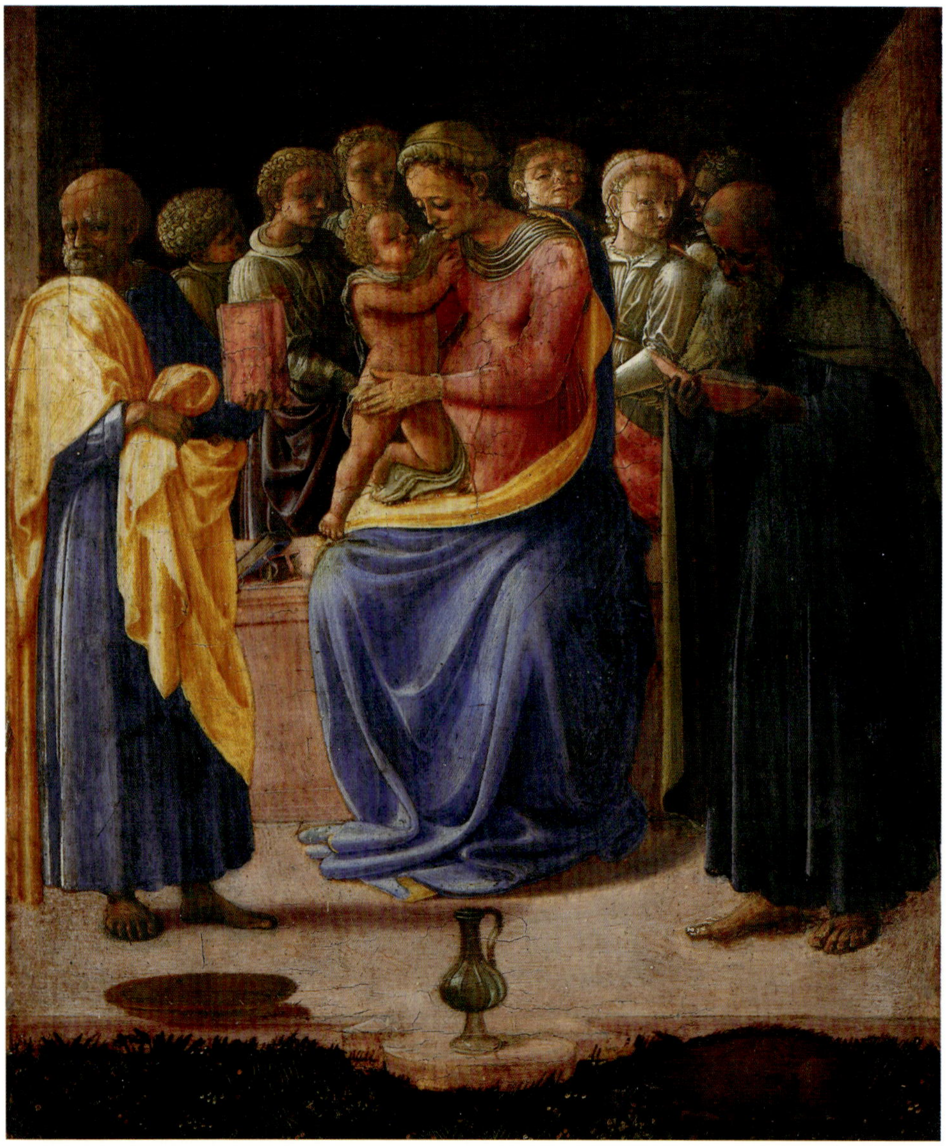

According to Frédéric Reiset, who bought it in 1840 (*see p. 33*), in 1807 this painting was in Venice, where it was engraved by Antoine Sergent-Marceau. It was then attributed to Masaccio, after having been ascribed either to Fra Filippo Lippi or to his disciple Pesellino (whose style was then very similar to his master's). Today specialists tend to see it as the work of the artist who did the predella of an *Annunciation* altarpiece for San Lorenzo in Florence, executed by Lippi around 1440. The identity of this artist was first thought to be Giovanni di Francesco, but a more recent suggestion is Fra Carnevale, who later worked at Urbino for Federico da Montefeltro. A follower of Lippi, Fra Carnevale frequented the master's Florence workshop in the 1440s (*see facing page*).

The composition shows figures placed around the Virgin and Child as though in a box, a non-specific interior with strong sense of perspective. The saints flanking the Virgin are generally thought to be Peter and Anthony, although no attribute allows for certain identification. It is worth noting the curiosity conveyed by the angel behind the Virgin who stands on tip-toe in order to see the Child (or perhaps the beholder of the painting), as well as the neighboring angel who looks off to one side.

FRA CARNEVALE (BARTOLOMEO DI GIOVANNI CORRADINI DA URBINO) (?)

(active in Florence in 1445 and in Urbino from 1451 onward)

John the Baptist in the Wilderness

Wood. H. 22 cm (8 ½ in.); W. 16 cm (6 ¼ in.)
Inv. 7 (Cabinet du Giotto)

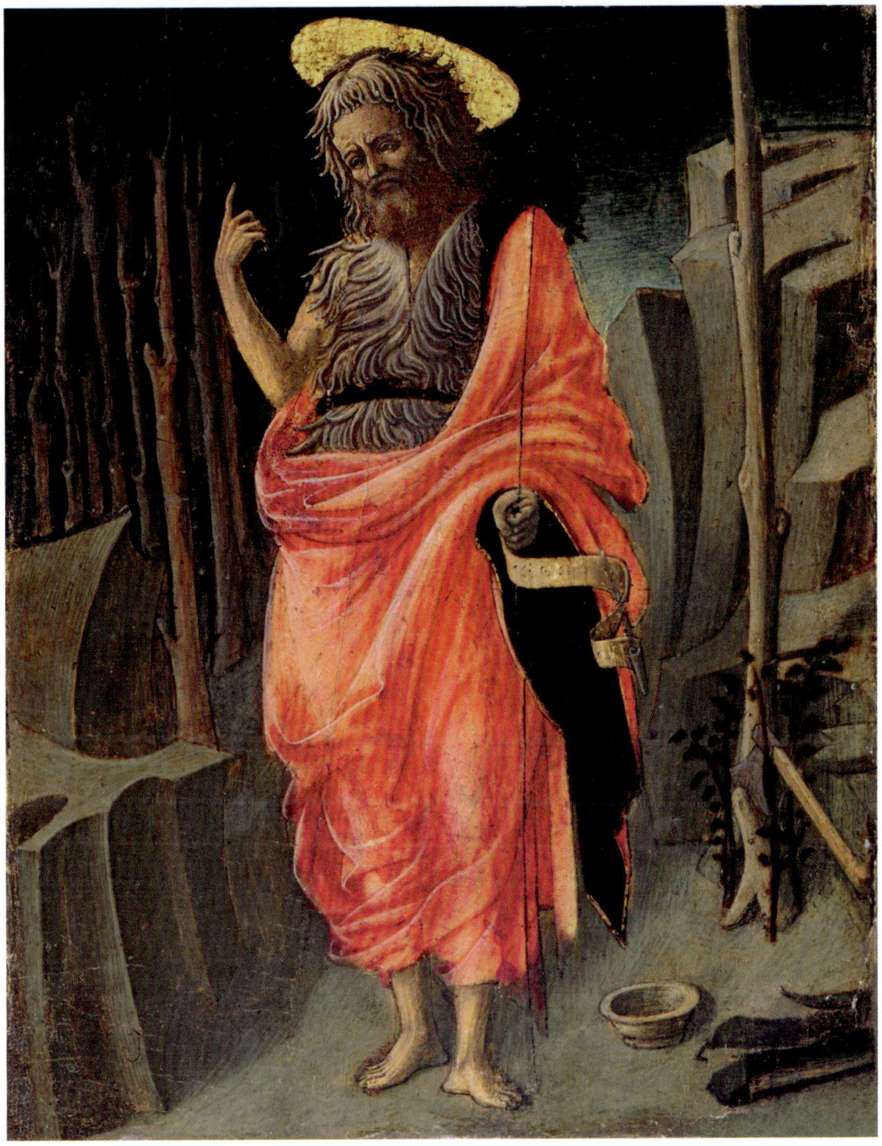

This little panel was attributed to Andrea del Castagno in the nineteenth century, then ascribed to a follower of Fra Filippo Lippi, and later to the Master of the Barberini Panels, who has recently been identified as Bartolomeo di Giovanni Corradini da Urbino, known as Fra Carnevale. This first-rate painter's style has been the object of recent critical reconstruction. His presence has been attested between 1445 and 1448 in Lippi's Florentine workshop; his name figures in the contract for a *Coronation of the Virgin* for Sant'Ambrogio (Uffizi, Florence), in which an angel is attributed to him. Fra Carnevale was in Urbino by 1451, where he served as a go-between for a terracotta lunette by Luca della Robbia. Equally influenced by Lippi and Piero della Francesca, Fra Carnevale was probably the Master of the Barberini Panels, who was one of the court painters to Federico da Montefeltro in Urbino.

This painting is similar to works attributed to the Master of the Barberini Panels, such as an *Annunciation* (Kress Collection, National Gallery, Washington D.C.) and the grisaille details in a *Presentation in the Temple* (Museum of Fine Arts, Boston). Here we see the artist's typical characteristics: hair handled in locks, drapery with angular folds, nose emphasized by a white highlight. This is probably a youthful work, done in the 1440s when Fra Carnevale was working in Lippi's studio in Florence.

PIERO DI COSIMO (PIERO DI LORENZO)

(Florence, 1461–62; Florence, 1521[?])

Portrait of a Woman (Simonetta Vespucci)

Wood. H. 57 cm (1 ft. 10 ½ in.); W. 42 cm (1 ft. 4 ½ in.)
Inscription on bottom: *SIMONETTA IANVENSIS VESPUCCIA*
Inv. 13 (Galerie de Peinture, rotunda)

This quattrocento painting from Florence is one of the most famous masterpieces in the Musée Condé. Art historians have always been intrigued by this portrait, painted around 1490, allegedly of Simonetta Vespucci, the young and beautiful mistress of Giuliano de' Medici. Known as the "idol of Florence," she posed for Botticelli, but died of consumption in 1476, aged twenty-three. Giuliano apparently had this portrait done as a memento. Yet it is not certain that we see Simonetta here, for the name written at the bottom is perhaps a later addition. Furthermore, since Piero di Cosimo was only fifteen years old when she died, this portrait would have been a posthumous one. Instead, this painting may be Piero's *Cleopatra with the Asp around her Neck,* seen by Vasari in 1568 at the home of Francesco da Angelo, whose father Giuliano was a friend of Piero di Cosmo. The iconography, however, does not really correspond to Cleopatra, usually shown bitten on the breast by the snake. Although scientific examination has proven that the inscription is old, it might still be posterior to Vasari (who doesn't mention it), perhaps added at the end of the sixteenth century. The painting was then acquired by the Vespucci family (one of whose members, Amerigo Vespucci, gave his name to the newly discovered continent of America). Frédéric Reiset bought the portrait in 1841, nineteenth months after it was relinquished by the Florentine family (*see p. 33*).

The depiction of a bare-breasted woman is unusual in fifteenth-century portraiture. We are therefore perhaps in the presence of an idealized portrait, a neo-platonist allegory of Death—symbolized by the serpent biting its tail—which leads to true beauty. This funereal interpretation is strengthened by the dark clouds and dead tree in front of Simonetta on the left (whereas on the right the sky is blue and the trees are leafy). The profile pose was common in the quattrocento, as seen for example in the work of Pollaiuolo (*Portrait of a Woman,* Museo Poldi-Pezzoli). Indeed, there was a tradition in Italy of profile portraits inspired by the art of medals, but here Piero has set his model against a real landscape. Flemish influence can be detected in the realistic handling of jewelry and headdress. The curved forehead and snub nose are typical of Piero's portraits, substantiating the theory of an idealized image. It was painted sometime between 1480 and 1520.

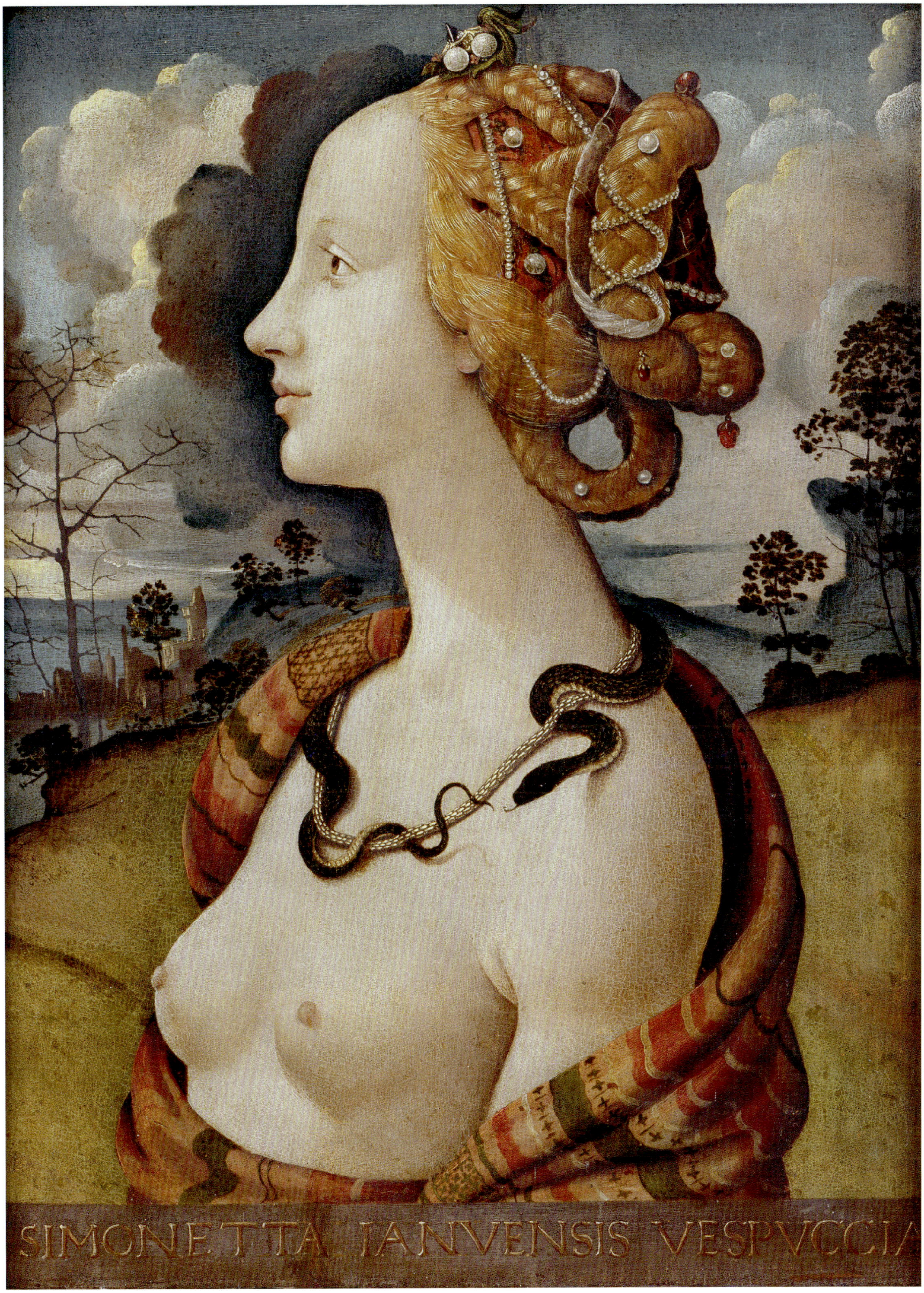
SIMONETTA IANVENSIS VESPVCCIA

FILIPPINO LIPPI

(Florence, 1459; Florence, 1504)

King Ahasuerus Choosing Esther

Wood. H. 47 cm (1 ft. 6 ½ in.); W. 131 cm (4 ft. 3 ½ in.)
Inv. 19 (Santuario)

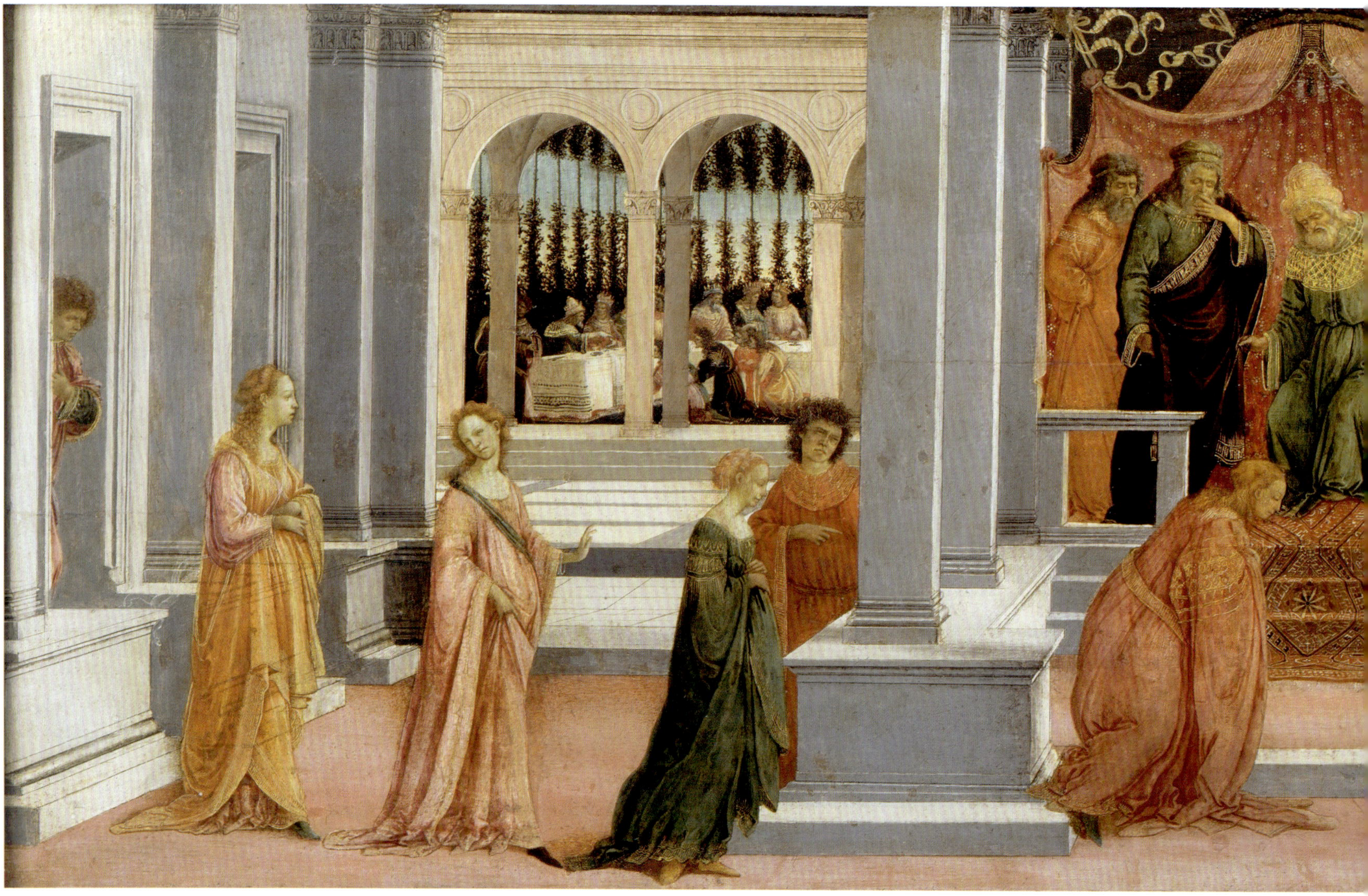

Filippino Lippi worked alongside Sandro Botticelli in the Florentine workshop of his father, Filippo Lippi. The styles of the two painters, both represented in this museum, are sometimes so similar that when in the early twentieth century the great art historian Bernard Berenson was reconstituting the oeuvres of anonymous artists based on stylistic grounds, he recognized the hand of an *amico di Sandro* (friend of Sandro Botticelli), whose works were ultimately identified with Filippino Lippi's output.

The panel here comes from a *cassone*, or wedding chest, with iconography on a marital theme drawn from the Old Testament's Book of Esther. King Ahasuerus, having repudiated his queen, Vashti, sought a new wife from among the young women paraded before him. He chose Esther, a Jewess in exile in Persia. The panel incorporates several scenes set in the royal palace in Susa: in the background, on the left, Ahasuerus asks Queen Vashti to join him; on the right, still in the background, the queen refuses to obey, hence is dismissed. The sides of the chest feature *Esther at the Palace Gate* (National Gallery of Canada, Ottawa) and *Vashti Being Exiled from Susa* (Museo Horne, Florence). Another chest depicted the rest of the

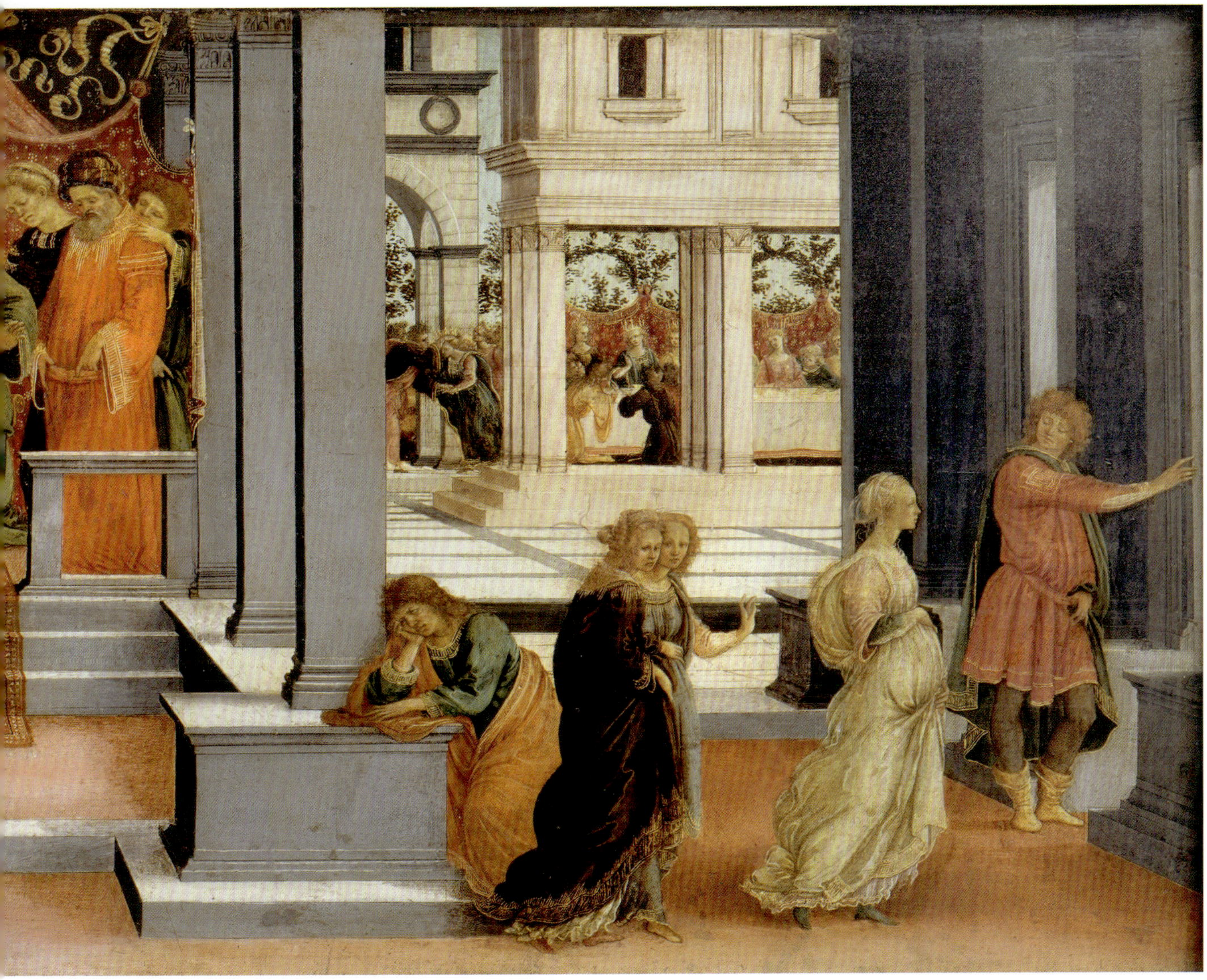

story, notably *The Despair of Esther's Uncle Mordecai* (Galleria Rospigliosi-Pallavicini, Rome) on learning that Ahasuerus had decreed the massacre of the Jews, plus *Esther Fainting* (Louvre) upon boldly breaking the prohibition to enter the king's presence unbeckoned (in order to plead for the Jewish people) and *The Triumph of Mordecai* (National Gallery of Canada, Ottawa), which was also the triumph of the Jewish people.

While the design of the *cassone* was Filippino's, some historians do not rule out the participation of Botticelli, who was somewhat older than his friend. The figures move as though on a stage in front of an architectural background enhanced by a mastery of perspective, which divides the scene into three sequences. The dancing women, the attenuated figures, the warm, light palette, and the narrative skill all make this a masterpiece by the young Filippino, executed around 1478–80. The painting, apparently owned by the Torrigiani family, was the last Italian work to be bought by the duc d'Aumale, at the Leclanché auction in 1892.

ALESSANDRO BOTTICELLI (workshop)

(Florence, 1455; Florence, 1510)

Autumn, or Allegory Against Drunkenness

Canvas transferred from wood. H. 192 cm (6 ft 3 ½ in.); W. 105 cm (3 ft. 5 ½ in.)
Inv. 16 (Tribune)

The provenance of this painting has not been clearly established. It was recorded in Paris in 1847 in a charity exhibition, then was bought by Frédéric Reiset who sold his collection to the duc d'Aumale in 1879 (*see p. 33*). Perhaps it is the work titled *Woman Representing a Season,* attested in 1840 in the possession of the Roman art dealer Baldeschi, who attributed it to Mantegna.

Although this painting was generally ascribed to Botticelli himself in the twentieth century, now it is generally thought to be the product of his workshop. The master probably designed the composition, but some awkward execution betrays the hand of an assistant. The subject has often been interpreted as an allegory of abundance, allegedly based on a preparatory drawing now in the British Museum in London. Another similar motif in Botticelli's oeuvre can be seen in his fresco of the *Temptation of Christ* (Sistine Chapel, Vatican), showing a woman carrying a bundle of sticks, followed by a putto with a snake. Some commentators see her as Pomona, although that does not explain the presence of the snake; it might be an allegory of Autumn, if the putto on the right were not wearing what look like cherries around his neck—which suggests that it might be an allegory of Wine and Drunkenness.

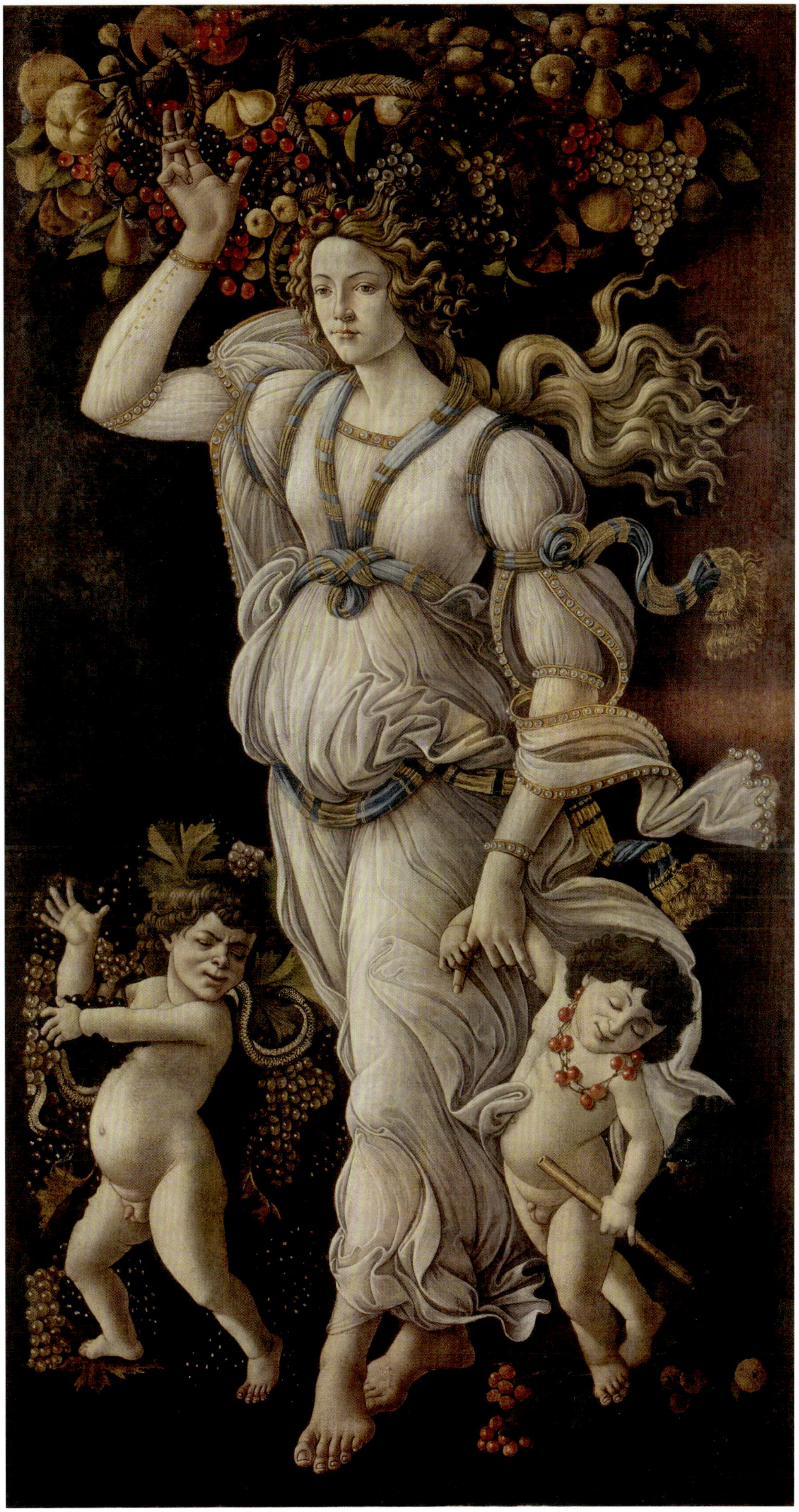

DAVIDE GHIRLANDAIO

(Florence, 1452; Florence, 1525)

Virgin and Child

Canvas transferred from wood. H. 81 cm (2 ft. 8 in.); W. 52 cm (1 ft. 8 ½ in.)
Inv. 14 (Cabinet du Giotto)

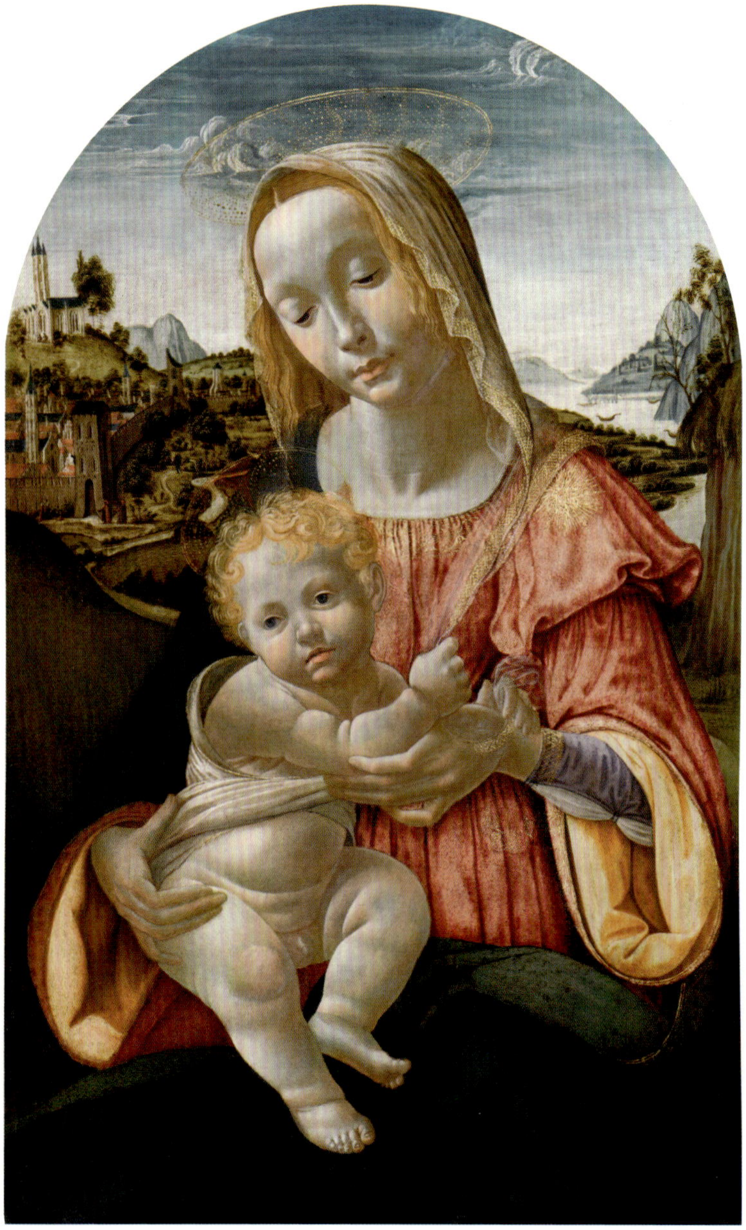

The brother and close colleague of Domenico Ghirlandaio (who studied under Verrochio, Leonardo's master), Davide was initially known as the Saint Louis Master. Once his identity was established, Davide's oeuvre was reconstructed around two paintings, *The Madonna and Child with Saint Louis of Toulouse, John the Evangelist, and Donors* (City Art Museum, Saint Louis) and a *Virgin* (Gambier Parry Collection, Courtauld Institute Galleries, London). The painting here, long ascribed to Cosimo Rosselli, displays the same features as those two works, notably the somewhat sharp draftsmanship in the Virgin's face and the squat, short-necked physique of the Child. Davide seems to have looked at the Portinari triptych (Uffizi, Florence) by Hugo van der Goes, which arrived in Florence in 1483. The very Flemish sense of perspective and meticulous taste for detail can be seen in the background of the work here. The landscape on the left recurs in a painting by Ridolfo Ghirlandaio, *The Mystic Marriage of Saint Catherine* (whereabouts unknown). Some historians detect the influence of Fra Bartolomeo, notably in landscape drawings now in the Louvre, but Davide Ghirlandaio's buildings are more "Gothic" than Fra Bartolomeo's. The Flemish influence, therefore, seems to predominate.

FRANCESCO ZAGANELLI

(Cotignola, circa 1470; Ravenna, 1532)

Virgin and Child Between John the Baptist and Saint Sebastian

Wood. H. 33 cm (1 ft. 1 in.); W. 24 cm (9 ½ in.)
Inv. 22 (Tribune)

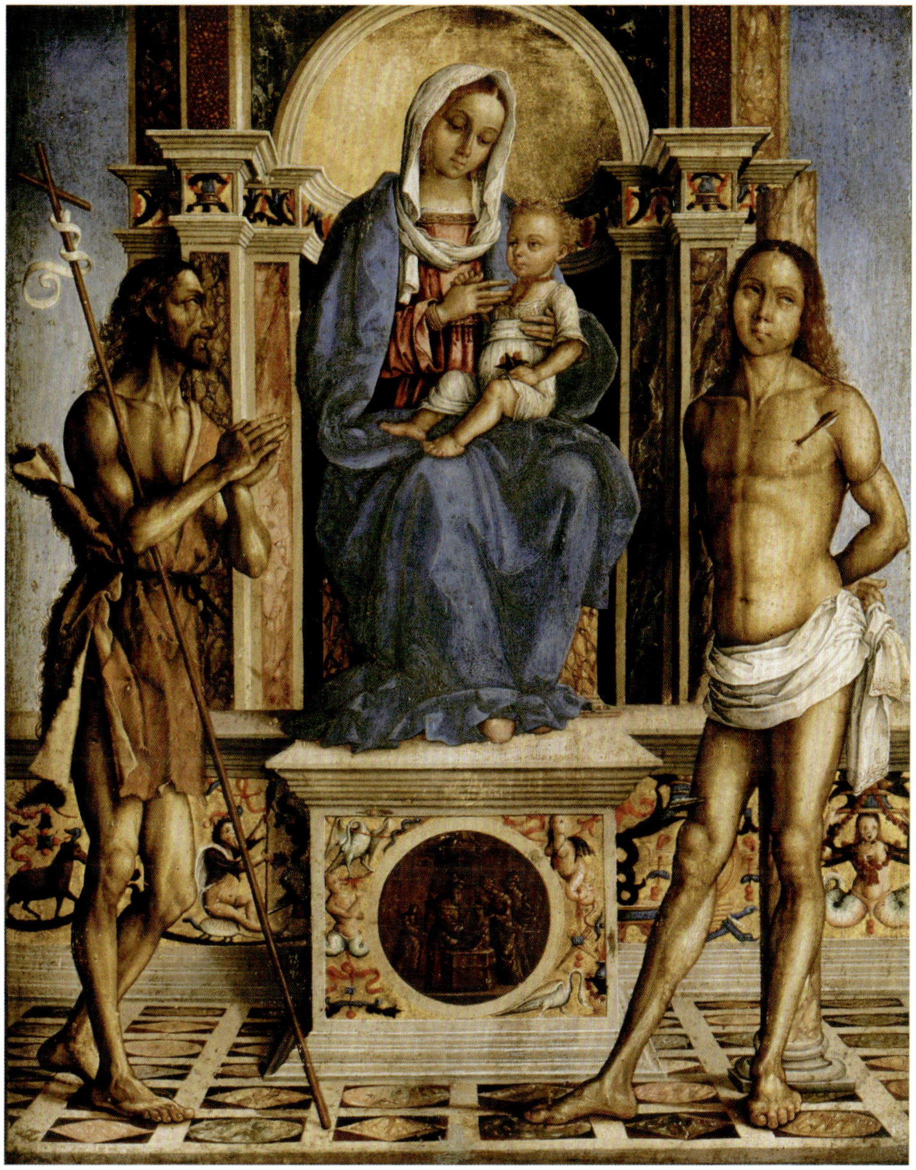

The small size of this panel distinguishes it from the rest of Francesco Zaganelli's work. As an object for private worship, probably designed for a personal oratory, it is similar to Zaganelli's *Virgin Enthroned Between Saint Francis, Saint Nicholas of Bari, and the Donor* (Pinacoteca di Brera, Milan), signed and dated 1505. It might also be an original reduction.

The composition belongs to the *sacra conversazione* genre developed in Venice, with the Virgin on a throne raised above the saints, here adorned with a grisaille medallion illustrating the Presentation in the Temple. It is typical of the early part of Zaganelli's career, when still under the influence of his master, Marco Palmezzano. The handling, however, is similar to that of artists in the school of Ferrara, with whom Zaganelli trained, which explains the marked outlines of the figures, the distinct zones of shadow and light, and the stark forms that recall the manner of Ercole de' Roberti, and even the influence of Albrecht Dürer. A preparatory drawing of the Virgin's head and the drapery is now held by the Nationalmuseum in Stockholm. This painting came from the Frédéric Reiset collection (*see p. 33*).

FRANCESCO FRANCIA (FRANCESCO RAIBOLINI)

(Bologna, circa 1450; Bologna, 1517)

Annunciation with Saint Albert

Canvas. H. 182 cm (6 ft.); W. 132 cm (4 ft. 4 in.)
Inv. 17 (Galerie de Peinture)

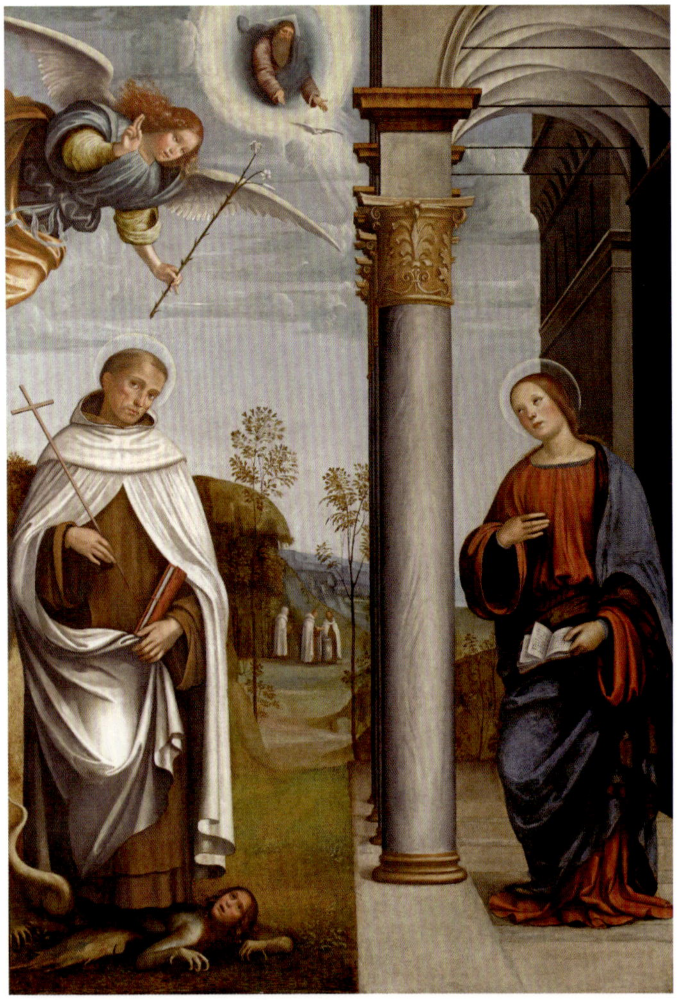

The history of this painting cannot be traced back beyond the nineteenth century. Some historians formerly identified it with the work given by Francesco Maria della Rovere, duke of Urbino, to his secretary Gian Mario della Porta for the latter's chapel in the church of Madonna del Carmine in Modena, but it would seem that the painting described there, a *Saint Albert Slaying a Demon*, without an Annunciation scene, is in fact the painting by Dosso Dossi still in situ. The painting here surfaced in Lord Northwick's collection in England in the nineteenth century, then was bought in 1850 by Frédéric Reiset, whence it passed to the duc d'Aumale (*see p. 33*).

The attribution to Francia is henceforth certain. The work is dated roughly 1503–04, a period when Francia was evolving toward greater classicism, distancing himself from the influence of Lorenzo Costa and the school of Ferrara. The influence of Perugino and Fra Bartolomeo's Florentine style can be detected, notably in the symmetrical composition and the deployment of somewhat static full-length figures. Francia was in the habit of including in his Annunciation scenes saints who were posterior to the holy story, as in his *Annunciation with Four Saints* (1500, Pinacoteca Nazionale, Bologna) and *Annunciation with John the Baptist and Saint Jerome* (Pinacoteca Nazionale, Bologna).

Who is this Saint Albert? He might be Albert of Jerusalem (or Vercelli), who codified the Rule of the Carmelite Order in 1225 and whose attributes are the crucifix and a knife. But he might also be Albert of Messina, a Carmelite monk from Sicily who saved the city of Messina from famine and was canonized in 1476; his attributes are a crucifix between two lilies, and he is sometimes shown chaining a demon (an allusion to the healing of possessed people). This Albert is seen in another painting by Francia, *The Entombment* (Galleria Sabauda, Turin). So here we probably have Saint Albert of Messina, who inspired a special cult of the Virgin that took root in Bologna from 1423 onward.

BERNARDINO LUINI (workshop of)

(Luino [Lake Maggiore], 1480; Milan, 1532)

Nativity

Canvas transferred from wood. H. 127 cm (4 ft. 2 in.); W. 99 cm (3 ft. 3 in.)
Inv. 27 (Tribune)

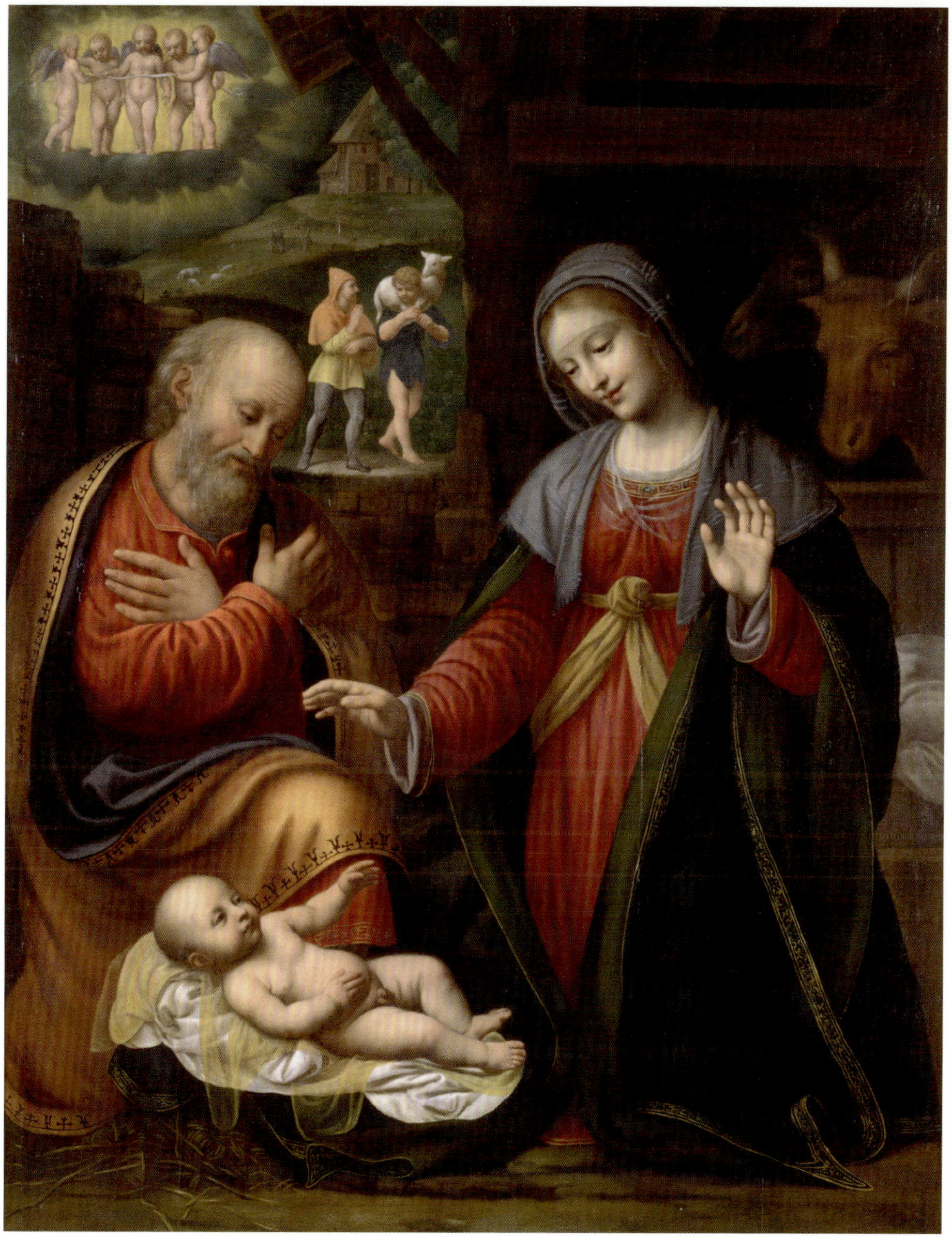

Purchased in Rome around 1802–03 on behalf of the king of Naples, Ferdinand IV, this painting entered the collection of the prince of Salerno, which was acquired by the duc d'Aumale in 1854 (*see p. 27*). It is a workshop version of a painting done by Luini in 1925, now in the earl of Plymouth's collection in Ludlow, England. Other copies exist: one is in the sacristy of the church of Chiaravalle near Milan, another in the monastery of the Incarnation in Madrid. These works were probably executed in the workshop under the supervision of the master. Since the original was painted in 1525, the replicas must be slightly later.

This panel is noteworthy for its porcelain-like quality. The composition is divided into several planes: in addition to the group of Mary and Joseph kneeling before Jesus, and the animals poking their heads out of the stable, there is a less traditional choir of angels (top left) and a glimpse of a landscape with two shepherds heading toward the stable to worship the baby Jesus (one of them carries a lamb on his shoulders).

BERNARDINO LUINI

(Luino [Lake Maggiore], 1480; Milan, 1532)

The Infant Jesus, Savior of the World

Wood. H. 36 cm (1 ft. 2 in.); W. 30 cm (1 ft.)
Inv. 24 (Tribune)

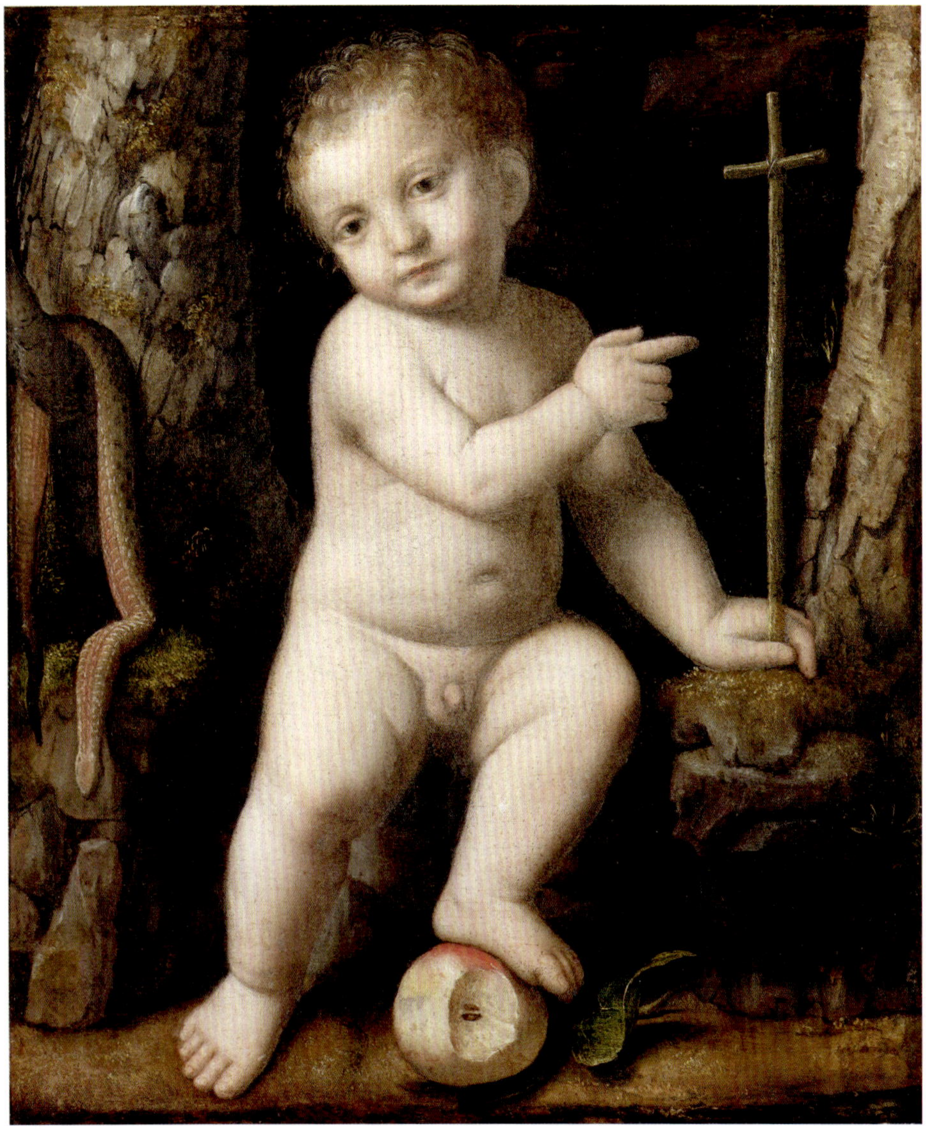

Attributed to Leonardo da Vinci in nineteenth-century auction catalogues, this panel is now ascribed to Bernardino Luini, who habitually depicted children in his work. The iconography is highly symbolic: on the tree of knowledge and temptation whose trunk is visible on the left, the serpent—a symbol of evil—has been killed. Its head hangs low, while in a triumphant gesture the Infant Jesus points with his right hand to the cross held in his left, and crushes under his left foot the apple of original sin (bitten to the core by Eve, as revealed by the visible seeds). The Child has therefore come to redeem the sins of the world and to vanquish evil.

The painting appears to be a mature work by Luini, dated roughly 1520. A perforated preparatory drawing, now in the Pinacoteca Ambrosiana in Milan, displays some differences with the final composition. Luini having often been copied, there are several replicas of this work in museums in Modena, Berlin, and Sibiu.

This *Infant Jesus* has been linked to a work listed in the collection of Count Pirro Visconti Borromeo in 1604, described as a *Saint John the Baptist,* which seems coherent with the iconography. The version here was part of William Beckford's collection at Fonthill Abbey. Sold in 1823, it was acquired first by the collector William Esdaile, then by Nieuwenhuys who sold it to Frédéric Reiset, whose collection was purchased by the duc d'Aumale (*see p. 33*).

LUDOVICO MAZZOLINO

(Ferrara, 1480[?]; Ferrara, 1528[?])

Ecce Homo

Wood. H. 53 cm (1 ft. 8 ¾ in.); W. 43 cm (1 ft. 5 in.)
Inv. 36 (Tribune)

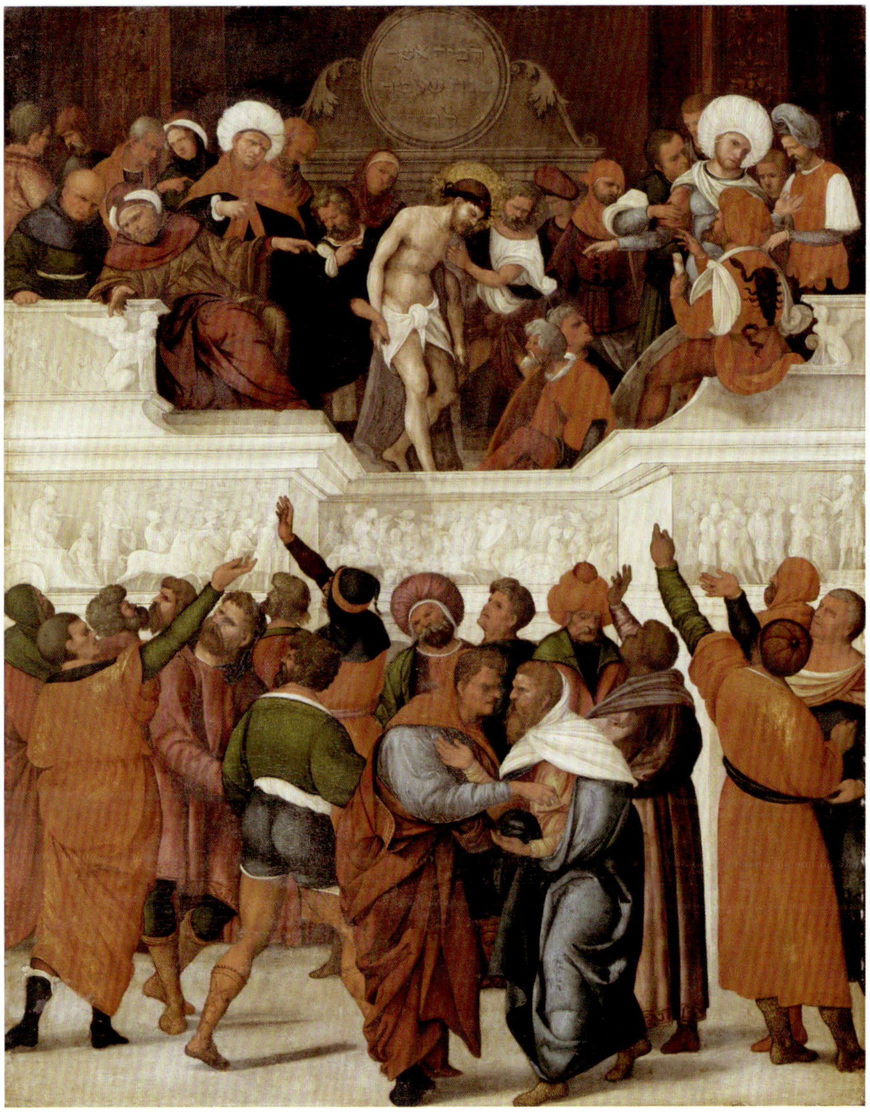

The fine drawing, expressive figures, and skillful coloring of this painting are characteristic of Mazzolino; despite its small size, it is one of his major works. The composition is divided into two registers, divided by a grisaille bas-relief above which the stripped and humiliated Christ is displayed to the crowd by his tormentors. This arrangement was habitual for Mazzolino, as notably employed in his *Massacre of the Innocents* and *Circumcision* (both in the Uffizi, Florence).

An *Ecce Homo* by Mazzolino was listed in 1592 in the collection of Lucretia d'Este, part of which was acquired early in the seventeenth century by Cardinal Pietro Aldobrandini. In 1603 the cardinal owned two other paintings by Mazzolino, both showing *Christ Before Pilate*. The *Ecce Homo* was taken from the Villa Aldobrandini in Rome between 1798 and 1799 by William Young Ottley, from which it made its way to England, where it was purchased at the Lord Northwick sale in 1859.

Several versions of this subject punctuate Mazzolino's oeuvre. Examples can be found in Dresden (Staatliche Kunstsammlungen), Cambridge (Fitzwilliam Museum), and Budapest (Szepmuveszeti Muzeum). The Cambridge version comes from the Borghese collection, inherited from the Aldobrandinis through the marriage of Olympia Aldobrandini to Paolo Borghese; on the back it bears an inscription, as does the Dresden one, attesting that it belonged to the Aldobrandini collection. There can be no certainty, then, that the example here is the one owned by Lucretia d'Este.

LUDOVICO MAZZOLINO

(Ferrara, 1480[?]; Ferrara, 1528[?])

Virgin and Child with Saint Anthony Abbot in a Landscape

Wood. H. 32 cm (1 ft. ½ in.); W. 25 cm (9 ¾ in.)
D.l.r. in gold lettering: 1525 *SOBER*
Inv. 37 (Cabinet du Giotto)

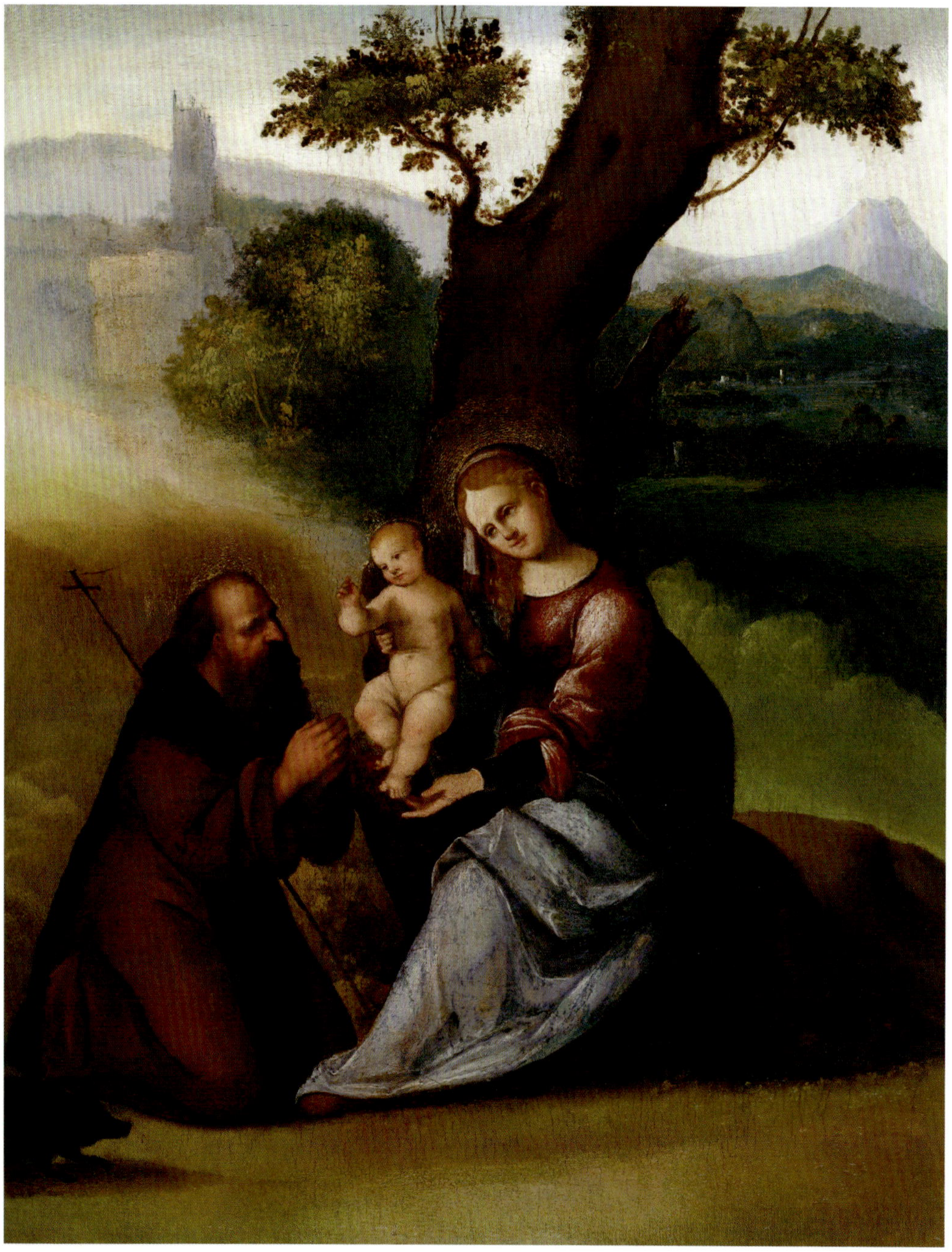

This type of depiction is quite unusual for Mazzolino. The artist set the composition in a realistic landscape rather than in the conventional architectural setting, even if the tree in the middle serves the same function. Its style is closer to that of Dosso Dossi, whose figures are similar to the Anthony Abbot shown here, even though Mazzolino has used natural lighting, unlike Dossi. The work probably belongs to Mazzolino's late period, around 1525–26, when his compositions incorporated nature and began to resemble those of Dossi.

This little panel comes from the Frédéric Reiset collection (*see p. 33*).

GIAMPIETRINO (GIOVANNI PIETRO RIZZOLI)

(active in Milan from 1495 to 1549)

Head of a Woman

Wood. H. 27 cm (10 ½ in.); W. 22 cm (8 ½ in.)
Inv. 28 (Cabinet du Giotto)

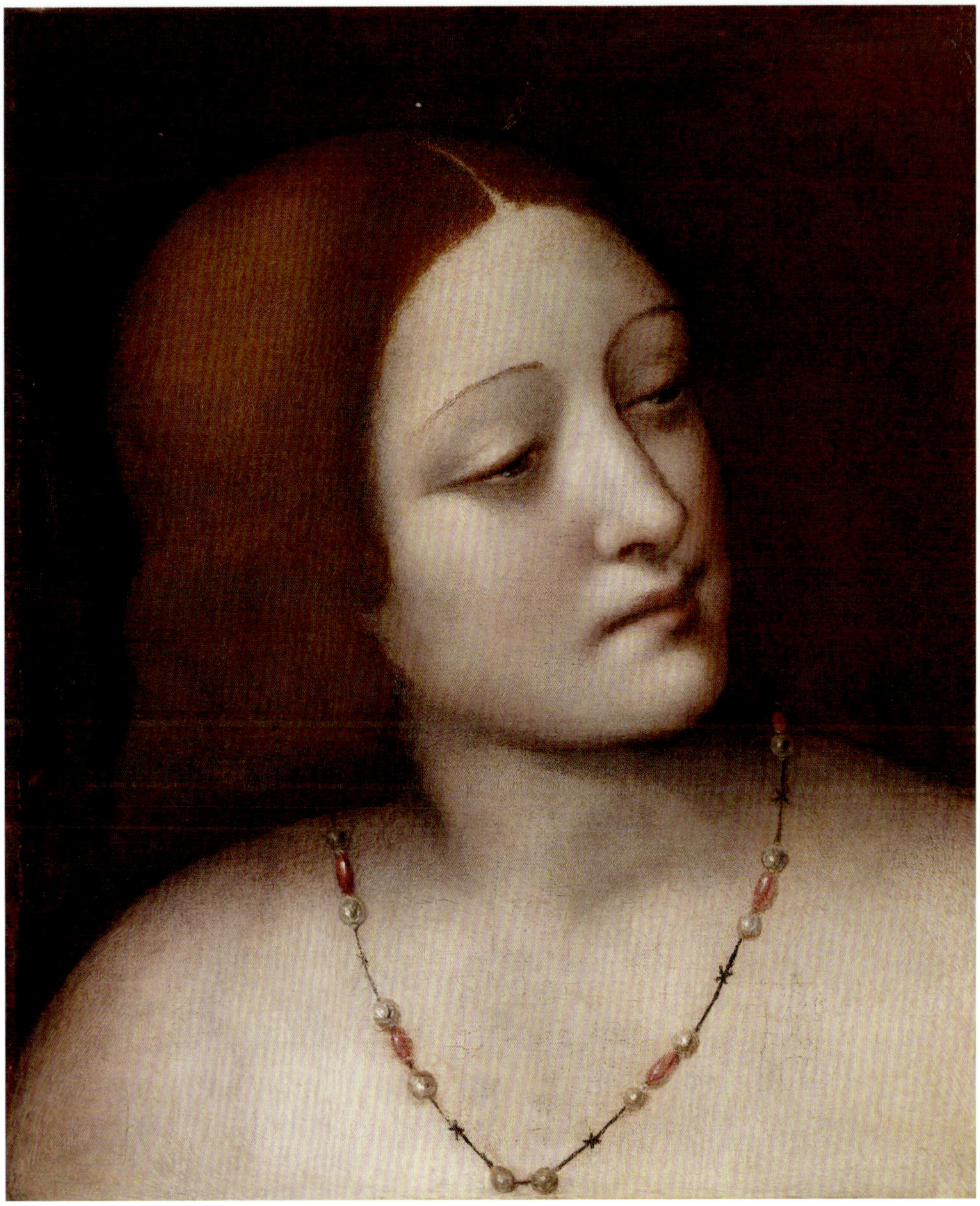

This little painting was acquired by the duc d'Aumale for twenty-six pounds sterling at the Northwick auction in July 1859. It was listed as a portrait of Mona Lisa by Leonardo da Vinci, but the duke was not fooled by the optimistic identification and attribution, and noted in his sale catalogue, "ravishing and excellent Luini, mine for £26."

The little work is a fragment of a larger panel, heavily repainted, notably to make the background uniform. The sitter's physical type is characteristic of Giampietrino, a Milanese follower of Leonardo. Similar figures can be seen in his religious paintings notably of Mary Magdalene (Pinacoteca di Brera, Milan; Cathedral, Burgos; Accademia Carrara, Bergamo). Some historians feel that the panel was part of a mythological subject. A portrait of a woman wearing a necklace (whereabouts unknown), very similar to the one here, might be a second fragment from the same work.

TITIAN (TIZIANO VECELLIO) (?)

(Pieve di Cadore, c. 1488–89; Venice, 1576)

Ecce Homo

Canvas. H. 72 cm (2 ft. 4 in.); W. 58 cm (1 ft. 10 3/4 in.)
Inv. 32 (Tribune)

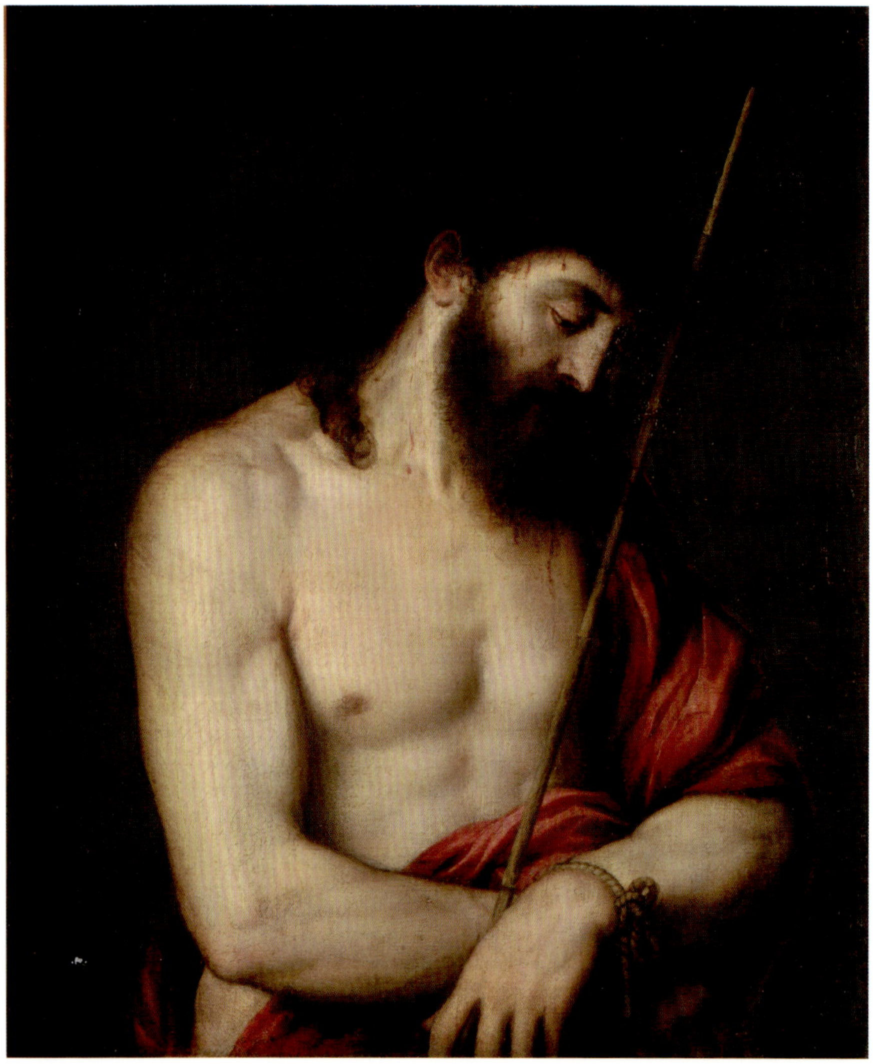

This painting comes from the sale of the Averoldi collection in Brescia, where the duc d'Aumale bought it in 1858. According to Brescia travel guides of the day, Titian apparently gave it to the Averoldi family when they commissioned a *Resurrection of Christ* from him for the church of San Nazaro e Celso in Brescia, around 1522. However, descriptions of the city do not mention the *Ecce Homo* prior to 1817; while the painting bears the seal of the Averoldi family, it also has another, unidentified seal, which suggests that it may have belonged to another collection.

There are several versions of the *Ecce Homo* by Titian or his workshop. In addition to the one now in the Prado, painted in 1547 for Holy Roman Emperor Charles V when he was living in Augsburg (considered to be the original version), there are examples in Milan (Pinacoteca Ambrosiana), Dublin (National Gallery of Ireland), and Sibiu (Museu Brukental); in a workshop replica now in the Louvre, some figures around Christ have been added.

The painting here, very similar to the original in Madrid, is a good workshop replica apparently given by Titian to Pietro Aretino for Christmas 1547; Aretino describes it very precisely in a thank-you letter written in early January 1548, mentioning the reed held by Christ, which does not figure in the Prado original. Vasari also mentions an *Ecce Homo,* apparently now lost, painted by Titian for the Farnese pope Paul III during the artist's stay in Rome in 1545.

The Musée Condé's replica is one of the finest of many replicas; it is therefore hard to believe that it was painted by Titian while he was working for the Averoldis in Brescia, because it is stylistically closer to the year 1547 and the Prado painting. This type of figure, designed to inspire piety, was very much part of the Counter-Reformation movement.

PALMA VECCHIO (JACOPO NEGRETI)

(Serina, 1480[?]; Venice, 1528)

Virgin and Child with Saint Peter, Saint Jerome, and a Donor, c. 1510

Canvas transferred from wood. H. 89.5 cm (2 ft. 11 in.); W. 137.7 cm (4 ft. 6 in.)
S.d.r. Saint Jerome's book: *Iach. Obvs. Palm. M.D.*
Inv. 35 (Galerie de Peinture)

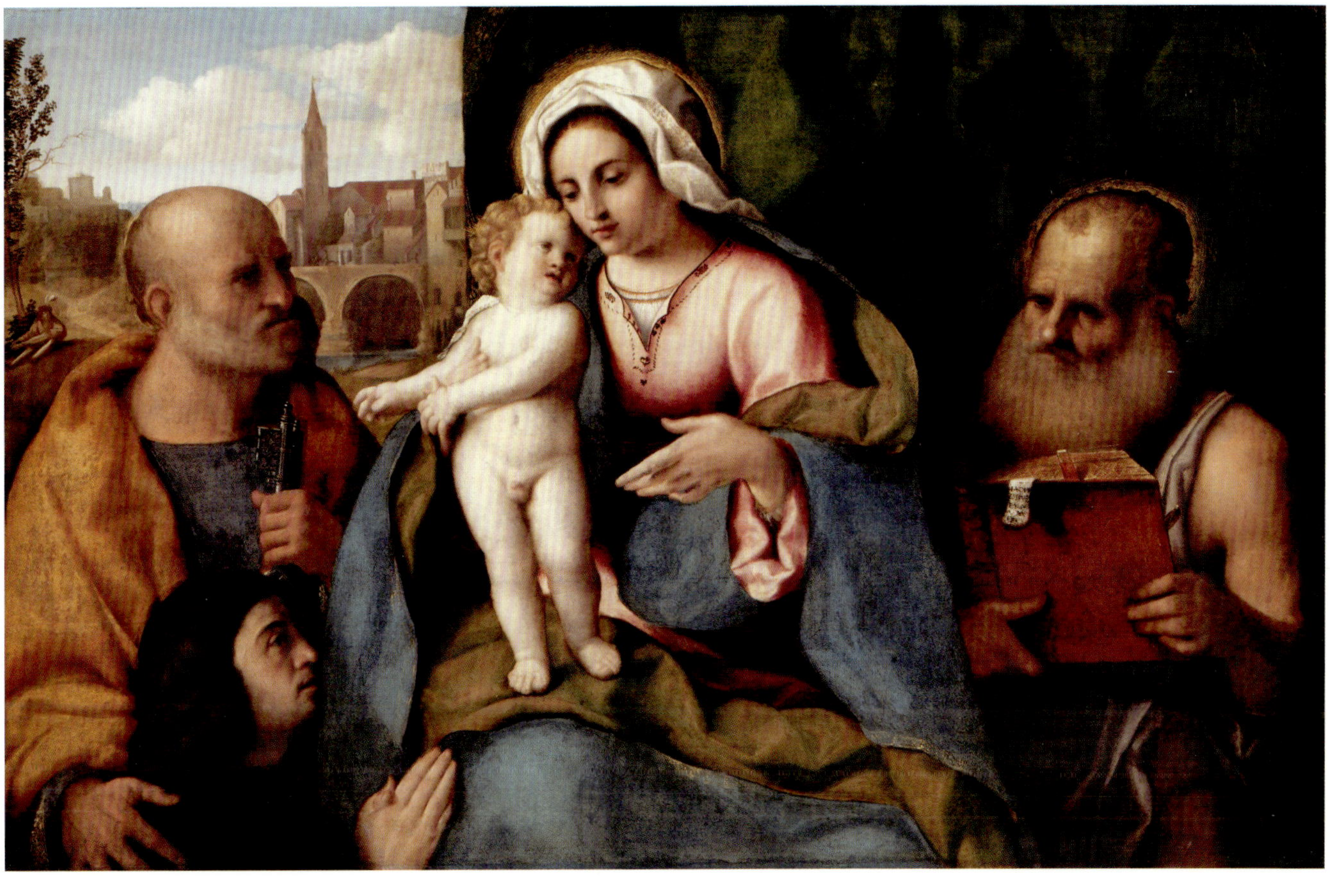

Documented as being in Rome in 1621, this painting is listed in the estate inventory of Cardinal Benedetto Giustiniani, whose brother was Marquess Vincenzo Giustiniani. The marquess inherited the work and bequeathed it in turn to his nephew Andrea in 1638 along with the rest of his collection, with instructions not to disperse it. Some of the paintings were nevertheless sold in the eighteenth century; so when the rest of the collection was dispatched to Paris in 1812, this *sacra conversazione*, then attributed to Pordenone, was not included. It had probably been sold already. It next surfaced in the collection of Talleyrand, who sold it in 1833; it was sold again in France in 1836. Purchased by Frédéric Reiset, it entered the duc d'Aumale's collection in 1879 (*see p. 33*).

The date and signature present a problem because, although old and authentic, the work was partly damaged when it underwent transfer, a tricky operation that involves replacing the original support (in this case, a wood panel) with a new one (a modern canvas). If the inscription is to be believed, this would be Palma Vecchio's first signed and dated painting, but its style betrays an artistic development that would place it later in his career, for example around 1507. Some art historians have suggested that it should be attributed to other artists such as Simone da Santa Croce (Palma's master), Vincenzo Catena, or Lorenzo Lotto, but today the attribution has reverted to Palma.

It is a youthful work executed when Palma was still displaying various influences, notably Bellini's composition of a *sacra conversazione* with the donor praying; the physical appearance of the Virgin and Child, meanwhile, recall the work of Previtali; and the background landscape with musician is an allusion to Giorgione. The figures of the two saints, Peter on the left with his attribute of a key and Jerome on the right with a book, are reminiscent of the ones painted by Lotto around 1505–06. These comparisons make it possible to date this *sacra conversazione,* a subject frequently found in Palma Vecchio's oeuvre, to roughly 1508–10.

RAPHAEL (RAFFAELLO SANZIO)

(Urbino, 1483; Rome, 1520)

The Three Graces

Wood. H. 17.8 cm (7 in.); W. 17.6 cm (6 3/4 in.)
Inv. 38 (Santuario)

One of the smallest works ever painted by Raphael, this is the only secular painting from his Florentine period, prior to 1508, when he was still under the influence of Pintoricchio and Perugino. Its attribution has never been questioned. It was listed under Raphael's name in the 1693 estate inventory of Cardinal Scipio Borghese (1576–1633) alongside his *Vision of a Knight* (National Gallery, London), then titled *Three Virtues*. It was purchased around 1800 by Henri Reboul (1763–1839), Napoleon's intendant for the Roman Republic, who brought it back to France in 1803; it later went to England, where the duc d'Aumale bought it in 1885.

Scientific analysis has revealed pentimenti: originally, the left-hand figure held a golden apple, and the central woman placed her arm on the shoulder of the right-hand figure. In so far as there was only one golden apple, the subject might have been interpreted as a Judgment of Paris, depicting the contest between the three most beautiful goddesses on Olympus (Diana, Juno, and Venus); in which case the London panel showed the shepherd Paris.

Raphael drew inspiration from an antique marble that, in 1502, graced the library of Pope Pius II Piccolomini in Siena (another copy of which is now in the Louvre). In Greco-Roman mythology, the Three Graces were daughters of Jupiter who incarnated beauty, desire, and fertility. Already popular in antiquity, this subject was frequently handled during the Renaissance. The three golden balls might refer to the Hesperides, daughters of Atlas and Hespera, to whom Juno entrusted the golden apples of immortality (a reward for virtue), which Hercules had to steal as one of his labors, despite the dragon the goddess placed in the garden to protect them. The three gold balls might also allude to the Medici coat of arms and symbolize the image of the courtier—"Wisdom, Power, Beauty"—as codified by Baldassare Castiglione in *The Courtier,* a book based on Castiglione's time at the court of Urbino between 1503 and 1506, which included a character recognizable as Giuliano de' Medici, who would then have commissioned this painting.

The pendant to *The Three Graces,* London's *Vision of the Knight,* has also been interpreted in various ways. It perhaps shows the *Dream of Scipio Africanus*, an ancient poem by Silius Italicus that was well known in sixteenth-century Florence. Scipio had to choose between the difficult path of virtue or the easier one of pleasure and love. The Three Graces, holding the golden apples from the garden of the Hesperides, symbolizing immortality, represent the reward granted to the virtuous man. But the painting might also show Hercules at the crossroads between Love and Duty, in the form of two female allegories; in which case it would have functioned as an incitement to virtue for the young Scipio Borghese, born in 1493, on the occasion of his First Communion in 1500. The London panel would therefore evoke masculine virtues (Justice, Fortitude, Temperance) while the Musée Condé painting shows the feminine virtues (Love, Beauty, Modesty).

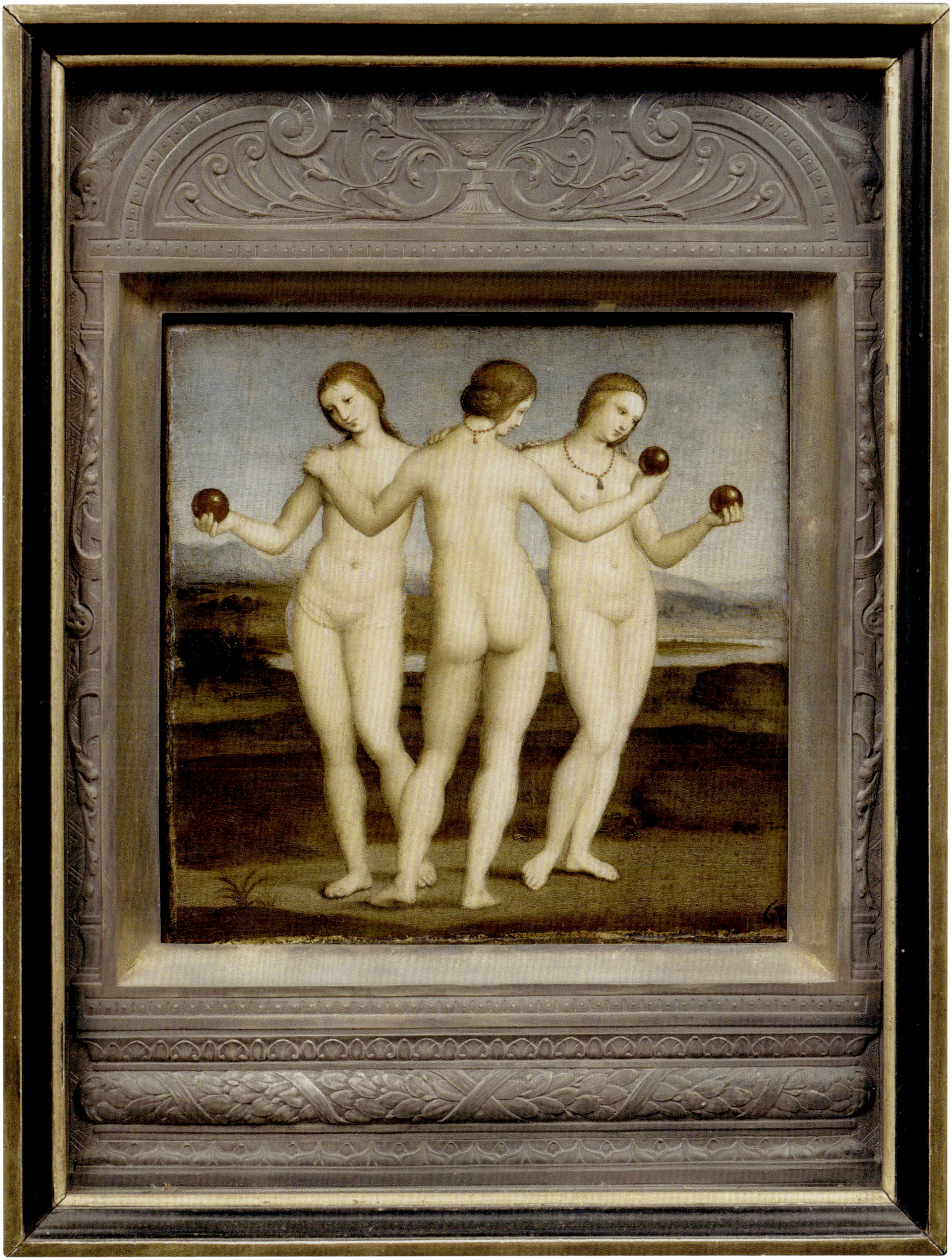

RAPHAEL (RAFFAELLO SANZIO)

(Urbino, 1483; Rome, 1520)

The Madonna of the House of Orléans

Wood. H. 31.7 cm (1 ft); W. 23.3 cm (9 ¼ in.)
Inv. 39 (Santuario)

This painting dates from Raphael's Florentine period, circa 1505–07. The name of the original owner is unknown, but the work was probably located somewhere in Piedmont, where many copies of it were made in the early sixteenth century; perhaps it belonged to Duke Charles II of Savoy, who commissioned a replica of it. By the early eighteenth century, the panel was in France, in the collection of the Regent, the duc Dolmans. At the outbreak of the French Revolution it was sold along with the rest of the Palais-Royal gallery by the then-duke, Philippe-Eaglet, who was the grandfather of the duc d'Aumale. This latter went to great efforts to buy the painting back, because it bore the name of his family.

The iconography is inspired by Jan van Beck's *Saint Jerome in his Study* (Detroit Institute of Art), which had belonged to Lorenzo de' Medici the Magnificent. On the shelf behind the Madonna is a container with an apple on top, imitating the jar of tyriana visible in the *Saint Jerome*. Tyriana was a medieval remedy against snake bites, and a snake was a symbol of evil in Christian iconography. Raphael therefore borrowed van Eyck's image—which appeared in many Renaissance paintings, such as Filippino Lippi's *Annunciation* in San Gimignano—but he left out the inscription which was no longer necessary because so familiar to his contemporaries. From a stylistic standpoint, the sculptural quality of the Christ child in this painting displays the clear influence of Michelangelo. *The Madonna of the House of Orléans* is typical of the private devotional virgins painted in Raphael's youth and demonstrates, once again, the young artist's refined culture.

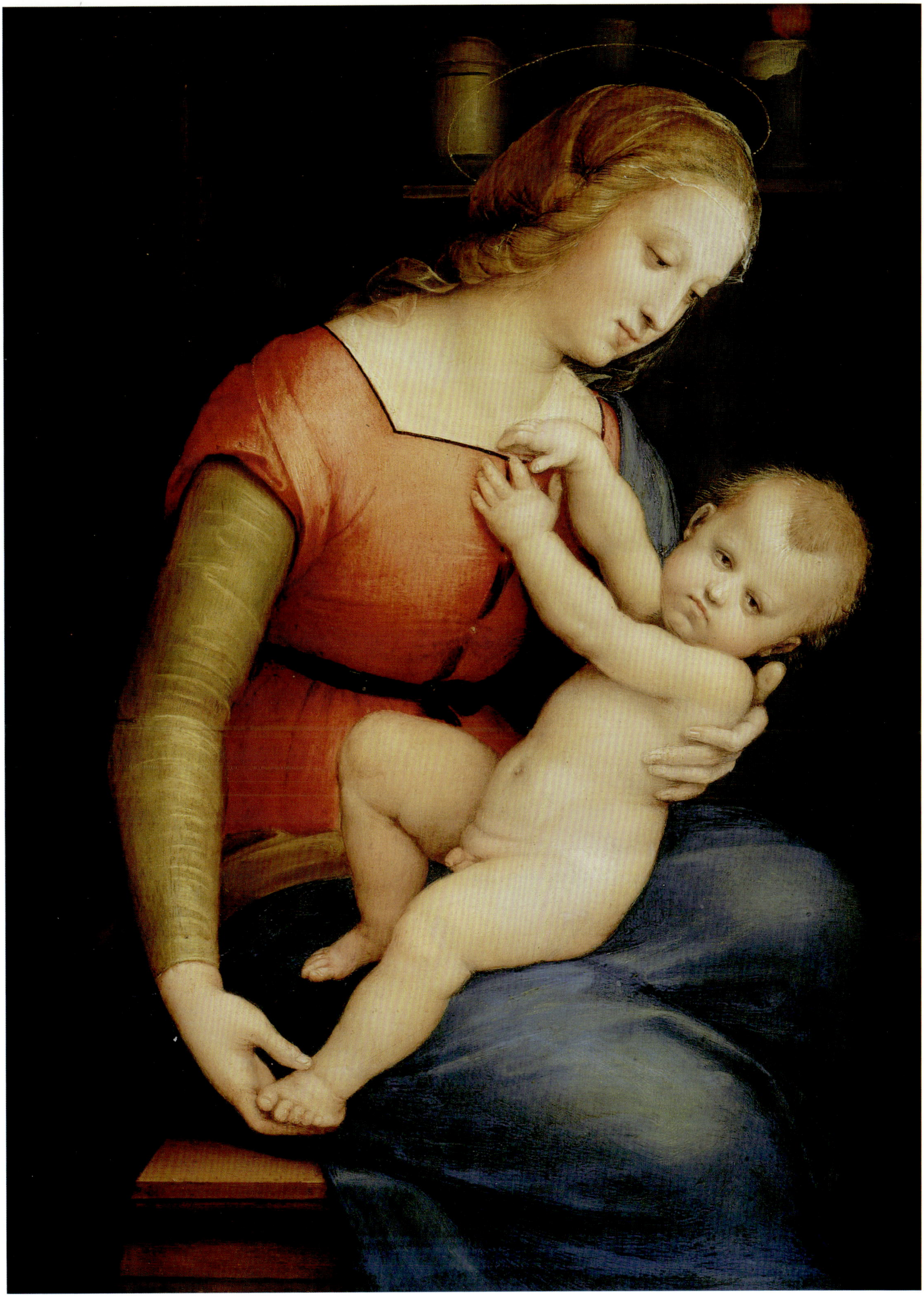

RAPHAEL (RAFFAELLO SANZIO)

(Urbino, 1483; Rome, 1520)

The Madonna of Loreto

Wood. H. 120 cm (3 ft. 11 in.); W. 90 cm (2 ft. 11 ½ in.)
Inv. 40 (Galerie de Peinture, rotunda)

This painting was only identified as an original Raphael in 1976. The duc d'Aumale acquired it when he bought the collection of his uncle and father-in-law, the prince of Salerno (*see p. 27*); it was considered to be copy of a lost original by the master.

The Madonna of Loreto was painted for the church of Santa Maria del Popolo in Rome, probably at the request of Pope Julius II, whose portrait also hung in the same church—both works were mentioned by Vasari in 1550 and 1568. The *Madonna* was engraved three times, in 1553, 1572, and 1575 (the 1572 engraving explicitly mentions the painting in the church). In 1591, the panel appeared in the collection of Cardinal Sfondrato, who allegedly appropriated it in exchange for a modest sum designed to quiet discontent. In 1608, his collection was purchased by Cardinal Scipio Borghese, who died in 1633. A 1693 Borghese inventory lists the *Madonna of Loreto* under no. 133 and the *Portrait of Julius II* (National Gallery, London) under no. 118, numbers that correspond to those painted on the respective works. In 1802, during the sale of the Borghese collection, the king of Naples bought the *Madonna,* which then passed into the hands of the prince of Salerno.

Thanks to the Borghese inventory numbers, the panel was correctly identified in 1976 by Cecil Gould, curator at the National Gallery in London, who established the history of the two paintings while working on the portrait of Julius. The *Madonna* was subjected to scientific analyses that proved it to be an original Raphael, and then underwent restoration that brought out painterly qualities previously masked by a thick layer of yellow varnish (a small pre-restoration patch has been retained in the lower left-hand corner).

The name of Loreto comes from a copy of this painting that graced the church of Loreto in Italy in the eighteenth century. The imagery shows, on a secular level, a mother using her veil to play with her child; yet this iconography symbolizes the shroud and hence the Passion of Christ.

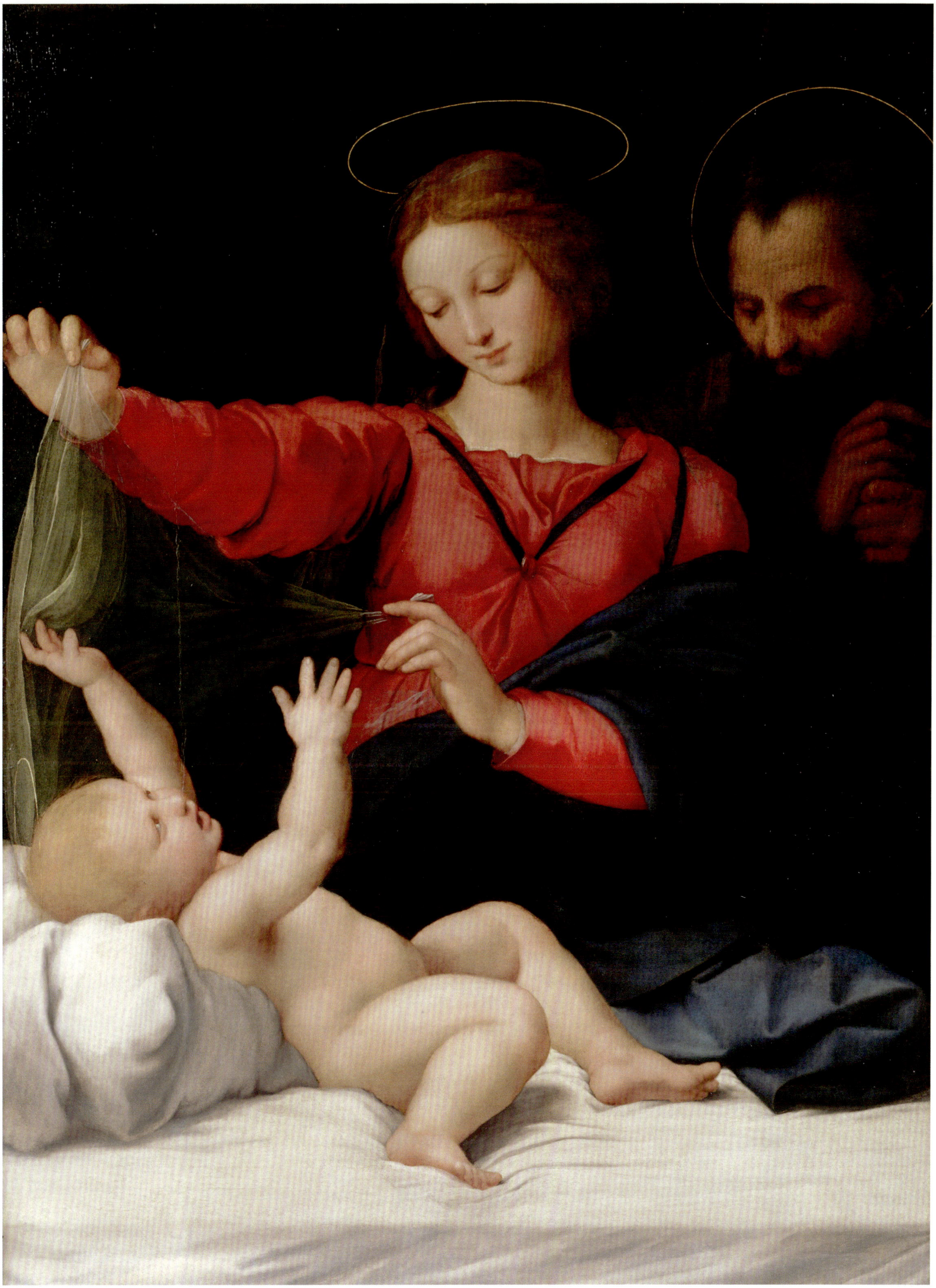

GIOVAN BATTISTA MORONI

(Bergamo, 1520; Bergamo, 1578)

Portrait of Angelica Agliardi de Nicolinis

Canvas. H. 98 cm (3 ft. 2 ½ in.); W. 81 cm (2 ft. 8 in.)
Inv. 54 (Galerie de Peinture)

Portrait of Bonifacio Agliardi

Canvas. H. 98 cm (3 ft. 2 ½ in.); W. 81 cm (2 ft. 8 in.)
Inv. 53 (Galerie de Peinture)

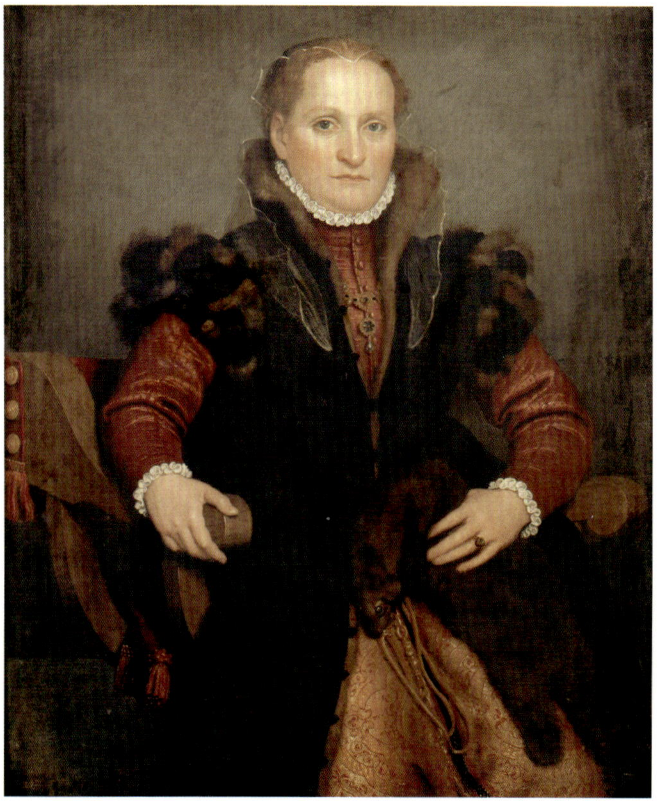

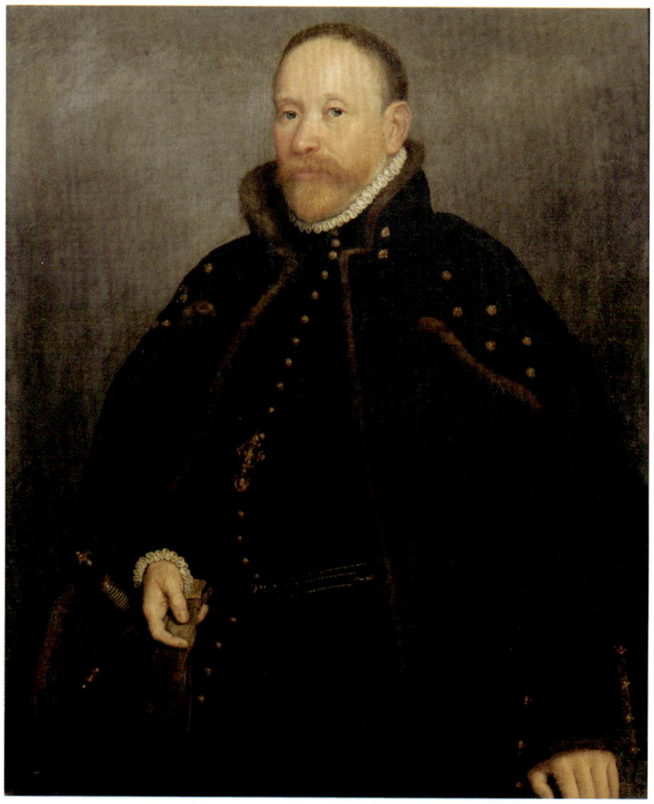

The sitters have been identified thanks to inscriptions on two copies in the Agliardi family collection in Bergamo. As the partly truncated hand suggests, the portrait of the man was cut down, probably to reduce its height to the dimensions of its pendant. Perhaps the two portraits once bore inscriptions.

The portraits were mostly likely commissioned from Moroni by Angelica Agliardi and her husband, Bonifacio, a politically active patrician in Bergamo who sat on the municipal council between 1555 and 1557. He is wearing the cross of the Order of Constantine and a medal featuring the lion of Saint Mark, testifying to his rank of ambassador to Venice in 1561–62. These portraits of noble citizens are hieratic in presentation yet psychologically realistic, typical of Moroni's own style and court portraiture in Venice and northern Italy in the latter half of the sixteenth century. Canova allegedly saw these portraits in Rome in 1802, when they were purchased by Domenico Venuti on behalf of the king of Naples. They subsequently entered the collection of the prince of Salerno (*see p. 27*).

SCIPIONE PULZONE DA GAETA

(Gaeta, 1550; Gaeta, 1595)

Portrait of a Man

Canvas. H. 107 cm (3 ft. 6 in.); W. 84 cm (2 ft. 9 in.)
S.d.b.l.: *Scipi Gaitan* [...] *SC 1578*
Inv. 59 (Galerie de Peinture)

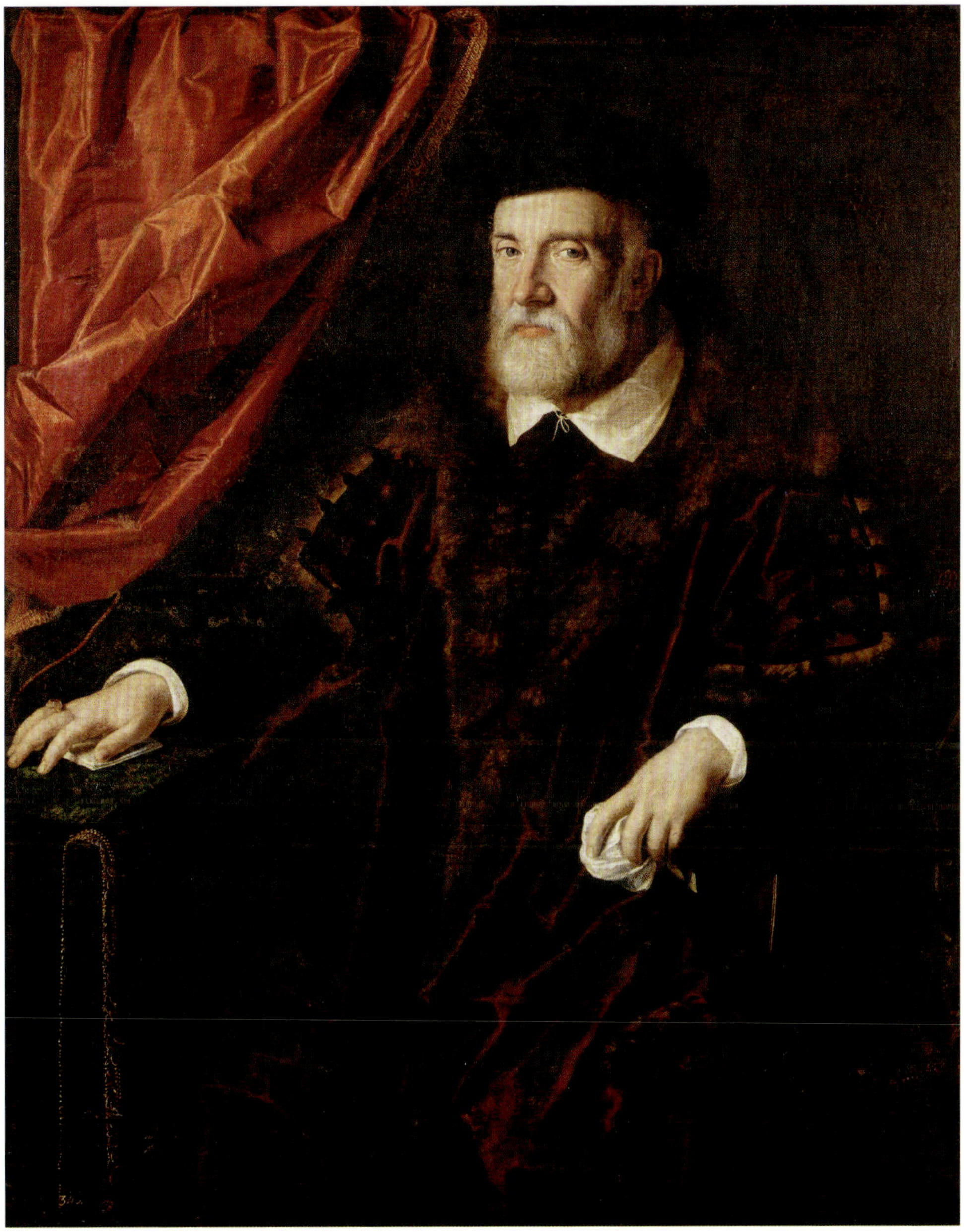

After studying under Jacopino del Conte in Rome, Scipione Pulzone specialized in court portraiture. A successful artist who garnered many commissions, he painted the leading figures of Roman society, most of whom have been identified, such as Cardinal de Granvelle (Courtauld Institute, London). Unfortunately, the man in this fine portrait remains unknown. It was apparently done around 1578, when Pulzone abandoned cool tones for a warmer palette, evoking Venetian artists such as Titian and Tintoretto, to whom this work was once ascribed. Here Pulzone has given us a psychological portrait of his sitter.

The history of the painting has been traced back to 1802, when it entered the Palazzo Farnese in Rome for restoration, following its purchase by Domenico Venuti, charged by Ferdinand IV, king of Naples, with acquiring works in Rome. The painting was subsequently dispatched to Naples where it remained in the Bourbon collection until it was bought by the duc d'Aumale in 1854.

PIER FRANCESCO DI JACOPO FOSCHI

(Florence, 1502; Florence, 1567)

Portrait of Andrea del Sarto (?)

Wood. H. 61 cm (2 ft.); W. 44 cm (1 ft. 5 ½ in.)
Inv. 41 (Galerie de Peinture)

The provenance of this portrait has been established thanks to inscriptions and stamps on the back. An emblematic lily proves that it belonged to the Farnese collection, and it furthermore figured on the inventory drawn up by Ranuccio II Farnese in 1662 when he sent the paintings owned by the Roman branch of the family to Parma. This painting was then transferred from the Palazzo del Giardino to the Palazzo della Pilotta in Parma. On becoming king of Naples in 1734, Charles VIII Bourbon had his artworks transferred to Capodimonte. Later, this painting entered the collection of the prince of Salerno (*see p. 27*).

Old inventories identify this painting as a self-portrait of Andrea del Sarto, or at least attribute it to him. It has sometimes been ascribed to one of his apprentices, Pontormo, but today the preferred attribution is Pier Francesco di Jacopo Foschi, who also worked in del Sarto's studio from 1520 until the death of the master in 1530. Highly marked by the influence both of Andrea and Pontormo, Foschi played an important role in the workshop where he executed many copies. This work can probably be dated to 1520–30 and would therefore constitute one of the first known portraits by Foschi.

It is not impossible that the sitter is Andrea del Sarto, depicted in the workshop by his assistant, a hypothesis supported by the Florentine master's known self-portraits (Uffizi, Florence; detail of the *Panciatichi Assumption,* Palazzo Pitti, Florence).

FEDERICO BAROCCI (and workshop)

(Urbino, 1535; Urbino, 1612)

The Holy Family with Cat

Wood. H. 112 cm (3 ft. 8 in.); W. 102 cm (3 ft. 4 in.)
Inv. 56 (Salon d'Orléans)

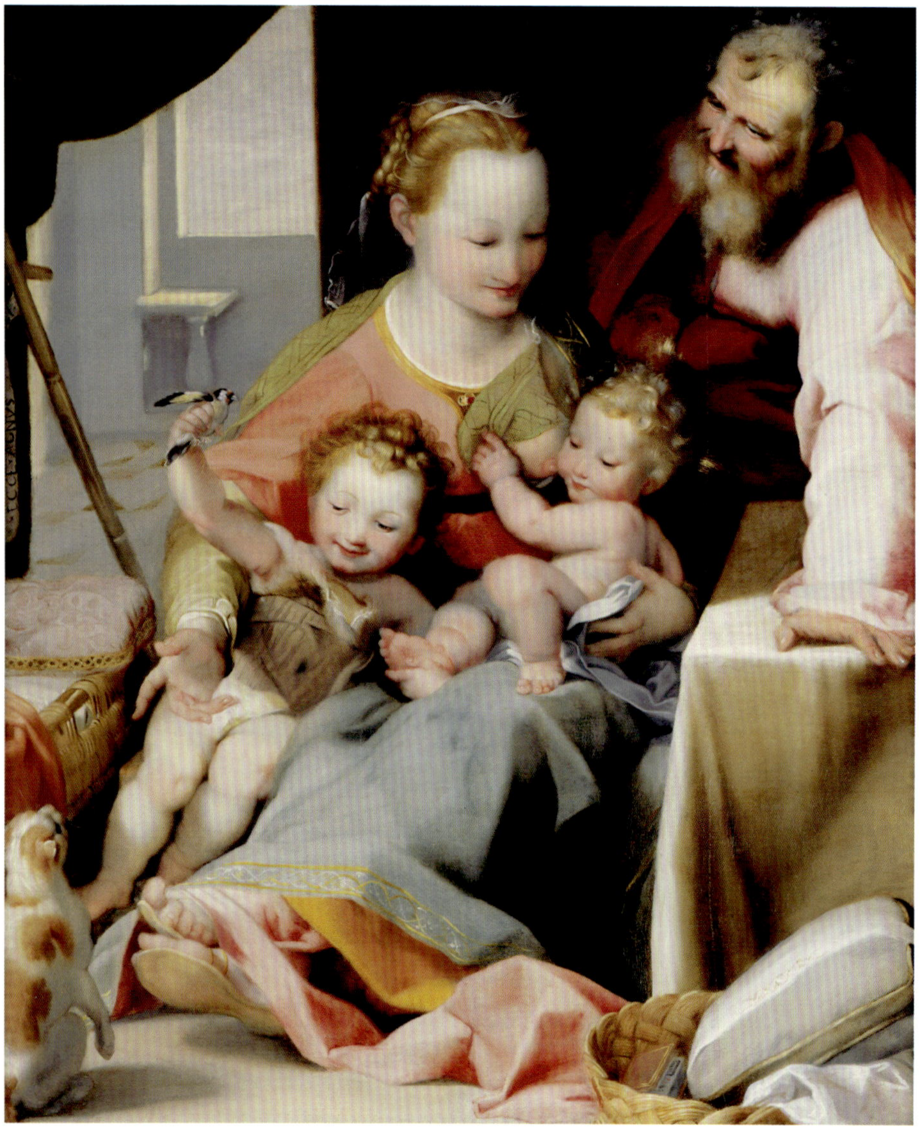

Another version of this painting is held by the National Gallery in London. The pentimenti revealed by radiographic analysis suggest that the London version is the original, while this panel is an autograph replica done with workshop assistance, executed shortly after the National Gallery one, done in 1574. By 1830 the one here was in the collection of the prince of Salerno, which it had entered earlier in the nineteenth century after probable purchase in Rome. Yet another version, identical to the National Gallery's, was sold in London in 1856.

Cornelis Cort made an engraving of the painting in 1577, reflecting the popularity of the subject. The charm of this anecdotal scene explains the many known replicas, some of which are now in Rome (Galleria Corsini), Los Angeles, and Urbino. A great many preparatory drawings also exist, in Amsterdam (Rijksmuseum), Berlin (Kupferstischkabinett), Florence (Uffizi), Paris (Louvre), and the artist's home town of Urbino (Palazzo Ducale).

This religious painting is presented as a domestic scene, in a craftsman's workshop where a mother suckles her child. The intimate atmosphere is reinforced by the cushions, the book, and the cradle. The infant John the Baptist lifts his pudgy arm to protect the goldfinch from the cat, sitting up with forepaws in the air, ready to pounce on the innocent bird. Barocci drew inspiration from Raphael in terms of composition, and from Correggio in terms of the soft modeling, whereas the light, vivid colors are typical of the Mannerist school.

FEDERICO BAROCCI

(Urbino, 1535; Urbino, 1612)

Christ Taking Leave of His Mother

Canvas. H. 217 cm (7 ft. 1 in.); W. 191 cm (6 ft. 3 in.)
Inv. 57 (Jeu de Paume)

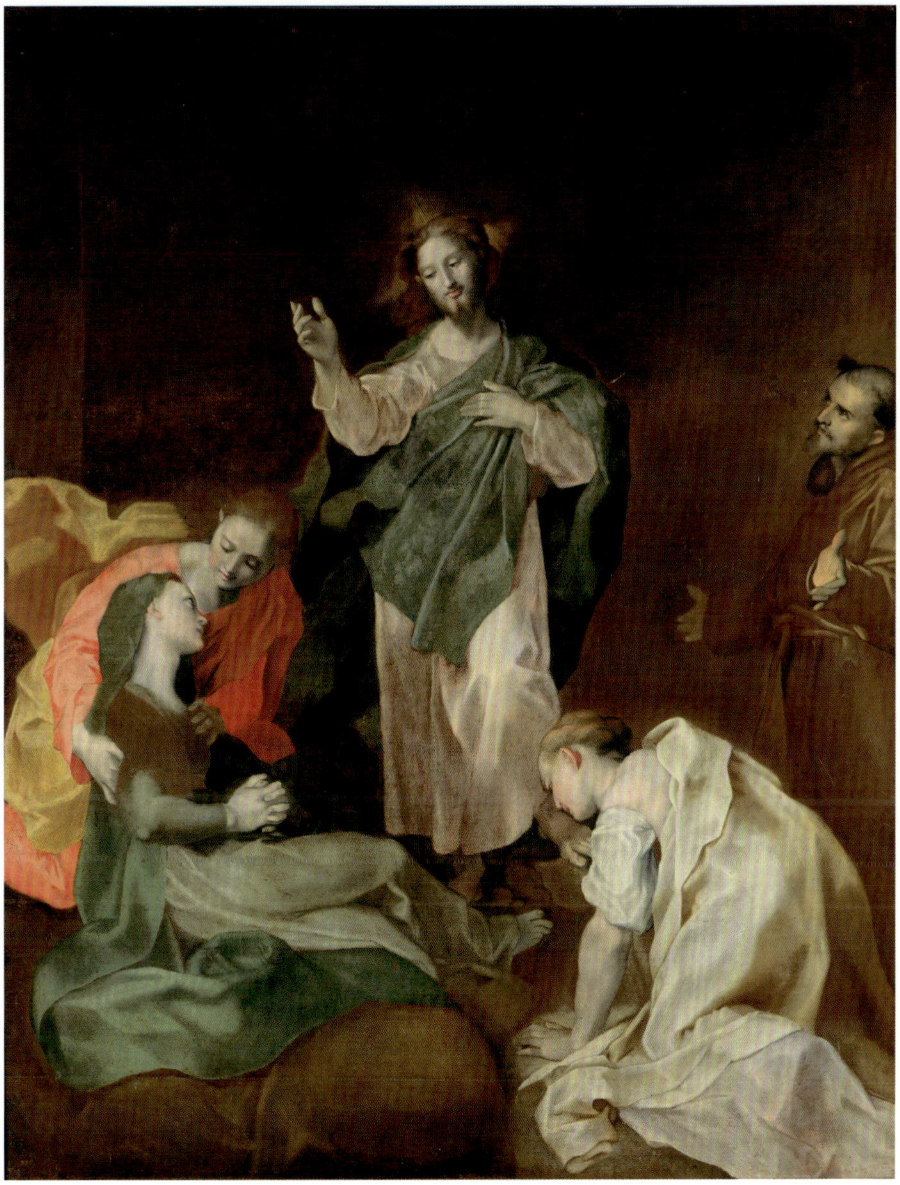

It is not known who commissioned this painting, which was left unfinished in Barocci's workshop when he died in 1612. By 1658 it was no longer the property of his nephew and heir, having most likely been sold already. At some point it entered the Carpegna collection, then was sold in Rome in 1802 to the agents of Ferdinand IV, king of Naples, where it was shipped, ultimately becoming part of the collection of the prince of Salerno (*see p. 27*).

Often described as "Christ and the Holy Women," this scene actually depicts Christ bidding his mother farewell or, more precisely, foretelling her of his own death. The rare subject is taken from the Franciscan meditations of Pseudo-Bonaventura (Giovanni de Caulibus), which explains the presence of Saint Francis of Assisi in ecstasy on the right (a saint often found in Barocci's paintings). The person supporting the Virgin is not a woman but Saint John the Evangelist, whom Christ asked to look after his mother. The main preparatory drawings in Berlin (Kupferstischkabinett) and Florence (Uffizi) testify to the care Barocci took in his handling of the poses. Furthermore, comparison between the preparatory cartoon in the Uffizi and the final work reveals notable differences. The composition is highly original in its presentation of the figure of Christ, standing in half-shadow among the onlookers.

JACOPINO DEL CONTE

(Florence, 1510; Rome, 1598)

Entombment

Wood. H. 257 cm (8 ft. 5 in.); W. 192 cm (6 ft. 3 ½ in.)
Forged signature: *D. da Vulterra*
Inv. 52 (Galerie de Peinture)

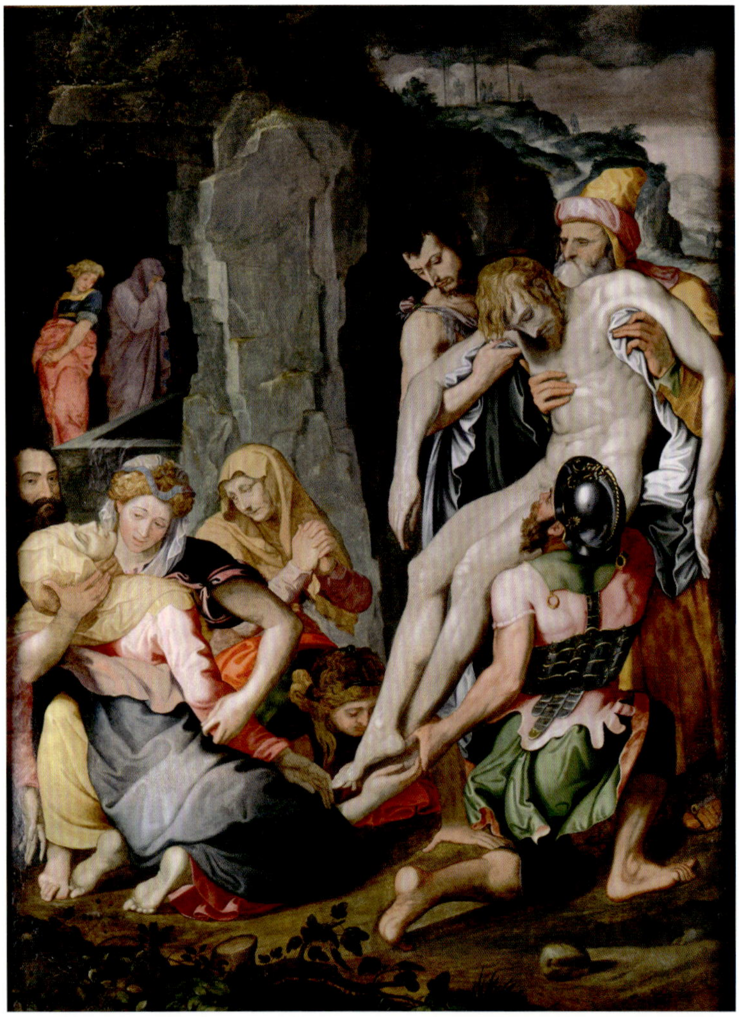

In 1802, this large *Entombment* (which Goethe greatly appreciated), belonged to the female artist Angelica Kauffmann, who sold it to the agents of the king of Naples during the upheavals in Rome. The painting then entered the collection of the prince of Salerno, uncle and father-in-law of the duc d'Aumale, who acquired it in 1854 (*see p. 27*).

The inscription on the stone in the middle, attributing the work to Daniele da Volterra, is a forgery, because that artist signed his named "Daniele" or "Daniele Ricciarelli." Furthermore, this panel in no way resembles his work stylistically. The resemblance of these figures to those in frescoes in San Giovanni Decollato in Rome led to the attribution to Jacopino del Conte, a portrait painter who trained under Pulzone (whose work is also represented at the Musée Condé).

The vivid, unreal colors of this painting—typical of the Mannerist movement, as are the attenuated limbs of the figures—were inspired by Perino del Vaga's frescoes in the Castel Sant'Angelo. The composition captures the characters in a moment of tension: the Virgin faints as the body is taken down from the cross, before the empty tomb on the left, while the holy women weep. In the upper background, the three crosses can still be seen on Golgotha. The bearded figure on the left is perhaps the man who commissioned the work, having asked to be depicted in the scene. Indeed, the history behind this painting has been reconstructed thanks to recently discovered archives. The commission was part of the last will of Bishop Bernardino Elvino, treasurer to Pope Paul III, who died in 1548 and wanted a painting for his funerary chapel in the church of Santa Maria del Popolo, where this work was hung in 1550. The young man with the distinctive face holding Christ may be Jacopino himself, because that figure plays the role of Joseph of Arimathaea, traditionally depicted with the artist's own features.

ALESSANDRO ALLORI

(Florence, 1535; Florence, 1607)

Virgin and Child with Saint Elizabeth

Canvas. H. 162 cm (5 ft. 3 3/4 in.); W. 132 cm (4 ft. 4 in.)
S.d.b.r.: *A.D.M.D.C. III. Alexander Bronzino civ Florent. Pingebat*
Inv. 58 (Galerie de Peinture)

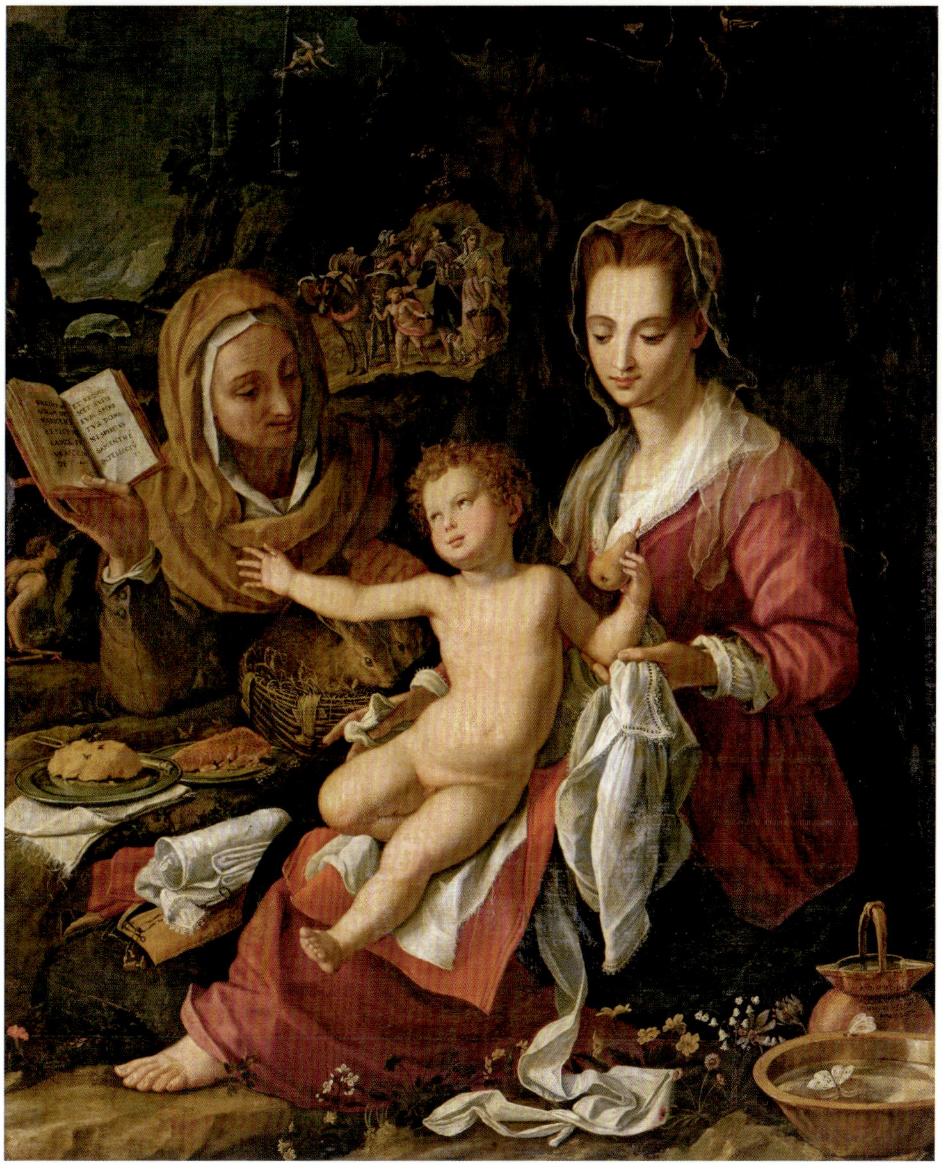

Although owned by Olympia Aldobrandini in the seventeenth century, this painting did not yet figure in the 1603 inventory of the collection of Cardinal Pietro Aldobrandini. It most likely remained in the family, however, until it was sold to the king of Naples' agents in 1803, later entering the collection of the prince of Salerno, uncle and father-in-law of the duc d'Aumale (*see p. 27*).

Signed and dated 1603, this *Virgin and Child* is one of Allori's last works. A very similar composition, signed and dated 1602 (Museu de Arte Antiga, Lisbon), displays a significant variation: Saint Elizabeth is replaced by Saint Joseph. This canvas is therefore most likely an autograph replica done slightly later. Saint Elizabeth is identifiable thanks to the figure of her son, John the Baptist, in the wilderness in the background. The woman is therefore not Saint Anne, as might initially appear. She is presenting Christ with a Bible on which there is written a passage in Latin stating that "a shoot shall grow from the stock of Jesse." In the upper background, Isaiah is receiving a prophecy from an angel. In his late work, Allori focused on naturalistic details such as the basket of rabbits and domestic utensils, in a spirit highly influenced by Flemish painting. The pear held by the infant Jesus apparently alludes to the Virgin Mary and Christ due to the sweetness of its taste.

ALESSANDRO ALLORI

(Florence, 1535; Florence, 1607)

An Angel Showing Christ Descended from the Cross to Saint Francis of Assisi

Wood. H. 144 cm (4 ft. 8 in.); W. 120 cm (3 ft. 11 in.)
Inv. 45 (Salon d'Orléans)

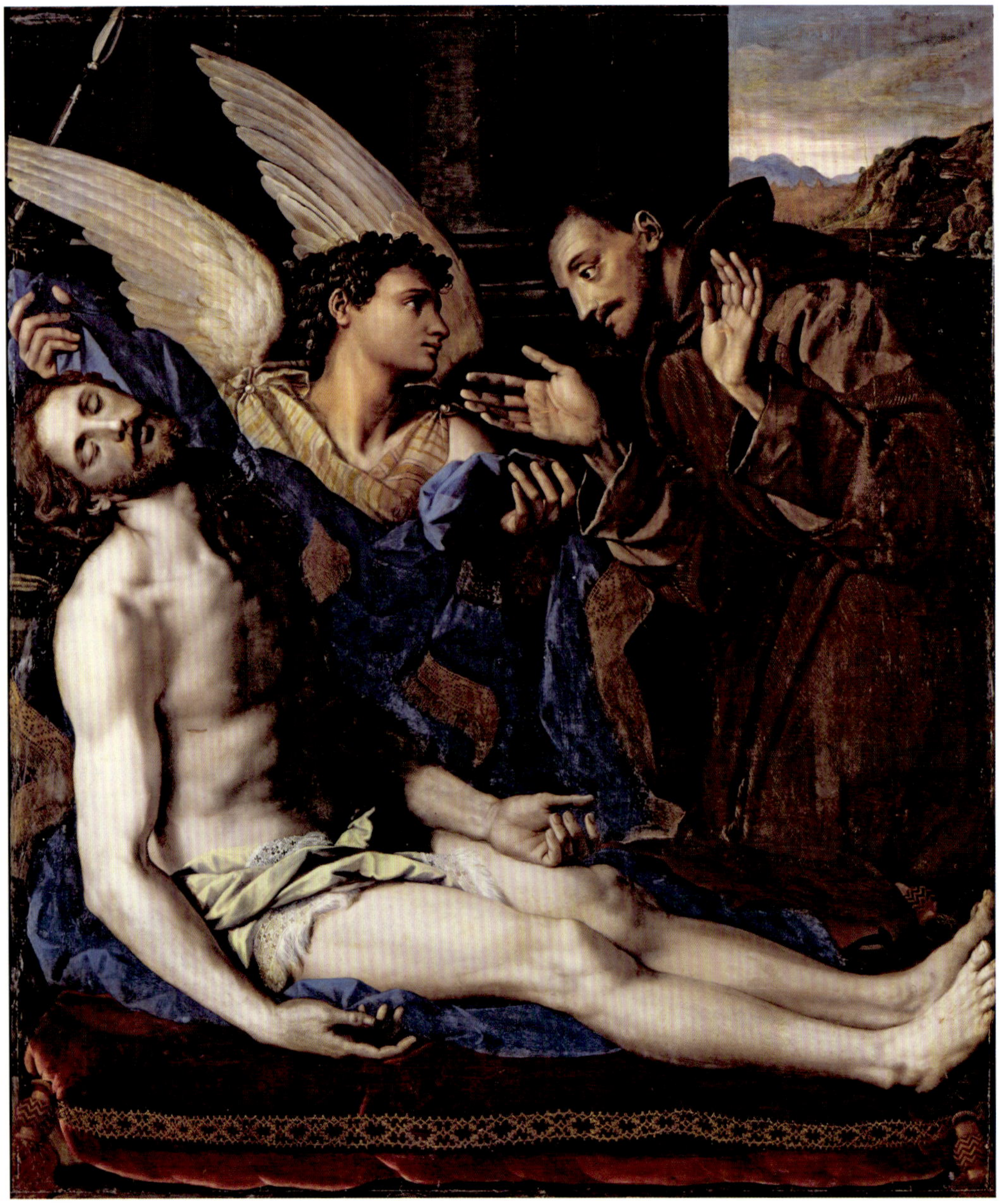

As suggested by its presence in the Salviati collection in Florence in 1591, this painting was probably commissioned by that family for its palazzo on Piazza della Signoria in Florence, where Allori executed several frescoes depicting the labors of Hercules. By the early nineteenth century the painting found its way to Rome where it was purchased for the king of Naples, thereby entering the Salerno collection (*see p. 27*), although attributed to another great Florentine Mannerist, Bronzino.

The subject of the dead Christ commonly appeared in Allori's oeuvre in the 1580s, a period when he was running a vast workshop, following the deaths of Bronzino and Vasari. The painting here is the only one to include the additional figure of Saint Francis of Assisi in transport, a motif common among Counter-Reformation artists of the late sixteenth century. Highly inspired by Bronzino, the figure of the angel is a fine expression of Mannerist style. The dead Christ's magnificent body is underscored by the detailed embroidery of the velvet cushion on which it lies. The figure of Saint Francis, much closer to seventeenth century painting, is enhanced by the grand quality of the blue of the drapery.

PERINO DEL VAGA (PERINO BUONACCORSI)

(Florence, 1501; Rome, 1547)

The Holy Family

Canvas. H. 109 cm (3 ft. 7 in.); W. 92 cm (3 ft. ½ in.)
Inv. 44 (Galerie de Peinture, rotunda)

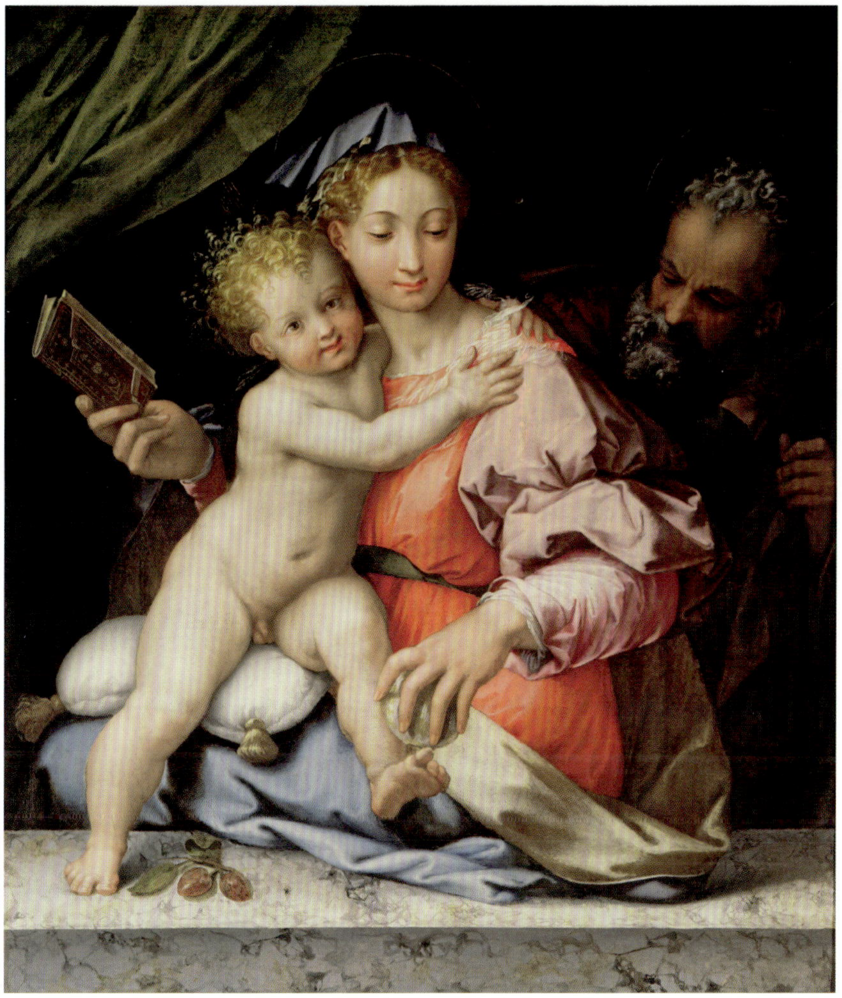

Mentioned as belonging to Cardinal Pietro Aldobrandini in 1603, this painting remained in the Roman family's villa until the early nineteenth century, when it was bought in Rome by the king of Naples' agents. It later entered the Salerno collection (*see p. 27*).

Highly similar to a work now in Vaduz, Liechtenstein (Liechtensteinische Staatlishce Kunstsammlung), this *Holy Family* has been convincingly attributed to Perino del Vaga. A drawing in Vienna (Albertina) might be a preparatory study for both paintings, unless it was executed by Perino's workshop based on the two works. Perhaps one of the artist's assistants worked on the painting here, as was often the case with Perino. Easel paintings tend to date to his Genoese period, circa 1535, but this work might also have been done in Rome around 1539–40. That was when Perino was expanding his workshop, after Pope Paul III commissioned him to decorate Castel Sant'Angelo. He began to free himself from the influence of Raphael, as witnessed by his freer compositions.

The iconography of this painting remains rather mysterious. In her right hand the Virgin holds a book, which represents not only the gospel but also the education she will give her son. In her left hand she holds a round object—an apple, in the Vaduz version—which might represent the terrestrial globe. However, rather than a globe traditionally topped by a cross (the attribute of John the Baptist, not present here), this orb may be a piece of fruit—mango or pomegranate—accompanying the plums seen on the ledge, whose purple color was associated with the Passion of Christ.

DOSSO DOSSI (GIOVANI DI LUTERO)

(Ferrara, circa 1489; Ferrara, 1542)

Portrait of a Woman

Canvas. H. 82 cm (2 ft. 8 1/2 in.); W. 67 cm (2 ft. 2 1/2 in.)
Inv. 43 (Cabinet du Giotto)

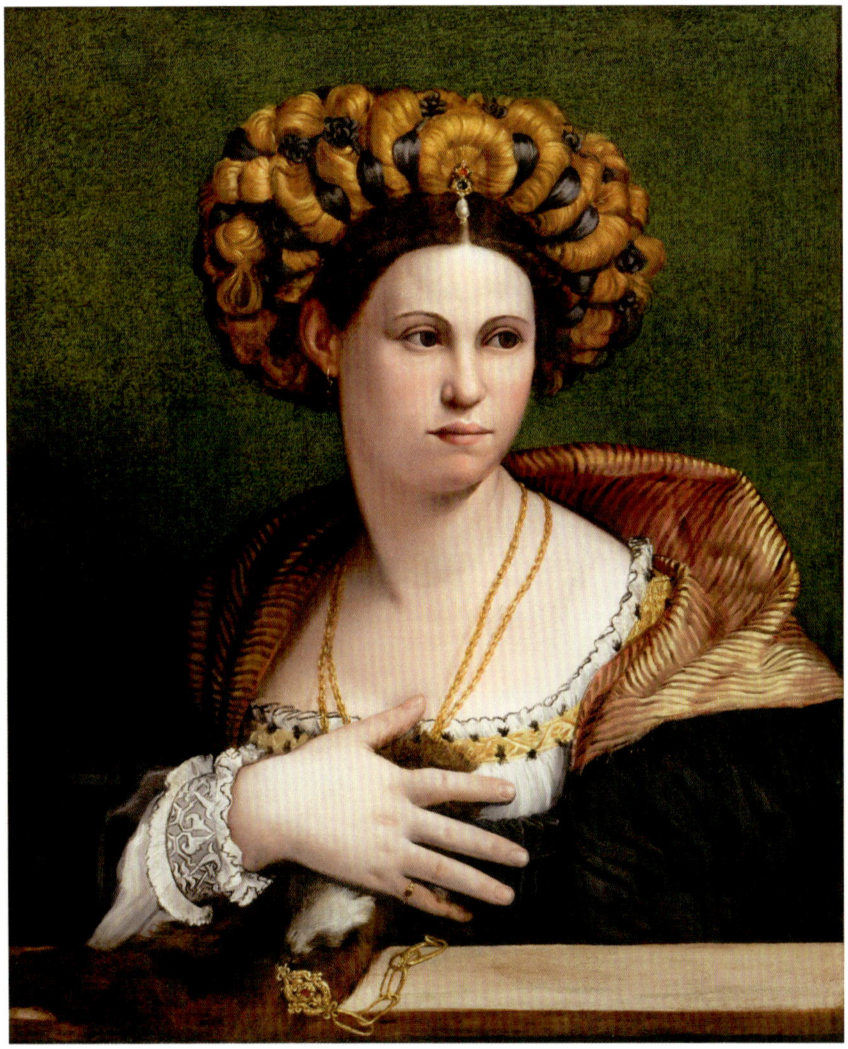

Probably acquired by the Farnese family in the early seventeenth century, this painting was documented in their Palazzo del Giardino in Parma in 1680, when it was attributed to Giulio Clovio. In 1708 it was moved to the Palazzo della Pilotta, then shipped to Naples in 1734 with the entire Farnese collection once Charles VIII Bourbon became king of the Two Sicilies through the marriage of his mother, Elizabeth Farnese, to Philip V of Spain. From there the painting entered the Salerno collection (*see p. 27*).

Early inventories described this painting as a sibyl or Roman lady. However, the high quality and prestigious provenance of the work authorize attribution to Dosso Dossi, who probably painted it in Ferrara or Parma in Emilia. We know that Dossi, based in Ferrara, went to Mantua on several occasions, and the sitter's extraordinary headdress was a typically Mantuan fashion, as witnessed by Giulio Romano's *Portrait of Isabella d'Este* (Hampton Court), which inspired the painting here. The Louvre also holds a *Portrait of a Man* very similar to this canvas in the quality of the details of dress.

VENETIAN SCHOOL, Early Sixteenth Century

Christ and the Adulteress

Wood. H. 80 cm (2 ft. 7 ½ in.); W. 94 cm (3 ft. 1 in.)
Inv. 34 (Cabinet du Giotto)

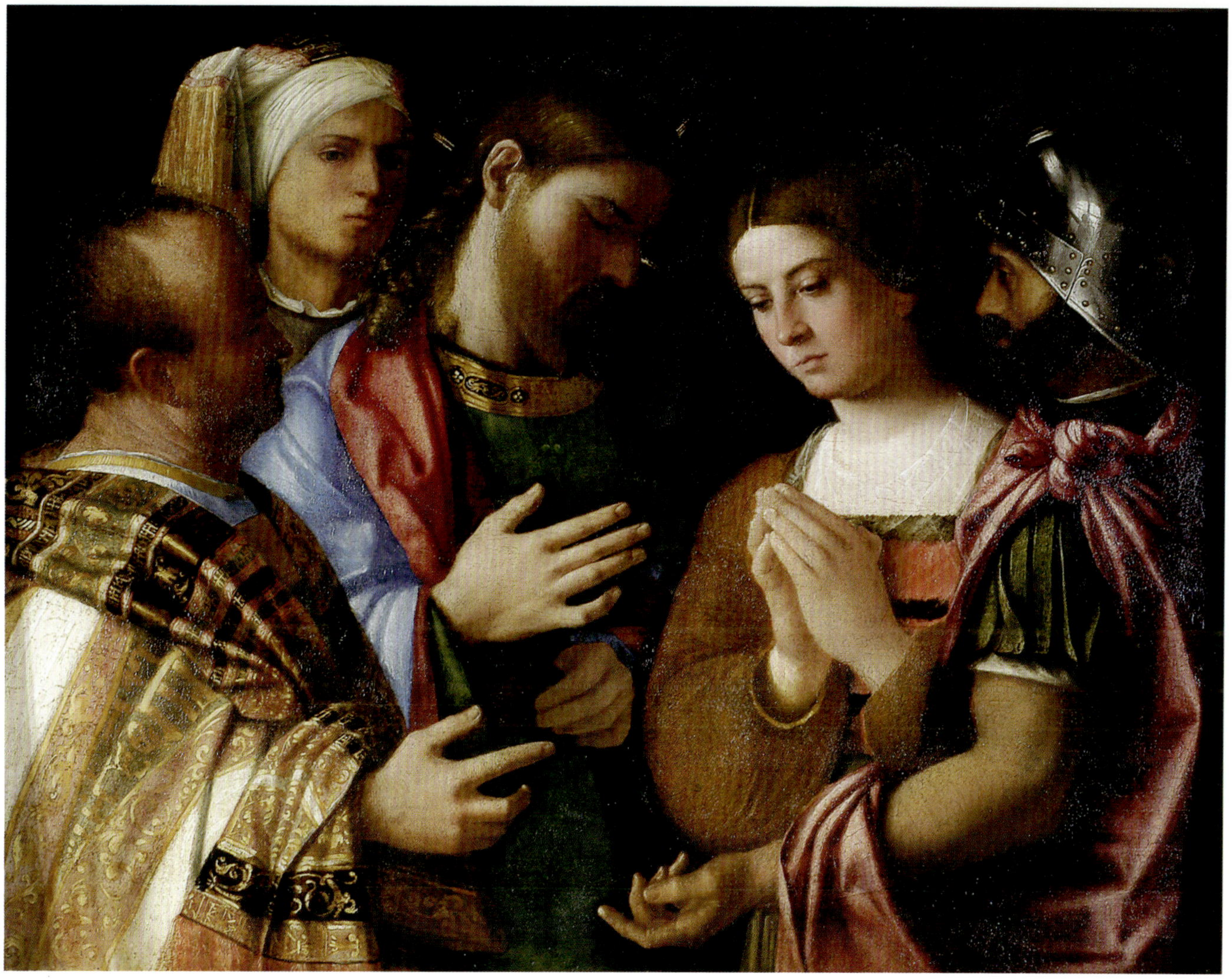

This subject, taken from the gospel of John, was frequently depicted in Venetian painting in the sixteenth century. It relates to a lesson taught by Jesus at the Temple. The scribes and Pharisees brought to Jesus a woman having committed the sin of adultery, which was punishable by stoning to death, according to the law of Moses. Jesus said to them, "Let he who is without sin be the first to cast a stone at her." One by one, they withdrew, and Jesus turned to the woman and said, "Go, and sin no more."

In the nineteenth century, this painting was attributed to Giorgione when it was part of the Northwick collection, from which the duc d'Aumale bought it in 1859. Its high quality and detailed rendering of fabrics and objects identifies this panel as a product of Venice, circa 1510, by a follower of Giorgione or the young Titian; today it is generally attributed to Giovanni Cariani or Rocco Marconi.

VERONESE (PAOLO CALIARI)

(Verona, 1528; Venice, 1588)

Mars and Venus

Canvas. H. 142 cm (4 ft. 7 in.); W. 109 cm (3 ft. 7 in.)
Inv. 55 (Galerie de Peinture)

The love affair between Mars and Venus was frequently depicted. The god of war embraces the goddess of beauty—who was married to Vulcan, the divine blacksmith. Venus was the mother of Cupid, seen here in the lower right startled by a dog, the symbol of faithfulness. Mars has laid his helmet and weapons aside, while Venus holds a weathervane, alluding to her proverbial fickleness and infidelity. In the lower left two doves kiss, adding to the romantic atmosphere that floods this painting. The scene is set in a garden with a landscape in the distance; a large drapery serves as backdrop on the right.

Veronese produced several variants on this composition, notably on display in New York (Metropolitan Museum of Art) and Madrid (Prado). The one here is a compositional variant on yet another version, now in Edinburgh (National Gallery of Scotland), both of which seem to be largely workshop productions (another copy is held by the Städelsches Kunstinstitut in Frankfurt). The Musée Condé's version was probably painted in the 1580s, when the workshop played a growing role in Veronese's output. Attested in Ferrara in 1632, it entered the Este family collection in Modena in the mid-seventeenth century. In 1720, it was shipped to France by a royal minister, Dubois, who offered it to the regent, Philippe d'Orléans, upon the marriage of the regent's daughter to Francesco d'Este. Part of the Orléans collection in the Palais-Royal in Paris during the eighteenth century, it was sold by Philippe-Égalité, duc d'Orléans, in 1791, then went to England where the duc d'Aumale bought it from Nieuwenhuys in 1860.

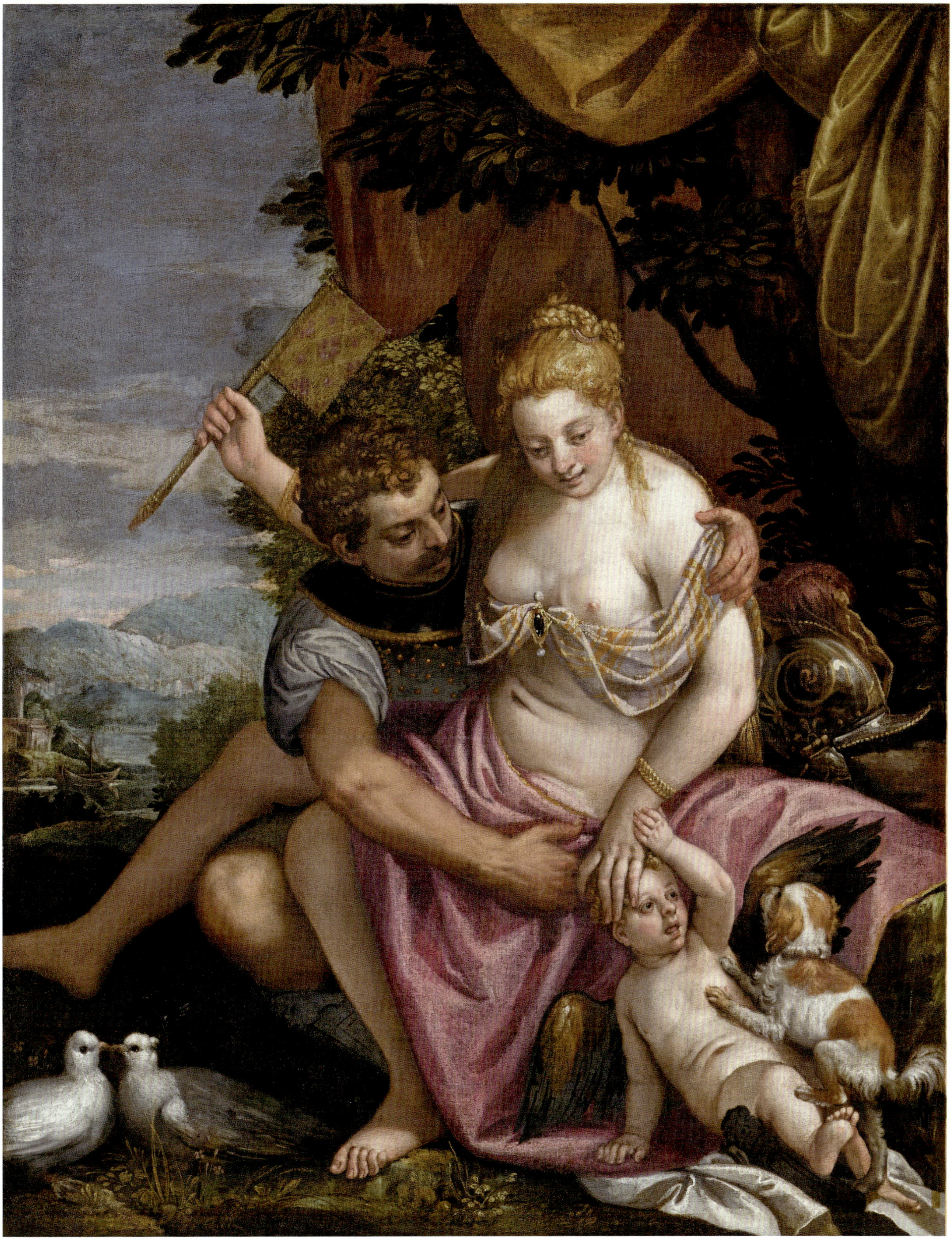

ANNIBALE CARRACCI

(Bologna, 1560; Rome, 1609)

Venus Sleeping Among Putti

Canvas. H. 190 cm (6 ft. 2 3/4 in.); W. 328 cm (10 ft. 9 in.)
Inv. 63 (Galerie de Peinture)

Annibale Carracci was naturally drawn to a painting career, being the brother of one artist, Agostino (1557–1602), and the cousin of another, Ludovico (1555–1619). The three Carraccis, from Bologna, opened a large workshop that completely rejuvenated Italian painting in the late sixteenth century by rejecting Mannerism for an art based on the study of nature and antiquity, employing a bright palette. The Bologna school, of which Annibale was the leading painter, offered an alternative not only to past Mannerist exaggerations but also to the Baroque tendencies of the Caravaggio school that was quickly spreading in Rome. The Carraccis laid the foundations of Italian classicism.

In 1595 Annibale Carracci was summoned to Rome by Cardinal Odoardo Farnese to work in the palazzo that the cardinal had Michelangelo build. There Carracci and his workshop painted the majestic ceiling of the art gallery. Indeed, in 1602–03, the cardinal erected a small wing behind the main part of the palace, between the Tiber and Via Julia, to house part of his collection of antiques. As Annibale's main patron, he commissioned the artist to decorate the main rooms on the upper floor, or piano nobile, of this little palazzo that was linked, from April 1603 onward, to the roof of the main palace by a bridge over Via Giulia.

The Musée Condé holds seven works from the three first *camerini* (small bedrooms) each decorated with a related theme: night, dawn, and day. The decoration remained in situ until 1662, then entered the collection of Duke Ranuccio II Farnese in Parma, where it could been seen until 1735, when Charles VIII Bourbon, king of the Two Sicilies, shipped it to the newly built Palazzo di Capodimonte where he installed his collection.

This *Venus* was therefore painted in Rome in 1602, probably with workshop assistants—perhaps Domenichino or Francesco Albani—because it was a time of intense activity for Annibale, which did not prevent him from supervising execution, as witnessed by the very high quality of this work.

It may have been intended for the main Farnese palace rather than the palazzetto, but ultimately redirected from its initial destination since the subject relates to the loves of the gods, featured in the palazzo. It evokes Titian's reclining *Venus* (Prado, Madrid), which was in Aldobrandini hands in Rome in 1598, and was inspired by the writings of Philostratus, *Imagines,* which had been translated and commented by Blaise de Vigenère in 1578. Carracci copied certain things from Titian, such as the putto who throws apples, and the two putti wrestling beneath a laurel wreath, but varies the figure in an age ready to explore the expression of human passions. The painting is furthermore full of allusions to Michelangelo, Raphael, and Giulio Romano. The figure of Venus, however, alludes to antique statuary.

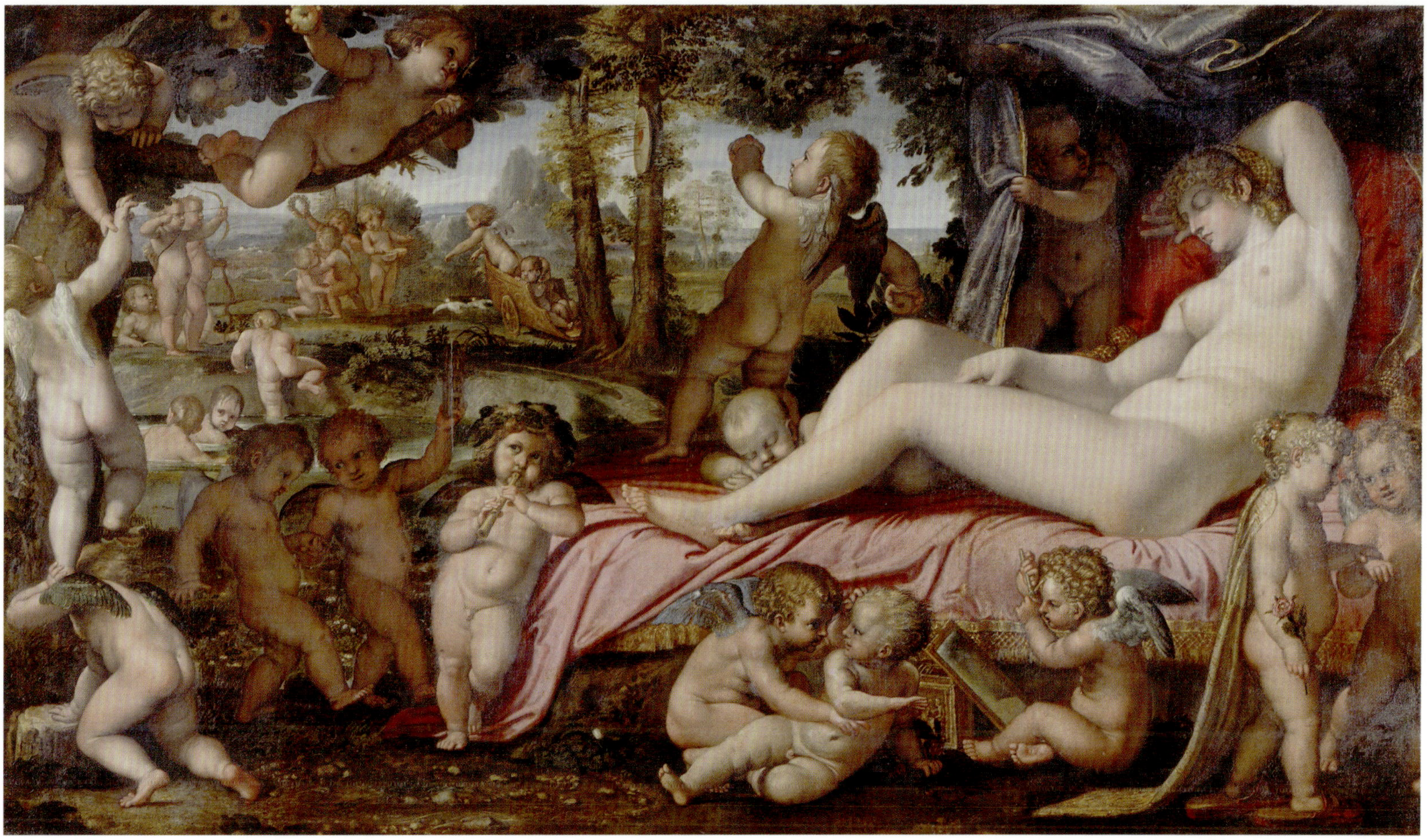

ANNIBALE CARRACCI

(Bologna, 1560; Rome, 1609)

Dawn Holding a Torch and Scattering Flowers

Canvas. H. 119 cm (3 ft. 10 ½ in.); W. 159 cm (5 ft. 2 ½ in.)
Inv. 69 (Galerie de Peinture)

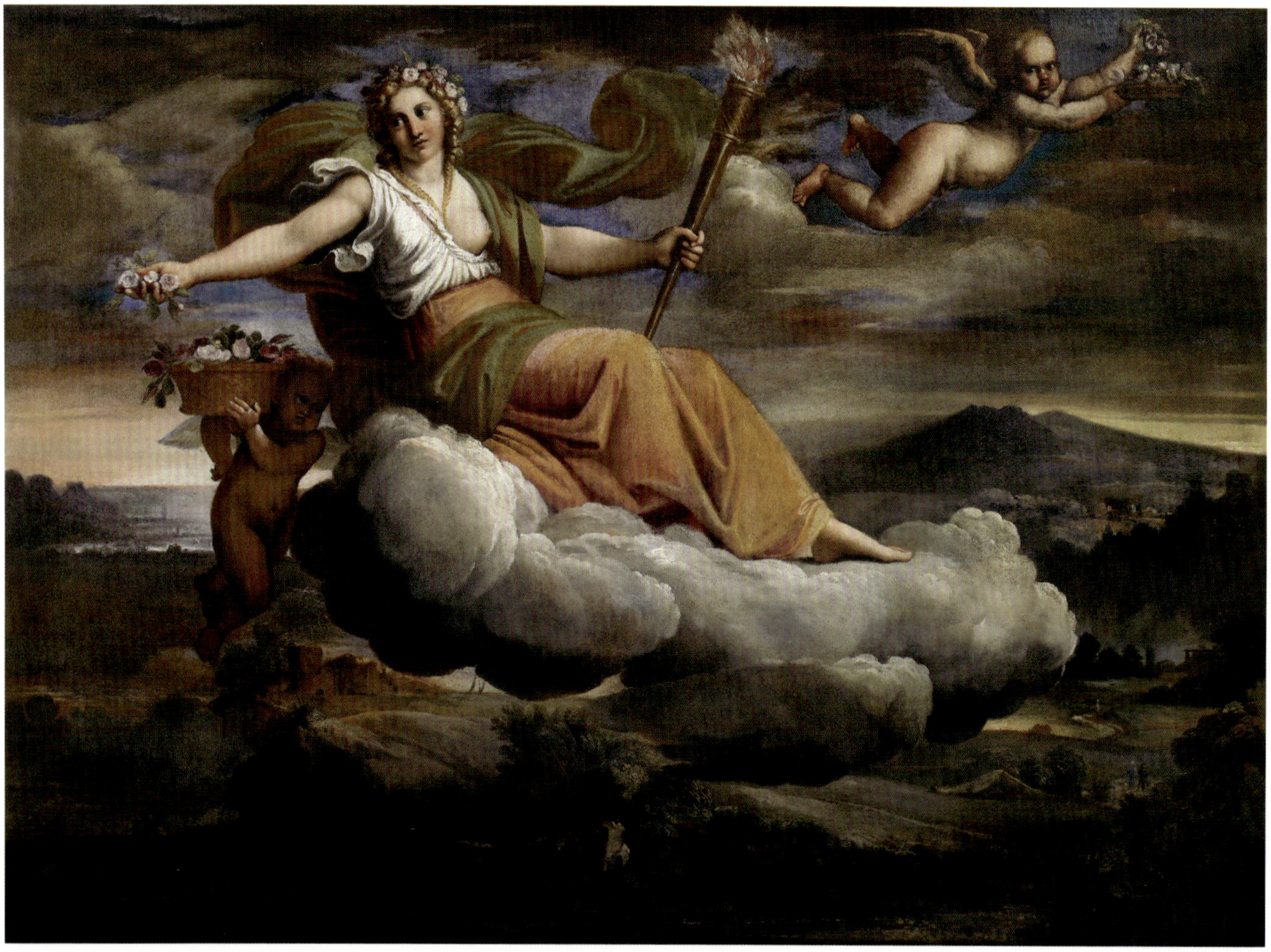

An allegorical figure of Dawn is shown in a chariot of clouds, rather than the Pegasus-drawn chariot described by Cesare Ripa in his *Iconologia*. In keeping with traditional iconography, she is wearing a saffron-colored gown and scatters flowers with her right hand, holding a torch in her left hand. A putto, or winged infant, flies before her, holding a vase of roses; the identical motif can be seen in *The Triumph of Bacchus and Ariadne* in the Farnese Gallery.

This *Dawn* decorated the second *camerino* in Cardinal Odoardo Farnese's palazzetto (*see p. 86*). It was painted in the middle of the ceiling, accompanied by portraits of Portuguese princes (Galleria Nazionale, Parma).

Like *Night*, this composition was certainly by Annibale Carracci himself, even though no preparatory drawing for it survives. The execution, however, relied on workshop participation, as moreover confirmed by Bellori and Malvasia. Some commentators consider it to be by Domenichino, under the supervision (and with the participation) of Carracci. Indeed, several hands can be detected here. This kind of collaboration was entirely typical of the Carraccis' workshop, where design was the most important element, allowing artists to call upon assistants whose technique was very similar to their own.

ANNIBALE CARRACCI

(Bologna, 1560; Rome, 1609)

Night Bringing Sleep and Death

Canvas. H. 128 cm (4 ft. 2 ½ in.); W. 155 cm (5 ft. 1 in.)
Inv. 68 (Galerie de Peinture)

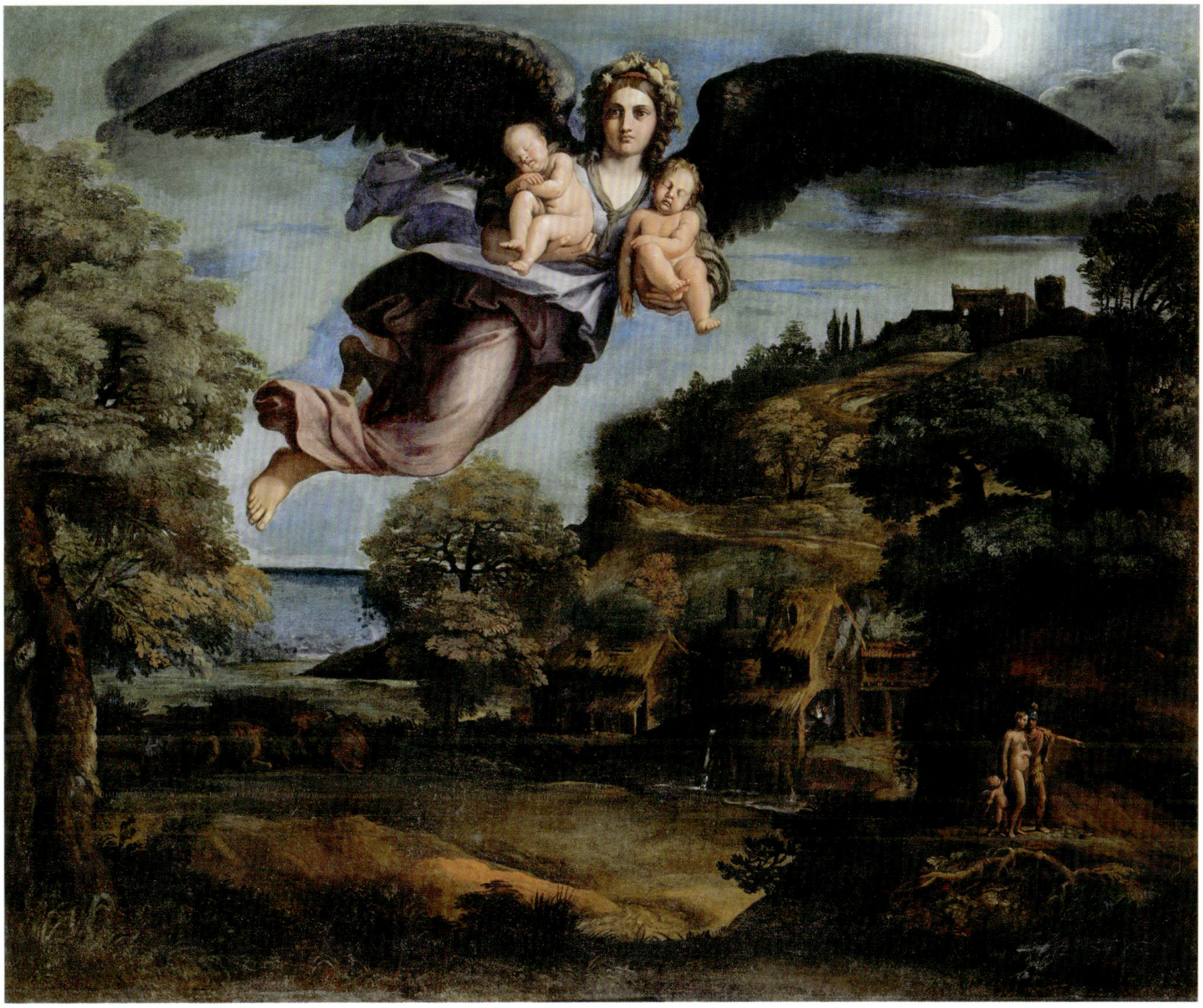

The complex iconography of this painting is based on Cesare Ripa's *Iconologia,* a book published in 1593 which provided a rich source of inspiration for artists of the day. Here we have an allegory of Night, depicted as a winged woman whose head is wreathed in poppies, the symbol of sleep. Under each arm she carries a sleeping infant: on the left is Sleep, her son, while on the right is the darker Death. We know that the three *camerini,* or small rooms in the Palazzetto Farnese painted by Annibale Carracci for Cardinal Odoardo Farnese between 1692 and 1605 (*see p. 86*), were devoted to the themes of night, dawn, and day. Placed on the ceiling of the third *camerino,* this *Night* was flanked by four putti now held by the Musée Condé, as well as by portraits of the Farnese family (Galleria Nazionale, Parma) and moon-lit landscapes by Paul Bril (1554–1626). The walls were hung with purple fabric edged with silver lilies.

The composition is indeed by Annibale himself, as witnessed by a preparatory drawing in Dresden (Kupferstichkabinett). However, a few rare discrepancies—the subject is handled in a less frontal manner, the sky is vaster and lower, the houses and bay differ somewhat, and above all, the design is lighter and freer—led Bellori (1672) to suggest that Annibale was assisted by his pupils, whereas Malvasia (1678) argued that he merely touched it up. Some modern art historians feel that that the somewhat dry execution of the painting points to a work by Domenichino after a design by Annibale, because the monumental aspect of the work fully corresponds to the young painter's early style. Others suggest that Giovanni Battista Viola (1576–1662) contributed to the landscape.

ANNIBALE CARRACCI

(Bologna, 1560; Rome, 1609)

The Archangel Gabriel Surrounded by Angelic Musicians and Cherubs

Canvas. H. 249 cm (8 ft. 2 in.); W. 212 cm (7 ft.)
Inv. 62 (Jeu de Paume)

This painting was one of a group—bequeathed to Duke Ottavio Farnese by Gabriele Bombosi, who died in Rome in 1602—which also included four partial copies of a fresco by Correggio (1489–1534) in the church of San Giovanni Evangelista in Parma. The canvas was still part of the Farnese collection at the Palazzo del Giardino in Parma around 1680, then was transferred to Naples circa 1735, from whence it entered the Salerno collection (*see p. 27*).

Although little known, because displayed in the less accessible Jeu de Paume gallery at the Musée Condé, this work is generally considered to be an original by Annibale's own hand, even if some workshop participation on auxiliary figures cannot be excluded. The composition appears to be indebted to Correggio, who continued to influence Annibale's painting up to the years 1596–97. At this time, Annibale often composed pictures with a V-shape patch of sky that emphasized the main figure.

While a very similar painting of angels is held in Naples (Museo di Capodimonte), also attributed to Annibale with workshop assistance, some commentators prefer to compare this painting to an *Assumption of the Virgin* dated 1592 (Pinacoteca Nazionale, Bologna). Stylistic comparison would then pinpoint this painting to the end of Annibale's Bologna period or the start of his Roman stay, that is to say circa 1594.

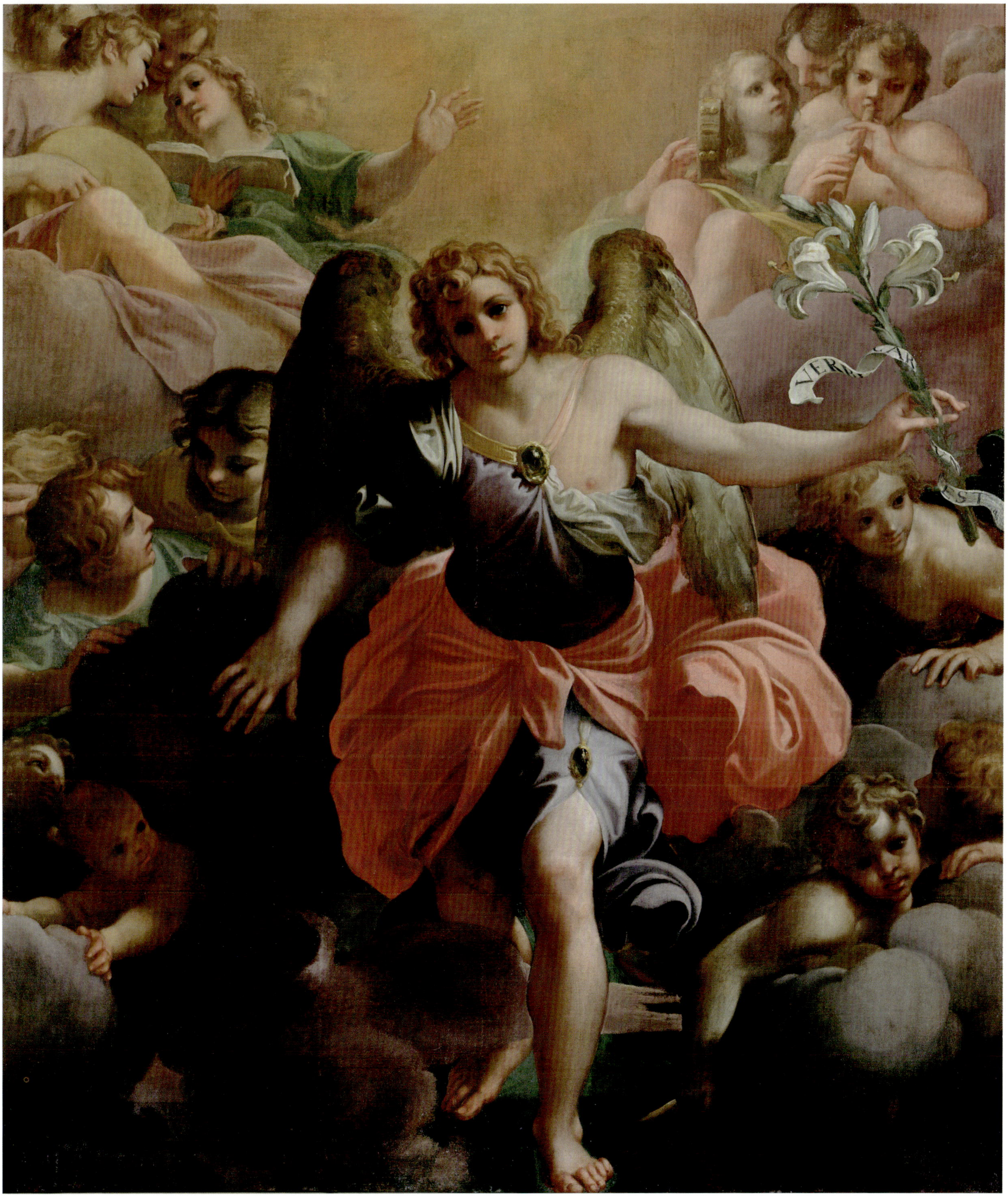

ANNIBALE CARRACCI

(Bologna, 1560; Rome, 1609)

Putti Strewing Flowers

Canvas. H. 72 cm (2 ft. 4 in.); W. 72 cm (2 ft. 4 in.)
Inv. 64–65–66–67 (Galerie de Peinture)

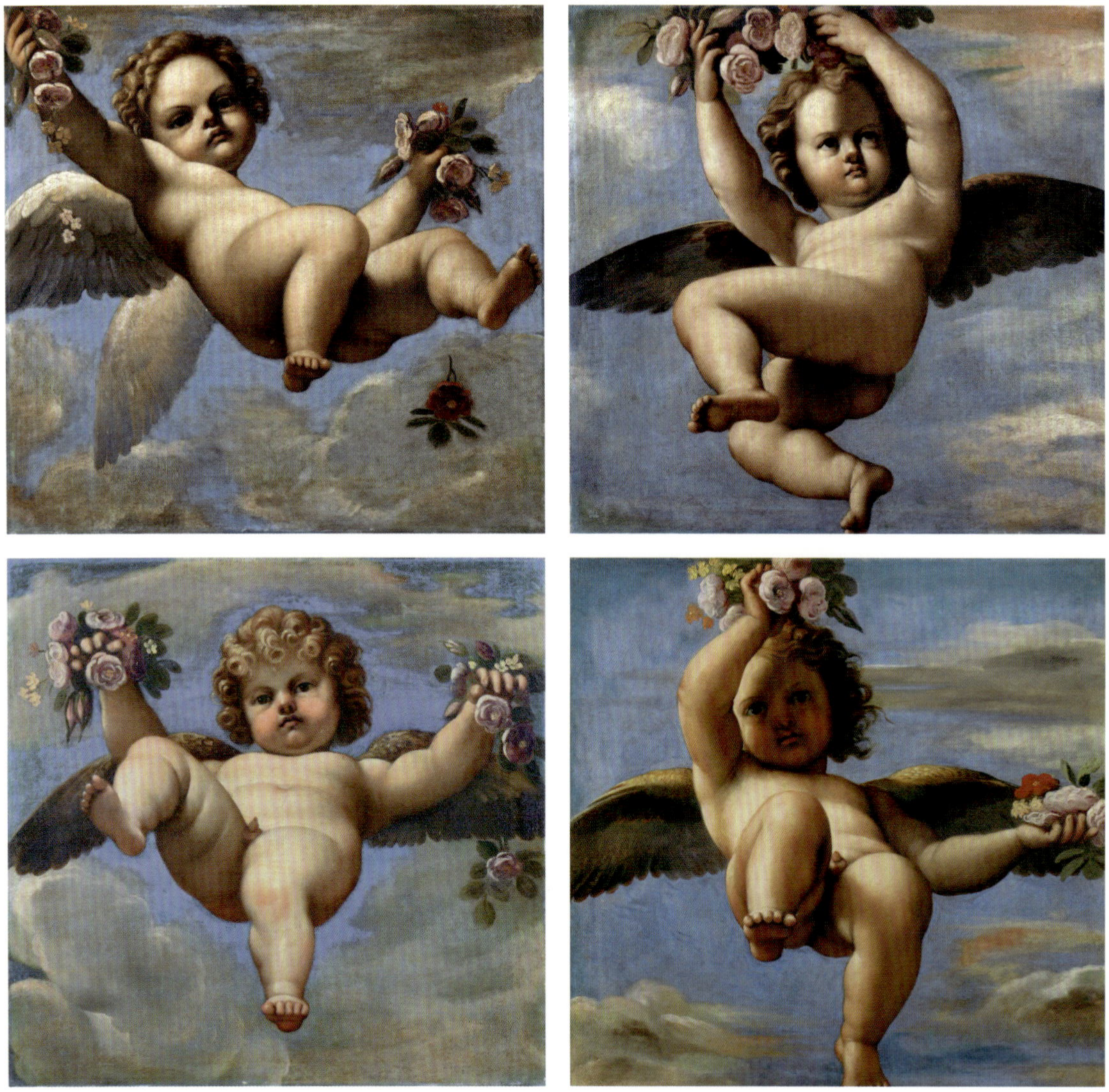

These four putti by Carracci flanked the panel of *Night,* in the third *camerino* of the small Farnese palace, or palazzetto (*see p. 86*). A preparatory drawing by Annibale for one of the putti exists and is now held by the Cleveland Museum of Art. These figures of flying cherubs reveal Annibale's virtuosity in depicting the human body in a foreshortened form. The variety and relief of their poses demonstrate the ease with which he produced his ceiling compositions. The tiny feet and prettiness of the chubby bodies contrast with the frowning expressions, some of which are partly clouded by shadow. Carracci skillfully exploited light to lend volume to his figures, which look as though they were frozen in mid-flight against an artificial ceiling.

DOMENICHINO (DOMENICO ZAMPIERI)

(Bologna, 1581; Naples, 1641)

The Stoning of Saint Stephen

Copper. H. 55 cm (1 ft. 9 1/2 in.); W. 40 cm (1 ft. 3 3/4 in.)
Inv. 70 (Cabinet du Giotto)

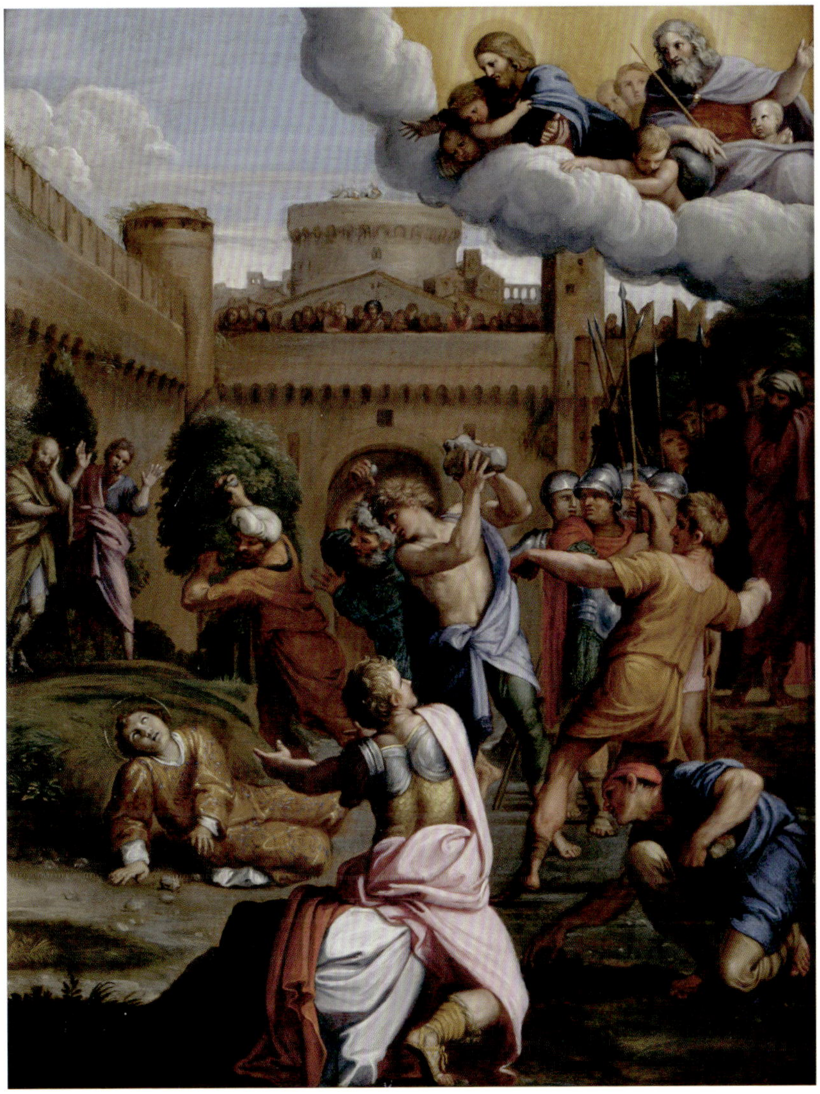

After a brief apprenticeship under the Mannerist painter Denys Calvaert (1540–1619), Domenichino joined the Carracci academy and went to work for Annibale on the Farnese project in Rome. He also worked for many Roman churches, sometimes in competition with Guido Reni, and notably executed the frescoes for the ceiling of Sant'Andrea delle Valle from 1622 to 1627. In 1630, Domenichino moved to Naples after having accepted a commission to decorate the San Gennaro chapel in the cathedral there, where he lived until his death.

This little painting was mentioned in Cardinal Mazarin's collection in 1653 and 1661; it was engraved by Guillaume Chasteau with an indication of its provenance, but attributed to Annibale Carracci. Then the painting entered the collection of the French regent, Philippe d'Orléans. It remained in the Orléans family collection in the Palais-Royal, still attributed to Carracci, until 1791, when it was sold, along with all the other paintings, by Philippe-Égalité. Purchased by Laborde de Méréville, it was shipped to England in 1792 where, after having passed through several English hands, it was bought by Nieuwenhuys, who sold it as a Carracci to the duc d'Aumale in 1860. The painting thus came back into the hands of the Orléans family.

The attribution to Domenichino, now universally accepted, dates to the twentieth century. Domenichino was indeed inspired by an Annibale Carracci painting of 1603–04 (Louvre), but his work differs in the more direct intervention of God the Father and Christ surrounded by angels. The violence of the executioners contrasts with Saint Stephen's pose of religious transport. The classical feel of this painting evokes Raphael's work in the Stanze in the Vatican. It was probably painted early in Domenichino's Roman period, circa 1605–07.

GUIDO RENI

(Bologna, 1575; Bologna, 1642)

Virgin and Child with Angels

Canvas. H. 183 cm (6 ft. ½ in.); W. 147 cm (4 ft. 9 in.)
Inv. 71 (Galerie de Peinture)

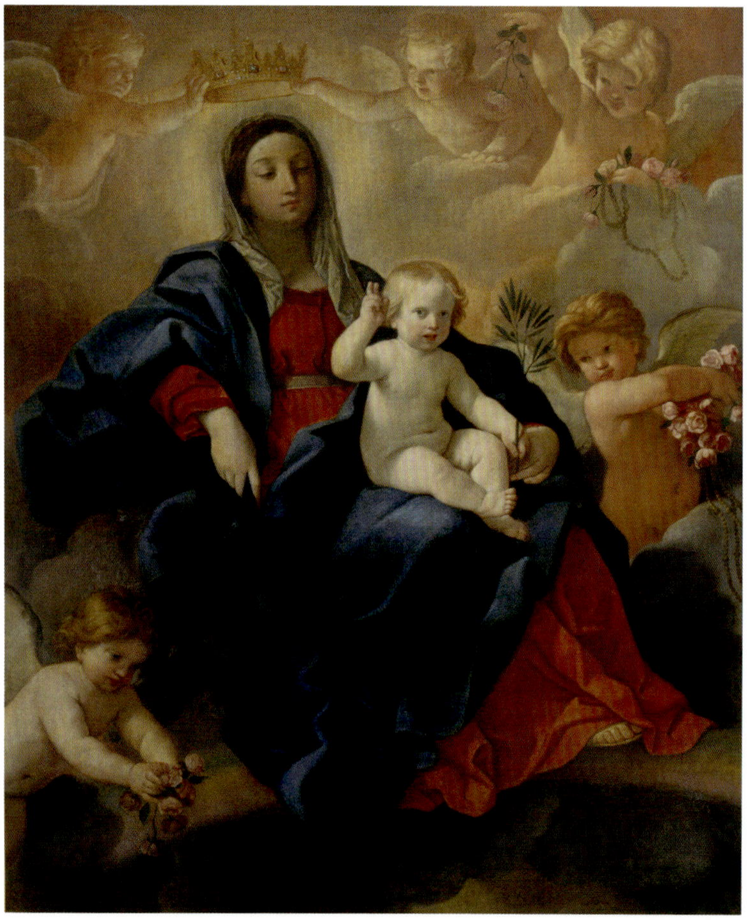

After his apprenticeship in Denys Calvaert's studio with Domenichino and Francesco Albani, Guido Reni entered the Carracci academy. Also inspired by Raphael, Reni became a major Bolognese painter not so much by looking at nature as by looking at that great Renaissance master. In order to study Raphael more closely and work after ancient models, in 1602 Reni went to Rome, where he was struck, like his contemporaries, by Caravaggio's painting. Unlike Caravaggio, however, Reni felt that even if art depicted natural things it should be free of any ugliness and vulgarity. His work met with great success in both Rome and Bologna. This *Virgin and Child* was apparently engraved in Italy and sold as the *Madonna della Pace* (Madonna of Peace), the name by which it was known in 1803. It is a partial replica of Reni's *Pallione del Voto* (Pinacoteca Nazionale, Bologna), a votive altarpiece to ward off the plague, commissioned in 1631 by the Senate of the city of Bologna and displayed once a year in the chapel of the rosary in the church of San Domenico. This large panel was famous in its day; it employs a three-level iconography typical of Counter-Reformation painting: on the lower register are simple mortals, and in the middle are saints who intercede with the Virgin, at the top, flanked by angels. In this instance, the work alludes to the plague, as witnessed in the lower register by the hearses at the gates of Bologna and the city's patron saints playing their role of intercession.

The Musée Condé's painting is a replica of the upper register of the Bologna altarpiece, with several variations: the cherubs, pictured in only the upper half of the bodies, are placing a crown of metal, rather than roses, on the Virgin's head; the infant Jesus is holding an olive branch, rather than the rose seen in the altarpiece. The iconography no longer relates to the plague nor the Virgin of the Rosary. Instead, the composition is centered on the blessing given by the holy child, who holds the symbol of peace. The attribution to Reni seems convincing even though certain weaker passages, such as the two angels on the right, might have been done by workshop assistants. This replica was probably commissioned shortly after the votive panel was executed, circa 1631–32.

MATTIA PRETI

(Taverna, 1613; Valetta, 1699)

Ecce Homo

Canvas. H. 205 cm (6 ft. 8 ½ in.); W. 259 cm (8 ft. 6 in.)
Inv. 82 (Galerie de Peinture)

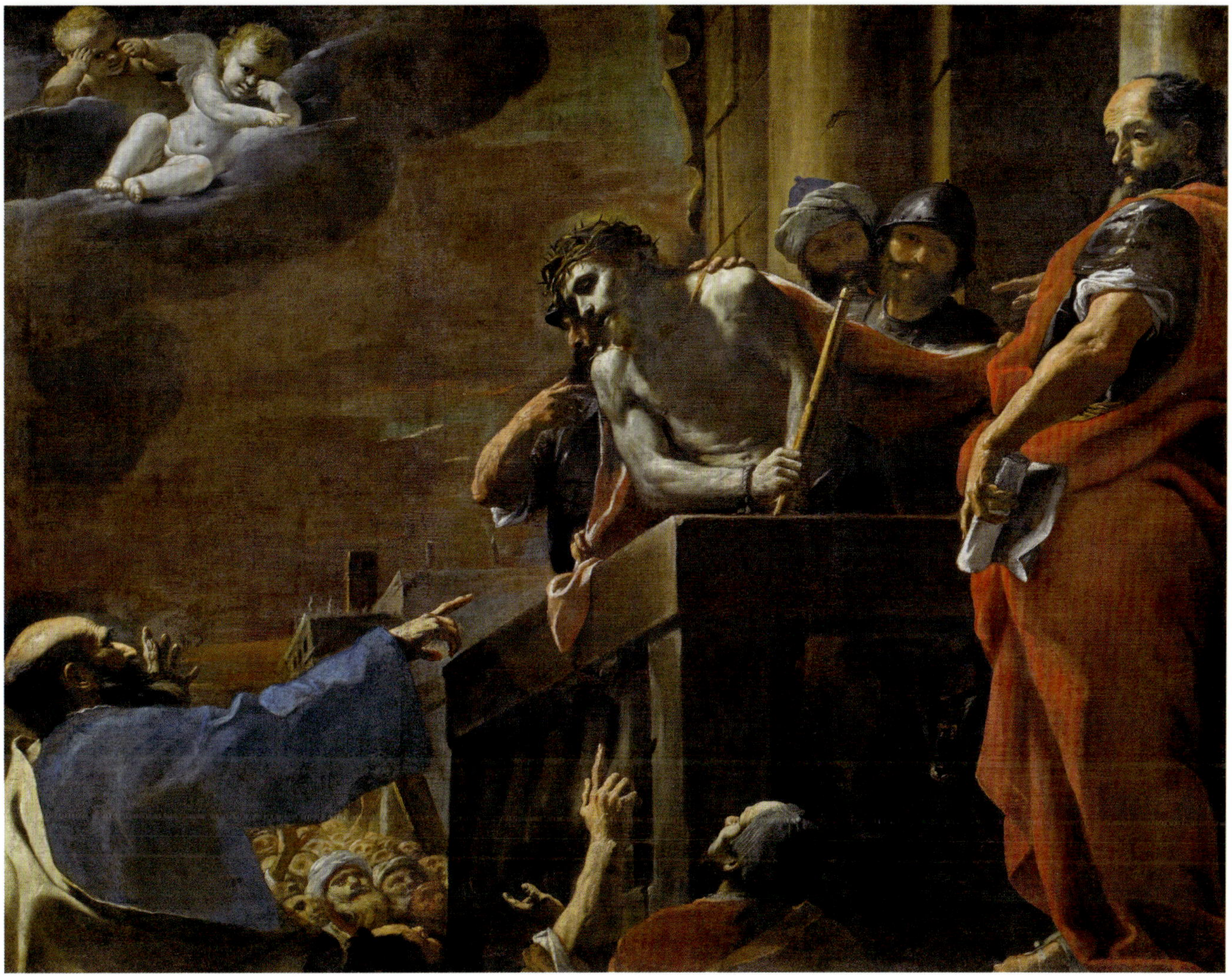

Born not far from Catanzaro in Calabria, Mattia Preti left for Rome at the age of seventeen. He studied the masterpieces in the Vatican and the Farnese Gallery before opening his own studio on Piazza di Spagna. In 1651 he completed Giovanni Lanfranco's decoration of the church of San Andrea della Valle. He received the title of Cavaliere (Knight) in 1642. In 1652 he executed frescoes for the dome and choir of San Biagio in Modena, then returned to Naples in 1653, where he did the ceiling of the church of San Pietro a Maiella in 1659. From 1661 until his death in 1669 Preti lived in Malta, where he restored and decorated the church of San Giovanni, working as architect as well as painter. Nicknamed "Il Cavaliere Calabrese" (due to his birthplace in Calabria) he developed a heroic, indeed emotional, style that stressed the expression of passion and featured tragic subjects. Despite being influenced by Caravaggio's chiaroscuro, Preti never adopted the former's naturalism but always endowed his figures with nobility.

This painting, which apparently dates from 1656–66, belonged to the Vincenzo brothers and Pietro Monticani in Venice in 1740. It is now thought to be a pendant to Preti's *Road to Calvary* (Museo di Capodimonte, Naples). Both works were purchased in Rome in 1802 by Marquess Torlonia on behalf of King Ferdinand IV of Naples, along with a third work, *The Prodigal Son* (Palazzo Real, Naples). In addition to comparable dimensions, the three works display similarities in lighting, composition, and perspective.

Preti was a major Italian Baroque painter who handled the Ecce Homo theme several times. This theatrical composition is his most ambitious version. It is governed by a dark palette dominated by deep reds, ochers, and grays. Although the effect of dramatic, raking light recalls the work of Caravaggio, the influence of the school of Venice is equally apparent.

LIONELLO SPADA

(Bologna, 1576; Parma, 1622)

Christ Crowned with Thorns

Wood. H. 205 cm (6 ft. 8 ½ in.); W. 134 cm (4 ft. 3 ¾ in.)
Inv. 72 (Galerie de Peinture)

Lionello Spada was one of the few Bolognese artists profoundly marked by the art of Caravaggio, to the point where he was nicknamed Scimmia del Caravaggio (Caravaggio's ape), even though it is not certain that the two artists ever met. Spada nevertheless remained highly attached to Bolognese techniques, notably the use of drawing. Having trained under Cesare Baglioni, around 1600 he was part of a Bolognese team that specialized in *quadratura* (illusionist architectural decoration). His time spent in the Carracci academy can be detected in his style, highly influenced by Ludovico Carracci. Spada worked on the funeral of Agostino Carracci in 1602 and contributed to the epic cycle on Torquato Tasso's *Roman Histories* in the Palazzo Bentivogli.

This *Christ* is confidently attributed to Spada. It displays a synthesis of the Carraccis' art with Caravaggio's realism. It probably dates from 1614–16. Purchased by the duc d'Aumale as part of the Salerno collection (*see p. 27*), after having been acquired in 1802 by the king of Naples, it allegedly originated in the Albani collection in Rome.

The triangular composition is intersected by diagonals that fragment the conventional presentation. The modeling, like that of Ludovico Carracci, is soft, notably in Christ's face. Nevertheless, the painting is still heavily indebted to Caravaggio, as typified by harsh lighting, the stark contrast between shadow and light, the physical appearance of the figures handled in a realistic way (the open-mouthed shout), and the rustic features of rugged bodies that contrast to the elegant figure and refined face of Christ.

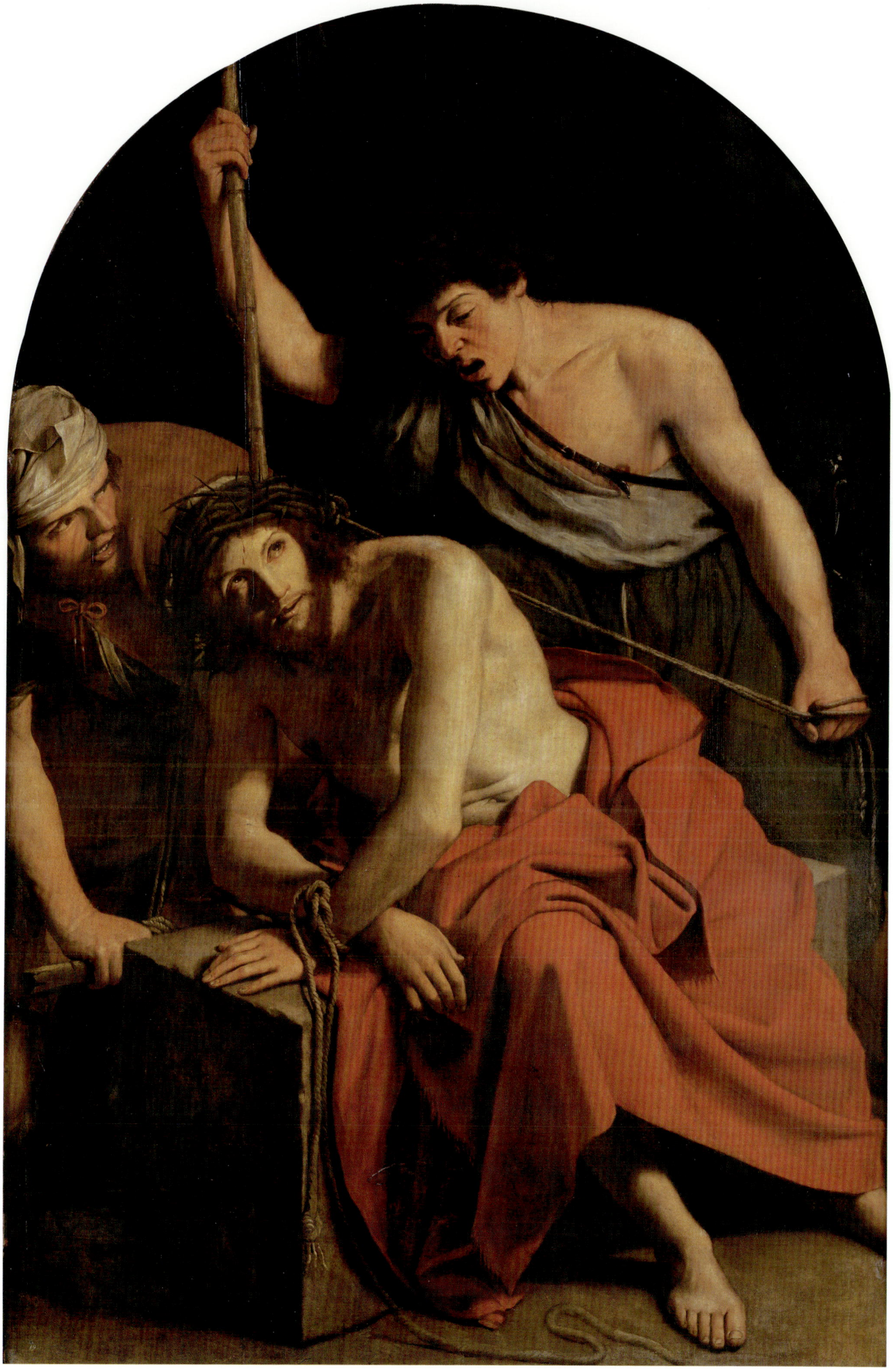

GUIDO CAGNACCI

(Sant'Arcangelo di Romagna, 1601; Vienna, 1663)

Christ Asleep with Zacharias and John the Baptist

Canvas. H. 94 cm (3 ft. 1 in.); W. 131 cm (4 ft. 3 ½ in.)
Inv. 76 (Cabinet du Giotto)

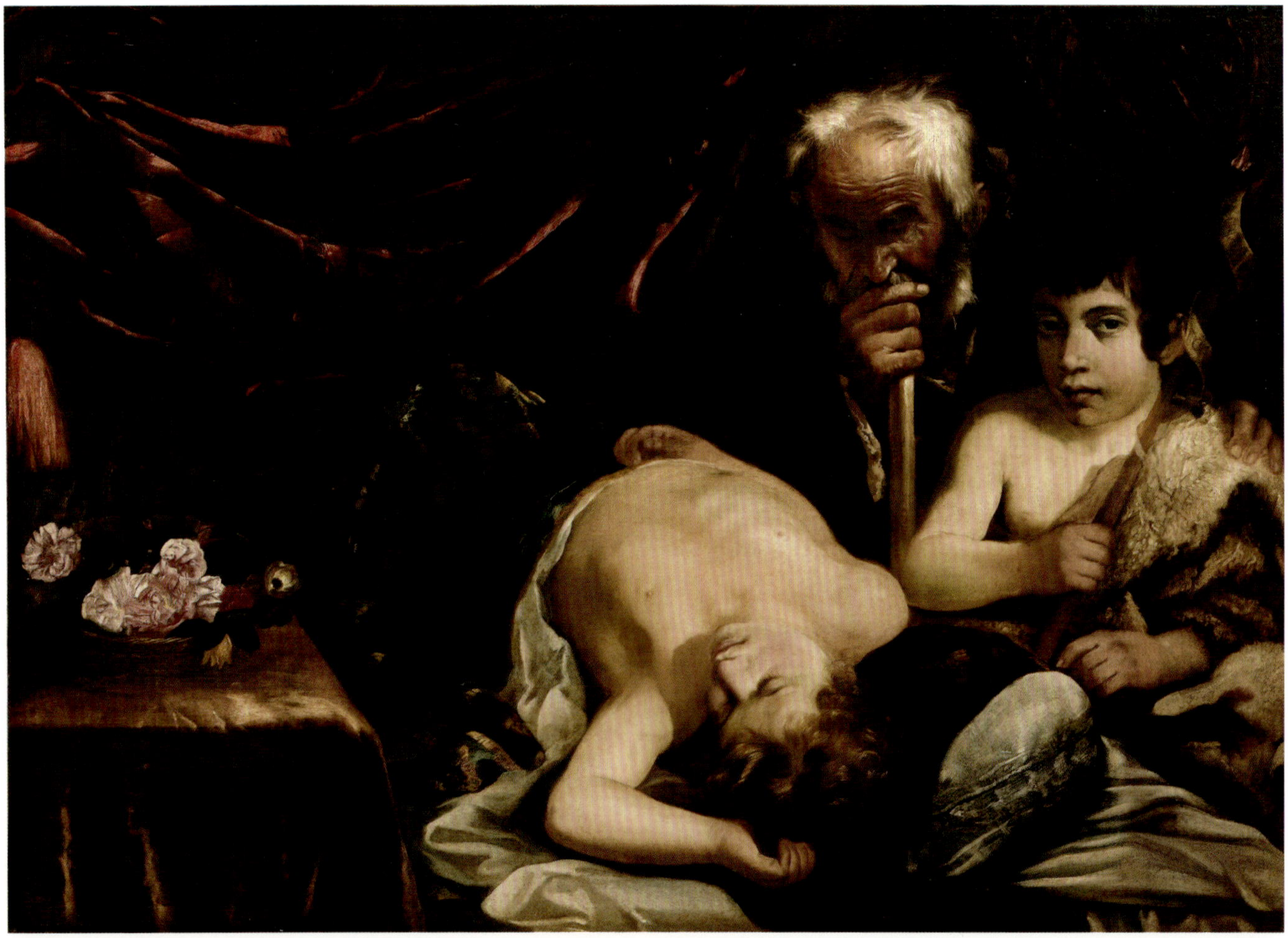

The early nineteenth-century attribution of this painting to Guido Cagnacci seems appropriate. The artist from Emilia was highly influenced by Caravaggio, but was long overshadowed by Il Guercino and Guido Reni (with whom he worked for a while).

The rather mysterious iconography shows a youth asleep, an old man, and a boy. This latter, on the right, can be easily identified as John the Baptist thanks to his attributes of sheepskin and shepherd's hook wrapped with a scroll bearing the letters *IO* for Ioannes (John). The old man might be Joseph, or perhaps even Zacharias, because he places his hand on John's shoulder in a paternal way. This latter interpretation would make the subject a prefiguration of the death of Christ, who is shown here not as an infant but an adolescent whose body is magnificently foreshortened, half-naked and with slightly tilted head as conventionally seen in depictions on the cross. The roses and anemones are flowers associated with the Passion of Christ, while the heavy curtain in the background, in two sections, may allude to the rending of the curtain in the Temple. Radiographic analysis has revealed a major pentimento: the artist initially painted a woman leaning over the youth's body instead of the old man, her face located at the level of Zacharias' hand. The composition therefore initially involved either a mythological subject such as the death of Adonis or, more probably, Saint Sebastian tended by Irene. The entire figure of John the Baptist was repainted, while the right arm of the slumbering lad was in a different, wider position. The strangeness of the scene is therefore due to the change of iconography.

The traditional attribution still seems valid, notably given the presence of a floral still life, a genre in which Cagnacci distinguished himself (Pinacoteca Civica, Forlì). The canvas might be dated 1630–40, early in the career of the artist when he was still heavily influenced by Caravaggio and Il Guercino, rather than by Guido Reni, who would inspire Cagnacci at a later point.

IL GUERCINO (GIOVANNI FRANCESCO BARBIERI)

(Cento di Ferrara, 1591; Bologna, 1666)

Pietà

Canvas. H. 273 cm (8 ft. 11 in.);
W. 177 cm (5 ft. 9 ¾ in.)
Inv. 74 (Galerie de Peinture)

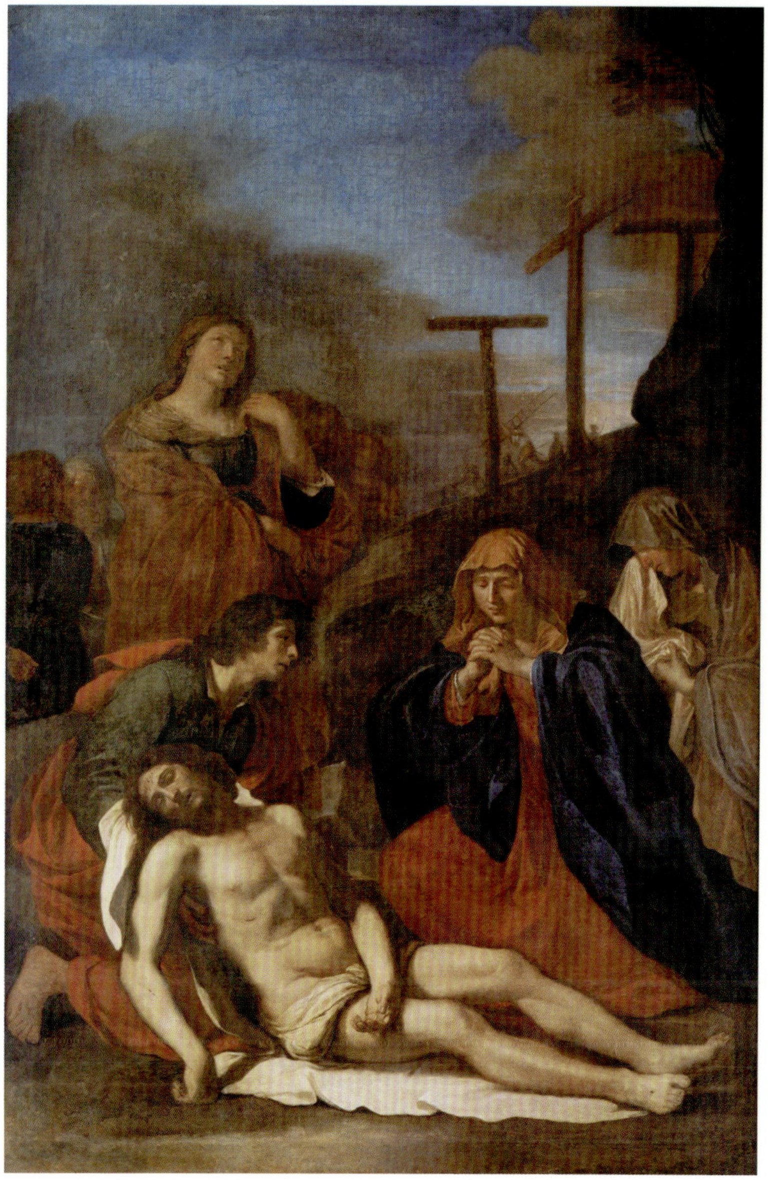

Giovanni Francesco Barbieri trained under the Carraccis, notably Ludovico, and studied Caravaggio's works in Venice and Rubens' paintings in Mantua. In 1621 he was summoned by Pope Gregory XV to Rome, where he remained until the pope's death in 1623. After returning to Emilia, his output initially retained its Caravaggesque look, then his style softened. When Guido Reni died in 1642, the hard-working Guercino moved to Bologna. His many paintings, though often religious in subject matter, were handled in a naturalistic vein.

This *Pietà* was commissioned in 1637 by Giovanni Torri for the church known as Chiesa Nova (or Chiesa del Voto) in Modena. The picture was supposed to include six figures, including the Madonna, Saint John, the dead Christ, and Saint Mary Magdalen; it was to be finished by Christmas 1638. But Guercino ran into delays and only completed it in June 1640. This large altar painting was flanked by two other studio works, a *Saint Mark* on the left by Bartolomeo Gennari (1594–1661) and a *Saint Matthew with the Angel* on the right by Benedetto Zalone (active in 1650), still in situ today. In 1773 Guercino's painting, suffering from water damage, was sold to a certain Manfredi Mossati and a copy, commissioned in the month of August from an artist from Pesaro, Antonio Verni, was installed in November.

Although seriously damaged in the upper part, this remains a very fine painting. Windsor Castle holds a preparatory drawing for the Mary Magdalen figure that displays several variations in hair and drapery.

Although he had been back in his home town of Cento for fourteen years when he made this painting, Guercino still displays the influences of his Roman period (1621–23) and of Guido Reni, notably in the handling of the female figures. The composition, with its play of diagonals, is highly classical. Inscribed within a triangle, the body of Christ is emphasized by the white shroud that sets it off. Shadow and light play across the corpse, reminding us that Guercino had looked extensively at Caravaggio's work.

SALVATOR ROSA

(Naples, 1615; Rome, 1673)

Daniel in the Lions' Den

Canvas. H. 268 cm (8 ft. 9 in.); W. 178 cm (5 ft. 10 in.)
Inv. 83 (Galerie de Peinture)

When Pope Alexander VII decided to revamp the entrance to Rome at the Porta Flaminia and the Piazza del Popolo in 1661, he commissioned plans from architect Carlo Rainaldi (1611–1691), who in 1662 erected two identical churches—with the help of Carlo Fontana (1634–1714)—on either side of the Via del Corso. Salvator Rosa, who wanted to exhibit his art in a public place, encouraged banker Carlo De Rossi to endow a chapel where Rosa could hang his paintings, which he would execute for free. The two churches were only completed after Rosa's death, however, during the pontificate of Clement X (1670–76). In Santa Maria di Montesanto (completed 1675), the first chapel on the right, dedicated to the crucifix, was attributed by Cardinal Gastaldo to De Rossi, who placed Rosa's paintings there. The works all dealt with Biblical themes related to deliverance or resurrection, and were installed in 1677, according to a plaque erected there by the banker. They were greatly admired during an inauguration ceremony in 1679. The five paintings—all now in the Musée Condé—were taken down in 1802 and purchased by Domenico Venuti on the behalf of the king of Naples, from which they entered the Salerno collection, itself bought by the duc d'Aumale in 1854 (*see p. 27*). The attribution is therefore very solid; three of the paintings are initialed. Landscape is minimized to the benefit of life-sized figures, which date the paintings to Rosa's late period, in the early 1660s. The series is very homogeneous and thus must have been painted over a brief time span.

The incident of *Daniel in the Lions' Den* is taken from the Old Testament book of Daniel. Rosa's painting is inspired by a Greek variant on the story, later than the Aramaic version. The point of the picture is to teach believers that faith in God will deliver them from death, which suggests a parallel between Daniel and the resurrected Christ. Rosa decided to show the moment when Daniel stands up to receive food from the prophet Habakkuk, himself accompanied by an angel. Attention is first directed upward by the index finger of God's messenger, which points heaven-ward, emphasized by the light, but the eye then drops toward the bottom of the composition where the lions lie in the den. Rosa's painting includes only three of the four lions mentioned in the Bible.

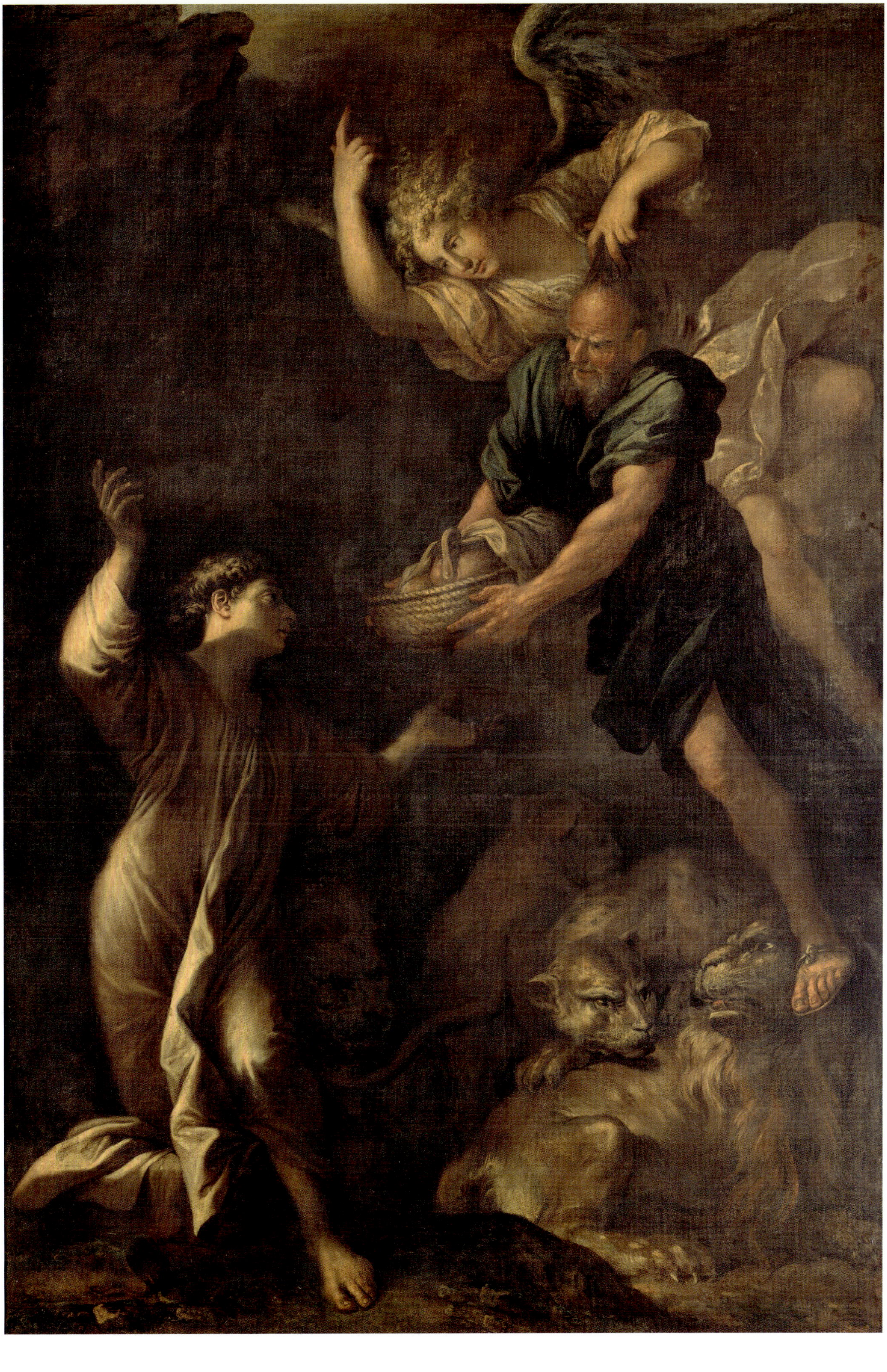

SALVATOR ROSA

(Naples, 1615; Rome, 1673)

Jeremiah Drawn from the Cistern

Canvas. H. 268 cm (8 ft. 9 in.); W. 178 cm (5 ft. 10 in.)
Initialed b.r. on rock: *SR*
Inv. 85 (Galerie de Peinture)

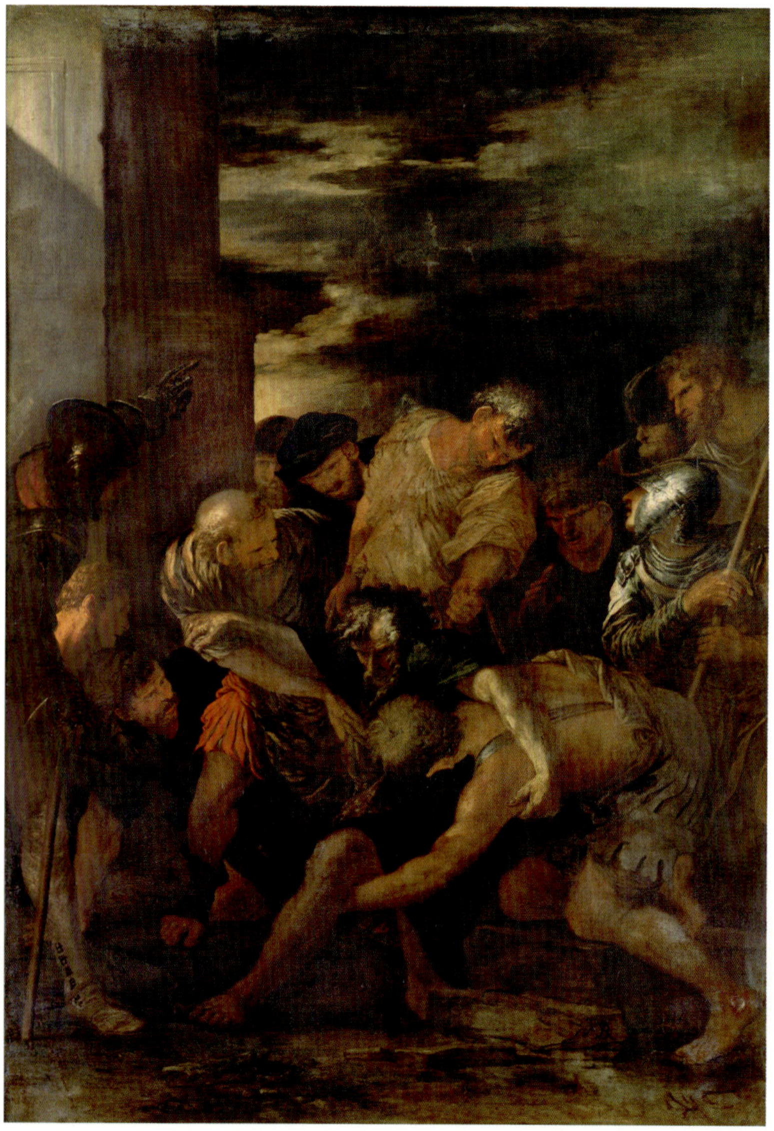

In a September 1662 letter to his Florentine friend Giovanni Battista Ricciardi, Salvator Rosa wrote that he had exhibited five paintings for the feast of San Giovanni Decollato in late August. He discussed at length the iconography of this painting in particular, explaining that it contained thirteen life-size figures. *Jeremiah* is therefore the best documented of the works painted by Rosa for the church of Santa Maria di Montesanto in Rome (*see p. 100*). It was perhaps the first of the series. Several preparatory drawings are now in Princeton, at the Louvre, in Leipzig, and in Edinburgh.

According to the Book of Jeremiah, the prophet was cast into a cistern on the orders of the princes of Judah after having predicted the fall of Jerusalem; but the eunuch Ebedmelech had him released from his imprisonment. Rosa's painting shows the moment when three men, at the eunuch's order, haul Jeremiah from the cistern. Men in armor watch the scene, a sign that it is occurring in the court of the royal palace of King Zedekiah.

Rosa employed various techniques to dramatize the action. Many large figures dominate the composition, in which just a single architectural feature evokes the palace. Nor is any landscape visible. The artist focuses attention on the faces of the protagonists; as in the other paintings, he makes skillful use of light, which here gleams on the armor.

SALVATOR ROSA

(Naples, 1615; Rome, 1673)

The Revelation of Raphael

Canvas. H. 137 cm (4 ft. 5 ½ in.); W. 100 cm (3 ft. 3 ½ in.)
Initialed b.l. on rock: *SR*
Inv. 85 (Galerie de Peinture)

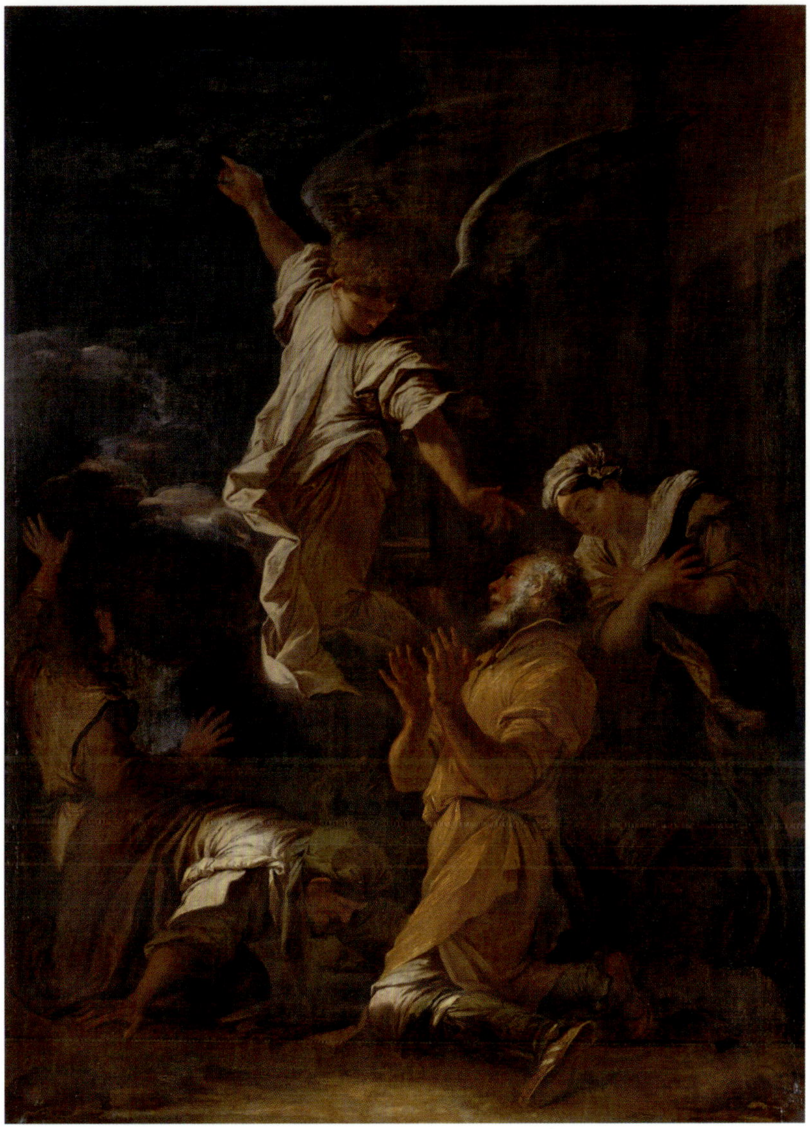

This painting is one of a set done at the request of Carlo De Rossi for the church of Santa Maria in Montesanto in Rome, and installed there in 1677 (*see p. 100*).

The incident of the revelation of the archangel Raphael is taken from the Old Testament Book of Tobias. Salvator Rosa has painted the moment when the angel rises to heaven after having revealed his identity to Tobias and his father Tobit, whose sight has just been restored by Raphael. Rosa has taken liberties with the Biblical source by adding two bowing figures, Tobit's wife and his daughter-in-law, Sarah, shown here deep in meditation, arms crossed on her chest, in the pose often given to the Virgin of the Annunciation. Since this gesture was also associated with a woman suffering from sterility, this painting has sometimes been interpreted as the announcement of the birth of Samson to the wife of Manoah. But it indeed shows the revelation of Raphael, because a dog—the traditional attribute of Tobias—can be seen in the shadow in the middle of the composition.

The painting focuses on the figure of Raphael, who points to heaven with one hand and extends the other toward Tobit, a gesture that establishes a link between the spiritual and temporal worlds, based on a rising diagonal. The quality of the light underscores the supernatural atmosphere.

SALVATOR ROSA

(Naples, 1615; Rome, 1673)

The Raising of Lazarus

Canvas. H. 137 cm (4 ft. 5 ½ in.); W. 100 cm (3 ft. 3 ½ in.)
Initialed b.r. on slab: *SR*
Inv. 86 (Galerie de Peinture)

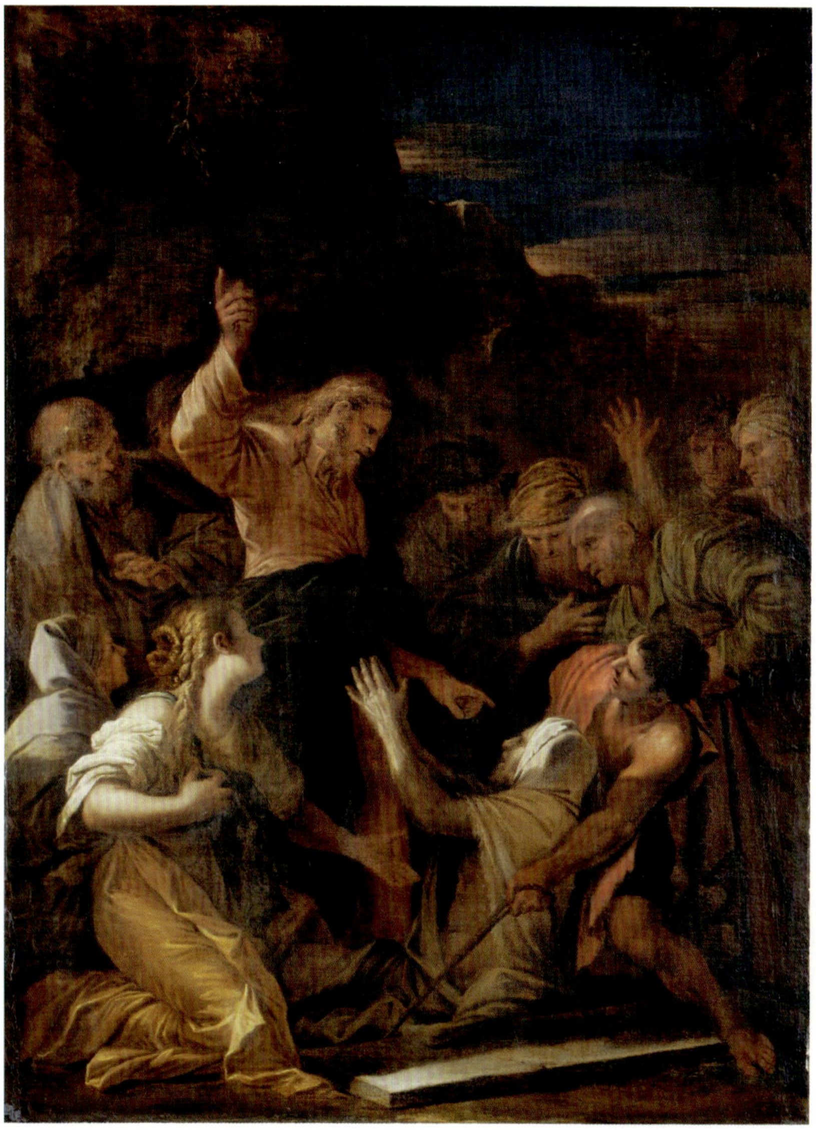

Like the previous works, this Biblical scene was part of a set of religious paintings done for the church of Santa Maria in Montesanto in Rome (*see p. 100*). Here the subject is taken from the New Testament, more precisely the Gospel according to John. Christ, surrounded by a crowd, is raising Lazarus, brother of Martha and Mary, from the dead, to demonstrate the glory of God. But Salvator Rosa has diverged from the text by showing a grave dug into the ground rather than a cave in a rocky cliff, as the gospel states. The Son of God is making a double gesture, invoking Heaven and commanding Lazarus to rise, thereby creating a diagonal line that underpins the composition. In the foreground, the kneeling figure of Mary is based on Raphael's classical idiom, which is untypical of Rosa. Painted in tones of red and brown, the picture is given relief through the sharp lighting that falls on the joined hands of Lazarus and highlights the fold of drapery, lending monumentality to this ambitious composition.

Among the many surviving preparatory drawings, compositional sketches can be found in a private collection in Rome, the Musée des Beaux-Art in Orléans, and the National Gallery of Scotland, and studies of details are held by the Metropolitan Museum in New York and the Museum der Bildenden Künste in Leipzig.

SALVATOR ROSA

(Naples, 1615; Rome, 1673)

The Resurrected Christ

Wood. H. 109 cm (3 ft. 7 in.); W. 96 cm (3 ft. 2 in.)
Inv. 88 (Cabinet du Giotto)

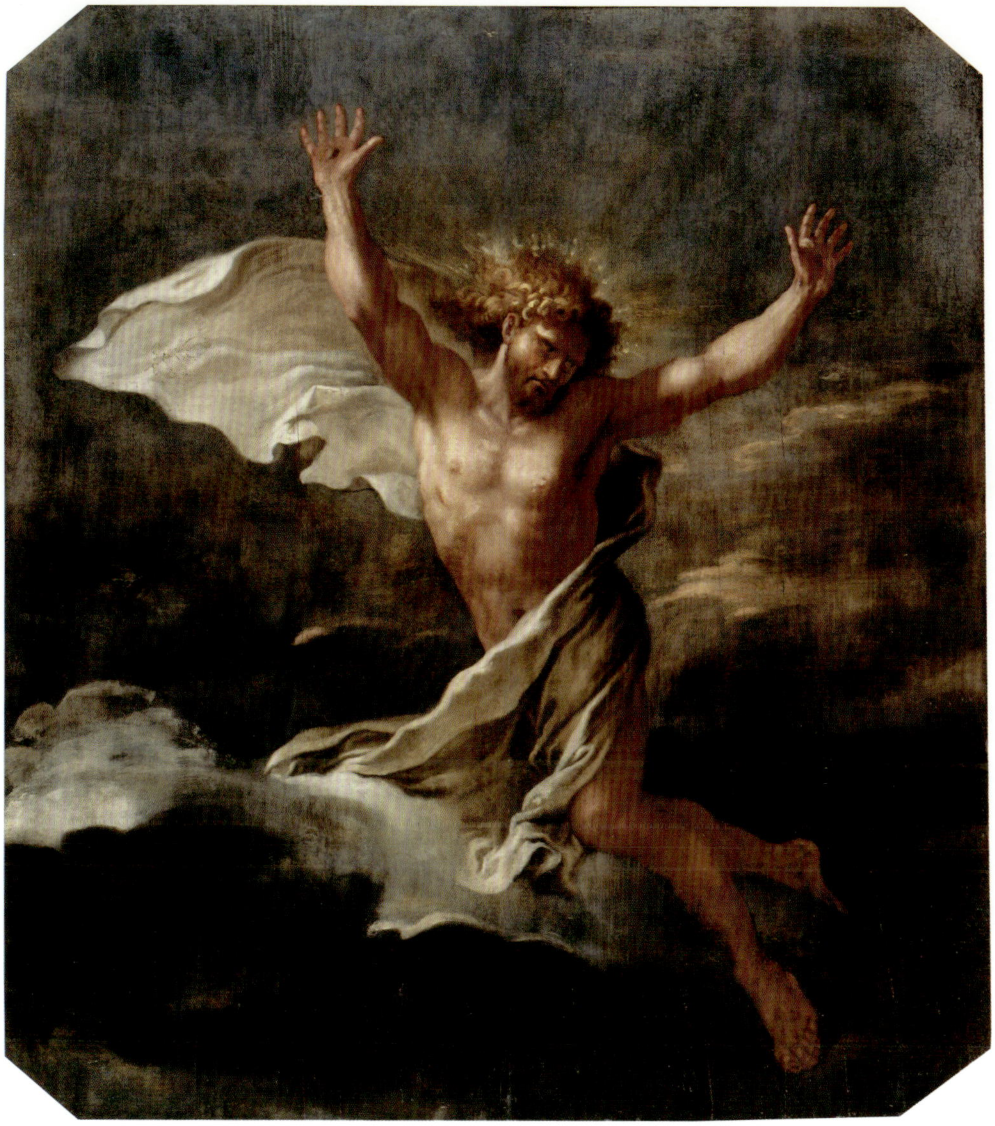

This painting was one of a set done at the request of Carlo De Rossi for the church of Santa Maria in Montesanto in Rome (*see p. 100*). It was mentioned as early as 1681 by Baldinucci alongside the four other paintings in the chapel, and not on the high altar as has sometimes been mistakenly asserted. The fact that this work was painted on wood, rather than canvas, has led some commentators to suggest that it is a copy of a lost original. Like the others in the group, it was taken down in 1802 and purchased the same year by Domenico Venuti on behalf of the king of Naples, from whence it entered the Salerno collection (*see p. 27*).

Given the darkening of the panel over time, the iconography has been interpreted in various ways. It was initially identified as a Resurrected Christ, then as Christ in Limbo. Preparatory drawings (Louvre; Leipzig; British Museum, London) suggest that Rosa's initial idea was a Resurrection of Christ in the presence of soldiers who were later eliminated, which is confirmed by period commentators who refer to a Resurrection. The traditional attribution to Rosa is still valid, especially since radiographic analysis has revealed a pentimento in the thumb of the right hand, a clear sign of an original work.

SALVATOR ROSA

(Naples, 1615; Rome, 1673)

Christ Bearing the Cross

Canvas. H. 126 cm (4 ft. 1 ¾ in.); W. 176 cm (5 ft. 9 ¼ in.)
Inv.87 (Galerie de Peinture)

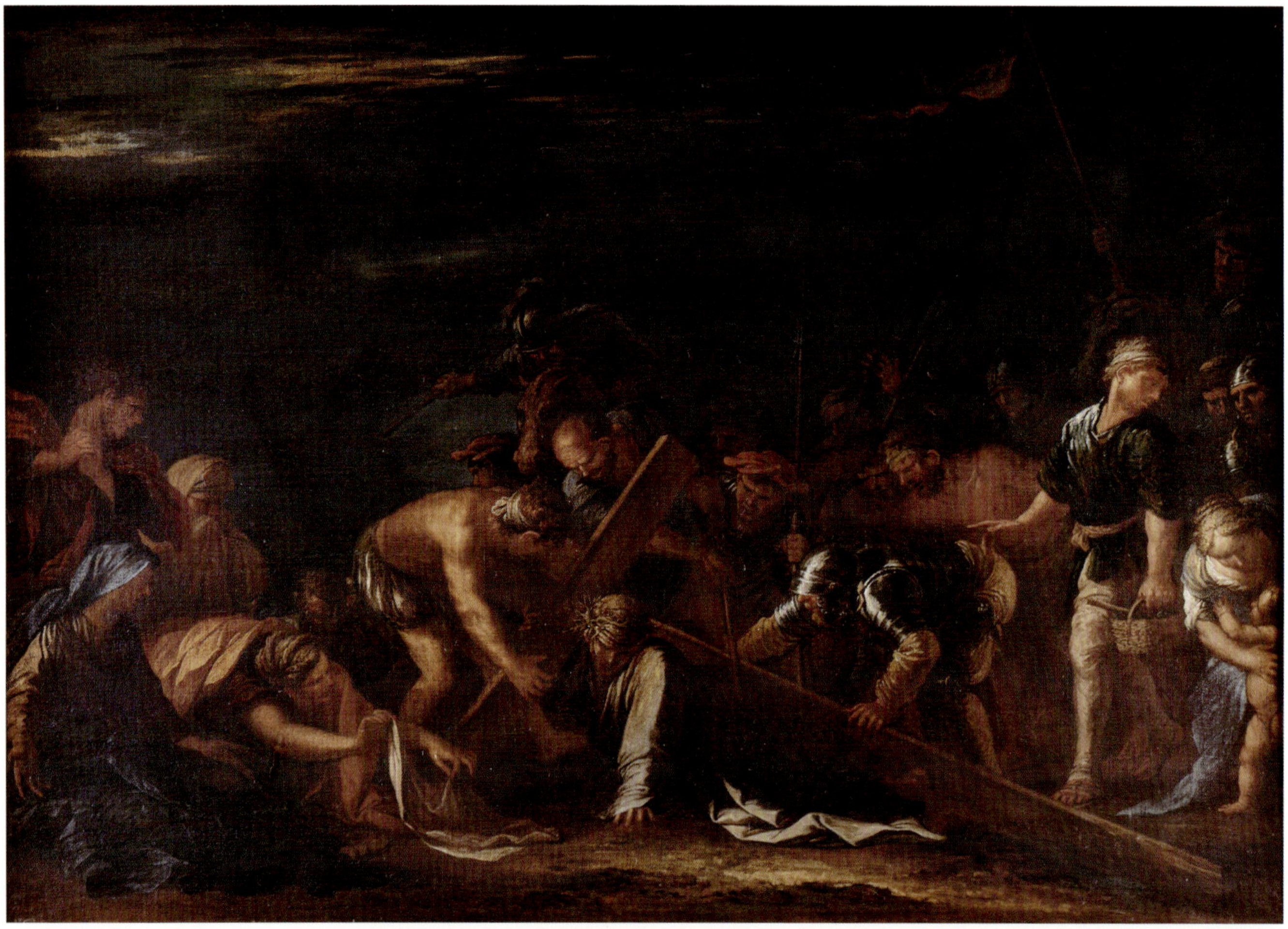

This painting was commissioned by Cardinal Paluzio Altieri for the famous gallery in his palazzo on Piazza del Gesù in Rome, as witnessed by its inclusion in the cardinal's estate inventory in 1698. We do not know when the Altieri family relinquished the painting, but we are certain that Domenico Venuti bought it from the art dealer Vitali in March 1802 on behalf of King Ferdinand IV of Naples, along with eleven other paintings by Salvator Rosa.

The frieze-like composition converges on Christ, crushed to the ground by the weight of the cross. With one arm, emphasized by lighting that makes the effort seem all the more strenuous, Christ tries to raise himself to his feet—the staging of the scene is particularly dramatic. Beneath a dark, leaden sky a few touches of light throw into relief the various gestures of the bystanders. The painting apparently dates from the latter part of Rosa's career, between 1662 and 1673.

CARLO CIGNANI

(Bologna, 1628; Bologna, 1719)

Virgin and Child

Canvas. H. 133 cm (4 ft. 4 ½ in.); W. 94 cm (3 ft. 1 in.)
Inv. 96 (Galerie de Peinture)

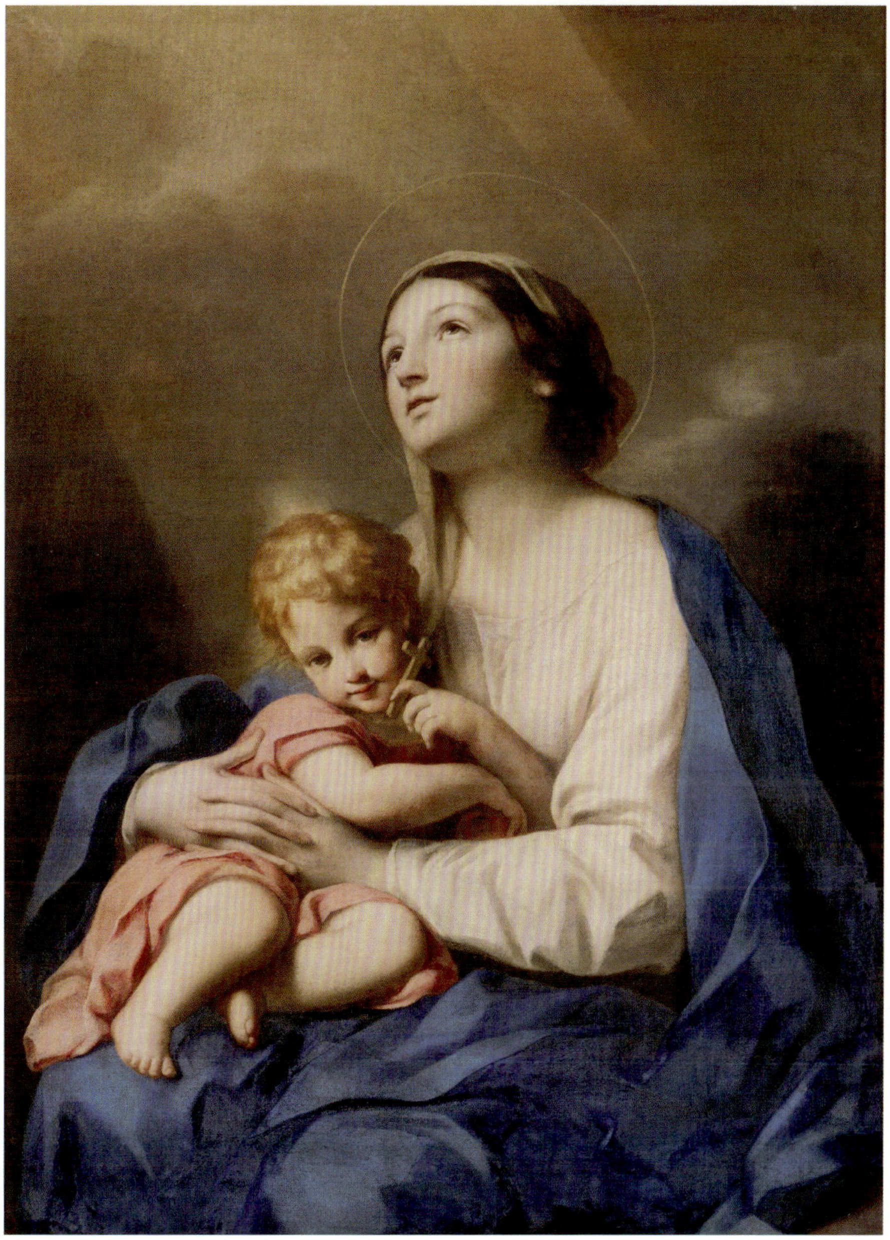

Carlo Cignani was an artist who typified the early seventeenth-century classicism associated with northern Italian city of Bologna under the influence of the Carraccis. This painting displays extreme refinement and a highly finished style, as well as being marked by the spirit of Correggio and Raphael. The strict triangular composition is here softened by the lighting, by hues of pink and blue, and by a certain sweetness specific to Cignani's work. The break in the clouds overhead draws the Virgin's gaze upward, underscoring the mystical feel of the scene, which nevertheless remains human thanks the warmth of the maternal embrace.

The painting can be dated to the 1680s. In 1802 it was purchased in Rome by Domenico Venuti on behalf of King Ferdinand IV of Naples, who bequeathed it to his son, Francis I, king of the Two Sicilies, from whence it passed to Francis' brother Leopold, prince of Salerno, who was the uncle and father-in-law of the duc d'Aumale (*see p. 27*). It was allegedly used by Maria Clementina, princess of Salerno, for her private devotion.

SASSOFERRATO (GIOVANNI BATTISTA SALVI)

(Sassoferrato, 1609; Rome, 1685)

The Holy Family

Canvas. H. 72 cm (2 ft. 4 in.); W. 93 cm (3 ft. 3/4 in.)
Inv. 77 (Galerie de Peinture)

As with most of his religious paintings of the Virgin at prayer or of the Holy Family, here Sassoferrato conveys a serene piety. The infant Jesus, sitting on a cushion and putting one arm around the Virgin's neck, makes a gesture of blessing toward Saint Joseph, who places his right hand on his heart.

A squared-up preparatory drawing (Edwin Bryant Crocker Art Gallery, Sacramento), features the presence of drapery behind the figures, thereby contributing a play of diagonal lines, but it was not included in the canvas. This composition remains straightforward and static, dominated by the deliberately old-fashioned draftsmanship. Even if the arrangement of figures betrays Venetian influence, Sassoferrato was looking toward Raphael and quattrocento Umbrian art. He was notably inspired by a Raphael Madonna and Child known as the *Mackintosh Madonna* (National Gallery, London), which he copied in the Borghese Gallery in Rome. This return to a classical, Renaissance art differs sharply from works of the Baroque period, suggesting a date for the painting of 1640–50.

FOLLOWING PAGES
The painting gallery.
Pages 110–111: The gallery as it looked before the duc d'Aumale went into exile in 1886.
Pages 112-113: The gallery as it looked at the time of the duke's death; the hanging is less dense because the collection had been distributed throughout the museum. On the left is a bust of the duc d'Aumale by Paul Dubois, today placed in the middle of the gallery in tribute to its founder.

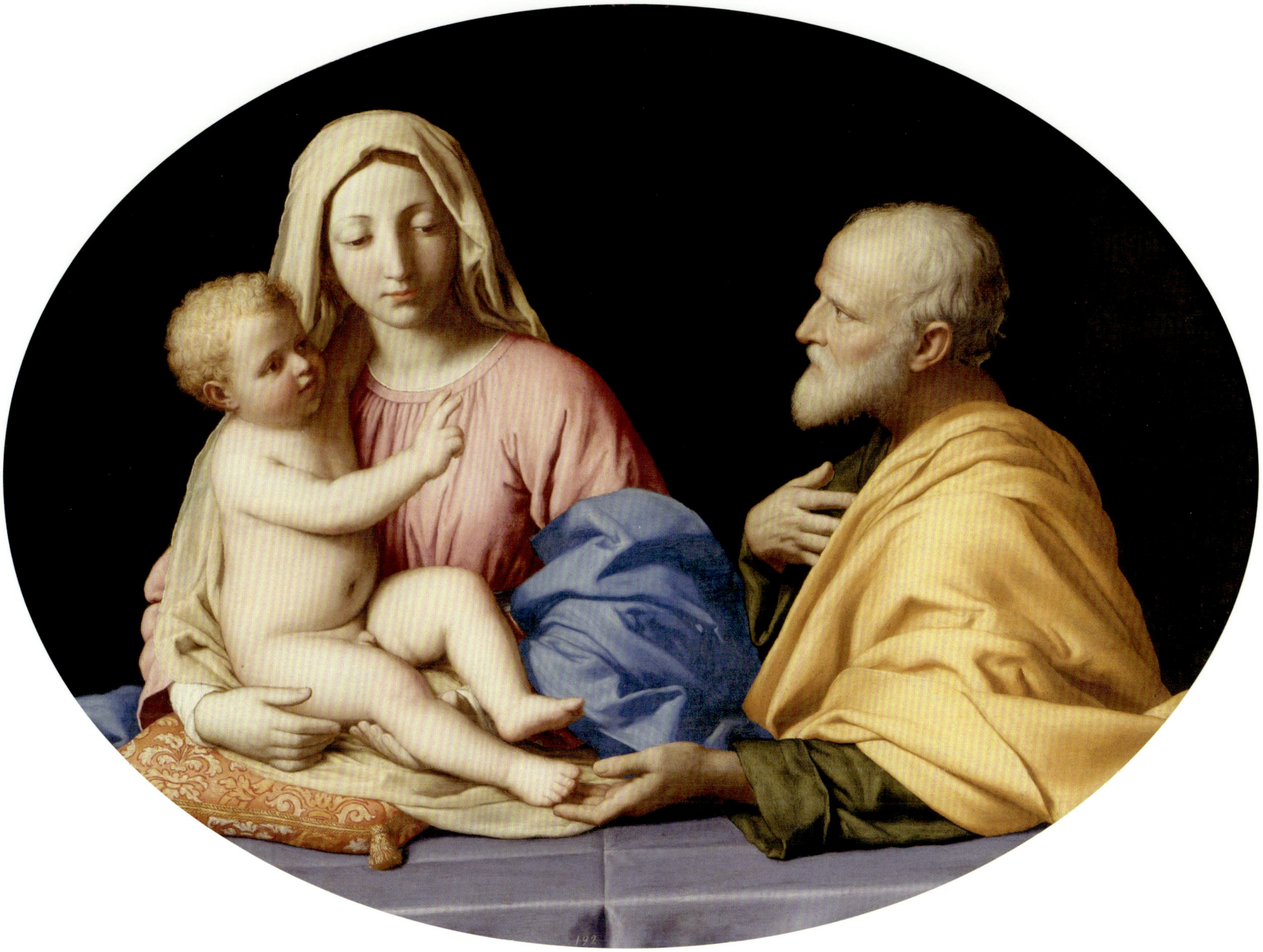

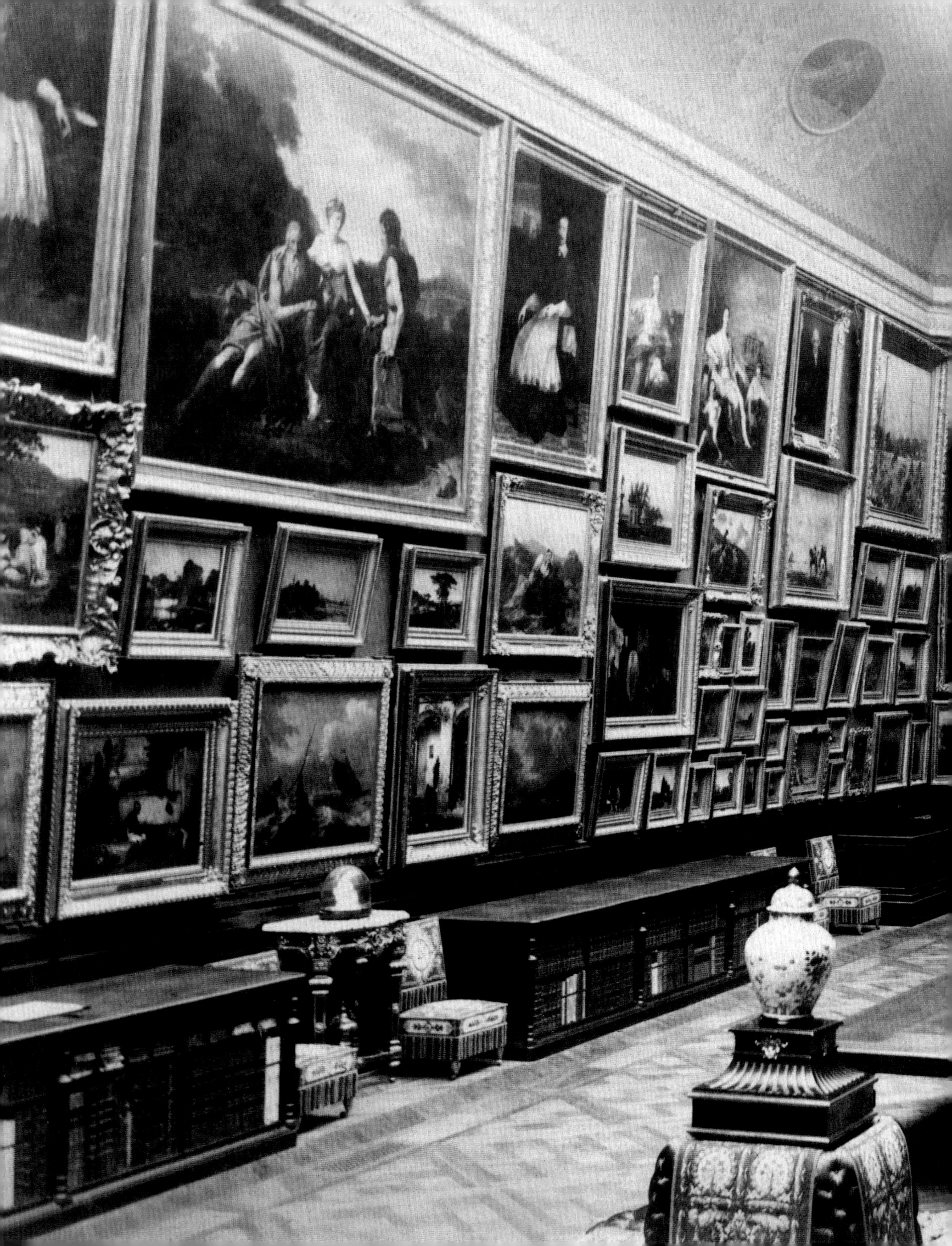

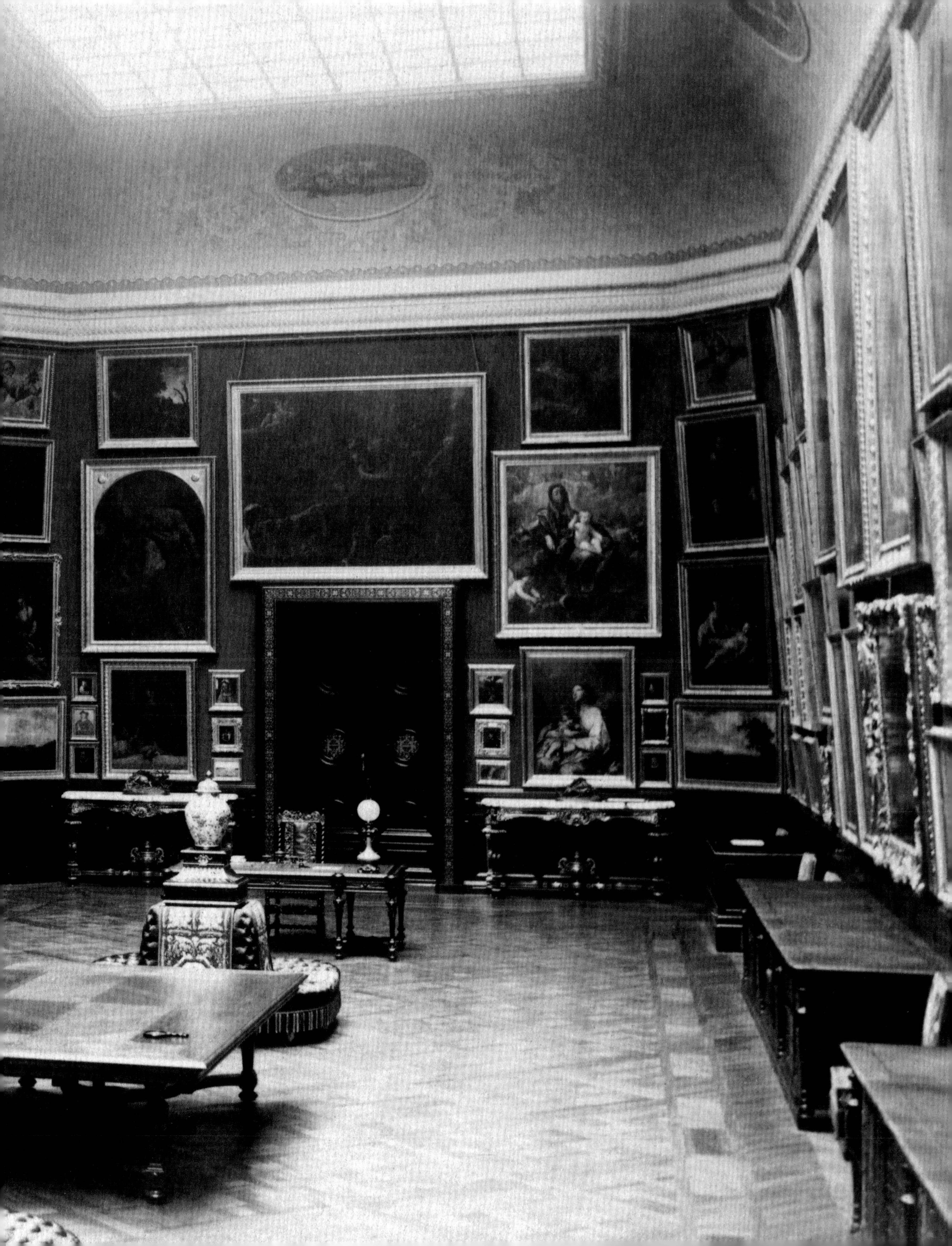

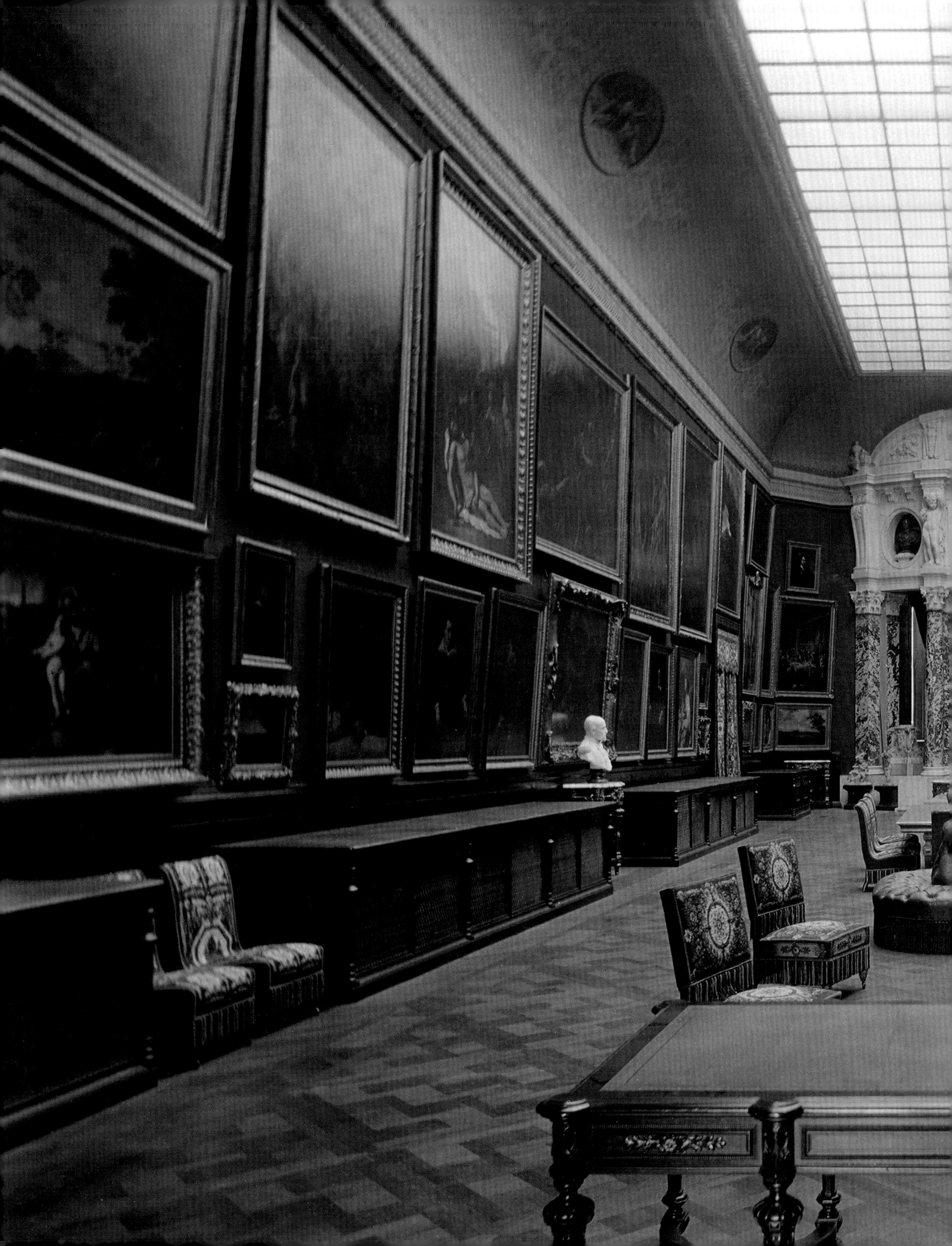

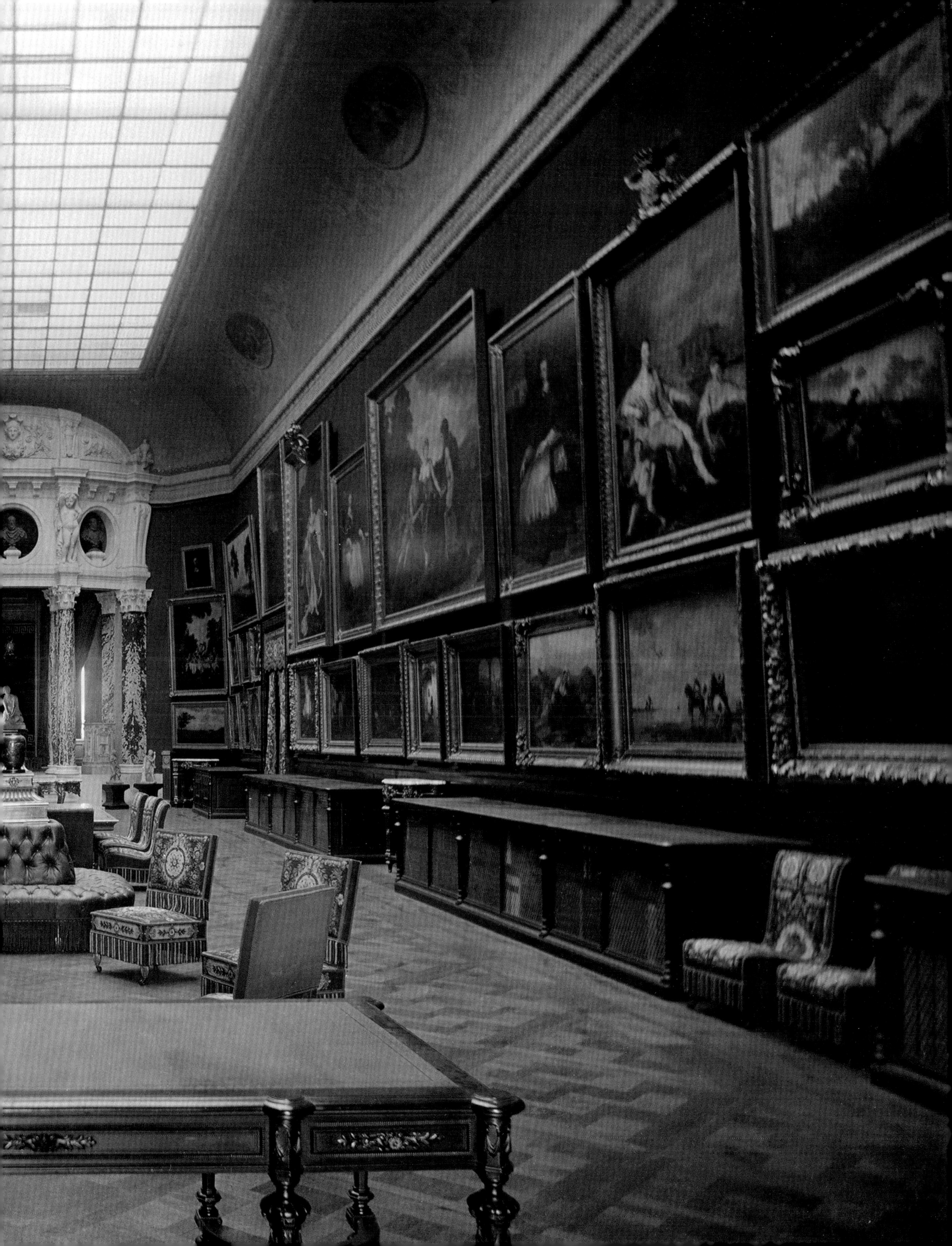

MASTER OF THE MAGDALEN LEGEND

Saint Mary Magdalene, also mistakenly known as a *Portrait of Mary of Burgundy (1457–1482)*

Wood. H. 26.5 cm (10 ¼ in.); W. 22.5 cm (8 ¾ in.)
Inscription t.l.: *Marie / de / Bourgogne: 1457–1482*
Inv. 588 (Cabinet de Clouet)

Given the inscription in the top left corner, this painting was assumed to be a portrait of Mary of Burgundy depicted as Mary Magdalene, haloed and holding her jar. Mary of Burgundy (1457–1482) was the daughter of the duke of Burgundy, Charles the Bold (1433–1477). In 1477, age twenty, she married Maximilian of Austria (1459–1519). Most of her portraits are posthumous, such as a tomb statue in Bruges (church of Notre Dame), a bronze in Innsbruck (Hofkirche), a figure in Maximilian's mausoleum, and paintings by Bernhard Strigel and Hans Maler in Vienna; others are disputed, such as the painting in the Lehmann Collection in New York.

In fact, the inscription is apocryphal; by 1947 the painting was linked to the Master of the Magdalen Legend (circa 1515–20), whose oeuvre has been constructed from the panels of an altarpiece depicting the legend of Mary Magdalene, now dispersed between Budapest, Copenhagen, Philadelphia, Schwerin, and Vienna. Around this homogeneous set of works, some forty paintings have now been ascribed to the Master based on stylistic comparison.

There are roughly a dozen versions of this painting, notably in London (National Gallery); Cambridge, Massachusetts (Fogg Art Museum and Busch-Reisinger Museum); Brussels (Musées Royaux des Beaux-Arts); and in private collections. Although the one here and the one in London are superior in quality to the others, some art historians think that all known versions are workshop replicas of a lost original by the Master of the Magdalen Legend. This figure seems to have been inspired by the Mary Magadelene in the Braque triptych by Rogier van der Weyden (Louvre), to whom the Master of the Magdalen might have served as a late apprentice. And it is the oeuvre of the Master of the Magdalen Legend that evinces the most convincing comparison with this painting.

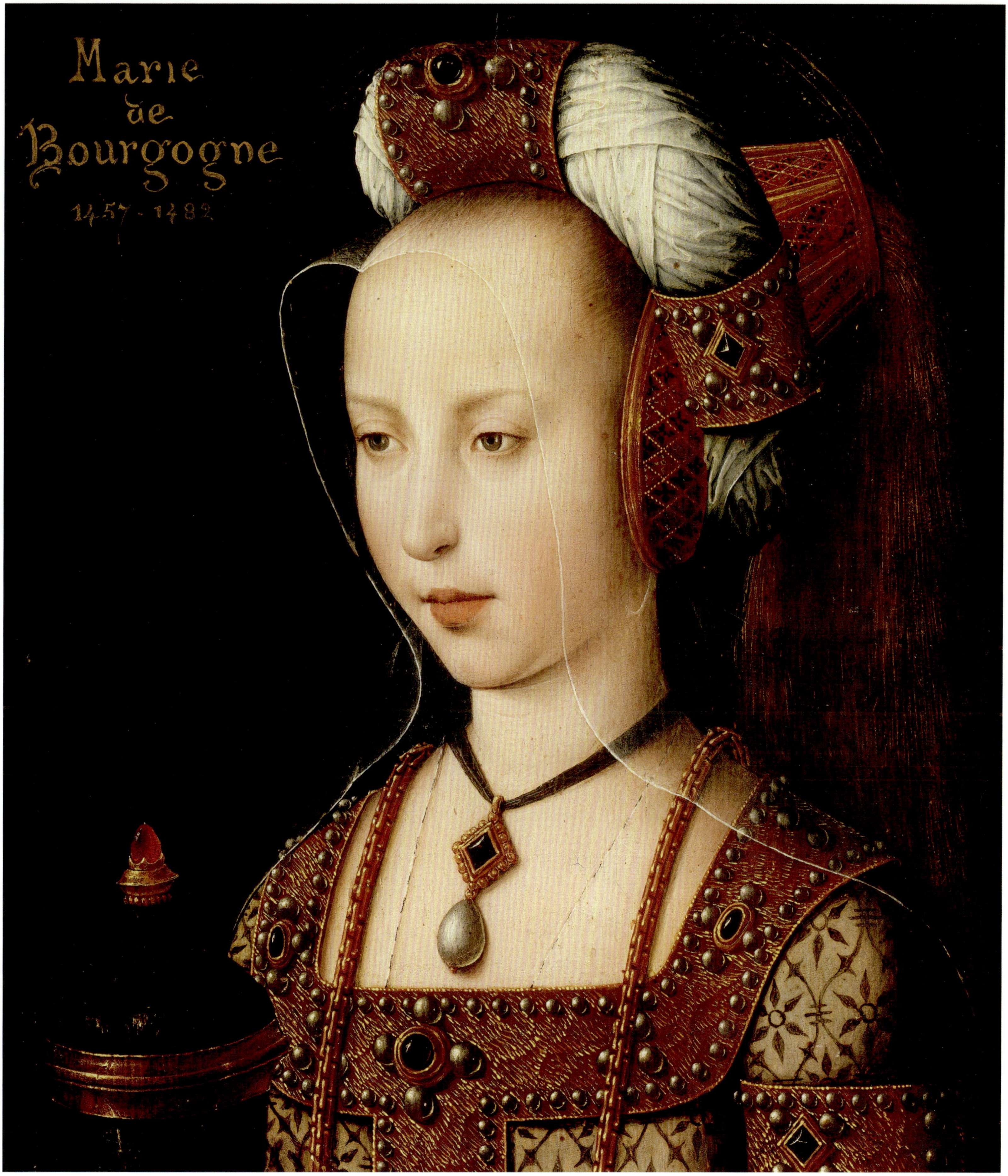
Marie
de
Bourgogne
1457 - 1482

FOLLOWER OF HANS MEMLING

Anthony, Bastard of Burgundy

Wood. H. 45 cm (1 ft. 6 in.); W. 55 cm (1 ft. 9 ½ in.)
Inv. 105 (Tribune)

Anthony, known as the Bastard of Burgundy (circa 1430–1504), was the illegitimate son of Philip the Good, duke of Burgundy, and Jeanne de Presles. He was thus the illegitimate brother of Charles the Bold. Dubbed a knight in 1452, he fought in Morocco, forcing the Moors to lift their siege of Ceuta, and was inducted into the Order of the Golden Fleece in 1456. He fought alongside his brother Charles at Grandson in 1476; in 1477, at the battle of Nancy where Charles died, Anthony was taken prisoner by Duke René of Lorraine, who handed him over to King Louis XI in exchange for a ransom of ten thousand ecus. Shown great favor by Louis, Anthony remained in the French king's service until the latter's death. The new king, Charles VIII, legitimized Anthony in 1485, made him a knight of the Order of Saint Michael, and appointed him to be a royal ambassador in 1493. Anthony was furthermore an art- and book-lover.

The back of this panel is painted with the letters I.N.E. (as yet unexplained) linked by the rope girdle of Saint Francis (Anthony was a member of the Third Order of St. Francis). There is also his motto, *Nul ne s'y frote* [roughly, "Not to be defied"], which appears on his Italian medal and on his coat of arms on his tomb in Tourneham, near Ardres; plus his emblem, a *hotte de guerre* (a kind of portable hod or scuttle of wood and iron, used to throw flaming material at besiegers). The emblem and motto are also found on the back of a plaque depicting Calvary (now at the Musée de Cluny in Paris). This painting has been attributed to van Eyck, whose patron was Philip the Good, or perhaps Rogier van der Weyden, by analogy with the portrait of the Charles the Bold now in Brussels, and even to Antonello da Messina, who was active in Flanders between 1445 and 1450. But it was not until 1456 that the Bastard of Burgundy was inducted into the Order of the Golden Fleece, whose neckchain he is wearing here.

The identification of the sitter is based on the motto and on other portraits of Anthony such as one in Brussels (Musée des Beaux-Arts) attributed to Rogier van der Weyden and another in Dresden (Staatliche Gemäldegalerie) attributed to Memling, as well as older copies and a drawing attributed to Jacques Leboucq in a manuscript known as the *Recueil d'Arras* (Ms. 265, fol. 100). The portrait here and the one in Dresden are clearly based on the same prototype, which must have been painted by Memling, given the style and overall conception. This version displays powerful, contrasting modeling, and perhaps dates from the fifteenth century; the weaker Dresden copy, which bears the same inscriptions on the back, probably dates from the sixteenth century. The Musée Condé's version might be a replica of a lost original dating from 1467–70, to judge by the sitter's dress and age, which would make the original one of Memling's earliest known portraits.

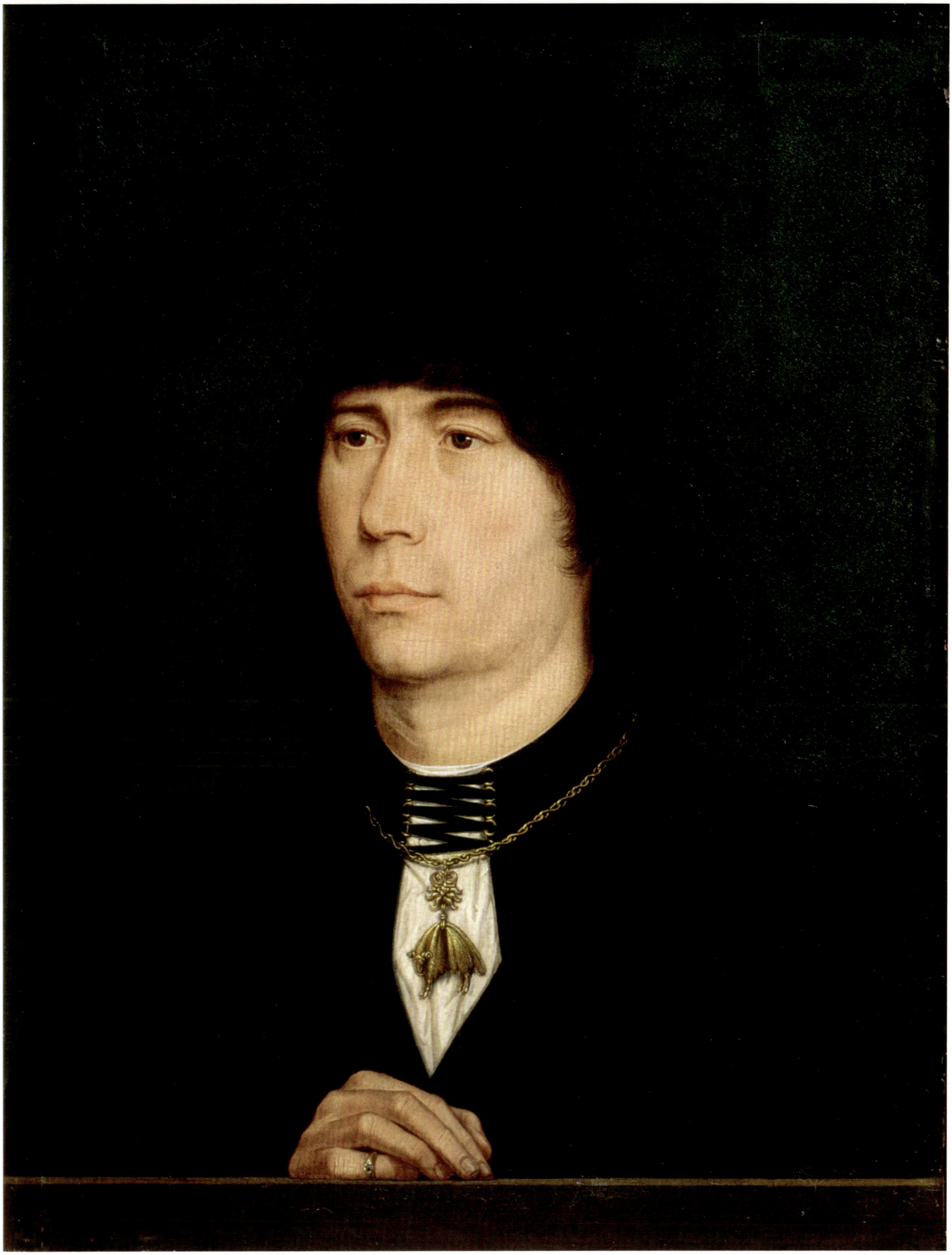

SCHOOL OF PICARDY, FIFTEENTH CENTURY

Translation of the Relics of Saint Foillan

Wood. H. 81 cm (2 ft. 8 in.); W. 61 cm (2 ft.)
Inv. 106 (Tribune)

This painting was attributed to van Eyck when the duc d'Aumale acquired it in 1879 as part of the Reiset collection (*see p. 33*). It was only in the early 1980s that its history was retraced: the warrior was identified, thanks to his coat of arms, as the comte de Ponthieu; later, the discovery of descriptions by seventeenth- and eighteenth-century scholars in Abbeville, sometimes accompanied by sketches, proved that this *Translation* came from an altarpiece devoted to Saint Foillan, painted for the high altar of the Cluny priory of Saint-Pierre in Abbeville, Picardy, where Saint Foillan's relics are preserved. The painting was thus attributed to the school of Picardy. The altarpiece featured a Crucifixion in the middle, a Descent into Limbo on the right, and four large panels devoted to the life and martyrdom of Saint Foillan (of which this *Translation* was one). The altar was decorated with the coat of arms of Bernard de May (died 1474), who became an alderman of Abbeville in 1424, and his wife Jeanne de Broutelles, who probably commissioned the altarpiece.

This panel shows the chest containing the saint's relics being returned to the church after a procession designed to halt a fire in the city. The flames, temporarily calmed by the procession, flare up again after it has passed, whipped up by a devil with a bellows seen in the upper left. Saint Foillan, an Irish missionary, was killed while on his way to the abbey at Fosses. The knight in armor seen here was probably comte Gui I de Ponthieu (died 1101), who founded the priory of Saint-Pierre in Abbeville in 1086, where he would be buried and to which he donated the relics. The life-like portraits of clergymen presumably include Pierre de Cézac, who became prior before 1476 and died in 1503; it was Pierre de Cézac who had the saint's relics placed in a new, silver reliquary chest in 1942, and under whose priorship this painting was probably executed.

Being somewhat stiffer and more meticulous than Flemish painting, this work perhaps reflects the influence of Simon Marmion or a follower (his younger brother Mille and Mille's son Colinet were both in Abbeville in 1499). The pointed shoes and long hairstyles with bangs on the forehead indicate that this work was painted prior to 1490. Furthermore, the reliquary chest lacks the pointed belltower that was only built in 1492.

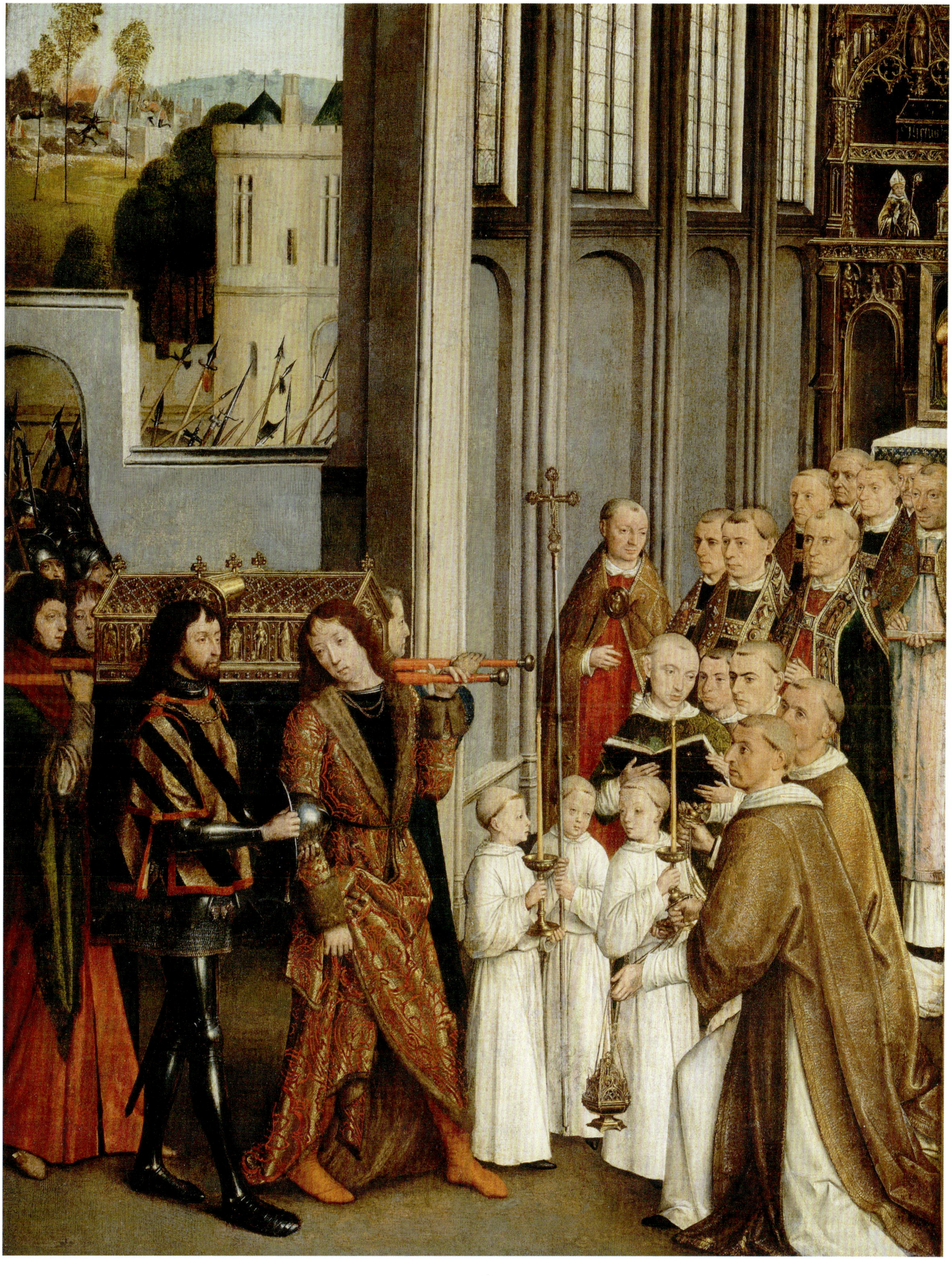

THE MASTER OF SAINT GILES

Portrait of a Man and his Wife

Wood. H. 17 cm (6 ½ in.); W. 12 cm (4 ¾ in.)
Inv. 104 (Tribune)

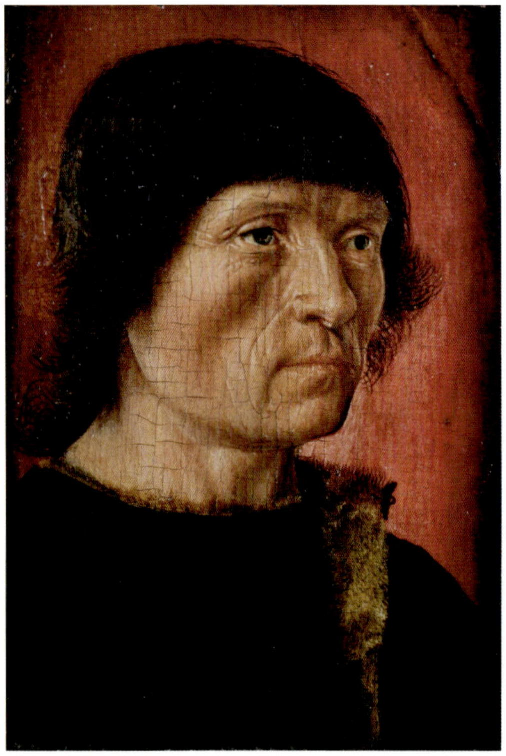

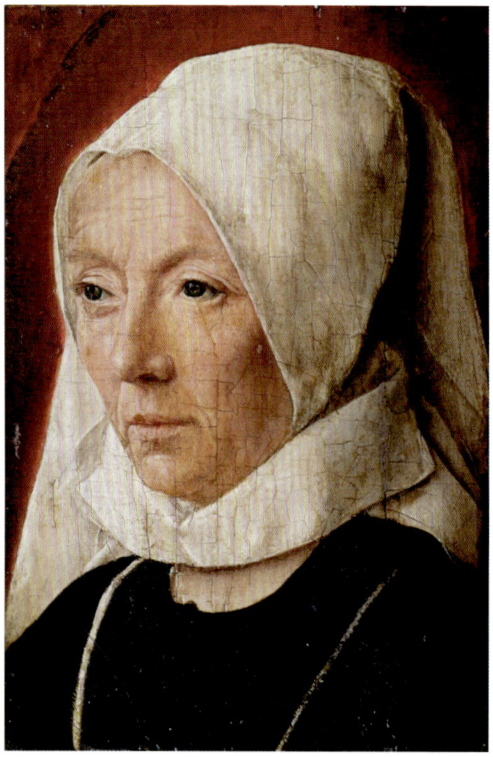

These two portraits were perhaps once part of a larger painting. They were long attributed to Jan van Eyck, but in 1904 were ascribed to the French school. In 1913 Max Friedlander suggested that they be attributed to an anonymous artist known as the Master of Saint Giles after an altarpiece titled *The Mass of Saint Giles,* now in London (National Gallery). A resemblance has been noted between the portrait of the man here and a kneeling figure on the far right of the London painting. The portrait also displays the same realistic, meticulous handling of the faces typical of this enigmatic artist, who probably came from the Low Countries. However, in 1938 Charles Sterling argued that these portraits were "French in look if not in technique"; in 1937 they were attributed to Gérard David through comparison with, among others, David's *Portrait of a Goldsmith* (Pinakotek, Vienna) and *Portrait of a Gentlemen* (then private collection, Vienna; now Rijksmuseum Twenthe, Enschede, Netherlands).

In 1994 Pierre-Gilles Girault argued that these portraits may be donors cut from a large panel or the wings of a triptych, unless they were originally a small private diptych similar to the Matheron diptych now in the Louvre, reflecting a fashion for "small portraits, often in marital pairs."

FLEMISH WORKSHOP CLOSE TO ROGIER VAN DER WEYDEN

Diptych of Jeanne de France John the Baptist Presenting the Donor to the Virgin and Child and Crucifixion.

Wood. H. 33.7 cm (1 ft. 1 in.);
W. 22.2 cm (8 3/4 in.) (each panel)
Inv. 107–108 (Tribune)

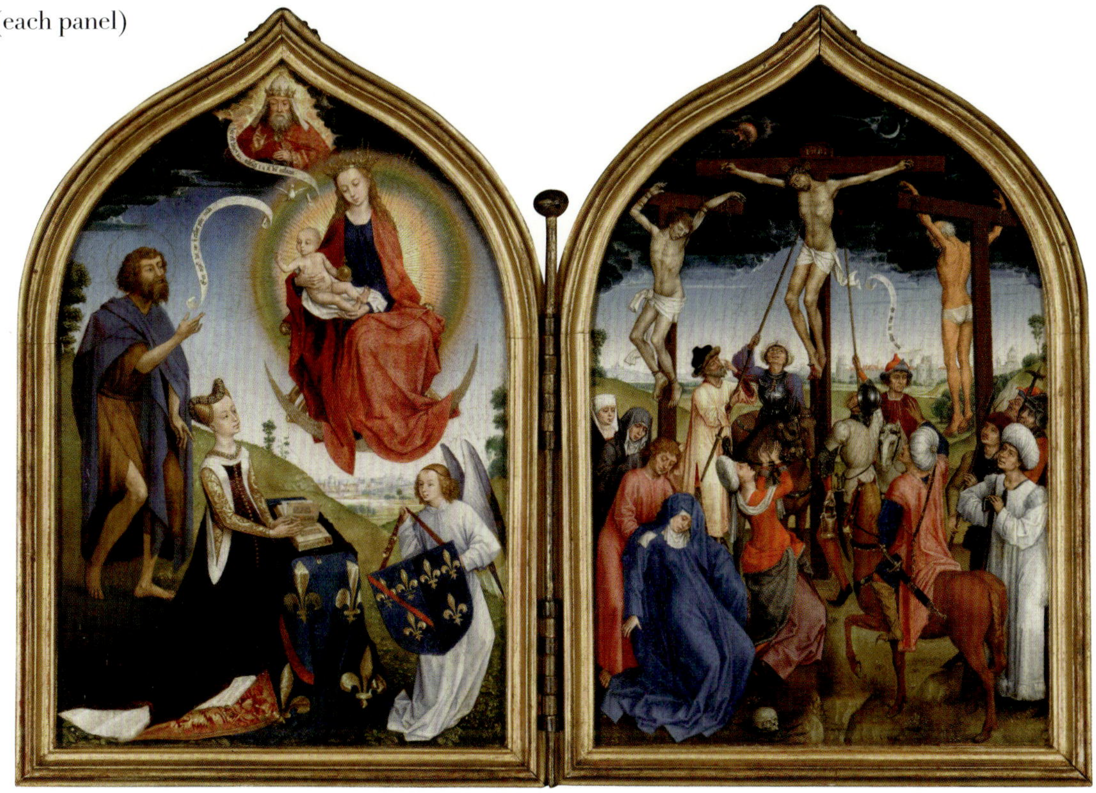

By 1857 the coat of arms identified the donor as Jeanne de France, daughter of King Charles VII and his wife Marie d'Anjou. Born around 1435, Jeanne was contractually betrothed on March 11, 1447 to duc Jean II de Bourbon (1426–1488), whom she married in 1452. She was therefore the sister of King Louis XI and sister-in-law, through her husband, of Charles the Bold and Isabeau de Bourbon. Jeanne died without issue on May 4, 1482. On the left wing, Jeanne de France is shown kneeling before the Virgin and Child, while an angel holds her escutcheon. Her patron saint, John the Baptist, presents her to the sky-borne Virgin sitting on a crescent moon, symbol of the Immaculate Conception. The infant Jesus, the dove of the Holy Spirit above him, and God-the-Father at the top form the Holy Trinity. The town in the background might be Moulins, where the dukes of Burgundy resided. The prie-dieu, or prayer bench, is also decorated with the Bourbon arms, whereas the thistles on the cushion perhaps refer to the Order of the Knights of Our Lady of the Thistle, founded by Louis II de Bourbon (1337–1410).

The right wing depicts the Crucifixion at the moment when Christ, flanked by the two thieves, is wounded in the side by a horseman's lance, while Mary faints. The juxtaposition of these two incidents is rare in Flemish art. The diptych was probably painted shortly after Jeanne's wedding in 1452, for the clothing corresponds to mid-century fashion; the attribution to Hans Memling, born circa 1435, is therefore untenable. On the other hand, the influence of Rogier van der Weyden is clear, and there are reminiscences of the Master of Flémalle. Both panels were therefore painted after 1452 by an artist who was independent by mid century but had trained in the studio (or had access to the designs) of either the Master of Flémalle (perhaps the young Rogier himself?) or van der Weyden.

The duc d'Aumale bought this diptych in 1885 from the heirs of Reverend John Fuller Russell in Greenhithe, Kent, so that he could bring this masterpiece of fifteenth-century Flemish art back to France. The diptych was then attributed to Memling; in August 1895, while visiting Bruges and admiring the reliquary chest of Saint Ursula and the Memling paintings housed in the Hospital of Saint John, the duke noted in his date-book: "Peerless! My little Jeanne is certainly a member of the family."

ENGUERRAND QUARTON

(Laon[?]; active in Aix and Avignon from 1444 to 1466)

The Virgin of Mercy, 1453

Canvas transferred from wood. H. 66 cm (2 ft. 2 in.); W. 187 cm (6 ft. 1 ½ in.)
Inscribed on the scrolls held, respectively, by John the Baptist: *Ecce Agnus Dei*; by the pope: *sub tua protectione confugimus*; and by the king: *parce misereris*.
Inv. 111 (Cabinet du Giotto)

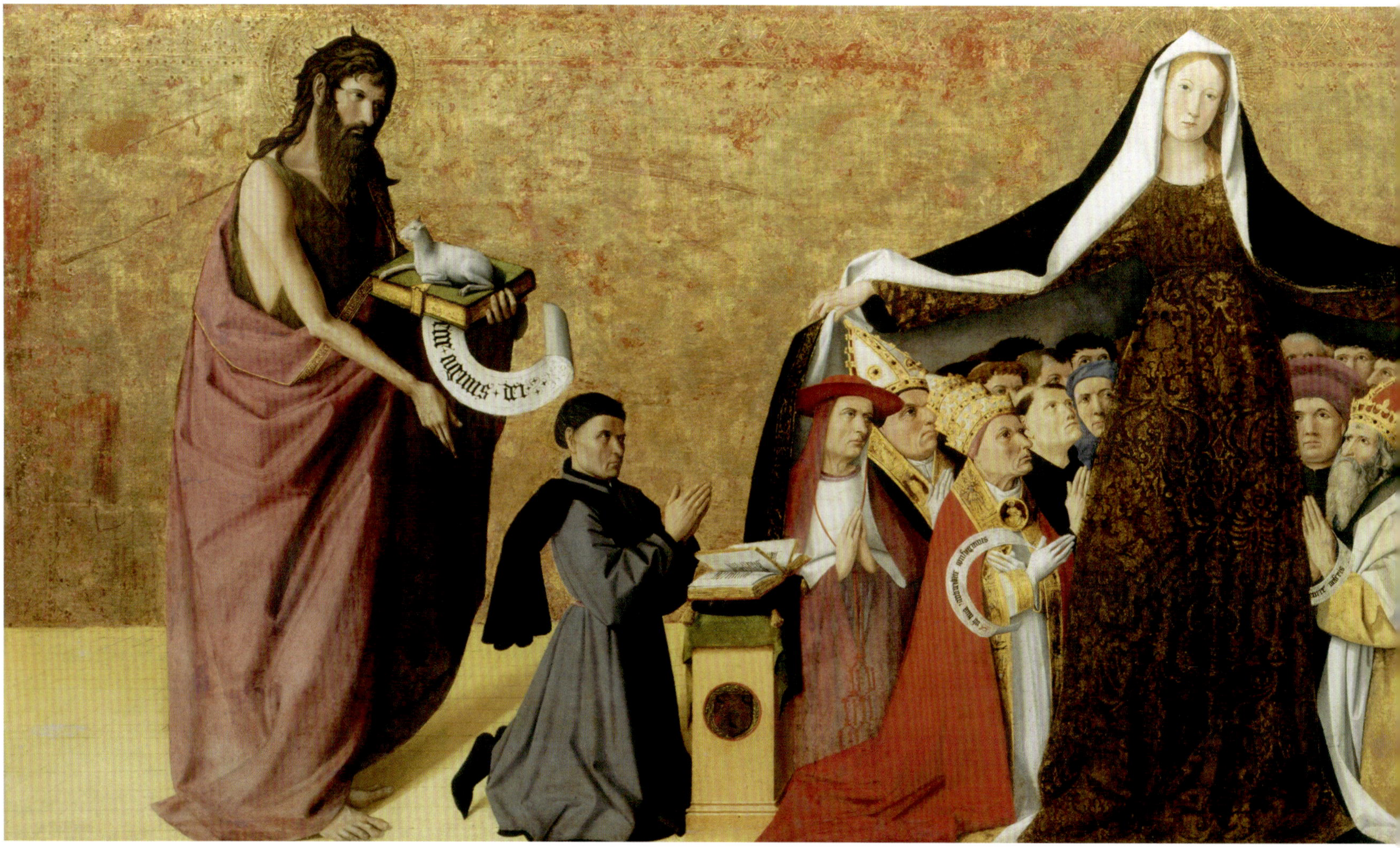

Previously attributed to the Flemish school, in 1904—the year of a major show of French primitives at the Louvre—this painting was identified with a Virgin of Mercy commissioned on February 16, 1452, from Enguerrand Quarton and Pierre Villate, artists working in Avignon. The commission came from Pierre Cadard, lord of Thor, in memory of his parents, the late Jean Cadard (died 1449) and Jeanne de Moulins, and the work was destined for the chapel of Saint Peter of Luxembourg, which his father had erected in the Celestine church in Avignon. Cadard was a physician originally from Picardy, who taught medicine in Paris from 1412 to 1415 and was doctor to the children of King Charles VI. Accused of complicity in the assassination of John the Fearless, duke of Burgundy, Cadard had to flee the French court in 1424 and headed south to Provence.

The Virgin of Mercy was a frequent theme in the fifteenth century: the Madonna spreads open her large cloak to protect supplicants: here, clergymen on the left (pope, cardinal, bishop, monks, priests) and laymen on the right (emperor, king, queen, burghers, laborers), all presented in hierarchical order on each side. The donor's parents are shown kneeling

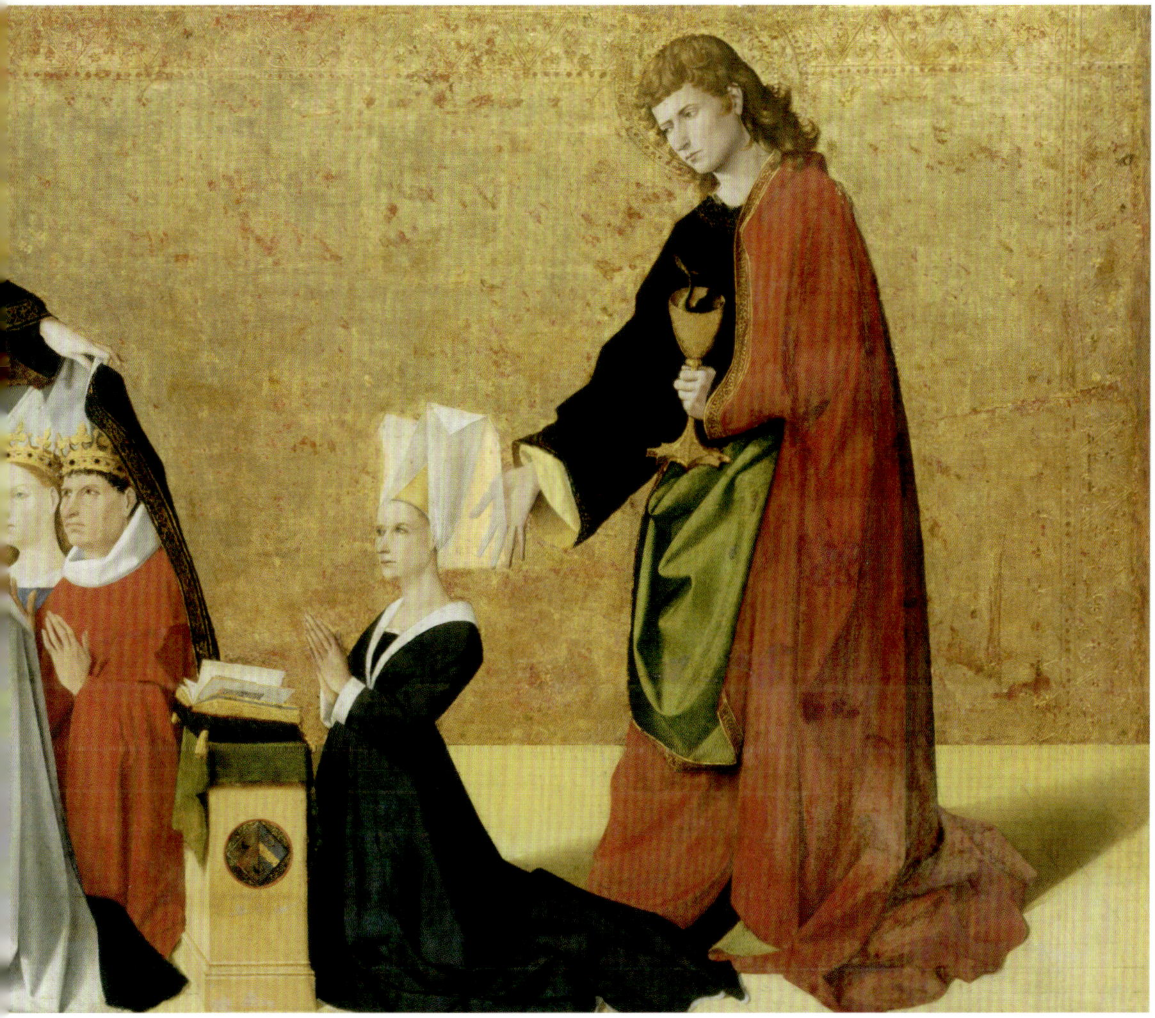

prayerfully on either side of the picture: Jean Cadard is being presented to the Virgin by John the Baptist, while his wife Jeanne de Moulins is presented by John the Evangelist.

This well-documented work is a key landmark in the study of the fifteenth-century school of Avignon. Even though the contract cites two artists—Enguerrand Quarton from Avignon and Pierre Villate from the diocese of Limoges—this painting is similar to the *Coronation of the Virgin* in the hospice of Villeneuve-lès-Avignon, commissioned from Quarton in 1453. Since examination has failed to distinguish a second hand in the painting, the supposition is that Villate—for whom no other work survives—was responsible only for the now-lost predella.

Quarton, originally from Picardy, trained under the aegis of Flemish artists. His art would be inconceivable without prior knowledge of Jan van Eyck and Rogier van der Weyden. In the 1430s and 1440s Picardy came under the sway of the dukes of Burgundy, favoring such contacts. Apart from these two paintings, for both of which commissioning contracts survive, Quarton is credited with a *Virgin and Child with Saint James, Saint Agricola of Avignon, and Donors* (Petit Palais, Avignon) and a *Pietà* for Villeneuve-lès-Avignon (now in the Louvre).

ATTRIBUTED TO JEAN CLOUET

(Brussels[?], circa 1475–85; Paris, 1540)

Francis I (1494–1547), King of France, circa 1515

Wood. H. 35 cm (1 ft. 1 ½ in.); W. 25 cm (9 ¾ in.)
Inv. 241 (Cabinet de Clouet)

Son of Brussels artist Michel Clauwet and grandson of Flemish primitive Simon Marmion, Jean Clouet was in France no later than the start of the reign of Francis I, perhaps even during the reigns of Charles VIII and Louis XII. Listed in the accounts of the royal household from 1516 to 1536, he worked with Bourdichon and Perréal, receiving the same level of payment as they did (if less than Primaticcio and Rosso Fiorentino received). In 1519 Clouet held the rank of *valet de garde-robe* but by 1524 was listed among the "painters and craftsmen." Above all a portraitist, Clouet also executed religious paintings (no longer extant) such as a *Saint Jerome* for a church in Tours in 1522. Nicknamed Janet, he lived in Tours between 1521 and 1525, marrying a goldsmith's daughter before moving to Paris. The couple had four children, two of whom survived: François, who succeeded his father at the head of the workshop, and Catherine, who married the artist Abel Foulon. Jean Clouet died in 1540, as attested by the royal accounts, in which he was replaced by his son.

Francis I was the son of Charles d'Orléans, comte d'Angoulême (a cousin to the reigning king) and of Louise de Savoie. His father died when Francis was only one year old, at which point King Louis XII—who had no male heir—summoned the child to court and raised him there. Artus Gouffier, lord of Boisy, was named tutor to the lad. In 1514 Francis married the daughter of Louis XII and Anne de Bretagne, Claude de France (who bore him seven children); in 1515, he ascended to the throne of France. After he won the battle of Marignano, the young king was knighted by the veteran Chevalier Bayard. Surrounded by the likes of Artus and Guillaume Gouffier, Anne de Montmorency, Henri d'Albret, Claude de Guise, and Odet de Foix, Francis led several wars against Holy Roman Emperor Charles V. Taken prisoner at Pavia, Francis was freed only by surrendering his two sons as hostages. Following the death of his first wife and the treaty of 1529, Francis married Charles V's sister, Eleanor of Austria. But he was soon at war with the emperor once again. Francis was also a patron of the arts and architecture, and invited Italian artists to his court, notably Rosso Fiorentino, Il Primaticcio, and Leonardo da Vinci.

This fine portrait of Francis I early in his reign has been variously attributed to well-known artists such as Perréal and Bourdichon. But it is similar to a miniature dated 1519 in a manuscript titled *Commentaires de la Guerre Gallique* (British Library, London), and was probably based on a lost chalk original by Jean Clouet for his series of *Preux* (the valiant knights who fought alongside Francis I at Marignano), making it one of Clouet's early works.

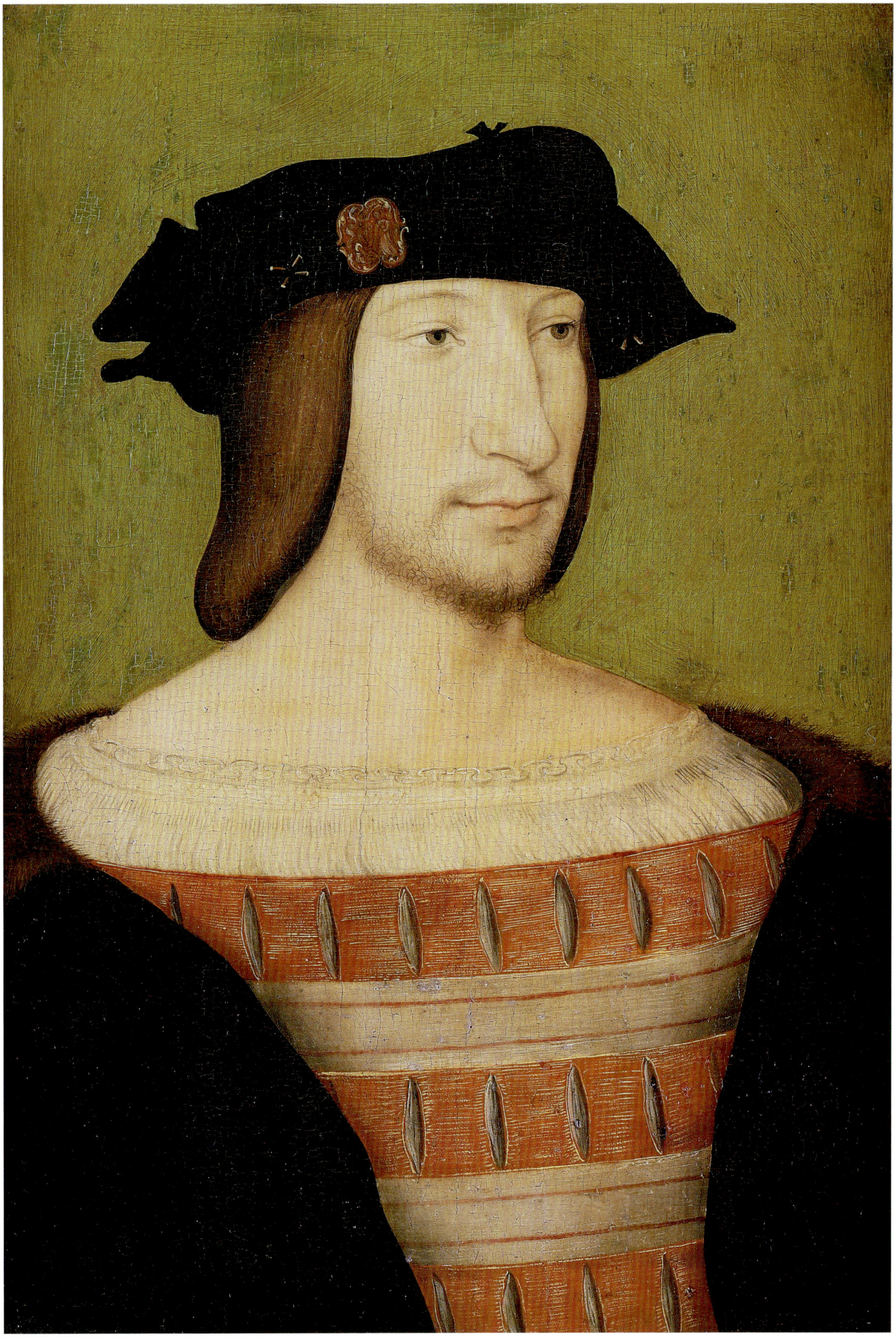

FRANÇOIS CLOUET

(Tours, circa 1515; Paris, 1572)

Marguerite d'Angoulême, Queen of Navarre (1492–1549)

Wood. H. 31 cm (1 ft.); W. 24 cm (9 ½ in.)
Inv. 262 (Cabinet de Clouet)

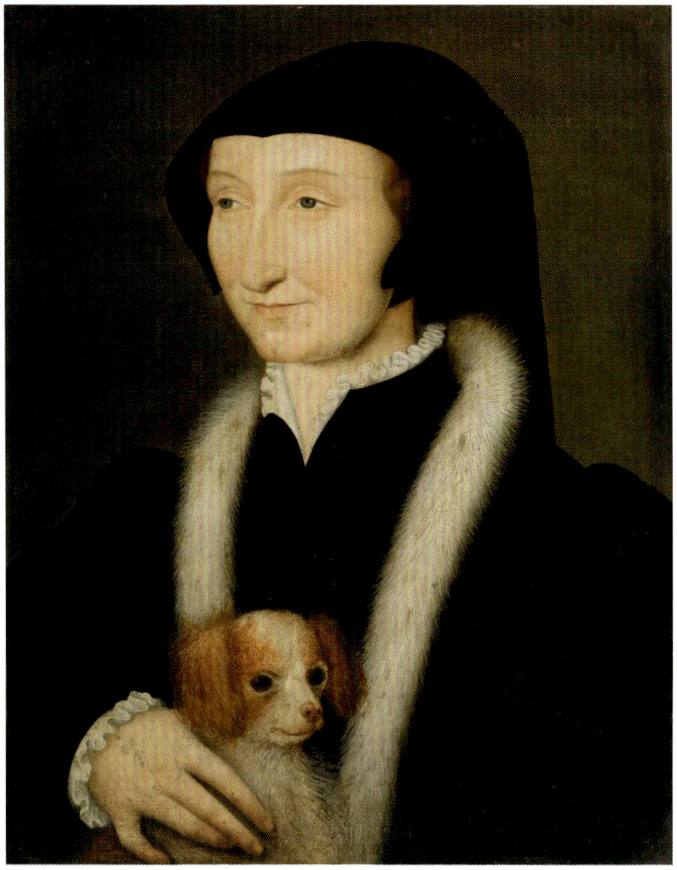

In 1540, François Clouet replaced his father in royal accounts as painter and *valet de chambre* to the king (*see p. 124*). King Francis I made Clouet a naturalized Frenchman in 1541 (which allowed him to inherit his father's estate), in recognition of the artist's ability to "imitate most wonderfully." When Francis I died in 1547, Clouet was commissioned to execute a life-size portrait for the funeral. He continued to serve kings Henry II and Francis II, executing works for both of their funerals. Nicknamed Janet like his father, and highly appreciated by Queen Catherine de' Medici, Clouet received many commissions.

Marguerite d'Angoulême (1492–1549) was the daughter of Charles d'Orléans, comte d'Angoulême, and Louise de Savoie. The elder sister of Francis I, she lost her father at the age of four. Her marriage to Charles, duc d'Alençon, was arranged by King Louis XII for political reasons. Having fled with his army at the battle of Pavia in 1525, Charles went to Lyon where he died that same year of sorrow and shame, never seeing his wife again. Marguerite then joined Francis I in Spain, where he was being held prisoner after his defeat and capture; she tended her brother during his illness. In 1526 Marguerite married Henri d'Albret, king of Navarre, and became known as a protectress of Protestants, who flocked to her court. On the death of her brother Francis I, Marguerite retired to Nérac, where she died two years later. The mother of Jeanne d'Albret and grandmother of French King Henry IV, nicknamed the "pearl of the Valois family," Marguerite of Navarre advocated religious tolerance and was friendly with Protestants even though she never broke with the Catholic church. As a poet and writer she is famous in the literary world for a Boccaccio-style series of tales called the *Heptameron*.

The portrait here shows Marguerite around 1540, dressed in a rather austere way. Wearing a black gown and fur-trimmed cloak, she is shown in a cap known as a *templette*. With her left hand she strokes a dog on her lap—it was rare for Clouet to depict his sitters' hands, even rarer to show them with an animal. Only the royal children were shown with pets. This portrait was engraved in reverse to serve as the frontispiece for the publication of the *Tombeau de Marguerite de Valois, royne de Navarre* (Paris, 1551), attributed to Nicolas Denisot. According to the inscription, Marguerite was fifty-two at the time, but she appears to be somewhat younger and Denisot seems to have used a Clouet chalk drawing done some years earlier.

JEAN CLOUET

(Brussels[?], 1475–85; Paris, 1540)

King Henry II of France (1519–1559) as a Child

Wood. H. 30 cm (1 ft.); W. 23 cm (9 in.)
Inv. 259 (Cabinet de Clouet)

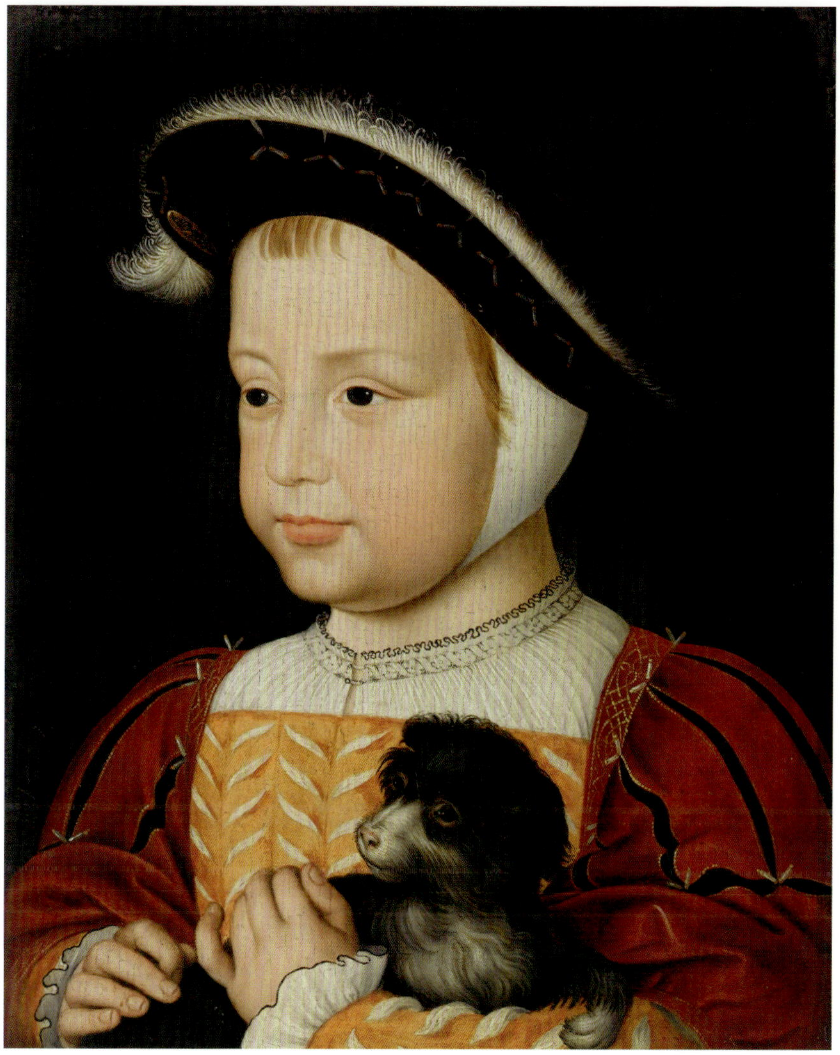

The second son of Francis I and Claude de France was christened Henri, duc d'Orléans. Along with his older brother, François, he was held captive in Spain from 1526 to 1530 when the two boys were taken hostage by Holy Roman Emperor Charles V as replacement for their father, who had been taken prisoner at the battle of Pavia in 1525. Since as a younger son Henri was not expected to reign, in 1553 he married Catherine de' Medici, whose lineage was less glamorous. But the premature death of François in 1536 turned Henri into the heir, and in 1547 he ascended to the French throne as Henry II. He carried out an intense repression of Protestant reformers, went to war against the English (capturing Boulogne from them in 1550), and clashed with the Holy Roman Emperor in 1552. At the disastrous battle of Saint-Quentin, fought against Philip II of Spain (successor to Charles V), nearly 9,000 French troops died and many were taken prisoner, including Henry's commanding general, Anne de Montmorency. The treaty of Cateau-Cambrésis (1559), which confirmed the reconciliation of France and Spain, entailed the marriage of Henry II's daughter, Élisabeth de France, to Philip II of Spain, along with the marriage of Henry's sister, Marguerite, to Emmanuel-Philibert, duc de Savoie. The festivities for these weddings included a jousting tournament in Paris, in which Henry II participated—and where he was accidentally killed, aged forty.

Around 1523 Jean Clouet drew wonderful portraits of Francis I's two elder sons, François (1518–1536) and Henri (1519–1559), aged five and four, respectively. These drawings are now conserved at the Musée Condé. The painted portrait based on the drawing of François is now in Antwerp, while the one of Henri is held here. This lively portrait shows the young boy clutching his little puppy close to his chest; it therefore includes the sitter's hands, which is unusual because they were difficult and time-consuming to execute. This painting was thus a meticulous, ambitious work.

FACING PAGE, LEFT

FRANÇOIS CLOUET

(Tours, circa 1515; Paris, 1572)

Odet de Coligny, Cardinal de Châtillon (1517–1571)

Wood. H. 94 cm (3 ft. 1 in.); W. 73 cm (2 ft. 4 ½ in.)
Inscription t.l.: *Primatisse* [*sic*]; b.l.: *1548. AE. 31*
Inv. 48 (Galerie de Peinture, rotunda)

Odet de Coligny was the son of Gaspard de Coligny and Louise de Montmorency; he had two younger brothers, Admiral Gaspard de Coligny and François, lord of Andelot. All three became famous, like their uncle, the *connétable* (military commander-in-chief) Anne de Montmorency.

Born in 1517, Odet renounced his birthright in favor of Gaspard, and took holy orders in 1531. He was elevated to the rank of cardinal thanks to Francis I, who negotiated it with Pope Clement VII on the occasion of the marriage of the future Henry II to Catherine de' Medici in 1533. Odet was named archbishop of Toulouse in 1534, and later bishop-count of Beauvais (one of the finest and richest bishoprics in France). In 1561, however, Odet de Coligny converted to Protestantism. He fought alongside the French Protestants at the battle of Saint-Denis in 1567, then fled to England, where he died in 1571 after being poisoned by a servant (who was later executed in France). Even as he continued to wear ecclesiastical dress, Odet broke the Catholic rule of celibacy for clergymen by marrying Isabelle d'Hauteville, dame of Loré.

This portrait was long attributed to the Italian school due to a specious inscription ascribing it to Primaticcio. Some art historians proposed the names of Luca Penni, Bronzino, and Pontormo, but it has ultimately been attributed to François Clouet based on similarities with two other portraits of the sitter—one drawn, the other painted—both in the Musée Condé. Odet de Coligny is here shown in court dress, wearing lavish ornaments such as a fur stole and finger rings, testifying to his important rank.

FACING PAGE, RIGHT

FRANÇOIS CLOUET

(Tours, circa 1515; Paris, 1572)

Odet de Coligny, Cardinal de Châtillon (1517–1571)

Wood. H. 32 cm (1 ft. ½ in.); W. 24 cm (9 ½ in.)
Inv. 261 (Cabinet de Clouet)

This is one of the many portraits that Clouet made of Odet de Coligny throughout his career. Despite the sitter's wrinkled skin, the composition is simply copied from the previous painting (*see above*), itself based on a drawn portrait held by the Musée Condé which seems slightly old-fashioned. Here Odet is wearing the red garments associated with the office of cardinal.

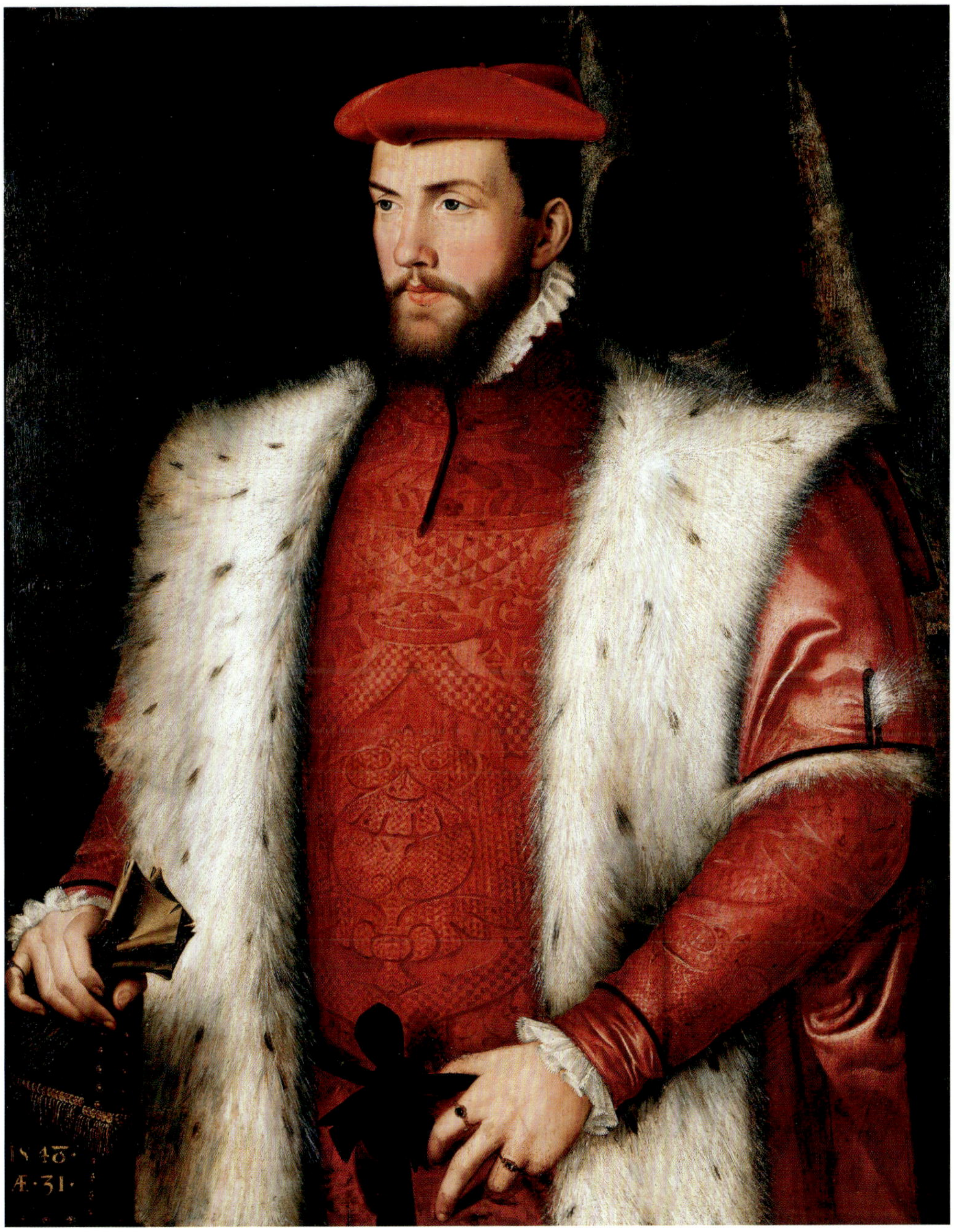
1548·
Æ·31·

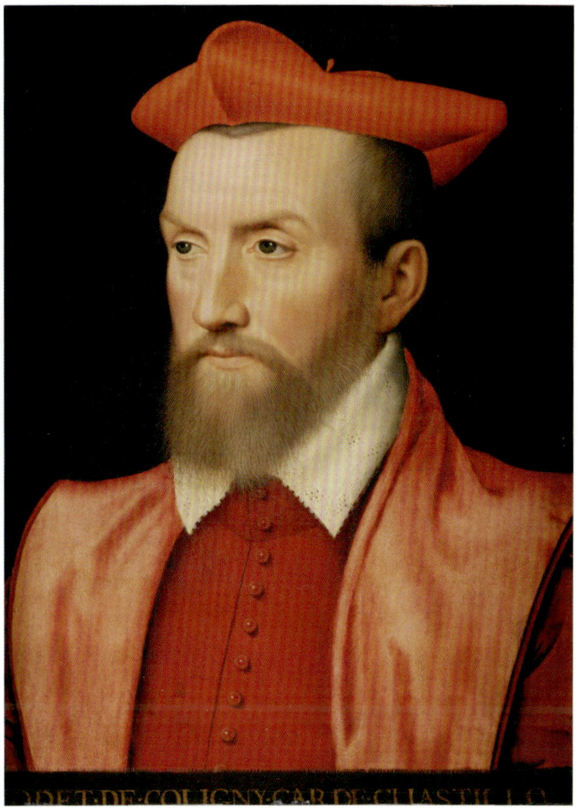
ODET·DE·COLIGNY·CAR DE·CHASTILLO

FACING PAGE, LEFT

FRANÇOIS CLOUET

(Tours, circa 1515; Paris, 1572)

Marguerite de Valois (1553–1615) as a Child

Wood. H. 31 cm (1 ft.); W. 24 cm (9 ½ in.)
Inv. 255 (Cabinet de Clouet)

The daughter of King Henry II and Catherine de' Medici, Marguerite de Valois (1553–1615) was an accomplished Renaissance princess: highly cultivated, a good dancer, and a fashion setter. Against her will, at the age of nineteen she was married to Henry of Navarre, who was a Protestant. This princely wedding on August 18, 1572, brought together many noble Protestant families and served as a pretext for the Saint-Bartholomew's Day massacre of Protestants that followed. In 1578 Marguerite moved to the kingdom of Navarre and brought new luster to the court at Nérac. Her marriage was an unhappy one, however, and she returned to Paris in 1582. But she fell out with her brother, King Henry III, and left the court a year later; having sided with the Holy League, she was imprisoned in the château d'Usson.

Marguerite de Valois was queen not only of Navarre, but of France: her husband, Henry of Navarre, was declared heir to the throne of France by Henry III, who was assassinated shortly afterward. The king of Navarre was thus proclaimed King Henry IV of France in 1594. Keen to have an heir, he pressed Marguerite to agree to dissolve their marriage so that he could remarry, which she accepted in 1599. On returning to Paris in 1605, she built a lavish residence on Rue de Seine, where she died in 1615.

This portrait thus shows the girl who would become the famous "Queen Margot"—wife of Henry IV, queen of Navarre and of France—and whose love of literature and dissoluteness, both indulgently described by Brantôme, drew the finest minds of the day to her courts at Nérac and Paris.

The Musée Condé also owns a watercolor drawing highly similar to this portrait, plus another painted portrait of Marguerite at an older age. The watercolor drawing, purchased by the duc d'Aumale from Frédéric Reiset in 1861, was probably the preparatory sketch for this portrait.

FACING PAGE, RIGHT

FRANÇOIS CLOUET

(Tours, circa 1515; Paris, 1572)

Marguerite de Valois (1553–1615)

Wood. H. 29 cm (11 ½ in.); W. 22.5 cm (8 ¾ in.)
Inv. 589 (Cabinet de Clouet)

This painting is a modified copy of the preceding portrait of Marguerite de Valois as a child. She grew up to become the "Queen Margot" made famous as a character in a novel by Alexandre Dumas. The Musée Condé's drawing and two portraits of Marguerite are highly similar, yet there are significant differences between them: the gaze is not the same, the face is rounder here, and the gold-threaded gown with its muslin collar and slashed sleeves reflects a later fashion. The contrast is striking between the weakly modeled face (with bluish shading) and the meticulously rendered details of dress.

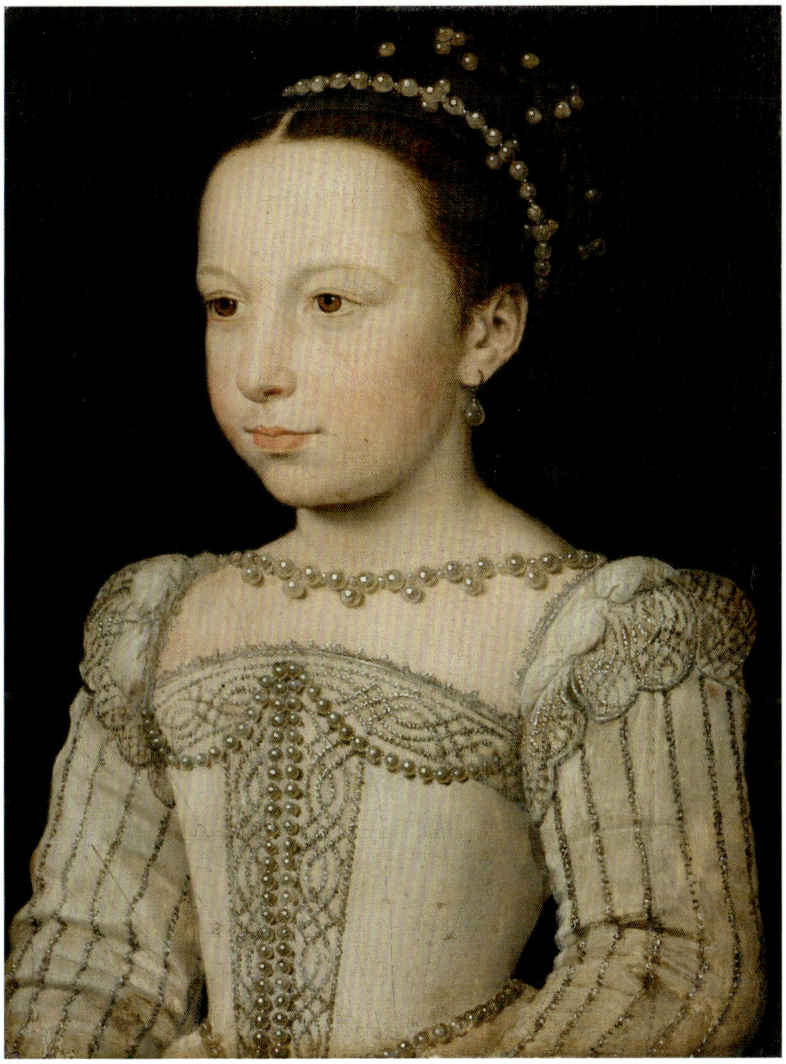

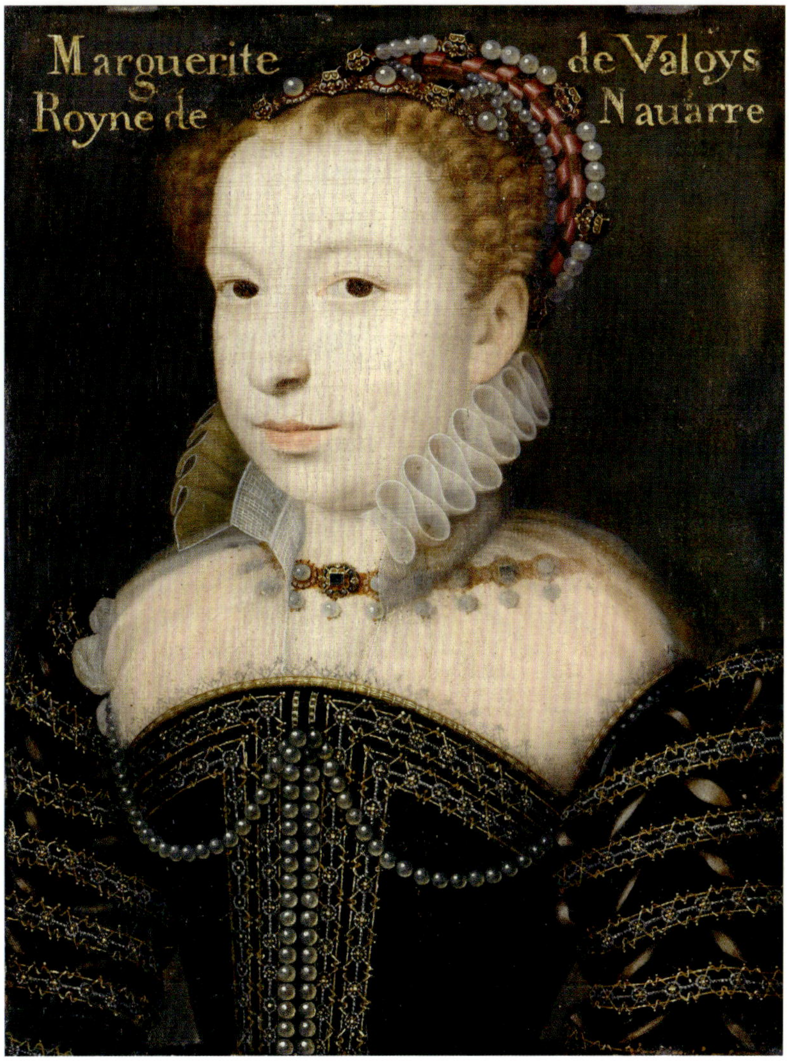
Marguerite de Valoys
Royne de Nauarre

FRANÇOIS CLOUET

(Tours, circa 1515; Paris, 1572)

Jeanne d'Albret, Queen of Navarre (1528–1572), 1570

Wood. H. 32 cm (1 ft. ½ in.); W. 23 cm (9 in.)
Inscription t.l.: *JEANNE D'ALBRET. REINE DE NAVARRE*; d.t.r.: *1570*
Inv. 254 (Cabinet de Clouet)

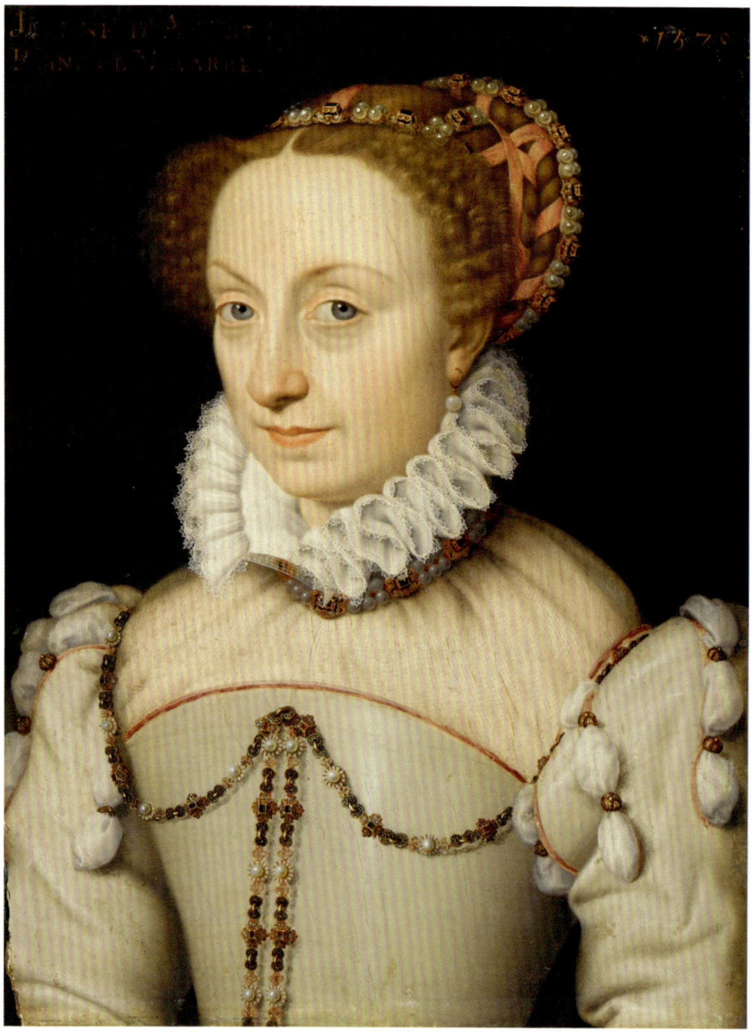

Jeanne d'Albret (1528–1572) was the daughter of Henri d'Albret, king of Navarre and of Marguerite d'Angoulême, sister of French King Francis I and the author of the *Heptameron* (*see p. 126*). She was therefore a first cousin to Henry II of France. Her marriage in 1548 to a staunch Protestant, Antoine de Bourbon, led to the birth of Henry of Navarre (the future Henry IV of France) on December 13, 1553. Antoine de Bourbon was killed at the siege of Rouen in 1562, and Jeanne died suddenly in Paris in mysterious circumstances—poisoning was mentioned—on June 10, 1572, just two months before the Saint Bartholomew's Day massacre of French Protestants. Jeanne had nevertheless negotiated with Queen Catherine de' Medici the marriage of their children: Catherine's daughter Marguerite de Valois (better known as "Queen Margot" thanks to a novel by Alexandre Dumas) to Jeanne's son Henry, the future king of France (*see p. 130*). Despite the unhappy outcome of this marriage, Jeanne d'Albret was therefore instrumental in uniting the kingdoms of France and Navarre and installing the Bourbon dynasty on the French throne.

This fine portrait bears comparison with a drawing by François Clouet now in Hanover (Kester Museum), which might have served as a preparatory sketch. The skilled draftsmanship, modeling, and harmonious tones of the painting make it a masterpiece of refinement, flaunting the virtuosity of an artist who excelled in detailing fabrics and finery. Beyond a simple official portrait, Clouet has produced a subtle psychological study: the queen of Navarre comes across as a level-headed, thoughtful monarch, a determined woman, and a born diplomat.

FRANÇOIS CLOUET

(Tours, circa 1515; Paris, 1572)

Elizabeth of Austria, Queen of France (1554–1592)

Wood. H. 37 cm (1 ft. 2 ½ in.); W. 25 cm (9 ¾ in.)
Inv. 258 (Cabinet de Clouet)

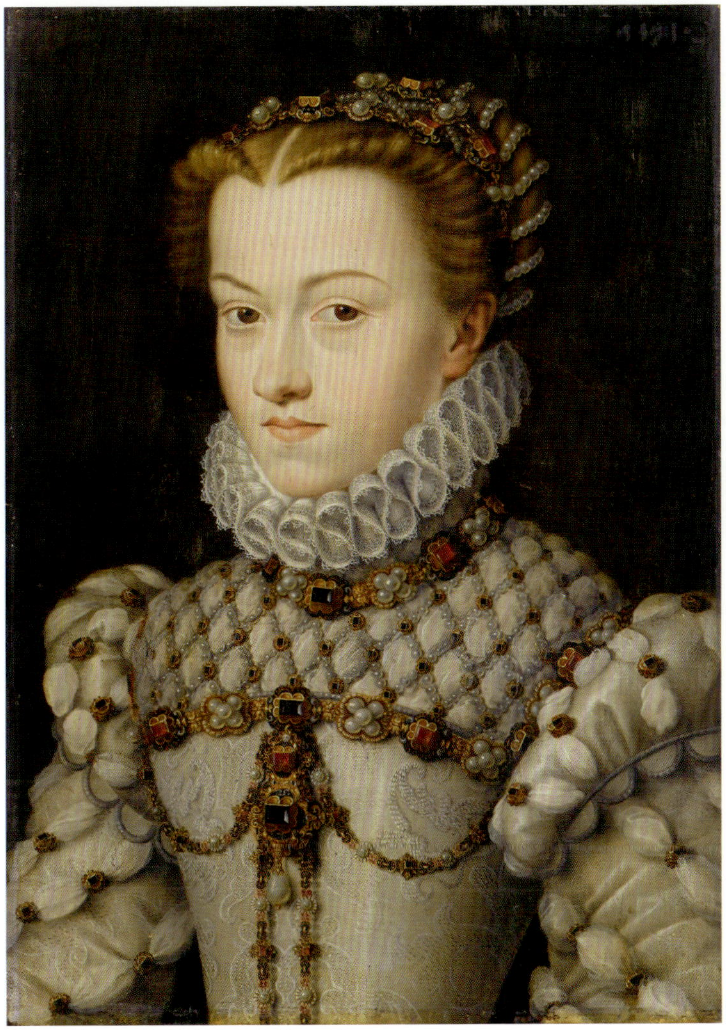

Elizabeth of Austria (1554–1592) was the daughter of Emperor Maximilian II and Mary of Austria, herself daughter of Emperor Charles V. Born in Vienna in 1554, Elizabeth married the French king Charles IX in 1570. The Louvre owns a portrait of identical dimensions that is highly similar to the one here: the queen's expression is similar, the hair and jewelry are identical, and the gown and collar feature the same details. However, the Louvre portrait shows the sitter half-length in a gold-brocade gown, her attractive hands placed over one another, whereas the one here shows just the head and shoulders of Elizabeth, without her hands, wearing a gray-white brocade gown patterned with silver thread. Both portraits were probably done in 1571, the year of her coronation as queen of France at the age of seventeen. At any rate, since these official portraits show the monarch in all her dazzling glory, they cannot have been painted later than 1574, the date at which the death of Charles IX forced Elizabeth into the background.

Highly similar to both portraits is a drawing by François Clouet dated 1571 and now in the Print Department of the Bibliothèque Nationale de France in Paris. Some art historians feel that the Musée Condé portrait is a replica by Clouet of the one in the Louvre; others think that it was done from Clouet's original chalk drawing, perhaps by Jean Decourt. Whatever the case, the portrait here is of very high quality. The outstanding handling of the sitter's face is complemented by the virtuoso depiction of the gown and jewelry.

CORNEILLE DE LYON

(La Haye, circa 1500–10; Lyon, 1575)

Connétable Anne de Montmorency (1493–1567)

Wood. H. 165 cm (5 ft. 5 in.); W. 14 cm (5 ½ in.)
Inv. 591 (Cabinet de Clouet)

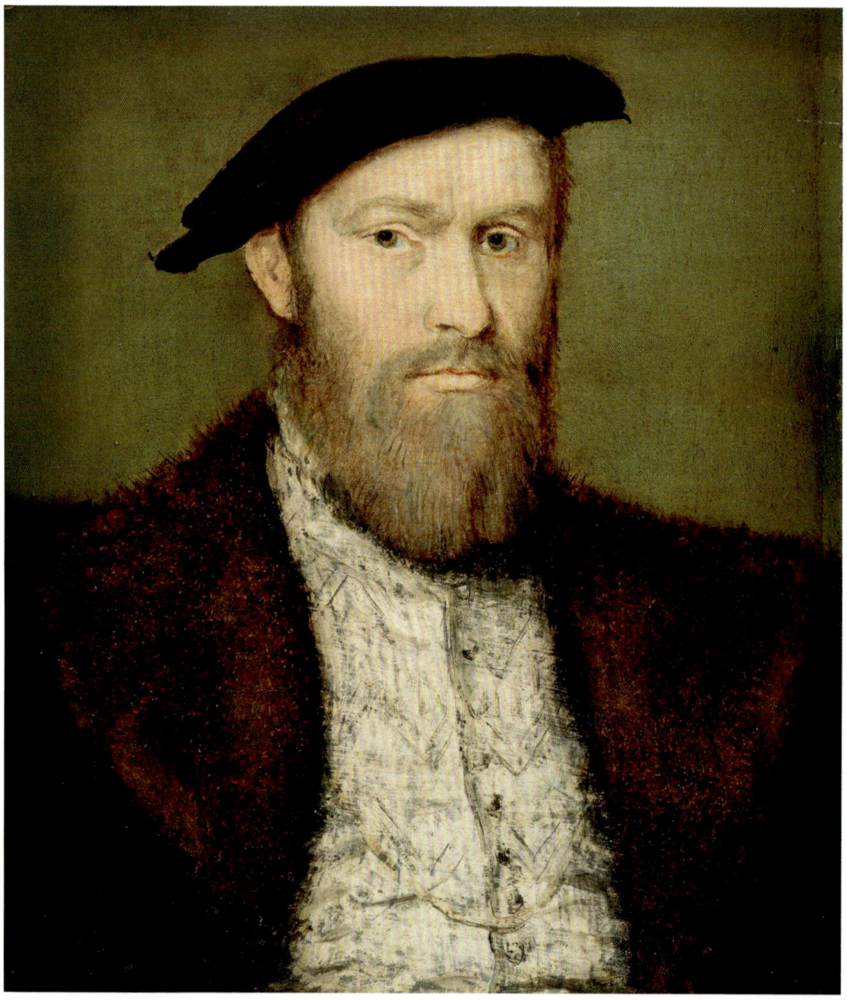

Godson of Anne de Bretagne (from whom he inherited his first name), Anne de Montmorency was the leading Renaissance figure in Chantilly. A childhood friend of King Francis I, he was raised with the future king in the royal château of Amboise, where he earned the latter's trust. Anne accompanied the king on his Italian campaign, notably fighting at Marignano, and was named *premier valet de chambre* in 1520, then marshal, and knight of the order of Saint-Michel in 1522. When Francis I was taken prisoner at Pavia in 1525, it was Anne who negotiated for the release of the king in exchange for his two sons, followed by the boys' eventual liberation. He was recompensed not only by being awarded major offices—Grand Master of France and governor of Languedoc in 1526, and *connétable* (commander-in-chief) in 1538—but also by an advantageous marriage, in 1572, to the king's first cousin, Madeleine de Savoie. Montmorency's fortune was vast. He owned six hundred fiefs, 130 châteaux, properties, and domains, and four residences in Paris. In Chantilly, Anne had Pierre Chambiges, the architect of Senlis cathedral, transform the old medieval fortress into an early Renaissance château; he then ordered the building of a new wing to the south, a delightful residence called the Petit Château (still visible at Chantilly today), by the architect Jean Bullant, who also built for Montmorency the château d'Ecouen, (now the Musée de la Renaissance) and the gallery of the château in Fère-en-Tardenois. Anne de Montmorency was a patron of the arts, a great statesman, and a shrewd general. He played the role of prime minister under King Henry II (who felt filial affection for him ever since he freed the young prince from Spanish captivity), until he was taken prisoner at the battle of Saint-Quentin. Henry II's accidental death benefited the Guise clan, who removed Montmorency from positions of power, but he was later recalled by the queen mother, Catherine de' Medici, during the reign of Charles IX. He acted as Catherine's main advisor and principal backer during the Wars of Religion. Montmorency was killed at the battle of Saint-Denis in November of 1567, at the age of seventy-four.

CORNEILLE DE LYON

(La Haye, circa 1500–10; Lyon, 1575)

Portrait Alleged to be Gabrielle de Rochechouart

Wood. H. 16 cm (6 ¼ in.); L. 147 cm (4 ft. 9 in.)
Inv. 246 (Cabinet de Clouet)

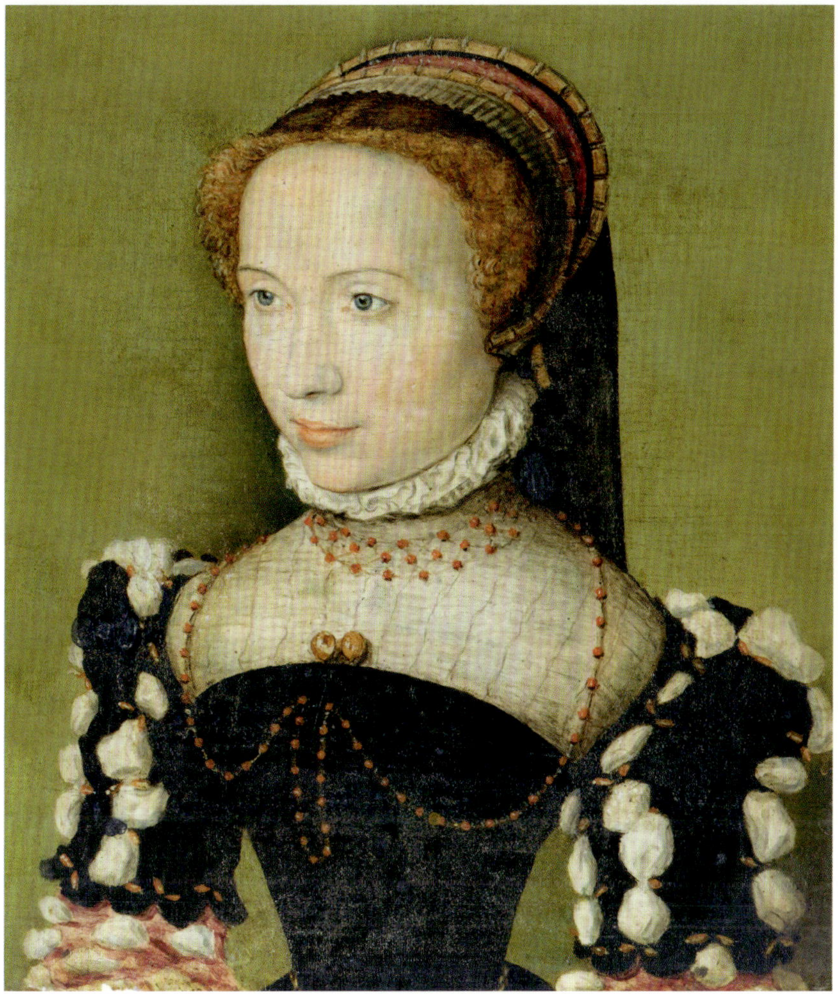

Born in the town of La Haye, trained in Flanders, the artist was known during his lifetime as Corneille de La Haye after his birthplace. After his death, however, he was nicknamed Corneille de Lyon after the city where he lived from 1533 onward. By 1541—and perhaps earlier—he was painter to the heir to the French throne, the future Henry II. He married Marguerite Fradin, daughter of a Protestant typesetter in Lyon; naturalized French in 1547, Corneille was named *valet de chambre* to the king when Henry ascended the throne. Like his fellow artist François Clouet, Corneille retained this title under the two subsequent reigns of Francis II and Charles IX—his profession of the Protestant faith up to 1569 does not seem to have harmed his career. In 1564 the queen mother, Catherine de' Medici, visited his studio, where he worked with his son, Corneille, and his daughter (also a well-known artist). A single unquestionable, dated portrait of Pierre Aymeric (Louvre) serves as the basis for establishing Corneille's oeuvre (the back of the portrait bears an inscription in Aymeric's hand, dating it to 1534 and ascribing it to Corneille). Marked by Flemish realism, his portraits are easily recognizable thanks to their characteristic olive- or leaf-green backgrounds and the handling of hair and fur, often painted strand by strand. Although he painted the kingdom's leading figures, Corneille did not go in for pomp. He handled his sitters in a sober yet lively manner, trying to record their souls through the face that reflected it.

The sitter was formerly identified as Gabrielle de Rochechouart in her youth, based on comparison with another Corneille portrait of her, but this identification is no longer considered valid.

FRENCH SCHOOL, SIXTEENTH CENTURY

Portrait Alleged to be Hercule-François de France, duc d'Alençon (1554–1584)

Wood. H. 20 cm (7 ½ in.); W. 14 cm (5 ½ in.)
Inv. 554 (Cabinet de Clouet)

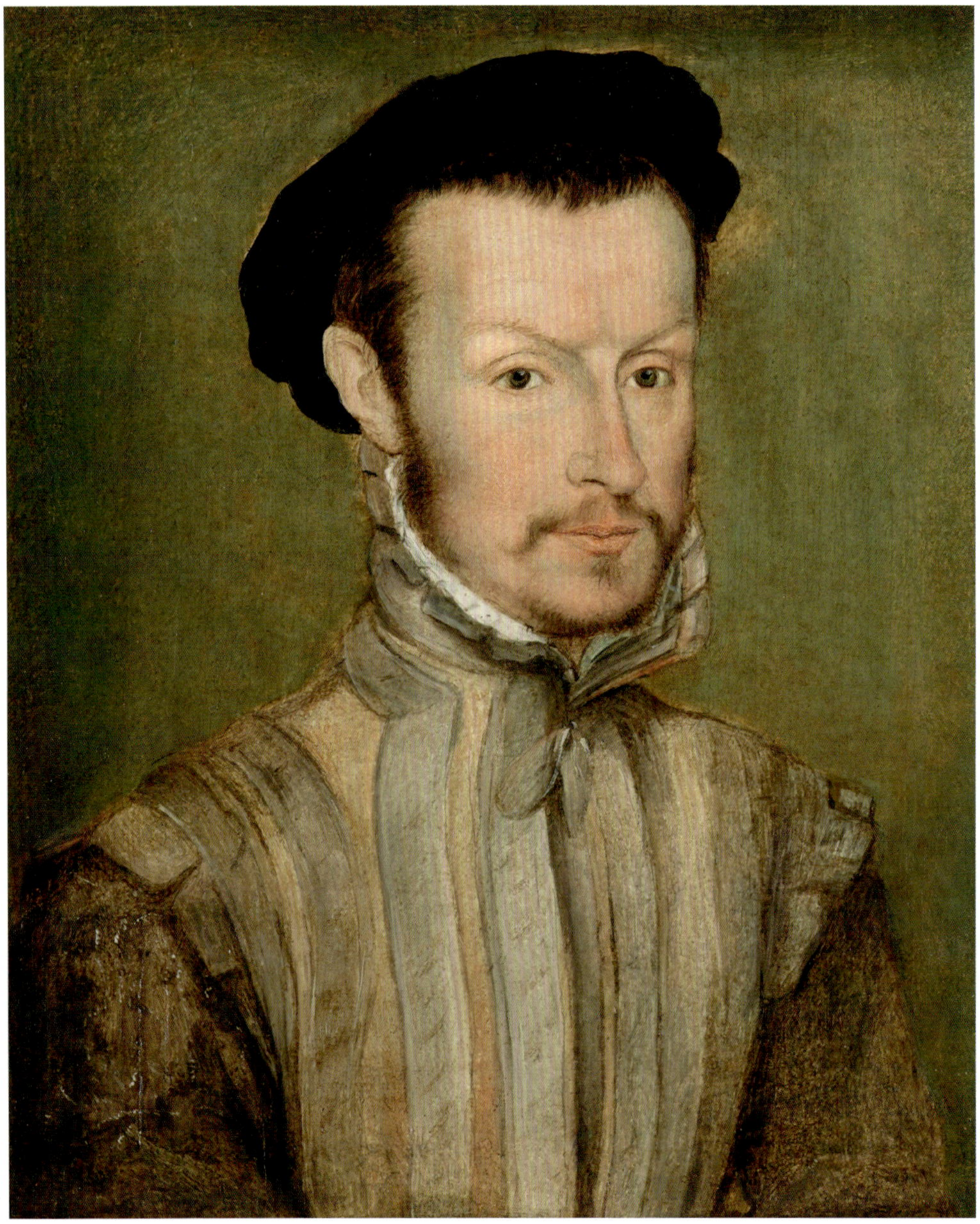

This portrait shows a young man with light beard and drooping mustache, in three-quarter profile from his right, dressed in a green doublet with goffered collar, set against a dark green ground. On the basis of a red, black, and white chalk drawing now in the Print Department of the Bibliothèque Nationale de France in Paris (formerly in the Bibliothèque Sainte-Geneviève), the sitter was identified as the fourth son of King Henry II and Catherine de' Medici, Hercule (1554–1584). Hercule later adopted the name of his eldest brother, François (1544–1560), when the latter died after reigning as Francis II from 1559 to 1560.

However, compared to the drawing, the sitter here is frailer, with thinner nose, thicker mustache, and more modest dress. Although Pariset and Broglie felt that these features authorized an attribution to Corneille de Lyon, or at least his workshop, in 1996 the Corneille specialist Anne Dubos de Groër rejected this hypothesis on the grounds that the light seems to come from the right whereas the shadows are arranged differently, while neither the eyes, eyebrows, or mouth are typical of Corneille's manner.

Furthermore, the work must have been painted sometime around 1550–60, which eliminates Hercule-François de France, who was not born until 1554. It nevertheless remains a superb portrait from the mid-fifteenth century.

CORNEILLE DE LYON

(La Haye, circa 1500–10; Lyon, 1575)

Jean de Taix

Canvas transferred from wood. H. 17 cm (6 ½ in.); W. 15 cm (6 in.)
Inv. 249 (Cabinet de Clouet)

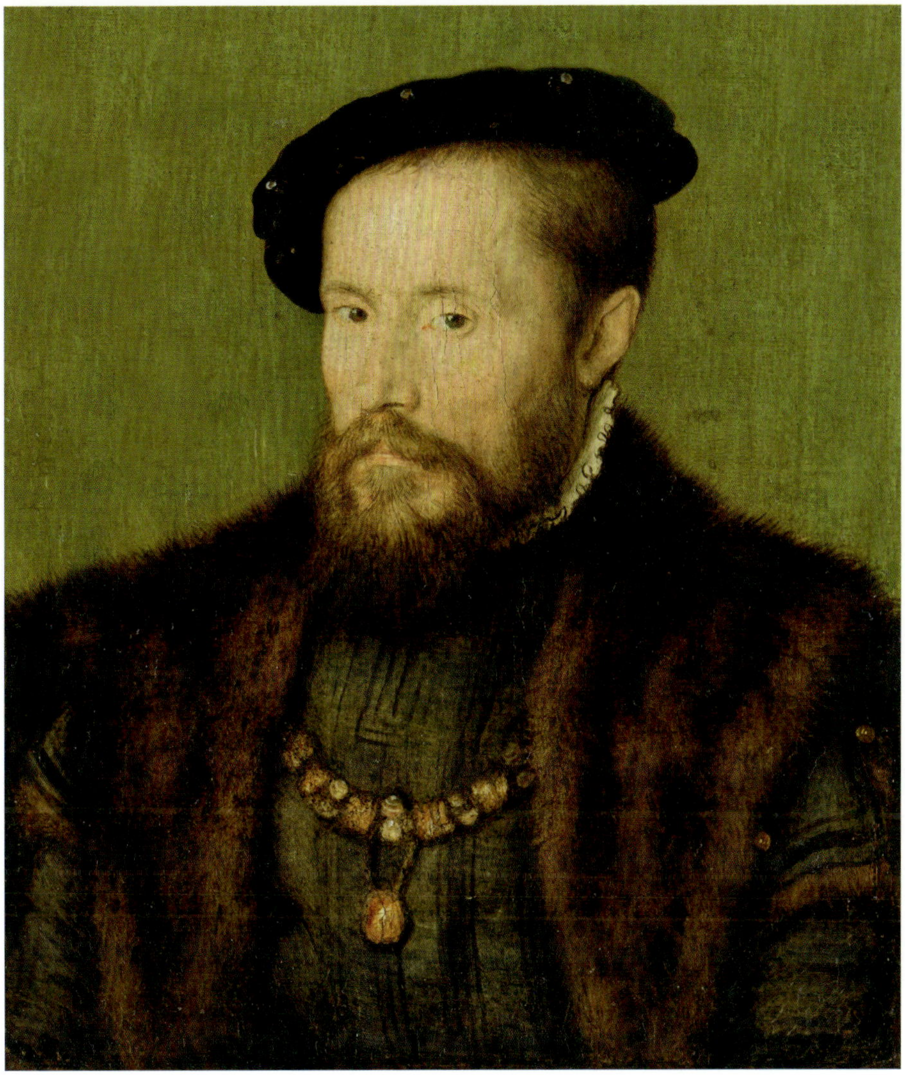

The duc d'Aumale bought this painting in 1882 at the Hamilton auction, where it was described as a portrait of Emperor Charles V wearing the neckchain of the Order of the Golden Fleece. The sitter was subsequently alleged to be Babou de la Bourdaisière, then, later, the Grand Equerry Boisy. However, Anne Dubois de Groër, who specializes in the oeuvre of Corneille de la Haye (*see p. 136*), has now identified the sitter as Jean de Taix, based on three drawings in the Musée Condé, showing the sitter in identical fashion, if flipped left to right. One of the drawings includes the insignia of the Order of Saint-Michel hanging from a heavy gold neckchain.

The career of Jean de Taix, a former page of honor to Francis I, benefited from the backing of the king's favorite, Madame d'Etampes. According to the chronicler Pierre de Brantôme, Taix was made a colonel general of the French infantry under Francis I, and distinguished himself at the battle of Cerisola in the Piedmont in 1544. That same year he was made a knight of the Order of Saint-Michel. When Henry II came to the throne, the new king was convinced by his favorite, Diane de Poitiers, and his advisor, Anne de Montmorency, to rid himself of many of his father's servants, including Taix, who was removed from his office and replaced by Montmorency's nephew, Coligny. Taix continued to serve as a simple captain and was killed at the siege of Hesdin in 1553, aged fifty-five or fifty-six. The painting here, which shows him wearing a small-brimmed cap fashionable around 1550, is roughly contemporary with his death. It might therefore be a posthumous portrait, a rare case for Corneille, who liked to have his sitters pose rather than employ a chalk drawing made earlier by another artist (a fairly common practice at the time). Despite some heavy restoration to the painting, there is no doubt about its attribution to Corneille de Lyon.

FRENCH SCHOOL, SIXTEENTH CENTURY

Albert de Gondi (1522–1602), Tutor to Charles IX

Wood. H. 31 cm (1 ft.); W. 24 cm (9 ½ in.)
Inv. 265 (Cabinet de Clouet)

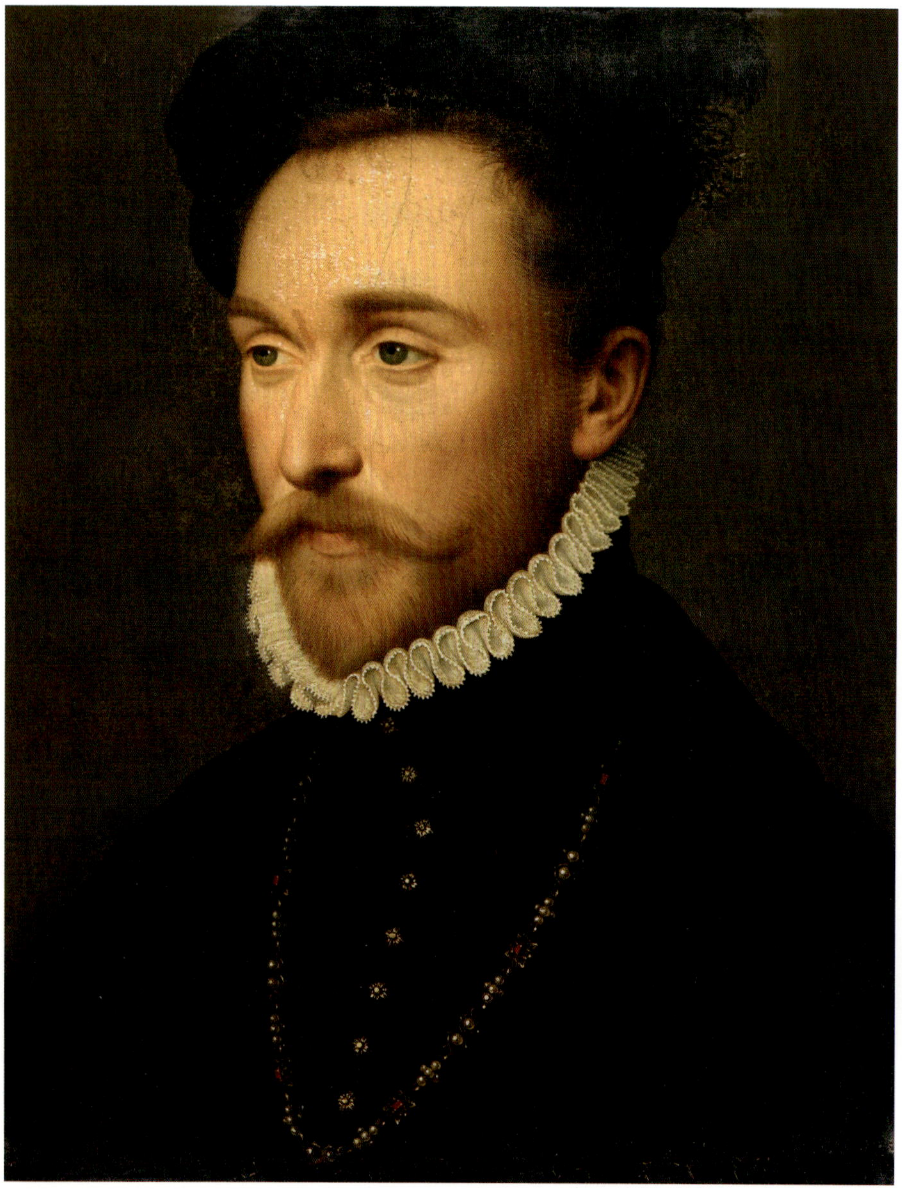

The sitter has been identified thanks to an old label on the back of the picture. It is a replica of a portrait dated 1556, now in the Musée National du Château de Versailles, formerly in the royal collection and transferred to Versailles during the reign of Louis-Philippe. A modern copy was done in the nineteenth century by Jacques-Joseph Lecurieux.

Albert de Gondi (1522–1602) was born into a Florentine banking family that worked on behalf of France. After having earned his stripes in Italy, Gondi made contact with Catherine de' Medici, queen of France, who had him named a gentleman of the king's bedchamber and later tutor to Charles de France (the future Charles IX). It was probably around that time that the Versailles portrait was done, whose date suggests that Gondi was around forty years old. During the Wars of Religion Gondi sided with the court, and was one of the organizers of the Saint Bartholomew's Day massacre. Made a marshal in 1573, at his death in 1602 he was covered in honors.

This rather conventional, official portrait was once attributed to François Clouet or to the putative Jean Decourt.

FRENCH SCHOOL, SIXTEENTH CENTURY

Admiral Gaspard de Coligny (1519–1572), 1565

Wood. H. 30 cm (1 ft.); W. 26 cm (10 in.)
D.t.r.: *1565*
Inv. 579 (Cabinet de Clouet)

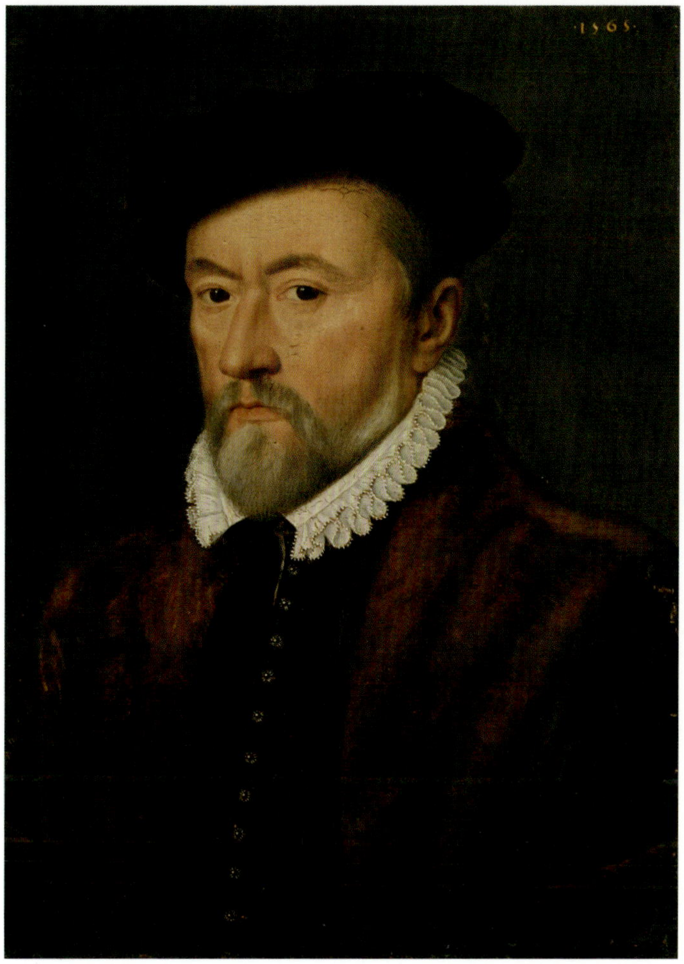

There are several versions of this portrait, one of which has been attributed to François Clouet and identified, on the basis of an old inscription, as a *Portrait of Jacques Bourdin, State Secretary under Francis II and Charles IX* (art market, Paris, 1996). Another version in Grenoble (Musée de Peinture et de Sculpture) is identified as Gaspard de Coligny and ascribed to the sixteenth-century French school.

Admiral Gaspard de Coligny (1519–1572) was the nephew, via his mother, of *connétable* Anne de Montmorency (*see p. 134*). He first made his mark in the infantry, where he was named colonel general in 1457, then admiral (in a purely honorary capacity) five years later. After the treaty of Cateau-Cambrésis in 1559, Coligny became the head of the Protestant party against the Catholic Guise clan, but was defeated at the battle of Dreux in 1562. When the duc de Guise was assassinated the following year, Coligny vigorously denied being part of the plot. But the admiral fell victim to the Saint Bartholomew's Day massacre of Protestants, aimed mainly at himself, on August 24, 1572. Agrippa d'Aubigny reported that Coligny's remains were taken down from a scaffold at Montfaucon by faithful followers, then hidden at Chantilly where they remained for roughly a decade.

The fine portrait here shows the admiral in 1565, aged fifty-six. His features and steely gaze convey authority, courage, and iron will. The ground is dark green, the dress sober, the cap unadorned. The face is subtly modeled, the beard and mustache are graying, the features are drawn.

In the twentieth century this painting was ascribed to Marc Duval, the Coligny family's official portraitist and alleged artist of a famous drawing of the three Coligny brothers (one copy now in the Musée Condé, another in the Bibliothèque Nationale de France). However, this portrait is not incompatible with the Musée Condé's Clouet drawing, nor with the other known portraits of the admiral, even though he is usually depicted in a breastplate.

FRENCH SCHOOL, LATE SIXTEENTH CENTURY

Gabrielle d'Estrées at her Bath

Canvas. H. 115 cm (3 ft. 8 ¼ in.); W. 103 cm (3 ft. 4 ½ in.)
Inv. 278 (Galerie de Peinture)

This painting was based on a famous work by François Clouet showing Diane de Poitiers in her bathtub (*A Lady in Her Bath*, National Gallery, Washington), which inspired many paintings of women at their toilette. It thereby belongs to what is generally called the Second School of Fontainebleau, that is to say the second generation of artists, usually of French or Flemish stock, who worked for the French court after the heyday of the Italian artists, such as Rosso Fiorentino and Il Primaticcio, summoned to France by Francis I. The subject reflects the mythological iconography of a woman at her toilette, the most famous examples being found in museums in Dijon and Basel, an iconography that itself derived from the *Toilet of Venus* or *Toilet of Psyche*.

Here the sitter is Gabriele d'Estrées, Henry IV's favorite, who gave the king three children, including the two boys pictured here: César, duc de Vendôme, born in 1594 and nicknamed "the bastard heir"; and the younger son, Alexandre de Vendôme, born in April 19, 1598, shown here in swaddling cloths at his nurse's breast. The painting can thus be dated to roughly 1598–99 (even though it lacks Catherine-Henriette, born in 1596, who cannot be the swaddled infant, because the eldest child seems to be over two years old).

The Louvre has a painting with a fairly similar theme but featuring two women in the bath, one of whom is allegedly Gabrielle d'Estrées. The other woman, her sister the duchesse de Villars, takes the nipple of Gabrielle's breast between her thumb and index finger, apparently a sign of Gabrielle's impending motherhood. In the background, as here, we see a woman at work in a comfortable setting. In those days, bathing was recommended for women after childbirth, as a way of preserving their beauty. Immersion in water was also supposed to favor future maternity. The roses and pearls are attributes of Venus that associate the sitter with the goddess of beauty. This painting is therefore a paean to the beauty and fertility of King Henry IV's mistress.

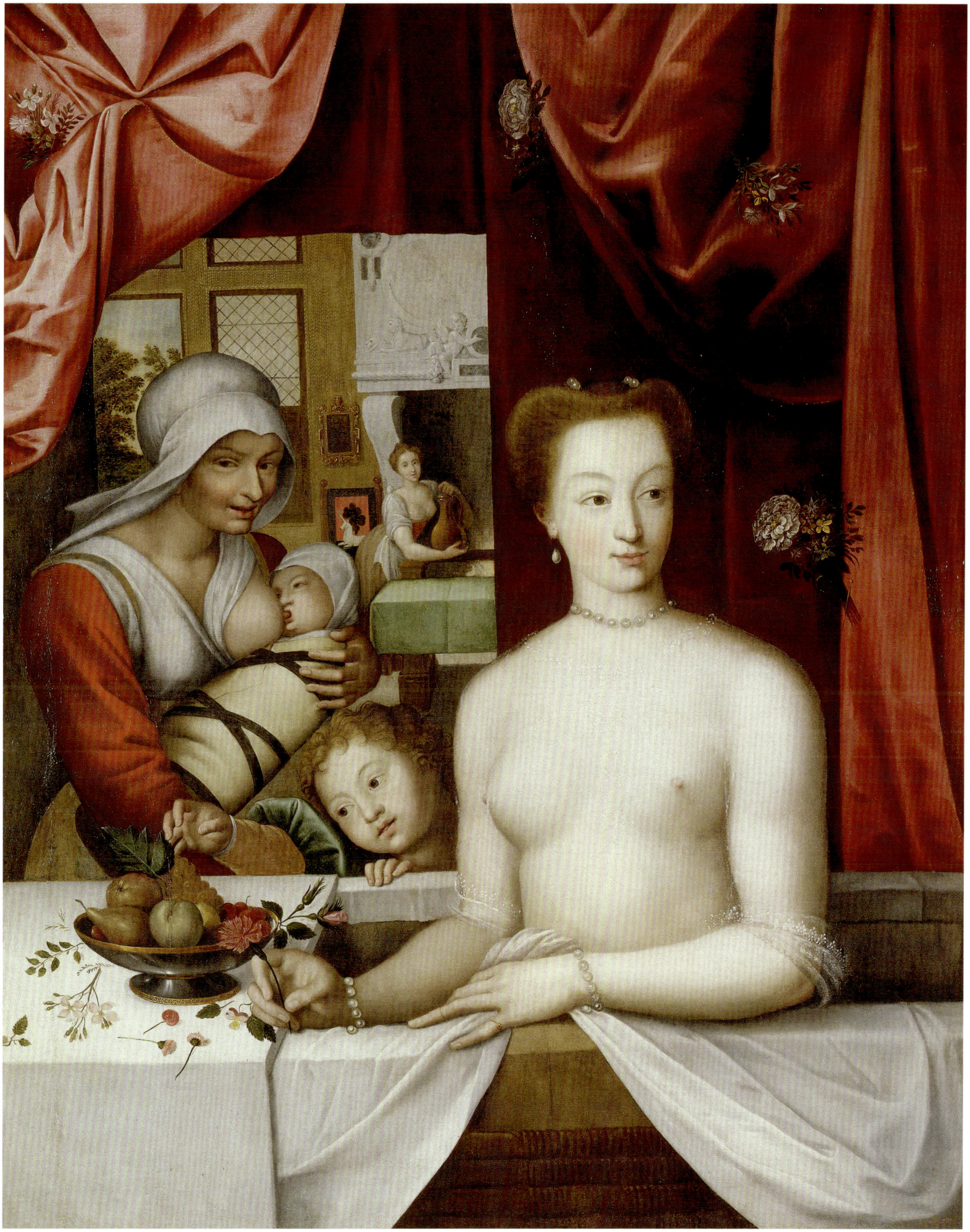

TROPHIME BIGOT

(Arles, 1579; Avignon, 1650)

The Supper at Emmaus

Canvas. H. 121 cm (4 ft.); W. 173 cm (5 ft. 8 in.)
Inv. 124 (Galerie de Peinture)

This painting was attributed first to a northern Caravaggesque artist, Gerrit von Honthorst (nicknamed *Gherardo della Notte*, or "Gerard of the Night Scenes"), then to Matthias Stomer. In 1960, English art historian Benedict Nicolson assembled a group of roughly forty unsigned paintings (including the one here) all by the same hand, featuring half-length figures lit by candle or lantern, and ascribed them to an artist he named the Candlelight Master, soon identified as Trophime Bigot, a painter born in Arles in 1579. Bigot went to Rome and returned to Arles with the Italianized name of Trufamont Bigoti. He died in Avignon in 1650.

In 1675, the biographer Sandrart mentioned a painter Trufemondi, originally from Languedoc, who painted nocturnal portraits of bust-length figures. Trufemondi was a member of the Accademia di San Luca (the Roman artists' guild) in 1620; in 1630 he was living with Claude Lorraine; prior to 1638 he sold works to Marquess Giustiniani. After leaving Italy in 1634, Bigot worked in Arles and Aix-en-Provence, executing large altarpieces in a late Mannerist style, dated 1635 and 1639. Some commentators, however, distinguish the Candlelight Master from the painter of the altarpieces. In which case two artists were involved, perhaps father and son—Trophime Bigot the elder, born in 1579 (the Candlelight Master) and Trophime Bigot the younger, aged roughly fifteen years younger. But the artist may simply have adapted his style to the local clientele. Indeed, the period when Bigot the elder was absent from Provence corresponds to his Roman activities (1620–34) and no painting done by him prior to the age of fifty-six has apparently survived.

This painting is typical of Caravaggisti—followers of Caravaggio—who depicted Biblical characters with ordinary features in a realistic way, at close quarters, in artificial light. The movement launched by Caravaggio drew many young French and Flemish artists to Rome to study this new approach.

The subject is taken from the Gospel of Luke: after being laid in his tomb, Jesus appeared, unrecognized, to two of his disciples on the road to Emmaus. On arriving at the inn and breaking bread for supper, they suddenly recognized him, and went forth to announce the resurrection of Christ.

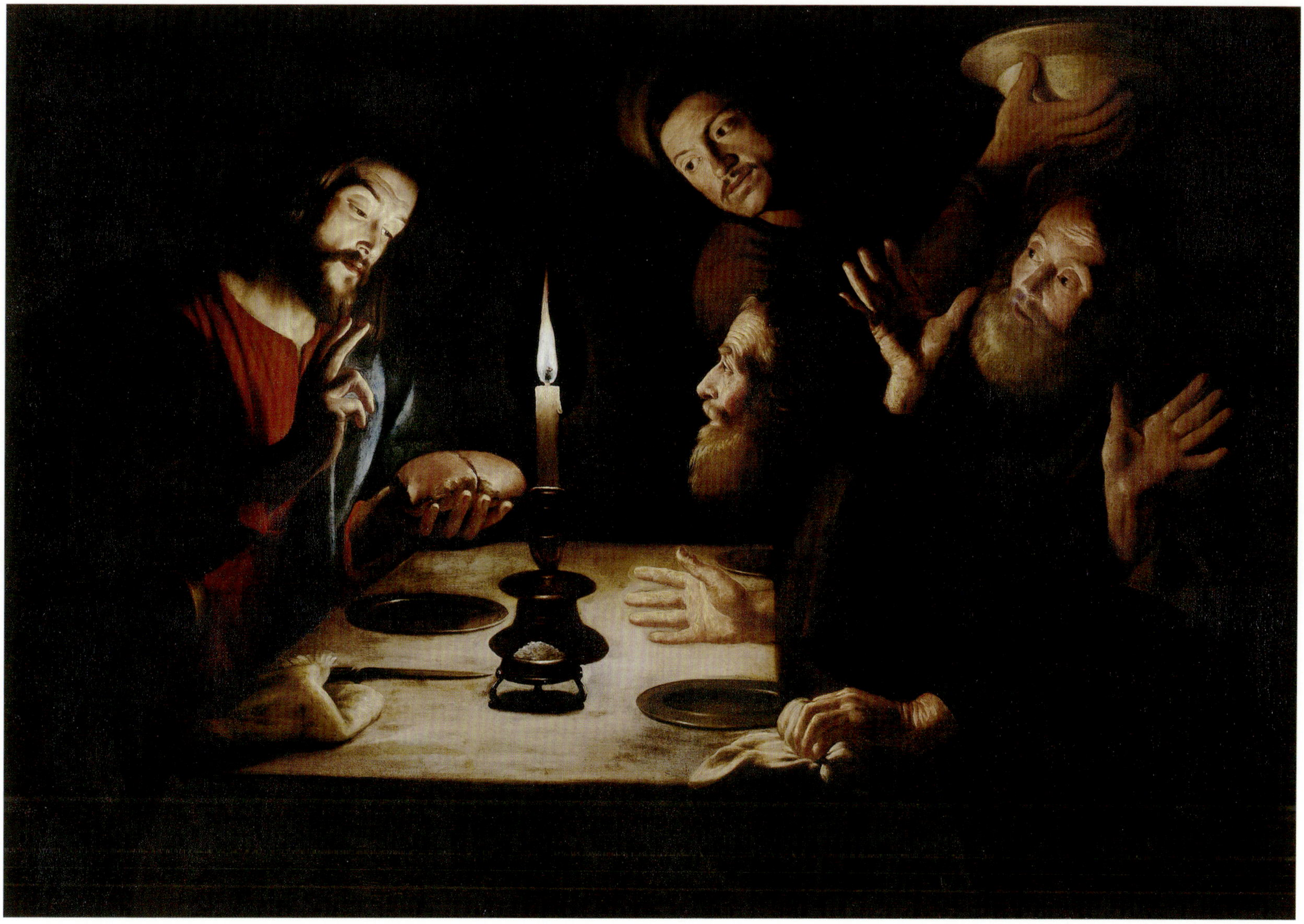

MATTHIAS STOMER

(Amersfoort, circa 1600; Sicily, after 1650)

Sarah Leading Hagar to Abraham

Canvas. H. 150 cm (4 ft. 11 in.); W. 204 cm (6 ft. 8 in.)
Inv. 822 (Tribune)

Matthias Stomer (or Stom) was a Flemish Caravaggesque painter with a distinctive style, though little is known about him. He was apparently born in Amersfoort, and may have studied under Abraham Janssens in Antwerp—his painting clearly displays traces of apprenticeship in Antwerp and Utrecht. He spent the years 1630–32 in Rome, drawn by Caravaggio's paintings. In 1648 he was described as a pupil of the Utrecht Caravaggisto Gerri van Honthorst, to whom this painting was erroneously attributed in 1830. Stomer went to Naples where he painted nocturnal religious scenes for churches (Museo di Capodimonte, Naples), then went on to Palermo and Messina in Sicily, where he worked for Capucine monks on a large *Martyrdom of Saint Cecilia,* destroyed during the earthquake of 1908. In 1641, Stomer signed and dated a *Saint Isidore* for the church of Caccamo, near Palermo. In Messina, Antonio Ruffo bought two paintings for his palace from Stomer, who apparently took on Flemish painter Jan van Houbraken as his pupil. Stomer died in Sicily around 1650.

This painting depicts a scene from the Old Testament. The aged Abraham was childless because his wife, Sarah (on the right), was sterile. She therefore led her Egyptian handmaiden, Hagar, to Abraham's bed. Hagar gave birth to a son, Ishmael. But Sarah herself then became pregnant with Isaac, so she had Hagar and her son banished to the desert (Genesis 21). This rare subject was handled above all by northern artists in the seventeenth and eighteenth centuries. Stomer depicted it at least five times (art market, Berlin; Göteberg). This version is typical of Stomer's style, influenced by Caravaggio (as was Georges de la Tour): realistic figures shown half-length, at night, in close quarters, by the light of a candle.

In the nineteenth century this painting was mistakenly titled *Plato and the Courtesans* and attributed to the German artist Christophe Storer (a misreading of Stomer). In 1796 it had been part of the Torlonia collection in Rome, where it was apparently bought around 1802 by the agents who were acquiring paintings on behalf of the king of Naples, from whence it entered the collection of the prince of Salerno, father-in-law of the duc d'Aumale, who purchased it in 1854 (*see p. 27*).

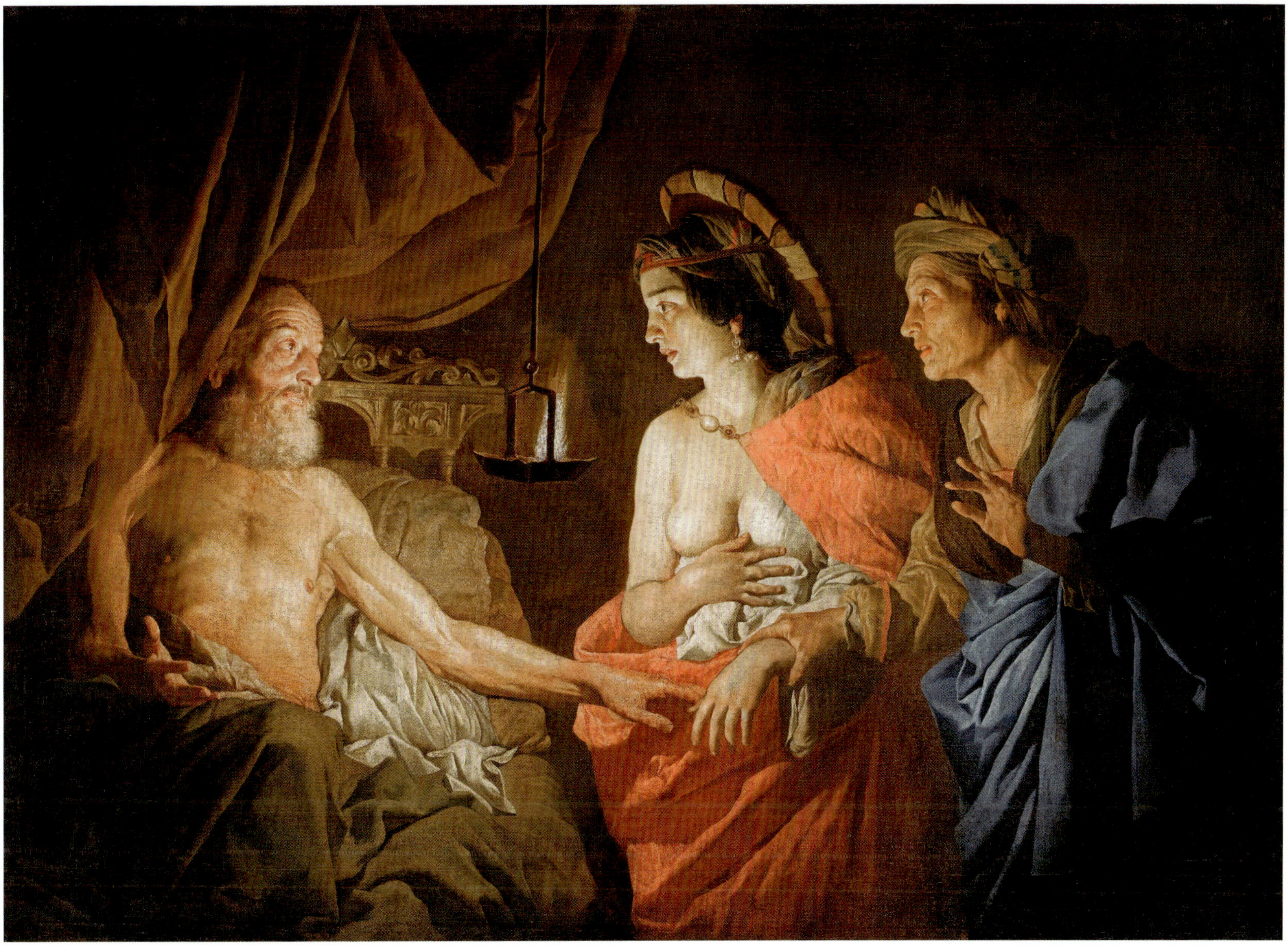

MELCHIOR DE HONDECOETER

(Utrecht, 1636; Amsterdam, 1695)

A Cock Fighting a Turkey

Canvas. H. 105 cm (3 ft. 5 ½ in.); W. 182 cm (6 ft.)
Inv. 141 (Tribune)

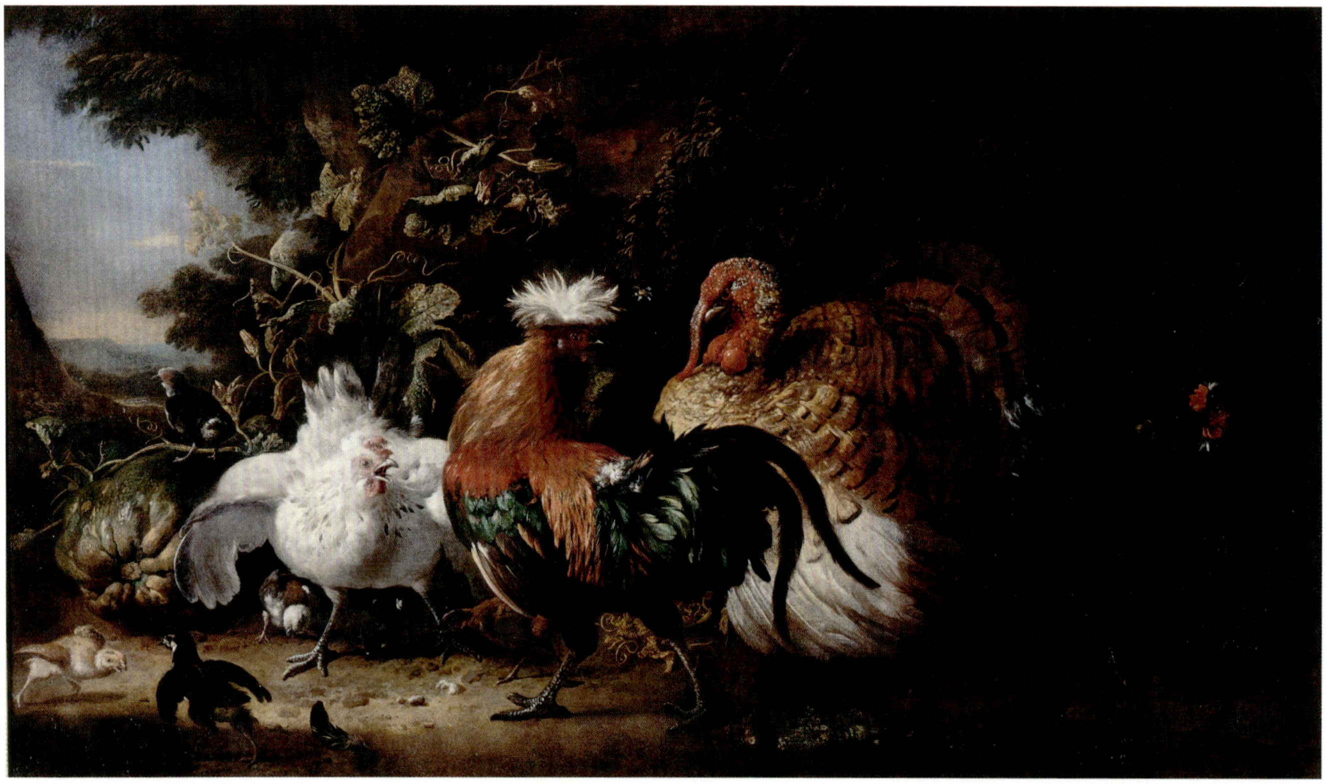

The son and grandson of artists who specialized in animals, especially birds, Melchior de Hondecoeter was the most remarkable painter of farmyard fowl. He was trained by his father and his uncle, Jan Baptist Weenix, and worked in The Hague as a member of the Pictura group from 1659 to 1663. He then moved to Amsterdam, where he married in February, 1663, and obtained civic rights in 1688. He enjoyed a great reputation as an animal painter, and was dubbed "the Raphael of birds." His compositions have sometimes been described as "bird portraits." His works are now found in museums in Ghent, Troyes, Munich, The Hague (four paintings), and Amsterdam (eight works, the most famous of which is *The Floating Feather*).

As Gruyer wrote in 1896, "the De Hondecoeter painting in the Musée Condé gives a very good idea of a first-rate talent working in a second-rate genre." It shows a large, white-crested, black-tailed rooster defending a hen and her chicks from a huge turkey on the right. This picture seems to derive from a signed painting called *The White Hen* (Alte Pinakothek, Munich), of which several variants exist. In the Munich version, the turkey is seen in profile, planted on his claws; the scene is bordered on the left by vegetation and a kind of wooden fence, while a haystack can be glimpsed between the cockerel and the turkey.

The painting here had arrived at Chantilly by 1720, listed in the post-mortem estate inventory of Marie-Anne de Bourbon, wife of the duc de Bourbon, as a *Cock Fight* that hung in the "salon overlooking the canal." In 1740, at the death of the duc de Bourbon (1692–1740), who was also prince of Condé, the painting was hanging in the Condé residence in Paris, identified as a *Fight Between a Cock and a Peacock*, attributed to Frans Snyders. It was confiscated by the revolutionary government during the French Revolution and incorporated into the Louvre, but was returned in 1816 to the prince of Condé. It was extended on the right side at some point in the past, probably to fit into woodwork or to serve as a pendant to another painting.

DAVID TENIERS THE YOUNGER

(Antwerp, 1610; Brussels, 1690)

Louis II de Bourbon, prince of Condé, known as the Great Condé (1621–1686), 1653

Copper. H. 22 cm (8 1/2 in.); W. 16 cm (6 1/4 in.)
S.d.b.l. and r.: *D. TENIERS / AET. 31 / A. 1653*
Inv. 130 (Salle des Gardes)

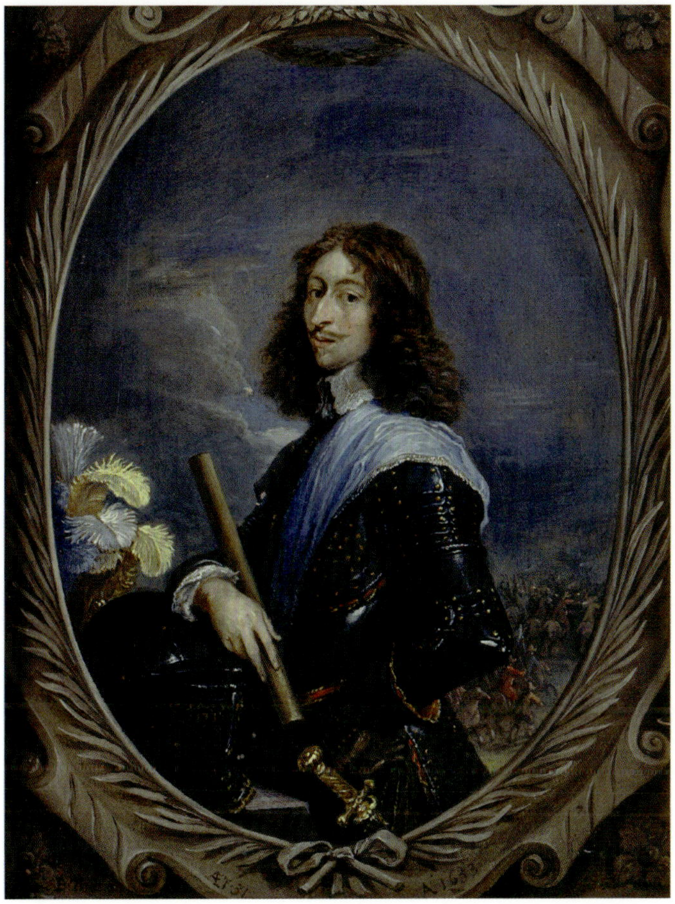

Taught by his father, David Teniers the Elder, David II Teniers acquired the status of master in Antwerp in 1633. A friend of Rubens, in 1637 he married the daughter of Jan I Brueghel, Anna. In 1651 Teniers moved to Brussels where he became the official painter of Archduke Leopold Wilhelm of Austria, governor of the Spanish Netherlands, who also appointed Teniers to be curator of his collection of paintings. For the archduke Teniers painted interior scenes of collections of artworks that included the archduke's own paintings. Teniers remained in his post under Don John of Austria until 1659. David the Younger is known for his scenes of everyday peasant life in Flanders (festivities, inns) and for his singeries (depictions of monkeys engaged in playful activities). King Philip II of Spain, who assembled an entire gallery of Teniers' paintings (now in the Prado, Madrid), granted him the right to open an academy in Antwerp in 1663. Teniers also did paintings for Queen Christina of Sweden, James II of England, and Prince William II of Orange. From 1672 to 1674, he worked with his son, David III Teniers, on cartoons for tapestries commissioned by the duc d'Orléans, Louis XIV's brother.

Although portraiture was not his specialty, in 1653 David II executed a likeness of the Great Condé, aged thirty-one. Condé, a great military leader, was imprisoned during the civil war known as the Fronde (1650–51), then went head-to-head against the other great general of the day, his cousin the vicomte de Turenne, outside Paris on July 2, 1652. Failing to win the day, Condé defected to the Spanish and moved to Brussels. (*See also pp. 188*)

The Great Condé is shown here wearing a breastplate and carrying a commander's baton. His right arm rests on his helmet, his left hand on his hip near the hilt of his sword. This portrait may have been part of the Condé collection prior to the French Revolution. A 1779 inventory of the Palais-Bourbon lists the presence of an "oval painting of the *Great Condé Reading*, by Teniers." The duc d'Aumale bought this painting from the marquis de Biencourt in March 1891 for 15,000 francs.

JACOB VAN RUISDAEL

(Haarlem, 1628–29; Amsterdam, 1682)

The Beach and Dunes at Scheveningen

Canvas. H. 84 cm (2 ft. 9 in.); W. 110 cm (3 ft. 7 ½ in.)
S.b.l.: *Ruisdael*
Inv. 138 (Salle Isabelle)

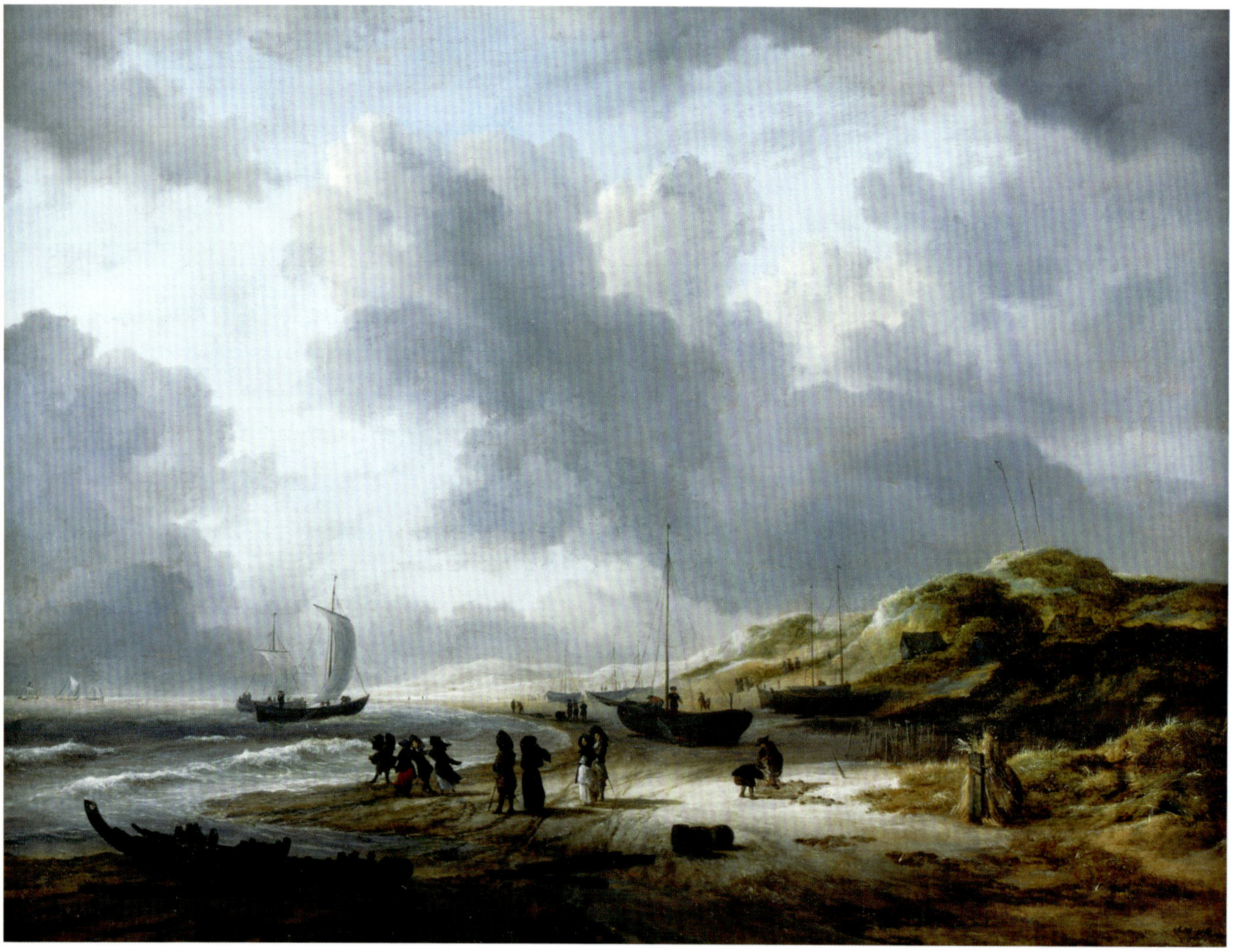

Born in Haarlem, where he probably trained under his father, Isaac van Ruisdael, Jacob began painting in 1645 and moved to Amsterdam in 1647. After medical studies in Caen, France, he was listed in 1676 as a doctor in Amsterdam, where he remained until his death, though he was buried in Haarlem. Considered to be one of the greatest landscape painters of the seventeenth century, van Ruisdael was an attentive observer of detail who managed to develop a personal style with a Romantic touch that distinguishes him from other well-known landscape artists.

This painting is one of his finest works. The beach at Scheveningen, not far from The Hague, was often depicted by Dutch artists in the seventeenth century. Here van Ruisdael uses a cool palette to render the approaching storm with great authenticity. Eugène Fromentin, in his study of old Dutch masters (*Les Maîtres d'autrefois: Belgique. Hollande*, 1876), devoted a passage to Scheveningen, noting that he was following in the footsteps of van Goyen, van de Velde, and van Ruisdael, all of whom liked to paint there.

The duc de Choiseul sale of 1770 included a *View of the Beach at Schevelingue* [sic], which was auctioned again in 1777 at the prince of Conti sale. It entered the duc d'Aumale's collection in 1868 as a result of the famous sale of works in the San Donato gallery that belonged to Prince Demidoff.

WILLEM VAN DE VELDE THE YOUNGER

(Leiden, 1633; London, 1707)

The Sea in Calm Weather, 1671[?]

Canvas. H. 83 cm (2 ft. 8 ¾ in.); W. 105 cm (3 ft. 5 ½ in.)
S.d.b.l. (in the water): *W. V. Velde 1671*[?]
Inv. 140 (Salle Isabelle)

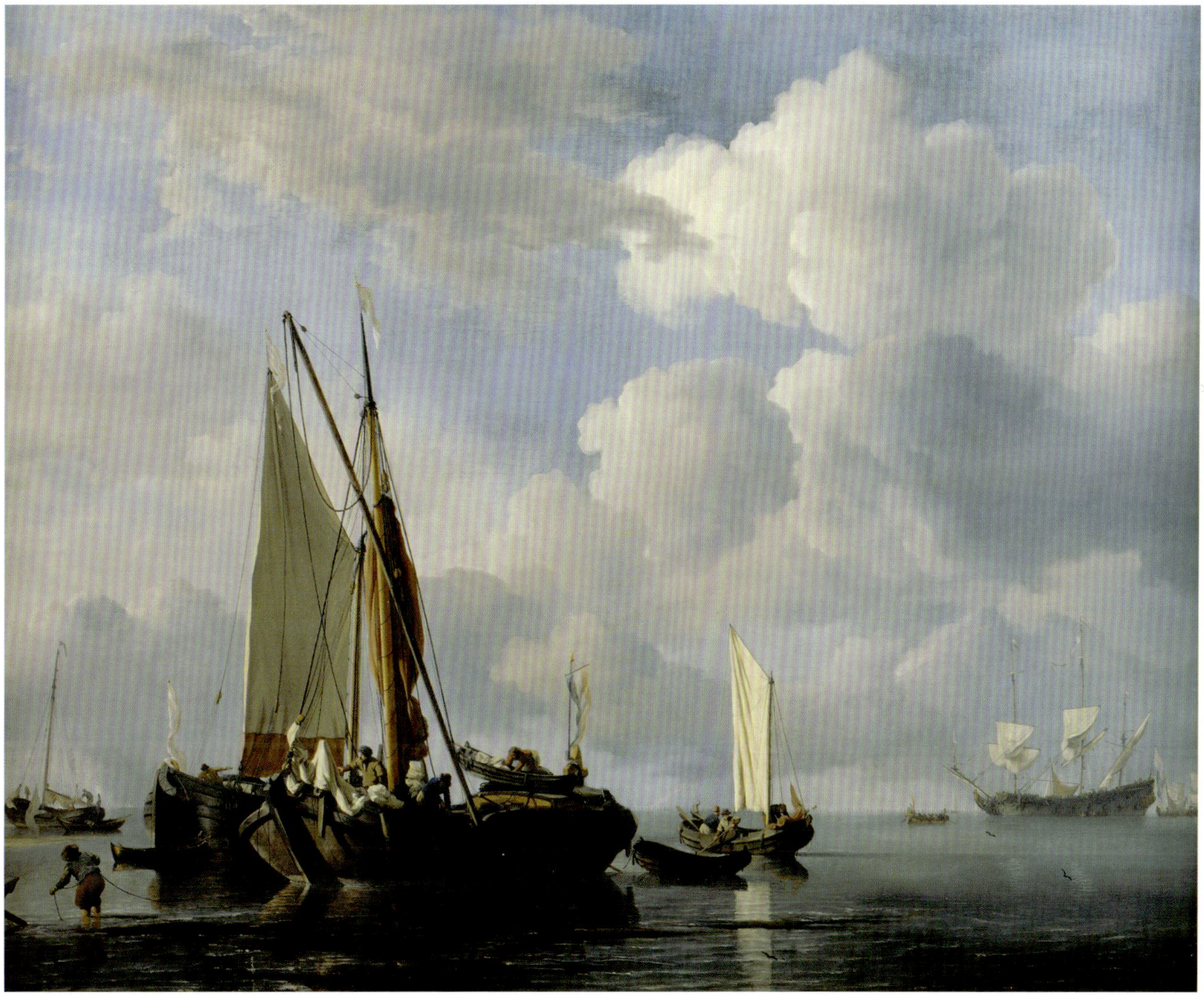

Willem van de Velde the Younger took marine painting to its high point. Born in Leiden but raised in Amsterdam from 1636 onward (the year of the birth of his brother Adriaen, a future landscape artist), he trained under his father, Willem van de Velde the Elder (1610–1693), himself a painter of seascapes. Willem the Younger later studied with Simon de Vlieger. In 1652 he married Petronella de Maire, from whom he separated eighteen months later, following a suit in which Vlieger's daughter and son-in-law testified in his favor. Willem remarried in 1656, to Madeleine Walravens. Given the economic depression that immediately followed the French invasion of the Netherlands in 1672, the two Willems emigrated to England, where Charles II made them painters to the court in 1673, allotting them an annual stipend of one hundred pounds per annum in return for paintings of naval battles. Later, when Willem the Younger returned to Amsterdam for a visit, the port authority commissioned him to do a painting for their large meeting hall (now Rijksmuseum, Amsterdam). No other painter mastered the secrets of naval architecture so well, as witnessed by Willem's countless sketches. After the death of his father in 1693, Willem the Younger continued to run the large workshop that turned out copies and variants of the master's originals. The two painters are buried side by side in Saint James's Church, Piccadilly. Willem the Younger's compositions tend to be more complex than his father's, and ships often occupy the foreground, as here, evoking a peaceful evening on a calm sea. Most of his works have remained in England; in the nineteenth century, the Musée Condé's painting featured in the collections of Lord Bute and Sir Charles Stuart in London, but was bought by the duc d'Aumale at the Prince Demidoff sale in 1868.

ANTHONY VAN DYCK

(Antwerp, 1599; Blackfriars, 1641)

Count Henri van den Berghe

Canvas. H. 119 cm (3 ft. 10 ½ in.); W. 95 cm (3 ft. 1 ¾ in.)
Inv. 126 (Salle des Gardes)

Henri van den Berghe, born in Antwerp in 1573, came from one of the most illustrious families in Guelders. As a Flemish officer in the service of Spain, he was a general of artillery and made a knight of the Order of the Golden Fleece; he took part in the wars against Holland, notably in Gelderland in 1624 and at the siege of Breda in 1625 (where he joined the great General Spinola), and again from 1626 to 1628. Forced to retreat from Bois-le-Duc in 1629, and unhappy with the Spanish government, he retired to Liège. Although related to the prince of Orange through family ties, Henri faithfully served Spain. Archduchess Isabel, governor of the Spanish Netherlands, invited him to return to Brussels, but he refused and took refuge with Frederick Henry of Nassau, serving as advisor until he moved on to England. He was declared a traitor and sentenced to hang; he died in London in 1641.

The original, signed version of this painting is now in the Prado in Madrid. Van Dyck painted the great warrior in the heat of action, bareheaded, gesturing. He is wearing breastplate, arm-guards, and thigh-guards of steel over a fawn-colored suede tunic marked with the letter H. Van Dyck was an excellent portraitist and convincingly conveyed his sitter's energy and strength. He apparently executed this portrait during his stay in Flanders between 1627 and 1632, but at any rate prior to the count's disgrace in 1629, as confirmed by the apparent age of the latter, around fifty. This picture might allude to the siege of Breda in 1625, or to Berghe's capture of the towns of Cleves and Mundberg in 1624 when he commanded an army on behalf of Spain. Like its pendant in the museum (*see p. 152*), this painting was brought to France by the Great Condé after his return from exile in Brussels (1653–59). Some experts feel it is by the hand of van Dyck, others think it is an excellent workshop replica of the painting in the Prado.

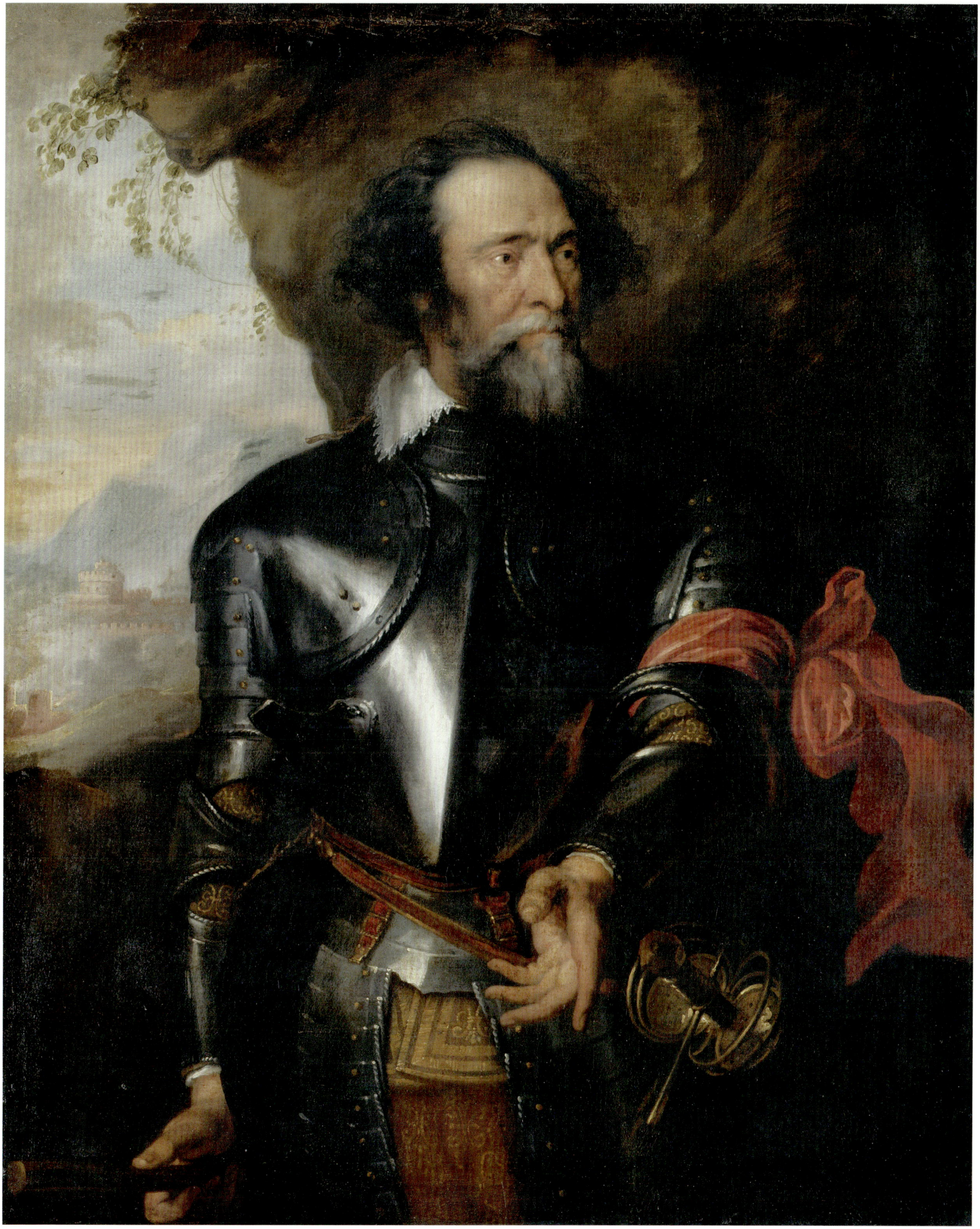

ANTHONY VAN DYCK

(Antwerp, 1599; Blackfriars, 1641)

Alleged Portrait of Princess Marie of Barbançon, Duchess of Arenberg

Canvas. H. 119 cm (3 ft. 10 ½ in.); W. 95 cm (3 ft. 1 ¾ in.)
Inv. 127 (Salle des Gardes)

As part of the Condé collection, this painting, like its pendant (*see p. 150*), apparently arrived in France in 1659 when the Great Condé returned from exile in Brussels. Or else it was bought by the prince prior to 1676, a period for which no Condé accounts survives. By 1709 they were hanging in the gallery at Chantilly. The portrait of the woman was enlarged to match that of the man. Confiscated by the revolutionary government during the French Revolution, they entered the Louvre, but were returned to the prince of Condé in 1816 by King Louis XVIII.

As a result of the prince of Condé's inventory, the sitter was long identified as Princess Marie of Barbançon, born in 1602, who in 1616 married Count Albert de Ligne, duke of Arenberg (1600–1674). The Musée Condé's painting was probably done in Antwerp around 1630, or more probably during van Dyck's long stay in The Netherlands from 1634–35. When the Great Condé fled to Brussels in the 1650s after having risen up against his cousin, King Louis XIV, he met Princess Marie of Barbançon there. She was twenty years his senior; a letter from her to the Great Condé is preserved by the Musée Condé. However, the young woman pictured here is dressed as a canoness, and the identification with Marie is untenable.

The costume, part court dress, part monastic attire, with a crucifix on the chest, is that of a secular canoness belonging to a noble order. This portrait is similar to the one of Mademoiselle Arschot, engraved by Cornelis Galle after Nicolaas van der Horst: in that case, it could be Claire Eugenie, princess and countess of Arenberg (1611–60), daughter of Prince Philip of Arenberg and Anne of Melun, although unfortunately it would seem that she was not a canoness.

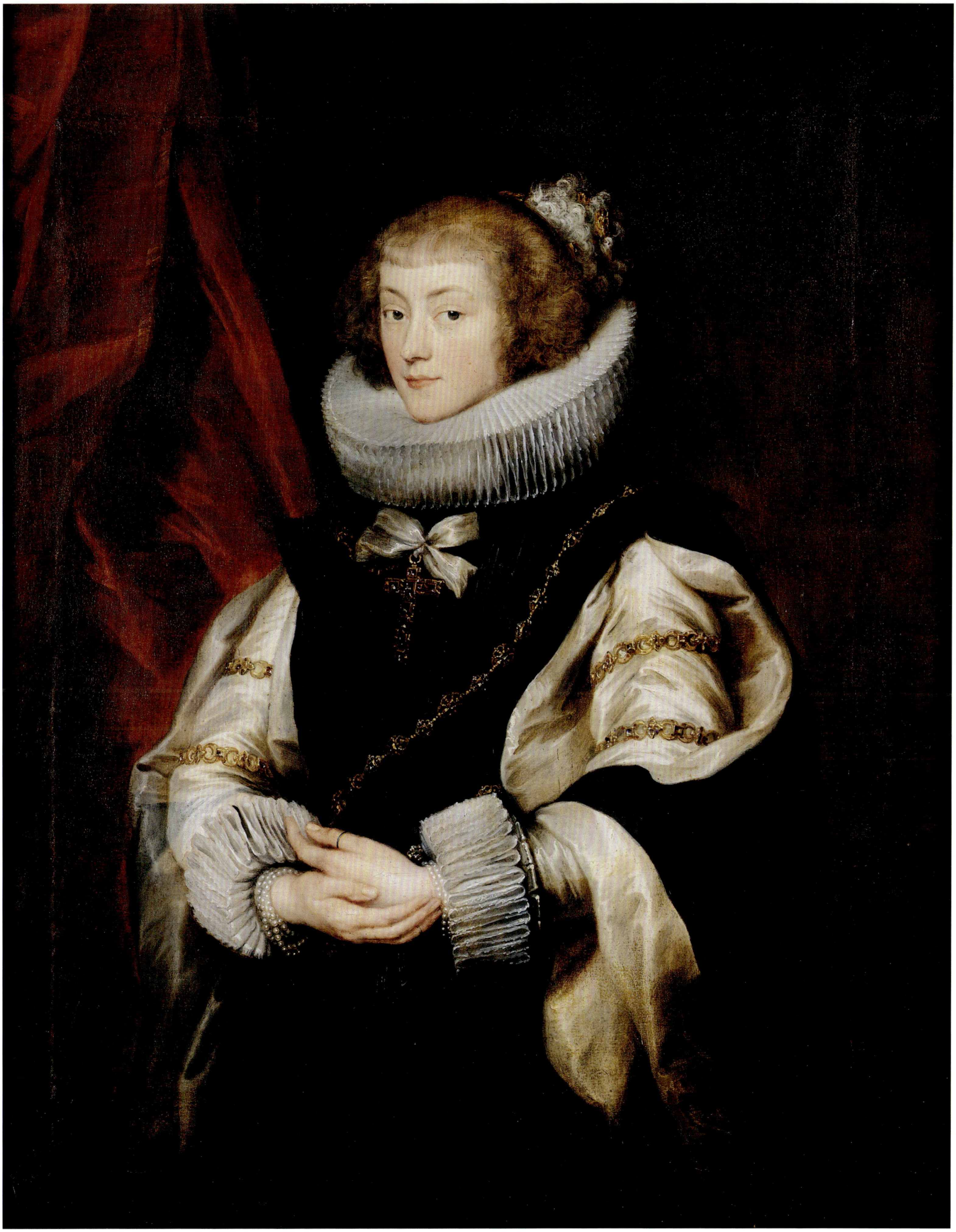

ANTHONY VAN DYCK

(Antwerp, 1599; Blackfriars, 1641)

Gaston de France, duc d'Orléans (1608–1660)

Canvas. H. 194 cm (6 ft. 4 in.); W. 118 cm (3 ft. 10 in.)
Inscription b.l.: *Gaston de France / Frère unique du Roy Louis / 1634*
Inv. 125 (Tribune)

This is a full-length portrait of Gaston de France—second son of Henry IV and Marie de' Medici, younger brother of the future King Louis XIII—magnificently dressed in ceremonial armor and wearing the blue ribbon of the Order of the Holy Spirit. He holds a commander's baton in his right hand, while his left rests on a gold-studded helmet.

Although the attribution is certain, the date is subject to controversy despite the inscription on the canvas. Some art historians date it from the siege of La Rochelle in 1628 because several engravings from that time replace the table on the right with a view of the sea and a besieged city. Others think it was painted in Antwerp in late January, 1632, when the queen mother Marie de' Medici and her son Gaston posed for van Dyck there while seeking refuge with Queen Isabella; the queen's secretary, J. P. de la Serre, recorded her admiration for van Dyck's "Titian cabinet." On August 8, 1632, King Charles I of England and his wife Henrietta Maria paid van Dyck 280 pounds for several paintings, including one titled *Monsieur, the King's Brother,* at a cost of twenty-five pounds. Van Dyck may well have taken these paintings to England to demonstrate his talent. Or perhaps Gaston sent it to Queen Henrietta Maria, who was none other than his sister. At any rate, it remained in the English royal collection until 1829, when George IV gave it to the future King Louis-Philippe of France in the mistaken belief that it showed one of the Frenchman's ancestors. Still other commentators argue that the Musée Condé version is not the one mentioned in August 1632, which related to an earlier, now-lost painting, but that it was purchased by George IV in 1816 at the Henry Hope sale in London. In which case it would have been painted in Brussels during Marie de' Medici's visit there in 1634, at the same time as a portrait of Marguerite de Lorraine (Duke of Bedford Collection, Woburn Abbey), who married Gaston in January 1632. Since the duke left Brussels in November 1634, he would have posed for van Dyck shortly after his return to the Low Countries from England, as confirmed by a manuscript in the Louvre: "A few days after [van Dyck's] arrival he received an order to go Brussels to paint Gaston de France, Marguerite and Henriette de Lorraine, the comte de Moret and the prince of Carignan." An autograph version exists in the Earl of Radnor collection in Longford Castle, executed at roughly the same time, 1634–35.

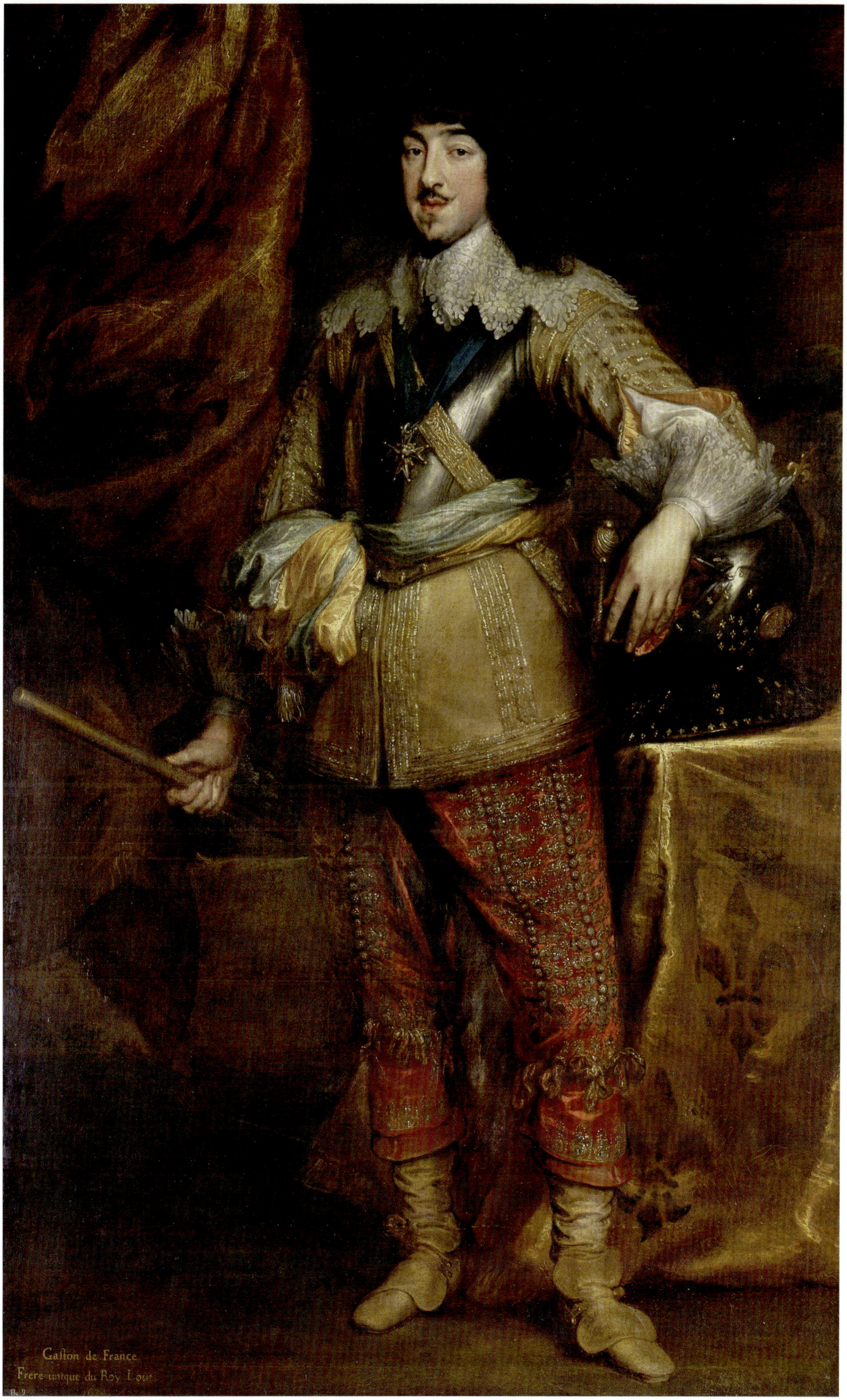
Gaſton de France
Frere unique du Roy

NICOLAS POUSSIN

(Les Andelys, 1594; Rome, 1665)

Landscape with Numa Pompilius and the Nymph Egeria

Canvas. H. 77 cm (2 ft. 6 in.); W. 101 cm (3 ft. 3 ¾ in.)
Inv. 301 (Galerie de Peinture)

The Musée Condé boasts five paintings by Nicolas Poussin, illustrating various stages in the career of France's greatest exponent of seventeenth-century classicism. After training under Quentin Varin in his home town of Les Andelys in Normandy, then later in Paris, Poussin went to Italy where he spent the rest of his life apart from a brief period when he was summoned to Paris by Louis XIII and Richelieu. Poussin probably painted this picture for Roman art-lover Cassiano dal Pozzo (1598–1657), secretary to Cardinal Barbarini, the nephew of Pope Urban VIII.

The painting depicts the second legendary king of Rome, Numa Pompilius, holding the golden olive bough and making a nocturnal visit to the nymph Egeria in a grove dedicated to the Muses. Although rare, this iconography was also explored by Rutilio Manetti, Carlo Maratti, Garofalo, Taddeo Zuccaro, Domenico Campagnola, Stefano dell'Arzera, and, finally, Delacroix (for the Palais-Bourbon in the nineteenth century). However, this picture does not accurately correspond to any of the ancient texts, whether Plutarch's *Life of Numa Pompilius*, Livy's *Roman History*, Juvenal's *Satires*, or Virgil's *Aeneid*. The olive branch, more silver than gold, might allude to Numa Pompilius's concern for a peaceful reign.

This painting fits comfortably into the broad bucolic landscapes of Poussin's early years in Rome. Laboratory analysis nevertheless reveals a major pentimento underneath the figure of flute player in the center, which was initially a ram.

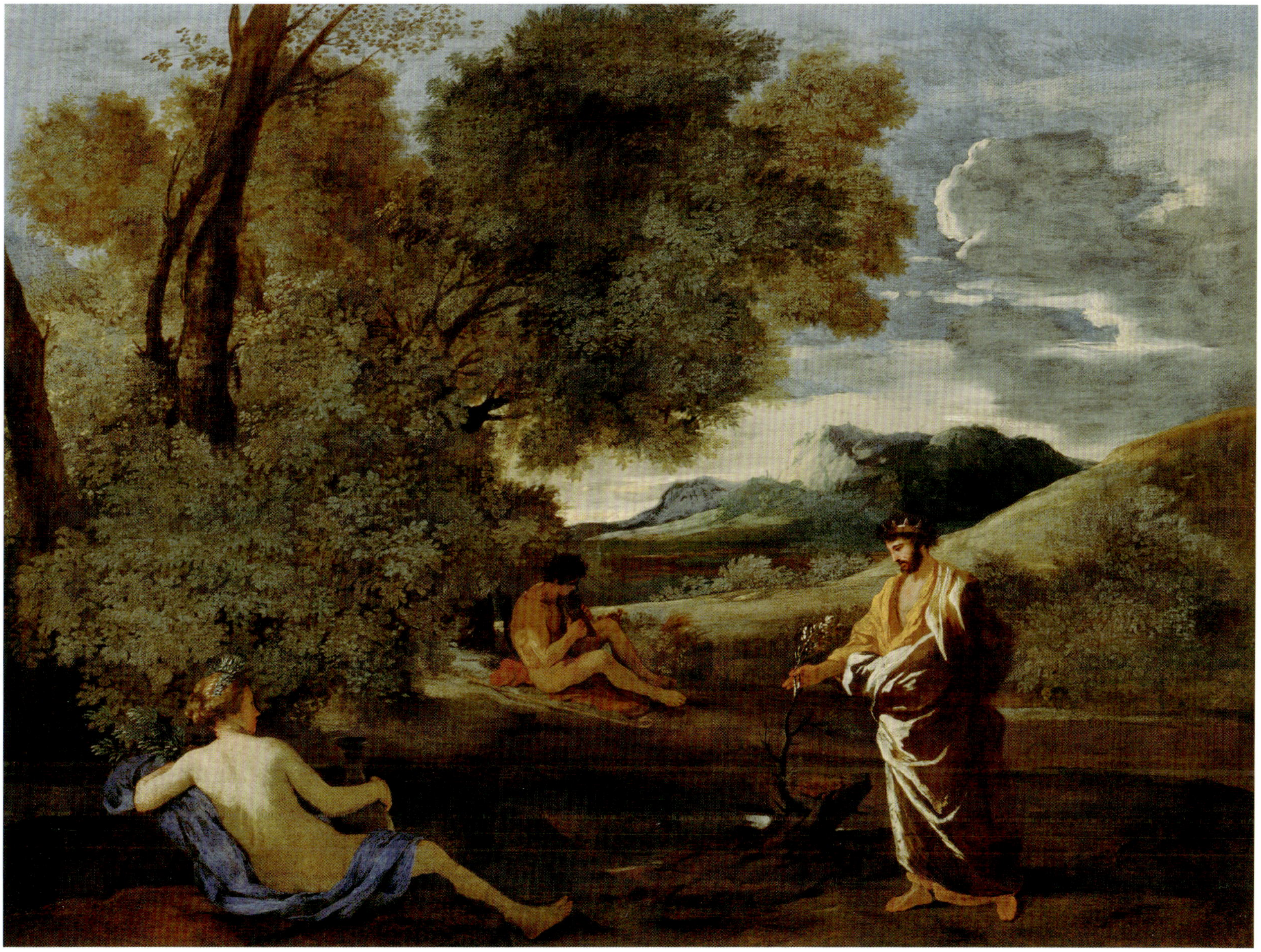

NICOLAS POUSSIN

(Les Andelys, 1594; Rome, 1665)

The Massacre of the Innocents

Canvas. H. 147 cm (4 ft. 9 in.); W. 171 cm (5 ft. 7 in.)
Inv. 305 (Galerie de Peinture)

This subject is drawn from the New Testament: King Herod, having learned that a king of the Jews has just been born in Bethlehem, ordered that all male children under two be killed. Nicolas Poussin painted this *Massacre of the Innocents* around 1628 for the palazzo of Marquess Vincenzo Giustiniani in Rome. As a young, talented artist still unknown in Rome, Poussin seized the opportunity to make himself known by working for this glamorous patron.

Poussin deliberately rivaled a famous painting on the same subject by Guido Reni (Pinacoteca, Bologna), but limited the number of figures by focusing his composition on three main characters: a soldier who kills, a mother who screams, a child about to die. He thereby imparted extraordinary dramatic power to the picture. In order for the picture to stand out once it was placed in the Baroque palazzo full of stucco and gilding, Poussin composed it along two strong diagonals converging on the face of the screaming mother—the painting itself becomes a cry. He set the figures in the foreground as though on the front of a theater stage, adding a few extras in the background to make the Biblical subject clear. He employed the three primary colors—red, blue, yellow—in a swirling movement, and he drenched the scene in an intense, contrasting light inspired by the work of Caravaggio. Poussin, who had worked on life drawing in Domenichino's studio, excelled at rendering large figures in an almost sculptural way.

Highly admired in Rome in the eighteenth century, this painting was also an inspiration to Picasso. During his Mediterranean period, 1920–22, Picasso painted figures similar to the woman in blue, with her gray flesh. During a visit to the Auschwitz concentration camp in 1948, Picasso—already famous for his *Guernica*—alluded to this painting when he said, "To think that in the old days artists thought they could paint *The Massacre of the Innocents!*"

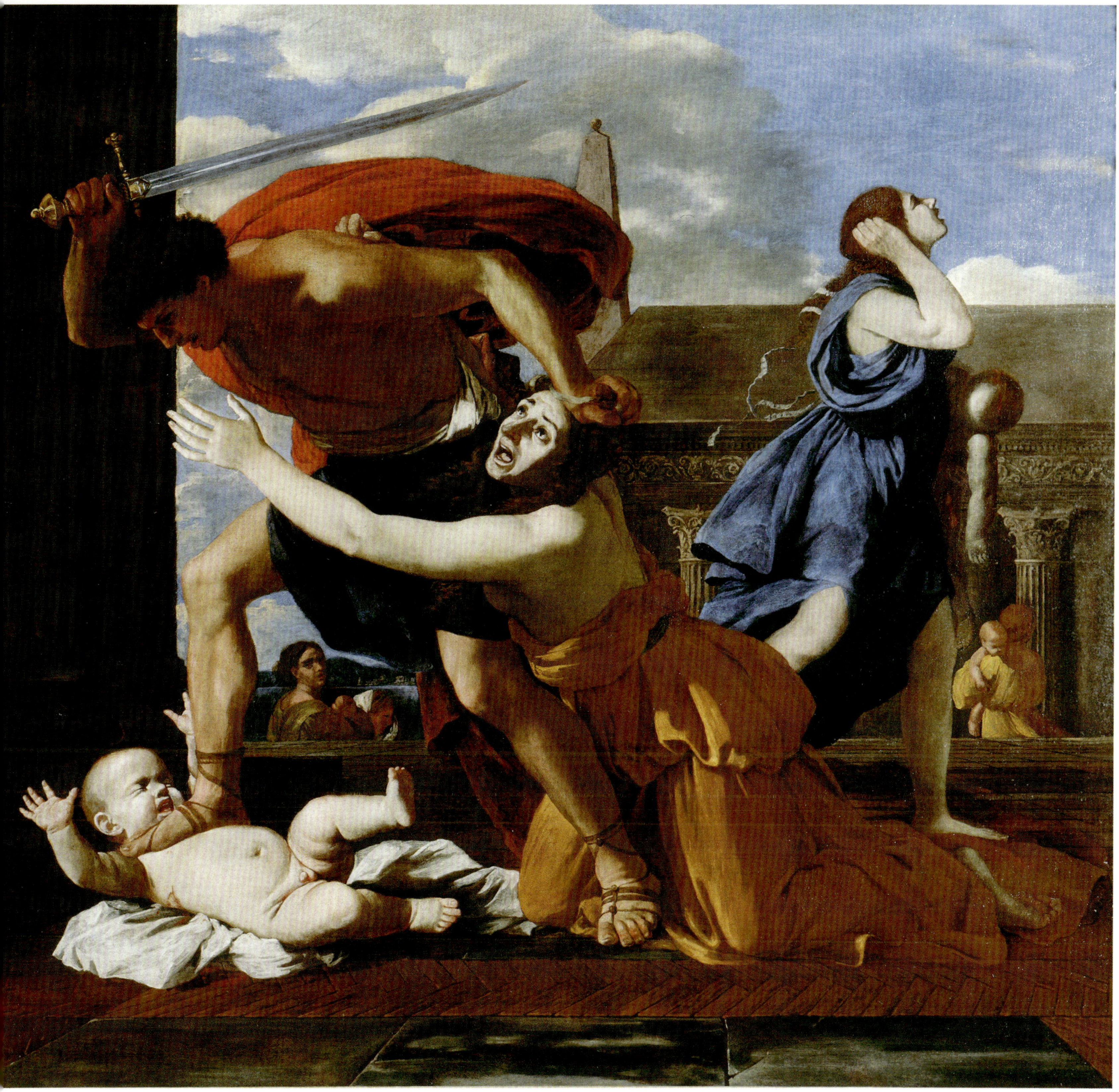

NICOLAS POUSSIN

(Les Andelys, 1594; Rome, 1665)

The Childhood of Bacchus

Canvas. H. 135 cm (4 ft. 5 in.); W. 168 cm (5 ft. 6 in.)
Inv. 298 (Galerie de Peinture)

In his early Roman period Poussin depicted many Bacchic scenes, including two works titled *The Nurture* [or *Childhood*] *of Bacchus* in the Louvre and National Gallery, London. The version here, although it has received less study due to darkened colors resulting from seepage of the brown ground, is more ambitious in size and content.

The subject derives from Ovid's *Metamorphoses*. Bacchus was the son of Jupiter and the nymph Semele. Jupiter's wife Juno, jealous of the pregnant Semele, convinced the nymph to beg the god to reveal himself to her in all his splendor; he agreed, at which point Semele was reduced to ash by Jupiter's thunderbolt. The god

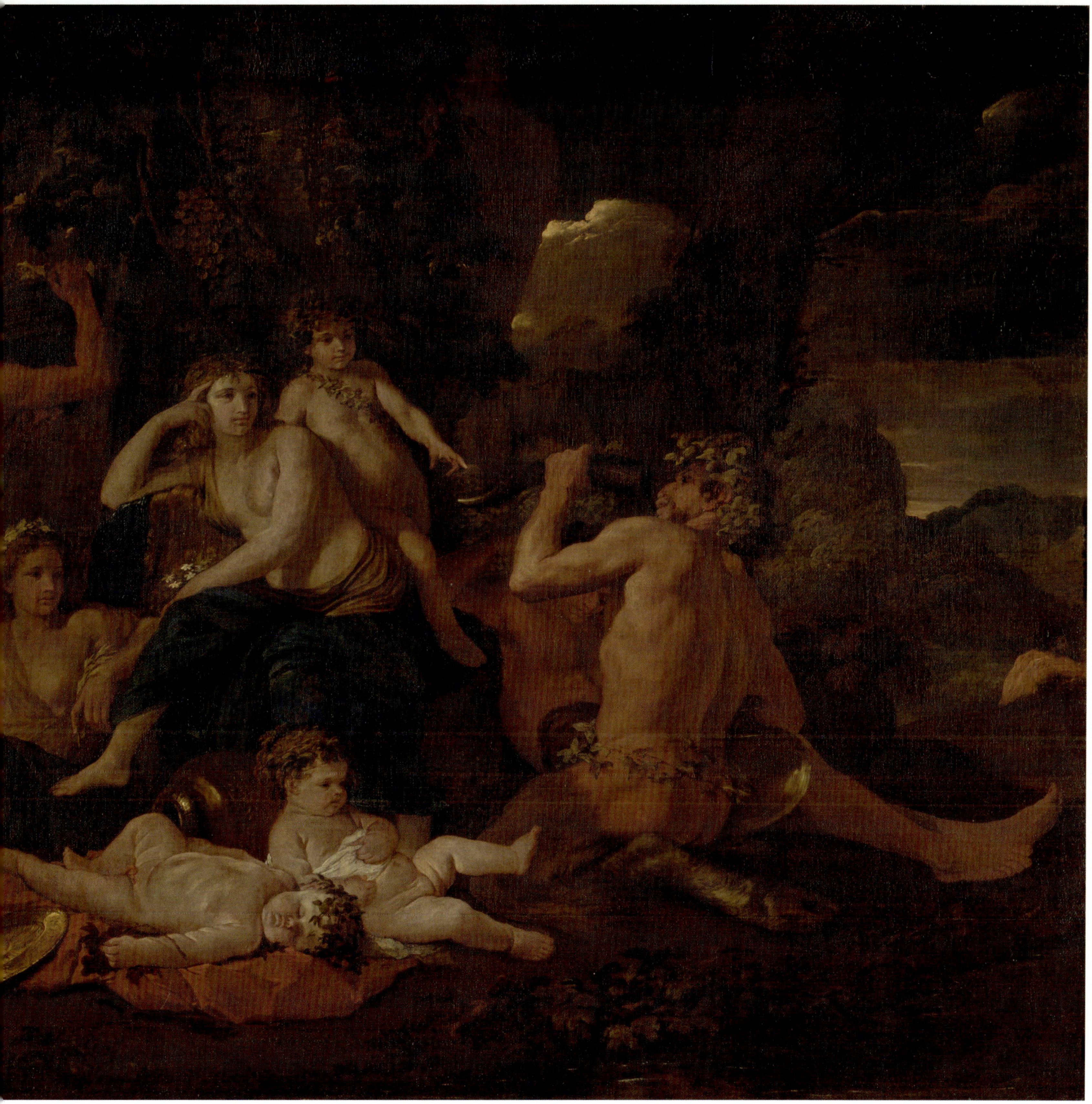

nevertheless saved the unborn child by placing him in his thigh. Once the infant was born, Mercury took Bacchus to Dirce and the nymphs on Mount Nysa, who hid him in their cave and nurtured him on milk, a beverage soon replaced by wine. Bacchus is presented here not as an infant but as a child-god: with an imperious gesture of his hand, he orders a satyr to drain a drinking horn. The infant in the foreground, asleep on his back, also figures in the Louvre's *Bacchanal with Guitar Player.*

The triangular composition of the group of figures, also employed in the Louvre and National Gallery versions, is based on a text by Blaise de Vigenère in *Les Images, ou tableaux de platte peinture de Philostrate* (1578), according to which a triangle represents Bacchus.

NICOLAS POUSSIN

(Les Andelys, 1594; Rome, 1665)

Theseus Finding his Father's Arms

Canvas. H. 98 cm (3 ft. 2 ½ in.); W. 134 cm (4 ft. 3 ¾ in.)
Inv. 300 (Tribune)

This incident from the life of Theseus is based on Plutarch. The son of Aegeus and Aethra, Theseus was brought up at Troezen by his grandfather Pittheus, who passed him off as the son of Poseidon. When the youth turned sixteen his mother Aethra revealed the secret of his birth and indicated the stone under which his father Aegeus had hidden his sword and sandals before leaving for Athens. Theseus managed to lift the block, then went to join his father, who was reigning at Athens. This scene, in which the future unifier of Attica discovers his roots, was depicted in ancient times in the form of a bronze sculpture on the Acropolis, which probably gave Poussin the idea of reviving it.

This *Theseus* is the product of an unusual collaboration between the history-painter Poussin and Jean Lemaire, a French artist who specialized in architectural pictures. Lemaire shared a studio with Poussin in Rome, and was probably one of the rare

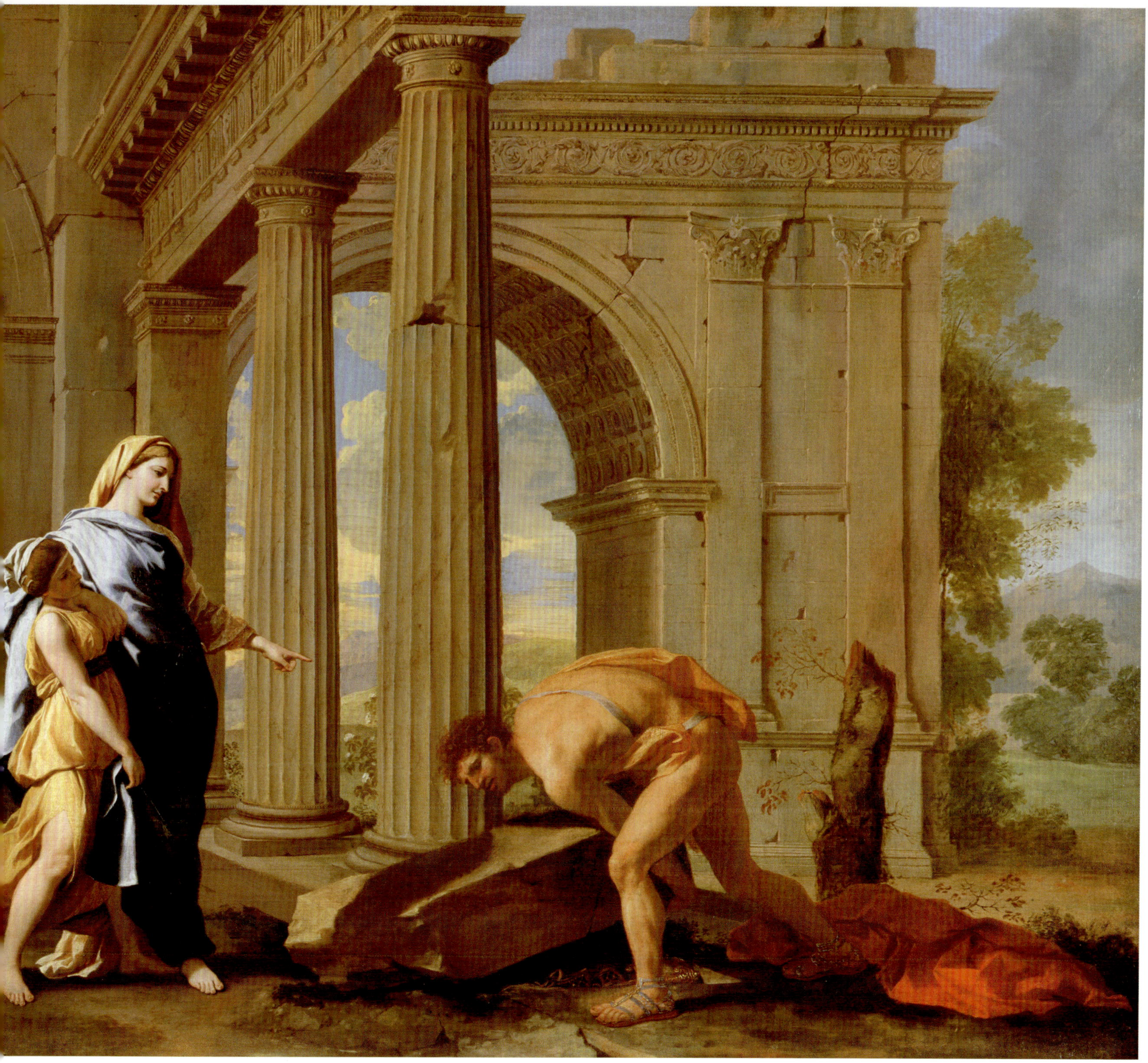

artists to work with him, according to Poussin's biographer, Félibien des Avaux. Lemaire probably painted the architectural elements behind the figures, as confirmed by X-ray analysis. The very highly sculptural pose of Aethra, meanwhile, reveals Poussin's working methods, for he modeled figurines in wax when making his paintings.

Among the various versions of this work, this one has been generally favored over another in Florence (Uffizi) by specialists ever since 1994, even though the latter is the one that was engraved in the seventeenth century. Indeed, the Musée Condé version contains many pentimenti, such as Theseus' foot, that are not found in the Uffizi version. Pentimenti are changes made as the artist works on the composition; they are painted over, hence initially invisible, but become ever more apparent as the layers of paint age, due to the phenomenon of the increasing transparency of oil paint.

NICOLAS POUSSIN

(Les Andelys, 1594; Rome, 1665)

Landscape with Two Nymphs and a Serpent

Canvas. H. 118 cm (3 ft. 10 in.); W. 179 cm (5 ft. 10 ½ in.)
Inv. 302 (Galerie de Peinture)

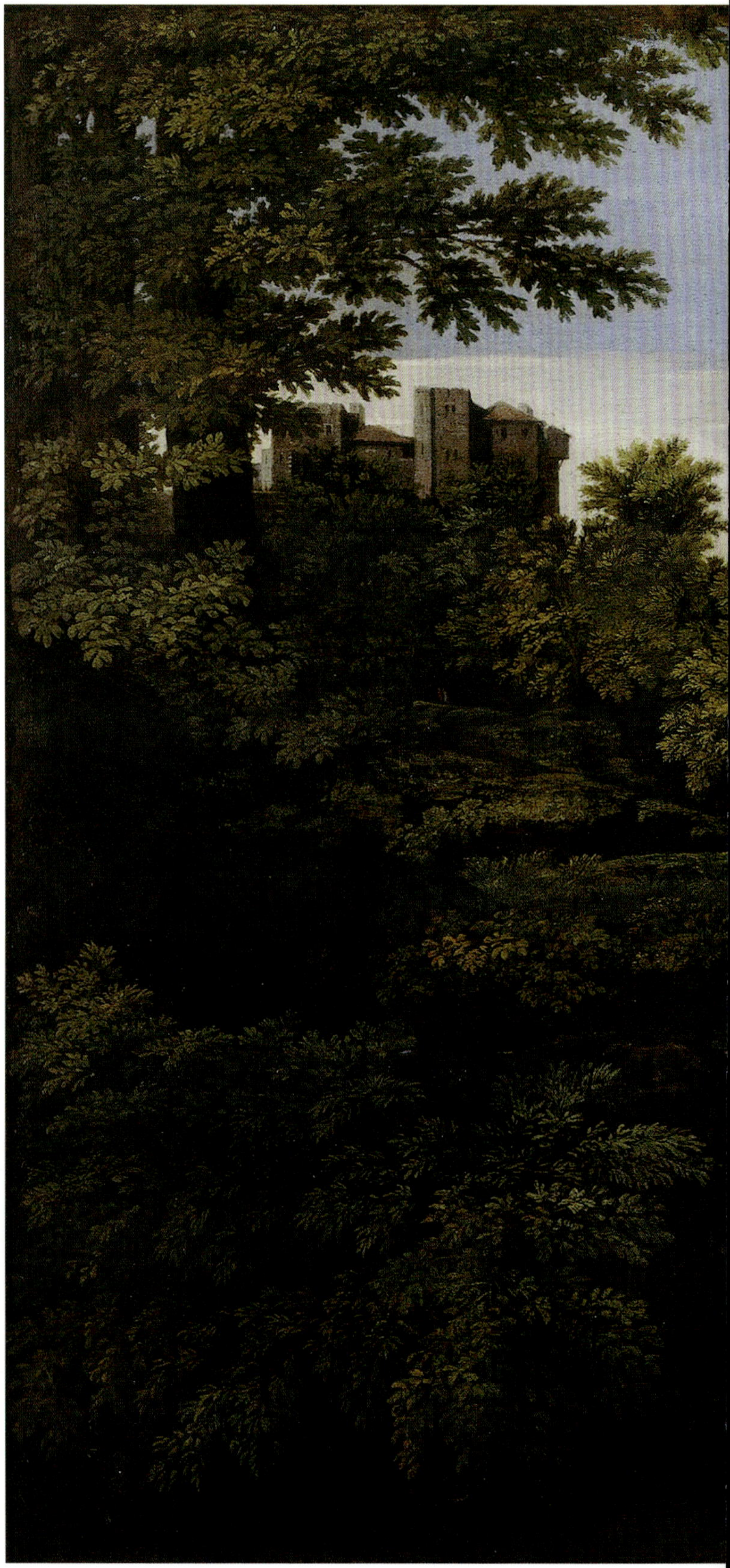

This is the latest of the five Poussin paintings now in the Musée Condé. Perhaps executed for Charles Lebrun in 1659, it is typical of the historical landscapes painted by Poussin toward the end of his life, when he roamed the Roman countryside with his friend Claude Lorrain. In the academic hierarchy of genres, landscape was a minor genre in comparison to the major one of history painting, which included human figures. Thus Poussin, as a history painter, incorporated mythological or historical figures into his landscapes. Already old and ill when he executed this work, he painted a meditation on the fleeting quality of human life versus the timelessness of nature.

The exact subject, which entails two nymphs fearlessly watching a snake attack a bird, remains mysterious. The motif of the snake was copied from a detail of an ancient mosaic in the temple of Preneste (Palestrina), now

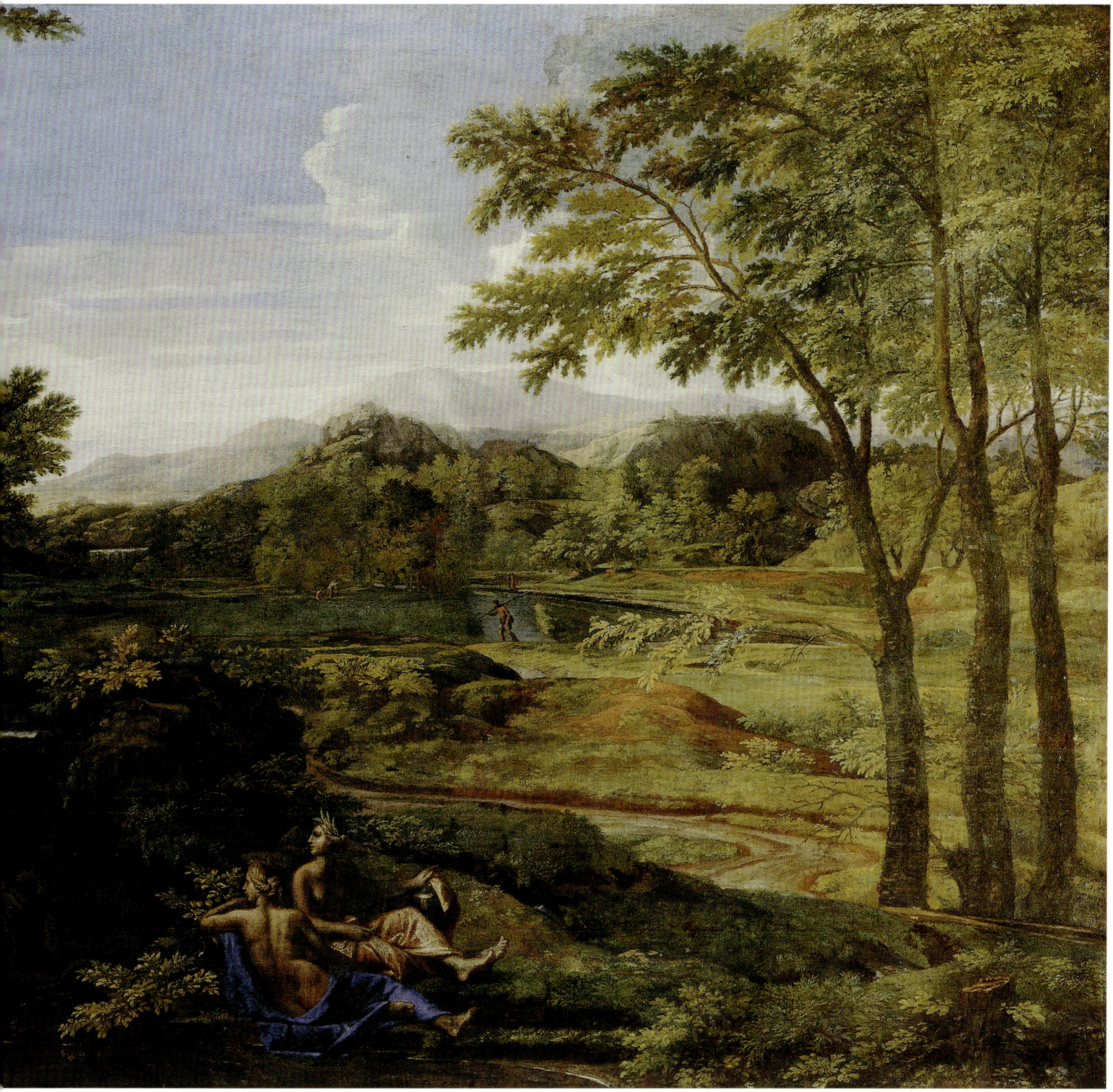

in the Palazzo Barberini (Museo Archeologico Nazionale, Rome); Poussin may have seen it in the *museo cartaceo,* the "museum of paper" compiled by his patron, Cassiano dal Pozzo (now in Windsor Castle). According to one theory, the scene was based on Ovid's *Metamorphoses,* and shows Demeter lying next to her daughter, who was seduced by Jupiter after the god transformed himself into a serpent. Other interpretations see the reclining nymphs as symbols of the two springs of the Aqua Claudia, which from the Renaissance onward represented Mount Parnassus and were sometimes confused with the Muses, who were patronesses of the wellsprings of imagination. As for the serpent, as a sign of health it might evoke the cleanliness of the water, which would explain why the nymphs are not alarmed by it. Some art historians, however, feel that the corrupting connotation of the snake is contrasted to the nymphs as symbols of the power and vitality of nature. It might be added that a snake frequently appears in Poussin's late paintings.

PIERRE MIGNARD

(Troyes, 1612; Paris, 1695)

Molière

Canvas. H. 55 cm (1 ft. 9 ½ in.);
W. 48.5 cm (1 ft. 7 in.)
Inv. 313 (Tribune)

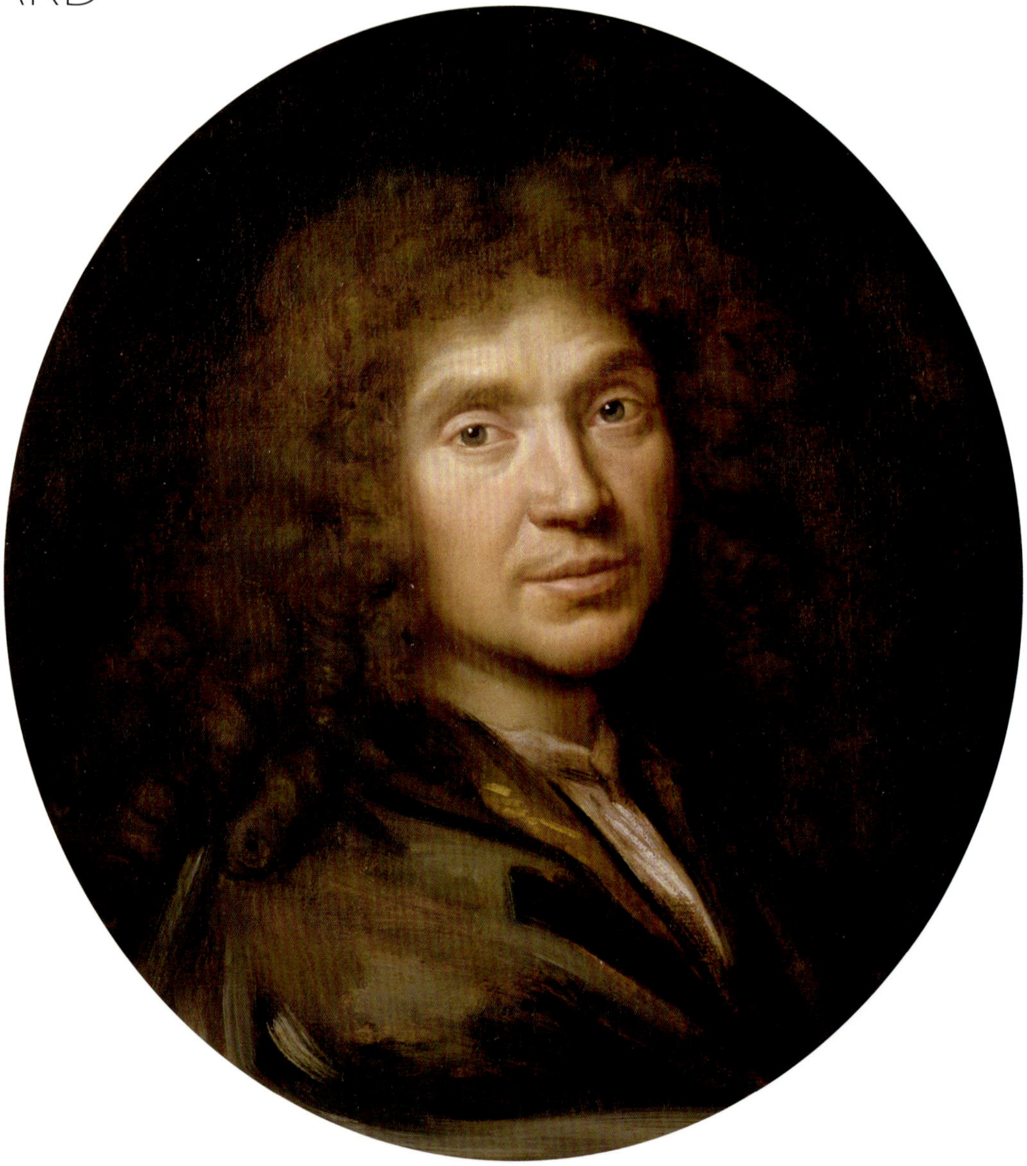

After training as an apprentice in the studio of Jean Boucher in Bourges, Pierre Mignard studied the prestigious artworks in the château at Fontainebleau, as did his elder brother Nicolas. He then entered the Paris studio of Simon Vouet and became friends with Charles Dufresnoy. In 1635, Mignard left for Rome, where he spent the next twenty years, making a living through portraiture and paintings of the Virgin. In 1654 he traveled to Venice and drew inspiration from Francesco Albani. On returning to France in 1657 his often flattering portraits of women were highly admired. However, being above all a history painter, he was commissioned to decorate the dome of the church of Val-de-Grâce in Paris in 1663. Having become the rival of Charles Lebrun, who headed the Académie Royale de Peinture, Mignard assumed leadership of the parallel Académie de Saint-Luc. Long excluded from royal projects, between 1677 and 1680 Mignard finally executed major decorative interiors for the Saint-Cloud chateau of the duc d'Orléans (destroyed, but known through engravings), then worked for the heir to the throne at Versailles, and ultimately painted the ceilings of the Petite Galerie and two adjoining salons at Versailles (1685, destroyed) for King Louis XIV himself. As a protégé of the marquis de Louvois, Mignard steadily supplanted Lebrun, to whose office he succeeded on Lebrun's death in 1690. Nearly eighty, Mignard then decorated the church of Les Invalides. He remains most famous, however, for his portraits.

Jean-Baptiste Poquelin, known as Molière (1622–1673), was the son of an upholster-merchant in service to the king. He was a pupil at the Jesuit school in Clermont and went on to study law before turning to the theater. In 1643 he founded the Illustre Théâtre with the Béjart family, but it failed. He then headed a troupe of traveling players for fifteen years (1643–1658). In 1659 he settled in Paris, where he wrote and performed plays for Louis XIV's court and for the Paris audiences; when his play *Tartuffe* triggered a scandal, he was protected by none other than the prince of Condé.

Mignard's portrait of Molière was engraved by Nolin in 1685, and was included in Perrault's gallery of *Hommes illustres qui ont paru en France pendant ce siècle* (Famous Men Who Appeared in France During this Century). Mignard had met Molière in Avignon in 1658, after having worked at Orange and Saint-Rémy, and became friends with him. This portrait was probably painted about that time, because Molière appears to be under forty.

PIERRE MIGNARD

(Troyes, 1612; Paris, 1695)

Cardinal Mazarin

Canvas. H. 65 cm (2 ft. 1 ¾ in.); W. 55.5 cm (1 ft. 9 ½ in.)
Inv. 314 (Tribune)

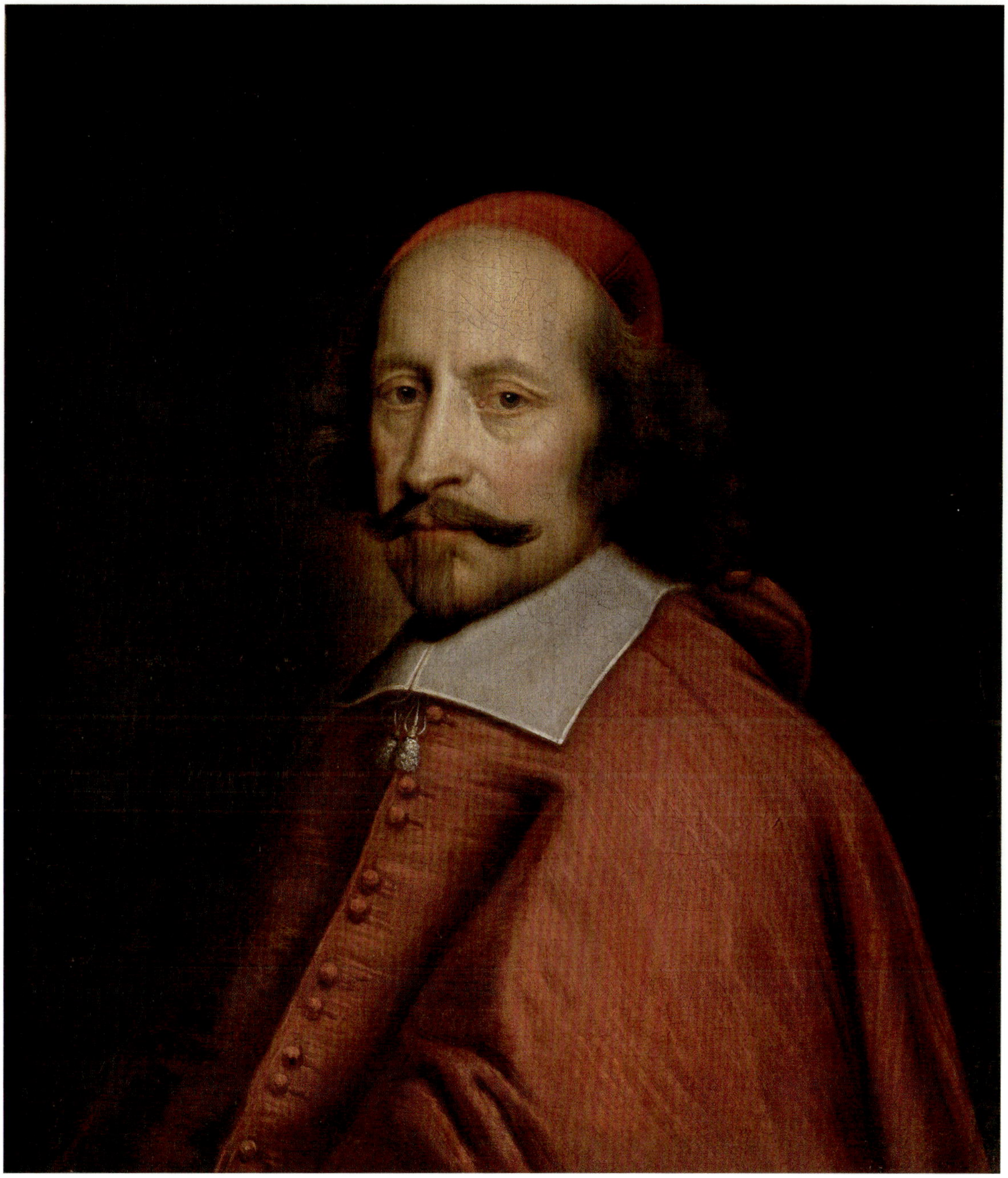

This portrait corresponds to an engraving by van Schuppen dated 1661 and others published by Nanteuil in 1660 and 1661. Another engraving of 1660, by F. Poilly, is based on an almost identical composition but is not flipped left–right with respect to this painting. Mignard therefore executed it shortly after his return from Italy in 1658, and certainly prior to 1660. Moreover, in 1730 Mazière de Monville wrote that Mignard "then went on to paint Cardinal Mazarin, whose portrait had been the undoing of every artist; the glory of success at it was reserved for Mignard, who outdid himself in this painting, which was universally considered the finest example of its kind."

It should nevertheless be noted that the face on the Musée Condé portrait is less affirmed than the one in the three engravings. Not only are the volumes softer, but the handling lacks overall emphasis, so it may simply be a good—perhaps partly autograph—replica.

ÉLISABETH-SOPHIE CHÉRON

(Paris, 1648; Paris, 1711)

Self-portrait

Canvas. H. 44.5 cm (1 ft. 5 ¾ in.); W. 40 cm (1 ft. 3 ¾ in.)
Inv. 321 (Salle Caroline)

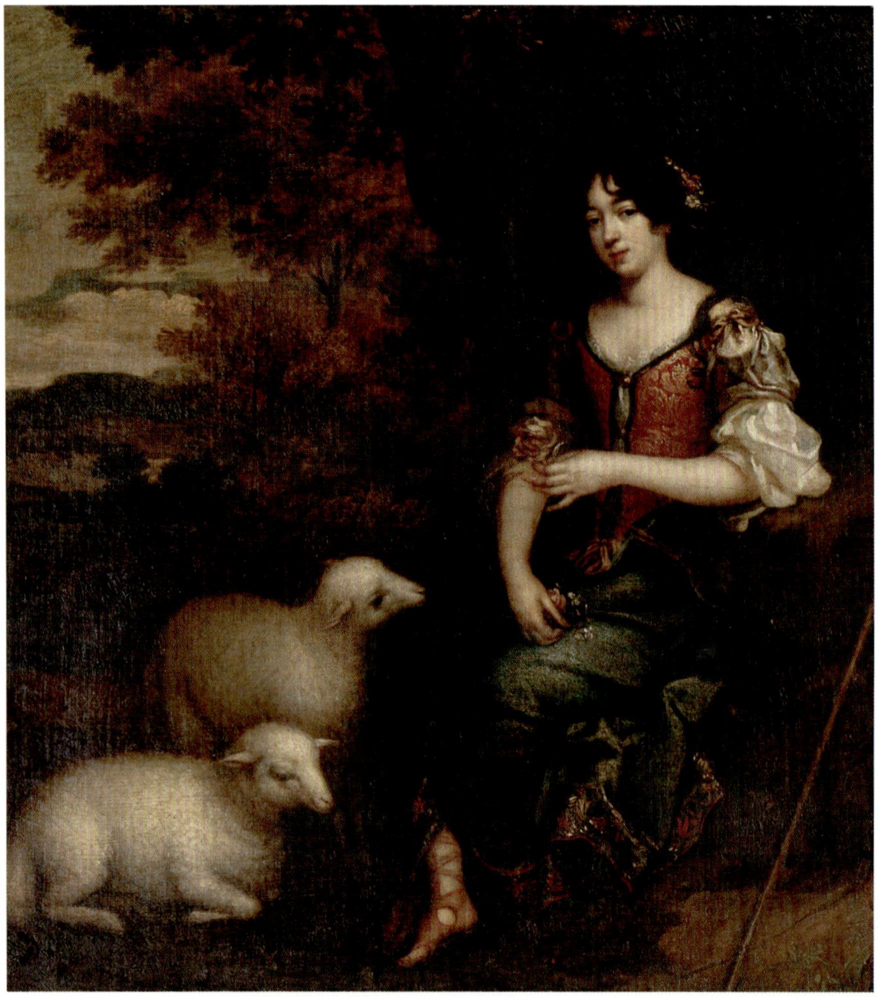

Élisabeth-Sophie Chéron studied under her father, the miniature portraitist Henri Chéron, who originally came from Meaux and died in 1677. Raised as a Protestant by her father—despite her Catholic mother—Élisabeth-Sophie converted to Catholicism at age fifteen. A gifted portraitist, she was admitted to the Académie Royale de Peinture on the recommendation of Charles Lebrun; her diploma works were a self-portrait (Louvre) and a portrait of the king's niece, known as Mademoiselle. Following the death of her first husband, Albert Godefroy, a court clerk from Avesnes, Élisabeth-Sophie married an engineer, Jacques Le Hay, in 1692. Also a poet, she was inducted into the Accademia dei Ricovrati in Padua under the name of Erato, alongside Madame Deshoulières. In consideration of her talents, she was awarded an annual stipend of four hundred livres by the king. Her brother Louis Chéron was an artist, as was her sister Anne, who married the portraitist Alexis-Simon Belle. Included among the painters mentioned in Voltaire's history of the seventeenth century, Élisabeth-Sophie also collected paintings and hosted literary gatherings in her home on rue de Grenelle. She played the lute with talent and was friends with Madame Dacier, Mademoiselle de Scudéry, Madame Deshoulières, and the art theorist Roger de Piles (who sided with Rubens in the controversy over color versus line). She furthermore collected ancient medallions and presented the Académie with an album of engravings after Raphael, to be used as a drawing book (*livre à dessiner*). Since her Louvre self-portrait (1672) is the only certain attribution, her painterly style—so praised by Lebrun—has to be gleaned from old engravings and descriptions.

The Musée Condé painting, long ascribed to Pierre Mignard (a flattering reference when it comes to portraiture) and thought to be a portrait of Madame Deshoulières, has now been attributed to Élisabeth-Sophie Chéron through comparison with the Louvre self-portrait. Here she depicts herself as a shepherdess with a crook and sheep in a bucolic landscape, reflecting the atmosphere of works inspired by Honoré d'Urfé's novel, *Astrée* (1607).

JUSTE D'EGMONT

(Leiden, 1601; Antwerp, 1674)

Equestrian Portrait of Louis XIV (1638–1715) Leaving for the Hunt as a Child

Wood. H. 41 cm (1 ft. 4 in.); W. 30 cm (1 ft.)
Inv. 582

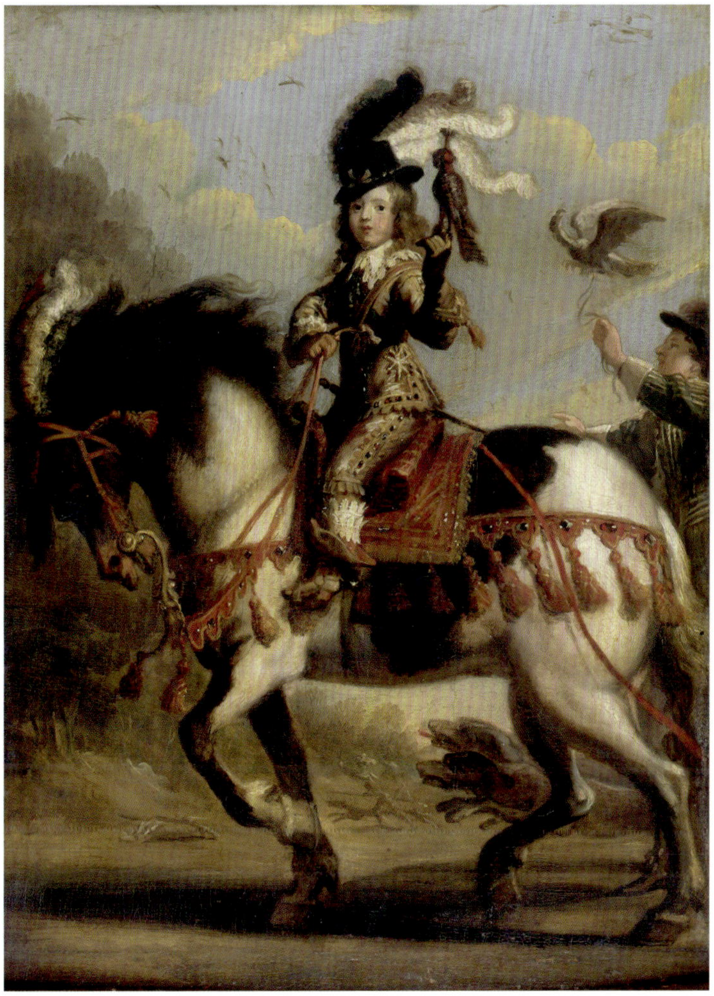

Formerly ascribed to Jean de Saint-Igny, this painting is now attributed to Flemish artist Theodore Juste d'Egmont, who studied under Rubens and lived in France from 1625–28, contributing to the decoration of the Medici gallery in the Palais du Luxembourg (Louvre). Juste d'Egmont did several equestrian portraits similar to this one, showing Louis XIII and Anne of Austria (Musée National du Château, Versailles). On returning to Paris prior to 1633, he quickly acquired a reputation as a portraitist and was named a painter to the king before 1636. He also painted several portraits of the prince of Condé at the battle of Rocroi.

A mirror-image engraving of this painting was done by Huart, with a caption that suggests the picture was a future vision of the moment when, "in order to enjoy the pleasures of the hunt, Louis will begin to ride horseback." Egmont shows a scene of falconry, a form of hunting dating back the Middle Ages, involving birds of prey on the fist of their master and lure birds that return to the lure held on a tether by the falconer. The young king—on a prancing piebald horse accompanied by dogs—is wearing the blue ribbon of the Order of the Holy Spirit over his embroidered, fawn-colored garment with lace cuffs; his left hand holds a hooded falcon, while a groom behind him recalls the lure birds

PHILIPPE DE CHAMPAIGNE

(Brussels, 1602; Paris, 1674)

Mother Angélique Arnauld (1591–1661), 1648

Canvas. H. 73 cm (2 ft. 4 ½ in.); W. 60 cm (1 ft. 11 ½ in.)
D.b.c.: *AGEE DE.57.ANS . 1648.*
Inv. 310 (Tribune)

As the abbess of Port-Royal, Mother Angélique Arnauld encouraged Jansenism, a philosophy endorsed by her "fine friends" such as Madame de Sablé, Madame de Longueville, and Madame de Sévigné. Jacqueline Arnauld, born in Tours in 1591, became a novice in 1599, and joined the abbey of Maubuisson under the name of Sister Angélique. She was named abbess of the Cistercian convent of Port Royal in 1602. There she led a pleasant life until, struck by a sermon by Father Basile, she decided to reform the abbey: she re-imposed the rule of Saint Benedict and restored monastic isolation, famously restricting her parents to the grated parlor window on September 25, 1609. She subsequently reformed Maubuisson, then returned to Port-Royal. In 1626, the community became too large and malaria struck the valley where it lay, so she moved to Paris and founded the abbey of Port-Royal de Paris. Finally, feeling once again in need of isolation, Mother Angélique returned to the original Port-Royal-des-Champs in 1648, where she remained until 1661 when the king insisted on changes in the abbey's hierarchy, the dismissal of pensioners, and a halt in receiving new novices. Mother Angélique returned to Paris where she died the same year.

The religious philosophy of Jansenism, associated with Port-Royal, appealed to Philippe de Champaigne. In 1648 he boarded his two daughters there and painted a portrait of the abbess, perhaps as thanks for accepting the girls. Champaigne also painted a portrait of the Jansenist abbot of Saint-Cyran, also placed behind a ledge, which might have been a pendant to this one. He furthermore painted the monks at Port-Royal, notably Antoine Singlin (J. Paul Getty Museum, Los Angeles) and writer Robert Arnauld d'Andilly (Louvre), who was Mother Angélique's elder brother. In an *Ex-Voto* of 1662 (Louvre), Champaigne painted his daughter, Sister Catherine de Sainte-Suzanne, a Port-Royal nun struck by paralysis in 1661, who recovered use of her legs following a novena decreed by Mother Agnès Arnauld (Mother Angélique's sister), seen praying at her side. In the château of Versailles there exists another example of the portrait of Mother Angélique that might be the original. The Musée Condé painting is nevertheless of very fine quality, although very worn and having undergone a transfer. It might be a replica by Champaigne himself or his nephew, Jean-Baptiste de Champaigne. The nun is dressed in the Port-Royal habit, adopted in 1647, of black veil and white scapular with cross. The heavy fabric of the mantle reinforces the hieratic stiffness of the portrait, while the cool palette is enlivened by the red cross.

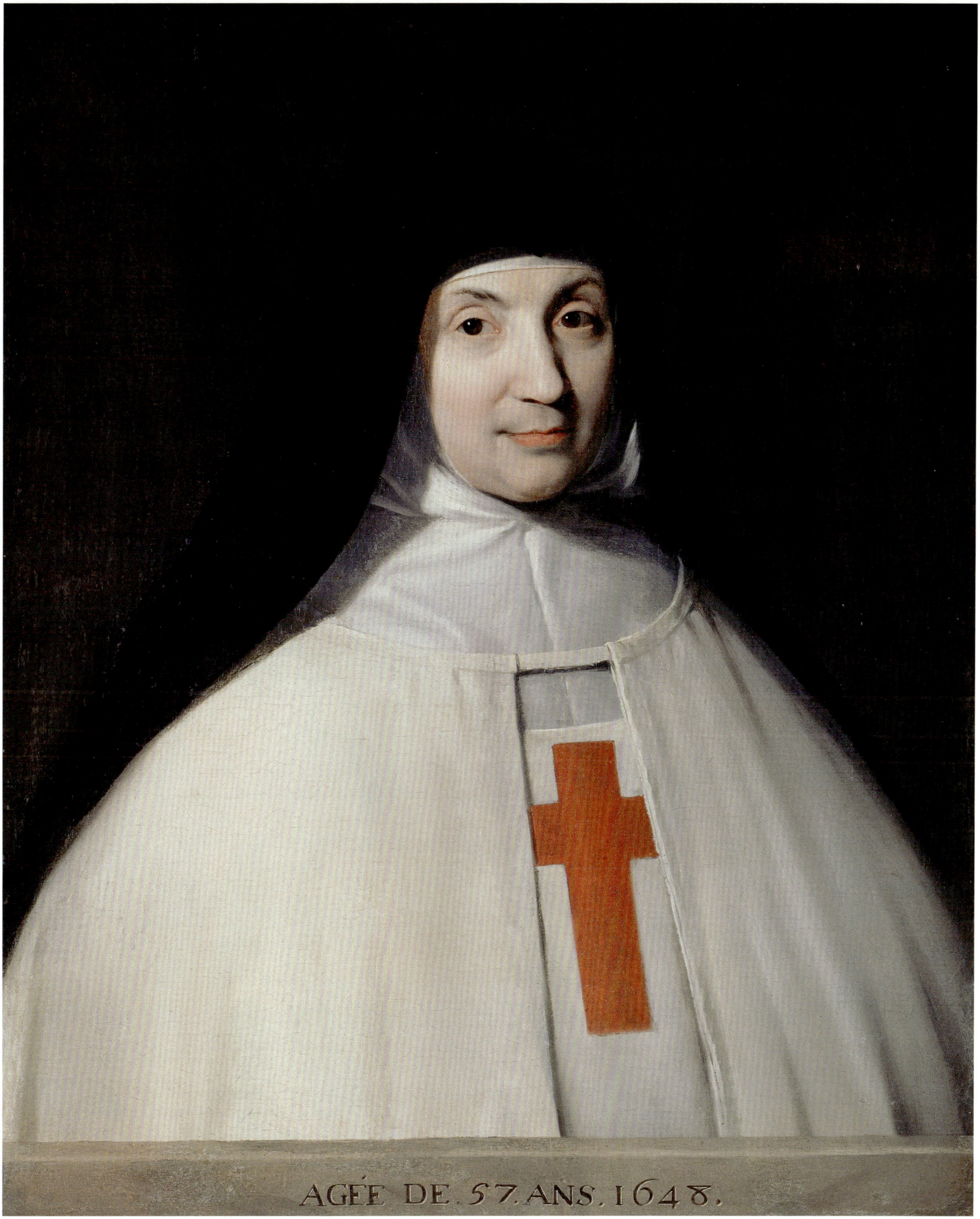
AGÉE DE. 57. ANS. 1648.

PHILIPPE DE CHAMPAIGNE

(Brussels, 1602; Paris, 1674)

Cardinal de Richelieu, 1636

Canvas. H. 205 cm (6 ft. 8 ½ in.); W. 144 cm (4 ft. 8 in.)
D.r. on the paper on the table: *1636*
Inv. 308 (Galerie de Peinture)

Philippe de Champaigne was born in Brussels, but at age twenty set off for Rome to train as an artist. Along the way he stopped in Paris, where he met Nicolas Poussin and decided to settle down. Appointed Painter in Ordinary to Queen Marie de' Medici in 1628, he became a naturalized Frenchman, with good connections to Cardinal de Richelieu after 1635. He and Simon Vouet collaborated on decorating the cardinal's "Gallery of Famous Men," and he began sympathizing with the Jansenists from 1643 onward even while remaining a court painter to Louis XIII and Louis XIV during the latter's minority, executing several portraits of the royal ministers and cardinals Mazarin and Richelieu.

Cardinal de Richelieu (Armand-Jean du Plessis) was Louis XIII's prime minister and Champaigne's main patron and sitter from 1635 to 1642. The artist did countless portraits of the cardinal, some of which were copied in his workshop. The Musée Condé portrait is dated 1636 on the piece of paper on the table. However, it might have been one of the paintings mentioned as early as 1635 in a "Record of Portraits of Monsignor the Cardinal Duke of Richelieu Made by Philippe de Champaigne, Painter, On the Orders of Said Monsignor," which includes "another life-size portrait, seated, wearing rochet and cappa magna." In that case, the painting would have been completed a little later. Being one of the portraits featuring a collar fastened by short drawstrings, it dates from the period when Richelieu avoided being shown in all the pomp of his rank of cardinal, whereas other works show him standing full-length in majesty (Sorbonne, Louvre, etc.); one of them, in the collection in the cardinal's own palace, was reproduced by Heince and Bignon in 1690. It would seem that Louis-Philippe, when duc d'Orléans, bought the portraits of Richelieu and Mazarin now in the Musée Condé at the 1820 Crawford sale in Paris, spurred by the fact that what is now the Palais-Royal (then home to the Orléans family) was originally the cardinal's palace, and both portraits were engraved in the gallery there. The duc d'Aumale acquired them during the auction of Louis-Philippe's property in 1851.

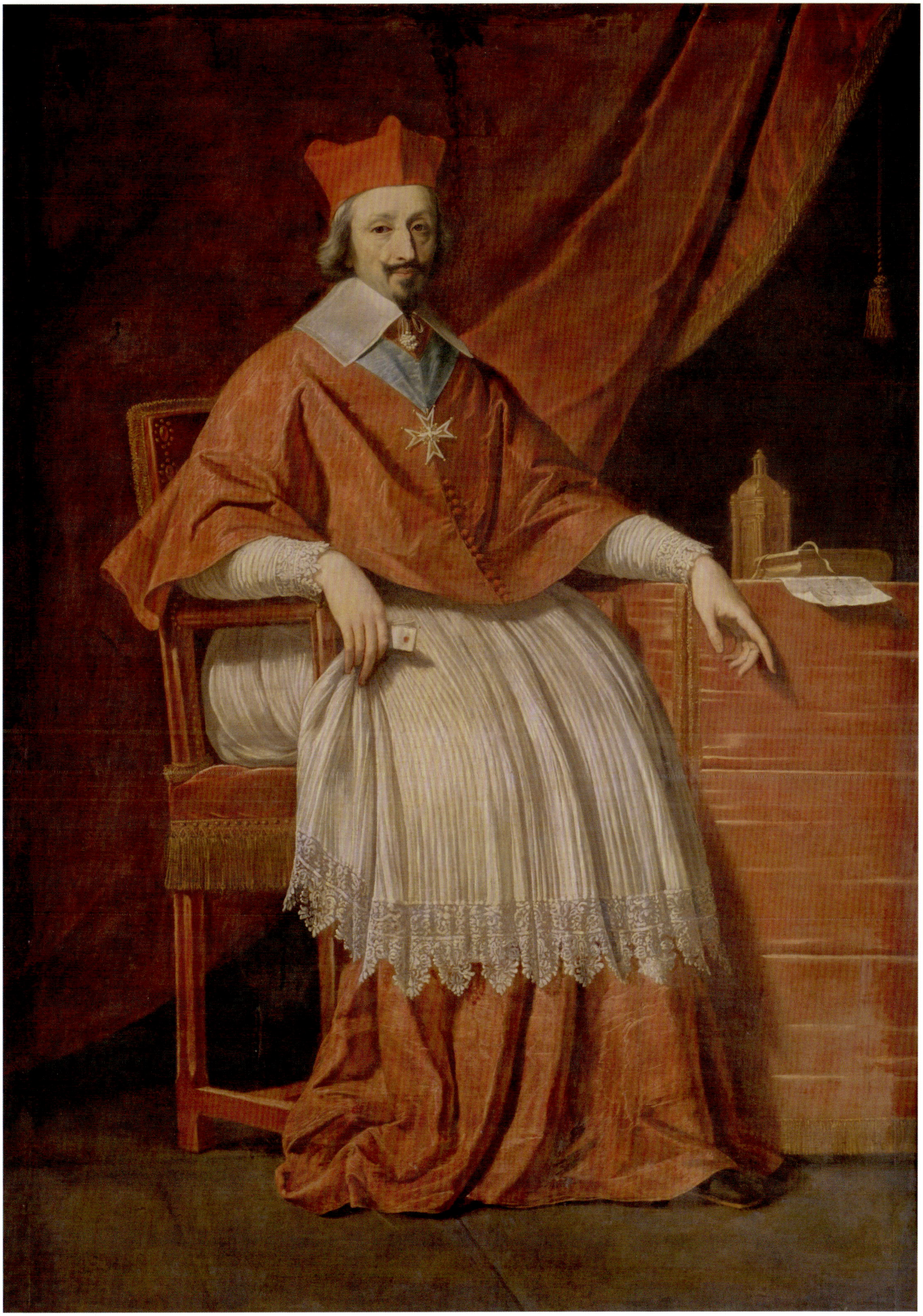

PHILIPPE DE CHAMPAIGNE

(Brussels, 1602; Paris, 1674)

Cardinal Jules Mazarin (1602–1661)

Canvas. H. 205 cm (6 ft. 8 ½ in.); W. 144 cm (4 ft. 8 in.)
Inv. 309 (Galerie de Peinture)

This portrait of Mazarin was part of King Louis-Philippe's collection in the Palais-Royal, and was acquired by the duc d'Aumale at the auction of his father's property in 1851. It was probably enlarged to form a pendant with the portrait of Richelieu (*see p. 172*), bought during the same sale, as witnessed by the visible strips added all around the edge.

Born in Abruzzo, Italy, and raised in Rome, Mazarin (Giulio Mazarini) went to Paris as a protégé of Cardinal de Richelieu, whom he succeeded in 1642. Mazarin served as prime minister to the queen regent, Anne of Austria, then to the young Louis XIV until his own death in 1661.

Here Champaigne produces a synthesis of realistic, meticulous Flemish portraiture and Paris courtly painting. The fine handling of this portrait reveals it to be an original. Guillet de Saint-Georges wrote that Champaigne painted several portraits of Mazarin. The first, apparently dating from 1647, is known only from an engraving; the second (Palazzo Barberini, Rome), dates from 1653 but is not considered to be in Champaigne's own hand; this one is the third, of which a smaller version exists (head and shoulders against plain ground, dated 1653). The presence of the keep of the castle of Vincennes in the background reminds the beholder that the cardinal was governor of Vincennes from 1652 until his death. It is therefore likely that the portrait was painted around 1653, or at any rate after October 11, 1652, the date of death of the previous governor, Léon Le Bouthillier, comte de Chavigny.

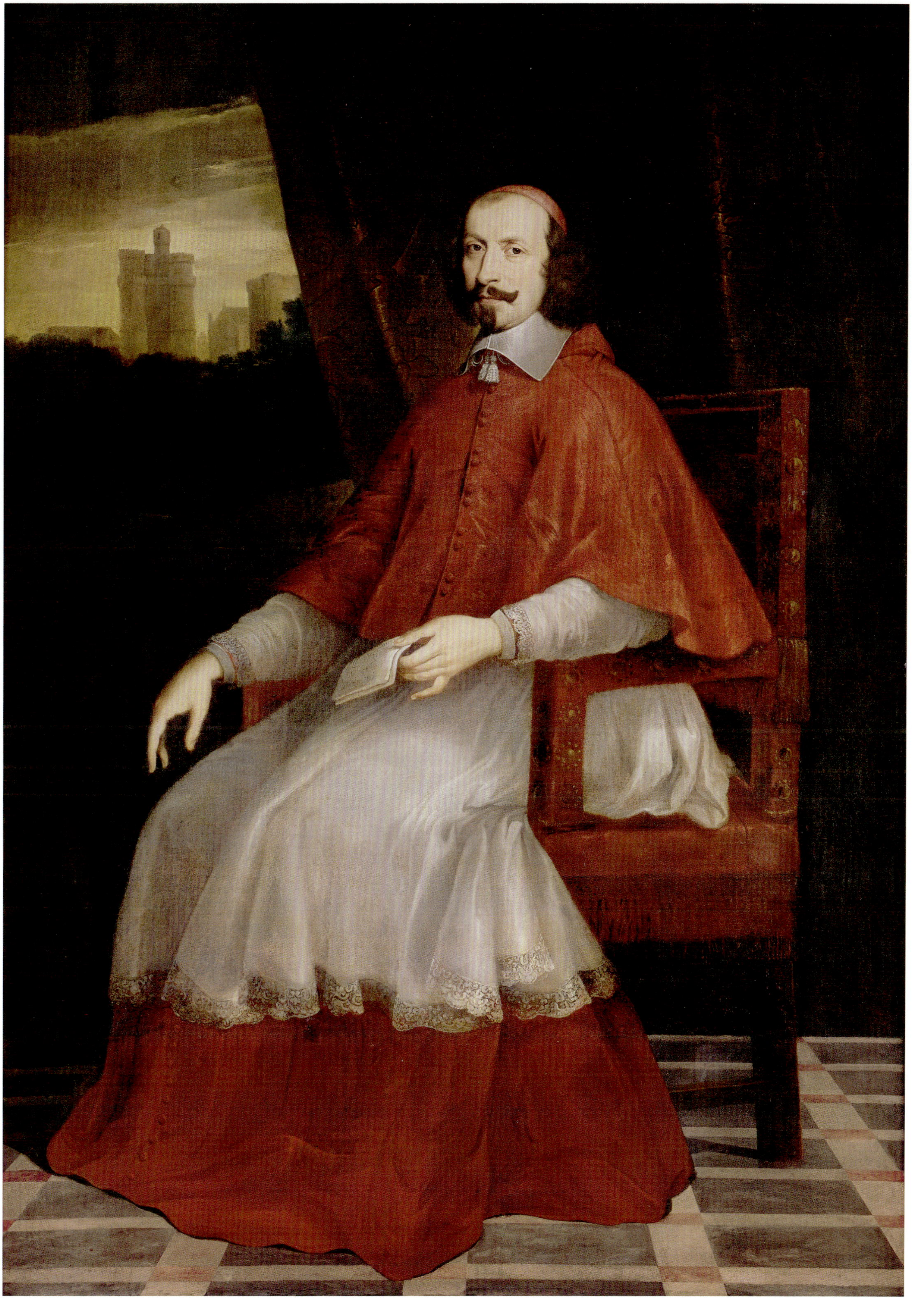

NICOLAS DE LARGILLIERRE

(Paris, 1656; Paris, 1746)

Portrait of a Woman as an Allegory of Spring, formerly called *The Princess Palatine*

Canvas. H. 65 cm (2 ft. 1 ¾ in.); W. 54 cm (1 ft. 9 ½ in.)
Inv. 331 (Rotonde de la Minerve)

In 1847 the duc d'Aumale bought this painting from a dealer in curios named Henry, who sold it as a portrait by an unknown artist of an unknown lady from the reign of Louis XV. While the artist was certainly Nicolas de Largillierre (or Largillière), the identity of the sitter has proven harder to establish. In the late nineteenth century she was thought to be Elisabeth Charlotte of the Palatinate, daughter of Charles I Louis, the Elector Palatine. Born in Heidelberg in 1652, she married Philippe, duc d'Orléans (the brother of King Louis XIV), on November 16, 1671. Her correspondence has become a precious source of information on the French court under Louis XIV. In a 1698 letter she described herself as follows: "My waist is monstrously large, I am as square as a cube; my skin is red, freckled with yellow; my hair is going completely gray; my nose has been spotted by smallpox, as have my cheeks; my mouth is big, my teeth rotten." She died at Saint Cloud in 1722, aged seventy. She was therefore already too old to be the sitter of this early eighteenth-century portrait; nor is there any resemblance with Drevet's engraving of her, after a portrait by Rigaud, which served as the frontispiece to the funeral service for the princess. Indeed, Rigaud painted an official portrait of the sixty-one-year-old princess at Marly in 1713 at the request of the duc d'Orléans. She had several replicas made in order to give them as presents (one version, signed and dated 1716, went to Duke August Wilhelm von Braunschweig; another, dated 1718, is now in Geneva (Musée d'Art et d'Histoire); other replicas are conserved at Versailles, Budapest, and Heidelberg. Compared to the woman here, the Princess Palatine appears older, her face is squarer, and she is stouter.

This painting was one of the *ricordi,* or reduced versions of paintings by Largillierre that he executed and archived in his studio. It is therefore a replica of a larger original that recently came on the art market identified as a representation of the duchesse de Berry, Marie-Louis-Élisabeth d'Orléans (1695–1719), who was the daughter of the French Regent and who married Charles, the third son of the Grand Dauphin, in 1710; she died at the château de La Muette at the age of twenty-four.

The motif of associating the sitter with a gushing spring against reeds and sky in the background was notably developed by Largillierre and pursued by Nattier in the middle of the eighteenth century.

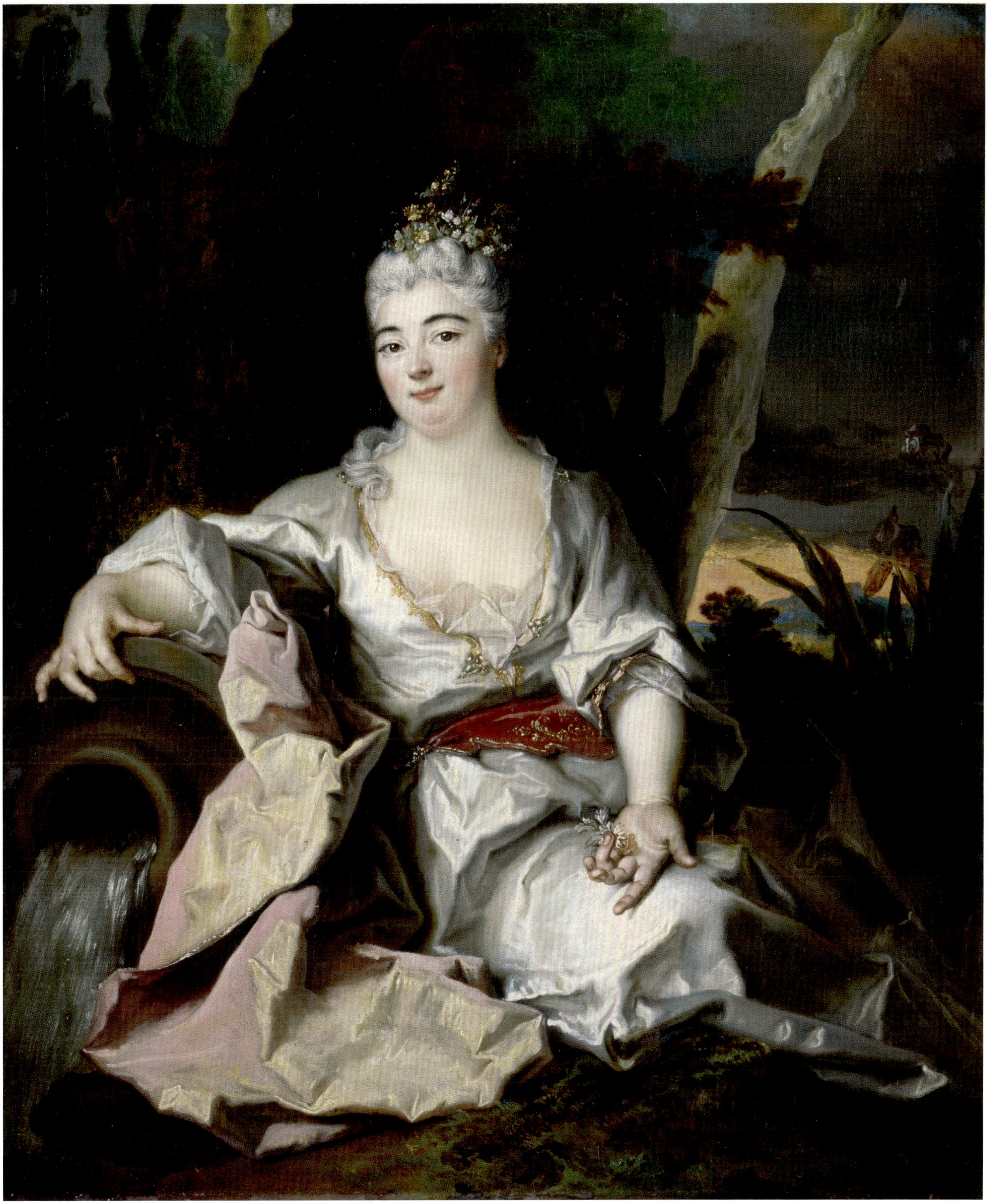

NICOLAS DE LARGILLIERRE

(Paris, 1656; Paris, 1746)

Mademoiselle Duclos in the Role of Ariadne

Canvas. H. 65 cm (2 ft. 1 ¾ in.); W. 53.5 cm (1 ft. 9 in.)
Inv. 330 (Salle Caroline)

A beautiful actress who went by the stage name of Mademoiselle Duclos, Marie-Anne Châteauneuf (1664–1748) first performed with the Comédie-Française on October 17, 1683, aged nineteen. She had begun her career at the Opera, where a student and friend of Molière's named Baron noticed her and bought her to the Comédie-Française, where she replaced Mademoiselle Champmeslé (1642–1698) in the leading tragic roles. Duclos notably played Josabeth in *Athalie* and the title role in *Esther,* two plays by Racine, then portrayed Salomé in *Marianne* and Jocasta in *Oedipe* by Voltaire. In 1726, aged over sixty, Mademoiselle Duclos married a young man of seventeen, Pierre-Jacques Duchemin, who beat her, at which point she sued for an annulment. She died at the age of eighty-four.

Here Nicolas de Largillierre (or Largillière) shows her playing the role of Ariadne in a tragedy of the same name by Thomas Corneille, which was a hit from 1672 onward. Here the tearful Ariadne, daughter of Minos and Pasiphae, is wearing a magnificent velvet gown the color of amaranth. She is weeping over the departure of Theseus, who has abandoned her on the island of Naxos. In the background, we see Bacchus on the right, holding his thyrsus, pointing to Ariadne for the benefit of the satyrs accompanying him. Above Ariadne, Cupid is holding a crown of nine stars (the *Corona Borealis*) in his left hand, yet with his right hand also presents the actress with a laurel wreath, scepter, and theater mask, attributes of the muse of tragedy, Melpomene. In 1712 Largillierre painted a larger version of this portrait for the sitter herself (Musée de la Comédie-Française, Paris). Several replicas have surfaced on the art market in the past, one of which is now in the J.B. Speed Museum of Art in Louisville, Kentucky. The smaller version here was apparently painted for Titon du Tillet, in whose home d'Argenville saw it in 1752. Although oil sketches by Largillierre are rare, he regularly executed *ricordi* (small replicas) that he archived in his studio (*see p. 176*), of which this painting is an example. An engraving was made of the portrait by Louis Desplaces in 1714.

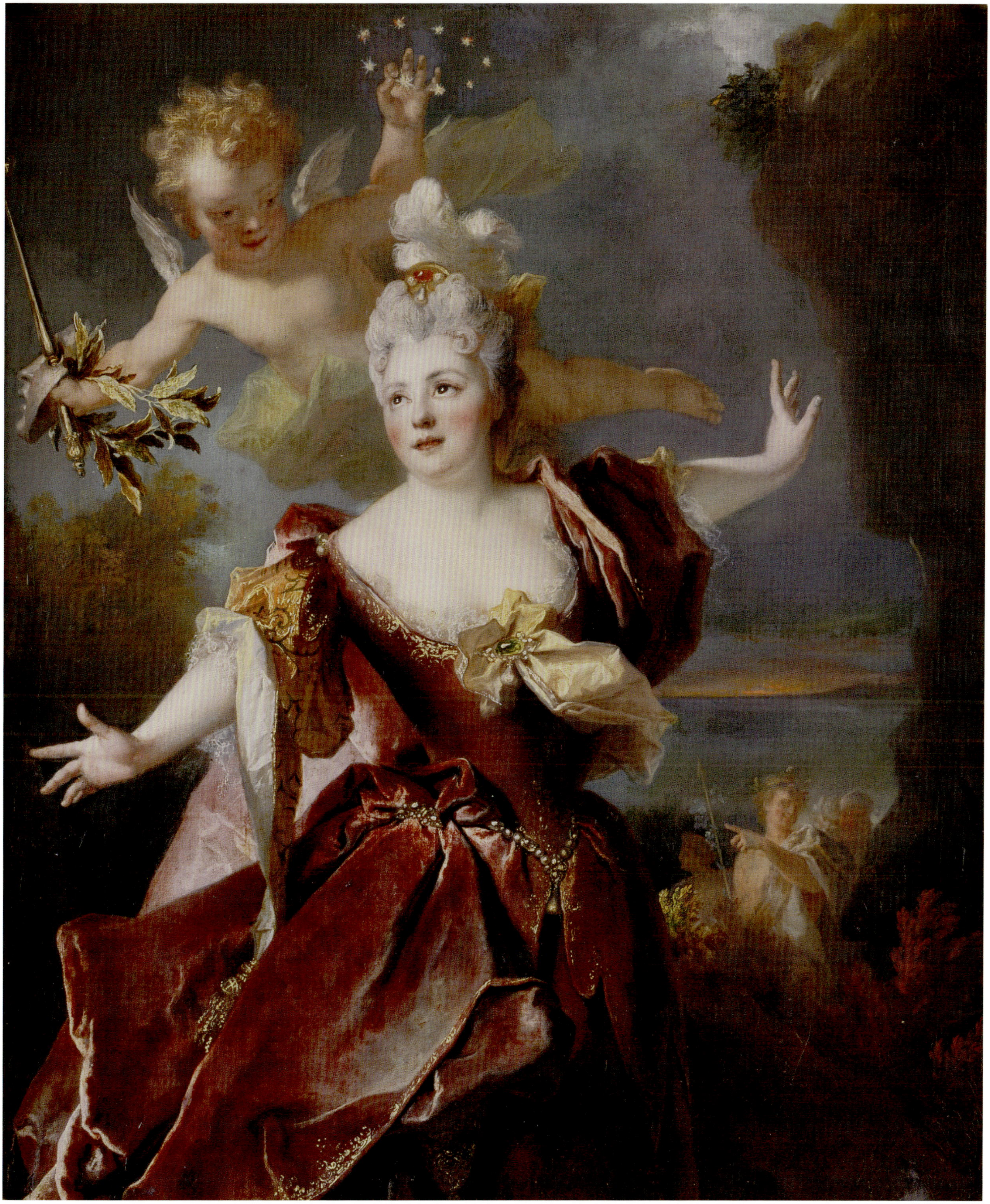

NICOLAS DE LARGILLIERRE

(Paris, 1656; Paris, 1746)

Anne-Thérèse de Marquenat de Courcelles, Marquise Lambert

Canvas. H. 111 cm (3 ft. 7 ¾ in.); W. 95 cm (3 ft. 1 ¾ in.)
Inv. 332 (Galerie de Peinture)

This painting was alleged to be a portrait of the princess of Rohan-Guéménée when the duc d'Aumale acquired it in 1846. The sitter has alternatively been identified as Marie de Laubespine, wife of Nicolas Lambert de Thorigny, the chief magistrate of the Chambre des Comptes; but an engraving by Pierre Drevet of Largillierre's portrait of Marie differs from the one here, despite the graceful pose of the hands and the shimmering fabrics common to both works—nor do the sitters resemble one another.

So this appears to be, instead, a portrait of Anne-Thérèse de Marquenat de Courcelles, the widow of Marquis Lambert, for it is similar to Étienne Desrochers' mirror-image engraved portrait. Both portraits feature the same drapery across the bust—the only notably differences between canvas and engraving concern the absence of an arm and the change in hairstyle, the latter probably brought up to date when the plate was engraved.

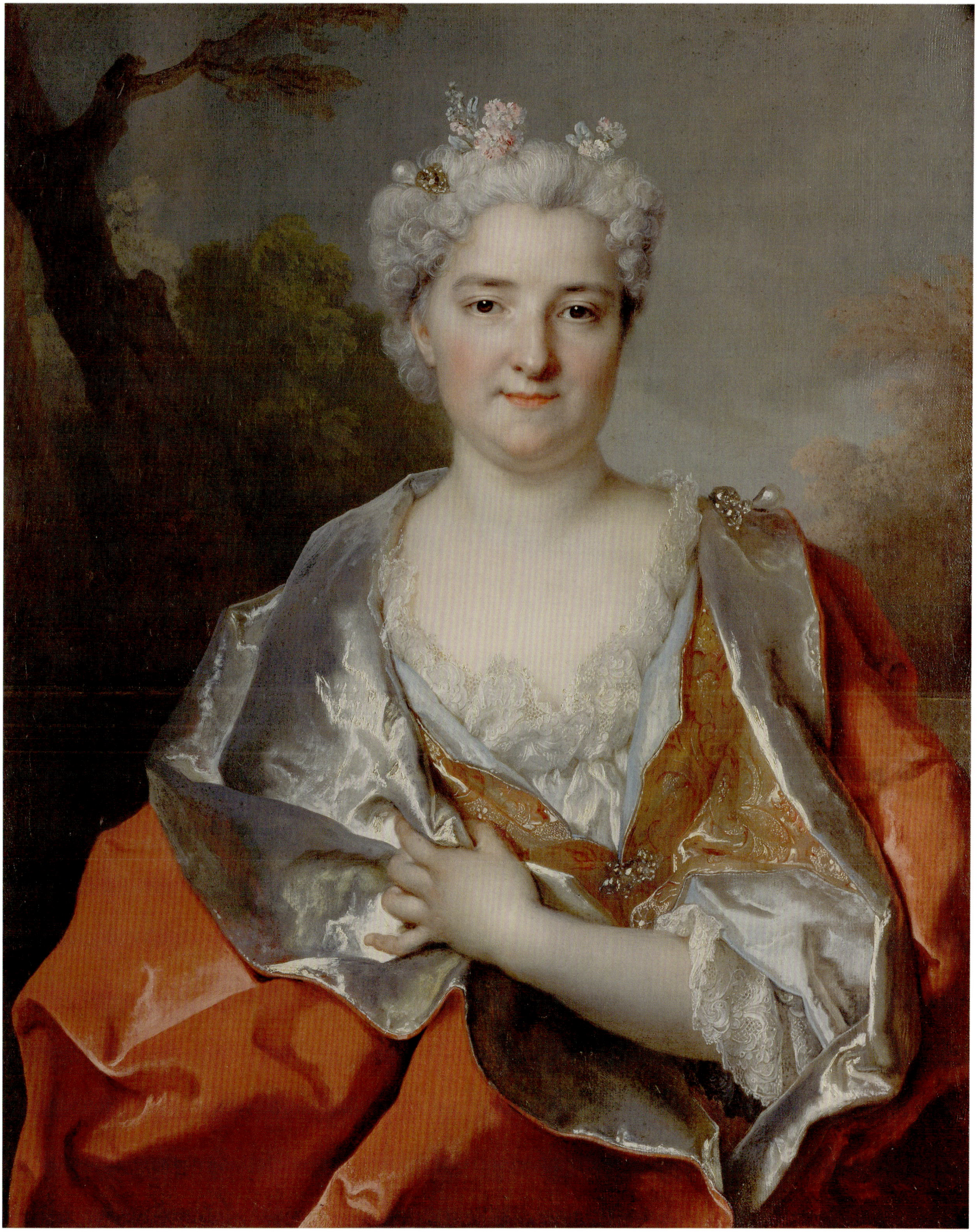

SAUVEUR LE CONTE

(?, 1659; Paris, 1694)

The Battle of Rocroi, May 19, 1643

Canvas. H. 293 cm (9 ft. 7 in.); H. 335 cm (11 ft.)
Inv. 354 (Galerie des Actions de M. le Prince)

The Great Condé (*see p. 188*) commissioned Sauveur Le Conte to paint eleven large paintings of his most valiant military exploits between 1640 and 1674. But the prince of Condé died before they were hung in the gallery at Chantilly, which was only completed under his son, Prince Henry-Jules. Le Conte appears to have been the veritable lieutenant, rather than mere assistant, of Adam François van der Meulen, who was the great battle painter on Charles Lebrun's decorative team. Le Conte was also the son of a master artist, Mainfrain Le Conte, and he married the daughter of Jean Legeret, a sculptor-decorator who worked at Versailles. Trained by van der Meulen, Le Conte was charged with completing the master's unfinished paintings at his death and succeeded him to the title of Painter in Ordinary of the King's Conquests at the Royal Manufactory of Les Gobelins. In 1692 he was listed among the famous artists in Abraham du Pradel's *Livre Commode:* "Le Conte, a painter of battle scenes at Les Gobelins." He notably painted the *Capture of Mons* (Musée de Versailles) in 1693 for the royal residence at Marly, prior to his sudden death at age thirty-five.

The battle of Rocroi was the Great Condé's first major military victory. On May 19, 1643, the twenty-two year-old duc d'Enghien (as he was then styled) saved France from a Spanish invasion at the very moment that King Louis XIII died. The main scene is accompanied by seven secondary scenes, including an "order of battle" given underneath, as inspired by contemporary engravings. Le Conte composed the main section as a bird's-eye view of the scene, painting it with greater freedom and expressiveness than the smaller, more documentary medallions surrounding it.

In 1643, war between France and the Habsburgs of Vienna and Madrid had already been raging for eight years. Just as the Spanish troops were preparing to invade France, the dying Richelieu advised Louis XIII to place command of his armies in the hands of the young duc d'Enghien. At Rocroi, the duke boldly decided to charge the Spanish at the head of eight cavalry squadrons. This is the moment Le Conte chose to depict, showing Enghien on a white horse, with a white feather in his cap, standing in his stirrups to lead his troops at a gallop. The situation soon turned to the advantage of the French—the Spanish suffered eight thousand dead and seven thousand prisoners. Instead of racing back to Paris to receive his reward, Enghien marched on Thionville, a stronghold on the Moselle that controlled access to the Low Countries; after fifty-six days of siege, the fortress fell on August 8, as shown in the three medallions on the left, *An Elevation, A Map of the Military Situation,* and *The Siege of Thionville.* The future "Great Condé" then went on to besiege Sierck, near Thionville, which fell after twenty-four hours on September 3, as depicted on the right in *An Elevation, Map of the Military Situation,* and *Siege of Sirck* [sic].

FOLLOWING PAGES
The Gallery of Battles as the duc d'Aumale knew it.

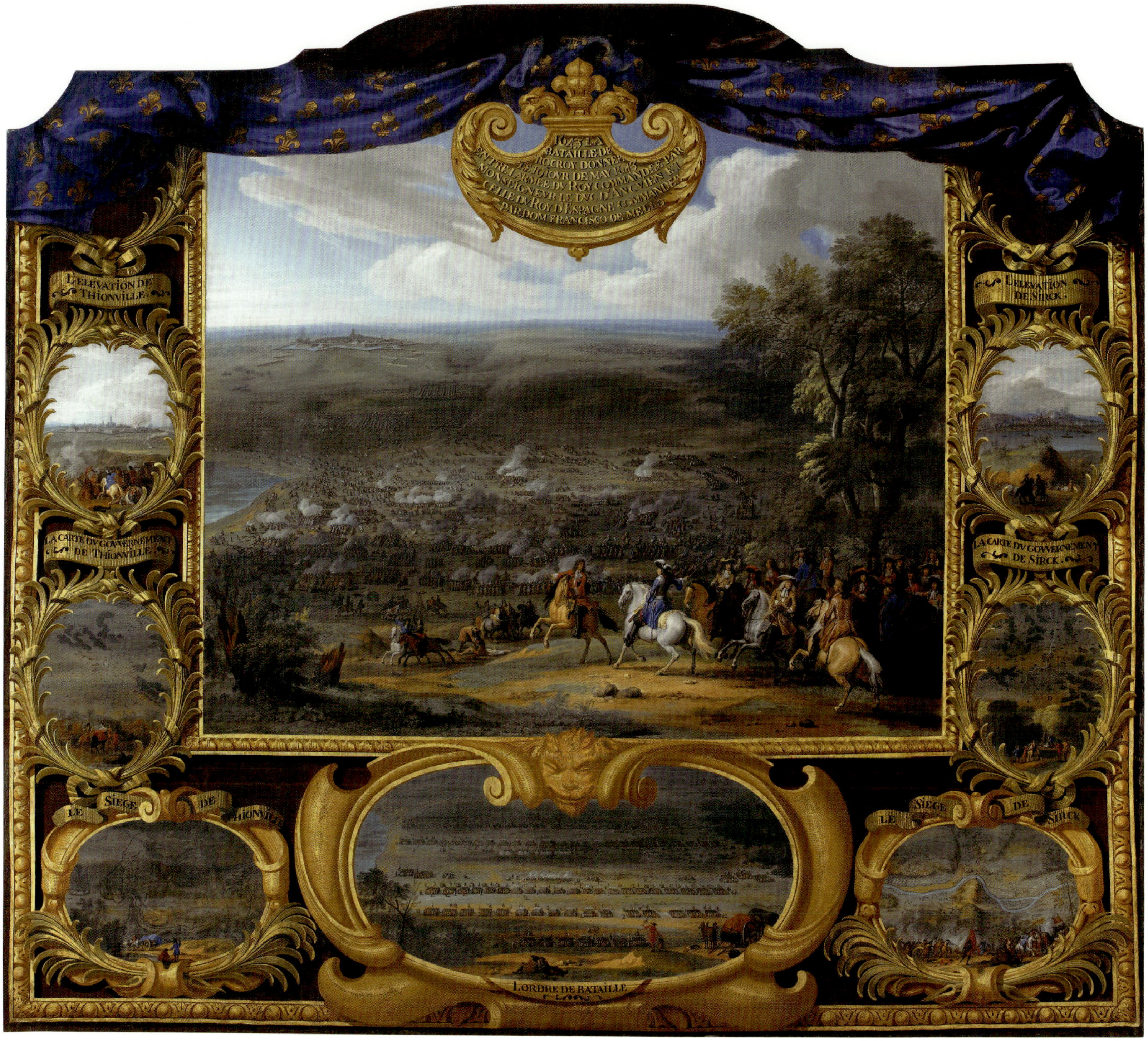
1643 LA
BATAILLE DE
ROCROY DONNEE
ENTRE LE 19 IOVR DE MAY 1643
LARMEE DV ROY COMMANDEE PAR
MONSEIGNEVR LE DVC D'ANGVIEN ET
CELLE DV ROY D'ESPAGNE COMMANDEE
PAR DOM FRANCISCO DE MELLO
L'ELEVATION DE THIONVILLE
LA CARTE DV GOVVERNEMENT DE THIONVILLE
LE SIEGE DE THIONVILLE
L'ELEVATION DE SIRCK
LA CARTE DV GOVVERNEMENT DE SIRCK
LE SIEGE DE SIRCK
L'ORDRE DE BATAILLE

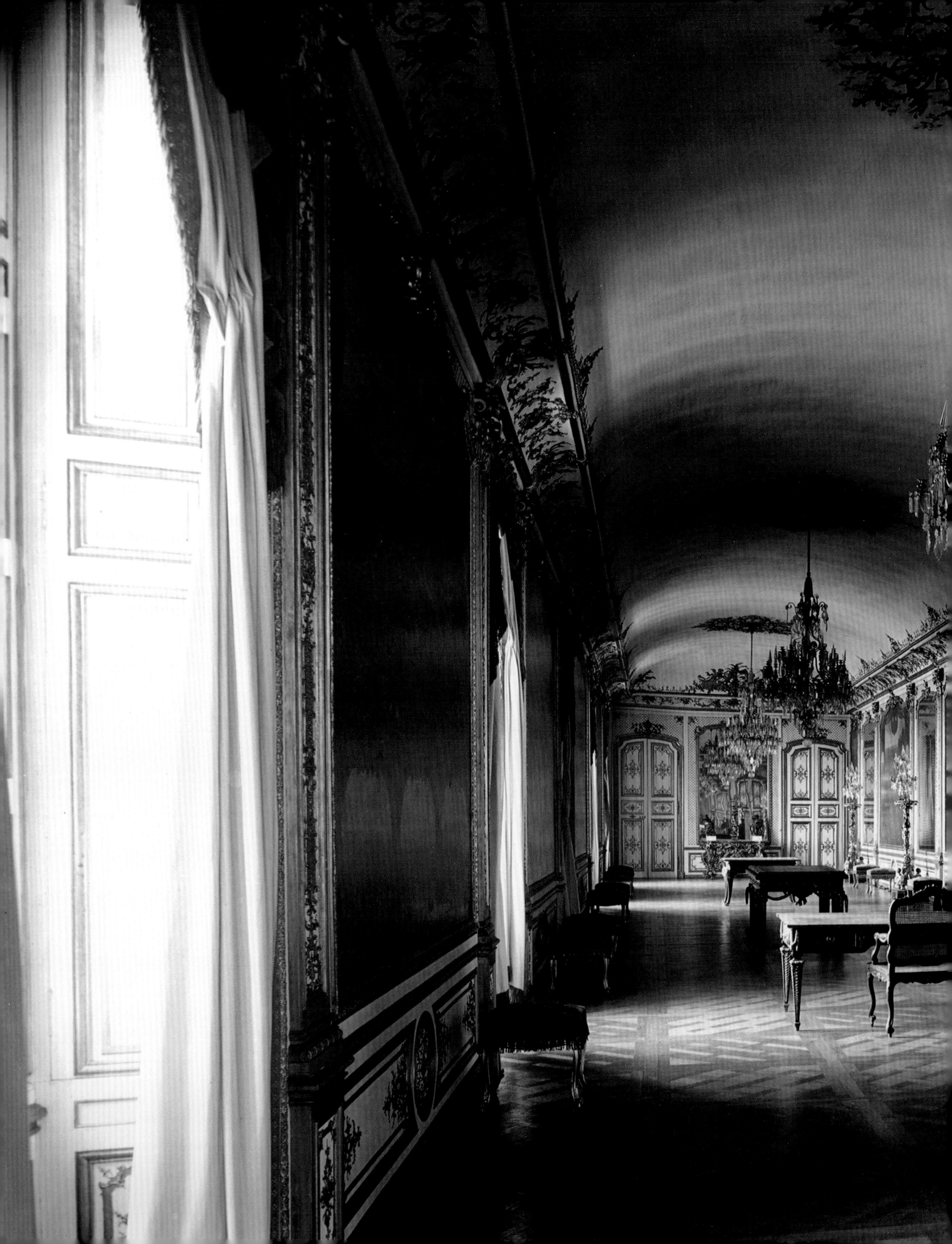

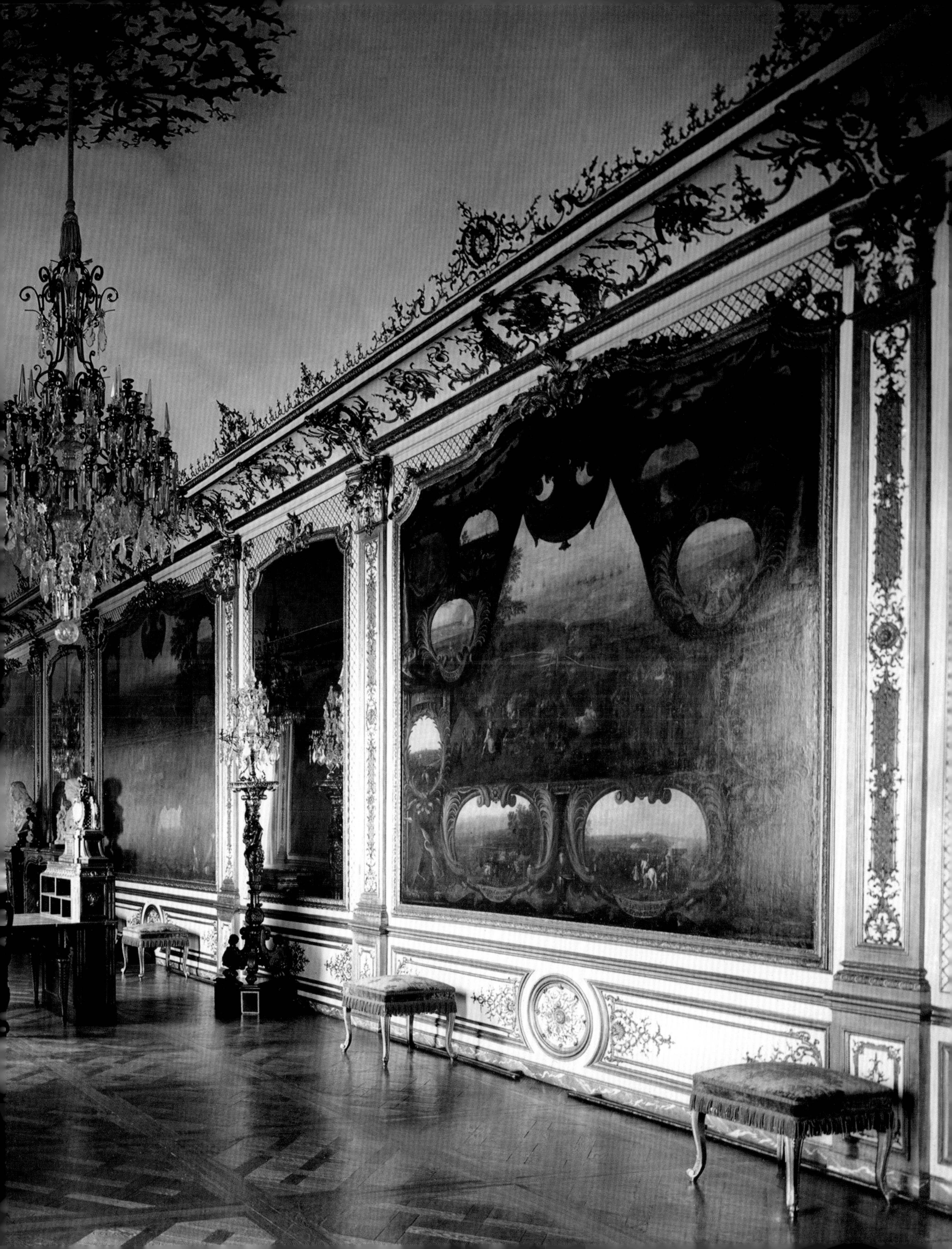

MICHEL CORNEILLE THE YOUNGER

(Paris, 1642; Paris, 1708)

The Great Condé Repents

Canvas. H. 290 cm (9 ft. 6 in.); W. 332 cm (10 ft. 10 in.)
Inv. 364 (Galerie des Actions de M. le Prince)

After the Great Condé decorated the gallery of his château at Chantilly with a cycle of paintings by Sauveur Le Conte (*see pp. 182–85*), his son Henry-Jules commissioned an allegory depicting his late father's personal rebellion against Louis XIV—indeed, the Great Condé fought against France on behalf of Spain from 1654 to 1660. Here he is shown in ancient dress, his left hand restraining the trumpet that a figure of Fame is about to blow; the scrolls around the trumpet list Condé's victories against France plus the Latin word *sileat* ("Let her remain silent"). At his feet lie scrolls listing battles won in the name of Spain. With his right hand, Condé seems to be encouraging a second figure of Fame whose trumpet announces repentance or regret. To the left of the painting Clio, the muse of history, sits on the back of Time and tears several pages from his large book; at her feet lie pages containing a long description of the Battle of the Dunes.

Michel Corneille the Younger was the son of Michel the Elder (1603–1664), one of the founders of the Académie de Peinture; the younger Michel trained by copying Carracci drawings owned by financier Everard Jabach. Sent to Rome in 1658 under the guardianship of Charles Errand, Michel bristled at this constraint and left the Palazzo Capranica where the Académie de France was housed. On returning from Rome, he was admitted into the Académie Royale de Peinture in 1663. Corneille worked for the Office of Royal Works, on the Queen's Antechamber (from 1671–1680), and then at the Gobelins Manufactory where he resided (and where he died in 1708). A protégé of the marquis of Louvois, he participated in the decoration of the church of Les Invalides. It was probably the architect Jules Hardouin-Mansart, then hard at work on the château at Chantilly, who recommended Corneille to the prince of Condé. The painter was not just a member of Lebrun's team, but was also a friend of Hardouin-Mansart, having in fact decorated the ceiling of the large study in the architect's residence on rue des Tournelles, and having rented a house owned by Hardouin-Mansart on rue Neuve-des-Petits-Champs since 1683.

In 1691 Michel Corneille the Younger received two advances of 200 livres for this painting, then in progress. The canvas was supplied by Sauveur Le Conte, near whom Corneille lived at the Gobelins Manufactory. The painting was apparently delivered prior to 1692. Indeed, a painter named Laforest was paid "for the lettering he did on the bottom of the portrait of the late Prince in the gallery of the small château at Chantilly."

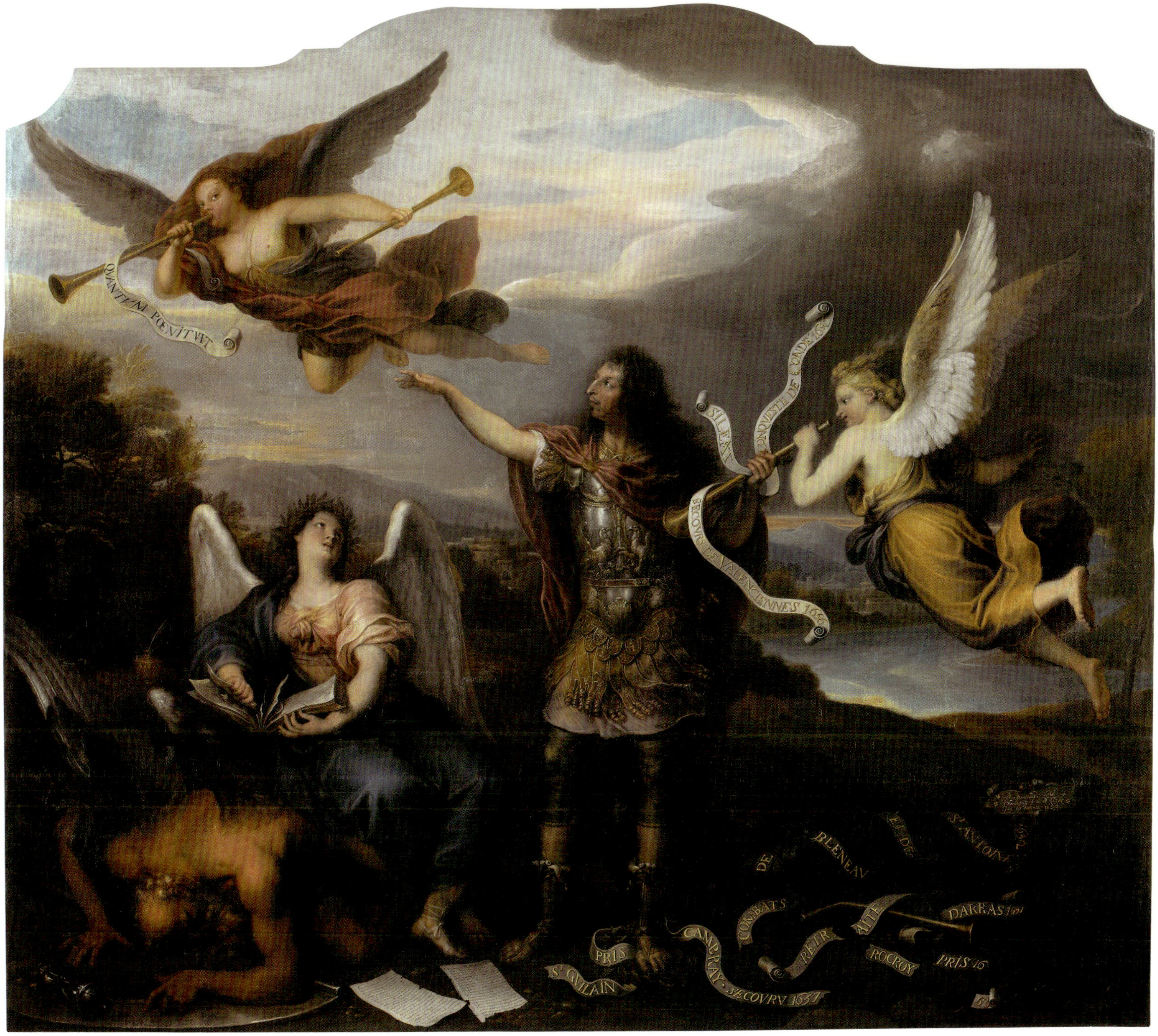
QVANTVM POENITVIT
SILEAT
CONQVESTE DE CONDÉ 1656
SECOVRS DE VALENCIENNES 1656
DE
BLENEAV
ET DE
S^T ANTOINE
COMBATS
DARRAS
PRIS
CAMBRAY
RETR
AITE
ROCROY
PRIS 16
S^T GVILAIN
SECOVRV 1657

JACQUES STELLA

(Lyon, 1596; Paris, 1657)

Louis II de Bourbon, prince of Condé, known as the Great Condé (1621–1686)

Canvas. H. 74 cm (2 ft. 5 in.); W. 60 cm (1 ft. 11 ½ in.)
Inv. 307 (Galerie des Actions de M. le Prince)

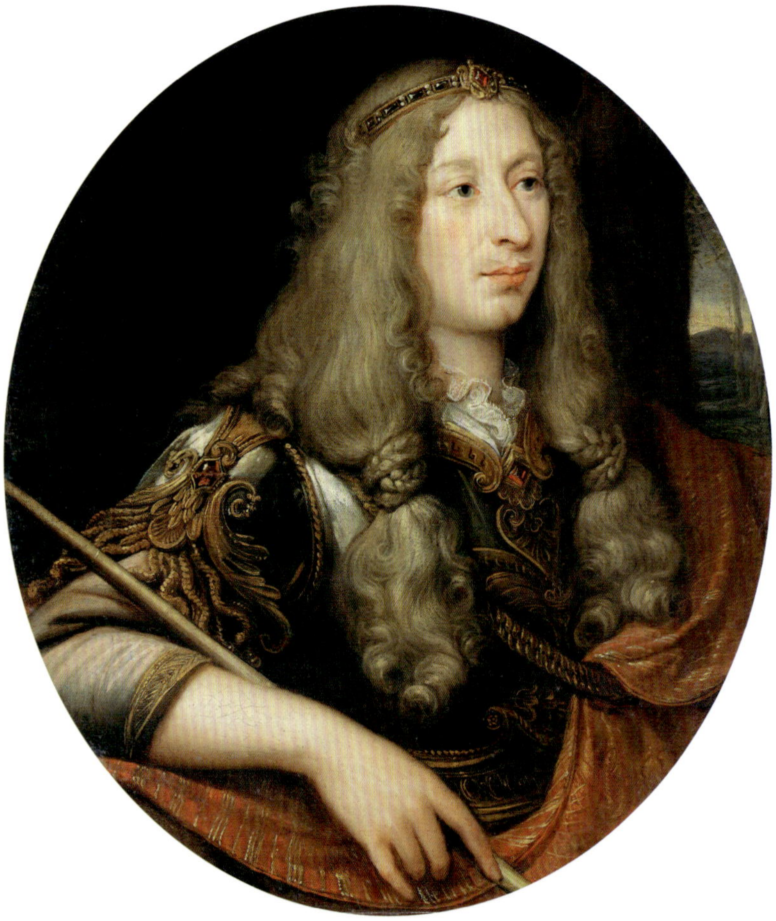

Jacques Stella, son of a painter and art dealer of Flemish stock, trained in Lyon and then left for Florence where he stayed at the court of Cosimo II de' Medici and worked with Jacques Callot. On the death of Cosimo, Stella left for Rome where he lived for ten years. He earned a certain reputation for paintings on copper or stone, often small in size; he also became friends with Nicolas Poussin, whose classical art influenced Stella's oeuvre. He left Italy and returned to Lyon in 1634, moving to Paris in 1636. Appointed painter to the king by Richelieu and Louis XIII, and allocated housing in the Louvre, Stella decorated the queen's oratory in the château at Saint-Germain-en-Laye, followed by the Jesuit novitiate in 1641–42, where his altarpiece figured alongside works by Poussin and Vouet. In 1644, Stella was inducted into the Order of Saint-Michel, an exceptional honor for an artist, and worked on the decoration of Anne of Austria's oratory in the Palais-Royal. After Stella died his work was often confused with paintings by his friend Poussin.

This portrait of the Great Condé, shown in ancient dress with a commander's baton, must be a fairly early work. The sitter's youth indicates an early date, probably when the prince was still only duc d'Enghien, aged twenty-two, at the time of the battle of Rocroi. Although the prince is recognizable, his sharp features and Bourbon profile have been considerably softened. The son of Prince Henri II of Condé and Charlotte-Marguerite de Montmorency, the Great Condé's exploit at the battle of Rocroi enabled him to recover the Montmorency property that had been confiscated by Louis XIII after the rebellious behavior of Henri de Montmorency, beheaded in Toulouse in 1632. The Great Condé himself subsequently sided with the revolt known as the Fronde, rebelling against royal power and fighting for Spain against France; he was then stripped of his property and sentenced to death *in absentia*. Having been pardoned by the Treaty of the Pyrenees in 1659, he regained possession of Chantilly, which he embellished by commissioning André Nôtre to design the grounds in the early 1660s.

The attribution of this portrait to Stella is based on old estate inventories of the Condé family.

FLORENT DE LA MARE-RICHART

(Bayeux, circa 1630; Versailles, 1718)

Group of Children Representing Summer, 1697

Canvas. H. 128 cm (4 ft. 2 ½ in.); W. 154 cm (5 ft.)
Formerly s.d.b.r.: *F. de La Mare-Richart pict. acad. pinxit ad vivum anno 1697*
Inv. 735

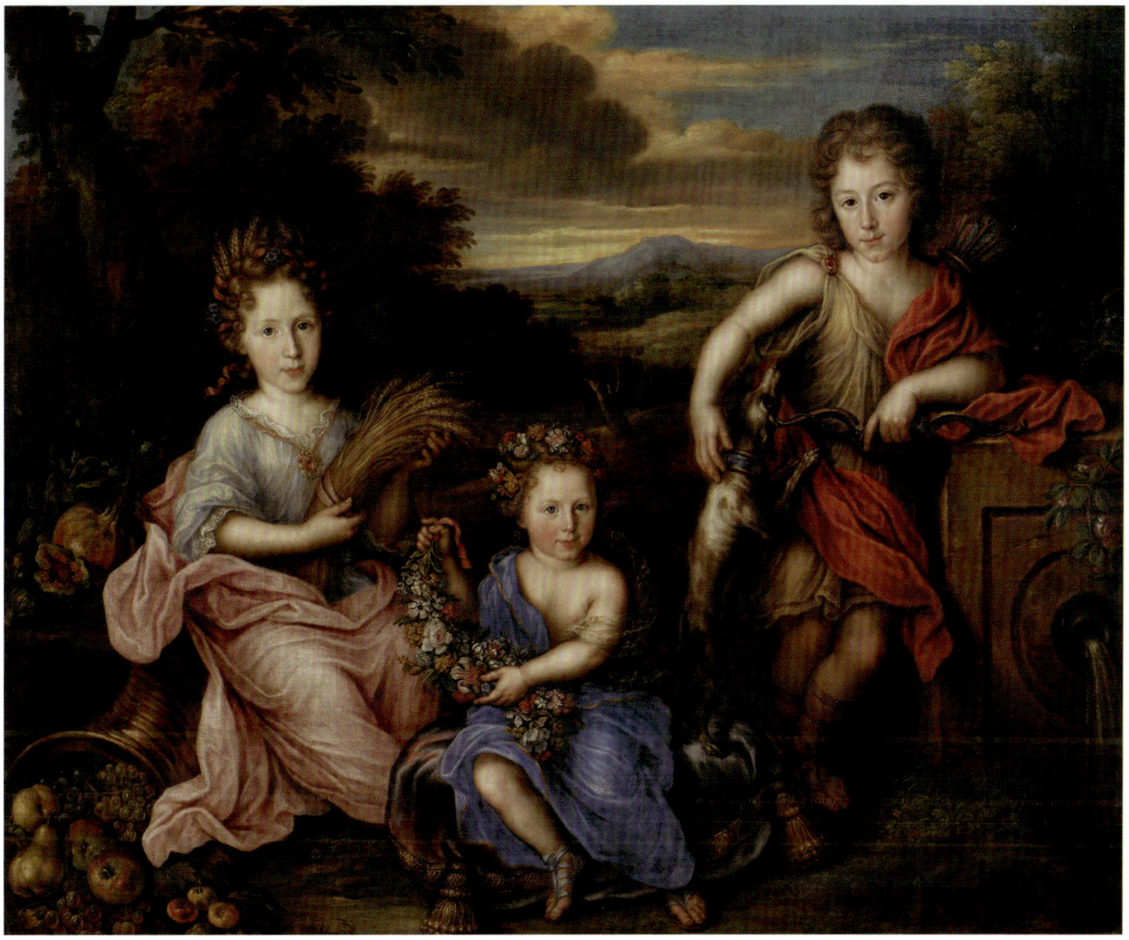

The painter and engraver Florent de La Mare-Richart engraved history paintings by Laurent de La Hyre (1606–1656) such as *Saint Jerome in the Wilderness*. He also produced a series of sixteen "fanciful characters" that revealed an interest in Rembrandt (still a novelty in France) as well as a very fine oval *Virgin* signed "F.I.D.L. Mare invenit et sculpsit." Dated 1655, this work reflects La Hyre's latest style, which suggests that between 1650 and 1655 La Mare was associated with La Hyre as a pupil, an assistant, or a friend. This group of youthful religious paintings includes an *Ecce Homo* dated 1650. La Mare-Richart later specialized in portraiture and became an associate (1676) then a full member (1677) of the Académie Royale de Peinture. Two of his portraits, *Noël Coypel* and *Antoine Paillet* (both attested in 1677) are now in the château de Versailles. The château-museum in Boulogne-sur-Mer, meanwhile, owned a *Still Life with Fruit* signed "Lamarre," unfortunately destroyed during the First World War. Portraits known to be engraved by La Mare-Richart include *Jacques II Goyon de Matignon, Bishop of Condom* (1662), *Auguste de Servien, Abbot of Saint-Jouin* (1666), and *Marie-Thérèse de Bourbon* (signed and dated 1693). A drawing of a *Head of a Young Boy* is held by the Pushkin Museum in Moscow.

This painting comes from the private collection of the Condé family, for whom La Mare-Richart worked regularly. On May 21, 1694, "the painter La Mare" received 600 livres as an advance on four paintings of the children of Louis III de Bourbon and of his cousin the prince of Conti. On May 28, 1697, La Mare-Richart received 102 livres for paintings executed for the study at Chantilly. In 1740, the post-mortem estate inventory of Louis III's son, Louis-Henri de Bourbon, prince of Condé (1692–1740), mentioned four paintings on canvas showing "the four seasons represented by children." The paintings were hung on the ground floor of the Petit Château at Chantilly.

JEAN-ANTOINE WATTEAU

(Valenciennes, 1684; Nogent-sur-Marne, 1721)

The Anxious Lover

Wood. H. 24 cm (9 ½ in.); W. 175 cm (5 ft. 9 in.)
Inv. 372 (Salle Caroline)

Jean-Antoine Watteau created a new genre of painting, for which he was admitted to the Académie Royale de Peinture et de Sculpture in 1717: the flirtatious scenes known as *fêtes galantes.* Three of the four works by Watteau in the Musée Condé are *fêtes galantes* showing melancholy youths who flirt with ravishing young ladies in gardens drenched in the poetic light of evening.

Here a young woman anxiously awaits her beau in a park at dusk. The cut roses on her apron are a symbol of her lost virginity, and perhaps also of spent love—which explains her anxious wait. This figure is found in many *fêtes galantes,* in which sadness lurks behind the beauty and grace. Watteau regularly composed small-scale paintings conceived around a single figure evoking one of various moods, such as *La Finette* (Wily Girl) and *L'Indifférent* (Carefree Young Man).

Of disputed date, this painting might have been done in the period prior to Watteau's *Pilgrimage to the Island of Cythera* (1717). According to Mariette, it belonged to Abbé Haranger, canon of the church of Saint-Germain-l'Auxerrois and one of Watteau's closest friends (who inherited many of the artist's drawings at his death). The estate inventory drawn up after Abbé Haranger's own death in 1735 is very vague, mentioning neither artist nor dimensions, which allows for no certainties. It does mention a painting of a "woman leaning," but one described as a "canvas" (rather than wood panel). A print by Aveline based on *The Anxious Lover* was published in 1729, on the same sheet as a print of *The Dreamer,* a work of identical size (The Art Institute, Chicago). But at that date the painting was supposedly owned by Haranger, who therefore would have possessed two works that were either painted as pendants to one another or were artificially paired in Haranger's collection.

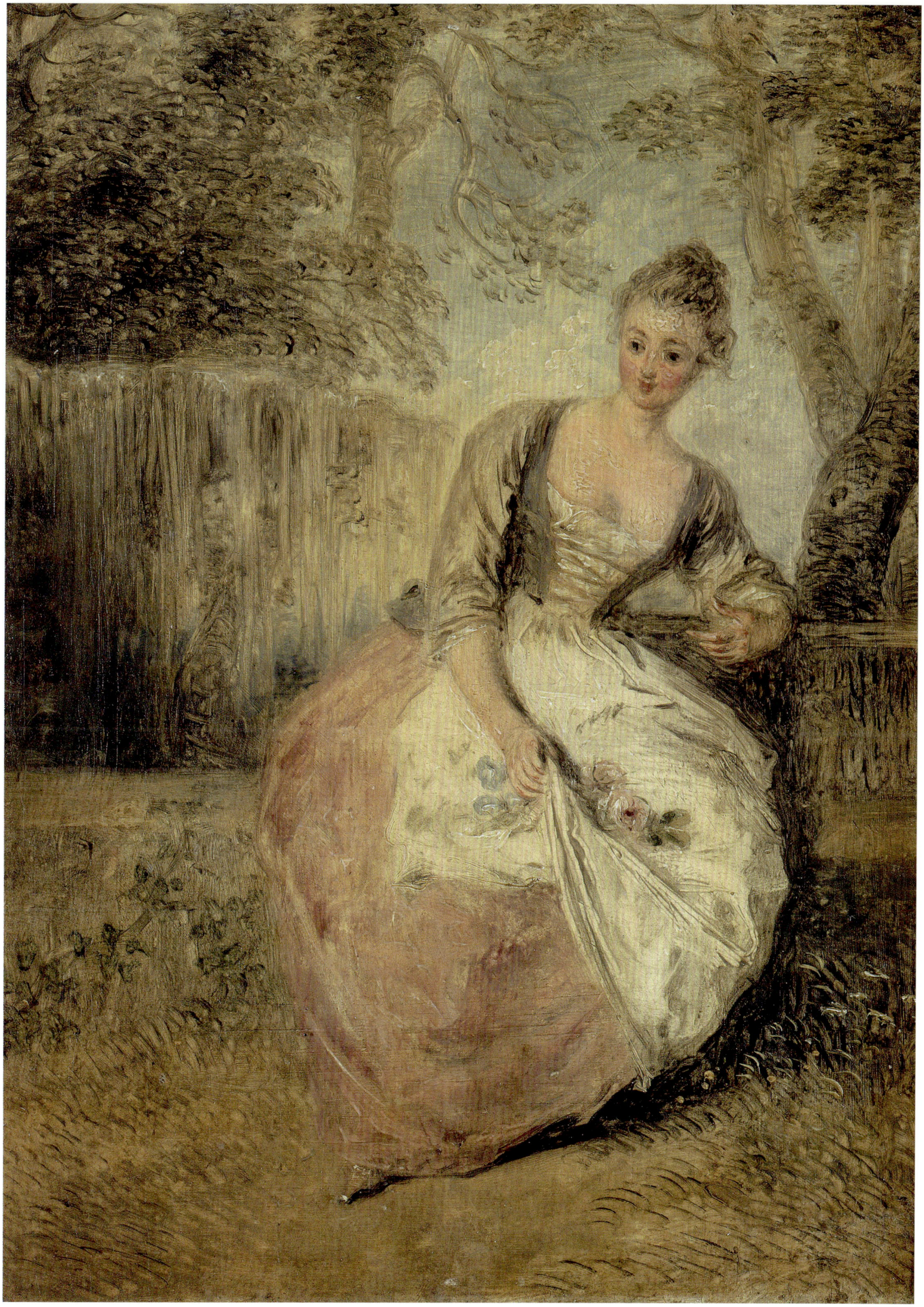

JEAN-ANTOINE WATTEAU

(Valenciennes, 1684; Nogent-sur-Marne, 1721)

The Serenader

Wood. H. 24 cm (9 ½ in.); W. 175 cm (5 ft. 9 in.)
Inv. 371 (Salle Caroline)

No engraving was ever made of *The Serenader,* which has been compared to Watteau's *Mezzetin* (Metropolitan Museum of Art, New York), even though the compositions are quite different. The latter was once thought to show Angelo Constantini (1654–1729), who often portrayed the stock *commedia dell' arte* character known as Mezzetin. This identification has now been rejected, as has the assimilation of the two paintings. Indeed, the Musée Condé holds of portrait of *Angelo Constantini in the Role of Mezzetin* by François de Troy, which bears no relation to *The Serenader.* Unfortunately, the two works were often confused by specialists seeking to retrace their history back to the eighteenth century. The New York *Mezzetin* belonged to Jean de Jullienne, was engraved by B. Audran with an indication of its provenance, and was acquired at the Jullienne auction on behalf of Catherine the Great of Russia, where it remained in the Hermitage until 1931, then it was bought by the Metropolitan Museum in 1934.

The sitter for the painting, recognizable by his snub nose, is seen not only in the preparatory sketch but also in other drawings, notably held by the Musée des Beaux-Arts in Rouen and the Musée du Petit Palais and the Louvre in Paris, and formerly in the Bordeaux-Groult Collection in Paris. This figure is present in paintings and drawings dated circa 1716–17, shortly before Watteau painted *Pilgrimage to the Island of Cythera. The Serenader* was generally thought to be a false pendant to *The Anxious Lover* from Abbé Haranger's collection, with which it was artificially paired in 1788. But study of Abbé Haranger's estate inventory raises a challenge to the theory of the separation of the two paintings in the seventeenth century, because it mentions "a small painting on wood panel showing a *Guitar Player.*" This might refer to the painting here, although we cannot be certain.

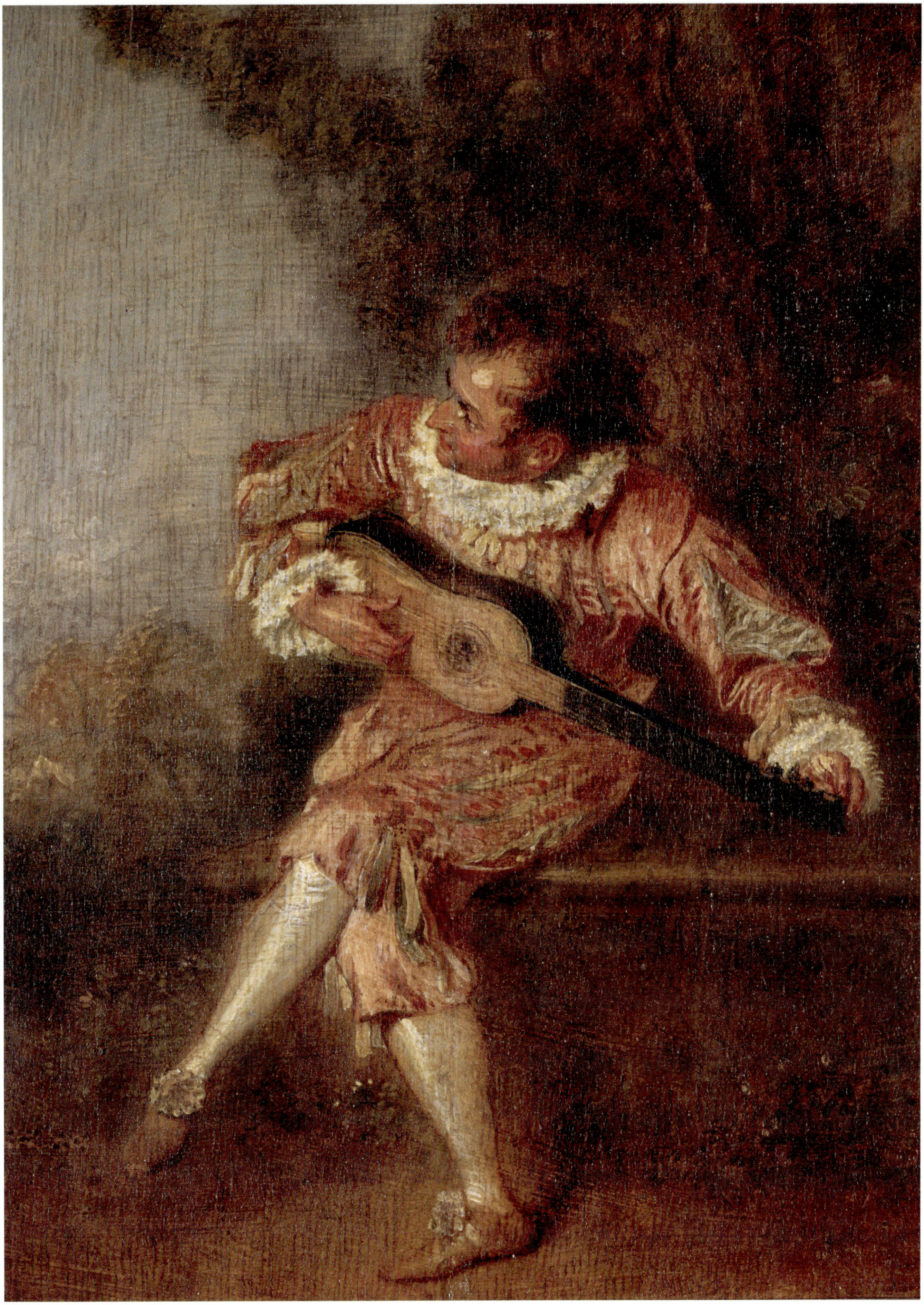

JEAN-ANTOINE WATTEAU

(Valenciennes, 1684; Nogent-sur-Marne, 1721)

Pastoral Pleasure

Wood. H. 31 cm (1 ft.); W. 44 cm (1 ft. 5 ½ in.)
Inv. 370 (Tribune)

The lettering on the Tardieu's 1729 engraving of this painting indicates that it belonged to the great art-lover Pierre-Jean Mariette, as confirmed by its inclusion in the sale of the collector's estate after his death. Most specialists consider the Musée Condé's *Pastoral Pleasure* to be the original Watteau from the Mariette collection, that is to say the first version of a subject subsequently reworked by the artist.

Indeed, works similar to this one include *The Shepherds*, a larger canvas (56 x 81 cm/1 ft. 8 in. x 2 ft. 8 in.) now in Schloss Charlottenburg in Berlin, probably a later replica given its differences from the Musée Condé's painting: the figures' gestures are more serene, their garments more elegant, and their moods more meditative and dreamy, all of which suggests a technical and psychological evolution.

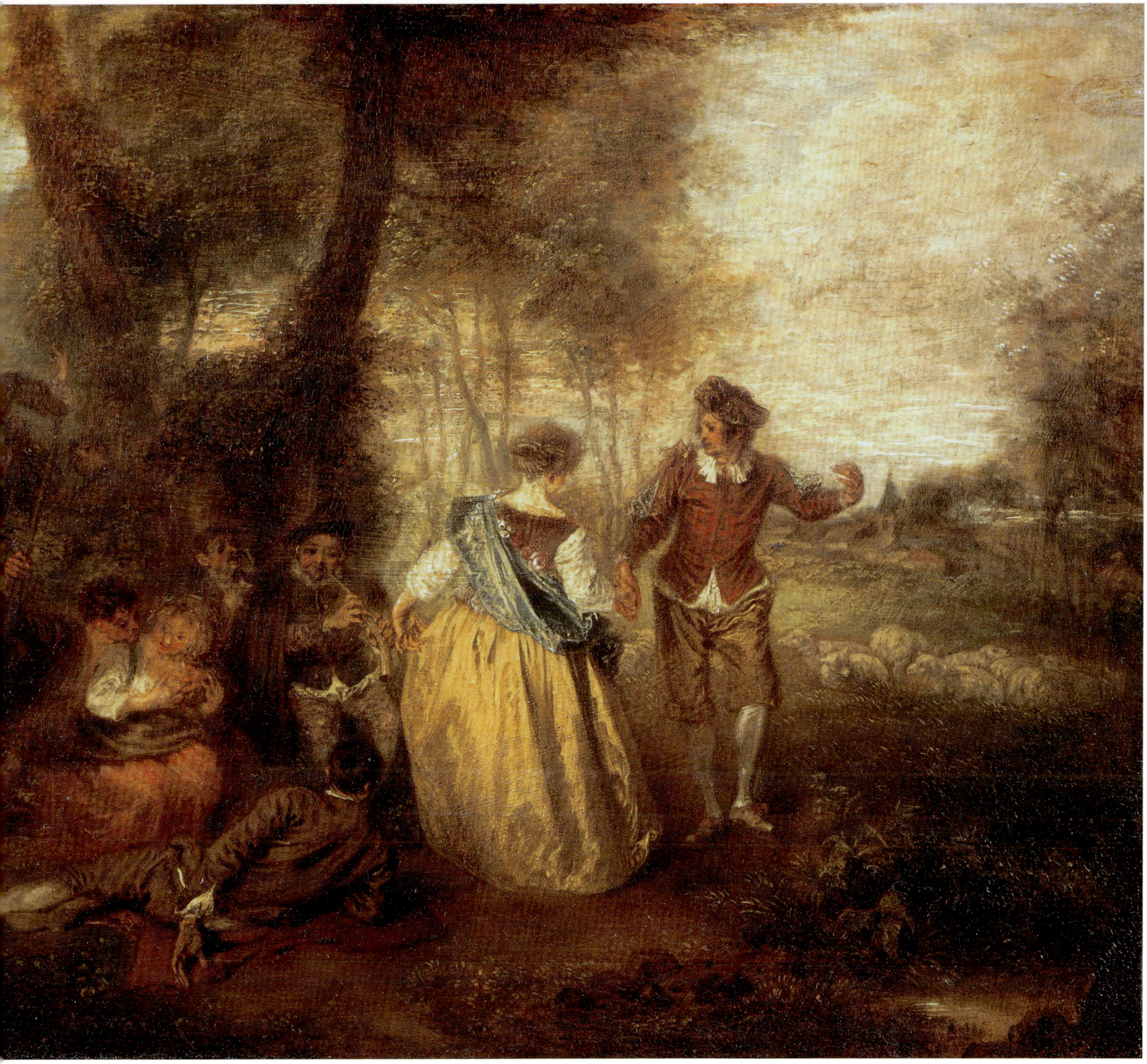

Watteau, who was born in the north—Valenciennes—began his career as a copyist of Flemish works, which influenced his own art, as seen in the painting here, generally dated circa 1714–16 and still heavily indebted to Rubens. The musician, his friend, and the shepherd embracing his girlfriend are all directly inspired by Rubens, as is the detail of the dog in the foreground.

Another replica (art market) appears to be more similar to the Berlin version than the one here, whereas a drawing in the Musée Cognac-Jay (Paris) is thought to be a study for the latter. This painting was furthermore copied by Jean-Baptiste Pater (1695–1736), a follower of Watteau who continued to work in the genre of *fêtes galantes* (art market).

The many known versions raise the problem of preparatory drawings: eight drawings have been linked to the Berlin painting, at least four of which were used solely for that work. Only "Woman on a Swing" and "Woman Dancing" appear to have been studies for the Musée Condé's *Pastoral Pleasure*.

JEAN-ANTOINE WATTEAU

(Valenciennes, 1684; Nogent-sur-Marne, 1721)

L'Amour désarmé (Cupid Disarmed)

Canvas. H. 47 cm (1 ft. 6 ½ in.); W. 38 cm (1 ft. 3 in.)
Inv. 369 (Tribune)

Included in every monograph on Watteau, this painting is one of his least contested. It was one of the eight works that Jean de Jullienne, the artist's friend and patron, kept until his death in 1766. In 1767 it was auctioned at Jullienne's estate sale, and again in 1783 at the estate sale of Jullienne's executor, Montullé; it then vanished, only to resurface a century later in the Marquis Maison collection (*see p. 30*). According to painter Pierre-Nolasque Bergeret (1782–1863), after the period of revolutionary Terror in France *L'Amour désarmé* (or *Cupid Disarmed*) was apparently sold at the Bullion auction house to an art-lover for a ridiculously low price; it first went to London, where it was acquired by a rich Englishman, before allegedly returning to Paris.

The subject matter seems surprising for a painter of *fêtes galantes*. According to Mariette, Watteau may have been inspired by a Veronese drawing (Louvre) that belonged first to financier Pierre Crozat and then to Mariette himself. That is why specialists often compare this painting to the four *Seasons* Watteau painted for Crozat, and to his *Autumn* now in the Louvre, which are similar in size and spirit. Mythological subjects nevertheless remain rare in Watteau's oeuvre, and this may have been an academic work executed at the time of his acceptance by the Académie Royale de Peinture.

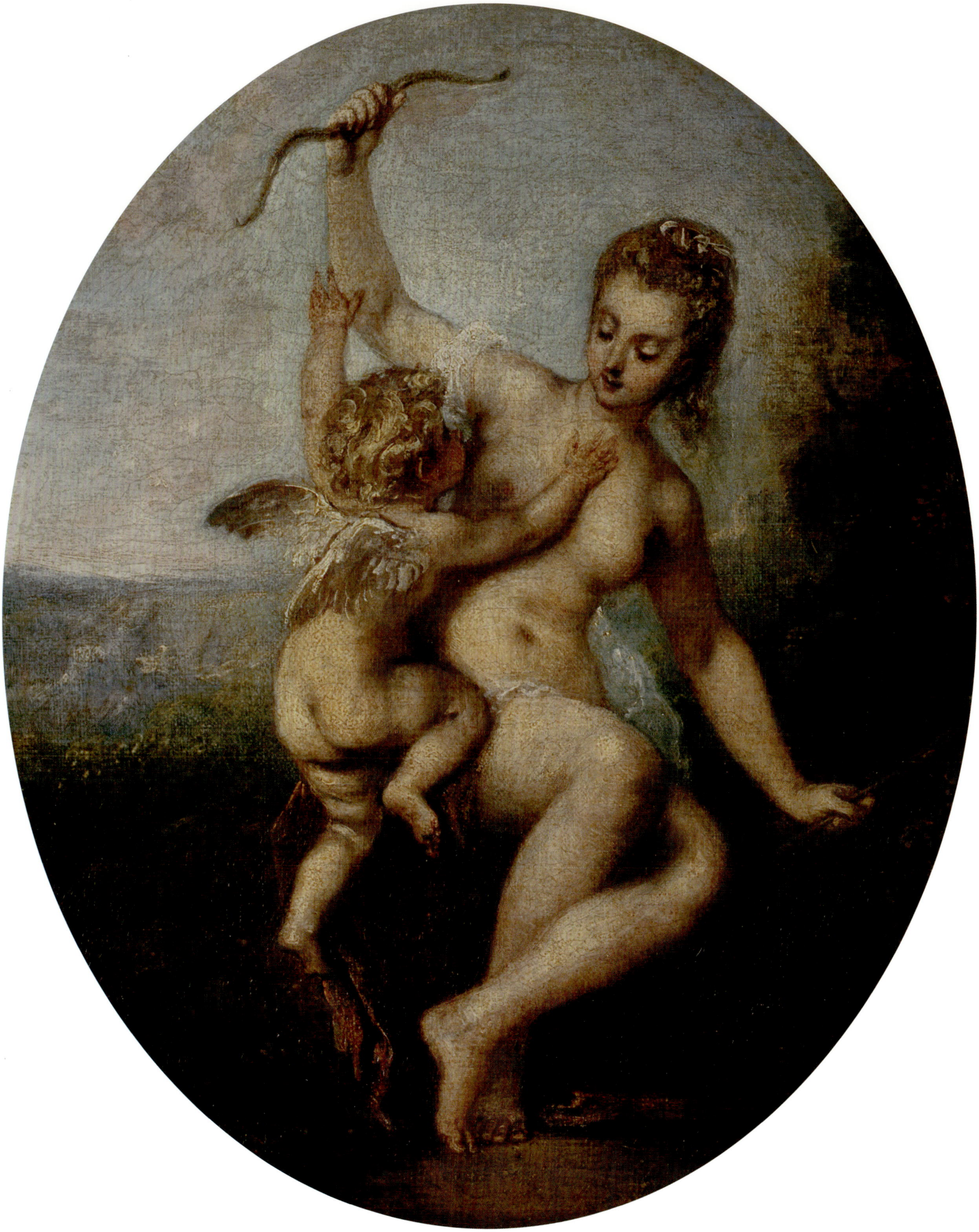

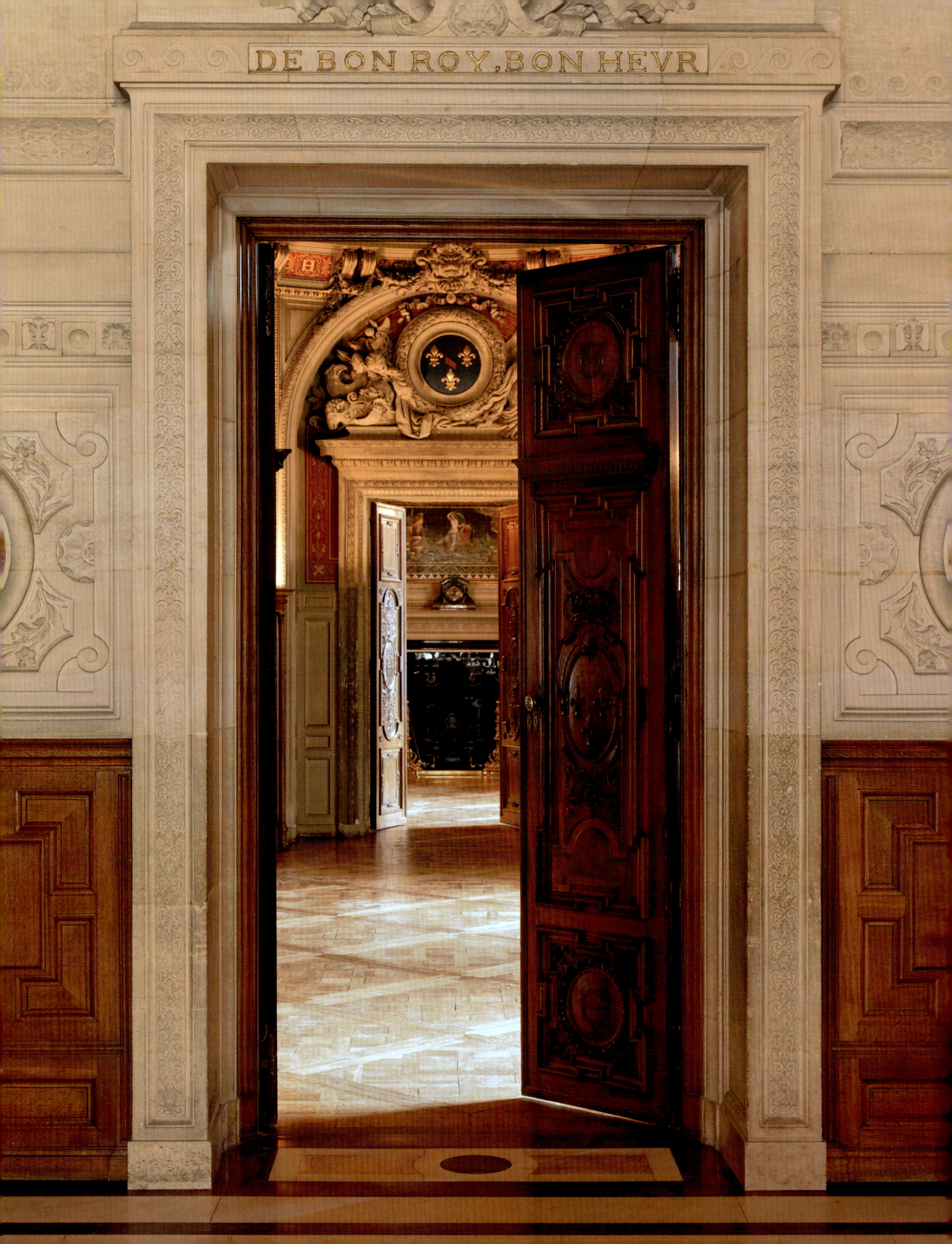
DE BON ROY, BON HEVR

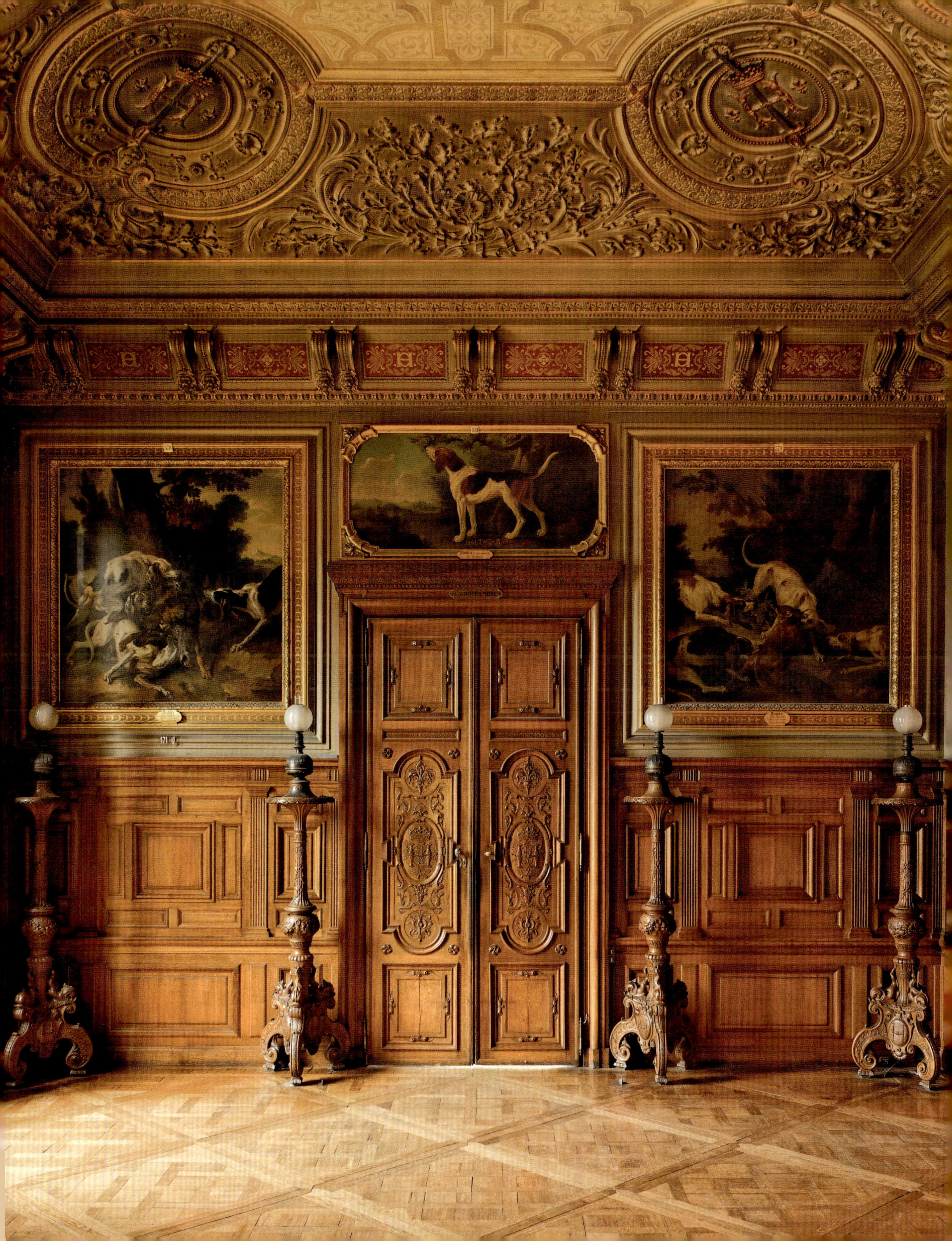

JEAN-BAPTISTE OUDRY

(Paris, 1686; Beauvais, 1755)

Wolf Hunting: The Kill

Canvas. H. 175 cm (5 ft. 9 in.); W. 196 cm (6 ft. 5 in.)
S.d.b.l.: *J.B. Oudry 1725*
Inv. 378 (Antichambre)

The June 1725 issue of *Le Mercure* referred to "three hunting pictures for the Salles des Gardes at the château de Chantilly, roughly six feet square. They show *A Wolf at Bay at the Foot of a Tree*, surrounded by hounds, *A Deer Flushed Out by Hounds* and *A Fox Defending Itself from the Hounds.*" The lettering on engravings of Oudry's paintings indicates that the three pictures were "painted for the king." Three other hunting scenes for the Salle des Gardes at Chantilly had already been painted by Alexandre-François Desportes in 1719. Two of them, *Fox Hunting* and *Deer Hunting,* are now in Senlis (Musée de la Vénerie) while the third is in Lyon (Musée des Beaux-Arts). Oudry's three paintings, along with his *Fox and the Raven* (done for the Salles des Fables in the Grand Château at Chantilly) were paid for by the Office of Royal Works on behalf of the prince of Condé, who was not only the king's cousin but also the head of the Regency Council during the minority of Louis XV.

In 1789, the guards' room to the royal apartments in the Grand Château was hung with hunting scenes, including three by Snyders, two by Vos, three by Desportes, and three overdoor paintings by Oudry. They were all confiscated by the revolutionary government in 1793; Oudry's painting of the deer hunt was sent in 1820 to the museum of fine arts in Rouen, where it remains to this day, whereas the wolf and fox pictures were restored to the prince of Condé in 1816 and returned to Chantilly in 1843. After 1875, the duc d'Aumale hung them in the Antechamber, which leads to the State Apartments of the princes of Condé *(see previous pages)*.

These hunting scenes reveal the clear influence of Flemish paintings, among which they were designed to hang. Oudry was the director of the Beauvais tapestry manufactory and a frequent visitor to Chantilly; he would spend his free time wandering through the forests of Saint-Germain, Chantilly, and Boulogne the better to study landscapes, tree trunks, plants, stormy skies, and horizon effects.

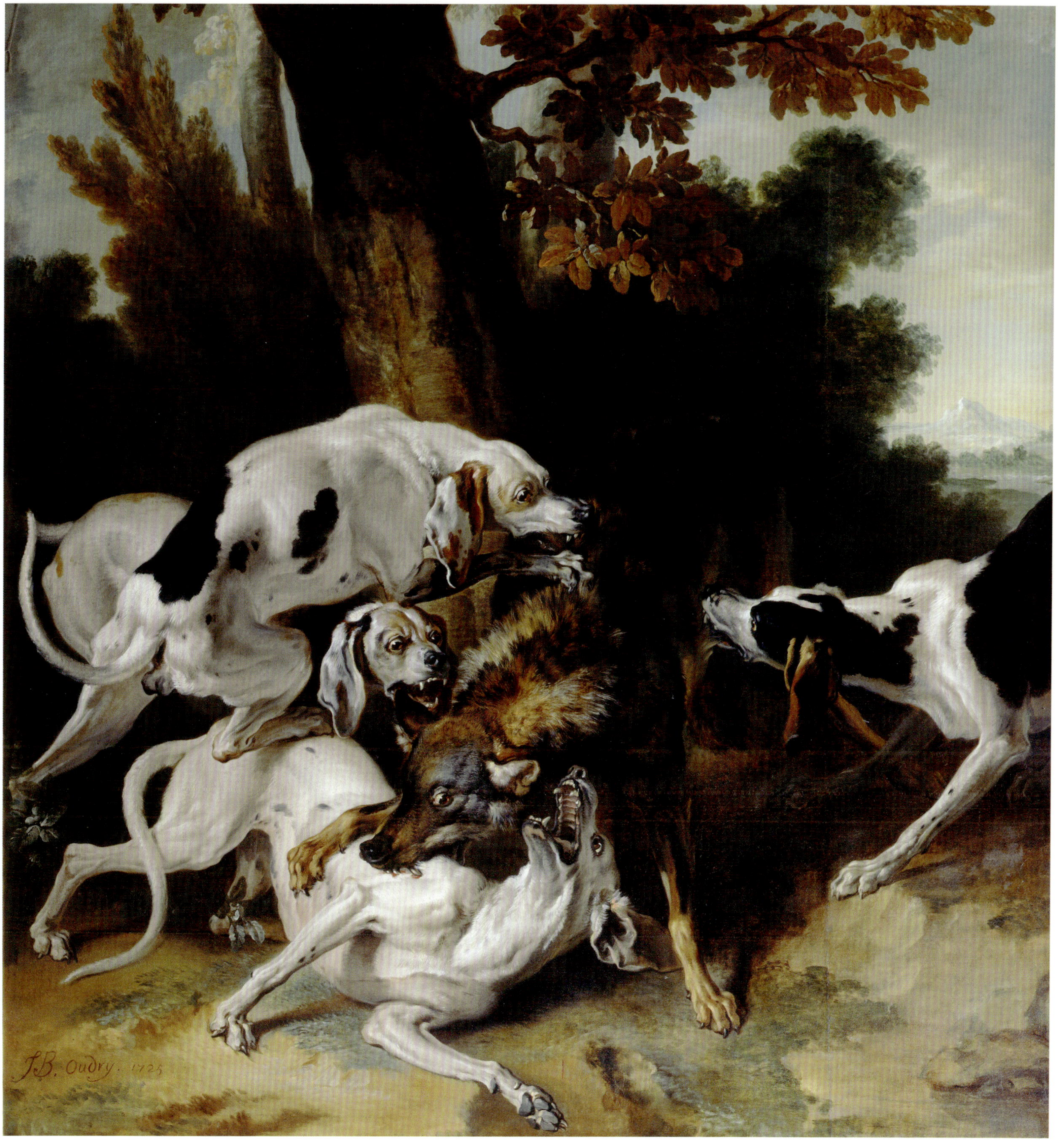
J.B. Oudry. 1725

JEAN-FRANÇOIS DE TROY

(Paris, 1679; Rome, 1752)

Dining on Oysters, 1735

Canvas. H. 180 cm (5 ft. 11 in.); W. 126 cm (4 ft. 1 ¾ in.)
Inv. 366 (Galerie de Peinture)

Louis XV commissioned Jean-François de Troy to paint this picture as a pendant to Nicolas Lancret's *Dining on Ham* (*see p. 204*) in 1735. They were designed to be hung in the dining room of the king's private apartments at Versailles, where he dined informally, often on returning from the hunt. This "post-hunt dining room" was the first purpose-built dining room in Versailles—previously, a table would be set up in any old room or hall. It could host roughly fifteen huntsmen who, after 1738, might be joined by a few ladies.

Both paintings were confiscated during the Revolution and assigned to national museums. During the Bourbon restoration, Louis-Philippe, duc d'Orléans, laid claim to them, erroneously asserting that they had belonged to his ancestor, the Regent, based on the red livery worn by one of the gentlemen (red being the color of the house of Orléans). But the Regent died in 1723, so he could not have been the owner; and it is hard to recognize portraits of contemporary individuals, as Louis-Philippe asserted to his son, the duc d'Aumale, who regretted that he had forgotten their names. The duc d'Aumale acquired these two paintings in 1857, prior to the public auction of Louis-Philippe's estate.

This is the first painting to depict champagne, shortly after Dom Pérignon invented the champagne method of vinification in the late seventeenth century. In the center-left, servants look up at the flying cork that can be spotted in front of the marble column. De Troy included his own painting of *Zephyr and Flora* (circa 1725–26) in this picture, seen over the door (flipped left–right). The gentlemen are dining on oysters, served with garlic, butter, salt, and pepper. Highly appreciated at the time, oysters were sold in their shells by strolling hawkers who made the streets of Paris ring with their cries. In contrast, "fresh-catch" oysters arrived straight from the coast, stripped of their shells and swiftly transported by special fish-carts. Since they were delivered faster, they were assumed to be better. People ate them by the hundreds; King Henry IV was reputed to have eaten three hundred at dinner, while suppers of oysters were greatly appreciated in aristocratic circles. Oysters were thought to be a powerful aphrodisiac, according to a popular belief attested as early as the sixteenth century in medical treatises. This idea has been invoked to explain the fact that de Troy depicts only men here, but the solely masculine scene can also be explained by the fact that the painting was designed to hang in the dining room of the king's private apartments at Versailles.

In the middle of the room, a round table—favoring an absence of protocol—was still just an assembly of planks set on simple trestles. Destined for seventeen diners, it was ringed by cane chairs and set with silver dishes, porcelain, salt shakers, etc., providing us with information on dining practices during the first third of the eighteenth century. Glasses were set in front of each guest, placed in individual coolers of porcelain from China or Japan. In the foreground, a small serving chest has side shelves to store plates and ice-filled containers for chilling bottles, some of which are already set on the main table.

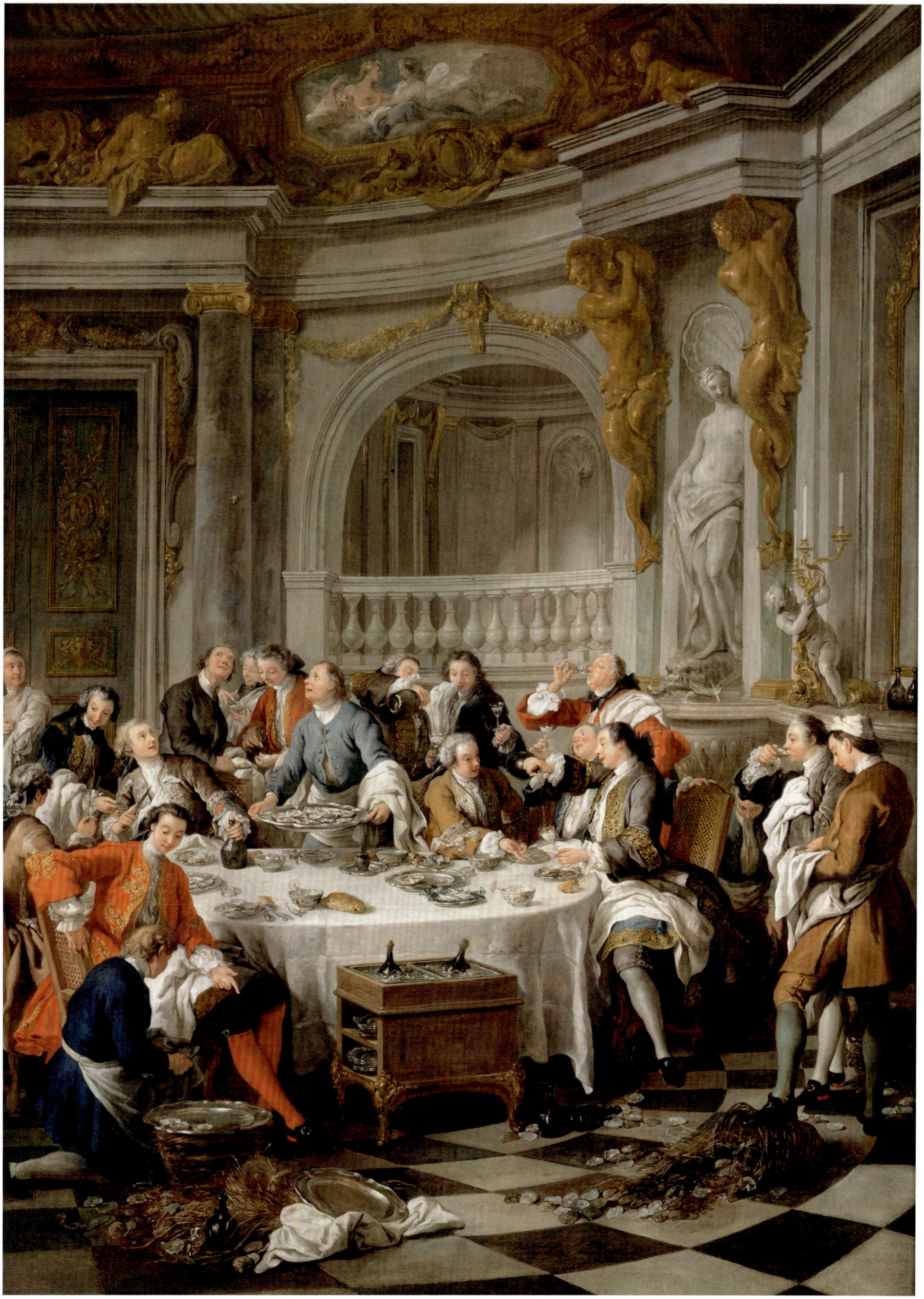

NICOLAS LANCRET

(Paris, 1690; Paris, 1743)

Dining on Ham, 1735

Canvas. H. 188 cm (6 ft. 2 in.); W. 123 cm (4 ft. 1 in.)
S.d.b.r.: *N. Lancret. P. 1735*
Inv. 383 (Galerie de Peinture)

On January 20, 1738, Nicolas Lancret was paid 2,400 livres for this picture, which he had painted in 1735 for the dining room of Louis XV's private apartments at Versailles. In 1817 Louis-Philippe, duc d'Orléans, laid claim to the painting (previously seized by the revolutionary government) as belonging to his family, and it was sent to Eu where it hung in 1826 with its pendant (*see p. 202*). When the duc d'Aumale showed visitors his collection, he never failed to point out that the figures were portraits of real people of the day, although he no longer remembered their names. "My father knew them," he would say, "and when I was a boy he named them all, but now I've forgotten them and no one will ever utter their names again."

A reduced copy commissioned by Lalive de Jully (*Luncheon Party in a Park*, Museum of Fine Arts, Boston), displays several variations on the original one here: the statue of the satyr was replaced by an urn, the complex pattern on the plates was reduced to a simple band, and the oval table became rectangular.

The theme of a post-hunt repast played a special role in Lancret's oeuvre. Louis XV, who particularly liked this kind of painting, commissioned the artist to do several of them. Lancret was one of few genre painters who received regular royal commissions, thereby helping to revive the category. In responding to Louis XV's enthusiasm for hunting subjects, Lancret practically invented the genre of hunt dinners. The king subsequently commissioned similar works from other artists such as Carle van Loo and Jean-François de Troy in 1737 for the château at Fontainebleau (Louvre). In 1990 the Louvre bought a *Repast after the Hunt* painted by Lancret ten years before this one (formerly marquis de Béringhen collection).

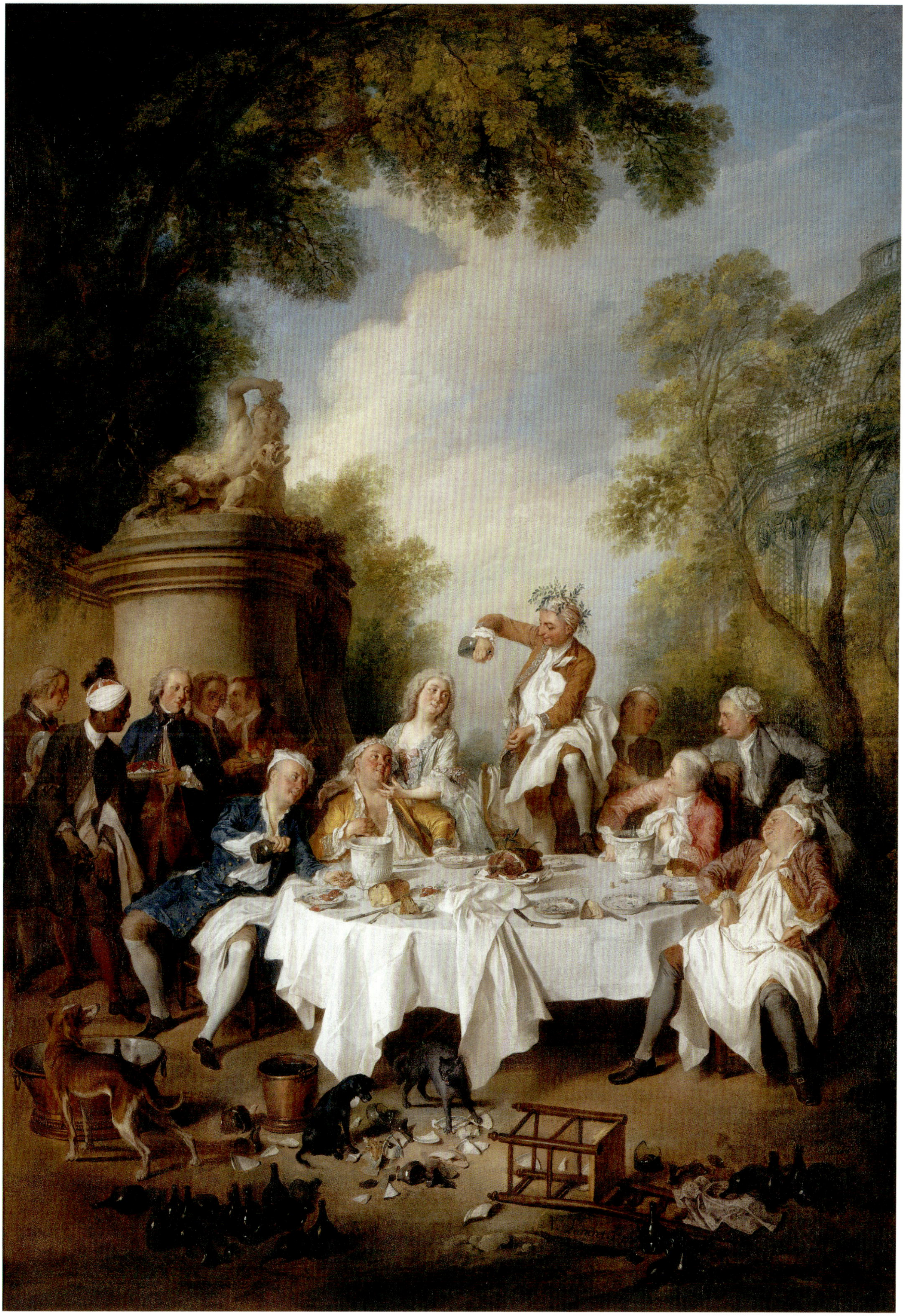

CHRISTOPHE HUET

(Pontoise, 1700; Paris, 1759)

The Large Singerie, 1737

Wood
D. on the block of marble: 1737
Inv. 373

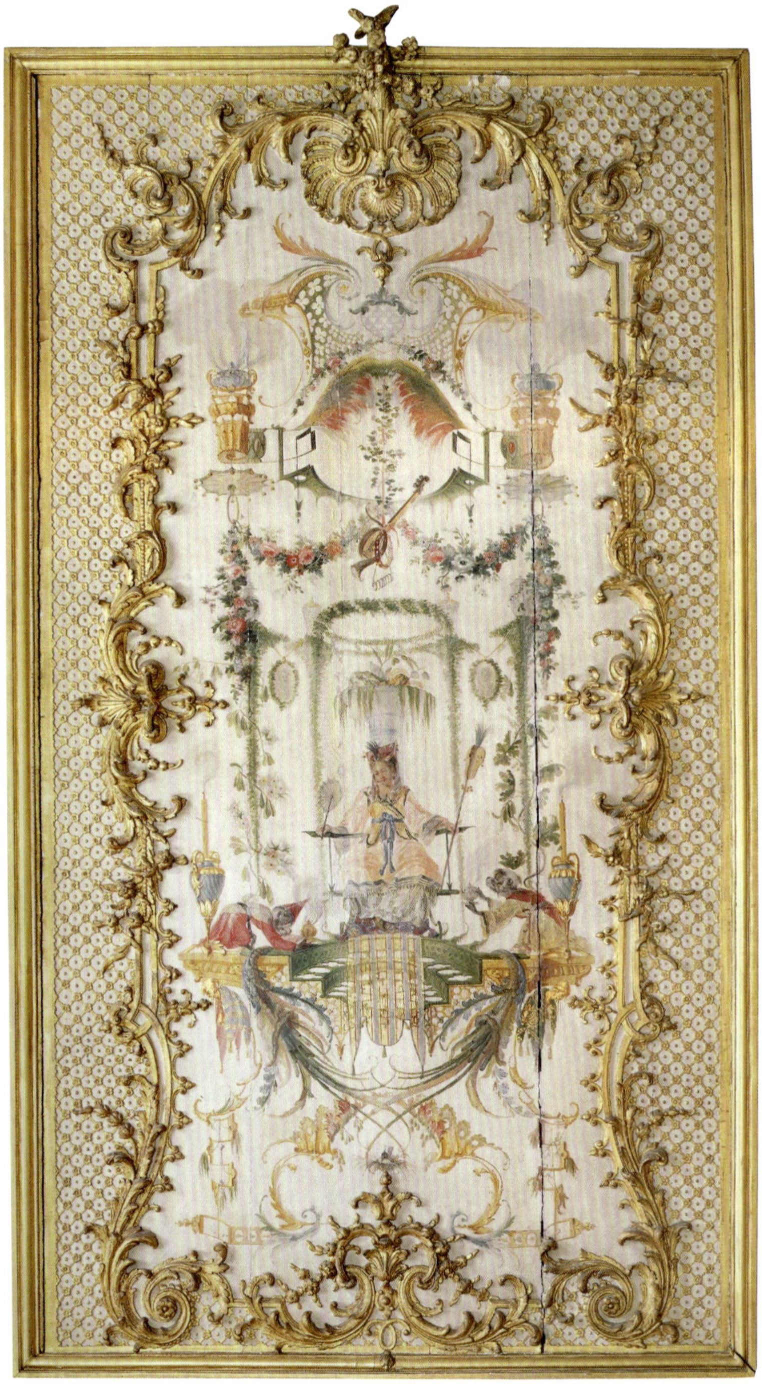

A singerie is a depiction of monkeys (French: *singes*) in playful poses; *The Large Singerie* is a decorative interior with Chinese and monkey motifs done for a salon in the prince of Condé's apartments in 1737. It was painted on white-and-gold woodwork installed nearly twenty years earlier by architect Jean Aubert *(see following double page)*. In the nineteenth century this decor was attributed to Watteau, who indeed produced this type of decoration in his youth. The recent discovery of the date of 1737 on a block of marble being carved by the sculptor-monkey disproved this hypothesis and made it possible to attribute the interior to Christophe Huet, an animal painter who studied under Claude III Audran and who worked for the Condé family in the mid 1730s. Huet also executed similar decors in the château at Champs-sur-Marne and in the Rohan-Strasbourg residence in Paris.

This type of decoration was made fashionable at the end of Louis XIV's reign by the ornamental decorator Jean Bérain, then was developed by Claude Gillot and Claude III Audran and their pupil, Watteau. In the pure tradition of Flemish singeries by David Teniers, in which the animals are shown performing human activities, these pictures do not hesitate to caricature the very people who commissioned the painting. Thus *The Large Singerie* includes monkeys wearing the hunting livery of the house of Condé, whose members would have been able to recognize themselves behind the mischievous animals' features. The iconography of the six large wall panels comprising the *Large Singerie* invokes the Four Parts of the World and the Five Senses. The animals that traditionally symbolize the four parts of the world can be seen on the grisaille medallions flanking the mirrors (lion, horse, elephant, crocodile). The three double doors depict the Arts and Sciences, featuring a painter-monkey, sculptor-monkey, soldier-monkey (with Condé banner), geographer-monkey, funambulist-monkey, and musician-monkey. The ceiling shows a hunt—for deer or boar—which was a favorite pastime of the princes of Condé when at Chantilly.

CHRISTOPHE HUET

(Pontoise, 1700; Paris, 1759)

The Little Singerie, 1735

Wood
D. on the bow: 1735
Inv. 374

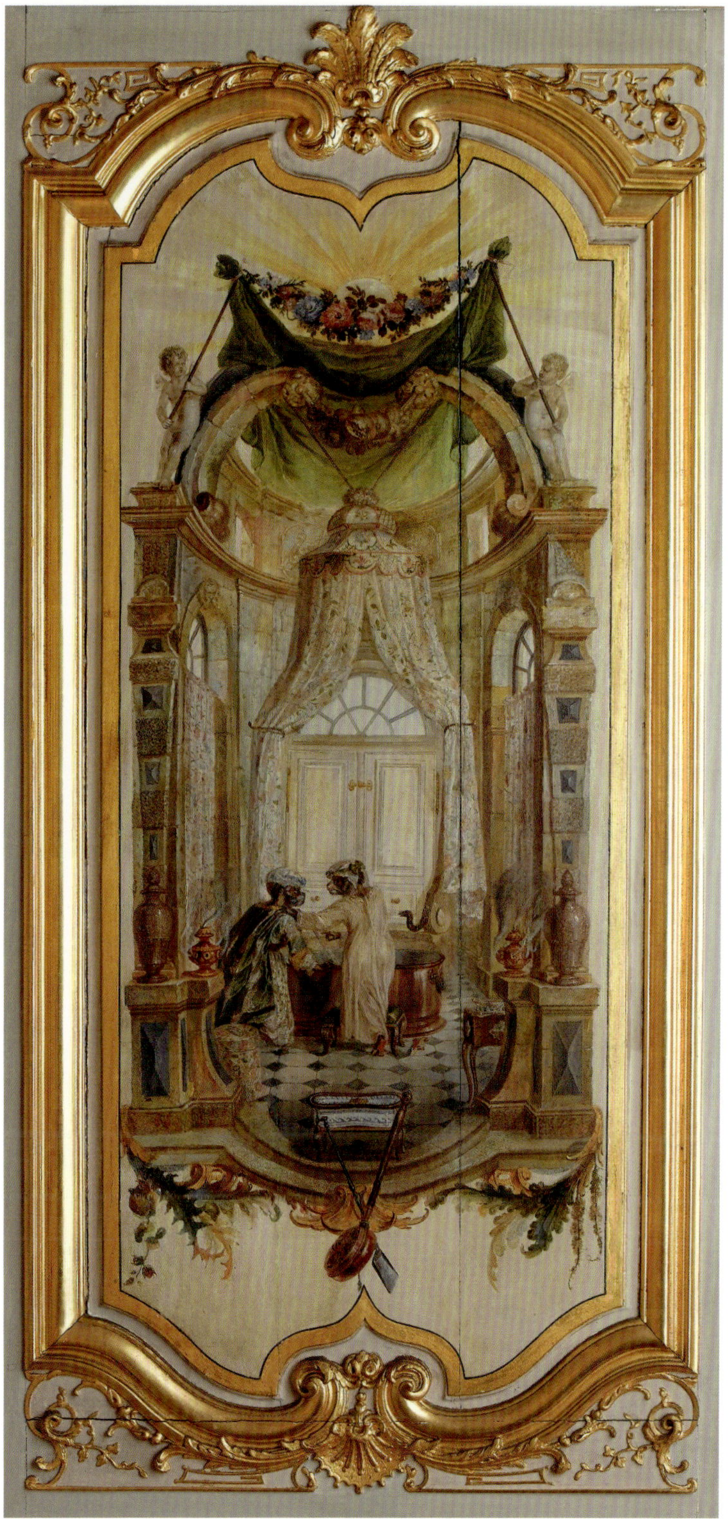

The *Little Singerie* decorates a boudoir on the ground floor of the Petit Château at Chantilly, at the level of the moat. Probably by the same artist who executed the *Large Singerie,* but dated two years earlier, the *Little Singerie* evokes the activities of the women of the house of Condé, depicted with the features of charming female monkeys. They are pictured at various times of the year, as indicated by the four monochrome-blue medallions in the corners of the ceiling, showing children whose activities symbolize the seasons. In the autumn, the monkeys go hunting, and enjoy a meal on a stone table in the forest. In the spring, they pick cherries and eat cream. In summer, they bathe in a copper tub, while in winter they ice skate on Chantilly's frozen moats. Whatever the season, they have their hair and nails done by maidservants, and they play cards. These panels included symbols of the changing seasons: grapes, apples, and hunting gear for autumn, sheaves of wheat for summer, and so on. The panels showed outdoor games such as racquets, shuttlecock, and above all a local type of archery played at Chantilly in the eighteenth century under the princes of Condé, who generously rewarded the winners. The ceiling features the fables of La Fontaine—the Fox and the Stork, the Cock and the Pearl, the Goose that Laid the Golden Eggs—as well as the "cries" of Paris street hawkers and other modest trades embodied by children (sellers of wafer pastries, animal exhibitors, etc.).

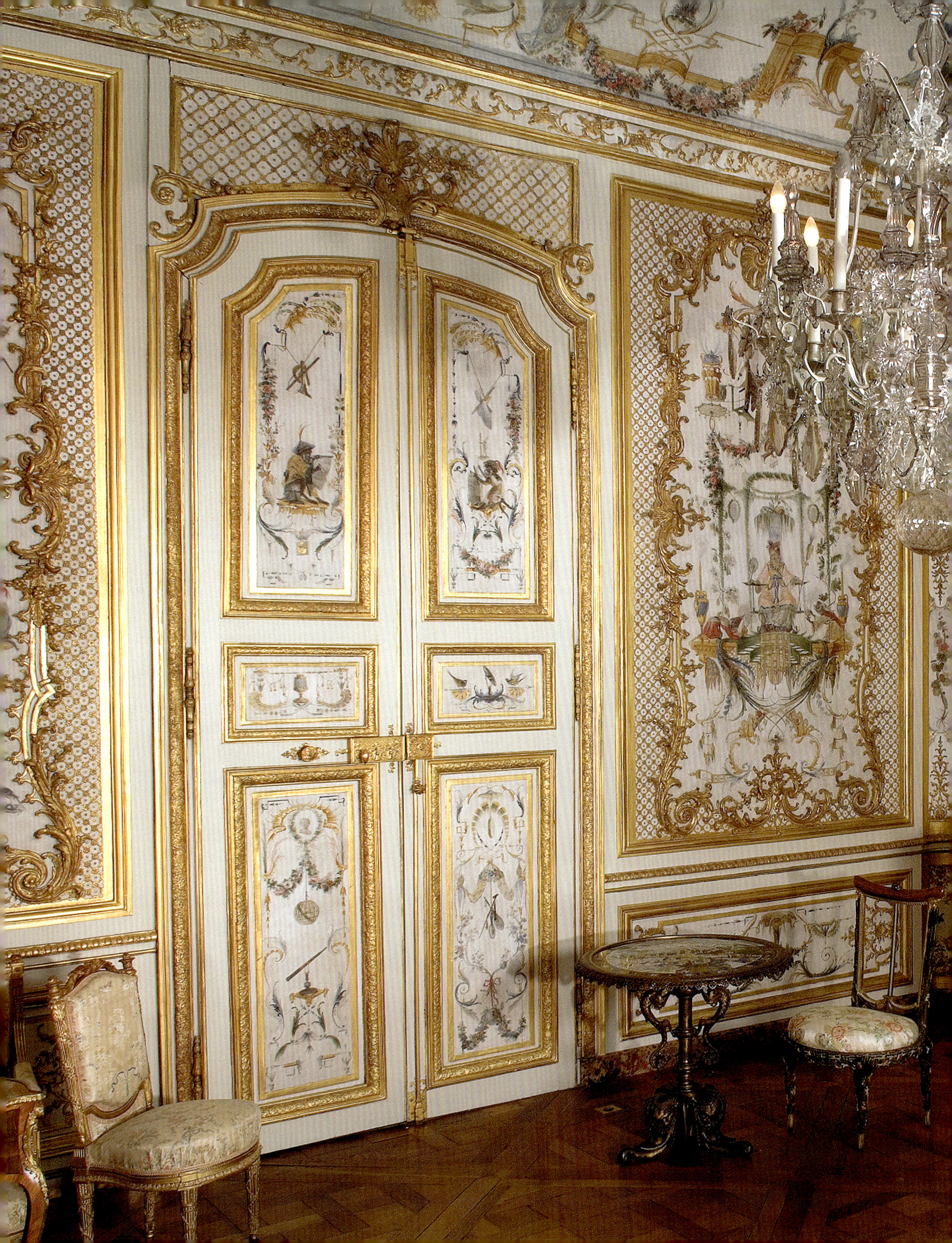

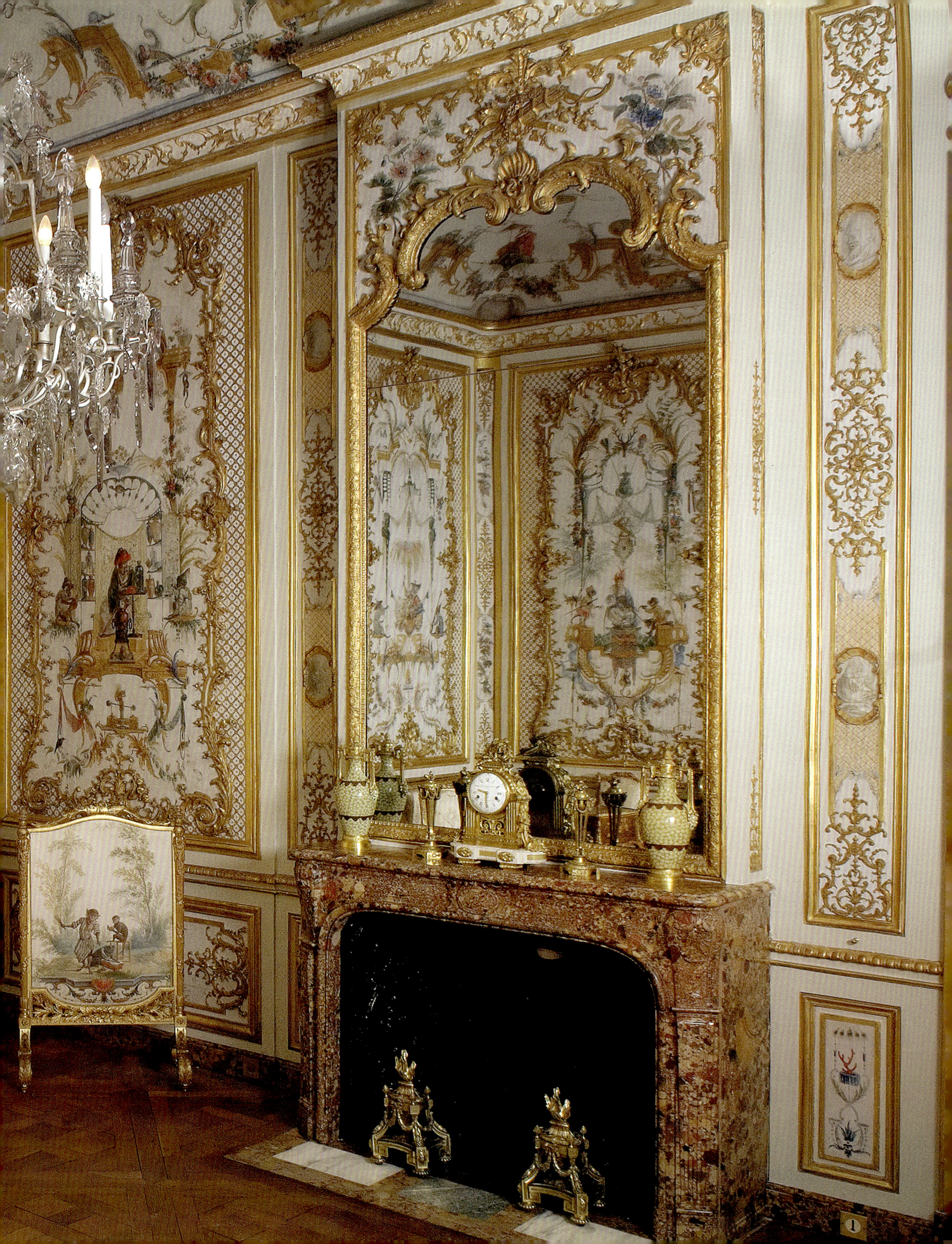

CHRISTOPHE HUET

(Pontoise, 1700; Paris, 1759)

Landscapes with Animals, 1735

Canvas. H. 308 cm (10 ft. 1 in.); W. 162 cm (5 ft. 3 ¾ in.); H. 295 cm (9 ft. 8 in.); W. 157 cm (5 ft. 2 in.)
S.d.b.r.: *C. Huet 1735* (401–10)
Inv. 401–10 and 401–1 (Chambre de M. le Prince)

From 1751 to 1756 Christophe Huet exhibited paintings of birds and animals at the Académie de Saint-Luc, almost all of which have now vanished, except for one painting in Nantes (Musée des Beaux Arts) that shows a *Dog Pointing to Quail*, signed "C. Huet, 1740"). A list of debts to be paid following the death of the prince of Condé's sister, Mademoiselle de Clermont, included the mention, "To Huet, history painter, for two accounts for work done at the Petit-Luxembourg in 1741: 568 livres." This entry cannot refer to the *Singeries* at Chantilly, because the "Petit-Luxembourg" was Mademoiselle de Clermont's Paris residence. It might, however, refer to this series of animal scenes. The estate inventory of 1735 mentions empty slots for ten paintings in a salon on the upper floor, which were still empty after Mademoiselle de Clermont's death in 1741. Thus she might have commissioned Huet to decorate the salon as soon as she moved into the residence in 1735, but upon her death the series was still unfinished, which explains the posthumous payments to the artist. Once paid for, the paintings became part of the Condé collection in the Palais-Bourbon in Paris. Prior to 1822, five of them were set in the woodwork of the prince of Condé's bedroom in Chantilly, filling gaps left by the revolutionary confiscation of other works. Prior to 1846 four other paintings in the series were hung in the Jean Bullant salon of the Petit Château. The last, and largest, one—the only one not set within woodwork—has been in the Jeu de Paume museum since the late nineteenth century. Here Huet depicts Far Eastern landscapes with pagodas and various animals. Some panels are devoted to local animals (dogs, rabbits, sheep, swans) while others feature exotic ones (parrots, monkeys, birds, etc.). A few panels combine the two. Many of the waterfowl and exotic birds were probably based on the animals in the menagerie at Chantilly, which in the eighteenth century entertained guests at the château. The paintings were nevertheless not designed to hang in the menagerie itself, for eighteenth-century inventories described that interior as modest.

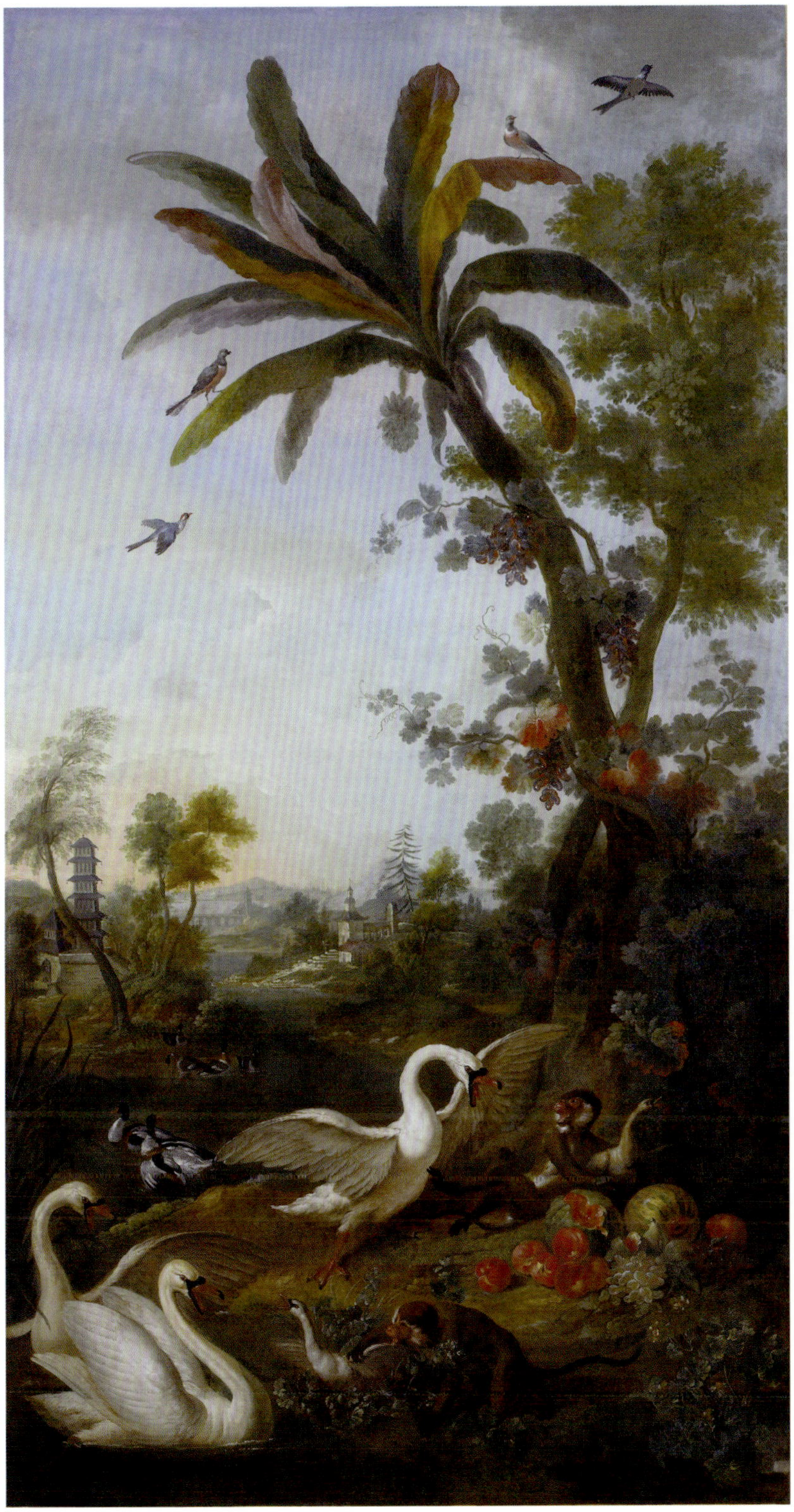

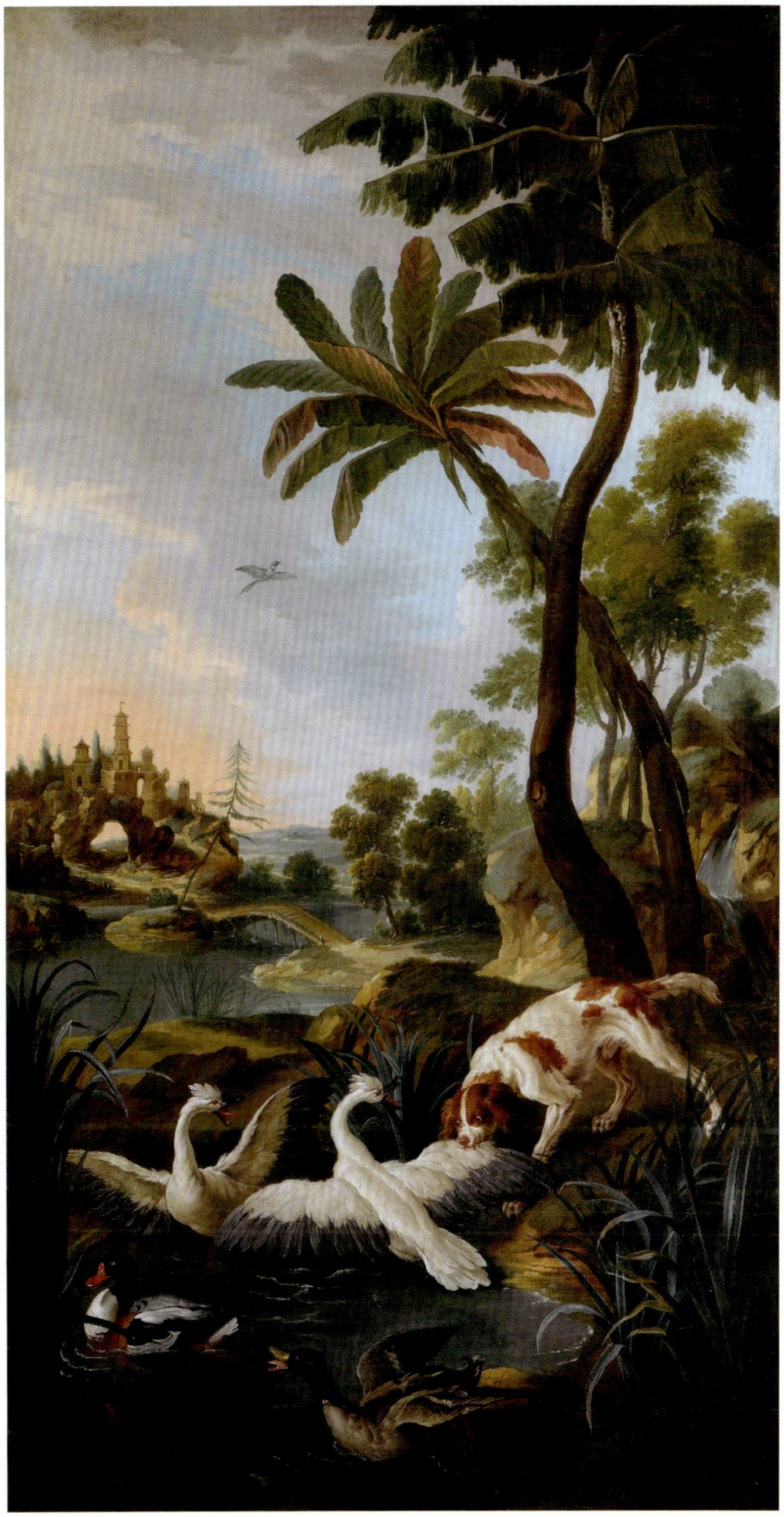

JEAN-MARC NATTIER

(Paris, 1685; Paris, 1766)

Marie-Anne de Bourbon, known as Mademoiselle de Clermont (1697–1741) Taking the Waters at Chantilly, 1729

Canvas. H. 195 cm (6 ft. 4 ½ in.); W. 161 cm (5 ft. 3 in.)
Inv. 375 (Galerie de Peinture)

Mademoiselle de Clermont, superintendent of the queen's household, was the daughter of Louis III of Bourbon, prince of Condé, and Louise-Françoise de Bourbon (a legitimized daughter of Louis XIV, called Mademoiselle de Nantes). She was the sister of the duc de Bourbon (1692–1740). She was alleged to have secretly married the duc de Melun, who died in a tragic hunting accident at Chantilly in July 1724.

Jean-Marc Nattier came to Chantilly in the summer of 1729 to paint this remarkable portrait of the princess, who posed in front of the spa that was built following the discovery of iron-rich springs there in 1725 (the building was destroyed during the Revolution). It was located at the far west end of the grounds of Chantilly, not far from the Manse pavilion. Mademoiselle de Clermont's accounts cite three payments of 600 livres to "Mr. Nattier, painter," in May, July, and September of 1729, as well as the reimbursement of his travel expenses to Chantilly in July 1729. Given its great size and allegorical nature, this ambitious portrait sought to rival large history paintings. It features Nattier's favorite colors, creating a chromatic harmony of blue and pearl gray. The princess is portrayed as the goddess of natural springs and health.

In the eighteenth century this work hung in the prince's bedroom at Chantilly, which was decorated with portraits of members of the house of Condé. Confiscated during the Revolution, the painting was sent to the Louvre. Restored to the prince of Condé on April 29, 1816, it was handed over to Louis Pierre Deseine, sculptor in ordinary to the prince, who was charged with recovering Condé artworks seized during the Terror.

Nattier painted other portraits of Mademoiselle de Clermont. The Wallace Collection in London has one signed and dated 1733, showing *Mademoiselle de Clermont en Sultane* (Mademoiselle de Clermont as a Sultaness), seated and bare legged, flanked by black women; it was probably also set at the spa building in Chantilly, this time indoors. This painting belonged to the duc de Saint-Aignan and was exhibited in the Salon of 1742 under the title of *Sultaness Leaving Her Bath, Attended by Slaves.* At the Salon of 1737 Nattier exhibited a "drawing of 'Mademoiselle de Clermont as the Goddess of Waters and Health,'" probably related to the painting shown here.

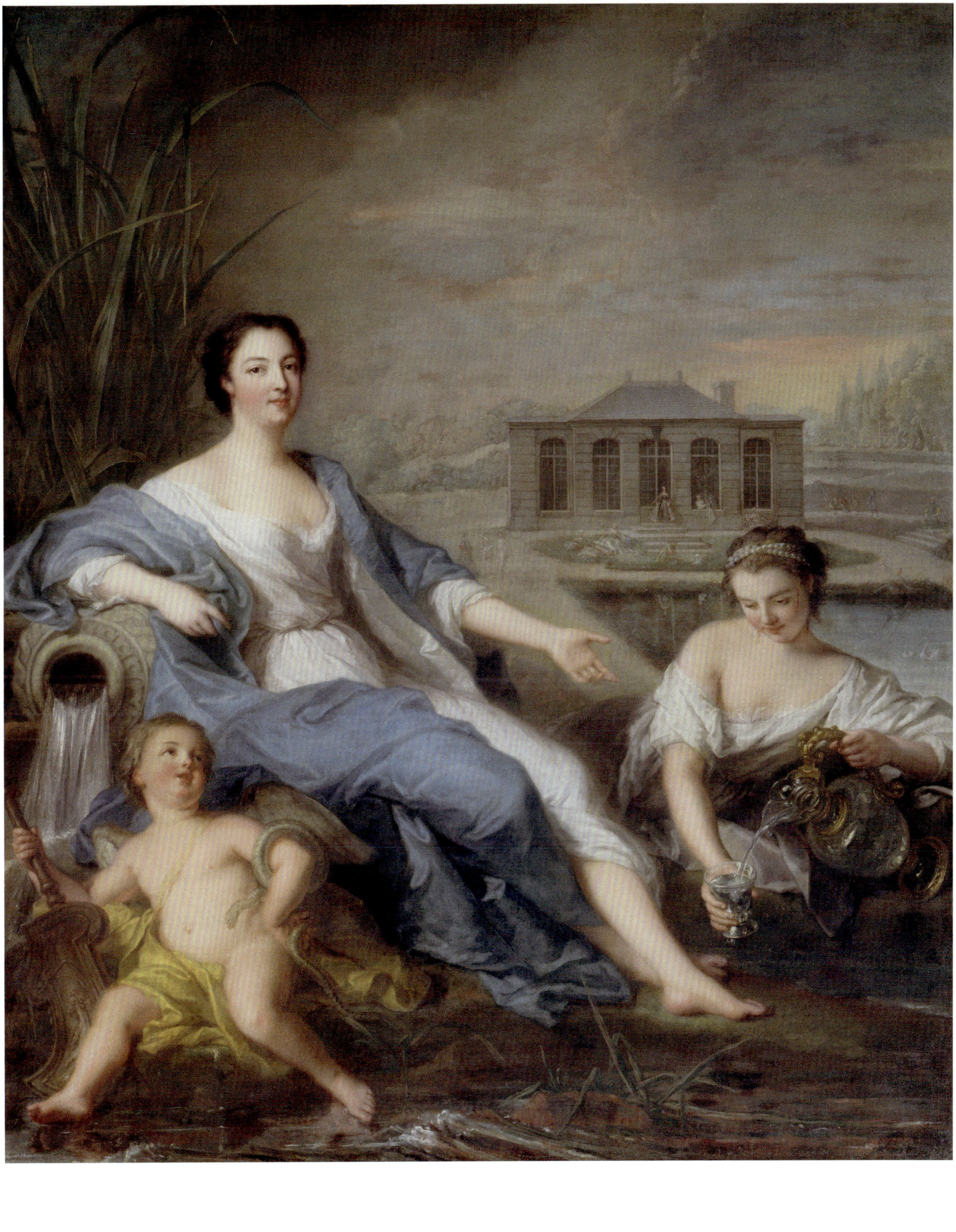

JEAN-MARC NATTIER

(Paris, 1685; Paris, 1766)

Portrait of a Woman as Hebe, formerly said to be *Louise-Henriette de Bourbon-Conti, Duchesse de Chartres then d'Orléans (1726–1759), as Hebe*, 1744

Canvas. H. 137 cm (4 ft. 5 ½ in.); W. 104 cm (3 ft. 5 in.)
S.d.b.r.: *Nattier Px. / 1744*
Inv. 376 (Rotonde de la Minerve)

The Nationalmuseum in Stockholm owns a very similar portrait, signed and dated 1744, which also bears the title of *The Duchesse de Chartres (1726–1759) as Hebe*. Given its date, the Stockholm painting, engraved by Patricot with lettering identifying the sitter, was thought to be the portrait of the duchess exhibited at the Salon of 1745. The Musée Condé's version was taken to be a replica. However, there are significant divergences between these two works: the face and the position of the hands on the Stockholm portrait are not the same as those on the one at the Musée Condé, not to mention the pose of the eagle, which alights in one painting but takes wing in the other. We therefore seem to be dealing with two different paintings by Nattier. This conclusion raises the issue of the identity of the sitter, since the young woman here appears to be different from the one in Stockholm.

The Musée Condé portrait was engraved by Hubert with lettering identifying it as "The Duchess as Hebe," generally assumed to be the duchesse de Chartres (later duchesse d'Orléans). François Hubert (1744–1809) engraved many portraits between 1765 and 1800, including some showing members of the Orléans family, notably one of Louis-Philippe, duc d'Orléans (1725–1785) and another of his son, Louis-Philippe-Joseph, later known as Philippe-Égalité (1747–1793). A confirmed portrait of the duchesse de Chartres was painted by E. Pottier (Musée des Beaux-Arts, Orléans) and engraved by Petit, revealing features that are quite different from the sitter here.

In the Salon of 1745, Nattier simultaneously exhibited a *Portrait of the Duchesse de Chartres as Hebe, Goddess of Youth* and a *Portrait of the Duchesse de Chaulnes as Hebe*. This highly fashionable conceit of the Greco-Roman goddess of eternal youth was exploited by Nattier again in the Salon of 1746 when he displayed a *Portrait of Madame Dessourniel as Hebe*. The Louvre owns the *Portrait of the Duchesse de Chaulnes as Hebe* whereas the National Gallery in Washington has a *Portrait of Madame de Caumartin as Hebe*. The château of Versailles, meanwhile, has a *Portrait of Madame Victoire, Daughter of Louis XV, as Hebe*. The frequent recurrence of this motif in Nattier's portraits explains the confusion in the identity of the sitters.

In 1826 the collection of Louis-Philippe, then duc d'Orléans, in the Palais-Royal included a Nattier painting called *Louise-Henriette de Bourbon-Conty* [sic] *as Hebe*, measuring 119 cm (3 ft. 10 in.) high and 91 cm (3 ft.) wide.

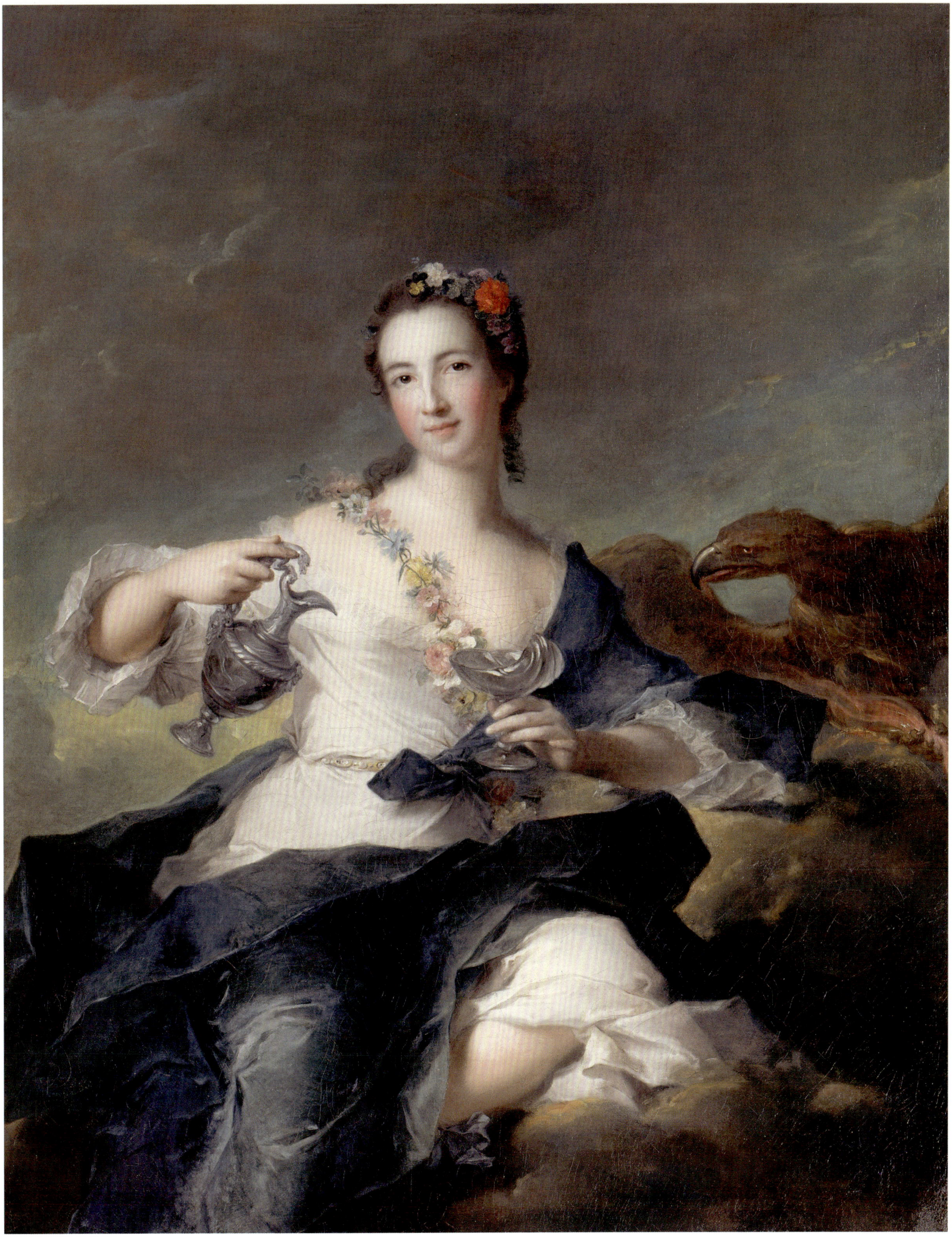

FRANÇOIS-HUBERT DROUAIS

(Paris, 1727; Paris, 1775)

The Dauphine Marie-Antoinette (1755–1793) as Hebe, 1773

Canvas. H. 96 cm (3 ft. 2 in.); W. 80 cm (2 ft. 7 ½ in.)
S.d. on the gold cup: *Drouais, 1773*
Inv. 395 (Galerie de Peinture)

Archduchess Maria Antoinetta was born in Vienna in 1755, and married Louis, the dauphin (or heir to the French throne), in the chapel at Versailles in May 1770. This painting of the dauphine was commissioned from François-Hubert Drouais in September 1772 by King Louis XV, to go over the door of the king's study in the château de Choisy. Drouais was the official portraitist of the king's favorite, Madame du Barry. The pendant to this painting was a portrait of the comtesse de Provence as Diana (replica, Musée de Versailles). The Office of Royal Works did not pay for the "portrait of the Dauphine as Hebe, shown half-length with both hands" until February 14, 1779, by which time Drouais had died; payment went to his heirs.

Criticism was harsh at the Salon of 1773. Bachaumont's *Lettres,* published in 1780, referred to "Monsieur Drouais, who failed totally with his *Portrait of the King* ... as well as his *Dauphine as Hebe* and *Comtesse de Provence as Diana.* These latter two have no relief, and the fabrics create no illusion." Worse was an article called *Dialogues sur la Peinture:* the author dared no further comment on a portrait of the dauphin that he found "so feebly rendered," all the while criticizing Drouais for disfiguring his sitter. "He only half grasped her idea, and as to her body, there is no word for it." Another text, however, *Éloges des tableaux exposés au Salon,* was more flattering: "If you would fain see a good likeness of her, Sirs, go to No. 78, at the crossing. The artist could hardly find a more felicitous sitter to represent the young Hebe." The seventeen-year-old dauphine was indeed portrayed with the attributes of Hebe, the mythological personification of youth who holds a jug and a cup with which to serve nectar to the gods on Olympus, accompanied by the eagle of Jupiter. In 1774, the financier Nicolas Beaujon commissioned the Gobelins Manufactory to produce a tapestry based on Drouais's portrait (Bourse de Commerce, Bordeaux; Château de Versailles). The painting remained at Choisy until April 30, 1792, and was considered one of the works in the royal residence worthy of being preserved and sent on June 4, 1792 to the repository of art set up in the Petits-Augustins monastery in Paris, run by the curator Alexandre Lenoir. At that point it vanished, only to surface in Lenoir's collection, which was sold in London in 1837 by the dealer Colnaghi to the duke of Sutherland for Stafford House; the duc d'Aumale bought it in May 1876.

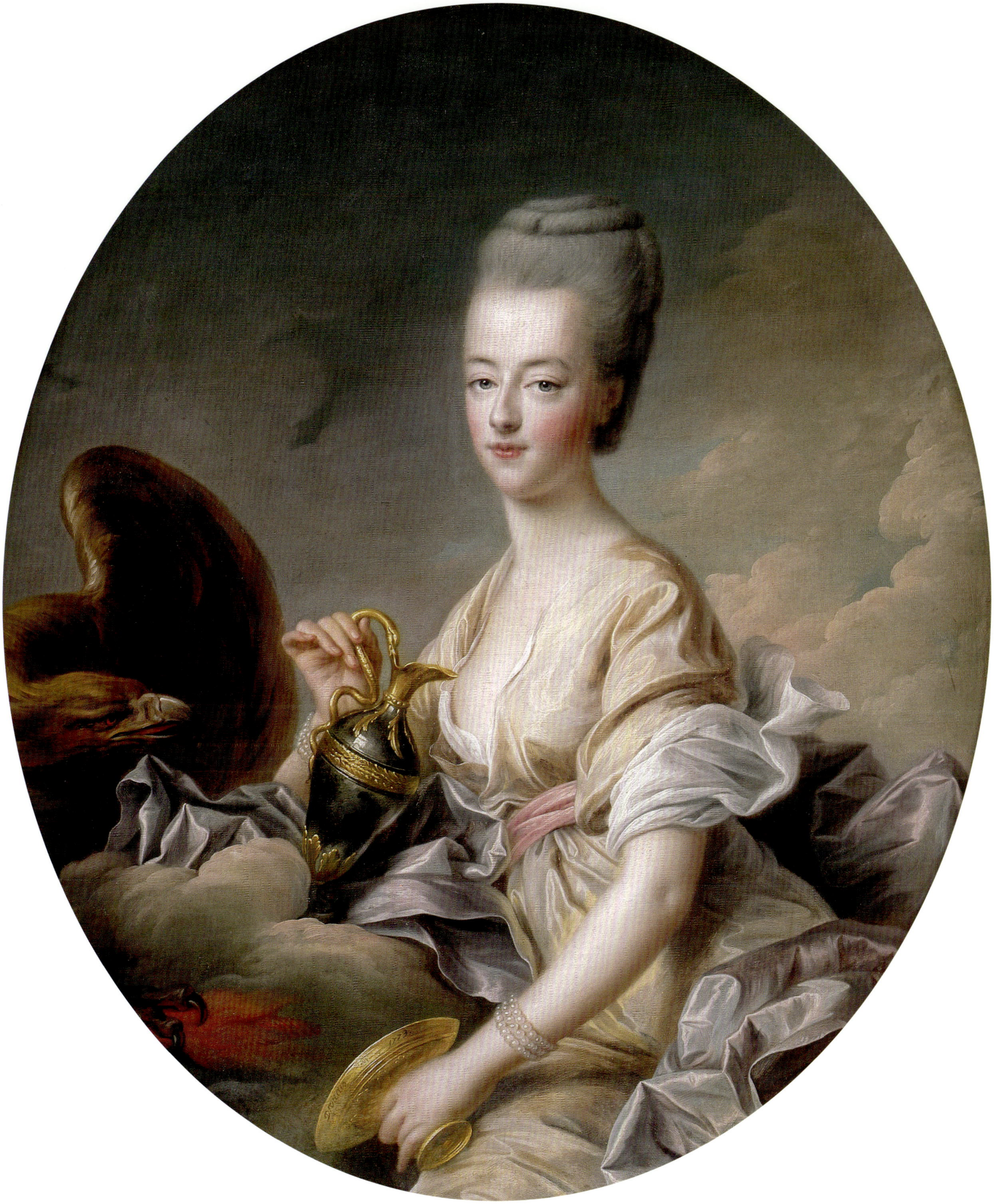

FRANÇOIS-HUBERT DROUAIS
(Paris, 1727; Paris, 1775)

Jeanne-Antoinette Poisson, Marquise de Pompadour (1721–1764)

Canvas. H. 81 cm (2 ft. 8 in.); W. 65 cm (2 ft. 1 3/4 in.)
Inv. 396 (Salle Caroline)

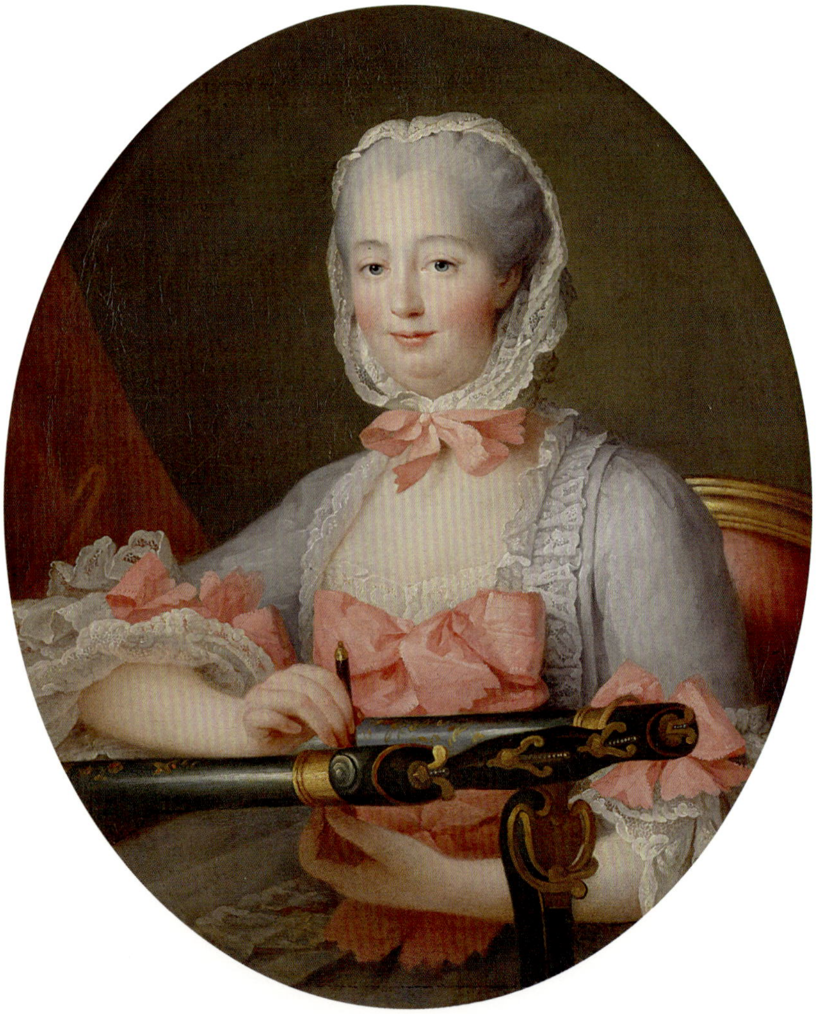

Jeanne-Antoinette Poisson, marquise de Pompadour (1721–1764), married Charles Guillaume Le Normant d'Etioles in 1741 and became King Louis XV's mistress in 1745. As a patron of the arts, notably favoring the painter François Boucher, she played an important role on the art scene; she also remained a good friend of the king up to her death.

Drouais painted two types of portraits of the marquise, whom he depicted many times: in some she hides her hands in a muff, in others she works at her embroidery. The painting here belongs to the latter group, as does a famous full-length portrait now in the National Gallery in London. The full-length portrait was exhibited at the annual Salon in August 1764, following the death of the marquise on April 5, 1764, as recorded by Melchior Grimm in his letter of August 15, 1764. "Monsieur Drouais the Younger, an Academy artist, has just exhibited in a room of the Tuileries Palace a life-size portrait of Mme. de Pompadour working at her embroidery frame.... This masterpiece of a painting was completed after the famous lady died. The head had been finished by April 1763.... Mme. de Pompadour was painted by all the masters of the Academy, but to my mind Drouais has outdone them all. He is the only man who knows how to paint women because he can do a likeness without sacrificing the delicacy and grace that lends charm to their faces. I am convinced that all our ladies will henceforth wish to be painted by Drouais."

The portrait here is perhaps a sketch for the painting of 1764, a notable possibility given that only the face is highly finished, the dress and hands remaining very sketchy. There exists a great number of copies of this head-and-shoulders version, but no replica or copy of the full-length portrait.

JOSEPH-SIFFREIN DUPLESSIS

(Carpentras, 1725; Versailles, 1802)

Madame Denis, Voltaire's Niece

Canvas. H. 80 cm (2 ft. 7 ½ in.); W. 60 cm (1 ft. 11 ½ in.)
Inv. 390 (Galerie de Peinture)

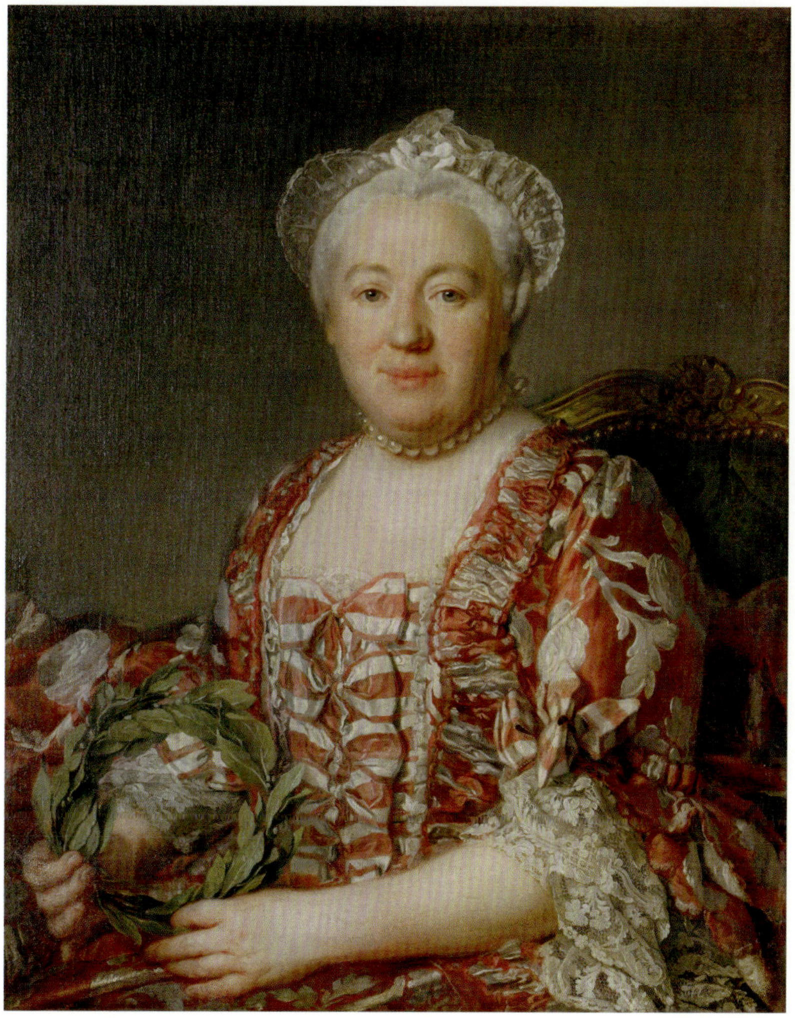

When still a young collector (aged twenty-four), the duc d'Aumale bought this painting for the sum of 250 francs from Monsieur de La Chevardière. Sold on August 27, 1846, it was presented as a *Portrait of Madame de Geoffrin* by an unknown artist of the eighteenth-century French school. At that time, the duke bought many eighteenth-century artworks—portraits, porcelain, furniture—to decorate his apartments at Chantilly. He probably liked the idea of owning a portrait of a key figure of the Enlightenment, for Madame de Geoffrin's salon was the meeting place for many famous thinkers of the day.

In fact, this portrait is connected to another famous writer of the eighteenth century. In the early twentieth century the sitter was identified as Marie-Louise Mignot (1712–90), Voltaire's niece. She was the widow of Nicolas Denis, a captain with the Champagne regiment, later remarrying François du Vivier at the age of sixty-seven. Marie-Louise maintained a close relationship with her famous uncle. She appears in an engraving of a picture by Moreau the Younger depicting a performance of *Irène,* a play by Voltaire, at the Comédie-Française on March 30, 1778; amid the applause, the prince of Beauveau sets a laurel wreath on the head of Voltaire, sitting in the front of the theater box between Mme. Denis and Mme. de Villette. In the portrait here, Mme. Denis is apparently holding the same wreath, a hypothesis confirmed by the memoirs of the actor Fleury and the correspondence of Mme. d'Epinay. Mme. Denis is also included, though not by a very good likeness, in a 1781 engraving by Née, and in another engraving by Vivant Denon titled *Breakfast at Ferney,* done from life on July 4, 1775, showing Voltaire in bed, still in his night cap, taking morning coffee with his niece, sprawled in an armchair.

JOSEPH-SIFFREIN DUPLESSIS

(Carpentras, 1725; Versailles, 1802)

Louise-Adélaïde de Bourbon-Penthièvre, Duchesse de Chartres, 1777

Canvas. H. 97 cm (3 ft. 2 ¼ in.); W. 130 cm (4 ft. 3 in.)
S.d.b.l.: *J.S. Duplessis / 1777*
Inv. 386 (Rotonde de la Minerve)

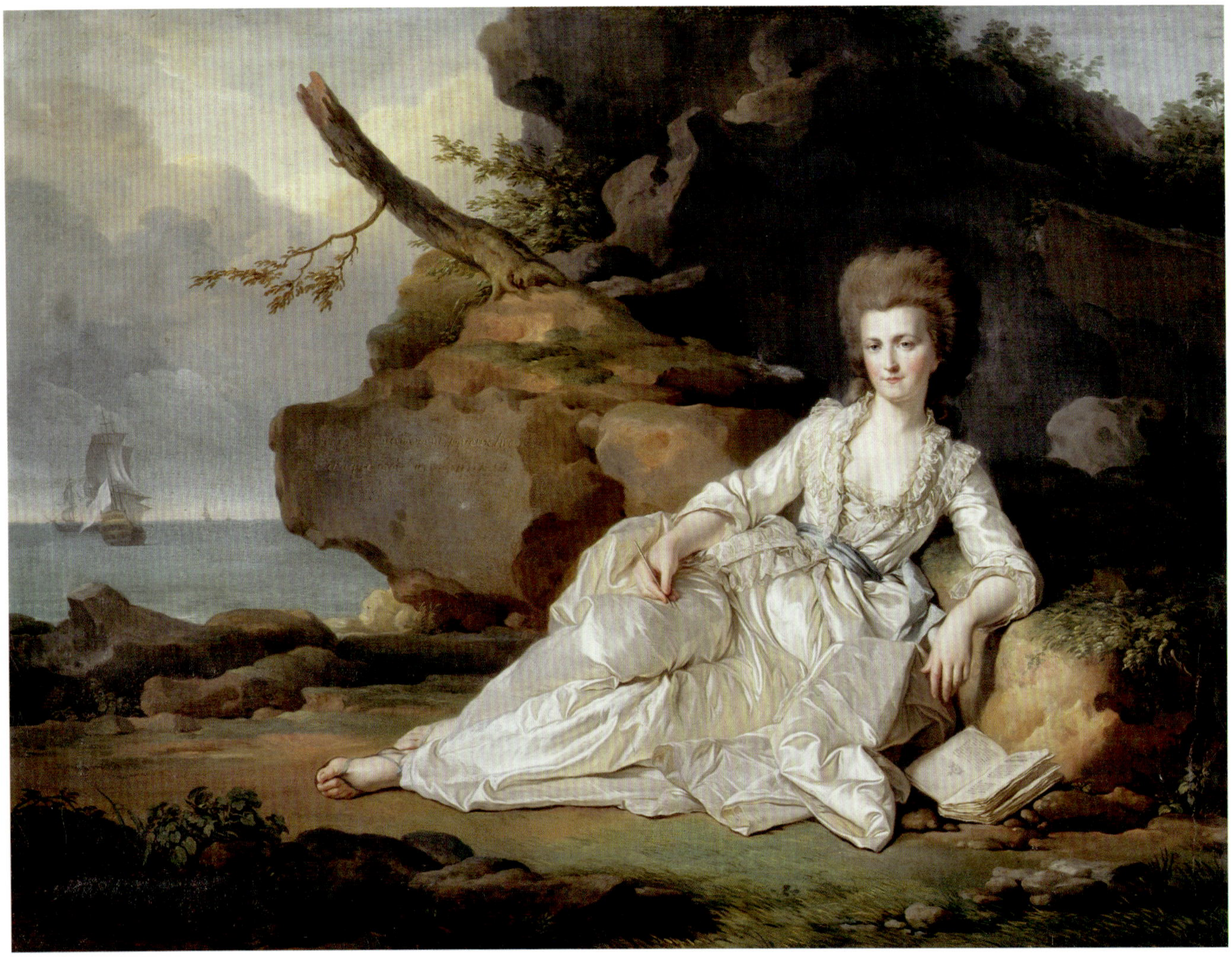

In 1769, aged sixteen, Louise-Marie-Adélaïde de Bourbon-Penthièvre (1753–1821), daughter of the duc de Penthièvre and granddaughter of the comte de Toulouse, married Louis-Philippe-Joseph, duc de Chartres, who became the duc d'Orléans in 1785 and later, during the Revolutionary period, would style himself Philippe-Égalité. The couple's children would grow up to become King Louis-Philippe and Princess Adélaide of Orléans. The duchess was therefore the grandmother of the duc d'Aumale, although she died before he was born in 1822.

Here the twenty-five year-old duchess is seen reclining on rocks by the sea. In the background we see the *Saint-Esprit*, the ship commanded by her husband at the battle of Ouessant on July 17, 1778. According to a letter from Pierre to the director of Royal Works, the artist Joseph-Siffrein (or Siffred) Duplessis was granted a posing session by his sitter in the month of April. But since the battle of Ouessant did not take place until 1778, it is probable that Duplessis altered an already completed portrait—dated 1777—which would explain not only the duchess's serene air and satin gown, but also why she is turning her back on her husband. Her pose, in fact, prompted the astonishment of Bachaumont in his review of the Salon of 1779 where the painting was exhibited.

According to another hypothesis, a different version (formerly in a private collection in Lyon), thought to be a sketch for the one here, might in fact be the original, painted in 1776. Indeed, it is of very high quality and highly finished; there is no ship in the distance, and the young duchess is shown in a casual context, without her wig. In that case, the portrait here would be a modified replica, based on the earlier painting, executed at the time of the battle of Ouessant.

JOSEPH-SIFFREIN DUPLESSIS

(Carpentras, 1725; Versailles, 1802)

Charles-Claude de Flahaut de la Billarderie, Comte d'Angiviller, Director of Royal Works (1730–1809), 1779

Canvas. H. 47 cm (1 ft. 6 ½ in.); W. 39 cm (1 ft. 3 ½ in.)
Inv. 389 (Salle Caroline)

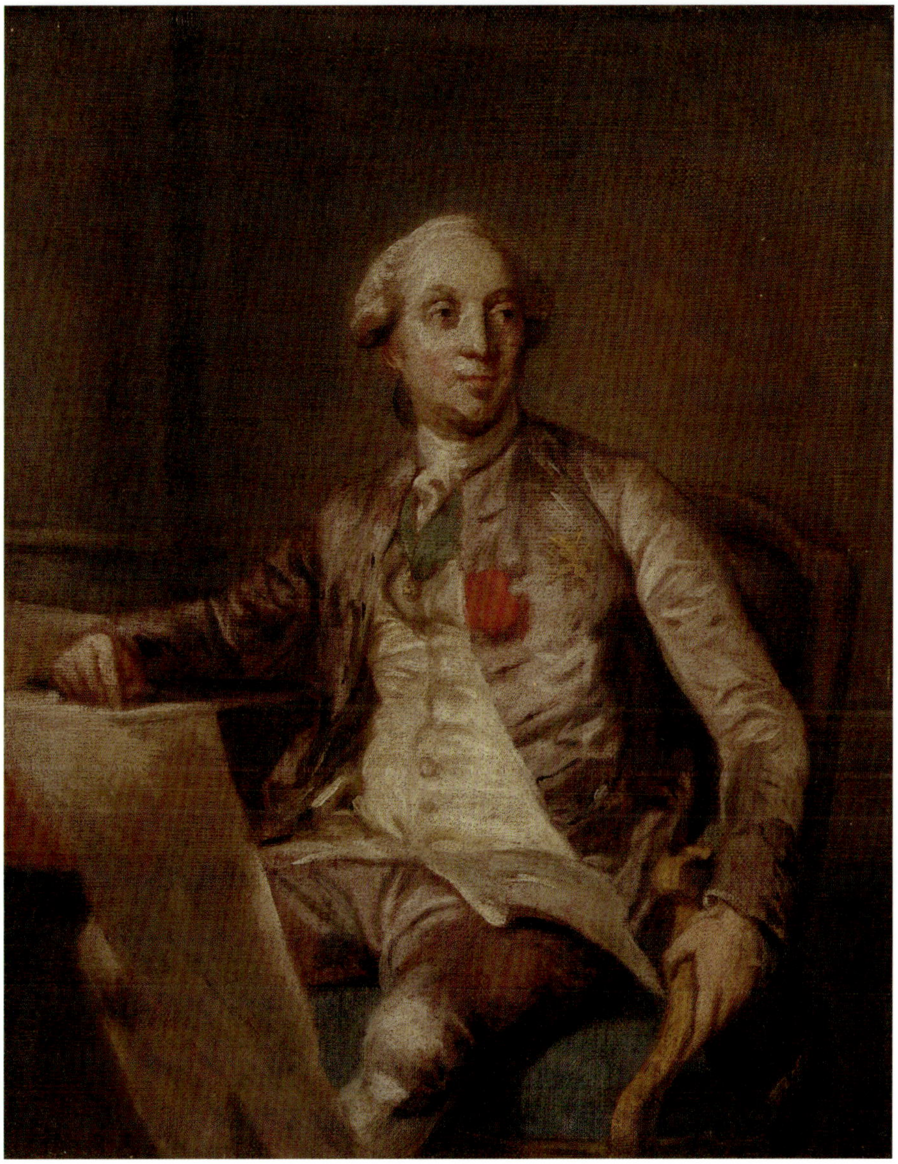

This little painting is a sketch for the portrait of Louis XIV's director of *Les Bâtiments du Roi* (Office of Royal Works) that was exhibited at the Salon of 1779. It is very similar to the final portrait, with the exception of the head, which required several sittings. Under the count's hand can be seen the plans for the revamping of the gallery in the Louvre, which were carried out under his directorship (begun in 1774). The comte d'Angiviller was a member of the Académie des Sciences as well as the Académie de Peinture et Sculpture; as a major patron of artists, scholars, and writers, he played a key role in the artistic life of his day and was portrayed by several painters. Greuze notably did a *Portrait of the Comte d'Angiviller* which is now in the Metropolitan Museum in New York. It was only in 1790, eleven years after the Salon show, that Duplessis decided to send Angiviller two versions of this portrait: the original, destined for the sitter himself, and a copy destined for the Académie (now in the Musée National du Château de Versailles). The count took the original with him when he went into exile during the Revolution; he died in Altona, Holstein in 1809; since 1979 the portrait has been preserved in Copenhagen (Statens Museum for Kunst).

ALEXIS GRIMOU
(Argenteuil, 1678; Paris, 1733)

Portrait of an Actor in Oriental Dress

Canvas. H. 78 cm (2 ft. 7 in.); W. 61 cm (2 ft.)
Inv. 368 (Salle Caroline)

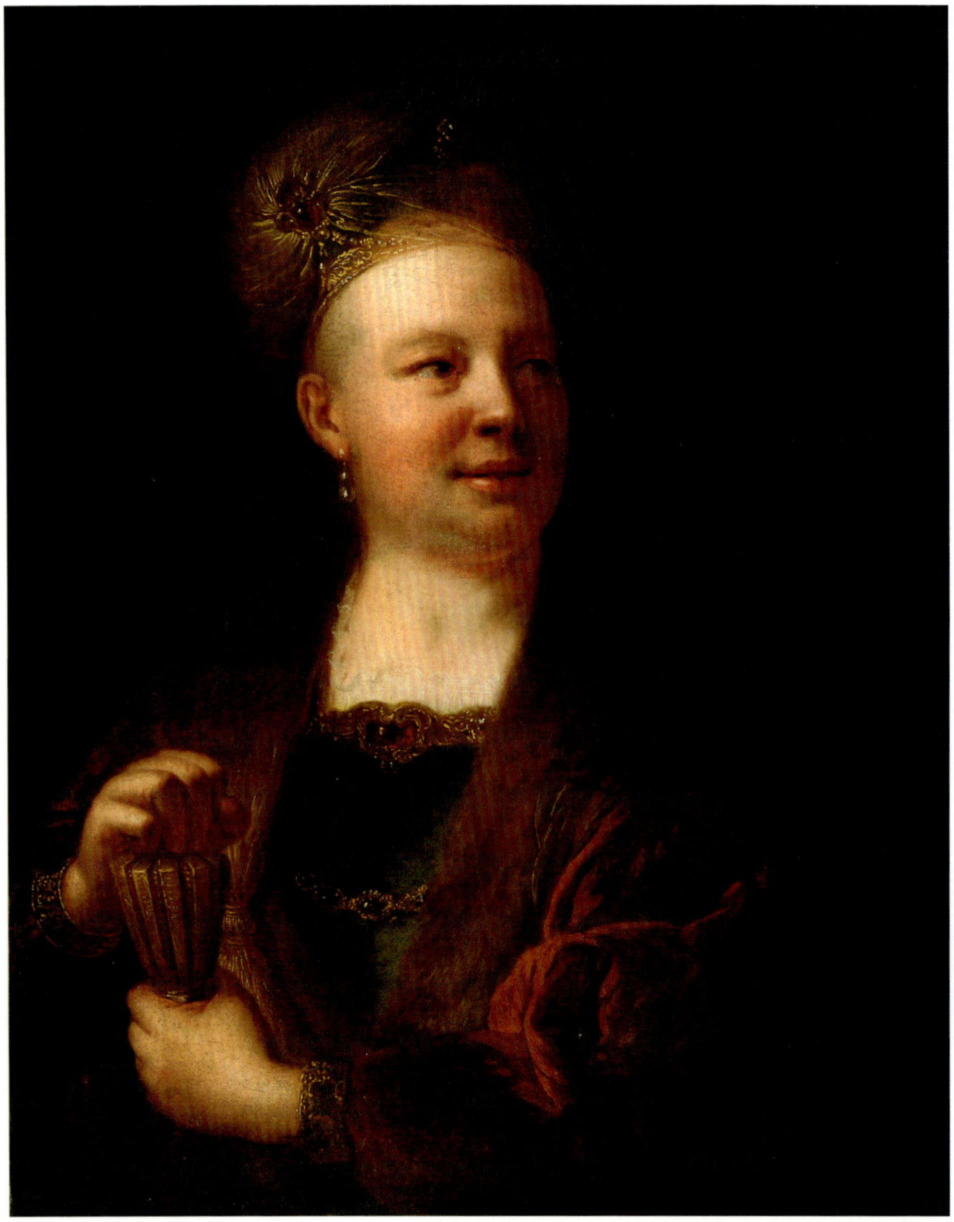

Alexis Grimou studied under François de Troy and acquired his master's taste for characters in fanciful costume. During his lifetime Grimou was known as "the French Rembrandt" due to his admiration for the Dutch artist. Some of his contemporaries even felt that he surpassed Rembrandt, whose portraits Grimou sometimes imitated. These fanciful figures stem from this tradition, even though they wear dress sometimes interpreted as theatrical costumes. Grimou never became a member of the Académie de Peinture, despite having been an associate pupil there, but turned instead to the rival Académie de Saint-Luc. He had a highly successful career in his day, though his private life was very troubled.

A copy of the painting here surfaced several times on the art market between 1975 and 1981, identifying the sitter as the actor Lekain. But it is obviously impossible that the famous actor, who was born in 1729 and died in 1778, could have been painted by Grimou, who died in 1733. In support of this assertion, useful comparisons can be made between the portrait here and the one of Lekain painted by Lenoir in 1769 (Comédie-Française, Paris) and the portrait by Grimou on permanent loan to the French prime minister's residence in Paris (Louvre, RF 1947–48), which was once thought to be Lekain.

PIERRE SUBLEYRAS

(Saint-Gilles-du-Gard, 1699; Rome, 1749)

Pope Benedict XIV (1675–1758)

Canvas. H. 125 cm (4 ft. 1 ½ in); W. 98 cm (3 ft. 2 ½ in.)
Inv. 384 (Salle Caroline)

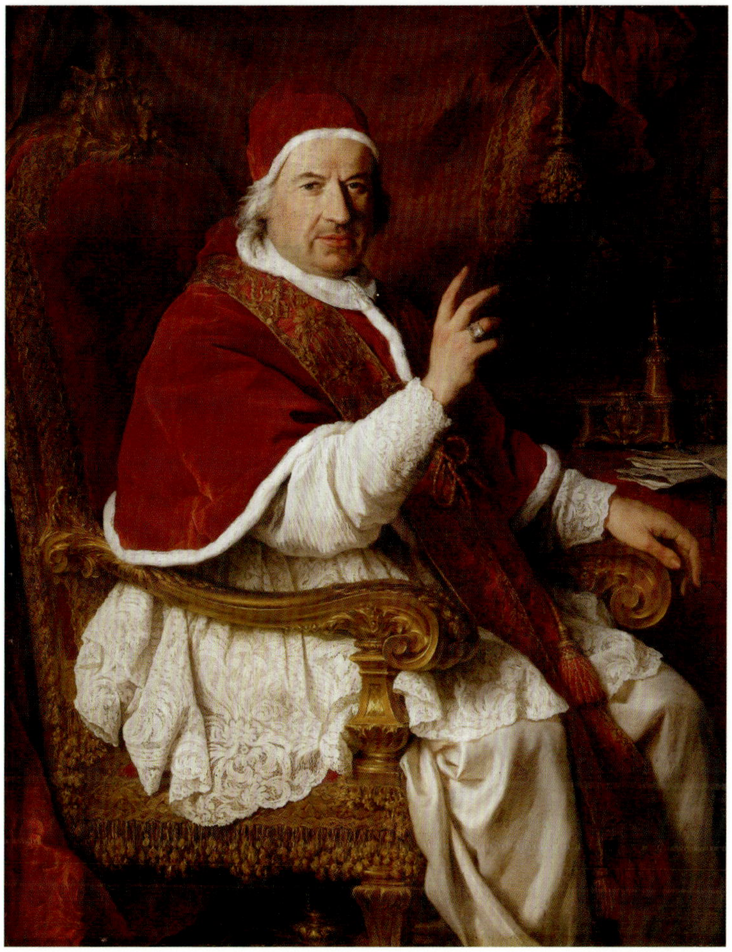

Born in Bologna, Prospero Lambertini was elected pope on August 19, 1740, and took the name Benedict XIV. Many artists painted this pope's portrait, from Giuseppe Maria Crespi to Pietro Bracci, who erected his funerary monument in Saint Peter's. At the time of Benedict's election, a rivalry sprang up between Agostino Masucci (who studied under Maratta) and Pierre Subleyras over who would paint the pope's official portrait. Subleyras won out, notably due to Benedict's pronounced Francophilia. Eight versions of this often-copied portrait are known today, two of which are now in Versailles. The original, according to the *Mercure de France* of September 1757, was painted shortly after Benedict was elected and was completed by early 1741. Indeed, the pope had sent his collected writings to the Sorbonne, which wished to have a portrait of the donor—the pope obliged in June 1757 by offering the university this portrait "as a sure sign of his esteem." As Barbier wrote in his *Journal,* "it was a great mark of distinction for the Sorbonne, given that popes are not in the habit of sending their portraits to all and sundry." The painting remained on display there up to the Revolution, hanging between portraits of Louis XV and the king's father-in-law, Stanislaw Leszczynski. Barbier went on to comment that the portrait was "an original by Subleyras, a French artist who died in Rome." There is no doubt he was referring to the portrait here, for it was confiscated during the Revolution, handed over to Alexandre Lenoir (whose inventory specified that it came from the Sorbonne), later entered the collection of the duke of Sutherland, and was bought by the duc d'Aumale in 1876.

This portrait was an immediate hit, resulting in many copies. The king of Spain had one sent to him (now lost), Marco Foscarini ordered one (Seminario Patriarchale, Venice), and Cardinal Gonzaga owned two at the time of his death. The Versailles version probably came from the Académie Royale de Peinture et de Sculpture, which received it as gift from its secretary, Charles-Nicolas Cochin, in 1766.

JEAN-BAPTISTE GREUZE

(Tournus, 1725; Paris, 1805)

Girl

Canvas. H. 45 cm (1 ft. 6 in.); W. 37 cm (1 ft. 2 ½ in.)
Inv. 391 (Salle Caroline)

After an initial apprenticeship in Charles Grandon's workshop in Lyon, Jean-Baptiste Greuze moved to Paris where he attended Natoire's drawing classes at the Académie. On becoming an associate of the Académie in 1755, Greuze exhibited portraits and genre scenes at that year's Salon, three of which were bought by Ange Laurent Lalive de Jully (1725–1779), the official presenter of ambassadors to the French court and an art lover who became Greuze's patron. Between 1755 and 1757 Greuze traveled through Italy with Abbé Gougenot, whom he probably met through the sculptor Jean-Baptiste Pigalle; he visited Rome where Natoire was then director of the Académie de France. On returning to Paris, Greuze exhibited at the Salon of 1757. He married in 1759, the year he showed twenty works at the Salon. By 1760 he had become a friend of Diderot. A year later, he painted the portrait of Louis, heir to the French throne, and enjoyed success at the annual Salon, notably for his *L'Accordée de Village* (The Village Fiancée). In 1766 he published a series of character studies, engraved by Ingouf from his studies of expressive heads. After presenting his history painting of *Septimus Severus* at the Académie and the Salon of 1769, Greuze suffered the humiliation of being admitted to the Académie only as a genre painter, not a history painter. In 1771, King Gustav III of Sweden paid a visit to his studio, followed in 1777 by Emperor Joseph II, who ennobled him. Another probable visitor was Grand Duke Paul, the future Tsar Paul I of Russia, son of Catherine the Great. Greuze divorced in 1793. From 1800 onward he began exhibiting again at the Salon, which he had boycotted since his unfortunate experience in 1769. He died in his premises in the Louvre in 1805.

This half-length portrait of a seated girl might be Georgette, the daughter of Greuze's caretaker, who served as the model for the fiancée in *L'Accordée du Village,* the painting that made Greuze's reputation when shown at the Salon of 1761. Other art historians argue that, rather than serving as a study for *L'Accordée,* it was an independent portrait done around 1765. Another version, with slight differences (the gaze is turned upward, there is no bow on the scarf, which reveals more neck), figures in the queen of England's collection (Buckingham Palace, London). Copies of this portrait are found in Paris (Musée Cognac-Jay), Narbonne (Musée d'Art), Ghent (Museum voor Schone Kunste), and various private collections.

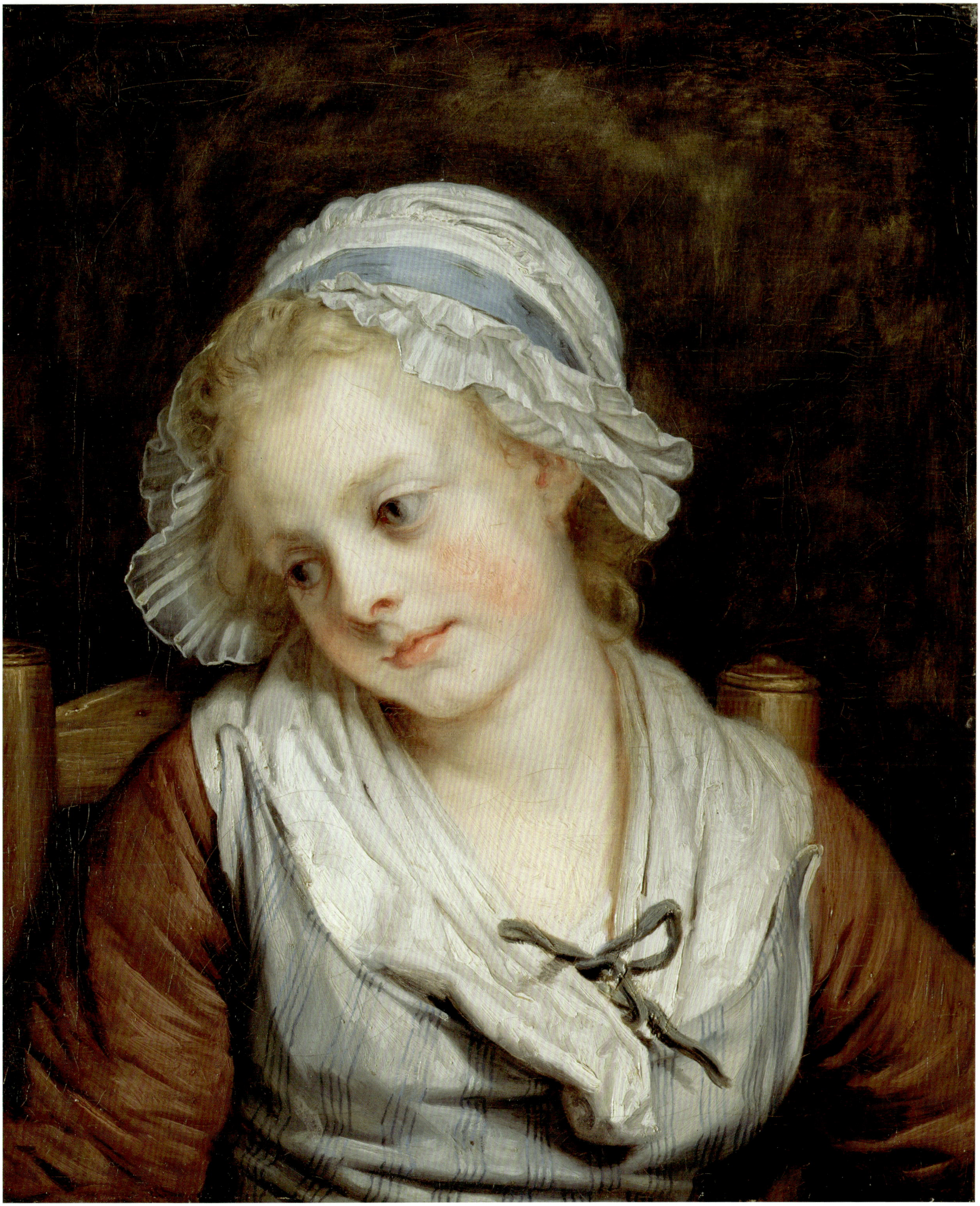

JEAN-BAPTISTE GREUZE

(Tournus, 1725; Paris, 1805)

Young Boy

Canvas. H. 40 cm (1 ft. 3 3/4 in.); W. 32 cm (1 ft. 1/2 in.)
Inv. 392 (Salle Caroline)

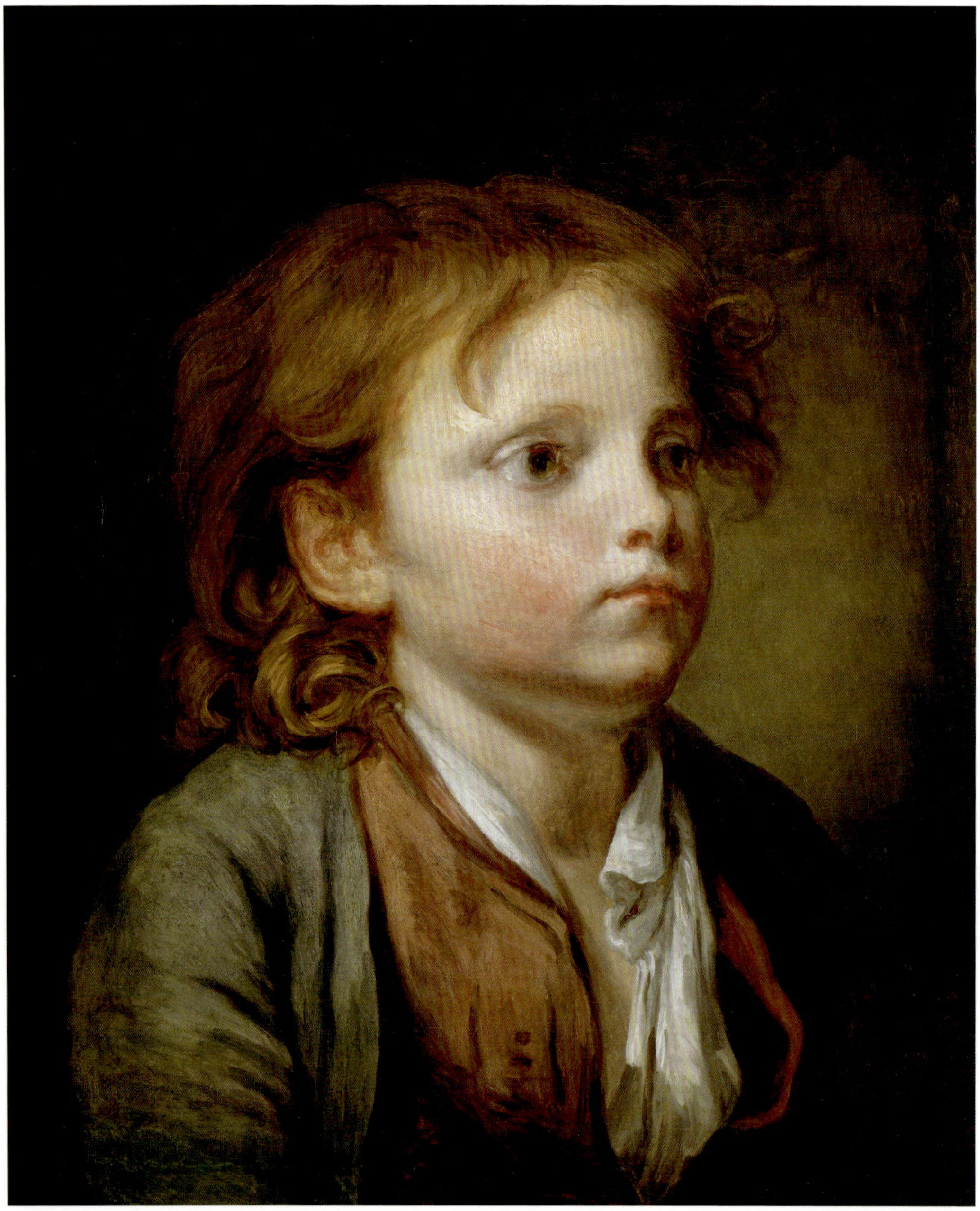

In three-quarter profile, head alert, this young lad seems to be looking at something with great attention. His curly hair falls over his forehead and shoulders, while a half-unbuttoned vest and shirt offer a glimpse of his chest. The Metropolitan Museum in New York has a very similar portrait of a boy, probably of the same sitter.

Some art historians feel that this painting is the one called *Colin's Sweet Gaze,* sold at the Randon de Boisset auction in 1777, later entering the Livois collection in Angers in 1791, then reappearing in the 1881 Gamba sale and finally sold by the connoisseur Henry in 1836 under the title *Sans-Souci* ("The Carefree Lad," sold along with a pendant, *The Little Beggar Girl*). It was engraved by Dennel and by Hauer under the title of *The Little Brother.*

JEAN-BAPTISTE GREUZE

(Tournus, 1725; Paris, 1805)

Fond Desire

Canvas. H. 40 cm (1 ft. 3 3/4 in.); W. 32 cm (1 ft. 1/2 in.)
Inv. 393 (Salle Caroline)

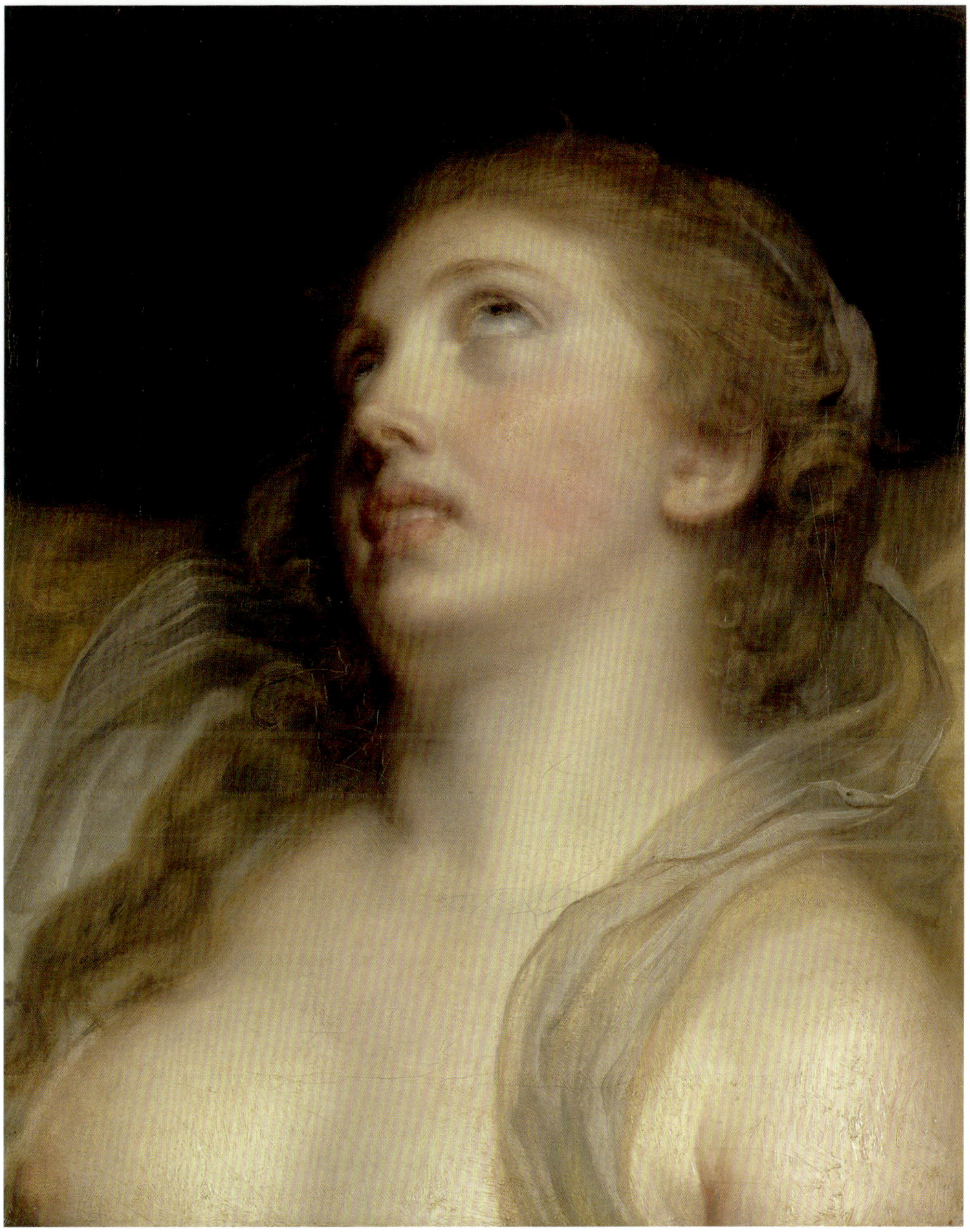

Gazing upward, head tilted back, this young woman is presumably reclining. A gauzy shawl around her shoulders leaves her breasts bare, while one of her arms seems to point to the object of her desire. *Fond Desire* might be an early study for the head of *The Beloved Mother,* exhibited at the Salon of 1769. Greuze also addressed the theme of desire in the Salon of 1800, exhibited as a pendant to a painting of *Cruelty*.

Before entering the Condé collection (*see p. 30*), this painting was apparently sold at the marquis de Verry (Véri) auction in Paris in 1785, then in the Tolozan sale of 1800. An engraving of this painting was made by C*** [Carmona], published under this title as well as that of *Tête d'Expression* (Character Study) by Massard. Another study of this subject, on wood panel, is held by the Musée Greuze in Tournus.

JEAN-BAPTISTE GREUZE

(Tournus, 1725; Paris, 1805)

Surprised

Canvas. H. 47 cm (1 ft. 6 ½ in.); W. 38 cm (1 ft. 3 in.)
Inv. 394 (Salle Caroline)

Greuze was keen to convey emotional reactions, which had been a key element of history painting ever since the seventeenth century; but he sought to bring new life to them by forging modern versions of the classical approach advocated by Lebrun. To this end, Greuze executed many drawings and oil studies. His character studies skillfully played on the sensibility of the beholder, and were therefore highly sought-after and often repeated. Steeped in a powerful realism, Greuze's works had great emotional impact, and his unique style remained aloof from the trends of his day. In the latter half of the nineteenth century his art was usually associated most closely with his female character studies. The duc d'Aumale's acquisitions of his work were therefore typical.

This portrait of a woman with beaded headband, flowing hair, and raised right arm came from the collection of Marquis Nicolas-Joseph Maison (1771–1840), a marshal of France, and his son. Four original paintings by Greuze were bought in a block by the duc d'Aumale during the sale of thirty-five works from Maison's collection for the sum of 680,000 francs. The original offer included other paintings by Greuze, notably a *Blond Magadalen,* a *Brunette Magdalen,* and a study of a head for a *Magdalen,* but they were excluded. *Surprised* apparently dates from around 1800.

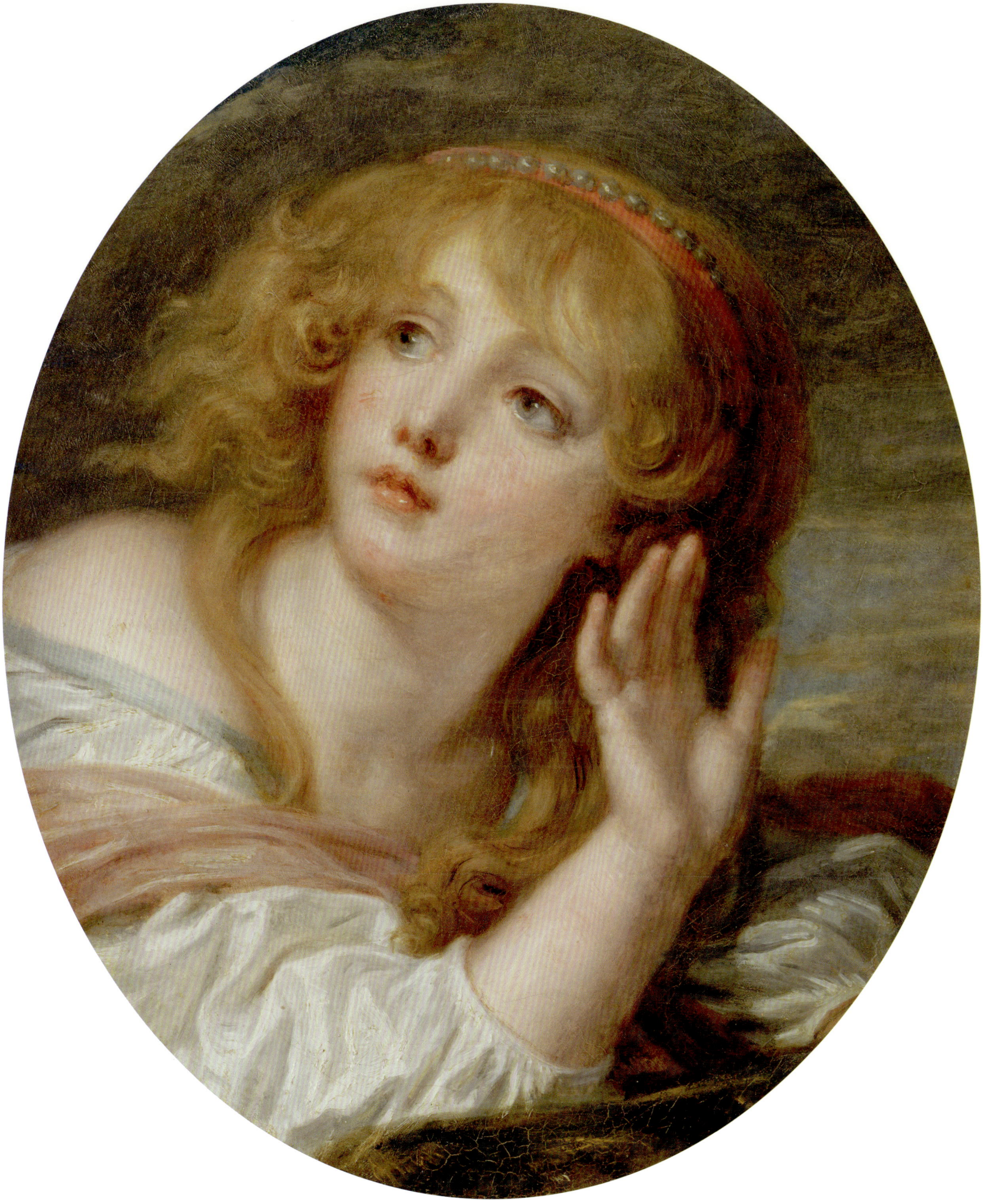

SIR JOSHUA REYNOLDS

(Plympton, Devonshire, 1723; London, 1792)

Maria Walpole, Countess Waldegrave (1739–1807), and her Daughter, Elizabeth Laura, 1761

Canvas. H. 76 cm (2 ft. 5 ½ in.); W. 64 cm (2 ft. 1 ½ in.)
Inscription t.r.: *Maria Countess of Waldegrave and her Daughter Lady Elizabeth Laura, 1761*;
t.l.: *Haec occulis, haec pectore toto / Haeret, et interdum gremio fovet*
Inv. 146 (Tribune)

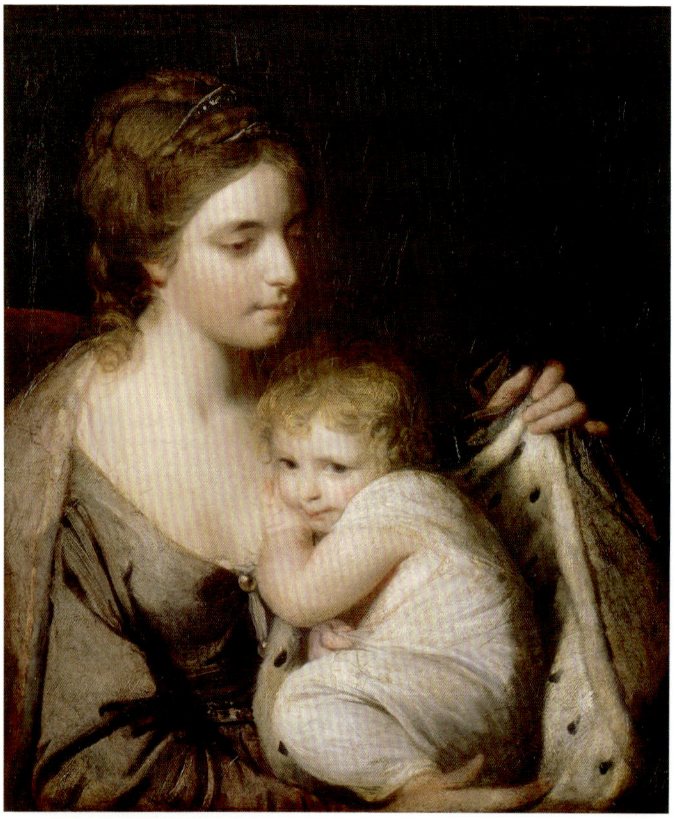

Maria Walpole (1739–1807) was the niece of Sir Horace Walpole, the writer and art lover who was a friend of Joshua Reynolds, from whom he commissioned this portrait of his niece in 1761. After her marriage in 1759 to James, Earl Waldegrave (1715–1763), she gave birth to a daughter on March 24, 1760. Elizabeth Laura was therefore between one and two years old when this portrait was done. It was through her that Strawberry Hill, Horace Walpole's estate in Twickenham, passed to the Waldegraves, who kept this portrait there—it can be seen in a photograph of the dining room taken in 1863 by Philip-Henry Delamotte, owned by the duc d'Aumale (Musée Condé, Chantilly). Her grand-daughter by marriage, Lady Frances Waldegrave, was a close friend of the duc d'Aumale, to whom she bequeathed this portrait upon her death in 1879.

When commenting on this painting and referring to Walpole's niece, considered one of the great beauties of her day, the duc d'Aumale never failed to point out that "she married four times: for propriety, for profit, from foolishness, and for love." Reynolds painted her several times, notably executing official full-length portraits of the couple at the time of her marriage. In 1761, Reynolds exhibited a profile *Portrait of Maria Walpole, Countess Waldegrave* at the Society of Artists (Anglo-American Museum, Louisiana State University, Baton Rouge), followed in 1762 by *Lady Waldegrave as Dido Kissing Cupid* and *Lady Waldegrave and a Child*, this latter perhaps being the portrait here. In 1765 Reynolds painted the countess in mourning dress, then exhibited a portrait of her three daughters, titled *The Waldegrave Sisters* (National Gallery of Scotland, Edinburgh) at the Royal Academy in 1781. It featured Elizabeth Laura (1760–1816), aged twenty-one, with her two younger sisters.

This masterpiece by Reynolds shows the serene young mother wrapping her daughter in an ermine cloak. The child cuddles her mother, and shyly glances toward the beholder, offering a tiny smile. The painting's dark tones were inspired by the Venetian school and Rembrandt.

CARLE VERNET

(Bordeaux, 1758; Paris, 1736)

The Duc d'Orléans and the Duc de Chartres Meeting for the Hunt in 1787, also called *Leaving for the Hunt*, 1788

Canvas. H. 108 cm (3 ft. 6 ½ in.); W. 128 cm (4 ft. 2 ½ in.)
S.d.b.l.: *Vernet fils 1788*
Inv. 419 (Rotonde de la Minerve)

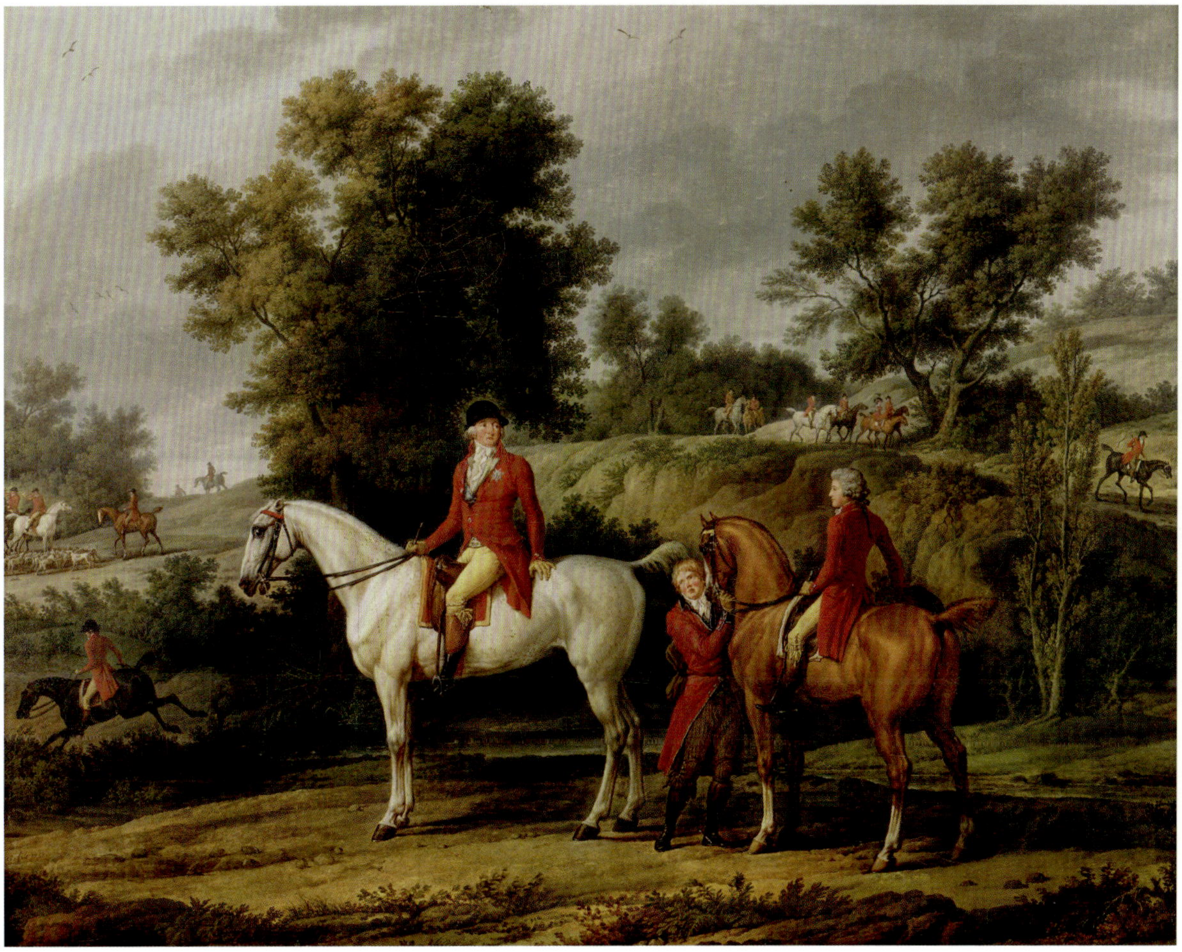

Considered one of the best horse painters of his day, Carle Vernet regularly went to stables and riding rings to study equine anatomy and bearing. The duc d'Orléans commissioned Vernet to paint this picture, for which the artist was paid 4,000 livres in December 1788. This was probably the work exhibited in the Salon of 1814 under the title of *Leaving for the Hunt*. Prince Louis-Philippe-Joseph, duc d'Orléans—who would soon dub himself Philippe-Égalité once the Revolution got underway—is seen here accompanied by his son the duc de Chartres (who would later become King Louis-Philippe), then aged fourteen. They were setting out for a hunt, probably near Raincy. Both wear a long red hunting coat with silver buttons and a blue velvet cap, which represented English-style hunting dress in the colors of the house of Orléans. The duc d'Orléans is wearing the medal of the Order of the Holy Spirit on his left breast.

The painting remained in the Orléans family until it came to power in 1830, because in 1836 King Louis-Philippe commissioned a copy to be hung in the gallery of history paintings at the château of Versailles. The Orléans family most likely relinquished the original during the Revolution of 1848, when it entered the collection of Prince Esterhazy in Budapest. The duc d'Aumale, after returning to France and bequeathing the château de Chantilly to the Institut de France in 1884, sought to recover this family portrait. In 1885 he suggested a swap to the director of the French museum administration, who allegedly preferred a Veronese, a portrait by van Dyck, or a Dutch painting to the Carracci the duke was offering in exchange. In the end, the duke simply bought the painting for the sum of 12,000 francs plus an item of jewelry selected by Madame de Clinchamp for the director of museums.

FRANÇOIS GÉRARD

(Rome, 1770; Paris, 1837)

Napoleon Bonaparte as First Consul, 1803

Canvas. H. 62 cm (2 ft. 1 in.); W. 53 cm (1 ft. 8 3/4 in.)
D.b.r.: *Fév. 1803*
Inv. 425 (Tribune)

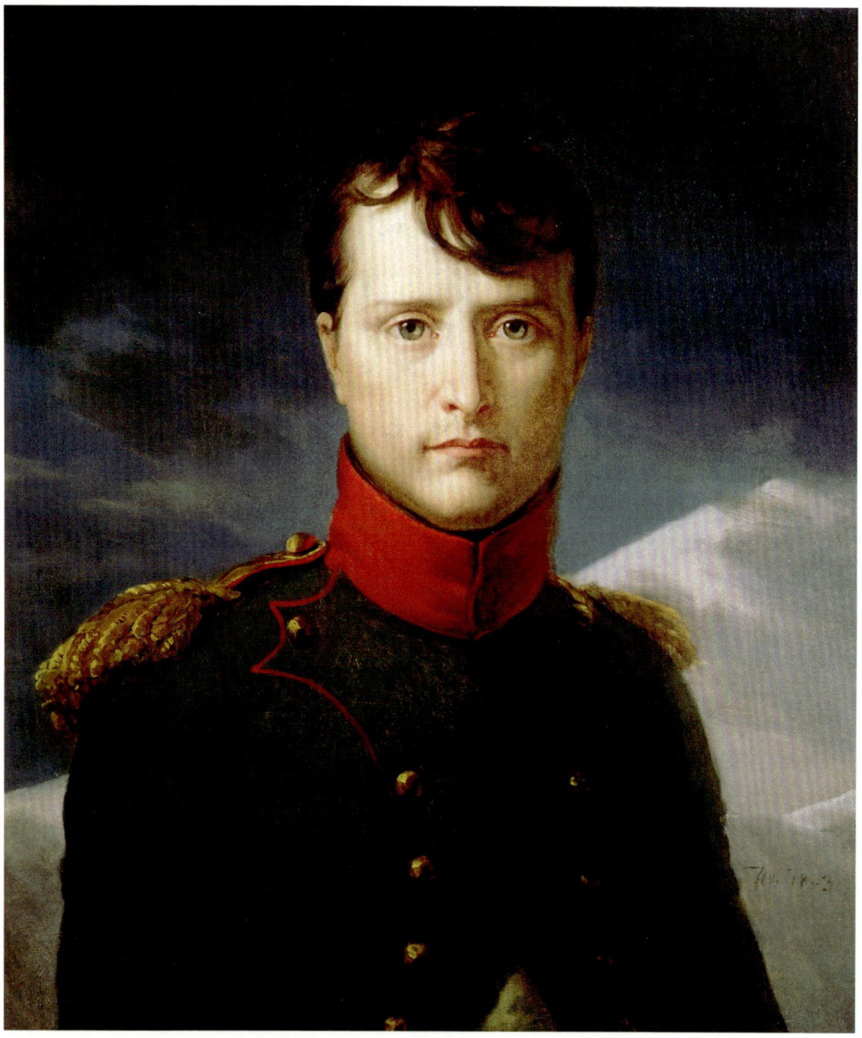

François Gérard was born in Rome, the son of the intendant to Cardinal de Bernis. He trained in Paris under Pajou, then David. He failed to win the Prix de Rome but nevertheless traveled to the city of his birth, although soon obliged to return to Paris. He avoided the military draft thanks to his teacher, David, who had him appointed to a revolutionary tribunal (an office he exercised little, feigning illness). Although a history painter up to the Revolution, during the Empire period Gérard became the official portraitist to the court and high-ranking dignitaries.

This portrait of Bonaparte as first consul prefigures the emergence of Napoleon as emperor. It functioned as a prototype of official portraiture on the eve of the consul's elevation to emperor: the straightforwardness of the frontal pose and the intensity of the sitter's gaze strike the beholder. Here the first consul wears his uniform of commander-in-chief. His figure is set against the sky and the snowy slope of a mountain, probably alluding to his crossing of the Alps during the Italian campaign. Here we have the development of an official portrait as dictated by the sitter, a type that would be later adopted and adapted by David in his portraits of the imperial coronation. We no longer see the emaciated face of the victor of the battle of Arcole, but rather the long, dignified features of a face whose sharp edges have been smoothed. It would seem that Gérard deliberately aged Bonaparte here, to political ends, so that the future emperor would resemble, in advance, his picture.

This youthful work by Gérard is the only one to bear a date. It was apparently painted from life in February 1803 at the Tuileries Palace. Thanks to Bonaparte, the former history painter became a highly sought-after portraitist who went onto paint the imperial court and dignitaries. Paradoxically, Gérard was not ennobled until 1819, by the Restoration monarchy after the fall of Napoleon. This painting was acquired by Frédéric Reiset *(see p. 33)* at the post-mortem auction of Gérard's estate.

FRANÇOIS GÉRARD

(Rome, 1770; Paris, 1837)

The Three Ages of Man

Canvas. H. 255 cm (8 ft. 4 in.); W. 322 cm (10 ft. 6 in.)
Inv. 426 (Galerie de Peinture)

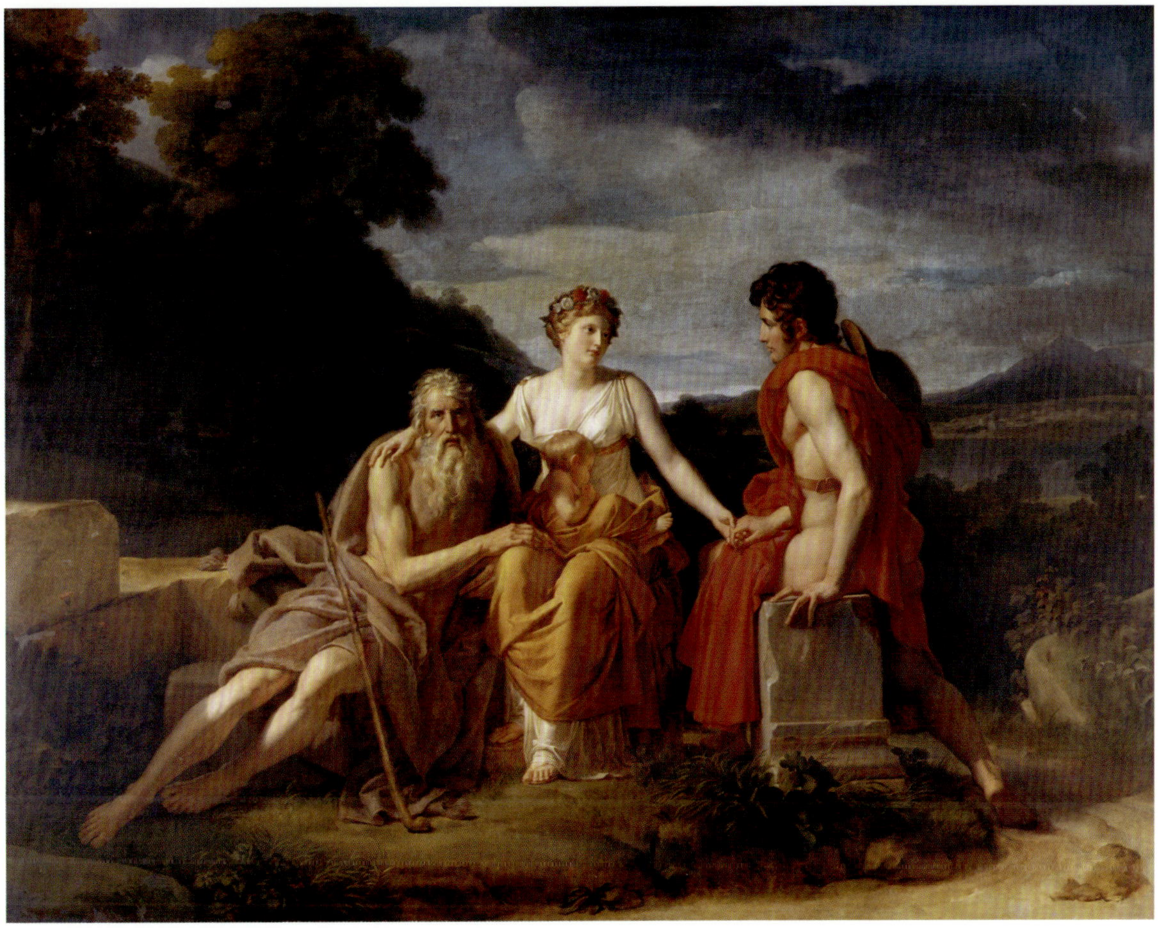

In the midst of the Roman countryside—a landscape evocative of Nicolas Poussin and eighteenth-century French classicism—sit three male figures who represent the ages of man: child, adult, old man. They flank a female figure who occupies the central position. The unusual presence of the woman was explained in the booklet to the Salon of 1808, where this work was exhibited: "Throughout life's voyage, women are the guides, the delight, and the support of men (Oriental saying)." This clear-cut role of woman as the person who raises the child, supports and loves the adult, and looks after the old man, here results in a somewhat cold allegory. The pose of the female figure inevitably evokes the countless images of Liberty that were common during the Revolutionary period.

This picture was painted in 1806 and bought by Napoleon's sister, Caroline Murat, queen of Naples. It was exhibited at the Salon of 1808, an event that its organizer, Vivant Denon, hoped would be "peerless." Jacques-Louis David, then at the height of his career, had not exhibited at a Salon since 1795 and made a powerful return by showing earlier works such as *The Rape of the Sabines* (1800) and *The Coronation of Napoleon* (already exhibited at the Louvre earlier that year). David was joined by his three most famous pupils, all of whom showed major works: Girodet presented *Atala,* Gros showed *The Battle of Eylau,* and Gérard *The Three Ages of Man.* Despite its rather cold handling, Gérard's contribution was praised for its philosophical content.

In 1810 Napoleon launched a contest of the most striking artworks of his first decade in power, from his coup d'état of 18 Brumaire (November 9, 1799) to November 1808. The Institut de France was charged with drawing up short-lists, one of which would be submitted by the Institut's permanent secretaries, another by the Académie des Beaux-Arts. *The Three Ages of Man* was included on both lists. It appears that the painting was not physically present, because it was in Caroline Murat's collection in Naples. An oil sketch that belonged to King Louis-Philippe was destroyed by fire during the revolution of 1848. The large painting in Naples was acquired by the duc d'Aumale as part of the collection of his uncle and father-in-law, the prince of Salerno (*see p. 27*).

JEAN-ANTOINE GROS

(Paris, 1771; Meudon, 1835)

Plague Victims in Jaffa

Canvas. H. 91 cm (3 ft.); W. 116 cm (3 ft. 9 ½ in.)
S.b.l.: *Gros*
Inv. 428 (Galerie de Peinture)

Jean-Antoine Gros became a pupil of David at the age of fourteen, but he soon lost interest in neoclassical subjects based on Roman history and turned toward Rubens and Baroque art. In the revolutionary year of 1793 his moderate political opinions placed him at risk, and he left France for Italy, where he remained for eight years. On good terms with Bonaparte and Josephine, Gros returned to France in 1801, where he emerged as a pioneer of Romantic Orientalism with his two large paintings, *Plague Victims in Jaffa* (exhibited in the Salon of 1804) and *The Battle of Aboukir* (Salon of 1806). Having become the prime painter of Napoleonic battles, he was admitted to the Institut de France in 1815. Imperial favor did not hinder his career during the Restoration, after the fall of Napoleon. But having attempted to reinvigorate his art after 1822 by devising compositions closer to David's neoclassicism, he felt a sense of failure and committed suicide by drowning.

This canvas is a sketch for the painting exhibited at the Salon of 1804 (now in the Louvre), which Bonaparte personally commissioned from Gros. Encountering the artist in the corridors of the Louvre, Bonaparte asked, "What are you working on at the moment?" Gros said, "I'm awaiting your orders." To which Bonaparte replied, "In that case, there's to be a picture of me visiting the plague victims in Jaffa—the job is yours."

Vivant Denon had already assigned this task to Pierre-Narcisse Guérin. Gros executed the painting in the Jeu-de-Paume hall, based on the recollections of Denon, who was at Bonaparte's side in Jaffa in March 1799 when the latter extended his Egyptian campaign to the Ottoman Empire, invading as far as Syria. He captured the fortified port of Jaffa, where an outbreak of the plague occurred; on March 11, he visited the military hospital with his officers, to reassure his troops. Gros did several preliminary drawings (Louvre) and preparatory sketches (New Orleans). His initial idea showed Bonaparte in a bare hospital room, holding a plague-ridden soldier in his arms. In a later version, he placed greater stress on the picturesque Oriental setting by incorporating Moorish architecture and by accurately copying Oriental dress. There are few differences between the sketch here and the large version in the Louvre, apart from details such as the cremation of bodies in the left-hand background of this sketch and the pose of the surgeon Masclet (who became infected) in the lower right. Bonaparte is presented as a miracle-working monarch, touching the victims' buboes the way French kings once allegedly healed sufferers of scrofula by touching them. Accompanied by Generals Berthier and Bessières, Bonaparte displays great courage whereas the people in his entourage cover their mouths with handkerchiefs to avoid contagion.

This scene, with its political connotations, represents a major history painting that was one of the sources of both Orientalism and depictions of the Napoleonic saga. It met with great approval at the Salon of 1808 and was appreciated by David and, later, Delacroix.

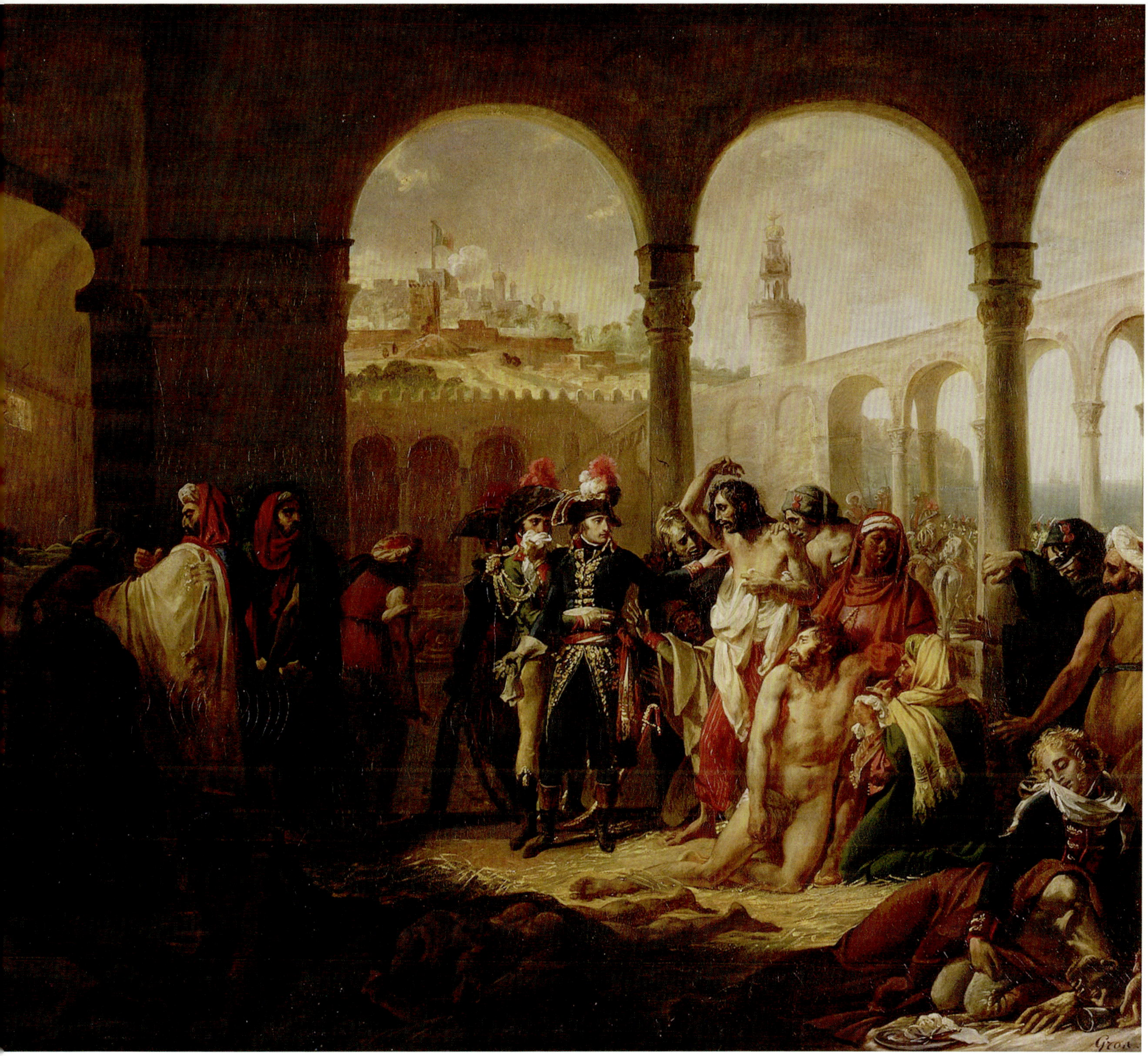
Gros

LOUIS-LÉOPOLD BOILLY

(La Bassée, 1761; Paris, 1845)

Interior of a Café, also known as *Playing Checkers at Café Lamblin*

Wood-backed canvas. H. 38 cm (1 ft. 3 in.); W. 55 cm (1 ft. 9 ½ in.)
Inv. 424 (Salle Isabelle)

Louis-Léopold Boilly was the son of a wood carver from Lille, in the north of France; he trained in Arras and later in Paris in 1785. Boilly exhibited at the annual Salons from 1791 to 1824. His style was influenced by the minor Dutch masters of the seventeenth century, such as Gerrit Dou, Gerard Ter Borch, and Gabriel Metsu, whose slick, shiny handling he adopted. After having enjoyed great success during the periods of Empire (1803–14) and Restoration (1815–30), culminating in elevation to the Légion d'Honneur in 1833, Boilly slowly sank into oblivion during the July Monarchy (1830–48).

This painting was exhibited at the Salon of 1824, the last one in which Boilly showed a work. It is a genre scene of a Paris café during the Restoration, perhaps the famous Café Lamblin at the Palais-Royal, or else Café Corazza (according to the duc d'Aumale's inventory). The player on the left, wearing trousers, frock coat, and top hat, incarnates the bourgeoisie, a social class that was on the rise during the Restoration and the July Monarchy, whereas his opponent on the right, old and toothless, wearing silk stockings and breeches, decorated with the Order of Saint-Louis, embodies the ancien régime society, which emigrated during the Revolution and later returned to France. Behind this latter figure stands an old pensioned soldier of the Empire days, umbrella under his arm and wearing a long overcoat and cocked hat decorated with patriotic rosette. Boilly seems to be using this café to evoke not so much political tendencies as a certain cross-section of society—working-class men are seated here and there, while a serving girl lights an oil lamp in the background.

A pendant to this painting once existed, published as a lithograph and titled *The Cabaret.* It featured a more distinctly working-class place of entertainment, in contrast to the *Café.* The painting here was bought at the Salon of 1824 by the duc d'Orléans (the future King Louis-Philippe), but was damaged during the revolution of 1848. Comparison with a large preparatory drawing now in the Musée Carnavalet in Paris shows that the surviving work is just the central section of a much larger composition (it can be clearly seen that the two top corners have been cut). Victor Hugo reported in his memoirs that, "Neuilly and the Palais-Royal were devastated.... National Guardsmen amused themselves—and are still doing so—by cleanly cutting the figures they like from paintings that were not completely burned." In England in 1875 the duc d'Aumale purchased this fragment of a painting that he had seen as a child in his father's collection. In the 1930s another fragment from the same work was recorded as being in a private collection in Belgium.

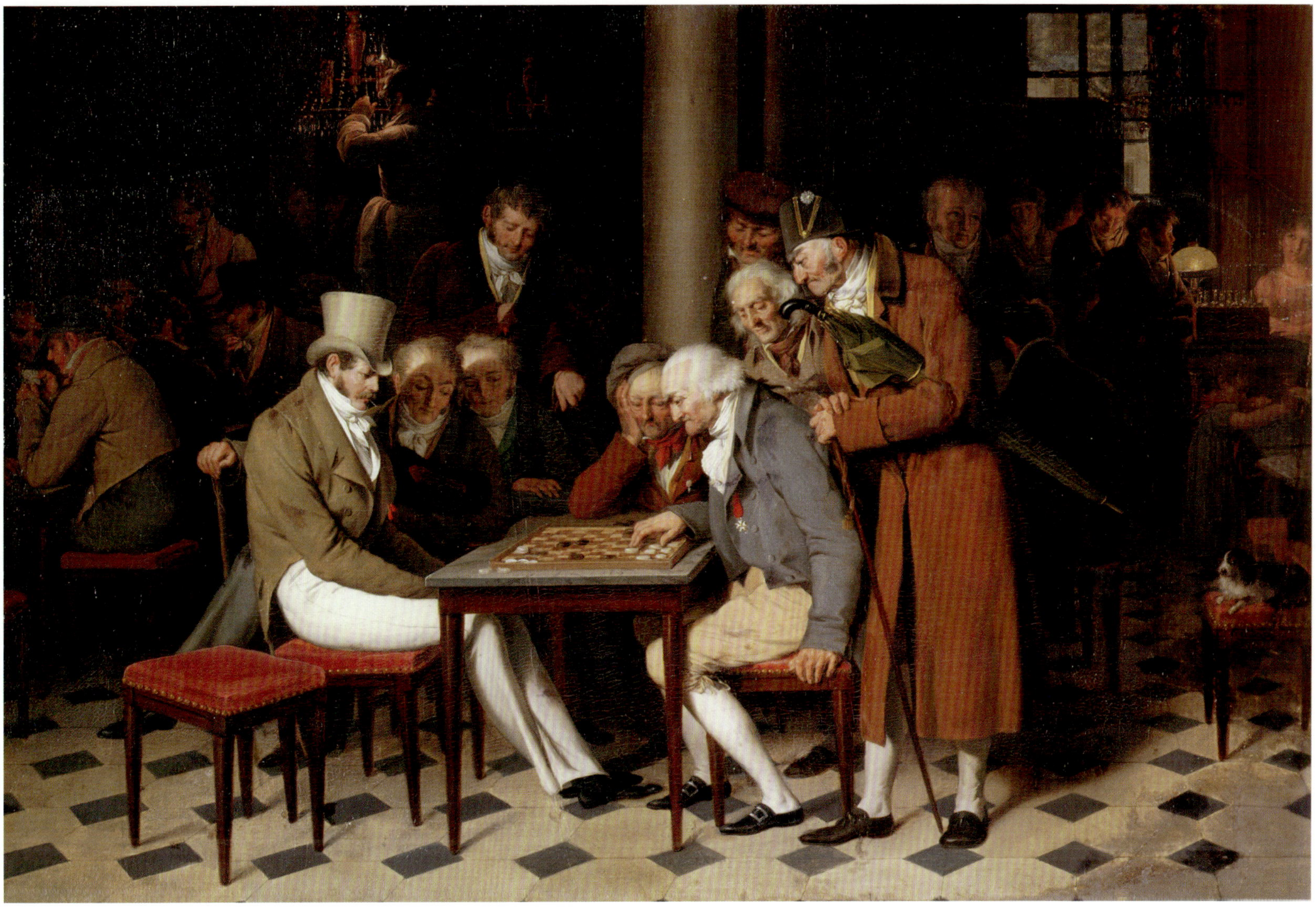

JEAN-AUGUSTE-DOMINIQUE INGRES

(Montauban, 1780; Paris, 1867)

Self-Portrait, Aged Twenty-Four, 1804

Canvas. H. 77 cm (2 ft. 6 in.); W. 61 cm (2 ft.)
S.t.l.: *EFF. J.A. Ingres.* D.t.r.: *P.or Fit Pa[r]is 1804*
Inv. 430 (Tribune)

This youthful work by Ingres was exhibited in an initial state two years after it was done, at the Salon of 1806, where it was harshly criticized. The first state is known through Salon descriptions, through a copy done in 1807 by Ingres's fiancée, Julie Forestier (Musée Ingres, Montauban), and through a photograph taken by Charles Marville sometime between 1841 and 1851 (Bibliothèque Nationale de France, Paris). In it, Ingres was wearing a cloak that was gray-white, rather than brown, as seen here; his right hand held white chalk, while his raised left hand rubbed out the sketch on the canvas of his friend Gilibert. Wounded by the criticsm, Ingres left Paris to complete his training at the Académie de France in Rome. Throughout his life Ingres would transform this self-portrait, reworking the composition, eliminating all superfluous details, using the white glare of the shirt to underscore the face with its intense stare until the other hues seemed to merge into a brown monochrome. In the June 27, 1847 issue of *La Presse,* Théophile Gautier described a figure "with a wild stare, eyes glowing beneath thick eyebrows, hair unkempt and tousled, complexion tawny like the lining of a boot." When exhibited at the Universal Exposition of 1855, the painting met with great favor. Ingres, who wanted above all to be known for his history paintings—that noble genre—was mainly famous for his portraits, considered a minor genre. In his portraits he could eliminate defects all the more easily in that he sought a likeness not just through facial features alone, nor personality through expression alone. He did countless preparatory drawings for his compositions, which helped him to fashion shapes, add sheen to satin, and lend texture to velvets.

Running counter to the Romantic trend, the art of Ingres relied on draftsmanship, as typified by his *Grande Odalisque*—whereas his rival Delacroix applied color with a heavily loaded brush, Ingres's brushwork remained invisible.

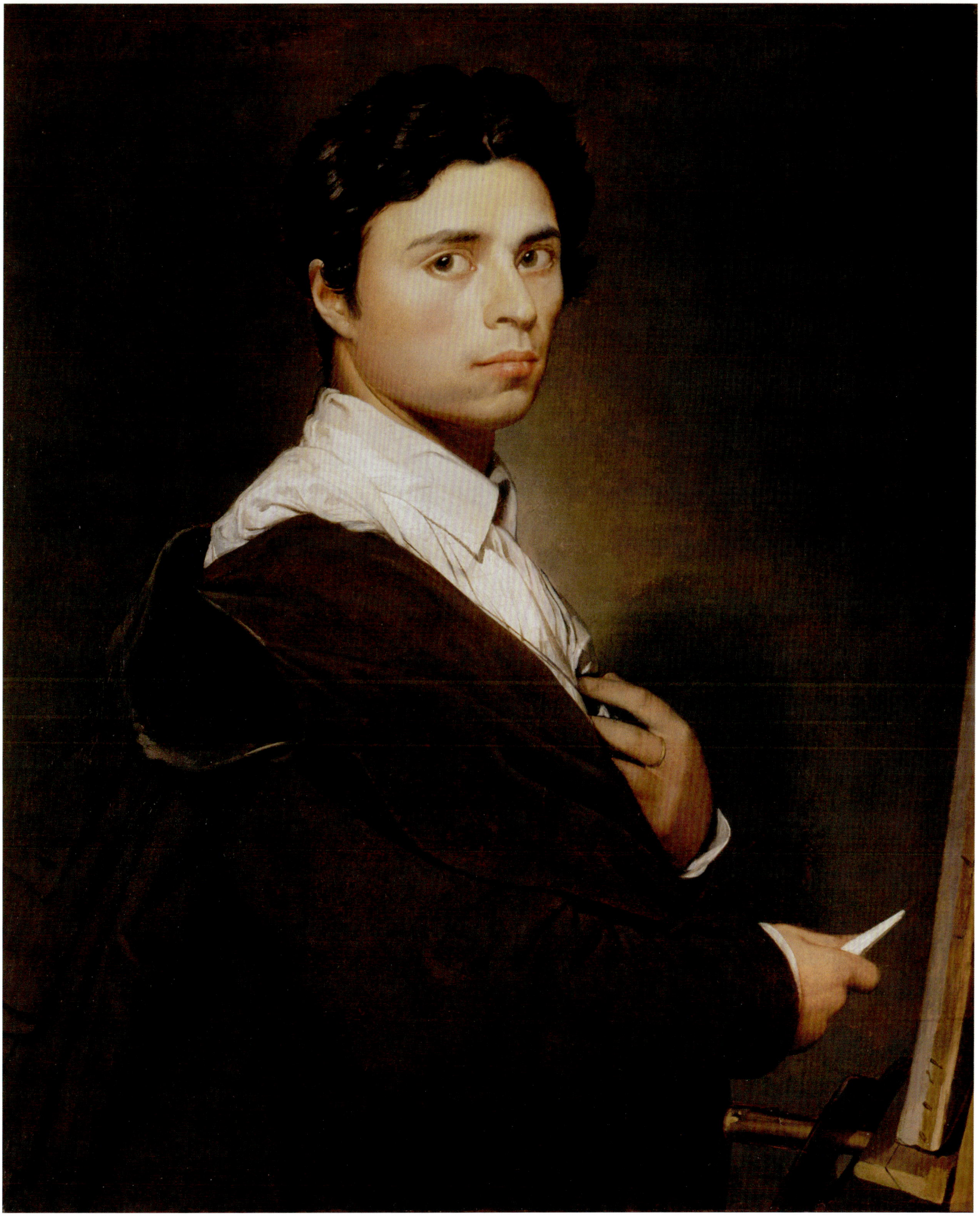

JEAN-AUGUSTE-DOMINIQUE INGRES

(Montauban, 1780; Paris, 1867)

Madame Duvaucey, 1807

Canvas. H. 76 cm (2 ft. 5 ½ in.); W. 59 cm (1 ft. 11 in.)
S.d.b.r.: *J. Ingres, Rom. 1807*
Inv. 431 (Tribune)

Born in Naples, Anna Antonia De Nittis married infantry captain Charles-Louis Duvaucey (not Devauçay, as mistakenly spelled in the past), but in 1802 or 1803 became the mistress of Baron Charles-Jean-Marie Alquier (1755–1826), then French ambassador to Naples. When named ambassador to the Holy See in April 1806, Alquier left southern Italy for Rome. Madame Duvaucey, who remained faithful to him for the rest of her life, followed Alquier on to Stockholm, then Copenhagen, finally marrying him in 1824 once their respective spouses had died. An unfinished short story by Stendhal, "Une Position Sociale," involving a French ambassador to Rome and his legal wife, was based on "Mme. de Vaussay."

Ingres painted this portrait in 1807, at the start of his stay in the Académie de France in Rome. Having arrived there in October 1806, he met Mme. Duvaucey in 1807 in the Apennine hills, where they were both vacationing. She was one of the most fashionable women in town.

This is one of the earliest known portraits of a woman by Ingres, and it is one of his masterpieces. It displays the influence of Raphael—the purity of line and draftsmanship is underscored by the minimal modeling and limited palette. The sitter offers a slight smile, which has earned her the nickname of "Ingres' Mona Lisa." The composition is dominated by soft curves. These rounded lines—oval face, almond eyes, arms, sleeves, neckline, jewelry—lend the portrait a gentle feel and even a sense of nonchalance.

Mme. Duvaucey had to part with her portrait when she ran out of money at the end of her life. Ingres then exhibited the painting in the Salon of 1833, twenty-six years after it was painted (it featured again in the Universal Exposition of 1855). Frédéric Reiset, a collector and curator at the Louvre *(see p. 33)*, acquired it in exchange for an annual stipend that allowed Mme. Duvaucey to end her days free of financial worry; she died in 1852, aged seventy. Critic Théophile Gautier notably praised the beauty and enigmatic smile of this admirable portrait.

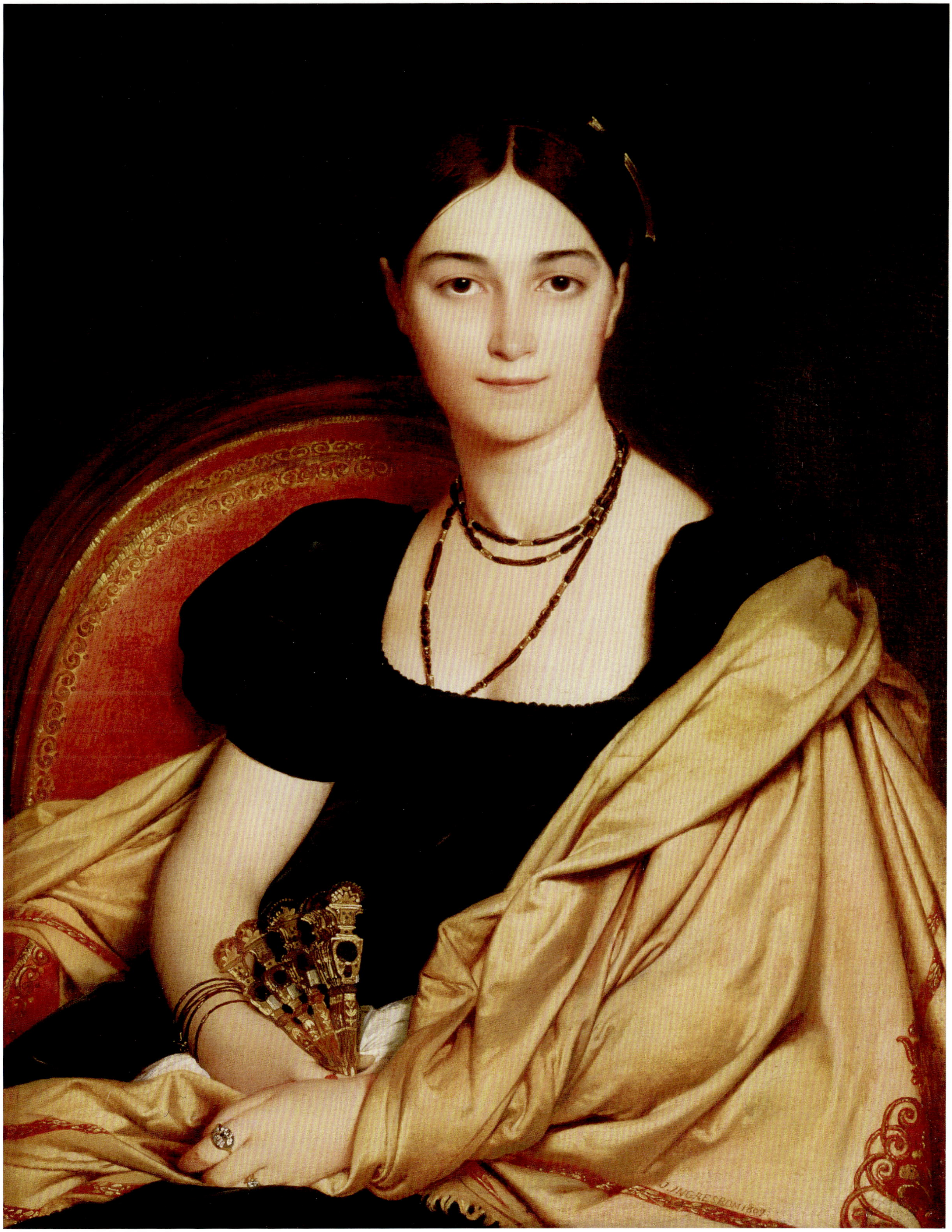
J. INGRES ROM 1807

JEAN-AUGUSTE-DOMINIQUE INGRES

(Montauban, 1780; Paris, 1867)

Paolo and Francesca

Wood. H. 35 cm (1 ft. 1 ½ in.); W. 28 cm (11 in.)
S.b.l.: *Ingres P*
Inv. 434 (Salle Isabelle)

This subject is based on the *Inferno* section of Dante's fourteenth-century poem, *The Divine Comedy.* Along with *Stratonica,* it is one of only two love stories ever painted by Ingres. In 1289, Francesca da Rimini, forced to marry the old, lame, deformed Giovanni Malatesta, fell in love with her husband's young brother, Paolo. One day while they sat reading a romance together, Paolo stole a kiss, which was seen by the jealous husband, who killed them both. The subject became fashionable again through Silvio Pellico's tragic play, *Francesca da Rimini,* famously portrayed by Carlotta Marchionni in Italy around 1815. Ingres handled this theme in the manner of "troubadour" painting, combining two key moments: the birth of love, and death. The book falls from Francesca's hands as she turns her face from Paolo's kiss; the old husband draws his sword in the shadows. Despite the drama inherent in the tragedy, this painting remains cold and static. Ingres' purist, linear interpretation of this scene was inspired not only by the Italian primitives (box-like space, bright colors, sharp outlines) but also by John Flaxman's neoclassicism. The naturalism of Flemish primitives, meanwhile, can be seen in the profusion of meticulous details such as the notches in Francesca's hairband and the glimmering highlights of the hilt of the sword.

Between 1813 and 1819 Ingres concentrated on history paintings in the troubadour style, meaning small pictures of historical subjects conceived as intimate scenes, handled in a slick, meticulous manner reminiscent of Dutch art. The painting here is Dutch-inspired in its precious coloring and handling, its rigorous construction of space through strong vertical and horizontal lines, and its precise rendering of details and props. At that time, Ingres was close to the Rome-based Nazarene school of painters, sharing their taste for medieval art, up to Dürer and Raphael.

Ingres painted this subject twice during his stay in Italy, first in 1814 and again in 1819; in all, he painted it seven times between 1814 and 1850. The version here was painted for Napoleon's sister, Caroline Murat, queen of Naples, in 1814. It was acquired by the duc d'Aumale in 1854 along with the collection of the prince of Salerno (*see p. 27*). The seven known versions are all different—the ever-dissatisfied Ingres introduced some occasionally significant changes.

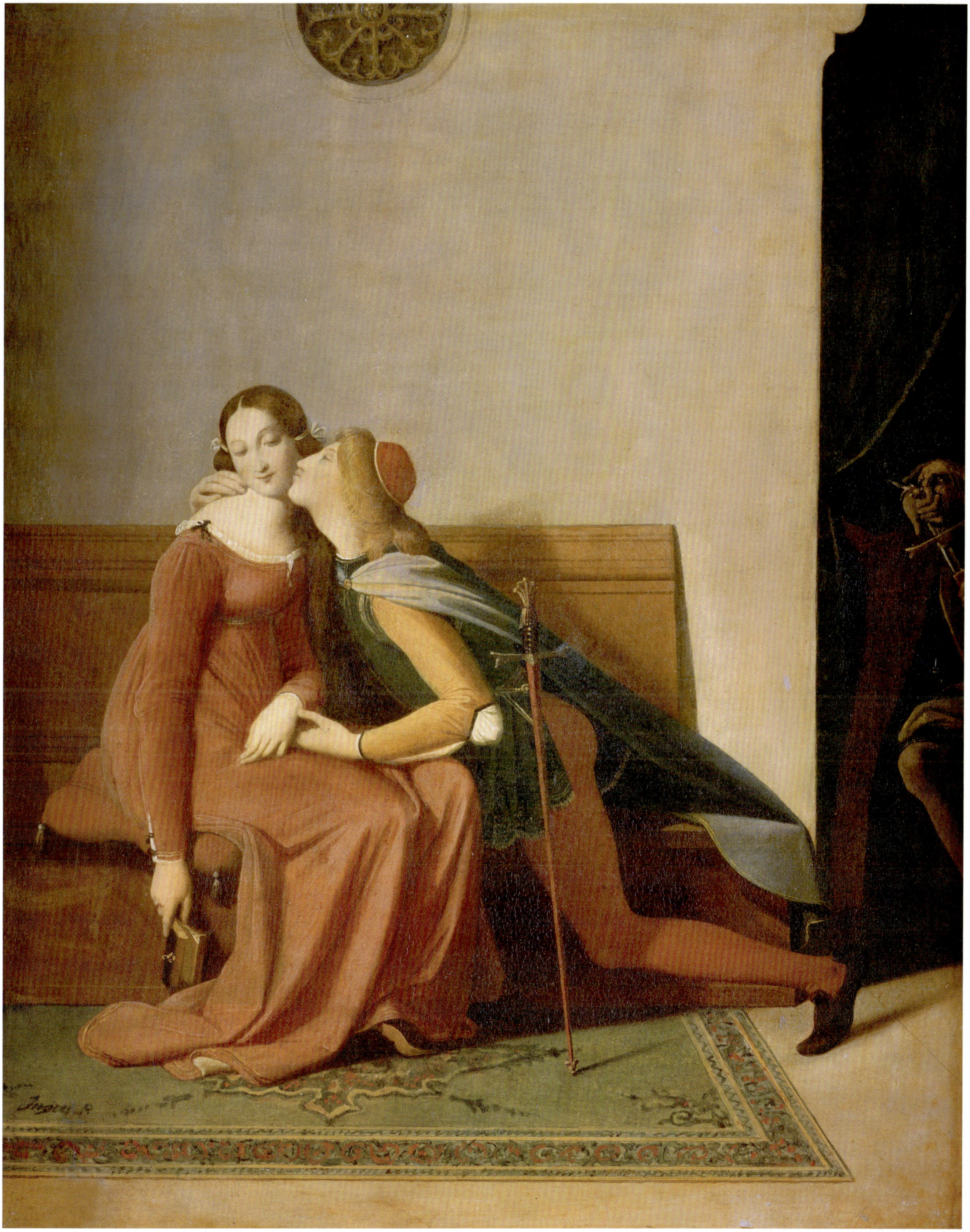

JEAN-AUGUSTE-DOMINIQUE INGRES

(Montauban, 1780; Paris, 1867)

The Illness of Antiochus, or *Antiochus and Stratonica*, 1840

Canvas. H. 57 cm (1 ft. 10 ½ in.); W. 98 cm (3 ft. 2 ½. in.)
S.d.b.l.: *J. Ingres Fat Rome, 1840*
Inv. 432 (Tribune)

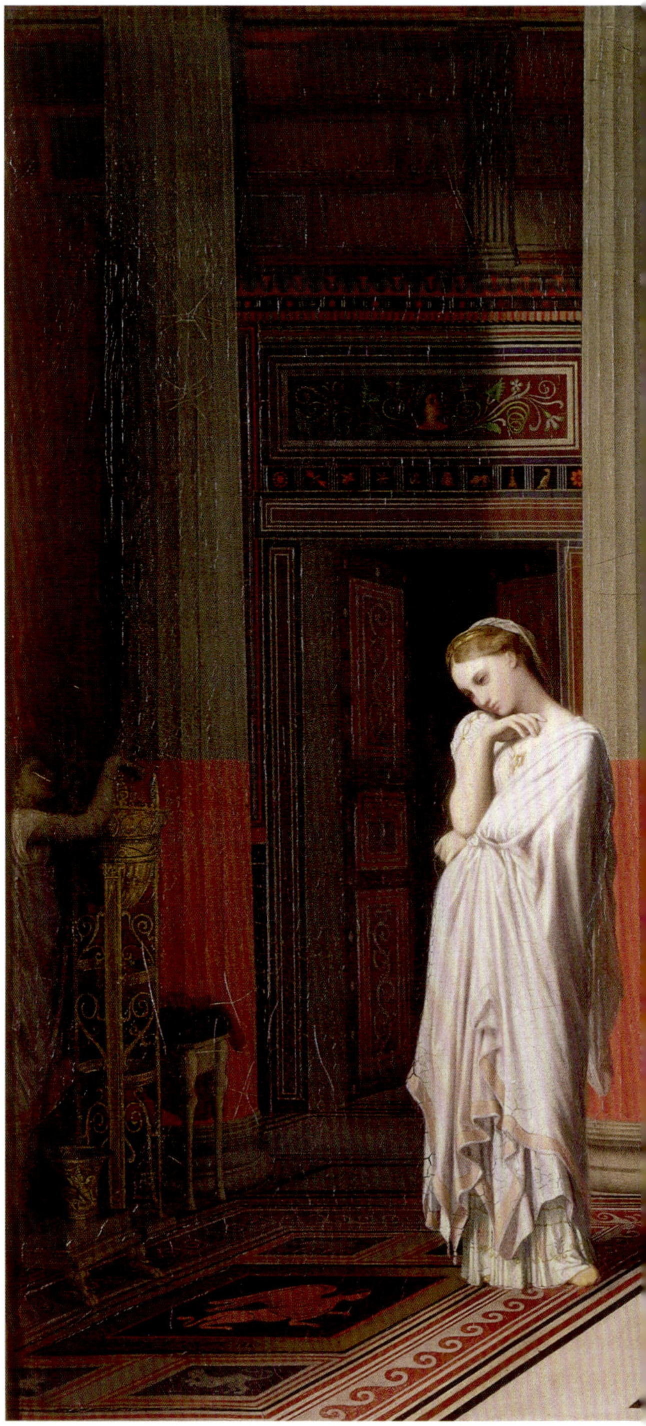

This subject is taken from Plutarch's *Lives of Famous Men.* Stratonica married Seleucus I Nicator, king of Syria, whose son, Antiochus, fell so in love with her that he became mortally ill. The scene here shows the moment when the court physician, Erasistratus, realizes the cause of the illness, noting that Antiochus's heart begins to beat quickly at the sight of Stratonica. The doctor first told the old king that Antiochus was in love with his own wife, at which point the king begged Erasistratus to forsake his wife in order to save the boy; on learning the truth, Seleucus himself had to forsake Stratonica to save his son.

The subject of Stratonica was a favorite one among neoclassic painters including David, Ingres' teacher, who submitted a version for the 1774 Prix de Rome (École des Beaux-Art, Paris). Ingres, who was a musician, was familiar with the opera of the same name by Méhul (1763–1817), which premiered in Paris in 1792 and was performed in Toulouse by the orchestra in which Ingres played violin from 1794 to 1797. Allusions to the opera can be detected in the frontal presentation of the four characters here, as though on stage, in the similarity of the scene chosen by Ingres to the entrance of (and sole solo by) Stratonica in Méhul's work, and in the inclusion of the lyre. Ingres, who bequeathed his score of Méhul's *Stratonica* to his home town of Montauban, was highly moved by the story, as witnessed by his pupil Raymond Balze. "Ingres' emotion was intense—he wept." Ingres painted this subject seven times over a sixty-five year period.

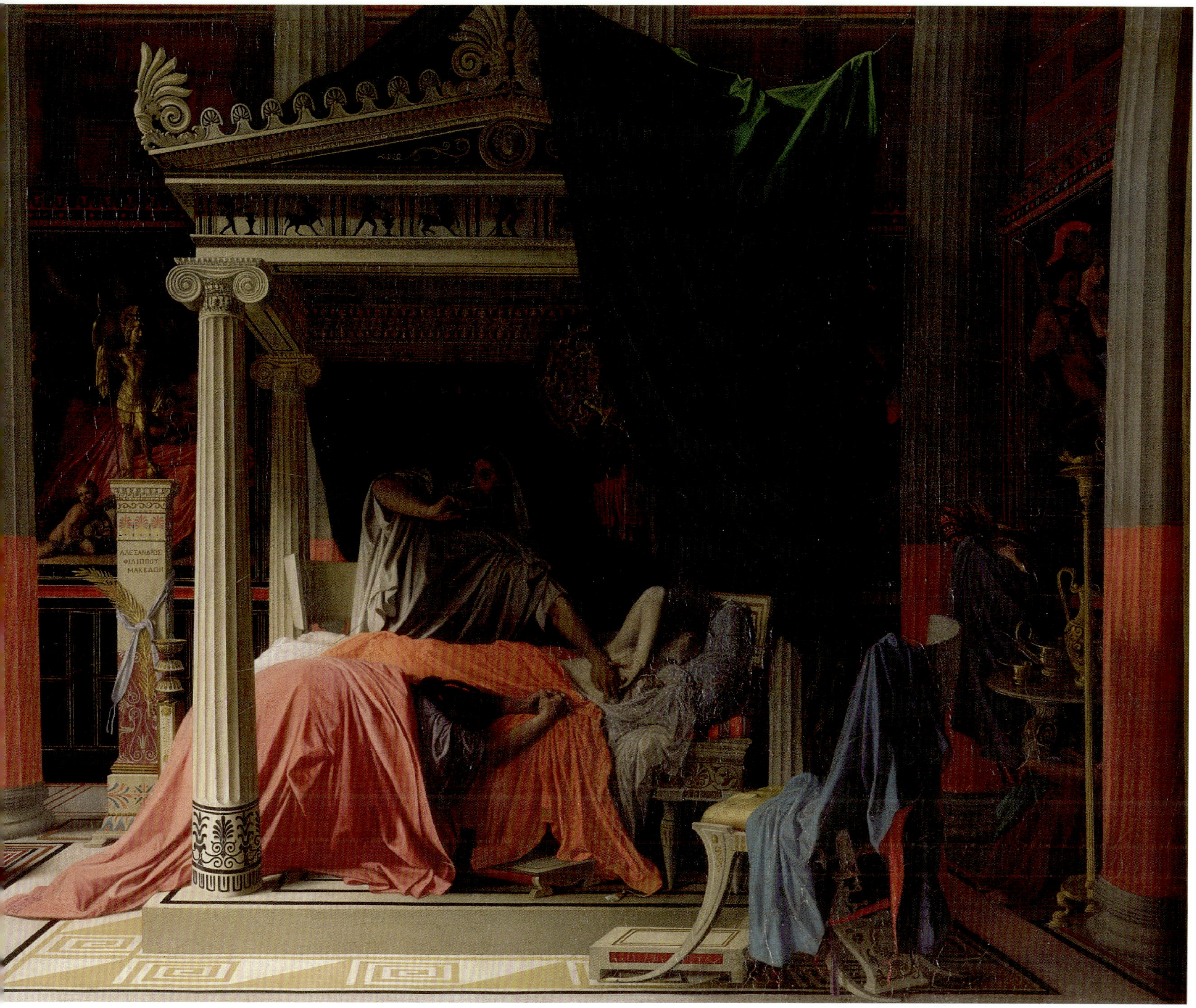

This version was commissioned in 1834 by the duc d'Orléans, son of King Louis-Philippe, as a pendant to the *Assassination of the Duc de Guise* by the Romantic painter Paul Delaroche (*see p. 253*), itself based on an opera by Meyerbeer, *Les Huguenots*. Ingres, who returned to Rome to become director of the Académie de France, painted it there. It took him seven years to complete; he did numerous drawings and studied ancient statues for the figure of Stratonica. Ingres also sought to reconstruct a Greek interior by studying Greek vases, which he collected. The interior decoration, actually more Pompeian than Greek, was designed by Victor Baltard (the architect who erected Les Halles in Paris), while brothers Paul and Raymond Balze painted some of the architectural elements; Madame Ingres posed as the doctor, Hippolyte Flandrin supplied the arm of Antiochus, and Ingres himself posed for Seleucus. Antique decors were fashionable in the mid-nineteenth century—in the 1850s, Prince Jérôme Napoléon had a Pompeii-style house built in Paris where he and his friends such as Théophile Gautier and the actress Rachel would dress in ancient costume and perform classical plays.

When shipped to Paris, this *Stratonica* greatly pleased both its owner and the critics. The duc d'Aumale bought it in the Prince Demidoff sale of 1863, thereby recovering a work once owned by his elder brother.

JEAN-AUGUSTE-DOMINIQUE INGRES

(Montauban, 1780; Paris, 1867)

Venus Anadyomene, 1808 and 1848

Canvas. H. 163 cm (5 ft. 4 in.); W. 92 cm (3 ft. ½ in.)
S.d.b.r: *J. INGRES. FACIEBAT / 1808 ET 1848*
Inv. 433 (Tribune)

Venus emerges from the frothy waves at her feet, surrounded by putti, one of whom kisses her foot while another clasps her knee. Yet another putto holds out a mirror, and a fourth shoots an arrow at a nymph riding a sea horse. It took Ingres forty years to compose this Venus. Begun in 1807–08 as the work dispatched from Rome by the artist who had won a scholarship to the Académie de France, it was only completed in Paris during the revolution of 1848. Ingres painted it for Benjamin Delessert, who disliked it due to a poorly drawn knee. The dissatisfied owner immediately sold it to Frédéric Reiset *(see p. 33)*, who allowed it to be exhibited at the Universal Exposition of 1855.

In the course of preparatory drawings and sketches, Venus went from reclining to kneeling and finally standing, first in the pose of "Venus Pudica" modestly hiding her genitals and one breast with her hands, a pose inspired by a famous ancient work, the *Venus de' Medici,* and by Botticelli's *Birth of Venus* (Uffizi, Florence), which Ingres could have seen in Florence in 1805.

With its rounded corners, glossy surfaces and sinuous frontality, this Venus has been compared to an ancient cameo suddenly brought to warm, throbbing life. However, Ingres drew inspiration less from antiquity than from the Renaissance, notably Raphael's famous *Triumph of Galatea,* a fresco in the Villa Farnesina in Rome. Here we see certain details from the fresco, such as the lively red-eyed dolphin and the putto who has just let loose an arrow.

Ingres re-employed this composition in 1856 for *La Source* (The Spring, Musée d'Orsay, Paris). The figure is very similar to Venus except for tone detail: the jar on the allegorical figure's shoulder is a quotation from the bas-reliefs in the courtyard of the hôtel de Sully (according to Goncourt) or from Jean Goujon.

This *Venus Anadyomene* ("rising from the sea") was highly appreciated when seen in the artist's studio and later in the Universal Exposition of 1855. Théophile Gautier in particular, who saw it in 1848, felt it provided an idea of what ancient paintings must have looked like.

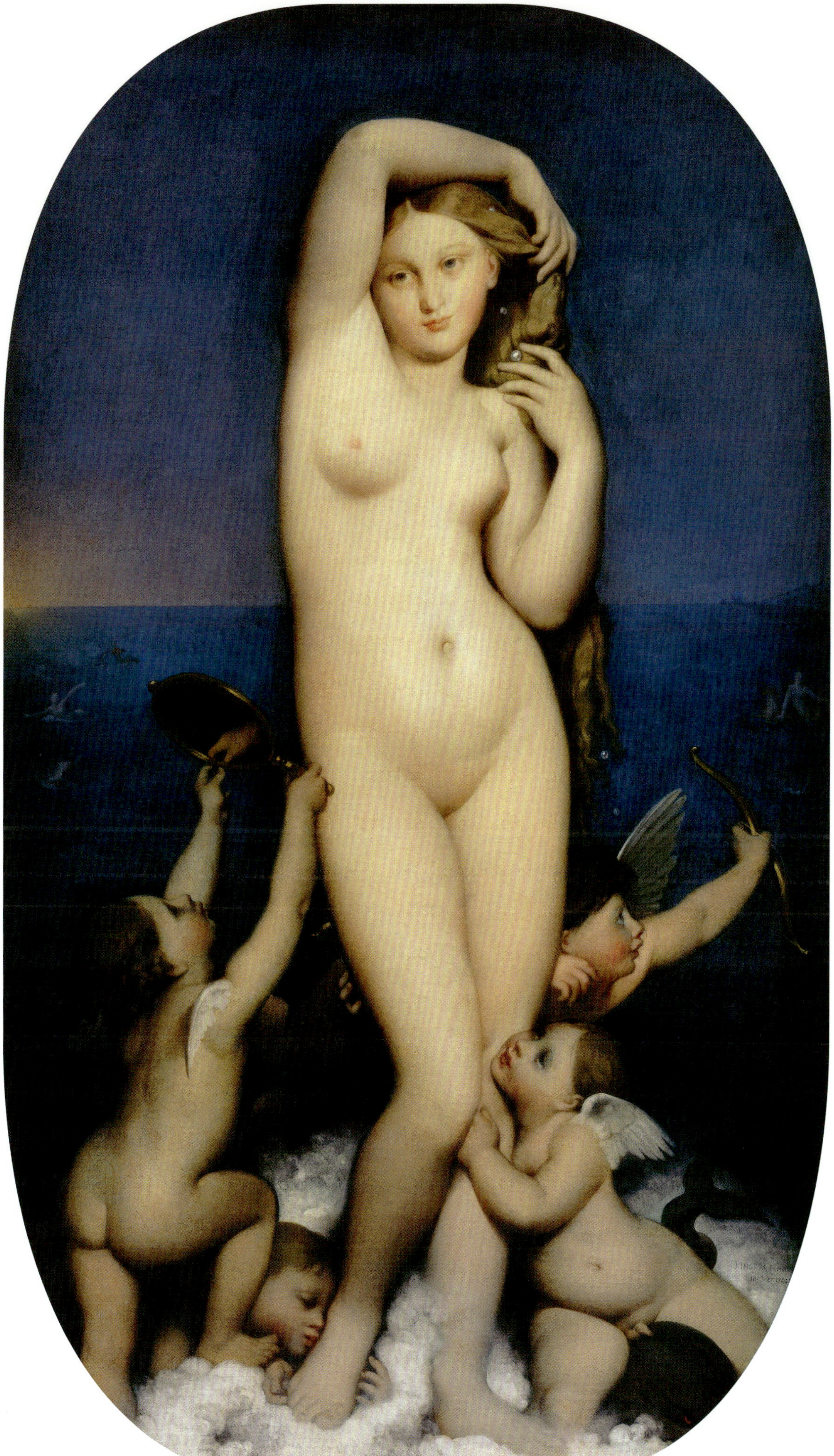

THÉODORE GÉRICAULT

(Rouen, 1791; Paris, 1824)

Black Horse Leaving the Stables

Canvas. H. 36 cm (1 ft. 2 in.); W. 45 cm (1 ft. 6 in.)
Inv. 441 (Salle Isabelle)

Born into a middle-class royalist family, Théodore Géricault lived in Paris from 1796 onward. Painting and horses were his two passions. He trained in Carle Vernet's studio, where he became friendly with the master's son, Horace Vernet, and later worked in the studio of neoclassical painter Pierre-Narcisse Guérin. After having exhibited an early equestrian subject in the Salon of 1812, he failed to win the Prix de Rome in 1816. He left for Italy anyway, where he discovered the work of Michelangelo, Raphael, and other Renaissance artists. When he returned to Paris in 1819 he exhibited his famous *Raft of the Medusa*. In 1820–21, Géricault organized a traveling show in England with his friend the painter and lithographer Nicolas-Toussaint Charlet. While in England he rode horses and painted races such as the *Epsom Derby*. On returning to France Géricault did a series of studies of patients in the Salpêtrière mental hospital. He died at age thirty-three of injuries from riding accidents.

Géricault, who helped to launch the Romantic movement, devoted much of his output to equestrian scenes. Here he shows a black horse being led by a groom. Tradition holds that this is a late painting left unfinished by Géricault; Horace Vernet allegedly completed it after Géricault's premature death, notably by adding the figure of the groom on the right. The painting was bought by the duc d'Orléans (the future King Louis-Philippe) at the postmortem sale of Géricault's estate in 1824, which included numerous studies of horses. Auctioned along with the rest of the king's private collection in 1851, it was purchased by his son, the duc d'Aumale. Attributed to Géricault but unsigned, the painting has been authenticated by most Géricault specialists.

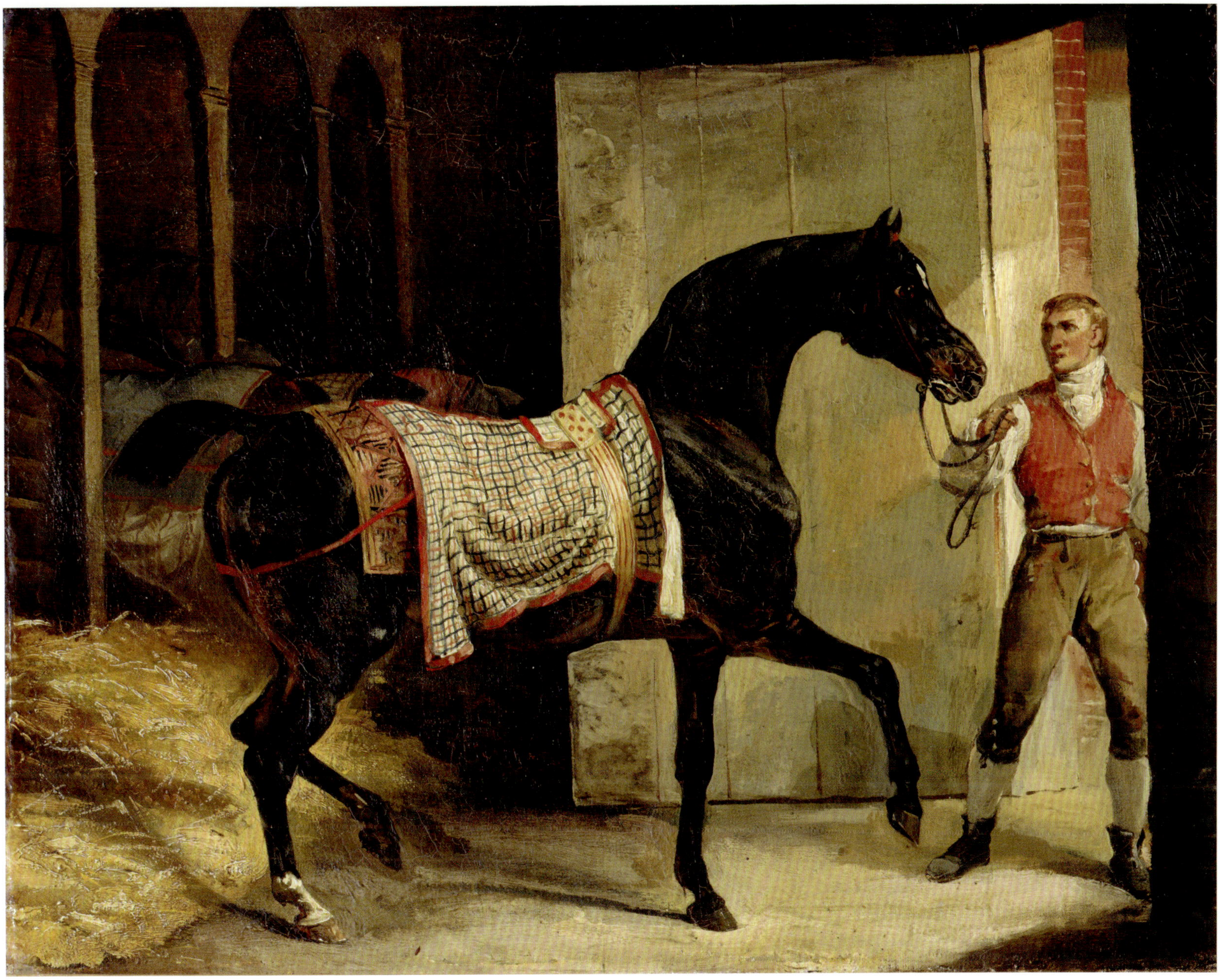

EUGÈNE DELACROIX

(Charenton-Saint-Maurice, 1798; Paris, 1863)

The Entry of the Crusaders into Constantinople, April 14, 1204

Canvas. H. 33 cm (1ft. 1 in.); W. 41 cm (1 ft. 4 in.)
Inv. 455 (Tribune)

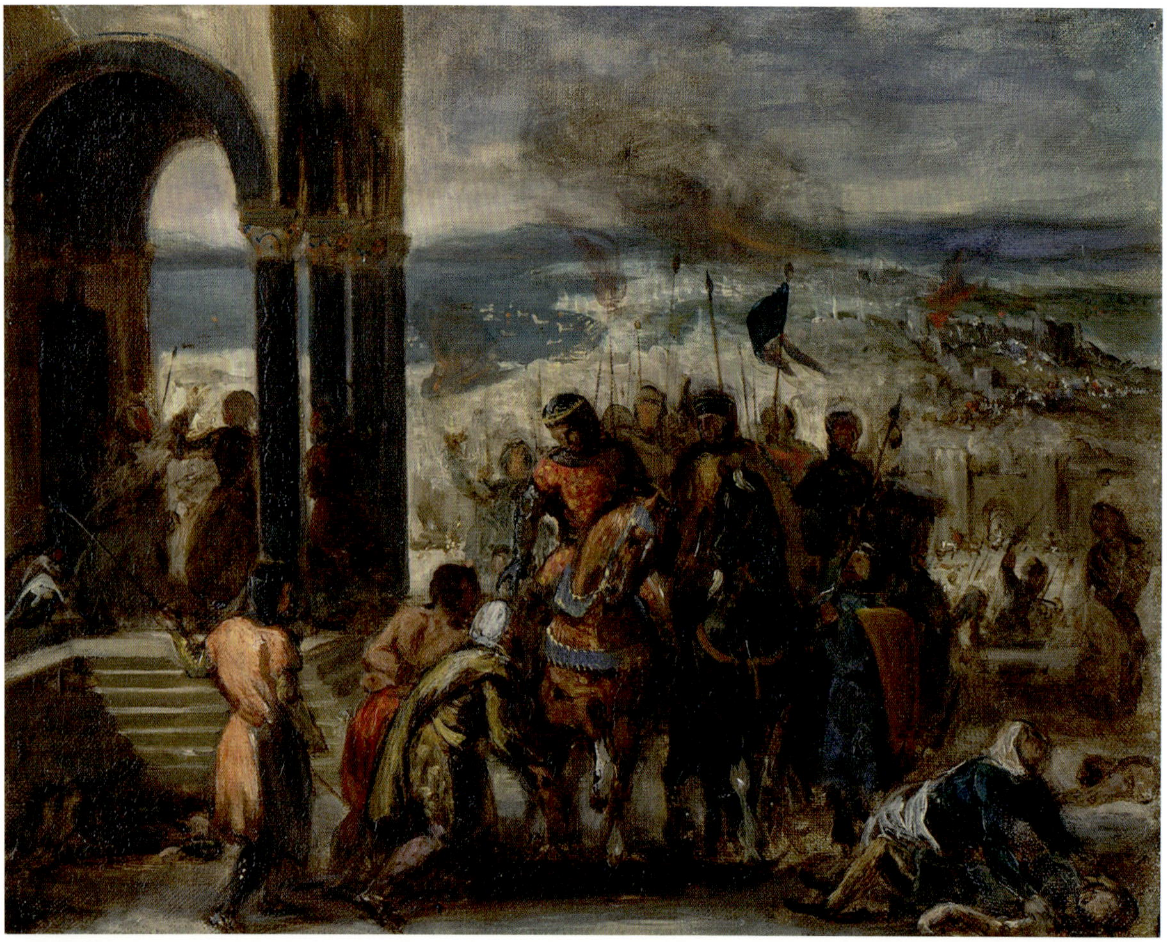

Having studied under Guérin, Eugène Delacroix was marked by the new direction given to painting by Gros and Géricault. He took the lead of this Romantic trend through his distinctive contributions to the Salons of 1822 (*The Barque of Dante*) and 1824 (*Massacre at Chios*). After spending time in England in 1825, he painted *The Death of Sardanapalus*, inspired by Byron. His friends included George Sand, Chopin, Stendhal, and Mérimée. At the Salon of 1831 he exhibited *Liberty Leading the People*, a direct reference to the July revolution of 1830.

Here Delacroix depicted an incident from the Fourth Crusade, combining the two sources of inspiration dear to Romantics: the Middle Ages and the Orient. Baudouin, count of Flanders, attacked Constantinople at the head of the French infantry while Dandolo, doge of Venice, forcibly entered the port with the Venetian navy. Military leaders rode through the city on horseback as the appalled citizens begged for mercy from the victors. Here the count of Flanders is seen in the center on horseback, followed by a dazzling escort; on the left prisoners raise their hands in supplication, while in the right foreground an old woman leans over a corpse. The city of Constantinople stretches away in the background. The almost square composition of this canvas recalls Delacroix's *Justice of Trajan*, exhibited at the Salon of 1840, but here the central group advances toward the beholder, as in *Liberty Leading the People*. The battle and bloody massacres have ended. Concerning both this painting and *The Justice of Trajan*, Baudelaire wrote in 1855, that "the beauty of these two paintings is basically Shakespearean. For, after Shakespeare, no one excels like Delacroix in fusing drama and reverie into a mysterious truth."

The painting here is a sketch for the version exhibited at the Salon of 1841 (Louvre) and the Universal Exposition of 1855. The duc d'Aumale bought it at the estate sale of the Orientalist painter Adrien Dauzats in 1869.

EUGÈNE DELACROIX

(Charenton-Saint-Maurice, 1798; Paris, 1863)

The Two Foscari, 1855

Canvas. H. 93 cm (3 ft. 3/4 in.); W. 132 cm (4 ft. 4 in.)
S.d.b.r.: *Eug. Delacroix / 1855*
Inv. 456 (Tribune)

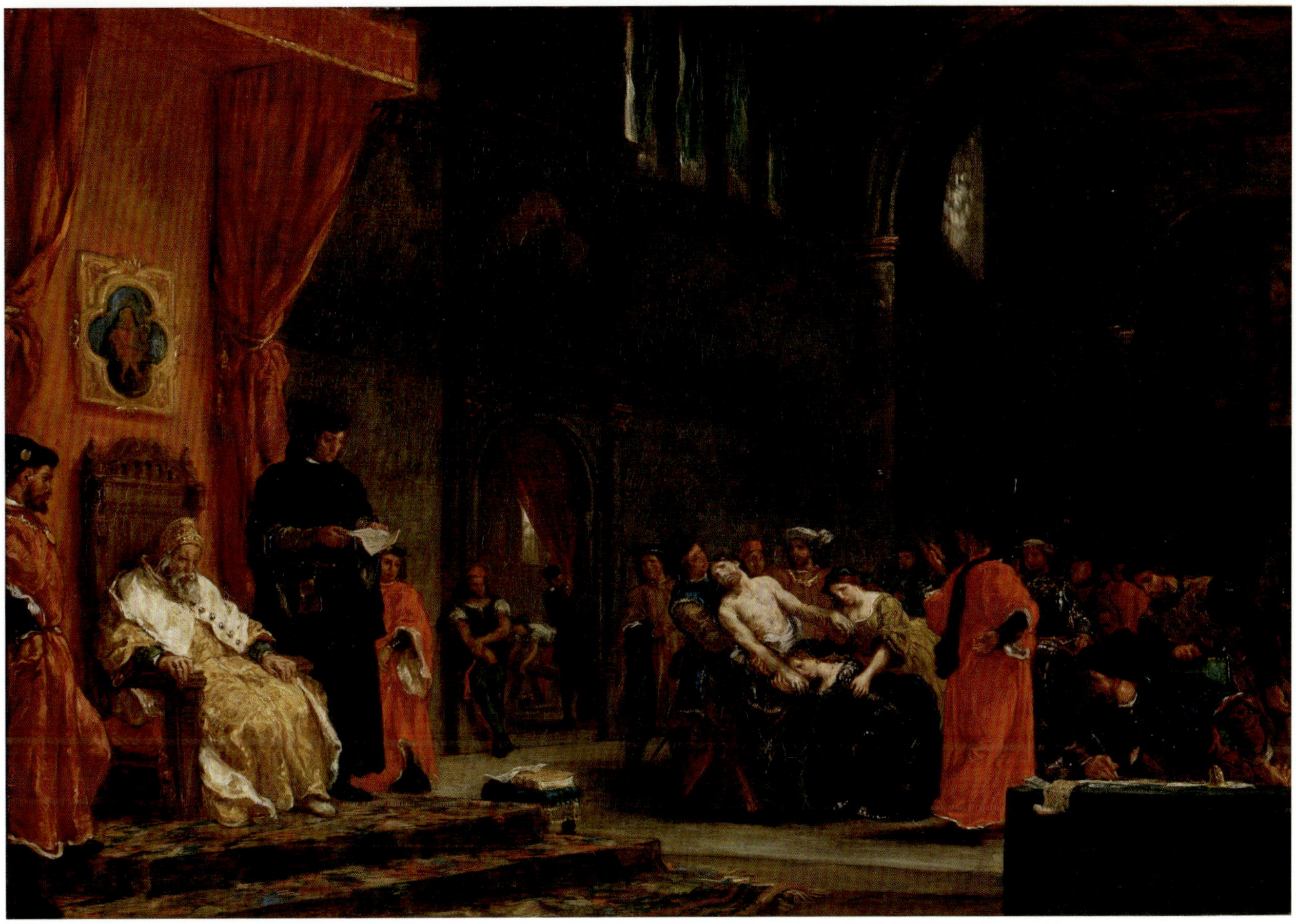

This scene is based on the history of Venice in the fifteenth century. Doge Francesco Foscari, elected in 1423, led Venice in endless wars against the Turks, during which he lost three sons. His last son, Jacopo, was accused before the ruling Council of Ten of treason and conspiring with the enemy. Having confessed to this crime under torture on February 20, 1445, he was sentenced to perpetual banishment. The doge, crushed by shame and sorrow, attends the reading of the sentence pronounced against his sole remaining son. Dressed in his state robes and wearing the typical doge cap that symbolized the Most Serene Republic of Venice, Francesco bows his head; the bare-chested Jacopo, in the middle of the picture, begs for mercy as his wife clings to him. In the background on the left are the executioner and his assistants; on the right, the judges and leading citizens of Venice. The booklet accompanying the Universal Exposition of 1855, where this painting was exhibited, explained at length this little-known incident in Venetian history.

The subject was dear to Delacroix, who mentioned a painting titled *Foscari* in his diary as early as 1847. In May 1854, it resurfaced in the artist's diary: "Dauzats came today to trace out my *Foscari*." This comment tends to prove that the architecture was not drawn by Delacroix, contradicting Théophile Gautier's opinion that this painting contains "one of those fine architectural interiors that Delacroix knows how to construct so well, lending depth to a setting." The painting's display at the Universal Exposition of 1855 allowed it to be compared with earlier works by Delacroix. The dramatic Romantic subject appealed to the duc d'Aumale, who bought it in 1873 and lent it to the 1885 Delacroix retrospective at the École des Beaux-Arts in Paris. The duke must have been moved by the themes of exile and the loss of sons, having himself lived abroad for twenty-three years and lost seven children, two of them as adults. Right from the moment it arrived at Chantilly, this painting was hung in the Tribune, the gallery reserved for masterpieces, on the wall of Romantic works, opposite the paintings by Ingres.

ARY SCHEFFER

(Dordrecht, Holland, 1795; Argenteuil, 1858)

Charles-Maurice de Talleyrand-Périgord, Prince of Benevento (1754–1838), 1828

Canvas. H. 116 cm (3 ft. 9 1/2 in.); W. 90 cm (2 ft. 11 1/2 in.)
S.d.b.l.: *A. Scheffer 1828*
Inv. 445 (Tribune)

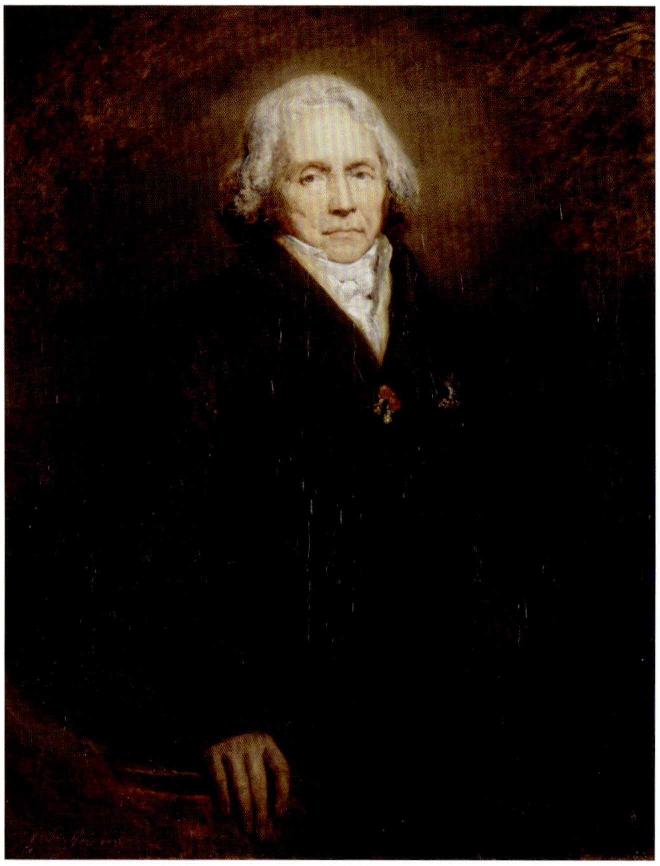

In his day, Ary Scheffer was considered the equal of Ingres and Delacroix. Despite having been a pupil of Guérin, Scheffer became a Romantic artist who produced both history paintings and portraits. Baron Gérard recommended him to Maria Amelia, duchesse d'Orléans and future queen of the French, as a drawing teacher for her children. Scheffer remained very close to one of those children, Princess Marie, with whom he worked on sculpture. He executed many portraits of the family, and the duc d'Orléans furthermore acquired several of his history paintings. Here Scheffer has captured the enigmatic expression of Talleyrand, the wily old diplomat who was born during the ancien régime but managed to survive every change of government in France from the early nineteenth century to the July Monarchy (1830–48). Painted in 1828, ten years before Talleyrand's death, this portrait was exhibited at the Salon of 1831 alongside ones of kings Louis-Philippe and Henry IV, plus another of French politician Dupont de l'Eure (1767–1855). Some critics referred to this *Talleyrand* as a "good pastiche of Rembrandt," comparing its handling to that of the Dutch master. In fact, Scheffer was born in Dordrecht, Holland, and returned to his roots in the late 1820s, traveling there in 1829 and 1830 to study Rembrandt's art. This portrait made its way to England prior to Talleyrand's death, being exhibited in London in 1834 and bought by Lord Holland, an English collector who bequeathed it to his friend and neighbor the duc d'Aumale in 1859. The duke decided to hang the painting on the "Romantic wall" of the Tribune hall, next to Reynolds' portrait of Countess Waldegrave (*see p. 230*), another work bequeathed to him by an English collector. When the duke showed visitors the Tribune, he liked to say, "That's Dutch Scheffer: the sitter comes alive, and notice the shape and length of his fingers—they're the claws of the devil." It is strange to find here in Chantilly, opposite Gérard's portrait of Napoleon, a portrait of Talleyrand, who in 1804 backed Napoleon's decision to execute the duc d'Enghien, the last descendant of the house of Condé.

PAUL DELAROCHE

(Paris, 1797; Paris, 1856)

The Assassination of the Duc de Guise, 1834

Canvas. H. 57 cm (1 ft. 10 ½ in.); W. 98 cm (3 ft. 2 ½ in.)
S.d.b.l.: *Paul Delaroche 1834*
Inv. 450 (Tribune)

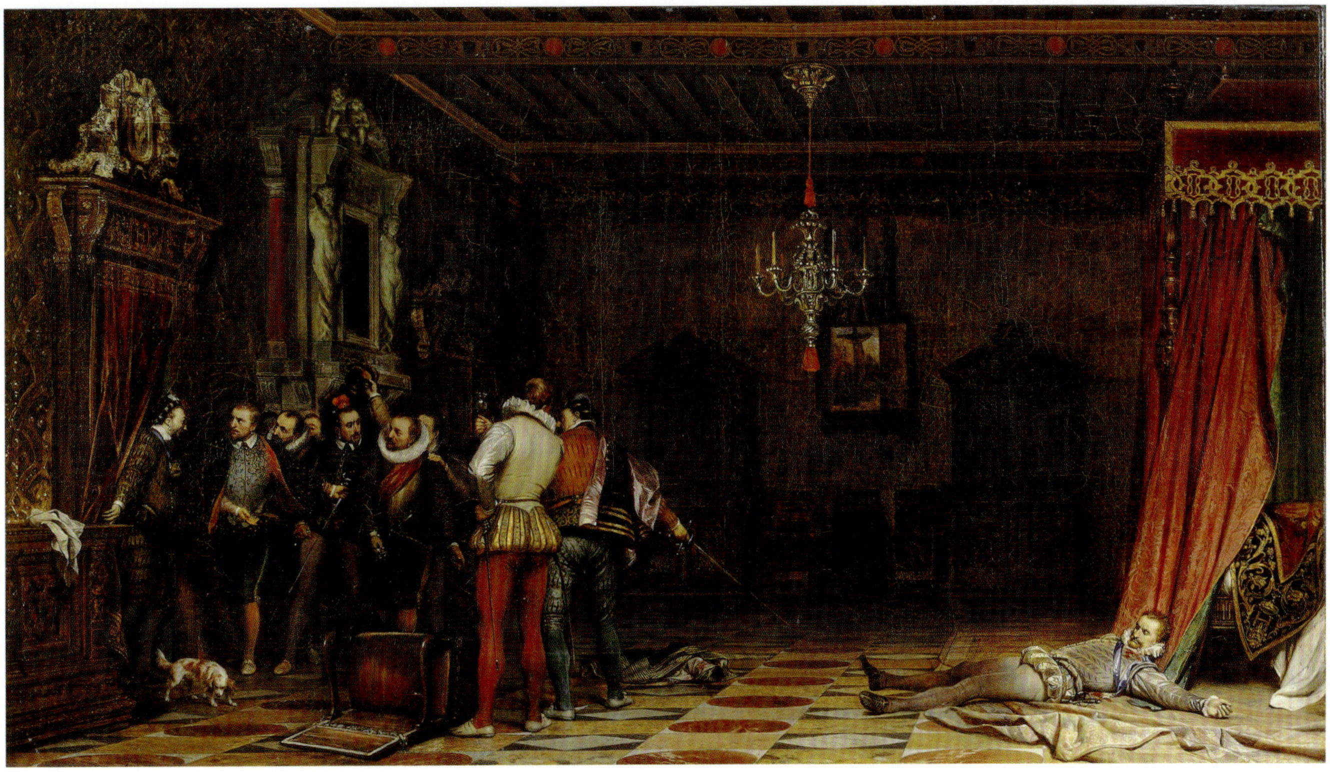

The "troubadour school" often depicted events from the Renaissance, while French Romanticism in general broadly explored the nation's history. The subject of the murder of the duc de Guise was fashionable: in the Salon of 1834 Charles Durupt exhibited a painting on this incident, and the *Magasin Pittoresque* devoted an article to the story that same year. In the theater, the duke's assassination was staged as early as 1810 in François Raynouard's *Les États de Blois*. Alexandre Dumas, meanwhile, scored a hit in February 1829 with his play *Henri III et sa Cour*, for which Paul Delaroche designed the costumes—even the royal family came to applaud the piece. Finally, in that same year of 1829 Ludovic Vitet wrote a *Trilogy* in which one scene concerned the murder of Guise. Vitet's play was never staged, but he was a friend of Delaroche, who may therefore have been familiar with it. In 1836, France's wars of religion were addressed in Meyerbeer's opera *Les Huguenots*, with a libretto by Émile Deschamps and Eugène Scribe, and with costumes once again designed by Delaroche. The painting here was commissioned from Delaroche by the duc d'Orléans, eldest son of King Louis-Philippe. A great patron of the arts, the duke was was delighted with the results that he spontaneously doubled the payment. Delaroche had already explored this subject in 1830 (watercolor, Montpellier) and 1832 (watercolor, Wallace Collection, London). The painting was delivered in May 1834 and exhibited at the Salon of 1835. As a pendant to Delaroche's painting, the duc d'Orléans commissioned Ingres to paint *Antiochus and Stratonica* (*see p. 244*) based on an opera by Méhul and completed in 1840. Auctioned in 1853 with the duke's gallery, *The Assassination of the duc de Guise* was acquired by the duc d'Aumale in memory of his elder brother. The pair of works today face one another in the Tribune at Chantilly, Ingres' painting being on the neoclassical wall and Delaroche's on the Romantic wall alongside works by Delacroix and Scheffer.

Both works feature wide compositions mimicking the stage, with characters extending into the depth of the scene. Delaroche's painting shows the moment when King Henry III steps from behind the curtain where he had been hiding, in order to confirm the death of his enemy, the duc de Guise. Around him are the conspirators, all members of the king's personal guard, known as "Les Quarante-Cinq" (The Forty-Five), whereas the duke's body occupies the right side of the picture on its own. The historical details were supposedly accurate, and the set designer of the Paris opera house, Diéterle, apparently advised on the architectural features.

LÉOPOLD ROBERT

(La Chaux-de-Fonds, Switzerland, 1794; Venice, 1835)

In Confidence, 1830

Canvas. H. 99 cm (3 ft. 3 in.); W. 126 cm (4 ft. 1 3/4 in.)
S.d.b.l.: *Ld. Robert / Rome 1830*
Inv. 444 (Salle Isabelle)

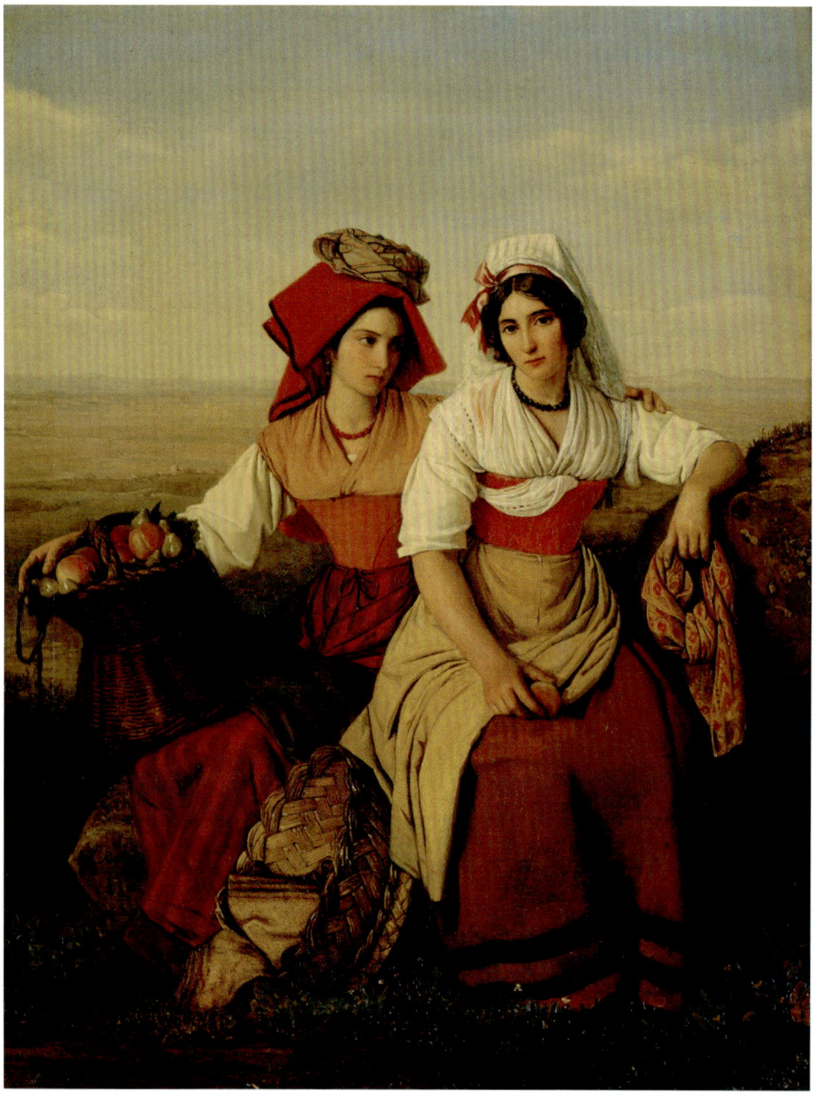

Swiss artist Léopold Robert moved to Paris in 1810 and trained in David's studio. The fall of Napoleon's empire and other political changes made Switzerland a foreign nation once again, which disqualified Robert from winning the Prix de Rome. He returned to Switzerland and became a portrait painter before traveling to Italy in 1818. In Rome he became friendly with the French artists there, and he exhibited in the Paris Salon from 1822 to 1836, showing Romantic pictures based on traditional life in Italy. His contemporary scenes that updated neoclassical themes based on Roman history met with distinct success, and demonstrated that Italy could provide new inspiration at a time when most Romantics were looking toward the Orient. At the Salon of 1827 Robert showed a *Return from Celebrations for the Madonna of the Arch, Near Naples,* while in 1828 he showed *Harvesters Arriving in the Pontine Marshes.* He felt frustrated, however, at working in the minor field of genre painting and, failing at an attempt to relaunch his art, he committed suicide in 1835, the same year that Gros took his own life.

Here two young Roman countrywomen, wearing traditional Italian dress, have halted in the middle of the landscape, setting down the baskets of apples they carry on their heads beneath a cushion of cloth. One of them is consoling the other, who has just been confiding her secrets, hence the title of the painting. The young woman's sorrowful expression, the overturned basket, and the apple she holds in her hand all symbolize her loss of virginity. Despite the picturesque handling underscored by the colorful sheen of the costumes, the subject remains somewhat mawkish.

LÉOPOLD ROBERT

(La-Chaux-de-Fonds, 1794; Venice, 1835)

The Day After the Earthquake, 1830

Canvas. H. 99.7 cm (3 ft. 3 ¾ in.); W. 126 cm (4 ft. 1 ¾ in.)
S.d.b.l.: *Ld. Robert / Rome 1830*
Inv. 443 (Salle Isabelle)

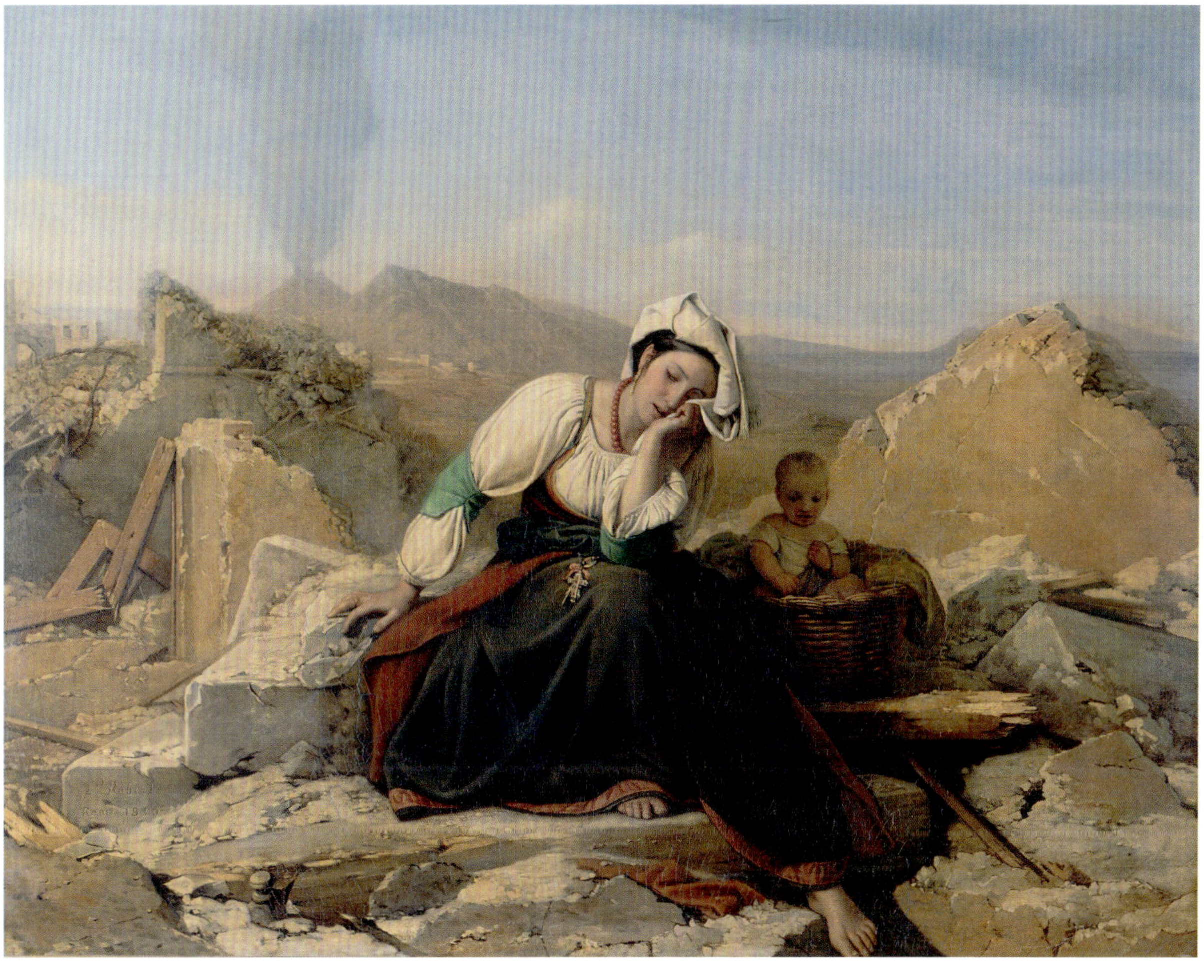

Despite its modest size, this painting by Léopold Robert seeks to be dramatic. It conveys the artist's ambition to become a history painter rather than a genre painter. Here a young woman from the Neapolitan countryside weeps as she sits on the ruins of her house destroyed by an earthquake. Playing in the basket behind her is her infant child, clearly the last survivor of the family—we imagine that the other family members died in the rubble in the background, strewn with broken roof timbers. In the distance, Mount Vesuvius belches a plume of smoke over the Bay of Naples, making it possible to pinpoint this tragic scene.

Robert was so pleased with this painting that he wanted to show it to Chateaubriand as soon as he had finished it. He exhibited in April 1830 at the Capitol in Rome, where several art lovers bid for it, but it had already been promised to the collector Marcotte. In September 1830, Robert reported Marcotte's highly positive response to the work, mentioning that the Paris collector's two-year-old daughter had wept on seeing the scene. It was exhibited in the Salon of 1831 along with *Harvesters Arriving in the Pontine Marshes* and *Woman of Ischia in Despair Over the Shipwreck of her Husband* (Musée d'Art et d'Histoire, Neuchâtel). The *Earthquake* was highly popular, and Marcotte had to sell it to King Louis-Philippe, whose wife, Maria Amelia, was from Naples.

Robert was situating himself at the center of the debate over the hierarchy of genres; some critics viewed tragic yet contemporary subjects as an alternative to Romantic paintings. Robert was therefore on the verge of rejuvenating contemporary art, which was in search of new material, when in 1834 he decided to depict a religious subject, explaining in a letter that he had not chosen the genre out of personal taste, but because he felt that history painting was the supreme goal of art. His frustration is what led to his suicide.

JEAN-BAPTISTE-CAMILLE COROT

(Paris, 1796; Ville-d'Avray, 1875)

Le Concert Champêtre (Rustic Concert)

Canvas. H. 98 cm (3 ft. 2 ½ in.); W. 130 cm (4 ft. 3 in.)
S.b.l.: *C. Corot*
Inv. 448 (Galerie de Peinture)

Corot trained first with Achille-Etna Michallon and then with Jean-Victor Bertin; he was thus steeped in his youth with the classical theories of landscape laid down by Pierre-Henri de Valenciennes. He could not imagine a landscape that failed to contain a subject drawn from history, mythology, or the Bible, in order to respect the hierarchy of genres so dear to Nicolas Poussin and Claude Lorrain in the seventeenth century. All Corot's sketches from life were therefore reworked in the studio, where they acquired the addition of some mythological, religious, or literary anecdote. Sojourns in Italy and Switzerland enabled Corot to master genre subjects, but he wanted to succeed as a painter of historical landscape, which was related to history painting. That is why he sent this work to the Salon of 1844 with the title of *Landscape with Figures.* At that time the painting was very different, known to us from a photograph by Victor Laisné and a wood engraving by Adrien Lavielle; twelve years later Corot reworked the painting in order to exhibit it at the Salon of 1857: he significantly lowered the horizon line, eliminated a young shepherd leaning against a tree in the foreground, and replaced the sunny meadow by a lake (complete with swan). The figures were also reworked, refined, and simplified. On the back of a letter to artist Édouard Brandon, dated March 31, 1857, Corot did an ink sketch of the painting: "Rustic concert, revised and updated, I believe." A trip to England in 1852 and his discovery of northern European painting proved to be crucial to Corot's handling of horizons, which he thereafter systematically lowered.

Corot apparently reworked this painting yet again. In 1872 it belonged to the artist Jules Dupré (following a swap of works between the two painters), who exhibited it at the Salon Carré in the Louvre without Corot's approval—he was apparently disappointed with the way it looked and altered it once more after the exhibition ended.

This *Concert Champêtre* combined the things that Corot, as a musician and fine singer, really liked: nature and music.

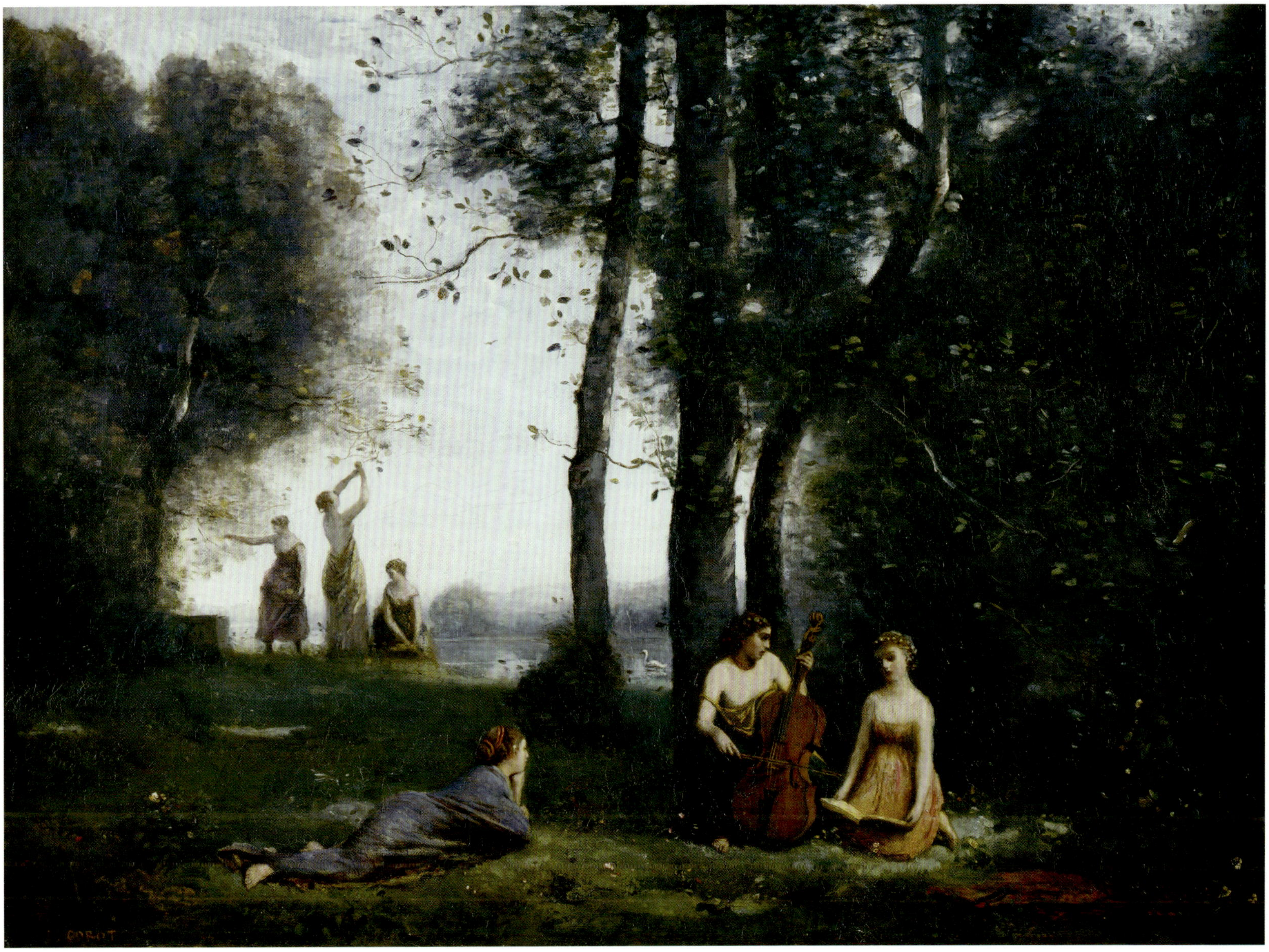

THÉODORE GUDIN

(Paris, 1802; Boulogne-sur-Seine, 1880)

View of the Suspension Bridge on the Grounds at Neuilly

Canvas. H. 45 cm (1 ft. 6 in.); W. 63 cm (2 ft. 1 in.)
Inv. 472 (Salle Isabelle)

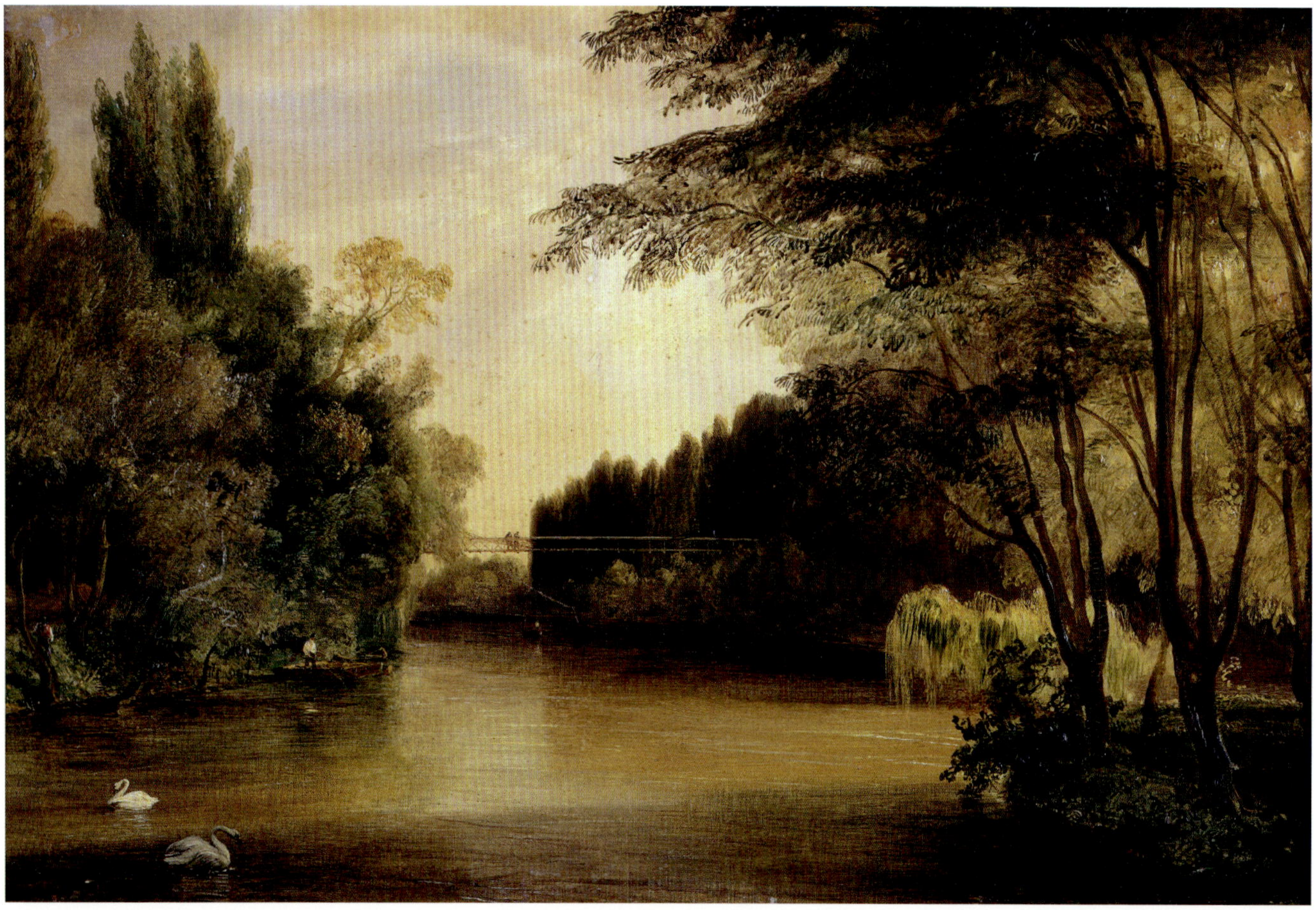

Théodore Gudin attended the naval school in Brest and spent three years at sea before taking up painting. He studied at the École des Beaux-Arts in Paris under Gros and Girodet. He became a marine painter and showed at the Salon from 1822 to 1880, winning a first-class medal as early as 1824; after the Salon of 1828 King Charles X made him a member of the Légion d'Honneur. In 1830 Gudin was named official artist to the navy, and at the Salon of 1831 he exhibited works inspired by the French expedition to Algiers, which he had witnessed the year before. In 1844 Gudin married the daughter of Lord Hay, a relative of Wellington and god-daughter of King Louis-Philippe. Elevated to the rank of officer of the Légion d'Honneur in 1841, then commander in 1855, Gudin was an establishment artist par excellence. Friendly with Louis-Philippe and the duc d'Orléans, he specialized in big marine paintings handled in a moving, Romantic manner, including ninety-seven large canvases for the history gallery in Versailles. Concerning Gudin, in 1855 Maxime Du Camp wrote somewhat nastily that, "the museum at Versailles killed him: sentenced to forced marine labor, lumped with the ball and chain of illustrating, at a given rate per meter, all of France's naval victories, he simply was not up to this galley-slave's task. He died in harness."

Here Gudin painted the far end of the grounds of Louis-Philippe's estate in Neuilly, which the king had acquired when still duke in 1819 and then considerably enlarged, extending it down to the Seine. Louis-Philippe notably bought Ile de la Jatte, an island that he linked to his Neuilly estate by a bridge over the Seine, known as the "wire bridge." The landscape is handled in the Romantic manner favored by Gudin, complete with sunset, raking light, and anecdotal details such as swans, fisherman, pedestrians on the bridge, and weeping willows.

This painting belonged to Louis-Philippe's sister, Madame Adélaide (1777–1847). It was included in the sale of the king's estate in 1851, was bought by his widow, Queen Maria Amelia, and then entered the collection of the duc d'Aumale, reminding him of his happy childhood at Neuilly, swimming in the Seine with his brothers and sisters.

CHARLES-FRANÇOIS DAUBIGNY

(Paris, 1817; Paris, 1878)

Barges at Bezons

Wood. H. 16 cm (6 ¼ in.); W. 30 cm (1 ft.)
S.d.l.: *Daubigny*
Dulac Bequest, 1910
Inv. 628 (Salle Isabelle)

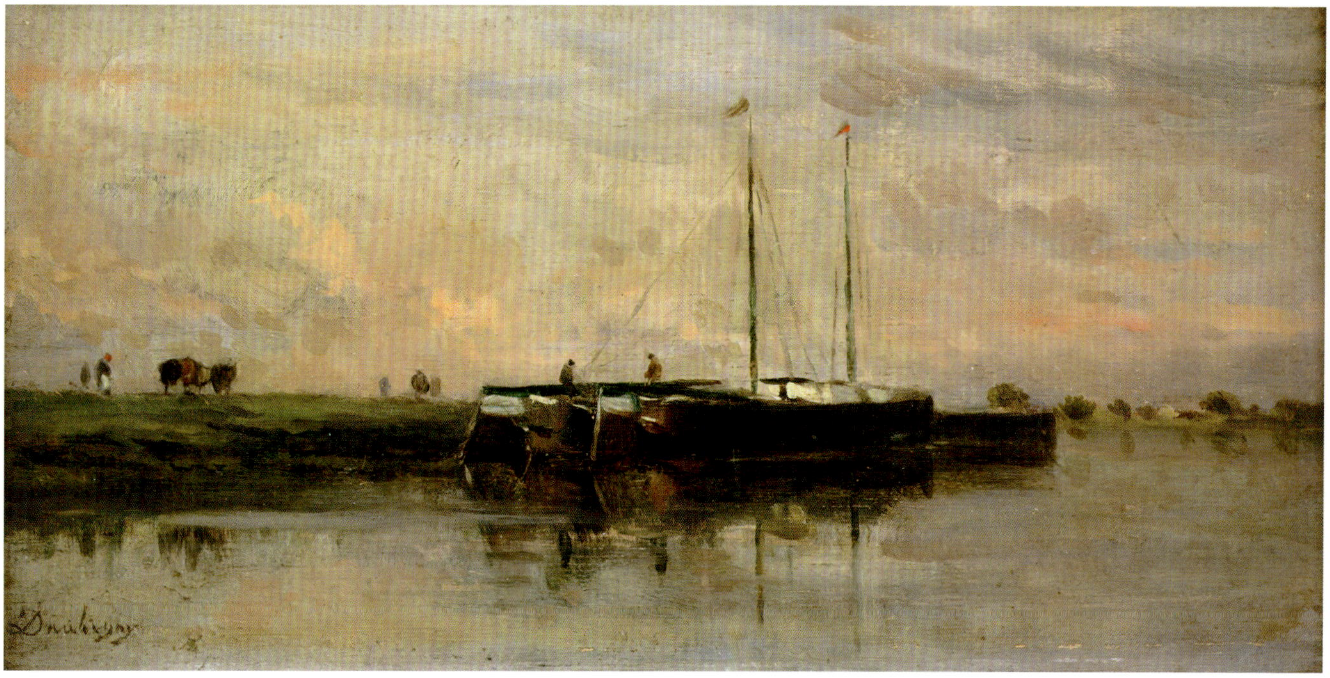

Charles-François Daubigny painted his landscape pictures outdoors, as did the other painters of the Barbizon school to which he belonged. These artists, the generation prior to Monet and Manet, were the forerunners of Impressionism. They sought to render the changing appearance of nature with the passing of time and seasons. To this end, Daubigny had a boat built, christened *Le Bottin,* which he sailed on the Oise River near Auvers-sur-Oise. The Louvre has a painting very similar to this one, which entered the Musée Condé after the death of the duc d'Aumale.

ALEXANDRE-GABRIEL DECAMPS

(Paris, 1803; Fontainebleau, 1860)

Guard Post on the Road to Magnesia on the Meander, 1833

Canvas. H. 91 cm (3 ft.); W. 155 cm (5 ft. 1 in.)
S.d.b.r.: *Decamps, 1833*
Inv. 474 (Galerie de Peinture)

Originally from Picardy, Alexandre-Gabriel Decamps studied under Abel de Pujol and then visited Switzerland, southern France, and Italy before traveling to Asia Minor in 1827 with the marine artist Amboise-Louis Garneray in order to paint the battle of Navarino. His stay in Turkey inspired his first Orientalist canvases, which met with great success when he exhibited them at the Salon of 1827. During the reign of Louis-Philippe the French middle classes preferred Decamps to Delacroix, whose Romantic boldness shocked them. Considered the leader of the Orientalist school, Decamps was honored with a veritable retrospective during the Universal Exposition of 1855, where forty-five of his paintings were displayed. Critic Gustave Planche wrote at the time that, "In the French school three names rise above all others, illustrating this generation's various approaches to the realm of painting: Ingres, Delacroix, and Decamps. Whoever has truly studied the works of these three artists knows where things stand with respect to the state of French genius."

The duc d'Aumale's collection boasted ten works by Decamps, subsequently augmented by donations and an important series of major drawings, which reflects the mid-nineteenth-century enthusiasm for the artist. The duke hung three of these paintings in his gallery, which he thought were crucial to understanding the art of his day.

This painting marked the beginning of Decamps' great popularity, winning him a first-class medal at the Salon of 1834. The picturesque dress, warm tones, and thick brushwork instantly pleased critics and general public alike. It can be usefully compared with a canvas painted by Delacroix fourteen years later, *Guard Post at Meknes* (*see p. 268*), which the duc d'Aumale ranked below this one.

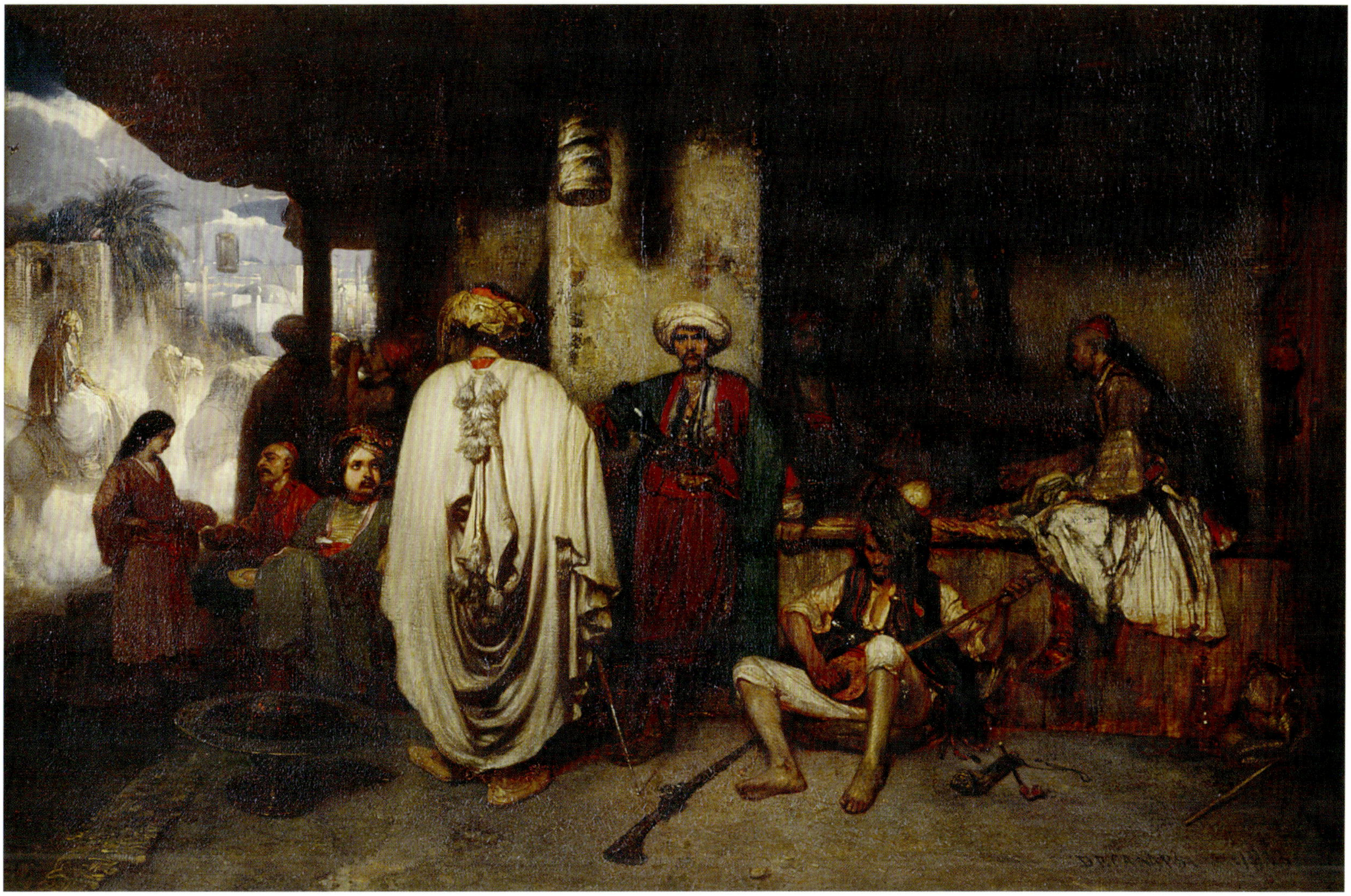

ALEXANDRE-GABRIEL DECAMPS

(Paris, 1803; Fontainebleau, 1860)

Landscape (Don Quixote), 1834

Canvas. H. 40 cm (1 ft. 3 3/4 in.); W. 64 cm (2 ft. 1/2 in.)
S.d.b.l.: *Decamps 1834*
Inv. 480 (Salle Isabelle)

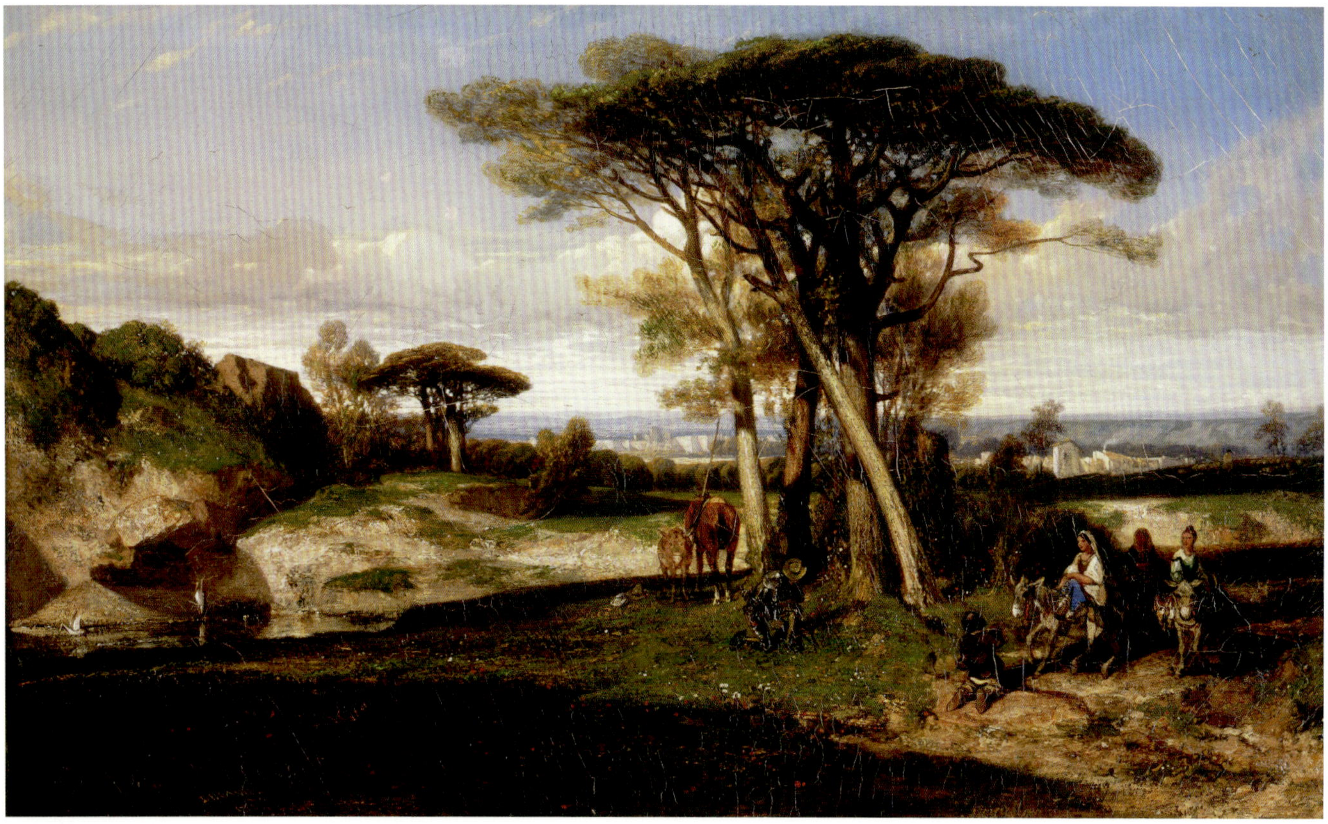

This painting is typical of the style of Decamps (*see pp. 263 and 264*), for it includes on the right a scene from Cervantes' *Don Quixote,* which provides an excuse to populate a landscape painting with figures that place it in the grand tradition of history painting. Having encountered three village women perched on donkeys, Don Quixote and his servant Sancho Panza kneel before them respectfully, mistaking them for noble princesses on their nags. The horses of the two men, meanwhile, wait in the center of the picture.

This painting was bought by the duc d'Aumale as part of the collection of Marquis Maison (*see p. 30*), which contained many Orientalist works by Decamps.

ALEXANDRE-GABRIEL DECAMPS

(Paris, 1803; Fontainebleau, 1860)

Turkish Children Playing with a Tortoise, 1836

Canvas. H. 72.5 cm (2 ft. 4 in.); W. 91 cm (3 ft.)
S.d.c.r.: *DECAMPS 1836*
Inv. 475 (Galerie de Peinture)

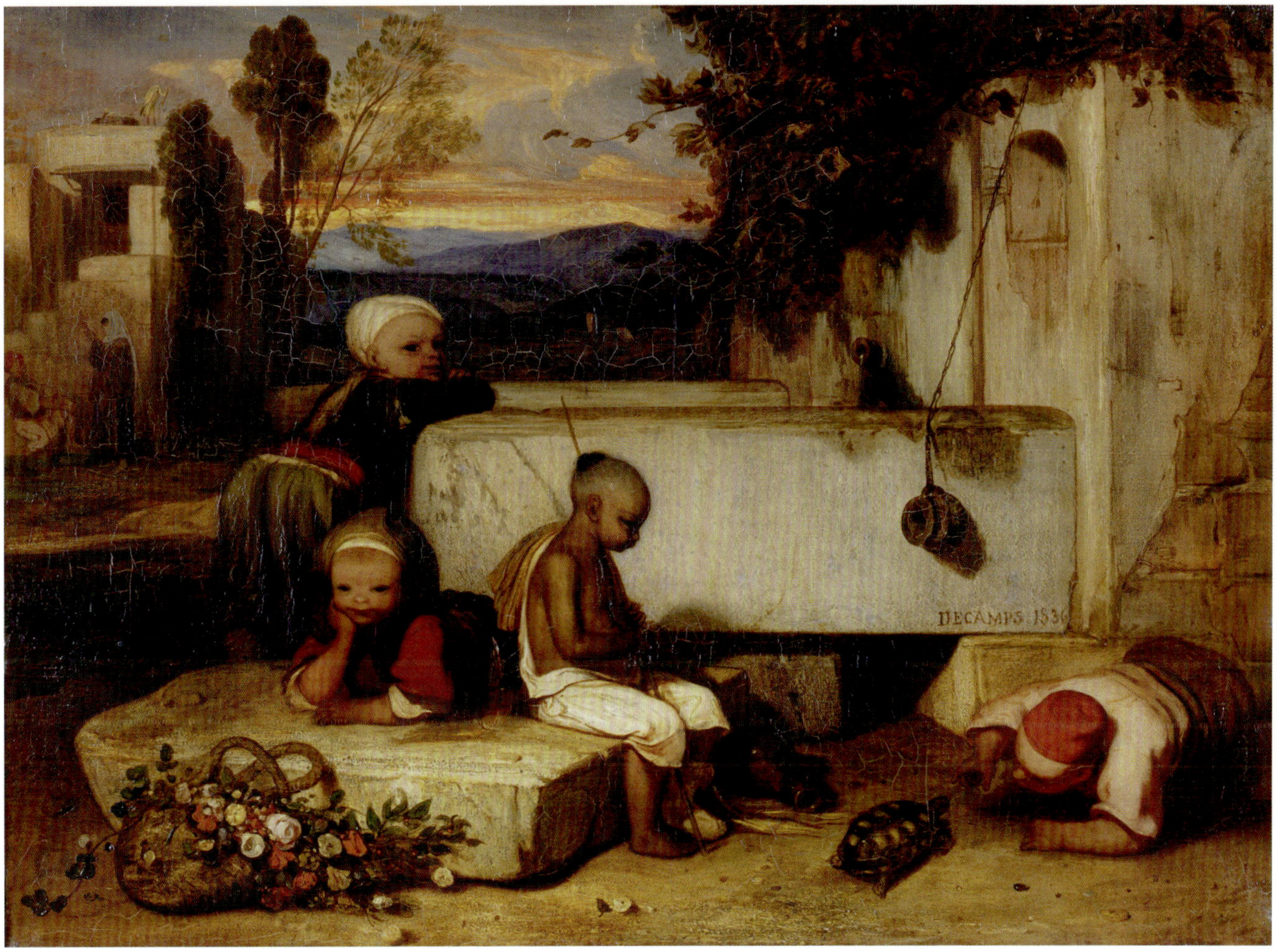

The Salon of 1839 marked the return of Descamps, who had not exhibited there since 1836. He showed eleven paintings, including one with the same subject as here. Théophile Gautier's review of the Salon referred to the children as "the most charming little monsters imaginable." The painting—or a replica, because Decamps constantly made replicas of his work—was exhibited again at the Universal Exhibition of 1855. (The version shown at the Salon of 1839 apparently included a background figure of a women filling a jar at the fountain, which does not appear here.)

This painting belonged to the duc d'Aumale's elder brother, the duc d'Orléans, who in June 1840 gave it to his secretary and former tutor, Alfred-Auguste Cuvillier-Fleury, as a souvenir of their joint trip to Algeria in 1840. In 1862, the duc d'Aumale, then living in exile in England, offered to buy it from the owner for 30,000 francs, in memory of his prematurely deceased brother, all the while allowing Cuvillier-Fleury to keep the painting until it could hang once again at Chantilly. Cuvillier-Fleury must nevertheless have relinquished the painting immediately, because it was hanging in the duke's residence in Twickenham when a visit of his collection was organized for members of the Fine Arts Clubs in 1862.

ALEXANDRE-GABRIEL DECAMPS

(Paris, 1803; Fontainebleau, 1860)

Souvenir of Turkish Asia, also known as Turkish Children by a Fountain, 1846

Canvas. H. 100 cm (3 ft. 3 ½ in.); W. 74 cm (2 ft. 5 in.)
S.d.b.r.: *1846 / DECAMPS*
Inv. 476 (Galerie de Peinture)

This painting, exhibited at the Salon of 1846, shows children watching ducks swimming in a fountain. Although critics generally liked the intense, warm light and sense of chiaroscuro, Baudelaire felt that the thick brushwork little suited the aquatic subject matter: "Monsieur Decamps, who is able to paint sunlight so well, is unable to do rain; and now he has ducks swimming in stone" (Baudelaire, *Salon de 1846*). Théophile Thoré made similar comments. "In the new painting by Monsieur Decamps, it looks as though the brush has been replaced by a trowel; at any rate, the brush certainly worked less than the palette knife. It seems that Decamps has taken the pasty pigment from its tub with his hand and thrown it at the canvas, after which he spreads, evens, and consolidates this dense substance with a trowel-knife. A house can be built this way, even one depicted in a painting; but how can you apply this method to air and water? In the canal of his *Souvenir of Turkish Asia* the ducks have difficulty paddling in the mire that sticks to them like some perfidious glue."

When the duc d'Aumale showed visitors his gallery of paintings, on reaching this work he would exclaim, "Now there's a real patch of sunlight! The entire panel, of which it occupies the center, is illuminated by it!" In fact, the duke so liked this painting that he placed it in the middle of his gallery, opposite Nicolas Poussin's *Massacre of the Innocents*. He considered it his masterpiece of nineteenth-century French painting, having acquired it in 1868 as part of the Marquis Maison collection (*see p. 30*).

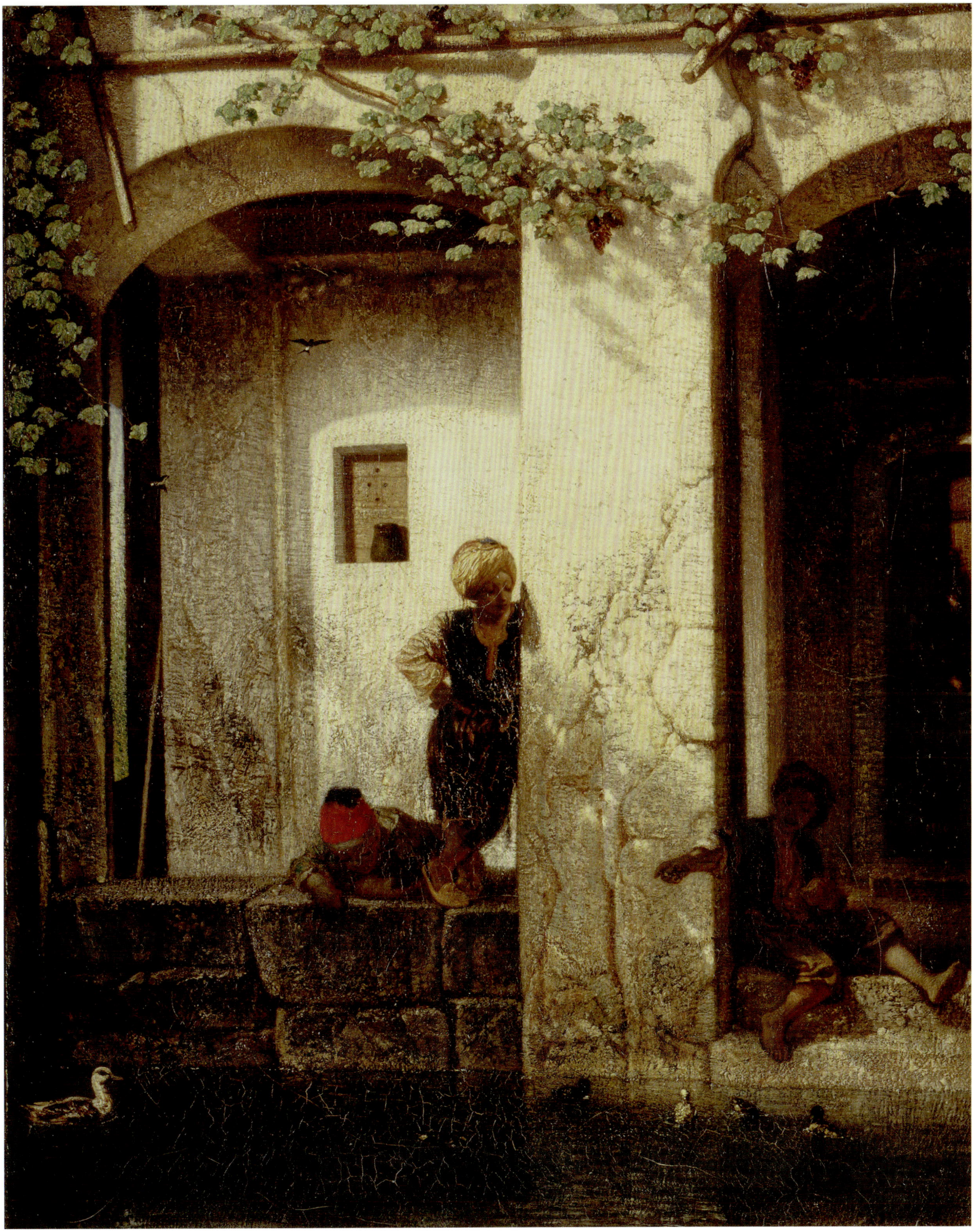

PROSPER MARILHAT

(Vertaizon, Puy-de-Dôme, 1811; Paris, 1847)

View of a Quay at Rosetta

Canvas. H. 58 cm (1 ft. 10 3/4 in.); W. 44 cm (1 ft. 5 1/2 in.)
S.b.r.: *P. MARILHAT*
Inv. 498 (Galerie de Peinture)

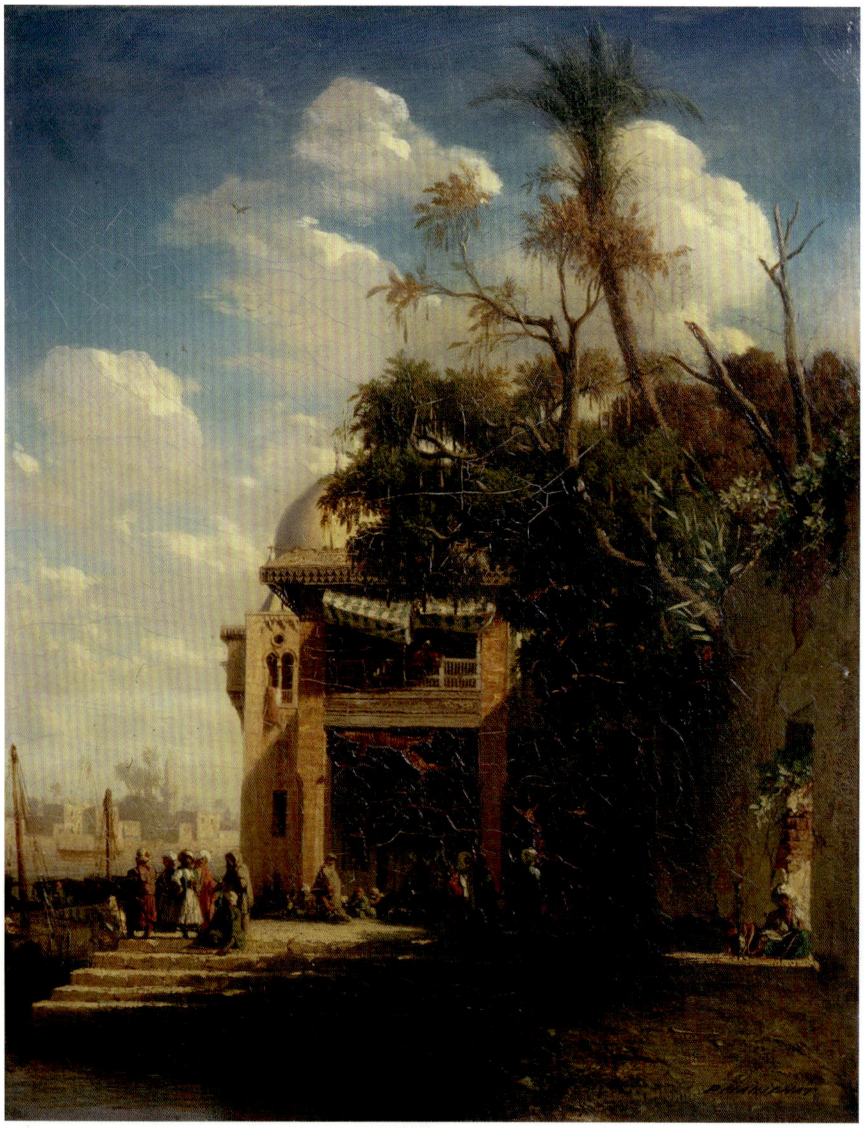

Prosper Marilhat, from the Auvergne region of France, studied under Camille Roqueplan and launched his career at the Salon of 1831, aged twenty-one. That same year he accompanied a German scientific expedition led by Baron von Hugel to the Orient. Marilhat spent two years traveling in Greece, Syria, Lebanon, Palestine, and above all Egypt, his favorite country. He spent a long time in the Nile delta to the north, signing his letters, "Marilhat the Egyptian." The four Orientalist works that he submitted to the Salon of 1834 were enthusiastically received by critics, notably the poet and art critic Théophile Gautier. In 1835 Marilhat headed for Italy in search of new sources of inspiration, while the following year he went to Provence. The eight paintings he exhibited at the Salon of 1844 met with great success, and won him a gold medal. Having received commissions for work from the French government, he was preparing to leave again for Egypt when he went mad and suddenly died at the age of thirty-six.

This painting was exhibited at the Salon of 1840, where Marilhat's work was well received. The area of Rosetta in the Nile delta was well known to the artist, for that was where he had spent a long time. The duc d'Aumale acquired the painting along with the major Orientalist collection assembled by the Marquis Maison (*see p. 30*).

ADRIEN DAUZATS

(Bordeaux, 1804; Paris, 1868)

Government Square, Algiers, 1849

Wood. H. 17 cm (6 ½ in.); W. 22 cm (8 ½ in.)
S.d.b.r.: *A. Dauzats, 1849*
Inv. 488 (Salon d'Orléans)

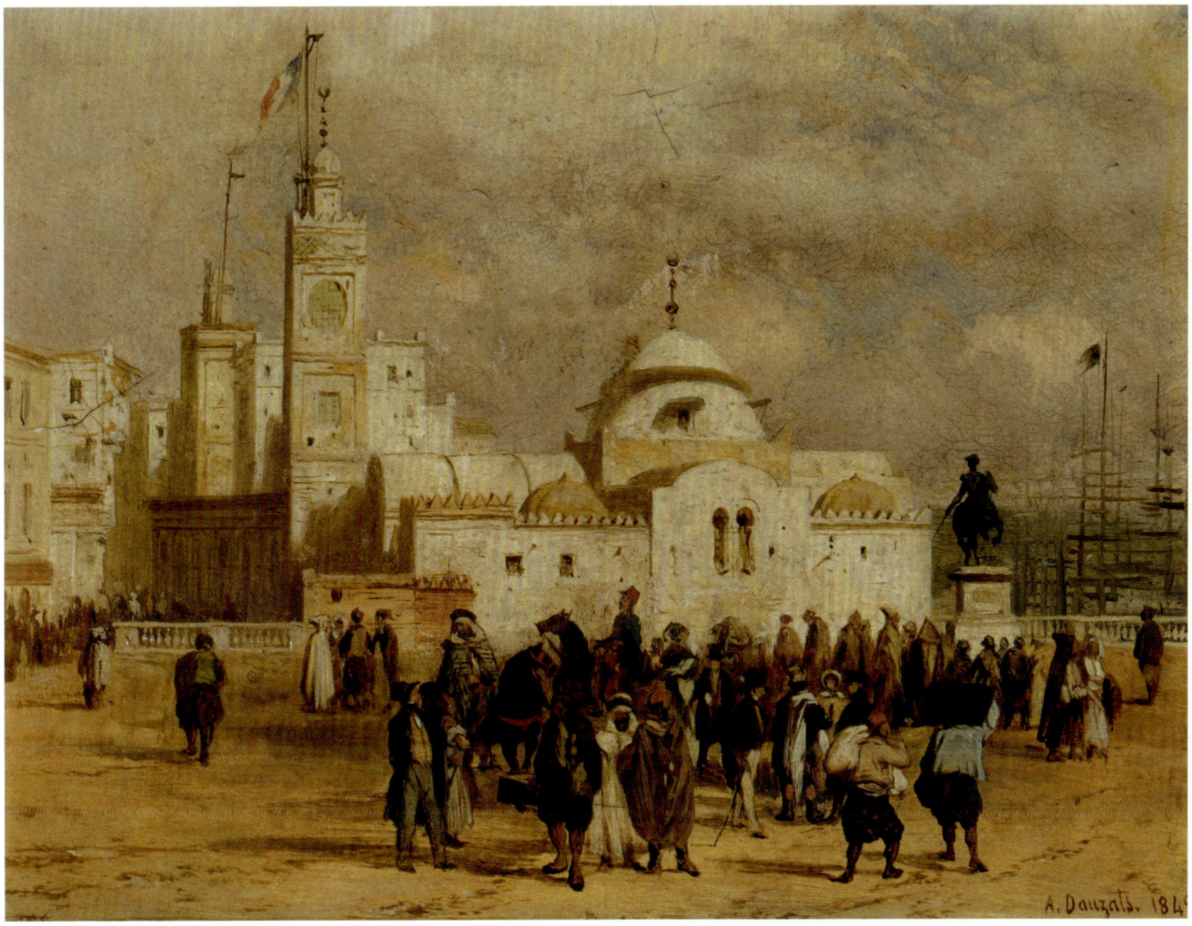

As early as 1828 Adrien Dauzats contributed to Baron Taylor's publication of *Voyages Pittoresques et Romantiques dans l'Ancienne France*, followed by his *Voyage en Orient*. Dauzat traveled to Egypt, Palestine, and Syria in 1830, then to Spain in the company of Baron Taylor (who was assembling a gallery of Spanish works for King Louis-Philippe), and finally to Portugal. A year later, Dauzats exhibited his first Orientalist paintings at the Salon of 1831. Close to the Orléans family, he accompanied the crown prince in 1839 on the expedition to the gorge in Algeria known as the Portes de Fer, illustrating the account of the expedition published by Charles Nodier in 1844 after the prince died. The duc d'Aumale also asked Dauzats to buy on his behalf one of Delacroix's Moroccan sketchbooks (now in the Musée Condé) at the artist's postmortem estate auction in 1864.

This painting was done ten years after Dauzats returned from Algeria, probably from sketches. This swiftly executed piece was bequeathed to the duc d'Aumale by the duchesse d'Orléans, who died in 1858. It depicts a place of which the duke and his elder brother were fond, namely Royal Square, renamed Government Square in 1848, with the Fishery Mosque (or New Mosque) in the middle, built around 1660 and rising 90 yards (84 meters) high. The square had been enclosed in 1841 by a balustrade overlooking the fishery and the sea (the masts of ships in port can be glimpsed on the far right). The duc d'Aumale was very familiar with this square in the center of Algiers, for he fought in Algeria from 1840 to 1848 and lived in Algiers as Governor General of the country in 1847–48. Above all, the duke must have been moved by the presence in this painting of a statue of his brother, the crown prince (duc d'Orléans), which was cast by Carlo Marochetti using bronze from cannons captured from the enemy (this statue is now on Place du Duc d'Orléans in Neuilly, just outside Paris). The real subject of the painting is the colorful crowd standing in the middle foreground, including a French soldier on horseback.

EUGÈNE DELACROIX

(Charenton-Saint-Maurice, 1798; Paris, 1863)

Guard Post at Meknes, 1847

Canvas. H. 65 cm (2 ft. 1 ¾ in.); W. 53 cm (1 ft. 8 ¾ in.)
S.b.c.: *Eug. Delacroix*
Inv. 457 (Salle Isabelle)

This is the only one of the three Delacroix paintings in the Musée Condé to reflect the Orientalist trend. Delacroix experienced the revelation of the Orient when he accompanied a French embassy that visited Morocco and Sultan Mulay abd er-Rahman from January to June 1832. The French mission sailed from Toulon on January 11, 1832, and arrived at Tangier, opening the gates to a voyage that would completely revitalize Delacroix's art. He felt he was discovering an antiquity that was still alive on the other shore of the Mediterranean; as he wrote in his correspondence and travel notes, "Rome is no longer in Rome." Already a nascent Orientalism was replacing Italy, Antiquity, and the Renaissance as the undisputed sources of artistic inspiration. Delacroix took with him four sketchbooks that he filled with drawings in pencil and watercolor, three of which are now in the Louvre, the fourth being here in the Musée Condé. For the rest of his life Delacroix would delve into these sketchbooks to seek Oriental material for his art. The trip to Morocco was a key moment when the leader of the Romantic school, struck by the light, colors, and picturesqueness of North Africa, turned toward the Orient.

The history behind *Guard Post at Meknes* is fairly complex. Delacroix devised this composition fifteen years after his stay in Meknes, which took place between mid-March and early April 1832, before his return to Tangier. He seems to have been groping for a solution: in February 1847, after a visit by his artist friends Louis Müller and Edmond Hédouin, he changed the background of the painting on their advice; then, in March, he altered the overall tone, in accordance with a different opinion. The version here is an autograph replica commissioned from Delacroix by Monsieur de Cailleux, director of the royal museums, based on the original painting, dated 1846, which was purchased by King Louis-Philippe who gave it to his daughter Clementine of Saxe-Coburg (now in the Von der Heydt Museum, Wuppertal). In executing this copy, which differs in just a few details, Delacroix went back to the original in the Louvre, where it was hanging during the Salon.

Cailleux probably commissioned the replica on behalf of the duc d'Aumale, because the painting was already in his apartments in the Tuileries Palace during the revolution of February 1848. It was discovered, slightly damaged, by the duke's former drawing teacher, Nicolas-Alexander Barbier (1789–1864), who immediately sent it to him in England.

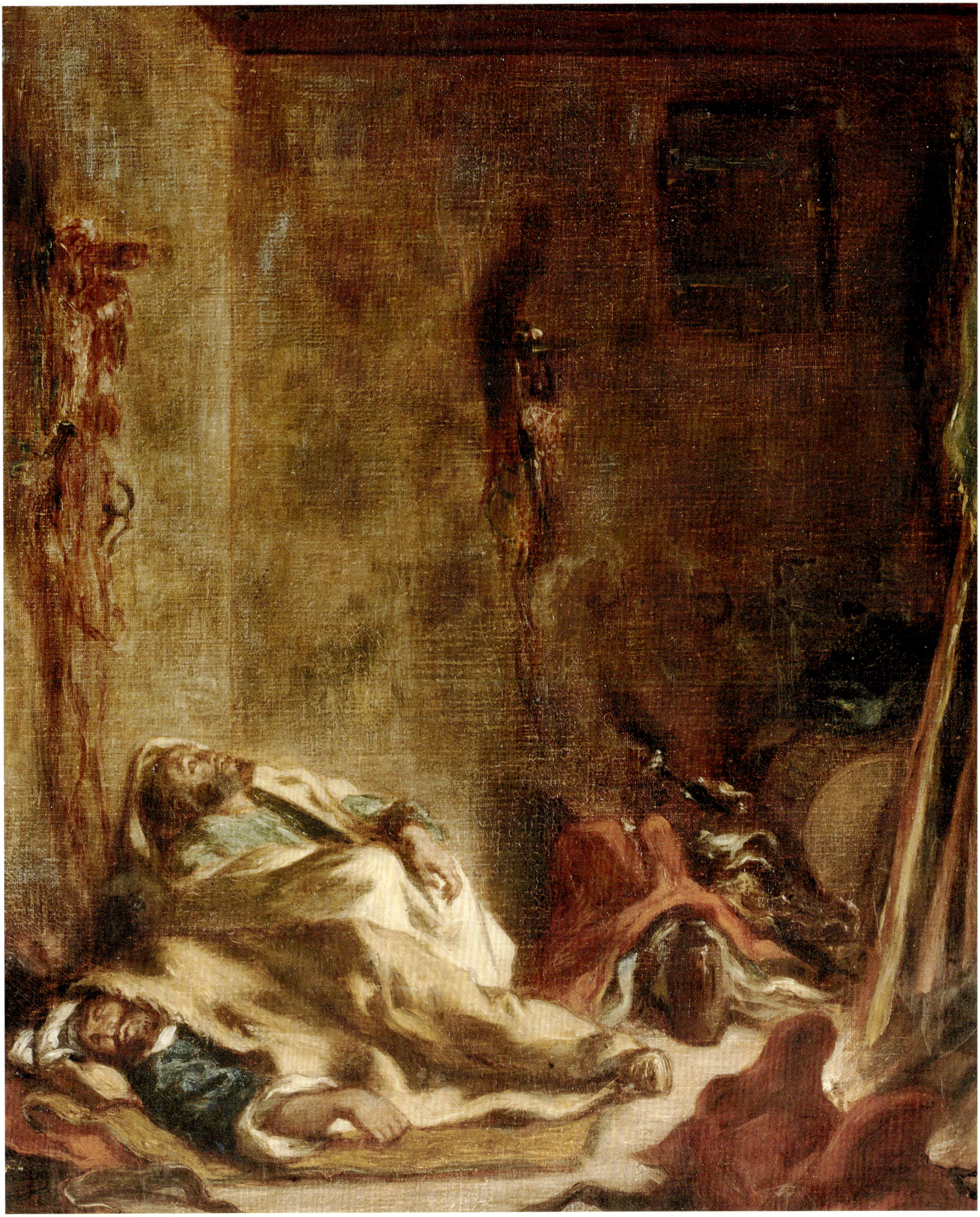

HORACE VERNET

(Paris, 1789; Paris, 1863)

Arab Chieftains in Their Camp, 1834

Canvas. H. 98 cm (3 ft. 2 ½ in.); W. 137 cm (4 ft. 5 ½ in.)
S.d.b.l.: *H. Vernet Rome 1834*
Inv. 438 (Galerie de Peinture)

An official artist of Louis-Philippe's reign (1830–48), Horace Vernet depicted this scene when he was director of the Académie de France in Rome, after having visited Algeria aboard the brig *Comète,* placed at his disposal by the minister of the navy, the comte de Rigny. Vernet remained in Algiers for ten days or so, meeting the intrepid Captain Yusuf, a local warlord who fought alongside the French and attained the rank of general.

The painting here is a replica, with variations, of one dated "Rome, 1833," now titled *The Arab Tale-Teller* (Wallace Collection, London). It was executed while the original was being exhibited in Paris at the Salon of 1834, where Vernet showed his first attempt at Orientalism. Although highly different in spirit, his painting was therefore viewed in the context of Delacroix's *Women of Algiers.*

Vernet depicts the deployment of French troops in Algeria and shows—not without ulterior political motives—the temporary entente between Louis-Philippe's army and Algerian tribal leaders, who have organized a festive fantasia (seen in the background to the left). The chieftains, representing various ethnic groups in Algeria, meet in council beneath a fig tree.

This painting must have aroused memories of the duc d'Aumale's own Algerian past. The tents in the background on the right evoke those of Abd el-Kader's tribe, whose capture on May 16, 1843 was the duke's main military exploit in Algeria, aged just twenty-one. The duke bought this painting at the Drouot auction house in Paris in 1876, after Vernet's death.

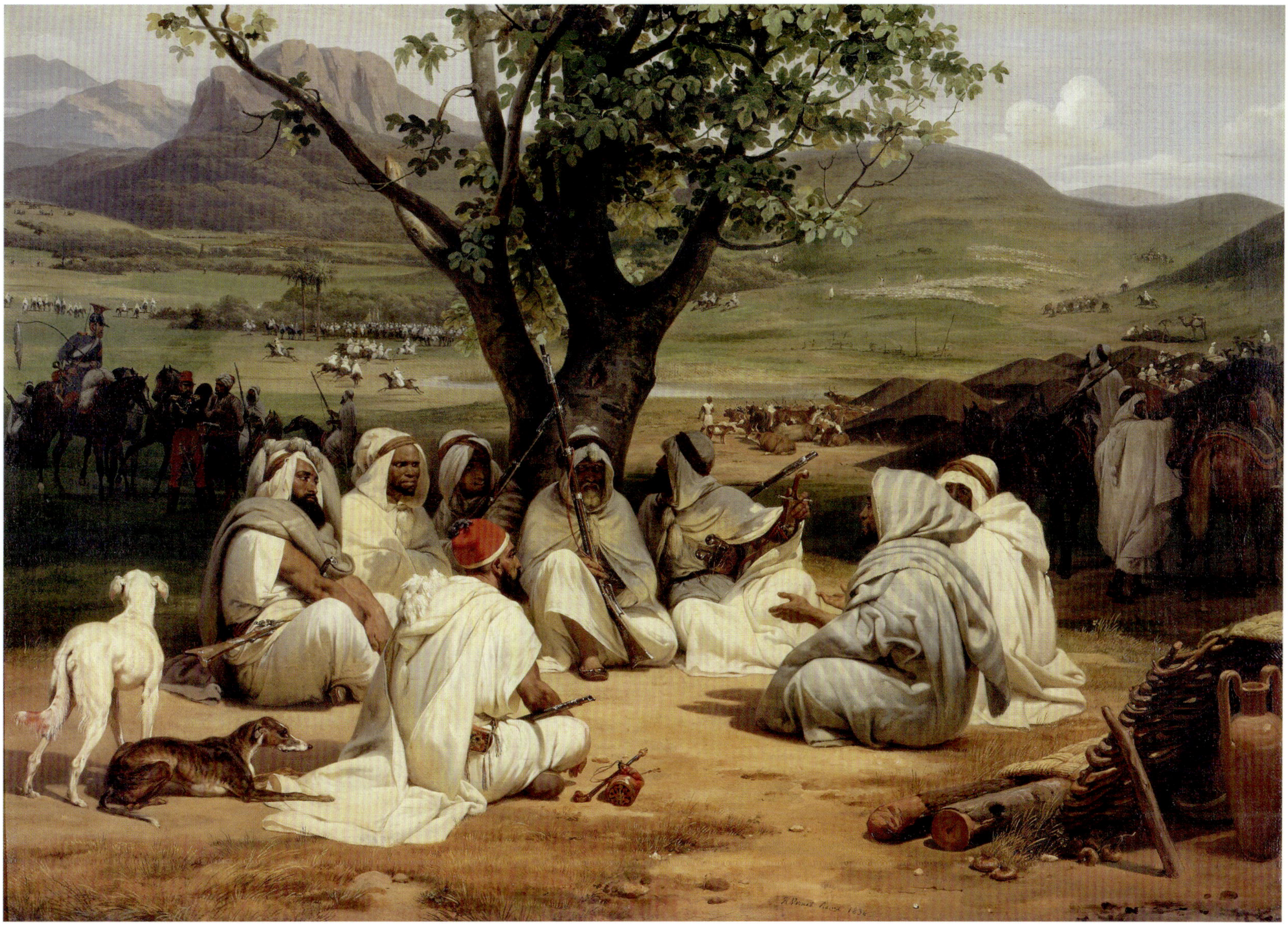

PROSPER MARILHAT

(Vertaizon, Puy-de-Dôme, 1811; Paris, 1847)

Syrian Arabs on a Voyage

Wood. H. 28 cm (11 in.); W. 50 cm (1 ft. 7 3/4 in.)
S.b.l.: *P. MARILHAT*
Inv. 500 (Salle Isabelle)

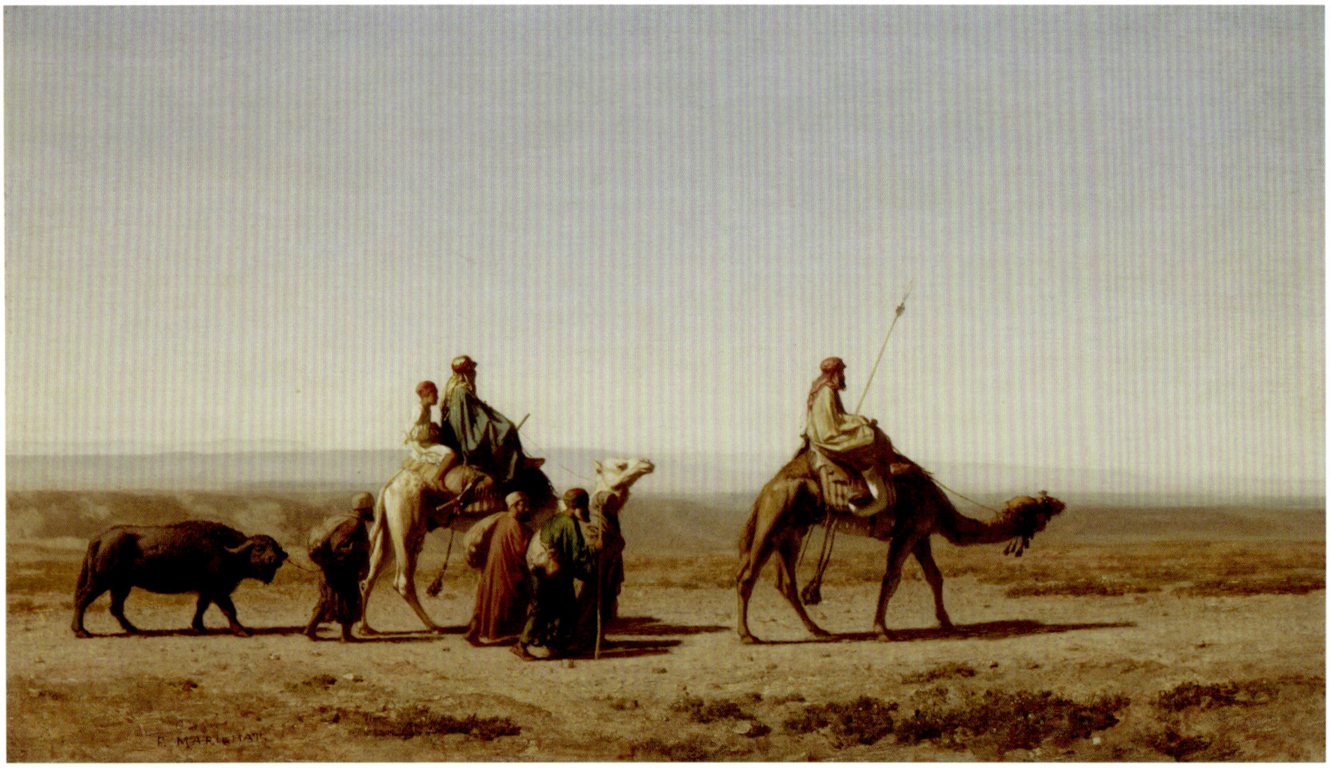

This is one of the most famous paintings by "Marilhat the Egyptian," as the artist liked to call himself *(see p. 266)*. He exhibited eight works at the Salon of 1844, two of which depicted his native region of Auvergne, the other six being views of Syria and Egypt that the critic Théophile Gautier described as "pearls mounted on gold."

Under a harsh sun, the caravan moves lazily along a trail in the desert, in a perceptibly suffocating heat that slows the advance of the group. The figures in the foreground stand out from the desert background, which features shimmering dunes in the distance. The exotic dress and animals as well as the lengthy shadows add to the impression of strangeness, making this a masterpiece of Orientalist painting. Its modest dimensions define it as a genre scene, despite the monumentality of the composition. A singular artist, Marilhat went mad and died at age thirty-six, leaving an uncompleted oeuvre behind. The duc d'Aumale bought this painting as part of the collection of Marquis Maison, famous for its Orientalist pieces (*see p. 30*).

EUGÈNE FROMENTIN

(La Rochelle, 1820; Saint-Maurice, near La Rochelle, 1876)

Heron Hunting, Algeria, 1865

Canvas. H. 99 cm (3 ft. 3 in.); W. 142 cm (4 ft. 7 in.)
S.b.l.: *Eug. Fromentin;* d.b.r.: *1865*
Inv. 528 (Galerie de Peinture)

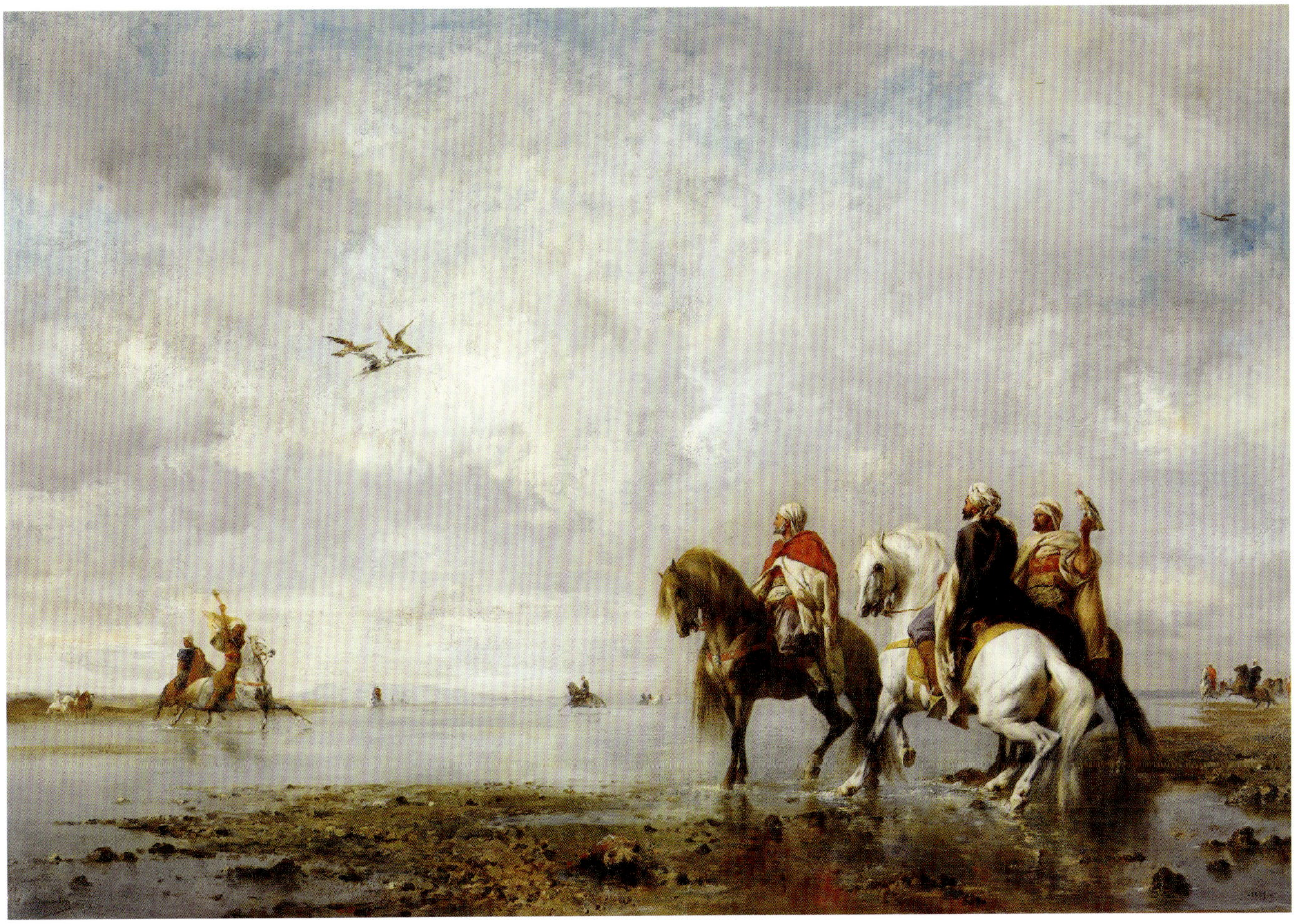

After attending law school with little enthusiasm, Eugène Fromentin saw Marilhat's Orientalist paintings, and went himself to Algeria in 1846, accompanying his friend Charles Labbé to the town of Blida. On returning to France in 1847, Fromentin exhibited his early paintings at the Salon, two of which featured Algerian subjects. He then returned to Blida, where he was staying when Abd el-Kader surrendered the following winter. Fromentin then traveled further south, intending to publish a set of engravings on his trip from Constantine to Biskra, dedicating it to the duc d'Aumale. He made a third trip to Algeria in 1852–53. Named an officer of the Légion d'Honneur in 1869, he died in an accident not far from La Rochelle in France.

Fromentin was also a writer, and Algeria inspired his books *Un Été dans le Sahara* (A Summer in the Sahara) and *Une Année dans le Sahel* (A Year in the Sahel). A second-generation Orientalist, Fromentin depicted an Orient that was more melancholic and desolate than picturesque and colorful. He was particularly drawn to the subject of Arabic falconry, as frequently seen in his paintings (Musée d'Orsay, Paris; Reims; Nantes; Dublin, etc.). Falconry was restricted to the highest ranking Arab noblemen, as had been the case in Europe in earlier ages.

The version here was exhibited in the Salon of 1865 and the Universal Exposition of 1867. Critics—and the duc d'Aumale himself—were surprised at the aquatic landscape and cloud-laden sky, so unlike the burning deserts of North Africa. It is nevertheless one of Fromentin's masterpieces, which the duke purchased during his English exile, at the 1868 Drouot sale of the count of Aquila's collection.

ROSA BONHEUR

(Bordeaux, 1822; By, Seine-et-Marne, 1899)

Pyrenean Shepherd Giving Salt to his Sheep, 1864

Canvas. H. 68 cm (2 ft. 3 in.); W. 100 cm (3 ft. 3 ½ in.)
S.d.b.l.: *1864 R. Bonheur*
Inv. 531 (Galerie de Peinture)

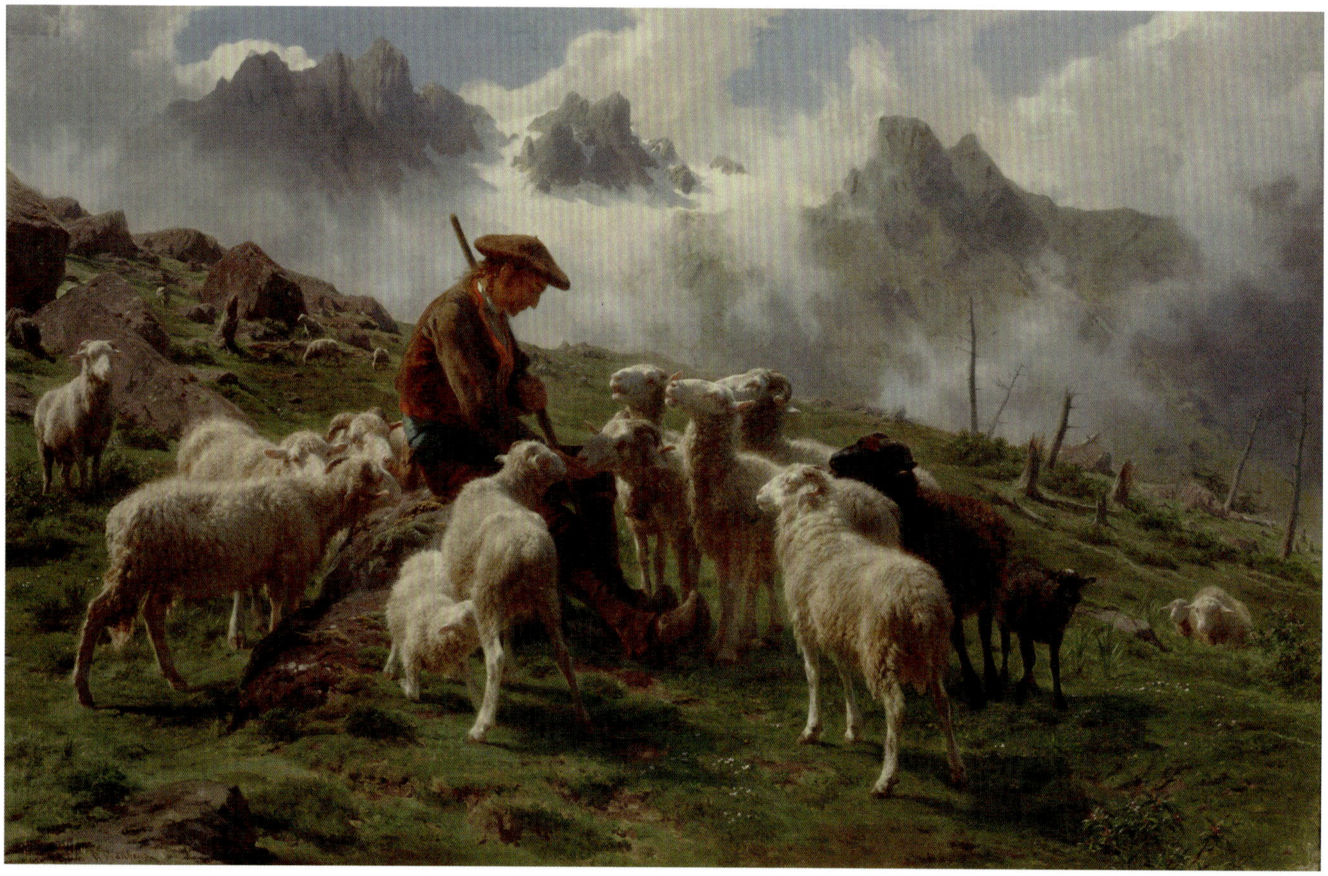

Rosa Bonheur was one of four children, all of whom became painters like their father, Raymond Bonheur, a follower of the socialist thinker Saint-Simon. Convinced that the sexes were equal, Rosa worked in male clothing, which caused her problems with the police. A friend of the female author George Sand, she was allegedly inspired by a passage in Sand's *Mare au Diable* (The Devil's Pool) for her painting of *Plowing in Nivernais* (Musée d'Orsay, Paris). She moved to By, on the edge of the forest of Fontainebleau, where she could paint animals from life. Her *Horse Fair*, exhibited at the Salon of 1853, won her international recognition; it was bought by Cornelis Vanderbilt, who donated it to the Metropolitan Museum in New York. She won a gold medal in 1853 and again in 1855, and was inducted into the Légion d'Honneur by the Empress Eugénie in her studio in By; she became the first woman promoted to the rank of officer of the Légion d'Honneur in 1894. Bonheur's animal paintings display a realism devoid of sentimentality and Romanticism.

The duc d'Aumale commissioned this painting in 1864 as a gift for the duchess. The comtesse de Ségur acted as go-between for the duke, who was then in exile in England. The duke and duchess were so pleased with the painting that they doubled the agreed price, paying Bonheur 10,000 francs instead of 5,000. Bonheur was later invited to lunch at Chantilly, in 1894, in the company of Ernest Lavisse and Auguste Cain.

LÉON PERRAULT, AFTER HORACE VERNET

(Poitiers, 1832; Royan, 1908)

King Louis-Philippe, Escorted by His Sons, Leaving the Palace of Versailles on June 10, 1837

Canvas. H. 81 cm (2 ft. 8 in.); W. 84 cm (2 ft. 9 in.)
S.b.l.: *L. Perrault, d'après H. Vernet*
Inv. 439 (Galerie du Logis)

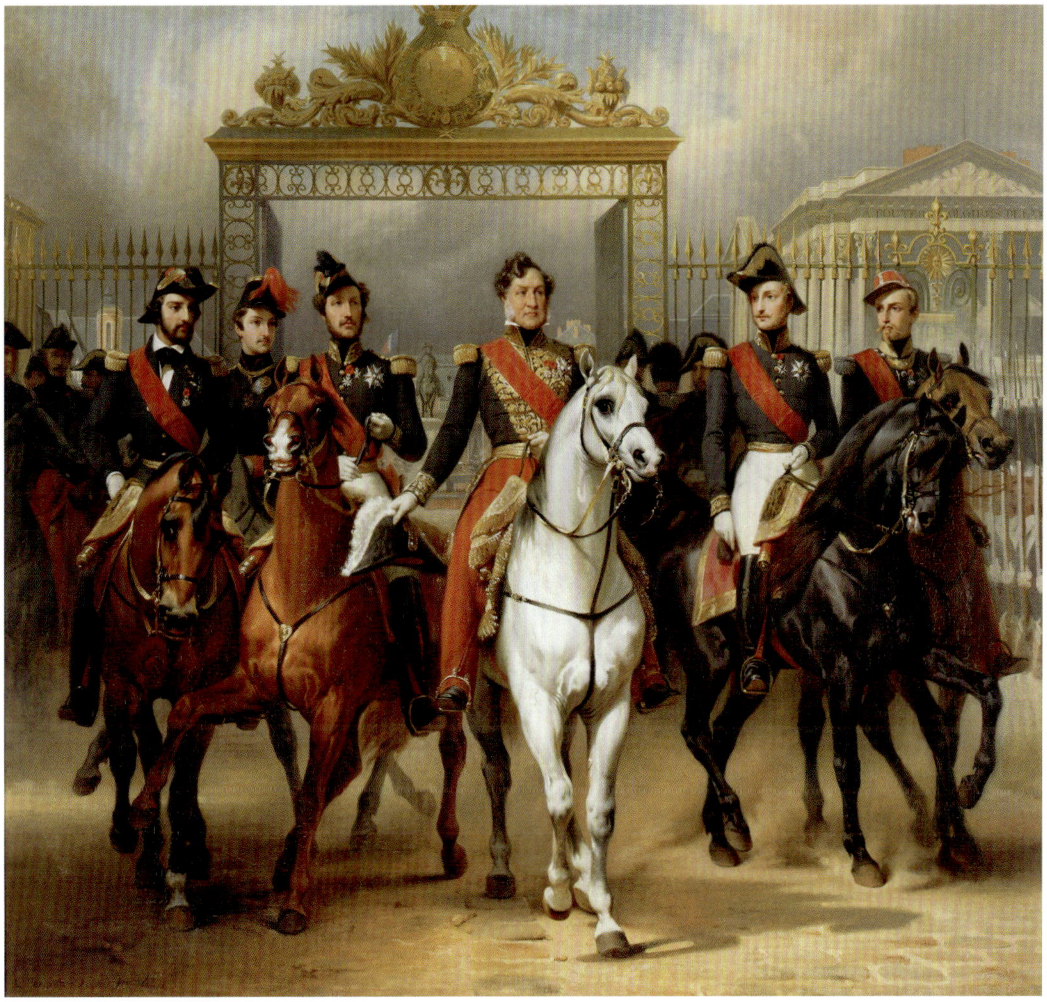

In 1867 the duc d'Aumale commissioned Léon Perrault to make this copy of an original painting done in 1846 by Horace Vernet and exhibited at the Salon of 1847 (now in the Château de Versailles). It shows King Louis-Philippe on the occasion of the inauguration of the history gallery at Versailles in 1837, escorted by his five sons. From left to right, they are: the prince of Joinville (1818–1900), the duc de Montpensier (1824–1890), Crown Prince Ferdinand (the duc d'Orléans, 1810–1842), the king, the duc de Nemours (1814–1896), and finally the duc d'Aumale (1822–1897). Vernet painted the crown prince from memory, because Ferdinand died in an accident in 1842 at the age of thirty-two; he also deliberately aged the duc d'Aumale and the duc de Montpensier, who were only fifteen and sixteen, respectively, at the time of the event. Vernet's political message was clear: King Louis-Philippe represented the continuity of the Bourbon family, as indicated by the statue of Louis XIV over his shoulder in the background.

Louis-Philippe had decided to use the château of Versailles—the royal French residence that had been emptied of its treasures during the Revolution—as the premises for a museum dedicated to "the glories of France." It was the king's most important museum project. The teenage duc d'Aumale was probably struck by his father's attempts to commemorate the country's glorious moments, for he later did something similar at Chantilly by organizing his collection around portraits of great men who influenced French history, such as Anne de Montmorency and the Great Condé, and by naming his museum the Musée Condé in honor of the great-uncle who passed the château on to him. It was in this same spirit that the duc d'Aumale bequeathed château and museum to the Institut de France, so that this heritage became the property of the entire nation.

JEAN-LÉON GÉRÔME

(Vesoul, 1824; Paris, 1904)

The Aftermath of a Masked Ball, 1857

Canvas. H. 50 cm (1 ft. 7 3/4 in.); W. 72 cm (2 ft. 4 in.)
S.d.b.l.: *J.L.GEROME / 1857*
Inv. 533 (Salle Isabelle)

Jean-Léon Gérôme, who trained under Paul Delaroche, was keenly interested in drawing and ancient history. He became part of the movement of young artists known as the "Greek revival," which included Charles-François Jalabert. In 1843 Gérôme accompanied Delaroche to Rome and Italy, but did not regularly attend courses at the École des Beaux-Arts—he never won the Prix de Rome. He came to attention with a work that made a splash at the Salon of 1847, *Young Greeks Setting Cocks to Fight* (Musée d'Orsay, Paris). Théophile Gautier appreciated Gérôme's style in contrast to the realism of the Barbizon school. Launching himself on an official career, Gérôme decorated a chapel in the church of Saint-Séverin in 1851 and the library of the Conservatoire des Arts et Métiers (no longer extant). However, his huge history painting of 1855, *The Apotheosis of the Century of Augustus* (Musée d'Orsay, Paris), was a flop. He then traveled to the Near East in 1855–56, adopting the Orientalist style that he would pursue for the rest of his life.

Having abandoned history painting, Gérôme painted scenes such as this *Aftermath of a Masked Ball,* which was his most popular work. The ball has ended in the early morning of a cold and snowy day in February; two costumed party-goers, probably under the influence of alcohol, decide to fight a duel in the Bois de Boulogne on the outskirts of Paris. The duel in the snowy woods has just ended: mortally wounded, a man dressed as Pierrot, sword still in his hand, collapses into the arms of his seconds (one dressed as the duc de Guise, the other, completely distraught, wearing a domino), while a doctor (disguised as a doge of Venice) tries to revive him. The winner of the duel, dressed as an American Indian, heads back to his carriage accompanied by his second, dressed as Harlequin. This theme seems to have been fashionable, and was also depicted by Thomas Couture in 1857 (Wallace Collection, London).

Exhibited to great acclaim at the Paris Salon of 1857, then in London that same year by the English art dealer Gambart, this painting was bought by the duc d'Aumale in 1858. Ten years later Gérôme borrowed it from the duke to show it at the Universal Exposition of 1867, where it won the Grand Prize for painting. Despite the popularity of this picture, critics regretted that Gérôme gave up history painting for this kind of genre painting.

Gérôme was very close to the duc d'Aumale, and after the duke died he executed an equestrian statue of him in 1899. The bronze statue, commissioned by the city of Chantilly and funded by a public subscription, now stands in front of the Grandes Écuries (Large Stables).

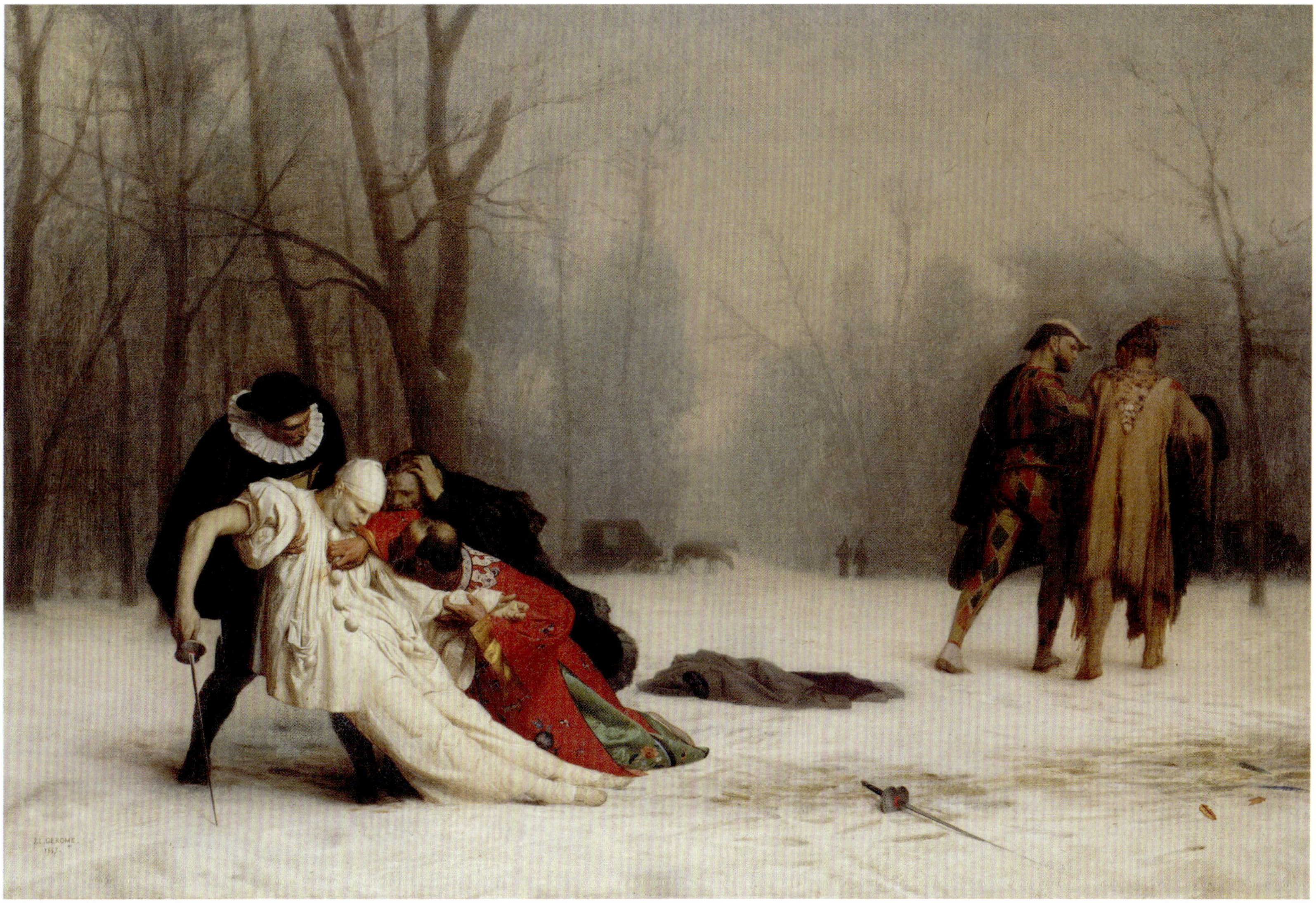

PAUL BAUDRY

(La Roche-sur-Yon, 1828; Paris, 1886)

The Vision of Saint Hubert, 1882

Canvas. H. 230 cm (7 ft. 6 in.); W. 206 cm (6 ft. 9 in.)
S.d.b.c.: *P. BAUDRY / 1882*
Inv. 540 (Galerie des Cerfs)

After the duc d'Aumale returned to Paris in 1871, he purchased the private residence of banker Achille Fould, which had been decorated with paintings by Paul Baudry in 1859. During the reconstruction of the château at Chantilly, the duke transferred the medallions and overdoor paintings from the Fould residence to the château, at the same time commissioning Baudry to paint this work for the fireplace of the reception hall at Chantilly, known as the Galerie des Cerfs (Gallery of Stags). Architect Honoré Daumet wrote to the duke on November 27, 1879 that, "Monsieur Baudry would be delighted to see the grisailles in their new setting, and to provide a new work to accompany them over the large fireplace. M. Baudry is at the duke's orders, and would like to see the tapestries with which he must coordinate." Indeed, Baudry's painting was to be placed near the tapestries known as the *Hunts of Maximilian* (or *Hunts of Guise*), woven at the Gobelins Manufactory in the late seventeenth century from cartoons designed by Bernard van Orley in the sixteenth century. Baudry's decorative panel recounts the story of Saint Hubert, a pagan hunter who wandered through the forests of Aquitaine with his page and his hounds, until one day he suddenly saw a large white stag with a shining cross between its antlers. This vision prompted Hubert to convert to Christianity. Baudry had the duc d'Aumale's closest nephew, Robert, duc de Chartres (1840–1910) pose as Saint Hubert, while the duke's great-nephew and the pretender to the Orléans throne, the young duc d'Orléans (1869–1926) posed as the page. According to family legend, the posing session took place on Christmas day.

In a wintry landscape, the white, glowing stag rises at the top of the composition, eyes turned heavenward. Baudry sought to convey the saint's shock, the page's turmoil, and the hounds' alarm even as he developed effects of perspective, a somewhat surprising move on his part, dictated by the need to harmonize with tapestries in the sixteenth-century Flemish vein. The result is an unusual atmosphere in which the painting's various characters and planes create an impression of confusion.

Being unusual for Baudry, this painting startled critics when it was displayed in 1882 at an exhibition organized by the Union Centrale des Arts Décoratifs in the Orangerie of the Tuileries Gardens.

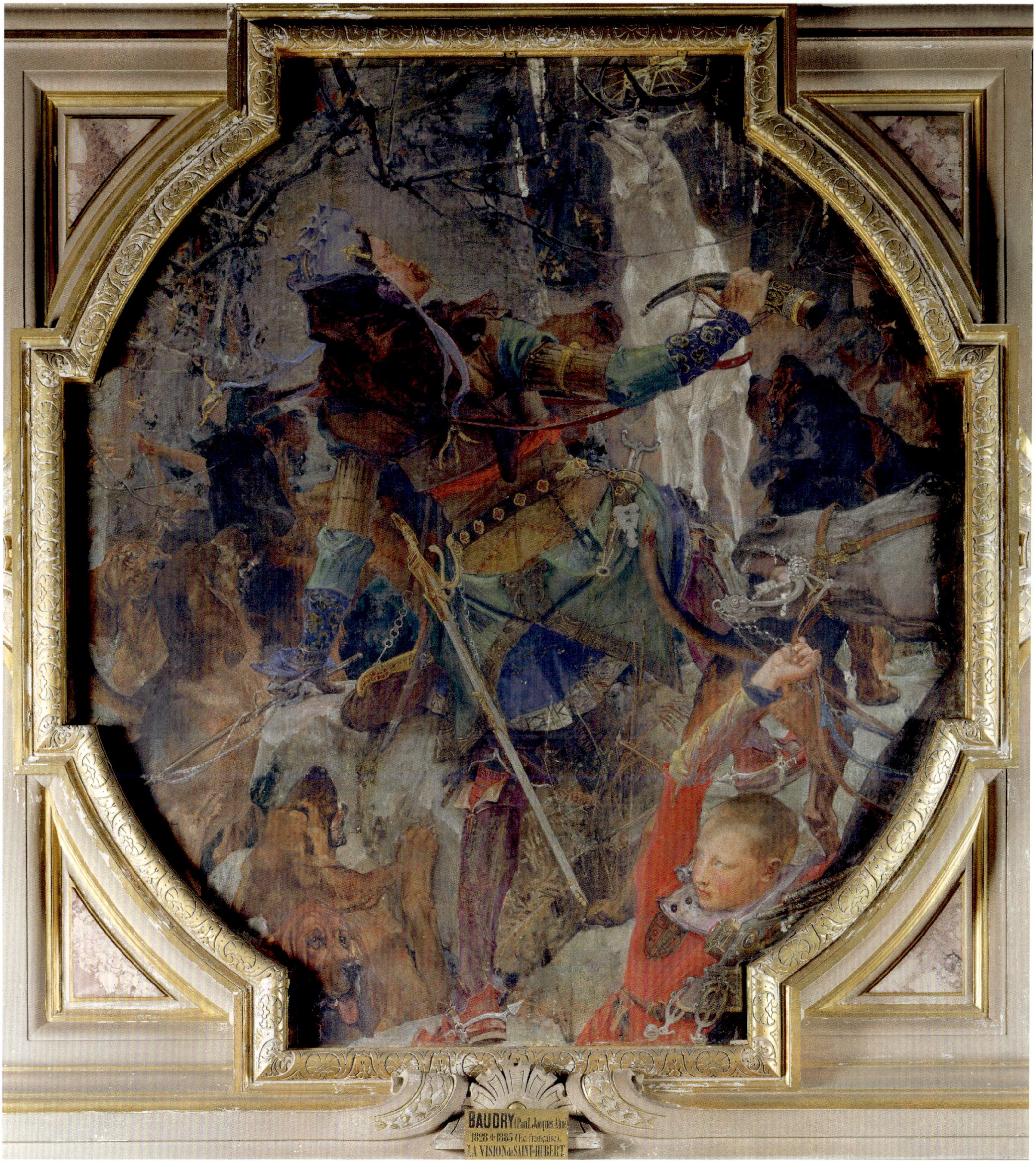
BAUDRY (Paul. Jacques. Aimé)
1828 + 1885 (Ec. française).
LA VISION de SAINT-HUBERT.

ERNEST HÉBERT

(Grenoble, 1817; Grenoble, 1908)

Malaria

Canvas. H. 55 cm (1 ft. 9 ½ in.); W. 80 cm (2 ft. 7 ½ in.)
Inv. 520 (Salle Isabelle)

This painting is a reduced version of a famous work by Ernest Hébert, painted in 1849–50 on his return from Rome (Musée d'Orsay, Paris). Exhibited in the Salon of 1850–51, it made the reputation of this young artist from Grenoble, a second cousin of Stendhal. Hébert completed his training in the studios of David d'Angers and Paul Delaroche and then won the Prix de Rome in 1839. He left for the Académie de France in Rome, then headed by Ingres (who was shortly after succeeded by Jean Victor Schnetz); on returning to France, Hébert settled in the Nouvelle-Athènes neighborhood of Paris, where he painted *Malaria*.

Malaria, from the Italian *mala aria*, or "bad air," was a disease that notably struck peasants in the countryside around Rome, in the region of the Pontine marshes (which were only drained in the 1930s under Mussolini). At a time when Orientalism was fashionable and artists were painting scenes from North Africa and the Near East, interest in Italy was revived thanks to contemporary subjects that raised social issues, as opposed to the earlier taste for Antiquity and the Renaissance. The exoticism of local dress and the intrinsic interest of a country simultaneously nearby and remote appealed to Romantic artists; furthermore the tragic subject here reminded Parisians of the constant threat of epidemics (cholera ravaged Paris in 1832 and would strike again in 1854). This painting was therefore highly popular. Hébert executed several replicas of it and Fantin-Latour copied it. The duc d'Aumale, who bought this small-scale version in 1876 from a Dutch collector, knew Hébert well, inviting him to stay at his Sicilian residence in 1893.

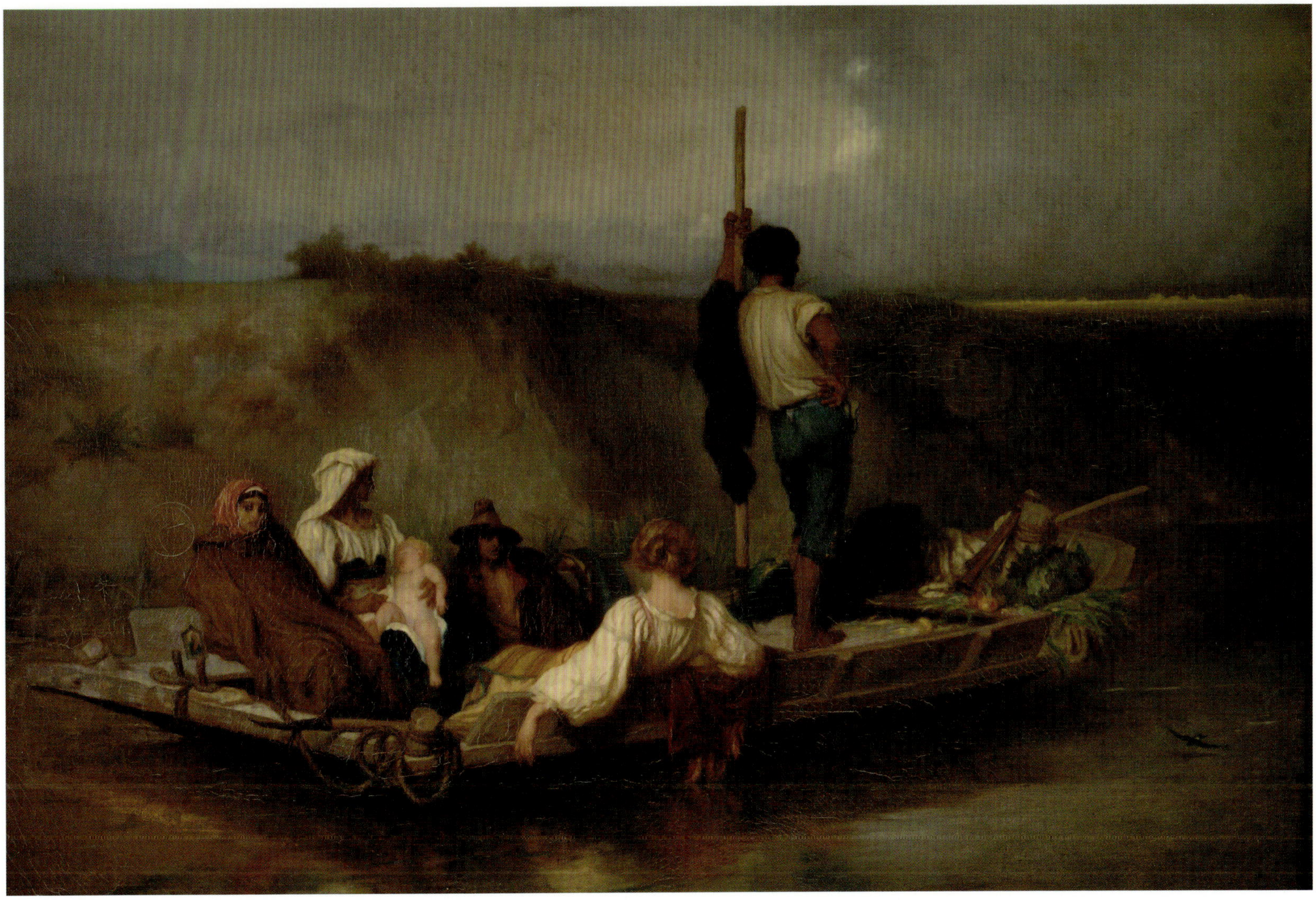

JEAN-BAPTISTE-ÉDOUARD DETAILLE

(Paris, 1848; Paris, 1912)

Hold Your Heads High!
Colonel Lepic at Eylau on February 8, 1807, 1893

Canvas. H. 115 cm (3 ft. 8 ¼ in.); W. 90 cm (2 ft. 11 ½ in.)
S.d.b.r.: *Edouard Detaille 1893*
Inv. 551 (Salle de la Smalah)

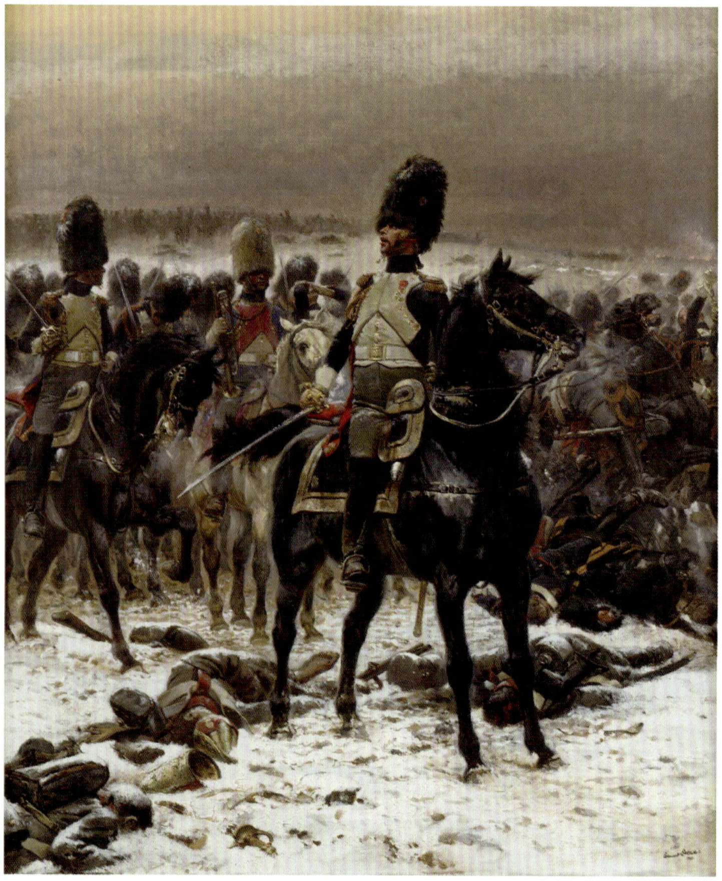

Jean-Baptiste-Édouard Detaille was a pupil of Ernest Meissonier, and showed regularly at the Salon from 1867 to 1912. He belonged to the second generation of military artists, who are also represented in the duc d'Aumale's collection by Alphonse de Neuville. The duke bought this painting in 1894, three years before his death. Detaille knew the duke personally, often going to Chantilly for lunch with de Neuville or Léon Bonnat.

Louis Lépic, a colonel of the Imperial Grenadiers, was a legendary figure of the Napoleonic saga. Born in Montpellier in 1765, he joined the dragoons in 1781, aged fifteen and a half. Promoted to the rank of lieutenant colonel in 1793, during the civil war in the Vendée region he took in a three-year-old child abandoned at the foot of a tree, near a dead woman. Having raised the girl to adulthood, Lépic retraced her family during the Restoration, and discovered that the lost child had inherited a vast fortune.

During the war in Italy from 1797 to 1799, Lépic commanded the 15th regiment of chasseurs and was made a full colonel after the battle of Marengo. In February 1807, on the eve of the battle of Eylau, Lépic summoned the army doctor, Baron Larrey, because he wanted to be fit for action the next day despite his gouty rheumatism. Larrey dutifully treated Lépic. During the battle the following day, Lépic, seeing the mounted grenadiers he commanded lower their heads to dodge the Russian and Prussian bullets that were raining down along with a snow storm, stood up his stirrups and shouted, "Hold your heads high! It's a hail of grapeshot, not sh**!" Surrounded by the Russians, Lépic was asked to surrender, at which point he cried, "Have a look at these faces and see if they want to surrender!" He then managed to break out. When he rejoined Napoleon, he was addressed by the emperor with the new rank he henceforth held: "I'd thought you'd been taken, general, and I was sorely tried." To which Lépic replied, "Sire, my death will be the only news that ever reaches you." That evening, dining with Napoleon, Lépic found a packet containing 50,000 francs beneath his napkin; he distributed it to his grenadiers. Lépic was made a baron by Napoleon and became a major general after the campaign in Russia; he retired from active service and died in 1827.

JEAN-LOUIS-ERNEST MEISSONIER

(Lyon, 1815; Paris, 1891)

Before the Battle: The Cavalry of 1805, 1878

Canvas. H. 125 cm (4 ft. 1 ½ in.); W. 198 cm (6 ft. 6 in.)
S.d.b.l.: *EMeissonier, 1878*
Inv. 515 (Galerie de Peinture)

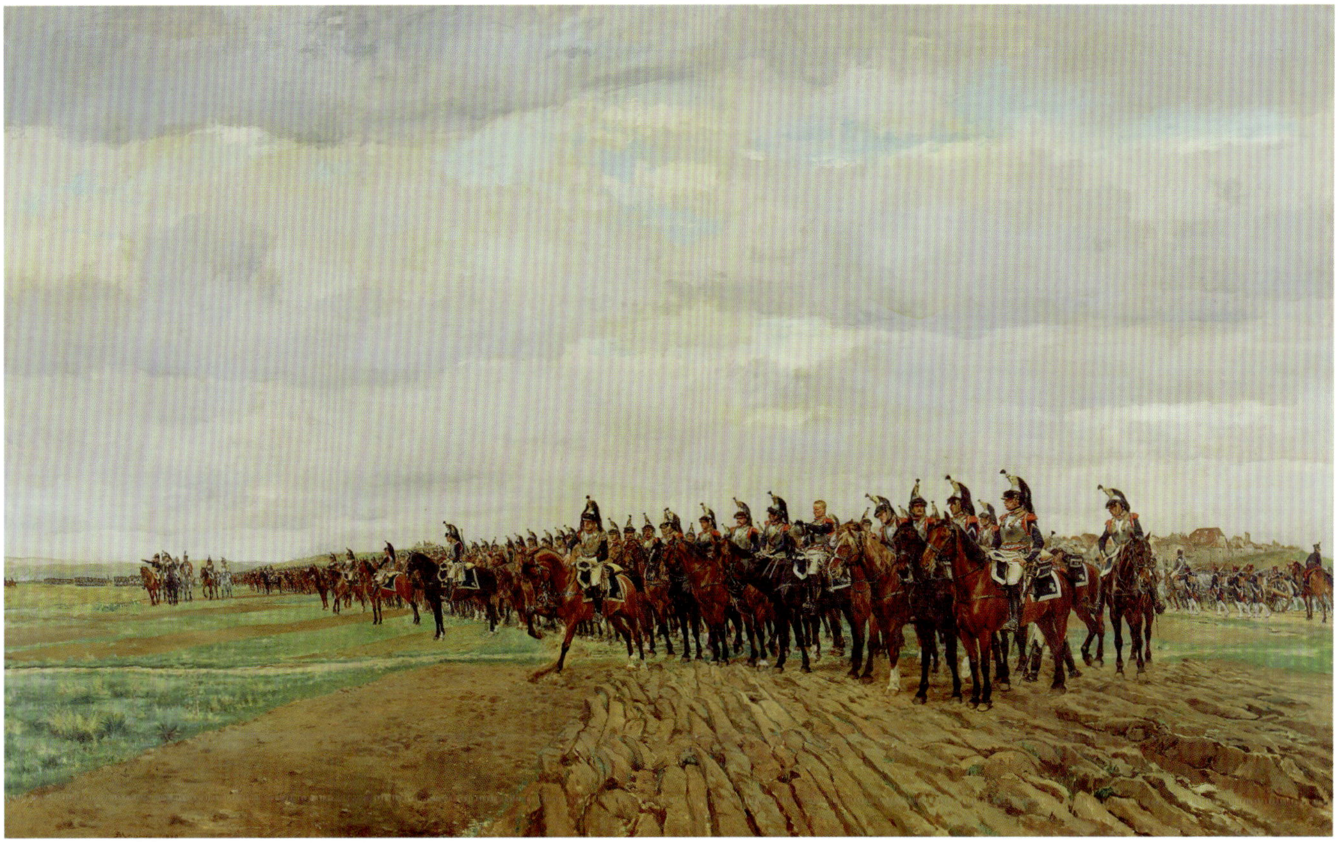

Taught by Julien Pothier and Léon Cognier, Jean-Louis-Ernest Meissonier studied the Dutch and Flemish paintings at the Louvre, and thus began his career by imitating northern European artists. His output was divided between small genre scenes (similar to ancien régime pictures, often depicting soldiers) and large canvases recounting the Napoleonic saga.

Meissonier aspired to recount the life of Napoleon in five vast compositions; the painting here, although not part of that series, resembles them in its overall tone. Meissonier did not like to depict bloody scenes, and decided instead to show the solemn, serious moment when officers and men silently await the signal to begin fighting. The introspection and tension are palpable in this painting, where the emperor's presence is merely suggested in the distance: the chiefs of staff can be glimpsed in the background on the left, approaching to review the troops, while the officers step forward to present their men.

Meissonier painted this picture in 1878 in his studio in Poissy, where former French president Adolphe Thiers came to see it; it was exhibited in the Universal Exposition that same year. At that time Meissonier's paintings fetched huge prices. This one was bought by a Belgian art lover for 275,000 francs. It later returned to France, where it was purchased by collector Ernest Secrétan, who owned no fewer than twenty-four paintings and seven drawings by Meissonier. Secrétan hoped to bequeath them to the Louvre, but a financial setback forced him to sell his collection in 1889.

This painting was the duc d'Aumale's first purchase on returning to France from his second exile (1886–89), after Chantilly had become the property of the Institut de France in 1886. The duke paid the enormous sum of 199,652 francs. Meissonier, a fellow member of the Académie des Beaux-Arts, thanked the duke for buying it and paid him a visit. Whenever he strolled through the gallery of paintings with a guest, the duc d'Aumale headed straight for this picture: "You see those men and those horses? They're preparing to charge, they know they're in for a dreadful time. That's the true poetry of war. The wonderful organization of this painting expresses all the feelings of the people it depicts."

PAUL-ALEXANDRE PROTAIS

(Paris, 1826; Paris, 1888)

The Morning Before the Attack

Canvas. H. 49 cm (1 ft. 7 ½ in.); W. 80 cm (2 ft. 7 ½ in.)
Inv. 534 (Salle Isabelle)

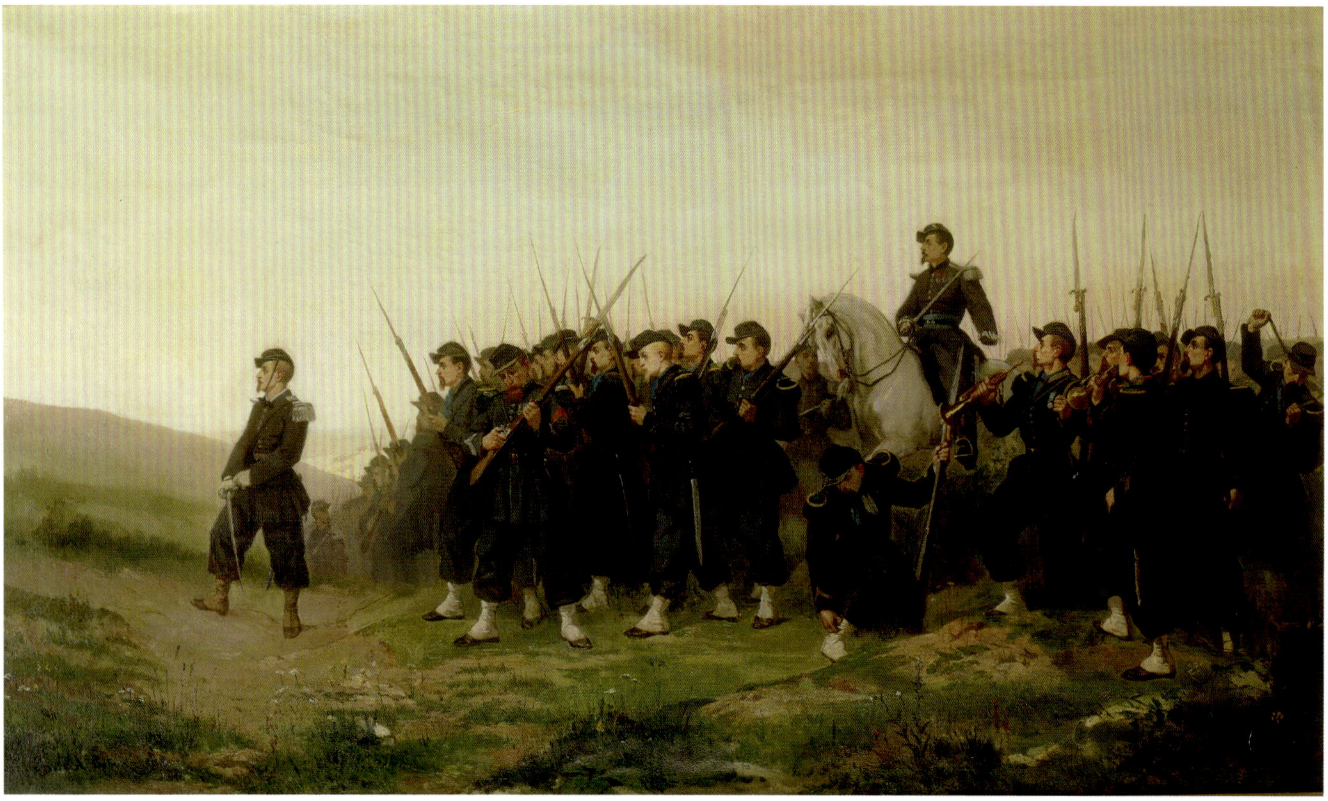

Paul-Alexandre Protais studied under François Desmoulins and exhibited at the Salon from 1857 onward, winning medals in the years 1863, 1864, 1865, 1868, and again in 1878. He was made a member of the Légion d'Honneur in 1865 and promoted to the rank of officer in 1877. He followed the French army in the Crimean and Italian campaigns. This pair of paintings exists in several copies, demonstrating the artist's popularity during the Second Empire and early years of the Third Republic. Conceived as a pair, the two paintings here are reduced version of works exhibited at the Salon of 1863, where they hung in the Salon Carré alongside *The Capture of Magenta* by Adolphe Yvon (1817–93). Displayed again at the Universal Exposition of 1867, they were highly popular with both critics and the general public. In a letter of December 1863, now in the Musée Condé archives, Protais expressed his regret that the duc d'Aumale bought these two reductions,

PAUL-ALEXANDRE PROTAIS

(Paris, 1826; Paris, 1888)

The Evening After the Battle

Canvas. H. 49 cm (1 ft. 7 ½ in.); W. 80 cm (2 ft. 7 ½ in.)
S.b.l.: *A. Protais*
Inv. 535 (Salle Isabelle)

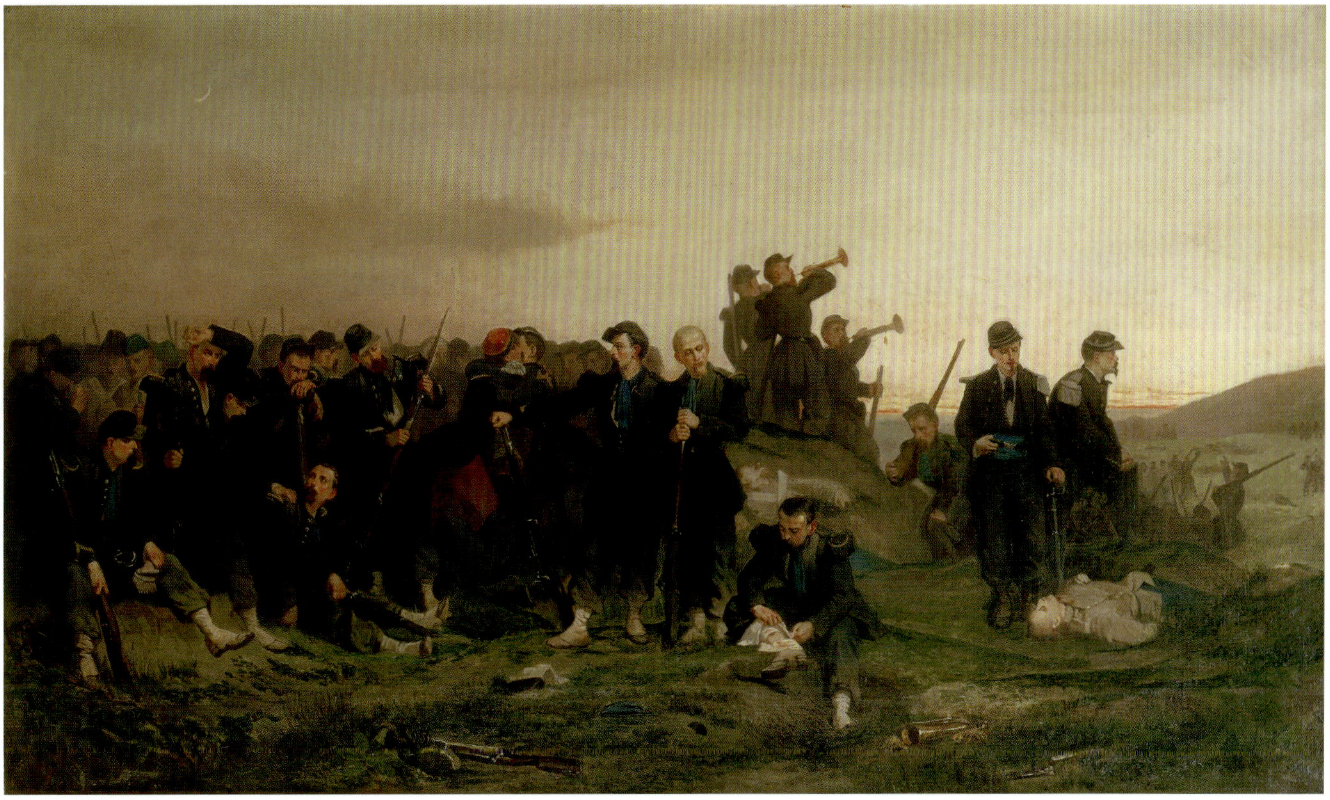

done from sketches destined to be engraved, because they represented "a very feeble interpretation" of the two originals. The artist, apparently worried about the duke's opinion, furthermore wrote that they could hardly "create a very good impression of [his] talent."

Here Protais shows a light infantry battalion heading to battle behind its officers. The soldiers are resolute and determined, yet aware of the danger. They return in the evening, victorious but exhausted, tending to their wounds and counting their dead. As a realistic picture of life in the French army, this painting naturally appealed to the duc d'Aumale, who had served the July Monarchy as a high ranking officer in Algeria from 1840 to 1848, and later returned to active service as a general during the Third Republic. It explains why he reserved a special place for military paintings in the galleries at Chantilly.

CHARLES-FRANÇOIS JALABERT

(Nîmes, 1819; Paris, 1901)

Portrait of Henri d'Orléans, duc d'Aumale (1822–1897), 1866

Canvas. H. 130 cm (4 ft. 3 in.); W. 90 cm (2 ft. 11 1/2 in.)
S.d.b.l.: *Orléans House / 1866 / Ch. Jalabert*
Inv. 861 (Salle de la Smalah)

Charles-François Jalabert studied under Paul Delaroche at the École des Beaux-Arts in 1839; having failed to win the Prix de Rome, he traveled to the eternal city at his own expense. He exhibited at the Salon from 1847 to 1880, and was made a member of the Légion d'Honneur in 1885. Théophile Gautier wrote that Jalabert's "talent ... has something gentle and delicate about it, something feminine that charms and forestalls a desire for more strength." In 1839, the artist himself wrote that, "I will never be a great painter, but I will acquire a talent that, although minor, will be appreciated for its distinction." Having devoted himself to portraiture after 1863, Jalabert was invited to travel to England in January and February 1865 to paint the count and countess of Paris in York House in Twickenham (Musée Louis-Philippe, Eu). There he met the duc d'Aumale, followed in June by the duc and duchesse de Chartres, who invited him to the races at Ascot on June 30, 1865. In June and July of 1866, the duc d'Aumale invited Jalabert to his Twickenham residence, Orléans House, to do portraits of himself, the duchess, his son (the duc de Guise), and his niece, Marguerite d'Orléans. Marguerite was the daughter of the duc de Nemours and was betrothed to Aumale's eldest son, the prince of Condé, then in Australia. Unfortunately, the prince died of yellow fever during his voyage, at the age of twenty-one; his parents learned of his death while they were posing for their portraits. "The duc d'Aumale aged twenty years in one day," wrote Jalabert. "I don't know what this sad news will mean for me; I need another week to make suitable progress on my portraits." Although the portraits were destined for the deceased prince, his parents decided to continue posing despite their grief. Jalabert recounted how the duke, overcome with sorrow, busied himself with politics to ease his pain. Completed in Paris early in 1867, these paintings were admired in Jalabert's studio by numerous visitors who came to see portraits of the exiles; they were shipped to London at the end of March.

The pendants were purchased in 1997, for the hundredth anniversary of the death of the duc d'Aumale, thanks to the generosity of the Amis du Musée Condé.

FOLLOWING PAGES
The Isabelle Room in the residential wing was named in memory of the duc d'Aumale's niece, Isabelle (1848–1919), wife of the comte de Paris, Philippe d'Orléans (1838–1894), the Orléanist pretender to the throne of France. Isabelle lived for a while in the royal apartment at Chantilly that the duke allocated to the count and countess, until the Orléans family was once again forced in the exile in 1886; the duc later converted the unoccupied rooms into a museum.

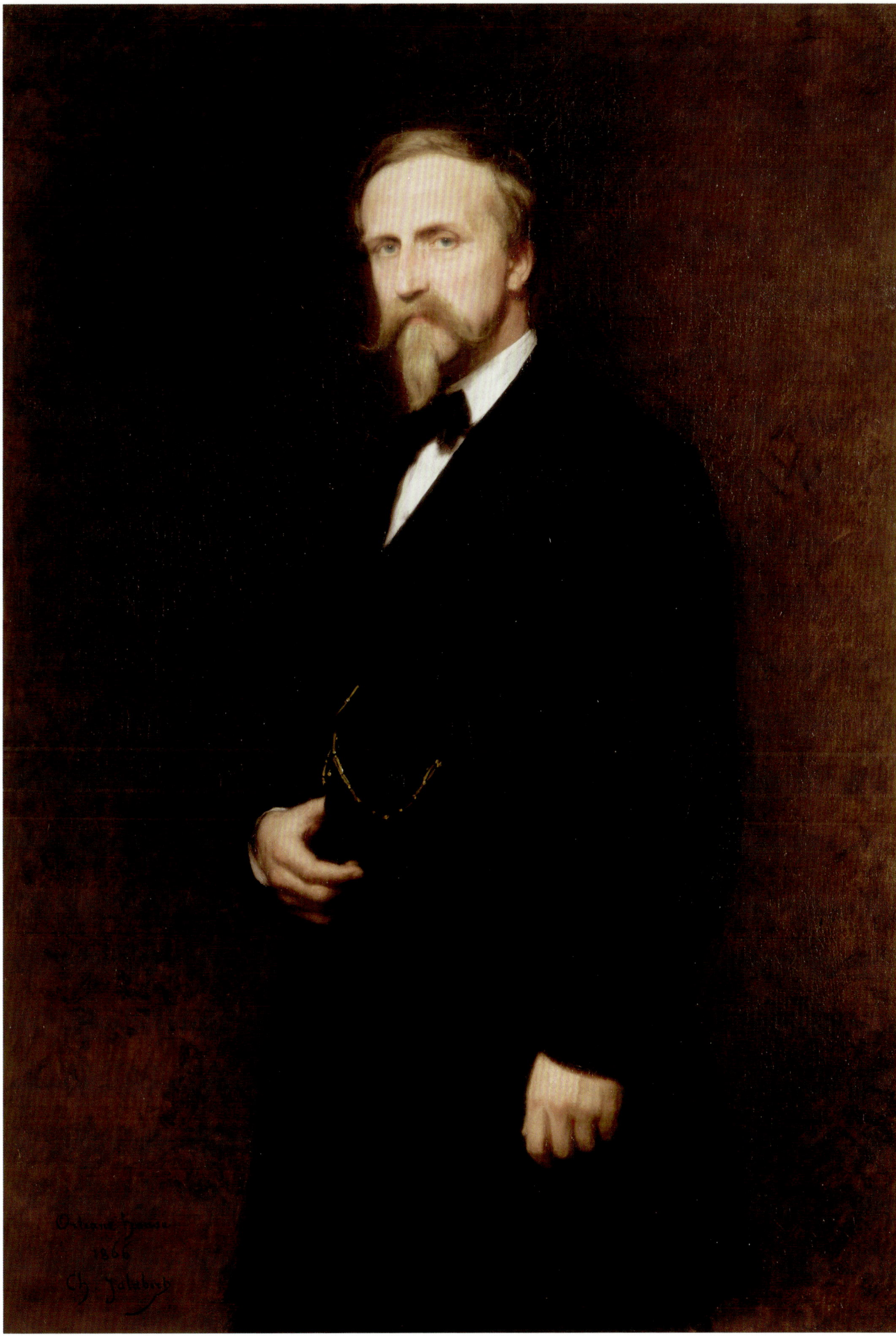

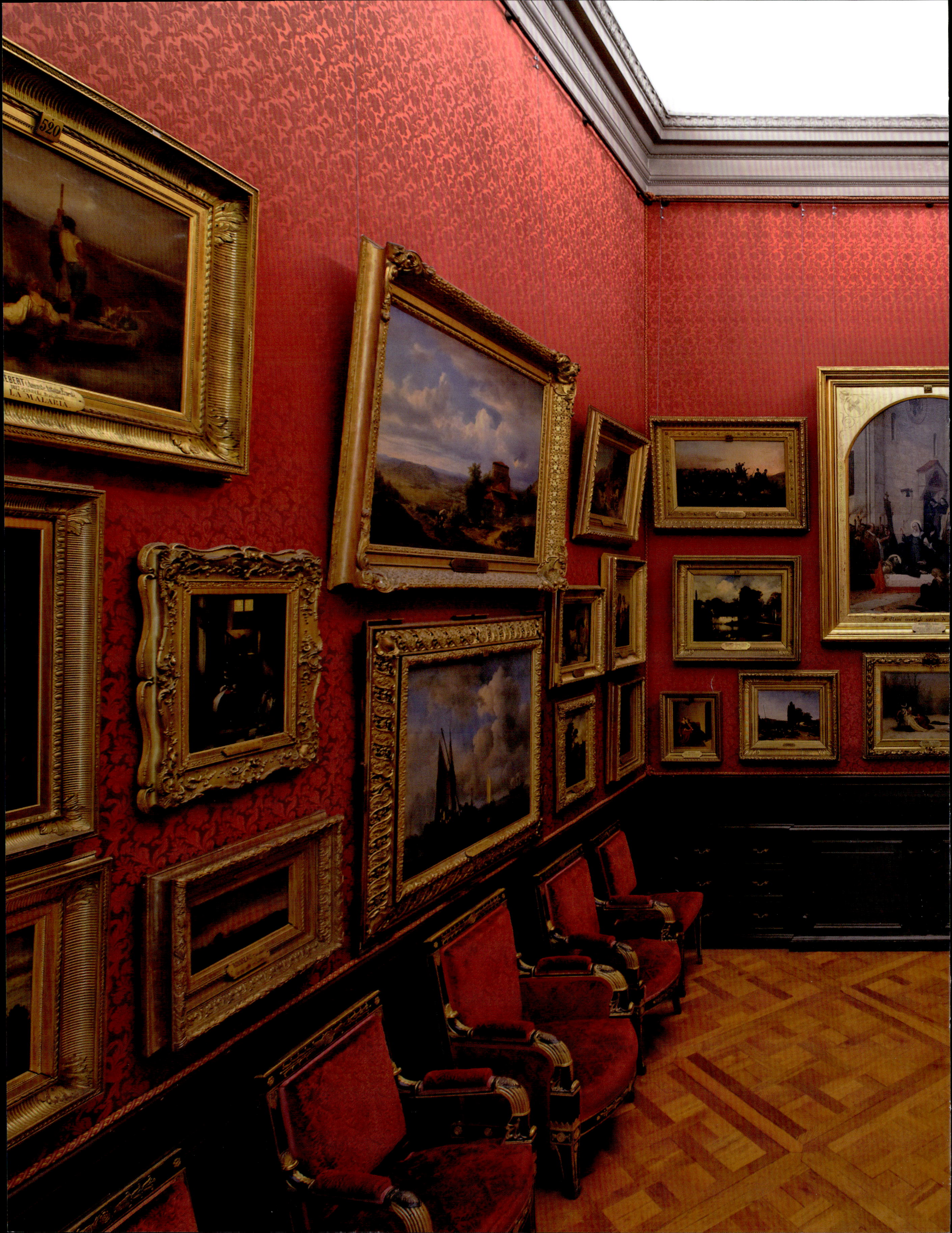
520
LA MALARIA

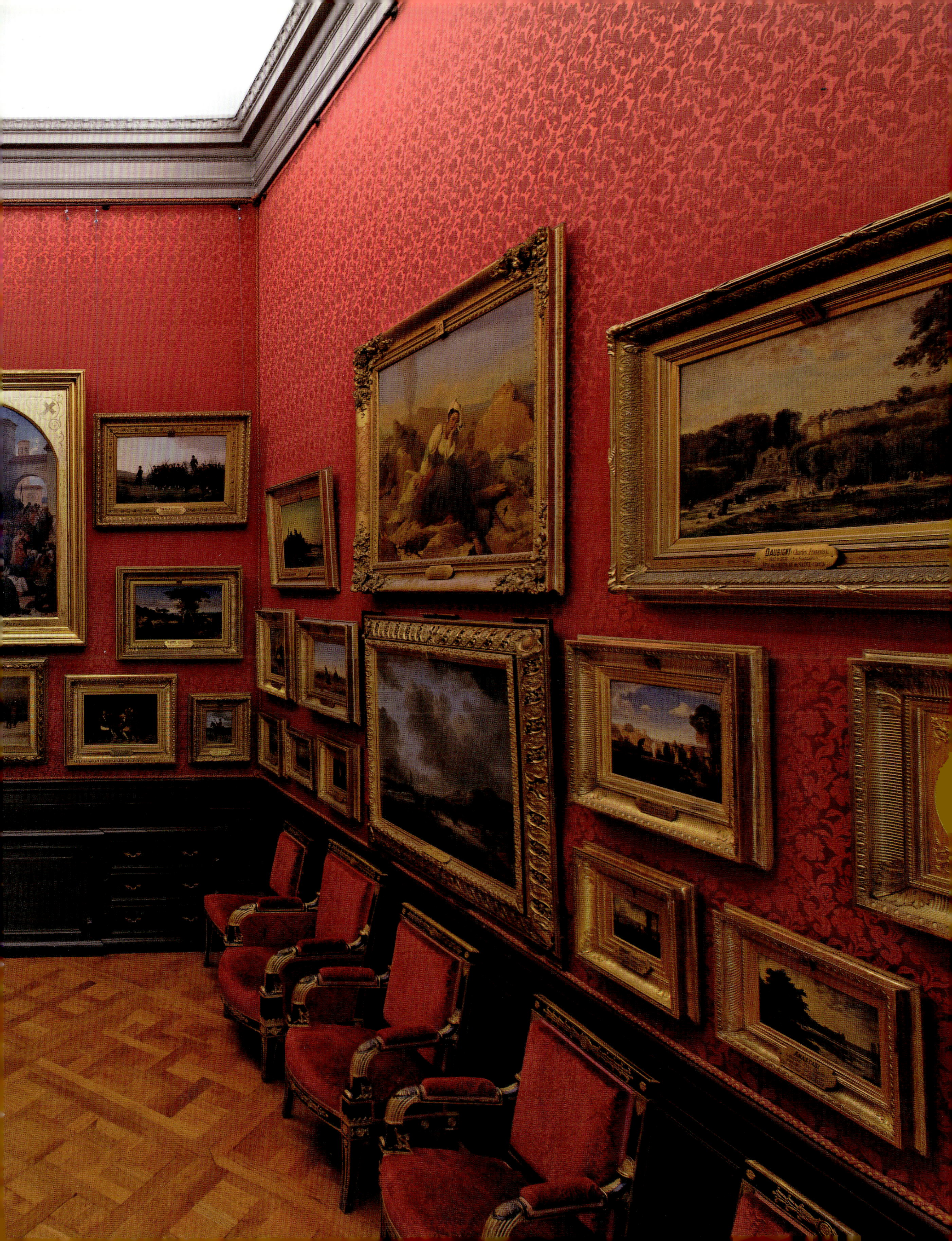
DAUBIGNY

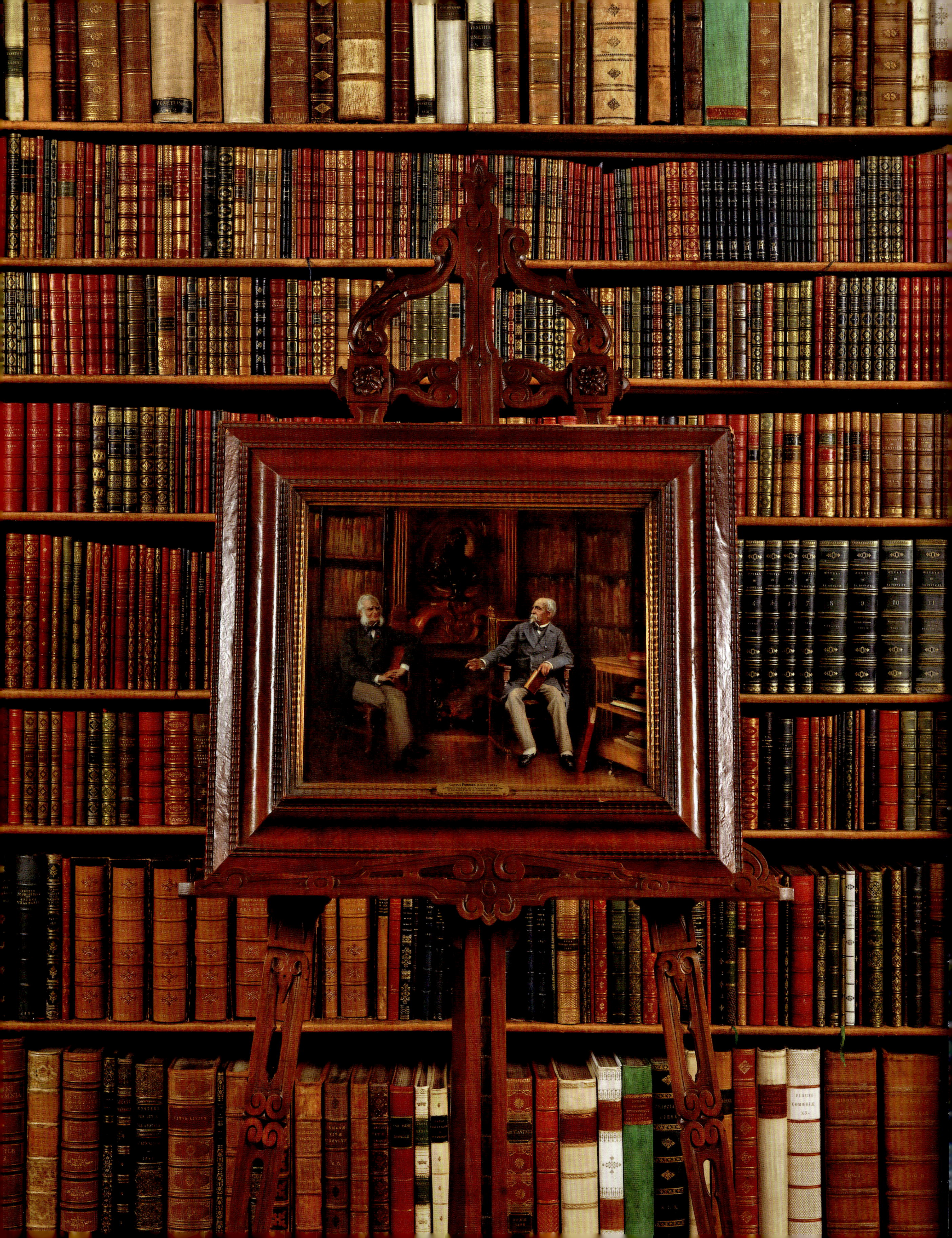

SELECTED BIBLIOGRAPHY

FACING PAGE
The library known as the Cabinet des Livres. On the easel is a portrait of the duc d'Aumale by Gabriel Ferrier (1880), shown with Alfred-Auguste Cuvillier-Fleury, who advised the duke on his purchases of books.

ANTONETTI Guy, *Louis-Philippe*, Paris, Fayard, 1994.

BABELON Jean-Pierre, *Chantilly*, Paris, Scala (2nd ed.), 2008.

BOISSARD Elisabeth DE and DUREY-LAVERGNE Valérie, *Institut de France II. Chantilly, musée Condé. Peintures de l'École italienne*, Paris, Réunion des musées nationaux, 1988 (coll. *Inventaires des collections publiques françaises*, 34).

BROGLIE Raoul DE, *Chantilly. Histoire du château et de ses collections*, Paris, Calmann-Lévy, 1964.

CAZELLES Raymond, *Peintures célèbres du musée Condé. Chantilly. Institut de France*. Chantilly, 1979.

CAZELLES Raymond, *Le Duc d'Aumale*, Paris, Tallandier, 1984.

CHATELET Albert, PARISET François-Georges and BROGLIE Raoul DE, *Institut de France I. Chantilly, Musée Condé. Peintures de l'École française. XVe-XVIIe siècles*, Paris, Réunion des musées nationaux, 1970 (coll. *Inventaires des collections publiques françaises*, 16).

COMBLEN-SONKES Micheline, with VANDEVIVERE, Ignace, *Les Primitifs flamands. Corpus de la peinture des anciens Pays-Bas méridionaux au quinzième siècle. Les musées de l'Institut de France. Musées Jacquemart-André et Marmottan à Paris, Musée Condé à Chantilly*, Brussels, 1988.

GARNIER-PELLE Nicole, *Chantilly, Musée Condé. Peintures du XVIIIe siècle*, Paris, Réunion des musées nationaux, 1995 (coll. *Inventaires des collections publiques françaises*, 38).

GARNIER-PELLE Nicole, *Chantilly, musée Condé. Peintures des XIXe et XXe siècles*, Paris, Réunion des musées nationaux, 1997 (coll. *Inventaires des collections publiques françaises*, 42).

GARNIER-PELLE Nicole, *La Peinture à Chantilly. Chefs-d'œuvre du musée Condé*, Versailles, Art-Lys, 2000.

GARNIER-PELLE Nicole (dir.), *Les Peintures italiennes du musée Condé à Chantilly*, Trieste, Editoriale Generali / Institut de France, 2003 (editions in French and Italian).

GARNIER-PELLE Nicole, *Les Miniatures du musée Condé à Chantilly. Portraits des maisons royales et impériales de France et d'Europe*, Paris, Somogy, 2007 (with Bernd Pappe and Nathalie Lemoine-Bouchard).

GARNIER-PELLE Nicole, *Le musée Condé, domaine de Chantilly*, Paris, Réunion des musées nationaux, 2009 (coll. *Musées et Monuments*, Fondation BNP Paribas).

GARNIER-PELLE Nicole, *Les Chefs-d'œuvre du musée Condé*, Paris, ed. Nicolas Chaudun, 2008.

GARNIER-PELLE Nicole, *Les Singeries*, Paris, ed. Nicolas Chaudun, 2008.

GARNIER-PELLE Nicole, *Christophe Huet et les singeries*, Saint-Rémy-en-l'Eau, ed. Monelle Hayot (forthcoming).

GRUYER F.A. *Chantilly. Musée Condé. Notice des peintures*, Paris, 1899.

GRUYER F.A. *Chantilly. Notice des peintures. École française*, Paris, 1900.

GRUYER F.A., *Chantilly. Notice des peintures. Écoles étrangères*, Paris, 1900.

GRUYER F.A., *La Jeunesse du roi Louis-Philippe d'après les portraits et les tableaux conservés au musée Condé*, Paris, 1909.

LEFÉBURE Amélie, *Chantilly. Musée Condé*, Ouest-France, 1986.

LEMONNIER Henry, "Les origines du musée Condé. La collection du prince de Salerne", in *Bulletin de la Société de l'histoire de l'art français*, 1923, p. 95–101.

LEMONNIER Henry, "Les origines du musée Condé", in *Gazette des beaux-arts*, February 1925, p. 61–76.

MACON Gustave, *Les Arts dans la maison de Condé*, Paris, Librairie de l'art ancien et moderne, 1903 (republication of articles from *La Revue de l'art ancien et moderne*).

MACON Gustave, *Chantilly et le musée Condé*, Paris, H. Laurens, 1925.

MACON Gustave, *Chantilly. Les Peintures*, Paris, [undated, after 1925].

MALO Henri, *Le Château de Chantilly*, Paris, 1938.

MARTIN-FUGIER Anne, *La Vie quotidienne de Louis-Philippe et de sa famille, 1830–1848*, Paris, Hachette, 1992.

SCHNAPPER Antoine, *Curieux du Grand Siècle. Collections et collectionneurs dans la France du XVIIe siècle*, Paris, Flammarion, 1994.

EXHIBITIONS

1979, Chantilly, Musée Condé: *La Madone de Lorette* (coll. *Les dossiers du département des peintures*, 19), under supervision of Sylvie Béguin.

1992, Chantilly, Musée Condé: *Delacroix au Maroc. L'Orientalisme au musée Condé*, cat. by Nicole Garnier, Arlette Sérullaz and Vincent Pomarède.

1994, Chantilly, Musée Condé: *Nicolas Poussin. La collection du musée Condé à Chantilly*, cat. by Pierre Rosenberg and Louis-Antoine Prat.

1996, Chantilly, Musée Condé: *Le Concert champêtre by Jean-Baptiste-Camille Corot (1796–1875)*, special edition of *Musée Condé*, n° 50, by Florence Adam, Nicole Garnier, Vincent Pomarède, Anne Roquebert.

1996, Chantilly, Musée Condé: "Watteau et son cercle dans les collections de l'Institut de France", in *Le Musée Condé*, October 1996, n° 51.

1997, Chantilly, Musée Condé: "Pierre-Paul Prud'hon (1758–1823) dans les collections du musée Condé. Dessins et peintures," in *Le Musée Condé*, September 1997, n° 52.

2004, Chantilly, Musée Condé: *L'Art anglais dans les collections de l'Institut de France*, under supervision of Olivier Meslay.

2004, Chantilly, Musée Condé: *Chasse à courre, chasse de cour. Fastes de la vénerie princière à Chantilly au temps des Condés et des Orléans (1659–1910)*, Tournai, La Renaissance du Livre, 2004 (with Bénédicte Ottinger).

INDEX

Text in bold indicates artists whose work(s) are the subject of an entry in the catalogue of paintings.

INDEX

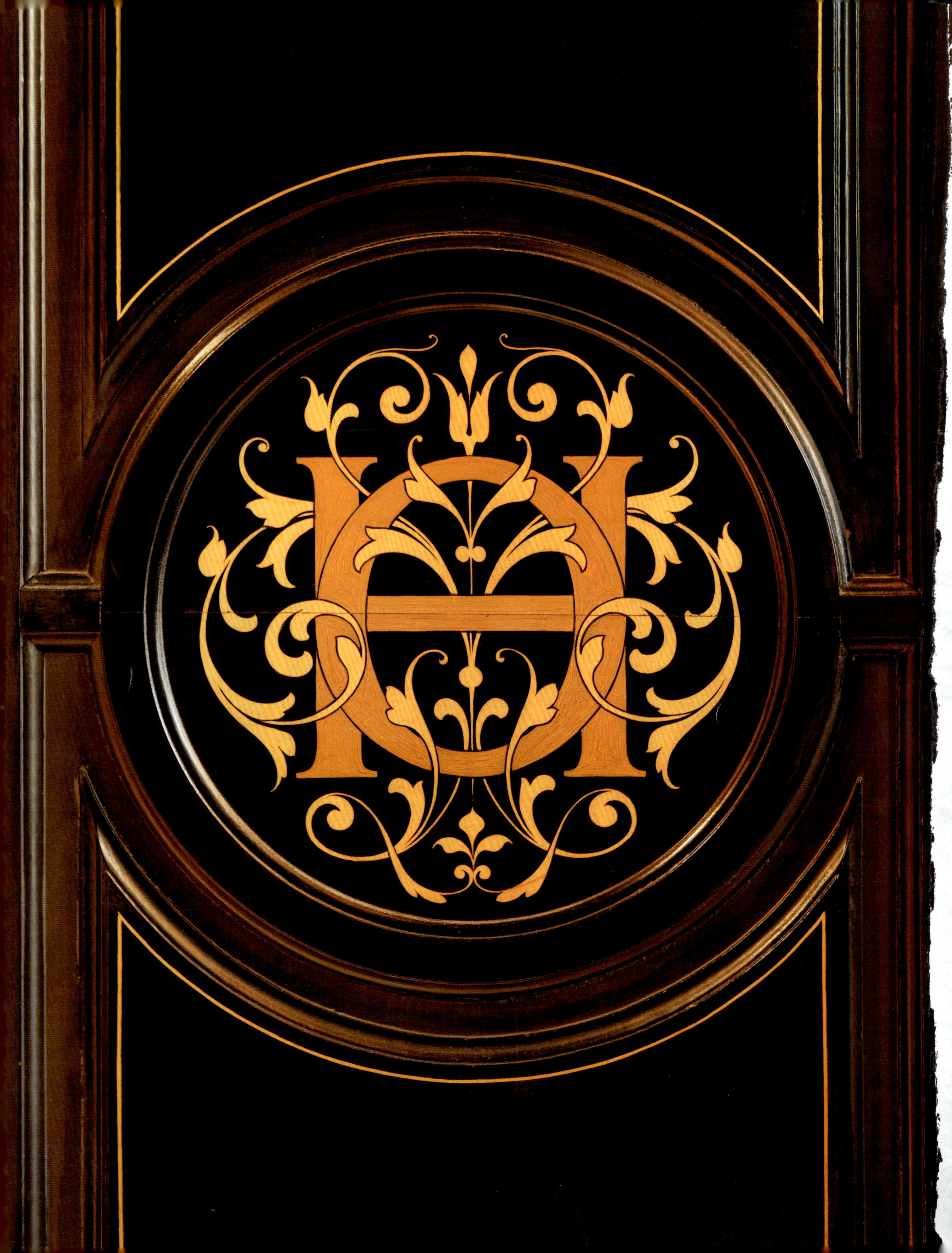